THE

BEST

OF

J.E. COLEMAN:

CLOCKMAKER

MR. J. E. COLEMAN

THE BEST

OF

J.E. COLEMAN:

From his "Questions & Answers" and
"Clockwise & Otherwise" columns over
the past forty years published in the
American Horologist & Jeweler.

Compiled and Edited by

Orville R. Hagans, CMW, CMC, FBHI, FNAWCC
6930 E. Girard Ave.
Denver, CO 80224

FOREWORD

Many men have a thorough knowledge of their profession. Only a rare few have the knowledge *and* the gift that allows them to share their ability with others for the benefit of the entire industry. Jesse E. Coleman had both the knowledge and the gift.

After spending four years as an apprentice to a competent, French-trained watchmaker, he eventually opened Coleman's Clock Shop, the Arcade Building, Nashville, TN. and ran it for 40 years before retirement. He shared his technical knowledge and his down-to-earth Southern sense of humor with his contemporaries through the pages of *American Horologist & Jeweler* magazine. His monthly column, "Clockwise and Otherwise" appeared for more than 28 years.

The unique question and answer format set up a communications link between Coleman and his magazine's readers that helped literally thousands of horologists to solve their day by day technical problems and to run a more lucrative, professional business, as well. He urged them to make the most of their talents in the "144-square inch world" that is the watchmakers bench.

He was an ardent researcher who spent many hours developing technical and background information so that he could lead his fellow horologists along more productive paths. He maintained that the successful watch/clockmaker should know "all" about the timepiece from its history to its technical operation. He urged the horologist to apply the same principles as the attorney or doctor and market their skills at a profitable figure just as other professionals do.

He did not confine his writings to AH&J alone. He also contributed informative articles to *HIA Journal, Horology, NAWCC Bulletin, BHI Journal, AWI News* and many other publications. He added to this constant flow helpful information by answering thousands of personal letters to solve specific problems.

In addition to all this involvement, Coleman found time to be active in association work. He was instrumental in founding the National Watch and Clock Collectors organization and contributed his efforts to unify the UHAA and HIA groups into forming the American Watchmakers Institute which is the only professional horological association in the United States today.

Jesse Coleman and Orville R. Hagans were friends for more than 40 years. They first met in 1932 and fell under the influence of William H. Samelius, "Dean of American Watchmakers." Samelius urged them to dedicate their lives to the advancement of horology in all its phases. They accepted the challenge and worked together for many years toward this goal. Coleman's contributions to AH&J were the results of a verbal agreement, sealed by a handshake with Hagans (who then owned the magazine) and lasted until Coleman's passing in 1975.

Despite his prolific output of articles and correspondence, or, perhaps, because of it—Jesse Coleman never got around to writing a book. As this publication goes to press, AH&J is still receiving requests for reprints or back issues containing Jesse's column. Spurred by this continued interest, and mindful of their mutual pledge to devote their lives to the advancement of horology, Orville Hagans has compiled these pages containing the bulk of Coleman's Clockwise and Otherwise" columns that first appeared in AH&J.

Most of the information is as valid today as it was when originally written. It is the hope of Orville Hagans, and all those connected with this project, that it will help to perpetuate the memory of Jesse E. Coleman and extend the benefits of his lifelong experience, research and friendly philosophy to guide horologists for generations to come.

Denver, Colorado
May, 1979

MAURY NORRELL

ACKNOWLEDGEMENTS

With sincere appreciation to my wife,
Josephine, and Harold J. and Charlill
R.Hansen for their invaluable assistance
in compiling, cross indexing and arranging
the questions and answers from more
than three hundred columns. Also to
Maury Norrell for his guidance, cooperation and writing the Foreword.

Orville R. Hagans

In order to preserve the authenticity of Mr. Coleman's writing, we have not deleted any references to firms or sources. It is possible that many of these references no longer exist or have undergone changes.

TABLE OF CONTENTS

GENERAL INFORMATION

CLOCK CASES

I have two French Granit clocks and the granit slabs have become loose. Can you tell me what material to use to fasten the slabs back in place and how?

A.

I have found that the common McCormick's Iron glue mixed with about 50 per cent water works fine. Also, the plastic adhesive called Casamite is quite satisfactory.

On any cement job of this nature it is well to remember the less cement used the better the job, because with a very thick layer of cement the object has, at the junction, no more rigidity than that of the cement itself. The greatest enemies of a good cement job are air and dirt. See that the surfaces are clean and spread the cement carefully and work it in to exclude all air possible. Marble and stone clock cases (cemented, and most are) should never be lifted and handled by the top. Always support the base.

I remember a while back you gave information as to how to go about restoring the original high lustre to the black marble French clock cases. We have tried various methods, but none succeeded.

A.

Practically all polishing operations at their finish wind up in the friction bracket. When this friction can't be applied mechanically, it means a lot of "elbow work".

Frankly, we've had no experience actually doing this type of work, but on one or two occasions, we have turned over marble cases to monument yards and have received an excellent polish job. I understand that they use an oxalic acid and paste known to their trade as "polishing putty". There must be a marble yard or monument yard near you; if convenient to drop by there, I'm sure they will gladly tell you something of marble polishing, and even

be glad to show you the complete operation.

A clockmaker friend tells me that he has obtained oxalic acid at the local drug store, cut pieces from an old felt hat and moistened the piece with the acid before folding it around a flat wooden block, and then went to work on the case with lots of rubbing. He says the results were satisfactory.

I bought an old clock with a black case which is either marble or onyx. I am trying to find something that will polish it and am wondering if you could suggest something to me. On the back of the clock is the inscription, "Medaille de Bronze, S. Marti Et Cie, 6."

A.

Yes, your clock is French, and you might be surprised to learn that Marti is still making clocks. Mr. R. Marti, now head of the firm Establissments S. Marti, 22 Rue General LeClarc, Montebeliard, France, writes that those movements marked "S. Marti Et Cie, Medaille de Bronze" were made from 1867 to 1869. Also, that movements bearing this mark are not now repairable by them. (Material is not available.)

Generally, black marble cases are polished with a mixture of the best beeswax and spirits of turpentine, as a thin paste. First clean the case thoroughly and cover lightly with paste; polish with a clean cotton cloth or piece of felt (an old hat may be used) on a block. The trick is plenty of "elbow grease."

The above is merely polishing—if the original finish has been worn off or roughed up, a little grinding sort of operation, using putty powder under the felt block, should precede the polishing.

GLASS

We've been asked several times whether or not there is a low-priced source of decorated clock glasses for American shelf clocks. "Tablets" was the name given them by the old-timers. In Chauncey Jerome's book we find the following: "The tablets were printed in the same manner (referring to dials printed by wood-cuts), the colors put on afterwards by girls, and the whole work on these beautiful tablets cost less than one-and-a-half cents: The cost of glass and work was about four cents." None of us could hope to replace a broken glass today for 4c and these broken and damaged glasses present the repairman with quite a problem.

There are several sources of fine hand-painted reproductions and such is unquestionably the proper method for the finer clocks such as the Terry "Pillar and Scroll" and museum pieces. But the making of such glasses requires the work of top-flight artists and because it must be done backward and the base is glass, it becomes a tedious, time-killing job placing the finished piece in a price bracket wholly impractical to include with the repair job of cheaper clocks.

Some clockmakers recommend to the clock owners that they secure a suitable print and insert same behind the glass as framing a picture or print, thereby completely dodging the "tablet" question in connection with the repair job. After all, it is to the interest of the repairman to hold the price down as much as practical simply because if the total figure gets too high the owner may decide not to have the old piece repaired at all.

With a little time and practice, you can make up a glass which we shall only call passable, and we would especially like to hear from other repairmen if they have a practical method of solving this problem.

From single strength window pane, cut "blank" to properly fit your door. Lay out on plain paper the exact size of this glass, a border of proportionate size as a guide when you lay the glass on top of it. This border to be painted around the edge of the glass in black. A thin gold line on the inside edge of the black border will add greatly to the looks of the finished "tablet." Scotch "wet-or-dry" masking tape does the trick. Simply mask off the inside line for the gold stripe, then a strip of tape placed approximately ⅛-inch toward the outside gives the desired space. Use Venus coach striping gold powder mixed with spar varnish and paint the stripe. Set aside to dry for 24 hours, remove the outside tape and paint on the black; another drying period and remove the inside tape.

For the center decoration, use a decal of some flower (obtainable at your 5 & 10) of suitable size for the opening; another drying period and back up the whole with white. Result: a passable substitute, not as cheap as Jerome made his but far below a handpainted special order job.

SUN DIALS

How to set up a sundial?

I'm a man who repairs watches but cannot set up a sundial. Someday, I will be greatly embarrassed if some friend asks me to set up a sundial and I'm forced to admit I am ignorant of this basic timekeeper.

Can you, therefore, give the necessary information in your column that will enable me to properly place a sundial? Also, if it is not asking too much, supply a few lines of the mechanics of the thing. I'm toying with the idea of building a sundial myself.

A.

The information necessary to set up a sundial would depend wholly on type of dial. For example, about 99% of all horizontal dials (surface flat and level) have the gnomon pointing directly to the North Star. Provided the dial was first built for that spot, you can readily see that if the dial surface remains flat and level, the angle of the gnomon as it related to that surface would have to equal the latitude of that place.

By all means, devote some time to the study of "dialing," or as it is sometimes called, "gnomonics." It includes astronomy, art, mechanics, mathematics, architecture and geometry, and is most interesting. You probably have (or can get it at your local library) a copy of Dr. Willis I. Milham's "Time and Timekeepers." Chapter two is devoted to the sundial. In the back of that volume is listed some 15 books that have been written on dialing. F. J. Britten's "Watch and Clockmaker's Handbook" has a short article. Both Milham and Britten give instructions for making a correct horizontal dial.

You can readily see that the mere fundamentals of dialing alone would fill several issues of a publication the size of A.H.&J. Many practicing watchmakers fail to recognize the sundial as a scientific instrument. It is—just as much as a watch or clock. The column would appreciate a nice, long letter telling of your study and including a photo of the dial you build. On the whole, bench mechanics ought to know more about sundials.

How Do You Set Sun Dial Accurately?

The other evening a group of us were discussing sun dials and their settings. Could you give us a few of the details concerning the placing of a sun dial in order to assure a reasonably accurate setting?

A.

"Dialing" is a far broader subject than most realize — there have been written a number of books upon the art of dialing; should you care to go into it I am sure that your local library has some and can assure you that it is very interesting.

Specifically, your question is: "How to set . . . ?"

Presuming that you refer to the common, flat, horizontal dial: it must be set level, and, the gnomon must point to the true North.

First, and foremost, if, one is considering accuracy, the sun-dial must be constructed for the exact latitude upon which it is to be set up. Both the angle of the gnomon and the dial lines are determined by its location (latitude).

Roughly (from map) Pittsburg is 40 degrees and 25 minutes North. This should be the angle of your gnomon, thus, you can readily see that a "flat" dial set level whose gnomon was cut to the location, i.e. 40 degrees, 25 minutes: the edge of that gnomon will be exactly parallel to the earth's axis. Set pointing to the true North, you ought to be able to sight along the top edge of the gnomon at the North Star (Polaris).

One writer has said: "Dialing or Gnomonics is considered by some a most interesting and intellectual avocation, as it calls to its use Astronomy, Geography, Geometry, Mathematics, Architecture, and Art."

DIALS

I am having trouble finding metal dials for old-time Seth Thomas weight clocks, 1-day and 8-day. They are the square type with Roman numerals. The dial part the numbers are on is convex and numbers are about 1 3/16 inches tall for 30-hour clocks and about 8 by 8 inches square overall. The 8-day dials are 10 inches wide by 9½ inches deep. If you cannot locate metal ones perhaps you could tell me where I could get the glazed paper ones in the style mentioned.

A.

There are a number of men throughout the country repainting these dials in the old manner, even making new zinc blanks where necessary.

The original dials were on zinc because paint forms a better bond with it than any other metal. If the old blank (metal) is in good condition on your clocks there is no reason to go the additional expense of having another made. Just send it for repainting. If it has been lost or you do not consider it usable, a new blank can be made to your drawing. Should you desire to save that expense, you might obtain some sheet zinc and cut your own blank to fit—key holes, etc., then just have that painted.

Setting the Moon
On the Grandfather Clock

How Does a Moon Phase Dial Operate?

You have straightened me out on several clocks, and now I need to find out about a moon phase dial. How is this disk supposed to operate? I notice a pin in the wheel next to the moon disk. I ran the hands around several times and this wheel turned very slowly. The disk has a moon on the top and one on the bottom; is this supposed to show the light and dark of the moon? By what I learned from examining it, the pin will carry the disc around when it comes in contact with the teeth in the disc. This is a new movement, German make (Nessalc, N.Y.).

A.

The moon dial is intended to show the age of the moon, only that. The two hemispheres on the dial are nothing more than decorative and the fact that they are circular and the one affording a pretty good imitation of the real moon is just a coincidence. You will note that there is a scale around the top, going from 1 to 29½. For all practical purposes, the Lunar month is just 29½ days. The moon disc is merely a solid saw-tooth wheel with 118 teeth cut upon it; driven by a pin in the hour wheel it gets kicked over two teeth every 24-hour day and thus makes one complete revolution in fifty-nine days.

With two moons painted upon it, one of them will pass through the half-circle opening in half the 59 days, or in 29½ days. Imagine a line drawn right through the center of the moon showing; the figure upon the top scale then tells you how many days old the moon is. To set the moon dial, simply turn either moon to the number of days since new moon.

These examples will make it clear: if the moon is new on the first day of the calendar month and the date you are setting it is the tenth, then set the moon to ten. Another: if the moon is new on the twelfth day of the calendar month and the date you are setting it is the twentieth, it is eight days old and you set it to eight. Completely forget the moon you do not see (one on the other half of the disc) it will automatically take care of itself.

MANY, IF NOT MOST, grandfather clocks have a moon age scale at the top of the dial. Often referred to as 'showing phases of the moon', and just as often confusing both the owner and repairer. In a manner, it does imitate the moon through its various phases, but this is a mere coincidence; the basic construction, like that of the clock, is to show the age of the moon (time of the moon in days).

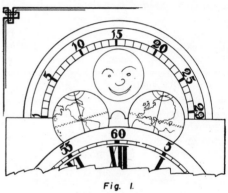

Fig. I.

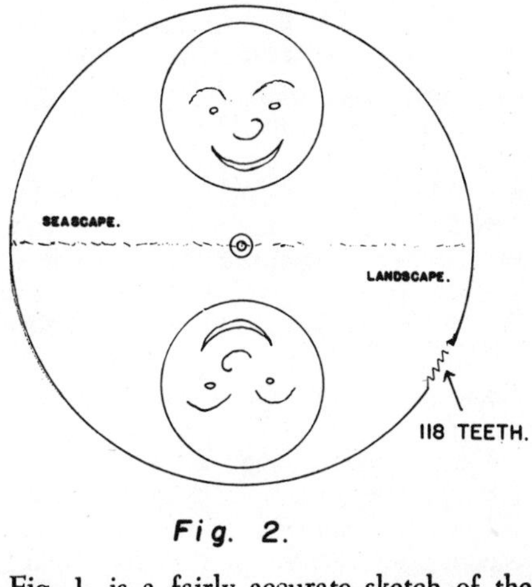

Fig. 2.

Fig. 1, is a fairly accurate sketch of the top portion of a grandfather dial with moon mechanism. Fig. 2 is the moon disc operating behind the dial — this disc has painted upon it two (2) moons; one usually has a sea scene for background and the other a

5

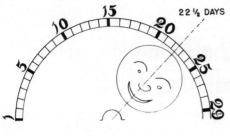

Fig. 3.

Fig. 4.

land scene. Cut into the edge of this disc are one-hundred and eighteen (118) teeth; it is ratcheted forward (clockwise direction) by one (1) tooth every twelve (12) hours.

The method varies slightly but basically it is the same. Upon some clocks a simple pin is set into the hour-wheel or the strike-snail if it happens to be mounted concentrically with the hour-wheel; on others, there is a projection or tab on the pipe of the hour hand. The pin and/or tab comes up under a lever pivoted to the sub-frame holding the dial, thereby lifting it (the lever) just enough to ratchet the moon disc forward by one tooth. Thus the moon disc gets moved forward by two (2) teeth every 24 hour day because the pin or tab revolves once per twelve (12) hours.

For all practical purposes the lunar (Moon) month is twenty-nine and one-half days (actually it is 29.53 days). Now, when the clock has ratcheted the moon disc forward for 29½ days, that is by fifty-nine (59) teeth, it has revolved the moon disc by exactly 180 degrees, one-half of the 118 teeth. As we have two moons upon the disc, the half rev (180 degrees) completes all that one moon shows behind the half-circle cut out of the dial. The scale painted around this half-circle is divided into 29½ divisions, and is so numbered; from this operation it is easily seen that this moon mechanism records the age of the moon.

One simply imagines a line drawn through the center of the moon acting as a hand, i.e. pointing to the date — some clocks have a little projection painted on top of the moon for this purpose. Fig. 1 shows a moon fifteen (15) days old. Fig. 3 shows the moon to be 22½ days old, while Fig. 4 shows a seven (7) day old moon.

To set the moon disc correctly, one turns to the calendar or almanac to determine on what day the moon was 'new'. Calculate from that day to the day of setting just how many days old the moon is, then turn the disc to that position. For an example, let's say the moon was new on the second of the month and you are setting the clock on ninth day of the calendar month, then on that day (9th) your moon is seven (7) days old and should be set as in Fig. 4.

Another example: let's say you've determined that the moon was new on the fifth (5th) of the month and that you are making the setting on the afternnon of the twenty-seventh (27th) it should be set on 22½ as in Fig. 3.

On those clocks with the tab on the hour-hand pipe, the disc is automatically ratcheted forward as the hour hand approaches twelve (12); those with a pin set into the strike-snail have it so set as to operate at the 12; those clocks with the lift-pin set into the hour wheel should have the hour-wheel set so as to make the one tooth forward ratched at 12. In this way your moon comes in at mid-night and moves into the second half of its day at 12 high noon — that is how one gets the half-day setting in the afternoon. Most almanacs give the exact hour, as: new moon on the 26th, 1:24 p.m., or new moon on the 28th, 1:16 a.m. Knowing that your moon disc moves or jumps by 12 hour periods and which of the two periods the moon changes in, it is easy to set it to the correct half-day.

6

ANTIMAGNETIC WATCH PATENTS

Last fall while pursuing a little horological research upon quite a different subject we ran upon one of the most unusual patent copies we've ever examined, titled Antimagnetic Watch.

Over the years we've read and/or examined many horological patent copies, and, have noted with a great deal of satisfaction that horological writers within the past decade have evidenced a greater use of them.

Among the early ones to make liberal use of patent copies was Joseph R. Oakley of 10 Audubon Lane, Poland, Ohio, 44514, in his "Text-Catalogue I" in which he reproduced about a dozen copies. That was about a decade ago and it is very noticeable that their use is upon the increase. The Millers'—Andrew and Dalia, 766 S. Street, Elgin, Ill., 60120, in their "Survey Of American Calendar Clocks,"

No. 831,561. PATENTED SEPT. 25, 1906.
H. S. MONTGOMERY.
ANTIMAGNETIC WATCH.
APPLICATION FILED MAY 9, 1905.

3 SHEETS—SHEET 1.

H.S. Montgomery, Inventor

Witnesses
Howard N. Orr.
B.G. Foster

By E.G. Siggers
Attorney

1972, utilized many patent copies. Ken Roberts in his "Connecticut Clock Technology of Joseph Ives," Box 98, Fitzwillian, NH. 03447, used several. Perhaps, the greatest use of patent copies is found in Warren H. Niebling's "History of the American Watch Case"—1971—in which some two/thirds of this work or 132 out of 192 pages are devoted to reproducing patent copies. We often refer to patent copies ahd have upon occasions utilized reproduced copies.

Before the turn of the century they took the horse from out front of the trolley and installed an electric motor; Mr. Edison perfected the incandescent light, and Mr. Bell gave us the telephone; it was about here that the American watchmaker was shoved into an electrical world and he immediately became interested in magnetism. The general thinking of the bench horologist during this era is a bit difficult to assess; treatises that came out towards the end of the era gave magnetism very short treatment, if at all. An outstanding example would be Grant Hoods "Modern Methods in Horology," 1903 which just about ignores it, though Charles Higganbotham's "Precision Time Measures" which came along in 1913 devotes one whole chapter to magnetism. Perhaps one good 'yardstick' for measuring the thoughts within the craft would be those letters to the editor — it was during this era bench horologists did a bit more 'sounding-off' than they do this date. Judging from those letters I'd say the trade was about evenly divided; many wrote in terms of 'rate' — that is, they were concerned with the way magnetism disrupted a good timekeeping rate; others seemed to be concerned only with main-spring breakage; blaming all breakage upon magnetism, etc.

The patent we refer to is: No. 831,561, titled "Antimagnetic Watch", issued to Henry S. Montgomery, of Topeka, Kan., Sept. 25th, 1906 — original application May 9th, 1905. Apparently Mr. Montgomery belongs to the later group as his invention seems to be directed toward protecting the main-spring. Webster defines 'anti' as a prefix meaning against or opposed to: thus I take it that Mr. Montgomery was patenting a device that opposed magnetism.

I well remember that my old mentor was most careful about magnetism; he would not tolerate the use of a little compass to detect it, saying that the bit of magnetism within the compass needle would be attracted by the vibrating balance and show a wiggle when no magnetism resided in the balance at all. He utilized a little device of his own making; a thin glass vial roughly half an inch in diameter and about three-fourths inch deep, in which he had hung a small piece of steel hair-spring wire cemented to a single strand of silk by shellac and suspended

7

from the center of the cork. Set upon the cork above a vibrating balance, this little bit of steel would do a nice 'wiggle' if there was the least bit of magnetism in that balance or hair-spring. Gently moved about over the main-spring any residue magnetism was immediately indicated.

It might be of interest to our younger readers to know that with all the attention paid to magnetism our shop did NOT have a demagnetizer per se — whether it was that inherent desire to stick by the old ways, or, to save the price of a demagnetizer I am not sure. Refering to an 1899 catalogue we see advertised: "Battery demagnetizer; accompanied with powerful solution battery, motor, coil, etc., $12.00." The going rate for watchmakers about that time was $10.00 to $12.50 per week of six ten-hour days, so you see any watchmaker equipping himself with a demagnetizer would be investing a full week's wage. Like our home-made detector, our demagnetizer was also home-made — it was simply a horse-shoe magnet suspended by a string — I'm not absolutely sure, but believe that our magnet was one taken from an old crank telephone ringer. The process was slow and tedious, but, it worked.

The principle was sound and used for many years up to a few short years back when the one-shot devices hit the market. That principle was: place the object — movement — to have it's magnetism extracted within a rapidly reversing magnetic field that could be slowly diminished to the zero point. This is exactly what happened when one used the little demagnetizers that plugged into the light circuit — you simply placed the movement within the coil; turned on the current and slowly withdrew the movement; the magnetic field created within the coil diminished the further away the movement was from it.

To use the horse-shoe magnet method the movement was placed upon a board or table— not on the bench as you do not want the magnet near tools — set the magnet astraddle of it and wind the string 30 or 40 turns; lift the magnet via the twisted string. The instant it is lifted it begins to spin, thereby creating a rapidly reversing field; then, continue to raise it slowly thus diminishing the field to the zero point. Carried through this routine two or three times generally did the trick; the watch was always tested again the next morning to make sure of no further magnetic build-up. Try it sometime when you have the yen to 'play'; you will enjoy the experiment.

Back to Mr. Montgomery's unusual patent: two pages of drawings and two pages of specs — too long to quote here in its entirety; I puzzled over this 'scheme' quite a little, and, asked a number of knowledgable old timers whether or not they had ever encountered such construction, or, had ever heard of it. All said they had not — perhaps, I should not become overly concerned at not being able fully to understand the scheme since the 'patentee' himself, confesses that he does not fully understand it.

Quote from line 54 of the specs: "While I am unable to fully explain the theory of the invention, in actual practice I select a throughly magnetized disc and determine, by means of a compass, the positive side thereof. I secure this disc with the positive side against one side of the barrel. I then determine, in like manner, the negative side of another disc and place this disc against the opposite side of the barrel. Said discs are connected by the arbor, which thus appears to form therewith a single magnet, the poles of which are upon opposite sides of the barrel. As a result a field of magnetism is produced about the barrel, and careful tests and experience have demonstrated that it controls an attack of magnetism when the watch is subjected to such influence by being introduced into a magnetic field."

Stripped of considerable wordage of the whole specs, this paragraph is the whole of his scheme; his drawings purport to show how these two magnetized discs may be applied to an "Elgin" watch.

He then goes on to say: "From the foregoing it is thought that the construction, operation, and many advantages of the herein-described invention will be apparent to those skilled in the art without further description." What the many advantages he deemed to be so apparent were, is left strictly to one's imagination for they are not otherwise mentioned by him; nor does he one time mention the balance and hair-spring or intimate that these members would be influenced if the watch was brought within a magnetic field. We must then conclude that his sole object was to protect the main-spring. Just how placing a magnet within a watch would make that watch "Antimagnetic" is still the $64 question, but, a still perplexing one is: the effect such a permanent magnet revolving within the watch would have upon its rate?

Though Mr. Montgomery did not succeed through the use of this most unusual invention, he did, via another patent about a decade later, become one of the best known men within the craft. That was the "Montgomery" dial — used by all the makers of ry. watches save just one, Webb C. Ball. As all know, the "Montgomery" dial was the one that had each minute marked with Arabic numerals from 1 to 60 just outside the minute track.

I am indepted to Mrs. Harrison Babcock, a long time Ball employee for this 'bit' — she tells me that Mr. Ball said: the numerals were small and therefore confusing, and, that trainmen almost never got to observe their watch in sufficient light, etc. The dial story is another good one and shall have to be told at another time.

CLEANING IVORY

Regarding the question of removing discoloration from ivory beads, I have never tried to remove color due to age, but if discolored by grease or perspiration, I have had good success by washing daily in pure Ivory soap leaving a film of soap on the beads, and then exposing them to sunlight. Usually in about a month's time all artificial discoloration is removed. Any good ivory with a nice polished surface will seldom discolor, only when the surface is rough or porous will it do so— personally I prefer the aged look in ivory to the pure white.

Ivory? First be sure it is ivory, and not "Parisian Ivory" (celluloid) or any of a multitude of plastics. You cannot tell by color, weight or smell, and various cleaners such as carbon tetrachloride, alcohol, ether, soap and ammonia, acetone, amyl acetate, etc., are apt to dissolve a plastic. Second, be sure it is not bone—a lot of people cannot tell the difference. Third, there are three kinds of ivory; 1—live ivory, the tusk or tooth of an animal killed within a few years of its use, and not exposed to heat or weather. 2—dead ivory, collected from the so-called "elephant graveyards" or found on the plains or veldt—being the long exposed remains of some animal wounded and lost, or one that died of natural causes. 3— mined ivory, prehistoric ivory or glacier ivory —this is the ivory of mammoth, mastodon, etc., of the Arctic that has been buried in ice, mud or dirt for a mere 50,000 years, or in the asphalt lakes of the Southwest.

Number one is the best, of course; number two may have decayed enough so that it is porous at least on the surface, and may have mineral or organic deposits or discoloration. These can be removed only by abrasives. Number three has mineral deposits, stress cracks, etc., and cannot be cleaned to the condition of number one.

De-grease with any such agent such as alcohol, carbon tetrachloride, benzene, Renuzit, or any of the detergents (used with caution).

To remove the yellow tinge due to age, dip in a mild solution of Chlorox to which about one-half as strong a solution of hydrochloric (muriatic) acid has been added; (example: 50% Chlorox plus 2% HCL) and place in the sun.

Let me suggest that anyone who attempts to clean ivory be very sure of what he has, and if it is at all valuable. As a means of testing, go to a music store and get some scraps of various old organ and piano keys, and experiment. Better to be sure than to be sorry. Hope the above is of some use to you.

JEWELERS SAW

The column has received a number of queries relating to Jewelers Piercing Saw Blades—finding this info a bit hard to pinpoint indicates that it just might be well to include same right here—in keeping with our long standing habit of throwing in elusive "bits"—below is a table from one manufacturer which appears to be approximate "standard."

Number	Length	Teeth per inch	Thickness & Width
6/0,	5"	80,	.007" X .014"
5/0,	5"	75,	.008" X .016"
4/0,	5"	65,	.009" X .018"
3/0,	5"	60,	.010" X .019"
2/0,	5"	57,	.010" X .021"
1/0,	5"	52,	.011" X .022"
1,	5"	47,	.012" X .024"
2,	5"	42,	.013" X .027"
3,	5"	39,	.014" X .029"
4,	5"	37,	.015" X .031"
5,	5"	35,	.016" X .034"
6,	5"	32,	.017" X .038"
6-6,	6"	32,	.016" X .036"
7,	5"	30,	.018" X .042"
8,	5"	26,	.019" X .045"
10,	5"	30,	.016" X .054"
10-6,	6"	30,	.016" X .054"
12,	5"	20,	.016" X .054"
12-6,	6"	20,	.016" X .054"
14,	5"	15,	.020" X .070"
15,	5"	12,	.020" X .085"

Despite the fact that the Jeweler's Piercing Saw is a very essential tool of the clockmaker, very little mention of it is included in horological literature. If saw questions continue to come in, they just might indicate that a whole column ought to be done on saw piercing. That factor when determining which blade to use is the stock to be sawed for better and easier work; the number of teeth per inch should be such as to have at least two teeth within the thickness of the stock. When sawing out clock hands, the more accurate the saw cut, the less filing and finishing has to be done, thus time is saved by using that blade best adapted to the stock.

WATCH INFORMATION

Tobias history

We've had quite a number of questions about English watches, made by "Tobias" at Liverpool. A good letter from Mr. Thomas Alker, Town Clerk of Liverpool, writes: "An examination of the only available Liverpool directories from 1796 onwards gives the following information concerning the family:

1796 No person by the name of TOBIAS resident in Liverpool.

1810 Miel J. Tobias, watchmaker, 5 Pool Lane.

1811 Same listing.

1811 Samuel Isaac Tobias, Silversmith and Watchmaker, 7 Upper Pitt Street.

1814 Miel Isaac Tobias, Watchmaker, 6 Great George St.

1814 Miel Isaac Tobias & Co., Watchmaker, 29 Lord Street.

1814 Samuel Isaac Tobias, Watchmaker, 8 Upper Pitt Street.

1834 Miel Isaac Tobias, Watch Manufacturer, 11 Great George Square.

1834 Miel Isaac Tobias, Manufactory, Dorans Lane.

1837 George Tobias, Watch Manufacturer, 21 Canning Street (firm of M. I. Tobias).

1837 Miel Isaac Tobias, same as above.

1839 Frederick M. Tobias, Watch Manufacturer, 11 Great George Street (firm of M. I. Tobias).

1839 George and Miel Isaac, as above.

1841 Same as 1839 except for the fact that the firm is described as Myer Isaac Tobias, of 6 Dorans Lane.

1845 The occupants of 11 Great George Square described as Elizabeth and Miriam and then there is no further trace of Miel Isaac.

1845 Other members of the family same as 1839.

1847 Edmund M. Tobias, Watch Manufacturer, 11 Great George Square.

1847 George W. Tobias, Watch Manufacturer, 41 Canning Street (both of the firm of M. I. Tobias of 6 Dorans Lane).

1849 No trace of Frederick M. Tobias.

1849 George Tobias and the firm M. I. Tobias, still at original addresses.

1851 Occupant of 11 Great George Square described as Elizabeth, (no further trace of above Edmund M.).

1857 The firm of M. I. Tobias, moved to 1 Dorans Lane.

1859 The firm of M. I. Tobias, spread to 3 Dorans Lane.

1865 George W. Tobias is described as a merchant living at 41 Canning Street, with a Myer Isaac Tobias, (presumably a son) described as a cotton broker at the same address.

1865 The firm of Myer Isaac Tobias described as merchants of 3 Dorans Lane.

1868 All trace of the firm Myer Isaac Tobias, on Dorans Lane has disappeared and George W. Tobias, is described as Gentleman, living at 41 Canning Street.

"It is obvious from the above that some time between the years 1865 and 1868 the family abandoned the watch manufacturing industry for the more lucrative American cotton trade which was then expanding rapidly here in Liverpool, more so than elsewhere."

"An old firm of clockmakers and jewelers, Messrs. Morath Bros., are at the present time in business opposite my office here in Dale Street. This firm which was established in 1838, whilst having no knowledge of the Tobias family or their watches, are making some inquiries

The Tobias family was very active exporting watches from both Liverpool and London. A great many are to be found in the U. S. A.

WATERBURY WATCH CO.

I have in my possession an American watch which I would like to know more about, such as where it was made, when, etc.

It is a 4-size Addison watch with the enclosed copy of a trademark on the upper plate. The escape wheel has 15 long teeth with 15 short teeth slightly bent upward. The first patent date on the movement shows Feb. 3, 1874 and the last patent date shows March 30, 1886.

I would like to know how to remove the upper balance jewels. The lower balance cap jewel may be adjusted by using a screwdriver—just as if one is to remove or replace the balance wheel in an alarm clock, but the upper balance setting has no slot for a screwdriver to remove the jewels.

Second, how can I tell that the watch is in perfect beat? Or should I say, how can I put it in perfect beat?

Any information that you can give me concerning this movement will be greatly appreciated.

A.

The monogram, "W.W.Co." is for the Waterbury Watch Company. This firm was first Benedict and Burnham and then incorporated as Waterbury Watch Company about 1880. The name was changed to New England Watch Company in 1898. The company failed in 1912 and was bought by Robert H. Ingersoll and Bro.; they failed in 1922, and plant was purchased by Waterbury Clock Co., which became U. S. Time Corporation in 1944.

The name, "Addison" and monogram, "W.W. Co." appeared upon series "K" New England Watch Company movements.

This is the duplex escapement—a French invention, but more favored in England than in France, and went into the largest production in the U.S.A. It is usually credited to Pierre LeRoy in 1750.

If you are not thoroughly familiar with this type of escapement, it may now be in beat. Remember, that like the "detent," the balance receives no impulse on the return stroke; this leads some to think the watch out of beat. The long teeth you refer to are usually called the "locking" teeth (escape-wheel) and the short ones the "impulse" teeth. If you have observed its action closely you should have noted that the long tooth rests (locks) against the body of the staff until the return stroke of the balance is completed; there it drops or passes into a small slot in the staff to be released as the balance wheel makes its forward stroke. At the instant the balance has revolved far enough to allow this locking tooth to escape, the impulse pallet on the balance wheel has been brought into position to be struck by the impulse tooth.

Adjustment of these escapements is rather delicate, and to properly cover it would require the space of several letters. Complete details are given in Higganbotham's "Precision Time Measures" and also in Eric Haswell's "Horology."

ELGIN

Please will you tell me if there is any difference in grade, model, of the 18-size B. W. Raymond, Elgin, and the 18-size Elgin Veritas watch, or are they all the same watch? If they are not the same, which is the best watch? The reason I ask is that I am considering purchasing an old model 18-size, and I want a little more information on this watch. Can you tell me in the series numbers of movement numbers of the 18-size Elgins, when the best were made?

I want a three-quarter plate bridge model, 23-jewel 18S, Elgin, and will be very glad if you can give me this information. I should also like to know which is the best size, the 18-size, the full plate bridge, or the 18-size, three-quarter plate bridge.

A.

Naturally you are going to find that a clockmaker is also a lover of 18-size watches. For all practical purposes, it is my thought that there is practically no difference between the 21-jewel B. W. Raymond and the 23-jewel Veritas. I quote descriptions taken from some Elgin literature of 1926:

"Veritas, O. F. Nickel. Lever setting for railroad service. Pendant winding. Twenty-three ruby and sapphire jewels. Gold setting. Barrel arbor pivots running

11

in jewels. Double roller escapement. Steel escape wheel, Exposed sapphire pallet stones. Compensating balance. Micrometric regulator. Adjusted to temperature, isochronism and five positions. Safety barrel. Patent recoiling click and self-locking setting device.

"B. W. Raymond, O. F. Nickel. Lever setting for railroad service. Pendant winding. Nineteen ruby and sapphire jewels. Double roller escapement. Steel escape wheel. Compensating balance. Micrometric regulator. Adjusted to isochronism, temperature and five positions. Patent recoiling click and self-locking setting device."

From this you can see that the two movements are virtually identical, save the twenty-second and twenty-third jewels. Since the prime purpose of a jeweled bearing is to eliminate friction, and the barrel arbor does not turn as the watch runs (keeps time) their qualities do not enter into its timekeeping. I regret that I cannot supply any data as to series numbers, and for all practical purposes, it would be safe to say either of these movements could be called the best timekeepers Elgin ever built. They did build a few "Father Time" movements that were "free-sprung." I doubt if they were ever in general commercial production; upon checking, I find that one I photographed was serial No. 21,825,070.

OTAY WATCH

Will you send me a synopsis on the Otay watch? I have picked one up and would like to know when the company was in existence, and about what year No. 1074 was made. How many were made altogether? What company made the Plymouth, and when?

A.

The generally accepted dates of operation of the Otay Watch Company are from April 15, 1889 to October 13, 1890. The former date was taken from a letter of Mr. Philip Henry Wheeler written to his family and dated March 25, 1889, in which he said everything was moving forward okay, and the factory would be completed by April 15. Mr. Wheeler had been signed on February 25, 1889 as general superintendent.

The late Major Paul Chamberlain (who showed this writer the first Otay I ever saw) probably devoted more time and study to the Otay story than any other man; besides contacting every known source, he actually visited the site of the factory, which is just five miles south of National City, California in San Diego County.

Of the serial numbering, he says, "If the Otay serial numbers between the lowest and highest were all made, the production would have been something over 29,000, a most creditable performance—personally I have seen or known of about twenty examples numbered between 1,208 and 1,340 and between 30,110 and 30,637."

If those numbers were followed consistently, there would have been 132 movements in the first group and 527 in the latter, a grand total of 659 watches. However, to date I know of no writer willing to stick his neck out far enough to pin the entire production down to the 659 figure.

A newspaper advertisement of August, 1888, stated that the capacity of the factory was to be 250 movements per day. Taking April 15, 1889 as the starting day, April 15, 1890 would be 365 days, and another 103 days would bring you to the closing date, October 13, 1890, or a total of 468 days. Allowing for some 67 Sundays, Otay must have operated about 400 days. Certainly they never reached that goal of 250-per-day.

The Chamberlain Memorial Collection contained movement No. 30,500, a P.H. Wheeler model, full-plate, 18-size, 15 jewels, with the Wheeler patented whiplash regulator. Dr. Karl Vogel, collector of New York City, has in his collection a similar movement, serial No. 1,419 (note that this is beyond the range mentioned by Major Chamberlain) and marked, "F.A. Kimball."

The Otay machinery was sold to a new firm organized to build watches, loaded upon a vessel in San Diego harbor and shipped to Alviso, California. The new firm was the San Jose Watch Company. Chamberlain says, "There is nothing to indicate that any watches were made at Alviso. Some of the Otay parts may have been assembled there, but none of the movements bear the name of the new company."

The San Jose Watch Company was incorporated May 8, 1891, and was as short-lived as the Otay. A Japanese syndicate bought the machinery, shipping it to Osaka, Japan. Movements made there were marked "Osaka Watch Co., Osaka, Japan."

Horology magazine, July, 1934 issue, carried a story from the San Diego Tribune titled, "Old Otay Factory Watch Going to Ford Museum." We quote a portion of that story:

"The watch is one of only six of its kind ever made, a make once designated by the late President Diaz as 'the official recognized railroad watch in Mexico.' It was acquired from Dale Smith, city clerk at National City, once an employee of the factory, by Jack Wooley, Long Beach general representative of the Ford Motor Company. In 1890 the factory produced the 'Overland Mail' movement, a 15-jeweled mechanism priced at $18 for the works only, but financial troubles overtook the factory and it was closed October 13, 1890, after only six 'Overland Mails' had been produced."

Mr. P. H. Wheeler was born at Sharon, Vermont, June 12, 1849, and died April 17, 1917 at Inglewood, California. He was described as a man of military bearing, about 6 feet tall, with brown hair, grey eyes, and weighing 200 pounds. He was possibly connected with more new watch factories than any other one man—he even went with the Otay machinery to Japan. A large volume could be written about his activities—it would be most interesting and would contain accounts of such factories as the Marion Watch Company, Springfield Watch Company, Columbus Watch Company, Rockford Watch Company, Otay, San Jose, Osaka, and others. His full life story has never been compiled. It awaits the pen and energies of some ambitious writer.

DEMAGNETIZING

We seem to have trouble demagnetizing watches, as our small demagnetizer does not seem to be able to free them.

What would you advise using for this work?

A.

Now that's just one more reason for being a clockmaker—one doesn't have to worry about demagnetizing.

Personally, we are using an old demagnetizer, a South Bend, I believe, of the early 1920s. These seem to be a little heavier than some of the late models. However, your difficulty can arise from improper operation as well as from a machine that doesn't work so well.

It is awfully easy to let go on the contact switch a little too early, i.e., before the watch being demagnetized is out of range, and it's just as easy to press it a bit early when inserting the watch.

The demagnetizing operation is one that must be watched closely. Be sure to have the watch centered within the magnetic field (in the center of the coil) before turning on the current. Don't jerk it—just withdraw it by a steady and continuous motion—bring it away straight; that is, in line with the coil opening and continue to the full arm's length before turning off the current.

Usually one well and completely carried operation, as above indicated, will remove all magnetism; however, it is always well to test the watch again the next morning when winding the rack.

If after 24 hours the watch shows traces of magnetism, repeat the operation and chances are no magnetism will be noted on the second morning. I've heard it said that a watch can be so heavily magnetized that it would have to be taken down and demagnetized, one piece at a time, but I have never had to resort to any such method.

Should you continue to have trouble, try another machine. This will quickly demonstrate whether it's the way it's operated, or the machine itself.

DANIEL QUARE

Having bought a watch at an antique sale, I would like to find out as much as I can about it. The watch is marked "D Quare London." No. 4177 fusee movement chain drive, double flag balance wheel. The movement is pinned and is in a double silver case. Enclosed is sketch of case marks.

A.

Daniel Quare, London (1649-1724) ranks among the most celebrated English makers of watches and clocks. If you have acquired one of his genuine pieces you now own a very fine watch.

It is rather difficult to compare your sketches which you sent with the hallmarks; the year mark which you say may be G or B most nearly resembles the G for 1762. This outdates the original D. Quare by some 38 years—we could be in error about the mark, and the movement could have been re-cased. Baillie says that the numbers on watches signed by Quare are known from 233 to 4989—here your number 4177 fits.

In 1707 Quare took an apprentice named Daniel, and evidently his Christian name must have been Quare too. There is that outside possibility that your piece could have been made by this second Quare and in 1762. It was only the "great" of the watchmakers who were imitated and there is also the possibility that the piece is pure forgery.

To actually determine, within reason, whether or not a piece is by the "master" always requires a close first hand examination and comparison, taking all the angles into account. First, I'd suggest that you get three or four good photos made, preferably by a good commercial photographer who with his equipment can give you "contact" (not enlargements) prints twice actual size. One view should be of the hallmarks, another of the back plate and signature, and one under-dial shot.

PERSONAL MAGNETISM

I am situated in a community where until we opened our store, the people had to mail their repair work out. The idea that some people cannot wear a watch because they have too much electricity in their bodies is widespread. It is, to my surprise, still advocated by some watchmakers in nearby towns. Can you suggest what might be the best argument to squelch this belief by my customers?

I have had some people testify that they are not successful in getting a watch to run properly until they buy a leather strap that goes under the watch. Is there any merit to this belief, and if so, why might it be true?

A.

This is an old one, and I'm sorry to have to admit that it is still being perpetuated right down into this atomic age. Ignorance or incompetence, sometimes a combination of the two, keep it alive. At the bottom of it is a simple play on words. "Personal magnetism" is a well-known phrase or term, and generally accepted by everyone without stopping to realize that it is not mechanical magnetism.

The word "magnetism" is used in a descriptive sense merely to indicate that someone has such a nature or disposition so as to attract others to him as a magnet attracts. Had it been made "personal attraction" instead of "personal magnetism," possibly these jokers would not have been able to keep the hoax alive so long.

Just before Christmas a friend came to me and said a watchmaker had told his wife the reason her watch would not run was because she had too much magnetism. We did our best to make a reasonable explanation (like above) and asked him for a bit of cooperation. This watchmaker had plainly fallen down on the job and was using the old magnetism hoax as an out. In view of the fact that he contended the watch was in order and that its failure to run was solely due to his wife's magnetism, we suggested that she have her sister and friends try it. Needless to say, after five tries on five separate people, the piece failed to tick more than a few minutes. The watch was a high grade one by one of our largest manufacturers and barely a year old. We then took it to a very good and careful man, had him pull it down and make an examination on the spot. He could not and did not find anything he could criticize. The watch was clean, well oiled (not too much or too little), there were no fingerprints, no burred screws or other tell-tale marks of the incompetent workman or botch.

We left and within an hour this last watchmaker phoned to say he had located the trouble when he started to reassemble it. The escape wheel was slightly loose on its arbor. It was delivered two days later with a nominal charge and on last check was running quite satisfactorily.

It's my guess the first mechanic may have honestly tried, leastways he turned out a good cleaning job. He could have carried it to another watchmaker for help, or he could have given it back to the customer with no charge, but he did neither—he delivered it and collected. I seriously doubt if he actually timed it or got any run on his repair-rack.

Any time they come up with a person who can't go near a surveyor's transit without deflecting its needle or can't get near a radio or television set without disturbing it, or whose car spark plugs won't fire as soon as he hits the driver's spot, then I'll begin to believe the magnetism hokum. There is absolutely no virtue, insofar as the mechanical action of a watch is affected, in placing leather or any other substance between the case and the wearer's arm. You (and all of us) have had customers come in with weird tales about timepieces (watches or clocks) with which certain incidents have taken place, and they deduce immediately that is what stopped the piece from running. It doesn't automatically follow that their deduction is correct or even mechanical. Remember the timepiece is mechanical. Investigate carefully some of these stories with that in mind, do a bit of logical reasoning on it and you will come up with quite a different answer.

History of Aurora Watch Co.

I have a nice 18S Aurora watch and I would like to know the history of it. The only engraving is "Aurora Watch Company, Aurora, Illinois," safety pinion, 15-jewel, serial number 131501.

The case was made by the Dueber Watch Case Manufacturing Company; 14k special gold-filled case. I would appreciate all the information you could give me.

A.

The Aurora Watch Company, Inc., Aurora, Illinois, 1883, began making watches in 1885, but failed a year or so later and the machinery was sold to the Hamilton Watch Company in 1892. We note that the serial number of your movement is 131501 and regret that we cannot give you the exact code which was used. I'm pretty sure the company never produced that many pieces, since their maximum production is generally conceded to have been about 100 a day. Check right under the balance cock for another number. This is said to be the true number.

Charles S. Crossman (1856-1930) began a series of articles in the summer of 1886 in one of the trade journals under the title of, "A Complete History of Watch and Clockmaking in the U. S.," and we quote here his article on the Aurora factory: "The conception of the Aurora Watch Company seems to have been with Mr. Wendell of the firm of Charles Wendell and Sons, doing business on State Street, Chicago. The organization of the company took place July, 1883, with a nominal capital of $250,000.00 in shares of $100.00 each payable in small monthly installments. The scheme was to interest one dealer in each town or city to the extent of making him a stockholder in the company and in turn give him the exclusive agency for the sale of the company's movements in his town or city.

"This appeared very plausible, for if enough dealers could be interested in the scheme, the company would have a guaranteed outlet for its production. The officers were Messrs. E. W. Trask of Aurora, president; Albert H. Pike of Kankakee, vice-president; Maurice Wendell of Quincy, treasurer and business manager. The directors were Messrs. M. Huffman of Quincy, E. W. Trask, Maurice Wendell, George F. Johnson and A. H. Pike. The scheme appeared auspicious and a considerable amount of stock was subscribed for in a short time.

"The city gave the company a plot of ground located in the southern part on which ground was broken immediately for a factory building. The machine shop was completed and occupied in September following when work was commenced on tools by a few men under Mr. Johnson as superintendent. The main building was commenced on September 1, 1883, and finished and occupied February 1, 1884. It was three stories and basement and is well suited for the purpose for which it is built.

"George F. Johnson, who is a practical man and one of the directors of the company, was appointed superintendent and commenced making parts of watches as soon as they were located in their factory. The movement is a regular 18S, full plate, of several grades in both nickel and gilt. They have a patent stem winding attachment made by Mr. Johnson. The first movements were put on the market in the fall of 1884 and were readily purchased by the stockholder dealers.

"Mr. Wendell afterwards severed his connection with the company and they then adopted the policy of selling their goods in open market, which plan if we may be allowed to pass an opinion, has made the company far more of a success than it would have been under the old plan. The company has usually employed 200 operatives, turning out about 150 watches per day. The greater part of them are low and medium priced grades.

"The officers of the company have changed somewhat, but for the most part remain the same as when first organized. They are at present as follows: Mr. Huffman, president; A. Somarindyck, treasurer; E. W. Trask, secretary; J. H. Webber, general manager; George F. Johnson, superintendent. They are all, with the exception of Mr. Johnson (who is a mechanical man), solid businessmen and all reside in Aurora, except Mr. Huffman, who is a leading jeweler of Quincy, and the success of the company may be said to be an assured fact."

This rosy outlook did not last very long, for I find in the American Jeweler for April, 1886: "At a meeting of the directors of the watch factory (Aurora)

lately, it was decided to lay off all hands except those in the finishing department. This department is behind the others in their work and it is expected that this will even up the work. Business stagnation,

George F. Johnson (Aurora)

caused by numerous strikes, has not tended to help the business of the company for several weeks past."

In the September issue we see a line stating: "The Aurora Watch factory now employs about 90 hands." Again we find Aurora mentioned in the April, 1889, issue: "There are 310 on the payroll of the Aurora factory. Two years ago the Aurora factory was making 20 movements a day; now, the number is six times that."

George F. Johnson (born January 26, 1851, died March 16, 1931) mentioned in the Crossman article as the mechanical man (and superintendent) had worked at the Rockford Watch Company before going with Aurora. After Aurora, he was a timepiece manufacturer (Waltham was first) in the U. S. for determining correct time and was the first to broadcast time by wireless for a watch factory.

He designed and built the telescope in the Illinois shops as well as supervising much of the electrical work in connection with the establishing of their broadcasting station—it was "9ZS." He was well known in most scientific circles, author of a number of articles and will be the subject of one of our "Stray Bits" articles toward the latter part of 1955.

George Prior watch history

The watch was made in England and is a key wind which has a chain that winds up on the mainspring barrel.

On the dial it has the name "George Prior" and at the bottom of the dial, "London." On the train wheel bridge the name "George Prior" appears again and a serial number which is 15569. The movement is encased in three separate cases.

A.

George Prior was a watchmaker of considerable note, having received two awards from the Society of Arts. He came of a watchmaking family. His grandfather, William Prior, and his father, John Prior, were watchmakers at Nessfield, a village about 15 miles northwest of Leeds, where George was born in 1782.

He moved to London in 1822, and died in 1830. Since your piece is London marked, it must have been made within that eight-year period. If we had a sketch or pencil rubbing of the hallmarks in the case, we might give you the exact year.

He made many watches for export to Turkey and this probably accounts for the three cases—seems that was popular in that country. Examples of his three-case watches are to be found in the Science Museum, South Kensington, the Victoria and Albert Museum, South Kensington, and the Metropolitan Museum of Art, New York City.

Old Home and Elgin watches

I have two key-wind watches and I would like to know approximately how old they are. One of them was made by the Home Watch Company, Boston, Massachusetts, and the serial number is 737873.

The other watch is an Elgin, serial number 733720. If you can give me any information on these watches, I will be very happy as I haven't been able to find much here.

A. Brooks Palmer records that the Home Watch Company was used by the American Watch Company of Waltham, and that number 5190283 was made about 1868. Now we have no further clue to their numbering and how much later number 737873 was made is anybody's guess.

Elgin made watch number 700,000 about 1880 and number 800,000 about 1881, thus your number 733,720 must have come out between those dates.

Fogg Patent Waltham Watch

My customer bought an 18-size Waltham watch, Fogg's patent, movement 426425, full-plate, double case 101016, with key wind. On the dial is "American Watch Co." Please, if possible, give me the age of the watch.

A.

The Waltham factory operated under the name The American Watch Company, from 1859 to 1885. An accepted listing of approximately how their serial numbers ran, says that 178,200 to 427,600 was used from 1865 to 1870. Your No. 426,425 must have come through in the latter half of 1869.

Mr. Charles W. Fogg was one of the leading mechanics at Waltham when they absorbed the Nashua Company. He was sent to Nashua to superintend the work there until another addition could be built at Waltham. Later, when the Nashua machinery was moved into this new addition, it was known as the Nashua department, and he continued to be superintendent over it.

Mr. Fogg was granted Patent No. 41,461 on February 2, 1864, covering a new type of regulator. This patent was assigned to the American Watch Company. The regulator had a pivoted lever with its bearings back near the base step of the balance cock. It vibrated between two adjustable points located where you now find the hairspring stud attached. He pinned his hairspring to the loose end of this lever and in operation, it worked between these stops very much as today's hairspring does between the regulator pins.

History of L'Epine Watch

A customer of mine would like some information as to the age of an old French watch that was carried by his great-grandfather while a member of the Prussian army in the 60's or 70's.

This watch has no movement markings whatever, except inlaid in the porcelain dial is the name "L'Epine, A Paris." It has solid or full plates, is chain driven, no jewels, and the balance wheel is about two-thirds the size of the upper plate. The balance bridge is hand-carved. In fact, the watch is hand made and key wound. with double case. The movement is about 16 lignes.

Any information you can furnish me from this meager description would certainly be appreciated.

A.

Jean Antoine L'Epine, Paris b-1720, d-1814, was a watchmaker of great ability and fame. About 1760 he introduced the "L'Epine caliber" in which separate bars or bridges were used instead of a one-piece top plate. He was the first to use a mainspring barrel supported at only one end and was probably the pioneer maker of thin watches.

L'Epine married Andre Charles Caron's daughter in 1756 and worked as "Caron et Lepine" until 1769. His father-in-law was a renowned mechanic and watchmaker to Louis XV. His brother-in-law, Peter Auguste Caron, whom we also know as Beaumarchais, maker of the small ring watch, bezel-wound for Madame Pompadour, was also the author of "Le Barbier de Seville" and "Le Mariage de Figaro" and watchmaker to the king.

L'Epine invented the virgule escapement about 1766. In 1783 he left his business to his son-in-law, Claude Pierre Raguet. It was continued under the L'Epine name, sold to J. B. Chaput in 1810, to Deschamp in 1827 and again to Fabre in 1832. It continued under the L'Epine name down to about 1916.

So much for the history of the name.

Pin-pointing your actual watch is another thing. Assuming the Jean went to work on his own at the age of 21, would make it 1741. Then to 1916 gives us a period of about 175 years in which "L'Epine, A Paris" appeared on watches. From your general description it must be an "oldie." One would have to judge from its construction, etc., as to the probable date, after making a close examination of the movement.

Data on Non-Magnetic Watch Co. of America

Recently I received a watch movement in an assortment that was new to me, and I wonder if you can supply some information about it and the company that made it. It is a 16 size, 17 jewel; marked Non-magnetic Watch Company of America, Paillards Patented Balance and Spring. No city is mentioned.

A.

An accurate answer on your watch is difficult, for the simple reason that the record of itself is confusing.

The Non-Magnetic Watch Co. of America was a sales organization rather than a manufacturer of watches. Thus, watches so marked were "contract" watches.

As early as 1884 "Palladium Balance Springs," inoxidizable, non-magnetic, made by C. A. Paillard of Geneva, Switzerland were being advertised in the British Horological Journal.

On page 215 of The American Jeweler for November, 1887, in the column "Trade Notes" we find what we believe is the first reference to your company, in this paragraph: "Our readers' attention is called to the advertisement of the Non-Magnetic Watch Co. goods in this issue. These goods are staple, but will prove especially appropriate as holiday gifts and we advise our readers to carry them in stock, as they are a novelty and will meet with a ready sale."

This was a full page ad—all wording, no cuts, headed in large letters "worth reading," containing a letter from

Ball Jewelry Store, 233 Superior St., Cleveland, Ohio, dated October 5, 1887: "Geneva Non-Magnetic Watch Co., 177 Broadway, New York. Gentlemen: The three non-magnetic movements came to hand this morning. I immediately took two of them out to the Brush Electric Co.'s factory where we subjected them to the severest test possible by placing them on the largest and most powerful dynamo machine made in the world. They were not affected a particle, and Mr. N. B. Possons, superintendent of the factory, pronounced them a perfect non-magnetic watch. One of the movements I had in an open-face gold case and the other was taken out of the box and handled without any covering whatsoever, and we were unable to detect a particle of variation in the motion of the balance. They are certainly the coming watch and I predict for them a grand future. Very Respectfully, (S) Webb C. Ball.

"These movements contain Paillard's patent non-magnetic compensation balance and hairspring, which are adjusted to temperature and are absolutely exempt from magnetic influences. For sale by all First Class Jobbers, Geneva Non-Magnetic Watch Co. (limited), 177 and 179 Broadway, New York."

In the following issue of The American Jeweler (December, 1887) we find the full page ad reproduced below. Note that no firm name is appended to this ad, yet the movement illustrated is plainly marked "Geneva Non-Magnetic Watch Co., Ltd., New York." Then in the next issue (January, 1888) we locate this full page announcement:

"Important To Watch Dealers. The Non-Magnetic Watch Company of America, organized under the laws of the state of New York (Capital $500,000.00) begs to announce that they have purchased the American business of The Geneva Non-Magnetic Watch Co., Ltd., and the exclusive right to use Paillard's Patent Non-Magnetic Compensation Balance and Hairspring for the United States and Canada.

"On or about Feb. 1, we will put on the market a full and complete line of 16-s., 3/4-plate stemwinding watch movements; nickel and gilt, hunting and open-

For Sale by Leading Jobbers.

face, in medium and low grades.

"These watches will be full jeweled, with Patent regulator and Safety Center Pinion. They will contain Paillard's Patent Non - Magnetic, Non - Oxidizable Compensation Balance and Breguet Hairspring; full non-magnetic escapement; will be accurately adjusted to temperature will be accurately adjusted to temperature, isochronism and positions, and will be unsurpassed for durability, workmanship and accuracy of performance.

"These watches will not stop or be in any way affected by magnetism, even when in actual contact with dynamos and powerful electro-magnets, and will be the best watches for the money ever placed on the American market. Every watch warranted and prices guaranteed.

"To be followed by a complete line of 18-s. full plate movements as soon as practicable. Very Respectfully, Non-Magnetic Watch Co., 177 and 179 Broadway, New York, January 5, 1888."

A check through the index to advertisers" of the Keystone for 1904, '05 and '06 shows no ads by this firm.

19

E. Harrison Watch

I wish to describe a silver, double-cased, key winding, fusee, chain-drive watch which I recently acquired. The movement is about 30 mm. in diameter with full plates. There is a verge escapement. The balance wheel is solid and is about 15 mm. in diameter. The balance wheel is back of the lower plate and the balance bridge is elaborately filigreed. On the lower plate there is engraved the following words: "E. Harrison, Warrington, 66." The dial is porcelain and the hands are gold.

The outer case has four hallmarks stamped inside. One is the profile of an entire lion. One is a full face view of a crowned head. One is an elliptical border surrounding initials which appear to be "C. W.," although the "C" is indistinct. The fourth is a shield with a device resembling a capital D. with a short "tail" projecting to the left from the vertical stroke of the D.

The inside case has six hallmarks. One is a rectangle with "W. H." inscribed within. One is the profile of a head and shoulders of a man. One is the profile of a lion exactly as stamped on the outer case. The other three marks are not distinct enough to describe accurately, although I am sure an expert could recognize them.

From this description, can you tell me something of the age of the watch and the life of its maker?

A.

It is most difficult to correctly identify hallmarks from a description. I would hazard a guess that the hallmarks in the outer case of your silver watch have the following meanings: 1. The lion indicates sterling silver quality. 2. The sovereign's head indicated that the duty had been paid. 3. The "C. W." are the maker's initials (case-maker). 4. The capital D on a shield is the date mark . . . a capital D was used for the year 1799. I have no explanation for the "tail" to the left of the D you refer to, unless it was a defect in the stamp.

Baillie lists an Edward Harrison at Warrington from 1770 to about 1795. These dates could easily be extended to 1799. Warrington was a town 15 miles east of Liverpool.

Stevens Watch

It is in a 14K hunting case, case serial No. 22912, Solidarity case. It is a 15-jewel movement; hand engraved on the plate is "J. P. Stevens & Bro., Atlanta, Ga." Movement serial number is 21196. It has a white enamel dial, Roman numerals, with "J. P. Stevens & Bro.. Atlanta, Ga." in black letters. It can be wound by key or crown, and has a slide-lever setting mechanism on the dial side of the case.

A.

Mr. J. P. Stevens was born on his father's plantation near Savannah, Georgia, March 23, 1852. At 20, he went to work in the largest jewelry store in Atlanta, Georgia. In 1882, when Mr. Ezra Bowman decided to discontinue the manufacture of watches at Lancaster, Pa., Mr. Stevens went to Lancaster and purchased the machinery and at the same time recruited 11 workmen for the factory he was going to establish in Atlanta. He soon found the Bowman machinery insufficient for the operation as he had planned it and purchased additional equipment from the John Stark Tool Co. at Waltham, Massachusetts.

In the spring of 1885, Mr. Stevens decided to abandon the manufacture of watches and the equipment was sold to Northern interests. On November 1, 1885, he notified his business associates that he wished to withdraw from the firm.

Jurgensen history

In my collection of fine movements, I have a few Jurgensens, among these are two key winders, 19½ ligne, 21 jewel, numbered Mt No. 6637 and Mt No. 6703.

Could you tell me if these are Danish or Swiss manufactured? I also have a beautiful 17 jewel, 20 ligne, key wind, Jules Urban, Neuchatel, just as beautiful as the Jurgensen's Mt No. 7170, which is similar in appearance.

Was there a family or manufacturing connection between Jules Jurgensen and Jules Urban? By movement numbers is there a general dividing line for Jurgensen Danish or Swiss manufacture?

I also have a 20 ligne, American Watch Company, Appleton, Tracey & Company, Waltham, Massachusetts, key wind, No. 36,207, and an Elgin, 18 size, B. W. Raymond, No. 4037, and an old E. Howard & Company, 18 size, No. 802.

A.

Your watch questions are a little difficult for this clockmaker, and it is further confused by your mention of Jules Urban, for we do not find a single Urban listed. However, I do know that you have some very fine examples of watch construction.

The connection between the Copenhagen and the Switzerland operation was so very close, it is practically impossible to absolutely distinguish between those pieces that are of Danish origin and those of Swiss origin. Major Chamberlain records that Jorgen Jorgensen and Isaac Larpent formed partnership and established a watch factory at Roeskelde. (27 miles from Copenhagen) where they produced about 1,500 watches. Later in his narative, the Major says: "Many cylinder watches bearing the name are to be found (carrying high numbers) which seem to have been made in Switzerland." Now, if we accept the theory that the high numbered pieces were made in Switzerland, it becomes a question of whether or not the six and seven thousands are to be considered high. They are certainly much higher than the 1,500 credited to Larpent & Jorgensen.

Probably the most famous of the Jurgensen family was Urban Brunn Jurgensen, born in 1776 and died 1830. The founder of this watchmaking family was Jorgen Jorgensen. It was Urban Brunn Jurgensen who changed the spelling from Jorgensen to Jurgensen. Jorgen was born in 1748, died 1811, married Anna Leith Brunn, daughter of Urban Brunn; thus Urban Brunn Jurgensen, their first child, was named for his mother's father.

Urban Brunn Jurgensen was exceptionally well trained in horology. At 15 he was placed in his father's shop, and after five years training, he was sent to Le Locle, Switzerland, to the shop of Frederic Houriet, where his father had received a part of his own training. After that, Urban moved on to Paris, and the shops of Berthoud and Breguet, thence to London, before returning to Le Locle to marry Sophie Henriette Houriet, daughter of his old instructor.

He arrived in 1801 in Copenhagen with his bride and went to work with his father. His first apprentice was his brother, Frederic (born 1785). A daughter was born to Urban and Sophie in 1803, but died two years later. A son was born in 1805, George Frederic, but lived only one year. While the third child, Louis Urban, was quite small, Urban and Sophie returned to LeLocle. There on July 27, 1808, another son, Jules Frederic Jurgensen was born.

This Jurgensen family returned to Copenhagen in November of 1809, bringing with them many tools, the "secret art of piercing jewels," and nine workmen. Jorgen died in 1811, and Urban brought his brother Fritz back from Geneva, Switzerland, to take charge of his father's establishment. They lost another daughter in 1813, another in 1817, and a son in 1822. Urban was bowed with grief and his health failed. In the early part of 1830, he wrote his autobiography and died May 14, not quite 54 years old. It is recorded that he repaired 160 chronometers, made 43 chronometers, and six astronomical regulators between 1819 and 1829.

He was a prolific writer, contributing to the Danish Societe Royale des Sciences and several journals. His two largest works were: "Principes Generaux de L'exacte Measure du Temps," 225 pages with 19 plates, published at Copenhagen in 1805, and "Memories sur l'Horlogerie Exacte, 1. Remarque sur l'Horlogerie Exacte et Proposition d'un Echappement Libre a Double Roue. 2. Del'Isochronisme des Vibrations du Pendule."

From this brief sketch, you can see that all the Jurgensens were Swiss trained, used Swiss tools, and employed Swiss workmen. Also that there was much travel between Copenhagen, Geneva, and Le Locle. So far as I know, no writer has ever listed any system of numbering, or any other method of distinguishing between Danish and Swiss movements.

Shortly after his father's death in 1830, Jules Jurgensen moved to Le Locle, (probably between 1832 and 1834) to establish the great business that bore his name. This is the Jurgensen so well known in the U.S.A., since we see many pieces from this firm. Jules died in 1877, but the house was carried on by his sons, Jules (1837-1894) and Jacques Alfred (1842-1912). It is now, we believe, the firm, Ed Heuer & Co., S.A. Bienne, Switzerland.

Your Appleton & Tracy, No. 36,207, was made about 1860. The Elgin No. 4037, about eight years later. The Howard must be the oldest of these three. We have no record of the Howard numbering below 20,000. They started with this number about 1859. The first Howard factory was at Roxbury about 1850, the second at Waltham in 1857. Though you may see some Howards marked Boston, the factory was at Waltham and the office was at Boston.

TRENTON WATCH CO.

I am most anxious to know how old a watch is that I now have in my possession. The only information I can supply you with is as follows:

The watch is a very old antique lever-set, approximately 18 size. The number on the movement is 455981, the case number is 389429, and the name on the dial is Trenton Watch Company. The Silverode case is very large and heavy. Attached to this same sheet are several pencil rubbings of the hallmark in the case.

A.

First of all, the pencil rubbing shows the trademark of the Philadelphia Watch Case Company, and is not a British hallmark. All that can be determined from it is the person who made it and the material from which it was made. "Silverode" was a trade name of their own for their nickel-silver cases.

This factory was first organized as the New Haven Watch Company by some New York City interests. It is presumed that they located in New Haven, to be near other eastern watch factories, on the 16th day of October, 1883. The capital stock was $100,000 and Mr. Aaron Carter of Carter, Sloan and Company, manufacturing jewelers of New York City, was elected president.

They started to make a regular 18 size, lever movement, and by the time that about one thousand of these had been completed, all the original capital had been absorbed and it became necessary to look about for a location where additional funds could be raised. The New Haven residents evidently did not become very interested in the project. Mr. J. Hart Brewer, a director in the corporation from Trenton, New Jersey, thought he saw the opportunity of doing something for Trenton, and suggested a move there. Through Mr. Brewer's efforts the capital was raised to $250,000 early in 1886 and three acres of land was purchased near the P. R. R. depot in Chambersburg, a suburb of Trenton, and a building was completed by December and they started moving in the machinery from New Haven.

In an article written by Mr. Charles Crossman sometime between the removal to Trenton and 1888, he said: "The capital has been increased to $300,000 and the present output exceeds 150 per day with a steady gain. They have 160 employees and the watches sell to the trade at $3.75 each and are sold direct to the retail trade by the company. Mr. J. Hart Brewer has succeeded Mr. Carter as president, and Mr.

George R. Whitaker has succeeded Mr. W. F. Van Camp as treasurer. The present Board of Directors is composed of J. Hart Brewer, Samuel K. Wilson, Lawrence Ferrell, General W. S. Stoyker, William Roberts and John Moses of Trenton and Theo. W. Burger of New York." Mr. Brooks Palmer records that they failed in 1886. Therefore your watch must have been made between 1884 and 1886.

How old is this Peoria watch?

I am writing you concerning a watch I own. It is an 18-S Peoria, Ill., watch, 15 jewels, Adj. grade, with coin silver case, double back with inner back marked, anti-magnetic shield, and movement has an anti-magnetic hairspring. The serial number is 21009.

A.

The Peoria Watch Co., opened in May of 1885, on Fredonia Avenue between Bradley and Malvern streets. Its doors were closed sometime in 1891. There is no way for us to tell from your serial number just where within this five-year period the watch was actually made.

This company was incorporated Dec. 19, 1885; E. D. Howard, president; Eustace H. Smith, vice president; William Smith, treasurer; J. F. Hoke, secretary; and C. M. Howard, manager. Directors were E. D. Howard, C. M. Howard, E. H. Smith, J. C. Woelfle, H. P. Smith, G. P. Benezat, and J. F. Hoke.

Writing of the Peoria Watch Company, in 1888 Mr. Henry G. Abbott said: "The company employs about 90 hands and the product is about 30 movements per day. These movements are all nameless and are known as Grade A, No. 1, Special, Grade C, Grade D, Grade A&K, and Nos. 1 to 6, inclusive. They are all 18 size, 15 jeweled, quick train."

In 1888 E. H. Smith was president, W. H. Smith, treasurer; W. W. Hammond, secretary; J. B. Greenhut, vice president; and Clarence M. Howard, manager. Ferd F. Ide was plant manager and his foremen were: T. M. Youngglove, jeweling; W. Earler, damaskeening; F. A. Hordon, gilding; J. Frazier, engraving; J. H. Burns,

train room; F. S. Wenk, balances; W. H. Murray, flat steel, escapement and screen; M. Clapp, adjusting, and J. B. Wormwood, machine shop.

To go back of "Peoria" the Howard brothers, E. D. and C. M., had purchased considerable watchmaking machinery from the assignees of several defunct watch factories, principally the Cornell factory at Grand Crossing, Ill., and the United States Watch Factory at Marion, N. J. In April of 1880 they organized the Independent Watch Company of Fredonia, N. Y., and started a factory with this machinery. Much time was spent finishing up old watch material. They underwent a sort of reorganization and with it brought out a new movement in the summer of 1883.

By the summer of 1885 this last effort had floundered and Mr. J. C. Adams (of Chicago, who had a hand in organizing Elgin) went to Peoria with a view to interesting citizens of that city in building a watch factory. In the fall a delegation of interested capitalists enthused by Mr. Adams' arguments went to Fredonia to inspect the factory there. A little later they bought the Fredonia plant for $150,000. A portion of the payment was stock in the new Peoria factory. We find the two Howards and W. H. Smith from the old Board of Directors at Fredonia, upon the new Board at Peoria.

In all likelihood, Mr. Abbott's figure of 30 movements per day in the fall of 1888 is the very top. Chances are that they did not exceed half that for the entire period, but for the sake of a rough look, let's speculate that they operated five years or about 1,500 working days. At 15 movements per day that would only be 22,500 movements, but we do not know where they began . . . one, 100, or 1,000. It would look as if your No. 21,009 must have come along towards their close.

John Moncas was a watchmaker

What can you tell me about an old watch I have? It is a key wind, fusee drive, right angle escapement, marked "John Moncas, Liverpool," bearing the number 2842. The case is silver and has a poorly defined mark: TE over HF, surrounded by several figures and the letter "D."

A.

John Francis Moncas, Liverpool, was active around 1820. This is as near as we can accurately date him.

Many Liverpool watches we see today are labeled with the name of the "merchant-seller." Apparently you have one under the name of the real maker, and G. H. Baillie certainly thought so or he would not have listed him. A watch by Moncas is in the famous Ilbert Collection.

Every maker had his own system of numbering — apparently used whatever method happened to strike his fancy. These have not been recorded except in rare instances of a few of the very top men like Breguet and Frodsham; therefore, your number 2842 has no meaning beyond being "the serial number."

What is a "Watchmaker's Watch?"

As an admirer of fine precision craftsmanship and accuracy, I have long been looking for a watchmaker's watch. The kind of watch that one could show to friends with pride, point out its finely made and adjusted movement (through a glass back) and feel that its timekeeping ability was of the highest order.

The Bunn Special model of the Illinois Watch Co. and the Hamilton Navigational Master watch have often been suggested as filling the above requirements.

I would appreciate your comments on these two watches specifically as well as your thoughts about other watches you feel may qualify and the reasons for your selections.

A.

You pose a difficult question—the term you use a "watchmaker's watch" could and does cover quite a bit of territory. Both the Bunn Special and the Hamilton Navigational you mention are fine pieces.

Shortly after World War I, Gruen brought out a special watch, I believe it was known as the "Pentagon" model. This was a specially adjusted, premium priced watch for presentations. Waltham Watch Co., about the same time or possibly a few years earlier produced a special movement and named it their "Maximus" model.

It has been my experience that a watch for "show" purposes, glass back so that the movement can be seen, etc., has to have some special features over and above superb top workmanship if you wish to impress your friends, laymen or watchmakers. In other words just keeping time does not seem to be enough.

I seriously doubt if there has even been a watchmaker (one who loves horology) that has not had the same basic idea expressed in your letter. Some go for minute repeaters, some for split-second timers, etc. At the risk of being personal I'm going to give you my own idea of such a watch; I've always wanted a well built tourbillon with detent escapement.

Both the detent escapement and the tourbillon carriage have certain draw-backs when it comes to hard everyday use. In all likelihood, your Bunn or Maximus would equal it for time keeping. Upon the other hand, the basic principle of the tourbillon action is something that excites watchmakers and laymen alike, and as for a conversation piece, it really makes it. Many watchmakers have never seen one and still fewer really understand them. For sheer workmanship, I know of nothing that exhibits it better than a well proportioned, "spidery" tourbillon carriage, correctly balanced once per minute in its jeweled bearings.

Unfortunately we live in an age that places a very light value upon correct time keeping. Its respect for a precision instrument capable of keeping time is rapidly approaching nil. For years I maintained a marine chronometer, checked daily against WWV by short wave radio, prominently displayed for the benefit of the public. Only a few (very few) old-timers would set by it. Most of the youngsters preferred to set by an electric, powered by a two-bit sync. motor. Some young squirts would actually put up an argument. Rather than expend time and effort defending the chronometer I just took it out and home, where I maintain it for my own satisfaction.

Lancaster Company was forerunner of Hamilton

A customer of ours would like to know the age of a New Era 185 watch, Serial No. 3465230, case No. 701272, case is hunting with double back with an arm and hammer in a diamond shape frame.

Perhaps you can give a little history of the company which would be appreciated very much.

A.

Your customer's watch was made by the Lancaster Watch Co., about 1879.

Adams & Perry Watch Mfg. Co., was organized at Lancaster, Pa., about 1874 and failed before it produced any watches. It was reorganized 1877 as the Lancaster Pennsylvania Watch Co., Ltd. This continued to May of 1879. They used "New "Era" and "West End" as names for their watches.

In May, 1879, it was again changed to The Lancaster Watch Co., failed in 1890, and was bought up by the Hamilton Watch Co., in 1892. Under the May 9, 1879, reorganization, James I. Hartman, was elected president; J. P. McCasky, secretary; K. D. Skyles, treasurer, and A. Bitner was appointed manager.

Data on an Illinois Springfield watch

I have in my possession a hunting case, 16-s watch of the following description: interior, Springfield, Illinois, keywind, key set, serial number 79302, monometallic balance, flat hairspring, single roller, 7 jewels.

I would like to know more about the origin, age, etc.

A.

The Illinois Springfield Watch Co. was organized in January of 1869, mainly through the efforts of J. C. Adams. Twenty-one months after starting to make the machinery, the first complete watches were produced in January, 1872.

At the end of the first years' work, $38,000.00 worth of watches had been made, they were producing watches at the rate of 25 per day, and had 125 operatives on the payroll.

The company began making their own balances in 1873 under the direction of John Leman. In that same year, they began to make their dials under the direction of John Regler and their own hairsprings under Daniel Currier. A Mr. Jelly headed a new jewel department. Previously all these items had been imported, so far as factory progress was concerned, they were advancing at a rapid rate.

Owing to a business depression, plus the fact that they were trying to sell their watches "direct," sales weren't so good. A large surplus, estimated at about $100,000.00, had accumulated by the end of 1873. In 1875 a new company was organized, the Springfield Illinois Watch Co., it absorbed all the liabilities of the old one. E. N. Bates was elected president. In 1879 came still another reorganization, the Illinois Watch Company with Jacob Bunn elected president.

According to the best information we have, they began 1873 with number 46,000, the next date is 1880 when they began with number 195,000, thus 149,000 were made in that seven-year period, or about 21,000 per year. Since your number 79,302 is but 33,000 past 1873 we may conclude it came through about a couple years later or very near 1875.

U.S. Watch Co. History

Could you tell me some information about the United States Watch Co.? I have an old key wind watch made in Marion, N.J., by Edwin Rollo of the U.S. Watch Co.—No. 4944 patented March of 1866.

Any information you could tell me on this subject would be greatly appreciated.

A.

At Marion, N. J., a suburb of Jersey City, work was begun upon the main building of The United States Watch Co., in August of 1864 — by late summer of 1867 they were putting watches upon the market — they were forced to make an assignment in 1872. The name "Marion Watch Co." was adopted (though never a corporate name) and they ran under it 'til the spring of 1874 when their bond holders foreclosed.

Their "Edwin Rollo" model, was named for a Mr. Edwin Rollo Pratt, one of their star salesmen. It was first manufactured under the superintendence of Mr. Wm. H. Learnerd, who was transferred from that position June 14th, 1869. It was a full plate, 18's, lever movement made in brass

—gotten out to compete with the P. S. Bartlett movement then being made by Waltham Watch Co.

Transferring superintendent Learnerd to the head of one of the departments displeased him very much; he resigned and brought suit against the company for breach of his five year contract; eventually winning the balance on that contract. It is interesting to note that while superintendent, Mr. Learnerd commenced a watch under the model name "United States," it was completed and produced under his successor, Superintendent H. J. Lowe, in the latter part of 1869. Pronounced the finest watch made in the U.S.A. at that time, it was listed to sell for $475.00. It was a 16's, three-quarter plate, 19 ruby jewels, three pairs of conical pivots, compensated balance, Breguet hair spring, closely adjusted to heat, cold, position and isochronism; nickel plate highly finished in damaskeen and frost work.

Back to your friend Edwin Rollo Pratt: towards the last, they brought out one ladies' model and named it "R. F. Pratt." Your watch should have a sort of 'butterfly' shaped opening in its top plate to give a view of the pallet action — perhaps you have noted that your balance is quite upon the large side — it is said that the model first submitted by Mr. Baldwin had conventional size balance but its rim cut directly across over the pallet action and that the directors (not watchmakers themselves) wishing visable pallet action, ordered the balance be made larger. In order to get temperature compensation Baldwin had to make the rim of the larger balance heavier than usual.

COLUMBUS WATCH CO.

I have a watch which to me is of great value. It has been handed down for two generations before. It's a Columbus No. 216 654, 6-size. Please give me some information on how old it is, what happened to the company, and how many of these watches they made.

A.

It is a natural thought that a maker, or company, for that matter, simply begins with No. 1 and consecutively numbers the pieces from there on out.

Unfortunately for those of us anxious to date accurately a special piece, this system was not followed in every instance, owing to mass production methods where a certain series was made to denote size, grade, etc. Then in many cases, where the numbering can indicate approximately the date of manufacture, records thereof have

neither been kept or made available to those compiling listings.

The Columbus Watch Company was organized November 18, 1882, and sold in 1902 to the South Bend Watch Company, South Bend, Indiana.

About 1876, Mr. Detrich Gruen and Mr. W. J. Savage formed a company at Columbus, Ohio, under the firm name of Gruen & Savage. They imported partly-finished nickel movements from Switzerland in 8, 16, and 18-sizes to fit American cases, and finished them and engraved them with the firm name. This continued until November 18, 1882, when the organization of the Columbus Watch Company was consumated, having for its object the actual manufacture of watches on the American plan.

The company started with a paid-in capital of $100,000.00, which was later increased to $150,000.00. Mr. D. Gruen was elected president, and Mr. W. J. Savage, secretary and treasurer. They secured Mr. Charles E. Mason for general superintendent, Mr. Philip H. Wheeler and Mr. W. W. Owen as division superintendents.

The new Columbus Company bought from Gruen & Savage an acre and a half of land at the corner of New and Thurman Streets on which Gruen and Savage had erected a two-story brick building, 23 by 80 feet, in 1881. A new brick building, 35 by 95 feet, three stories high, with engine house, was erected and connected with the old building by a hallway. This was known as the main building. It was finished by June of 1883.

Just nine months from its start, the Columbus Company turned out its first movement. They were able to make this remarkable speed toward production because they purchased so much of the required machinery ready-made. Some $10,-000.00 had been spent with the American Watch Tool Company of Waltham, Massachusetts. At the end of the first year they were producing ten watches per day and had employed 100 hands. Shortly, the number of employes was increased to 125, and they were producing about 45 watches per day. About half of the employees were women.

The model for the first movement differed from other American full-plate movements by locating the balance and balance bridge so that the mainspring barrel could be removed without taking out the balance.

It was designed by Mr. Gruen and Mr. Mason. The barrel had 72 teeth, the center wheel had 72; the center pinion, 11; the third wheel 60, with a pinion of 9. The fourth wheel had 70 teeth and a pinion of 8 leaves; the escape pinion had 7 leaves. While they were specializing on the 18-size at the beginning, they were also making eight grades of three-quarter plate movements, 16-size, and three grades of the ladies' 8-size. All were stem-wind. Your 6-size came later in their production.

The Columbus Company made no cases. They imported their mainsprings, hairsprings and jewels. They developed and perfected their own damaskeening process, a leaf polisher and a profile machine, but did not patent either of them. Mr. Gruen patented a "dust band," Mr. Owen a regulator, and Mr. P. H. Wheeler patented a micrometer regulator, No. 229,215, June 22, 1880; a stem-wind arrangement, No. 238,464, March 1, 1881; another regulator, No. 354,283 on December 14, 1886, and with Mr. Henry Barbier, a stem-wind and setting device, No. 361,658 on April 19, 1887, with all assigned to the Columbus Watch Company.

They adopted a concentrated plan for running a watch factory which proved very successful for a small factory. The plates, flat steel work escapements, and screws were all done in one room under one supervisor, Mr. W. W. Owen. It was known as the "escapement room." Mr. P. H. Wheeler, the other division superintendent, was over the "train room" where the damaskeening, wheel and pinion finishing and stem-wind parts were made.

Mr. Wheeler was advanced from division superintendent to factory superintendent on September 3, 1884, and there is record of a contract to run for three years, dated January 1, 1885, for $3,000.00 a year, signed by D. Gruen, president, and W. J. Savage, secretary and treasurer. As mentioned above, South Bend

bought the company in 1902. For round-figure dating, we might place your 6-size movement in the late '90s.

AMERICAN WATCH CO.

We have an American Watch Company 18S keywind, Foggs Patent #487491 movement number. Could you tell us something about the above watch like about the age. The case is coin silver and is a hunting case.

A.

American Watch Co., Waltham, Mass., organized Feb. 4th, 1859—that name used from then up to 1885. Absorbed the Nassau Watch Co., in April 1862. Entire factory rebuilt and enlarged 1878 to 1883. Name changed American Waltham Watch Co., in 1885, in 1906 became Waltham Watch Co., 1923 to 1925 The Waltham Watch & Clock Co., 1925 back to Waltham Watch Co., production was suspended 1950.

Roughly, they started with serial No. 427,600 with 1870, and, with 961,235 in 1875. Therefore your No. 487,491 must have been produced the first part of this five-year period. Waltham first began to make stem wind movements after 1870. Perhaps yours is among the last of the key winders.

According to a listing published by Waltham in 1954 serial numbers 486,001 to 488,000 were 18-size, 11-jewel, model 57 with expansion balance. Some marked William Ellery and some marked P. S. Bartlett. They take Waltham's grade "A" material.

The "Fogg Patent" evidently refers to a safety center pinion patented by Mr. C. W. Fogg, in 1865. A Mr. D. B. Fitts, of Holliston, Mass., patented a safety-center device Nov. 30, 1858, which safety pinion worked on the ratchet principle; it proved unsatisfactory and Mr. Fogg made one whereby the pinion head was screwed on. As you know, this is the very same principle employed this day on the Bendix starter pinion for cars. A suit at once grew out of the use of Mr. Fogg's pinion; the Elgin Watch Company claimed it infringed on their safety pinion patented by Mr. Burt. The Burt pinion head fit the center arbor friction tight and was held in place by a nut which unscrewed if the mainspring broke and kicked back. The infringement seemed plain but there was an amicable settlement and both companies agreed to permit the other to use their patented improvements.

"Hamilton Grade 613"

Designated "Hamilton Grade 613"—movement with calendar is grade 614—it is a 21,600 beat, seventeen jeweled movement, with KIF shock protection, unbreakable, self-lub mainspring, movable stud regulator, and a three-spoke screwless balance.

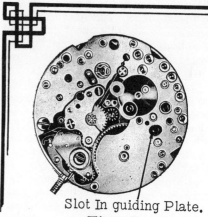

Slot In guiding Plate.

Fig. 2.

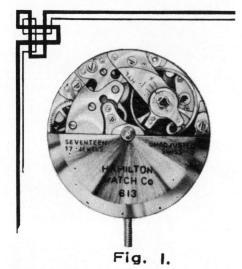

Fig. I.

Dick points out that the automatic winding train with its disc gear provides a roller bearing action virtually free from friction. Only the oscillating weight extends above the bridges. The wig-wag pinion, operating between large flat jewels, is constantly engaged with the oscillating weight gear; in conjunction with the stop click, it shifts automatically to engage either the winding up wheel or the reduction gear, adapting to the direction of the winding force each time the oscillating weight changes direction.

When dismantling remove the hands in the usual manner to assure correct engagement of the cannon pinion upon reassembly. Observe that this cannon pinion is free fitting and therefore must have a spring washer between the hour wheel and the dial. To release the mainspring's reserve power hold the crown and with a fine pick, press the lower pivot of the gear against the rear of the slot in the guiding plate. To disengage the gear from the ratchet

intermediate gear permit the crown to turn slowly backwards; see arrow in Fig. 2. Be careful with the pick to avoid damaging the slot in the guiding plate.

Next, remove the balance assembly. Then, after removing the two screws of the upper bridge of the oscillating weight, the complete oscillating weight assembly with its bridge can be lifted out of place. The assembly may be put into the machine for cleaning and after careful drying, fresh oil should be applied to the bearing. The rotor is permanently affixed to its axel. Never attempt to separate these parts as replacement includes the complete assembly.

The mainspring has been tested at the factory for the sliding of the brake spring at the correct torque and is self-lubricating. In the event of difficulty or damage, replacement of the complete barrel assembly is recommended. This ratchet wheel is located in the recess beneath the barrel. To make assembly easier, the ratchet wheel should be placed upon the square of the barrel arbor and the ratchet wheel and the barrel held together with tweezers while positioning them properly in the barrel recess.

With the barrel bridge and the upper bridge for the automatic device removed, the stop click and all gears of the automatic train are accessible except the ratchet intermediate gear. Exercise care to avoid damaging the fine wire spring of the stop click. The driving gear for the ratchet wheel, instead of meshing directly with the ratchet wheel, engages the ratchet intermediate gear which has been designed to separate manual from automatic winding. A spring, pre-loaded so that it brings the ratchet intermediate gear into working position during automatic winding, permits the gear to move back in the guiding slots when manual winding is used.

When checking the automatic mechanism, make sure energy is being transmitted to the ratchet wheel while moving the oscillating weight. Test in both directions. If there is any irregularity, examine the operation of the wig-wag pinion and the stop click. Also inspect the intermediate gear and rocking bar assembly for freedom, making sure that the respective springs have only enough tension to shift the engaging gears into working position. The interme-

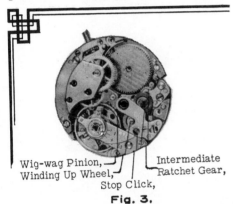

Wig-wag Pinion,⌐
Winding Up Wheel,⌐   Intermediate
                          Ratchet Gear,
        Stop Click,

Fig. 3.

diate wheel, usually referred to in conventional movements as the center or second wheel—sometimes dividing wheel, dividing hours and minutes—is located off center. The lower pivot has its bearing in the minute work cock. Tension—center friction—to the shaft of the wheel is a slip pinion which meshes with the minute wheel to drive the dial train. As with all center frictions it permits the dial train to turn separately when setting the hands to correct time. Light lubrication is required to keep the slip pinion from binding on the shaft.

The cannon pinion fits over a fixed post therefore loosely and is held in place by a spring washer between the hour wheel and the dial. The bearing hole for the pivot of the minute wheel is elongated. A spring pressing lightly against the pivot keeps the minute wheel closely meshed with the

cannon pinion and slip pinion to eliminate backlash. The rocking bar assembly, comprised of three gears, pivots on the hub of the winding wheel screw. During manual winding the intermediate winding pinion, permanently mounted on the rocking bar, is moved to engage the ratchet wheel by the rocking bar spring. This arrangement permits the pinion to move out of engagement whenever the ratchet wheel is driven by the self-winding mechanism. The other two gears mounted on the rocking bar are employed when setting the hands to time. The rocking bar is supplied only as a complete assembly.

Moebus "Synt-A-Lube" is recommended for all train pivots, balance jewels, upper and lower pivots of the self-winding train including the wig-wag pinion, and the break of the stop click. Do not lubricate the pivots of the stop click or pallet. Moebus 941 is used on the pallet stones. Moebius 8200 is used to lubricate the guiding slots of the ratchet intermediate gear and the working face of the ratchet intermediate gear spring. Also it is used on the lower pivot of the minute wheel and on the winding and setting parts, including the pivots of the gears mounted on the underside of the rocking bar assembly. This about covers all the new points and no special instructions are needed for the servicing of the movement proper—this might be added for the calendar mechanism of Grade 614— see Fig. 4. This calendar differs from other

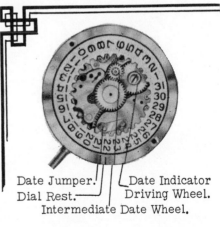

Date Jumper.⌐   ⌐Date Indicator
Dial Rest.⌐   Driving Wheel.
    Intermediate Date Wheel.

Fig. 4.

Hamilton calendar models. The date changes automatically at midnight with the start of change becoming apparent near 10:00 p.m. The date can be changed and/or set by rotating the hands clockwise through a 24 hour cycle, repeating until the correct date appears within the window; then the hands may be turned clockwise to the correct a.m. or p.m. time.

After removing the dial and dial rest, the mechanism remains intact, thus its operating may be plainly observed. Very simple in design, it is easy to take apart and assemble. The spring washer for the hour wheel is located under the date indicator guard and the date jumper spring fits into a recess in the underside of the guard. Observe that just one minute work cock screw is used because the screw in the other location is replaced by one of the indicator guard screws —see the arrow, Fig. 4. Making one rev. per 24 hours, the date indicator driving wheel does not require orientation. It is necessary only to install the hands to indicate 12 o'clock right after the completion of the date change cycle. Apply Synt-A-Lube sparingly and only to the center of the date indicator driving wheel and the intermediate wheel. This little 7¾ ligne, full rotor movement will shortly be coming to the "144" for servicing and these pointers will come in handy.

How to Uncase and Recase the Mido Multifort
Super-Automatic Powerwind Movements

A bent, flexible ring, placed in a groove of the cases of the 10½" and 6¾" Mido Multifort Powerwind series ref. 00916 P, ref. 00917 P and ref. 607 P is holding the movement tightly in the case. Neither case screws nor casing clamps are necessary.

UNCASING

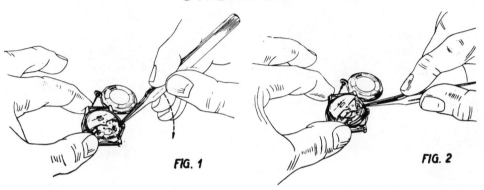

FIG. 1

FIG. 2

1. Unscrew back of case with proper wrench.
2. Pull out stem in handsetting position, loosen detent screw and remove stem.
3. Insert tweezer into stem hole of the movement (Fig. 1), lift movement (Fig. 2), now loose, out of the case.

RECASING

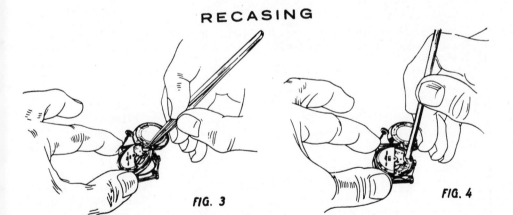

FIG. 3

FIG. 4

1. Hold and insert movement into the case opposite stem hole (Fig. 3) under the bent ring of the case.
2. Push movement strongly down into the case (Fig. 4), with a wooden stick on the barrel bridge.
3. Insert stem, screw on detent tightly, close the case, and check air and waterproofness with the Mido Superwatertest machine.

The 11" Powerwind series 0916 P—0917 P, the 12" Powerwind series 916 P and 917 P, are encased with the conventional movement ring.

31

TIMEX MODEL 87 MOVEMENT.

FRONT   BACK.

THE TIMEX MODEL 87 has been designated "Caliber 882." It is a 13½ ligne electronic movement, time drive has the usual miniature battery, hand setting and date indexing. Its case and crystal are identical to models 84 and 85.

On Model 87 the electric contact used upon model 84 has been replaced by an electronic thickfilm circuit consisting of two silicon planar transistors, one capacitor and four resisters.

The electronic circuit is connected to the

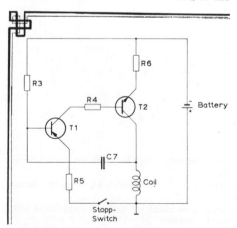

WIRING DIAGRAM.

moving coil on the balance wheel by a second small hairspring. This second hairspring controls the power supply from the battery to the balance wheel coil. A switch operated by the hand set mechanism disconnects the current in the electronic circuit when the crown set is pulled out to the set position. When the crown is in the set position, the watch is automatically stopped thus permitting the owner to set the watch to the exact second (hack). Also, it is clear that in this position the battery is not being discharged.

Timex Model 87 has an hourly beat of 21,600. The large balance wheel has a temperature compensating hairspring system and the rate may be adjusted in the usual manner by merely moving an orthodox regulator. The Timex electronic can be rated in all positions on any normal watch rate recorder. It can be dismantled and repaired with conventional tools and there is no need for special knowledge of electricity or electronics, nor any need for complicated electrical measuring or inspection devices, new tools, or microscopes. For checking the battery voltage, a high ohm voltmeter (about 20,000 ohms per volt), which is now in general use in most repair shops, is sufficient.

The first step in dissembly is to remove the battery followed by the movement from the case. To avoid damage to the case, the battery cap should be opened only at the spot indicated on the back of the case (arrow and words "lift here"). Check the voltage; any battery with a voltage of less than 1/5 volts, or which is known to have been in service in excess of one year, should be replaced. Avoid shorting the battery by metallic connections between the outer case and the negative pole, such a shorting will curtail the life of the battery.

Next, remove the crystal with any conventional crystal tool. The movement can be removed through the front of the case. See Figure 2. Note the locating notch in the bezel seat "A" and the corresponding key on the balance bridge "B".

The case back is fitted in place with epoxy resin and no attempt should ever be made to remove it. The crown set remains with the back. An automatic coupling device connects it with the setting stem when the movement is replaced. Should it ever be necessary to remove the crown, use the following procedure: "A" lift crown to 'stop' position. "B" Spread retaining spring with tips of tweezers and push the crown through the rear of the case, see Figure 3. If necessary the retaining spring and gasket may now be removed.

To examine place the movement upon a suitable movement ring and clamp the bat-tery in place with a battery retaining spring. This is the same as used upon Models 84 and 85 and is available upon your request to Timex Material Sales Division.

To assemble the battery retaining spring, loosen screws "A" and "B", Figure 10. Lift the switch insulation by a screw driver and insert the battery retaining spring between the switch insulation and the hand setting spring. Finally, tighten screws "A" and "B". One end of the battery retaining spring depresses the stopping spring fixed to the movement and allows the balance to be turned freely.

The negative pole of the battery must contact the connecting spring, No. 4160 on Figure 1, exploded view. Current from the negative pole flows through the connection to the connection yoke of the electronic circuit. These parts are insulated from the remainder of the movement. The positive pole of the battery contacts the battery retaining spring and thus flows to plate No. 100. Never use a metallic connection between the insulated and the uninsulated parts of the movement because this short-circuits your battery and curtails its service life.

Those electro-magnetic impulses given by the electronic circuit are transferred to mechanical driving impulses for the balance wheel in the very same manner as Model 84. The impulse current flows through the balance drive coil and the magnetic south pole of the coil is attracted by the north

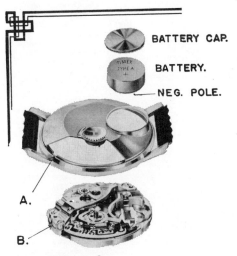

BATTERY CAP.

BATTERY.

NEG. POLE.

A.

B.

FIG. 2.

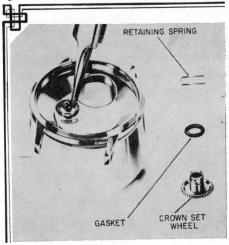

RETAINING SPRING

GASKET

CROWN SET WHEEL

FIG. 3.

pole and re-pulsed by the south pole of the permanent magnet system. The electronic circuit is triggered by the voltage which is induced in the coil of the balance wheel when moving through the permanent magnet system.

The permanent magnet system together with the shunt bridge can be rotated out of position so that the balance and hairspring are visible. To do this, remove one screw "C", Figure 4, if desired. This whole assembly may be removed by taking out both screws "C". After removal of the permanent magnet system from the movement the balance bridge and balance wheel can

the TIMEX model 87 movement (exploded view)

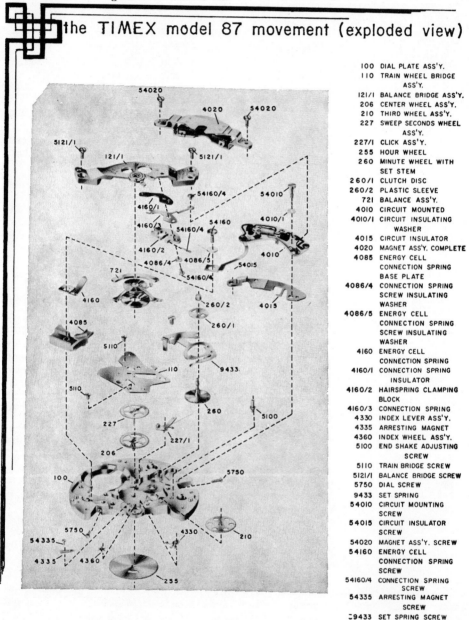

100	DIAL PLATE ASS'Y.
110	TRAIN WHEEL BRIDGE ASS'Y.
121/1	BALANCE BRIDGE ASS'Y.
206	CENTER WHEEL ASS'Y.
210	THIRD WHEEL ASS'Y.
227	SWEEP SECONDS WHEEL ASS'Y.
227/1	CLICK ASS'Y.
255	HOUR WHEEL
260	MINUTE WHEEL WITH SET STEM
260/1	CLUTCH DISC
260/2	PLASTIC SLEEVE
721	BALANCE ASS'Y.
4010	CIRCUIT MOUNTED
4010/1	CIRCUIT INSULATING WASHER
4015	CIRCUIT INSULATOR
4020	MAGNET ASS'Y. COMPLETE
4085	ENERGY CELL CONNECTION SPRING BASE PLATE
4086/4	CONNECTION SPRING SCREW INSULATING WASHER
4086/5	ENERGY CELL CONNECTION SPRING SCREW INSULATING WASHER
4160	ENERGY CELL CONNECTION SPRING
4160/1	CONNECTION SPRING INSULATOR
4160/2	HAIRSPRING CLAMPING BLOCK
4160/3	CONNECTION SPRING
4330	INDEX LEVER ASS'Y.
4335	ARRESTING MAGNET
4360	INDEX WHEEL ASS'Y.
5100	END SHAKE ADJUSTING SCREW
5110	TRAIN BRIDGE SCREW
5121/1	BALANCE BRIDGE SCREW
5750	DIAL SCREW
9433	SET SPRING
54010	CIRCUIT MOUNTING SCREW
54015	CIRCUIT INSULATOR SCREW
54020	MAGNET ASS'Y. SCREW
54160	ENERGY CELL CONNECTION SPRING SCREW
54160/4	CONNECTION SPRING SCREW
54335	ARRESTING MAGNET SCREW
9433	SET SPRING SCREW

FIG. I.

be removed. Screw "D" serves to adjust the end-shake of the balance and is fixed in place with epoxy resin. Before disassembling of the balance bridge, screw "E" which connects the electronic circuit to the balance bridge must be removed. Furthermore, the bronze hairspring must be removed by loosening screw "F". The hairspring stud can be pressed out of the balance bridge to separate balance and bridge. This bronze hairspring clamping block is insulated from the balance bridge. An insulating washer is located beneath the screw holding the bronze hairspring clamping block. Make sure that this washer is in place when re-assembling, otherwise a short circuit will occur. The crown set stem "G" is also the staff of the minute wheel, and, as such, is connected to the crown set on the case back through a clutch device.

On Figure 7, the crown set is depressed to its running position. The clutch disc is kept out of engagement with the stem and the setting spring depressed. In this position, the projection on the setting spring is kept out of engagement with the stopping finger of the balance wheel. The Nose "H" of the stop switch must touch the rivet "J" of the setting spring.

On Figure 6, the crown is in the set position. The clutch disc now engages with the square portion of the stem and couples the stem and crown-set, thus permitting the

disc is just out of engagement with the

ELECTRONIC SWITCHED OFF

FIG. 5.   K

ELECTRONIC SWITCHED OFF

FIG. 6.

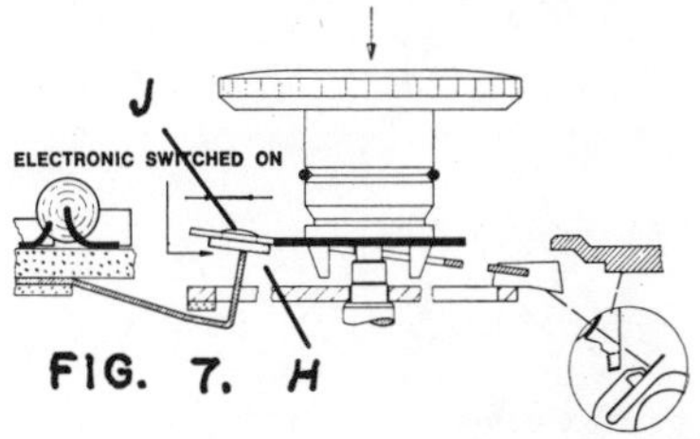

ELECTRONIC SWITCHED ON

J

FIG. 7.   H

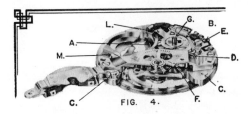

L.
A.
M.
G.   B.
E.
D.
C.
C.   F.
FIG. 4.

hands to be set. This position of the crown also allows the setting spring to move upward and butt against the stopping finger on the balance wheel, thus holding it. The nose "H" of the stop switch must be clear of rivet "J" of setting spring, thus interrupting the starting current of the electronic circuit.

Should the setting spring require adjustment, use the following procedure. Move the crown set upwards so that the clutch

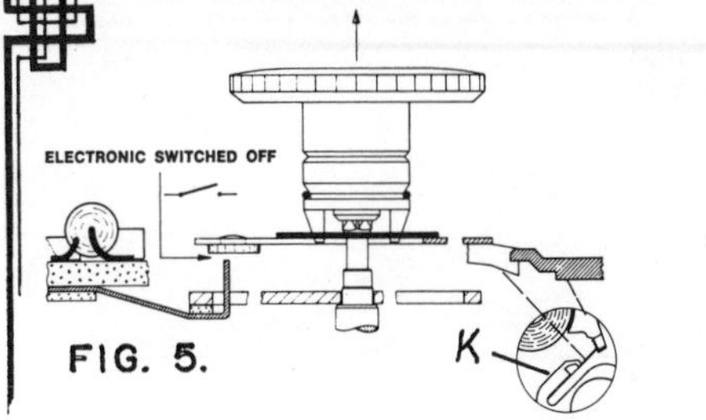

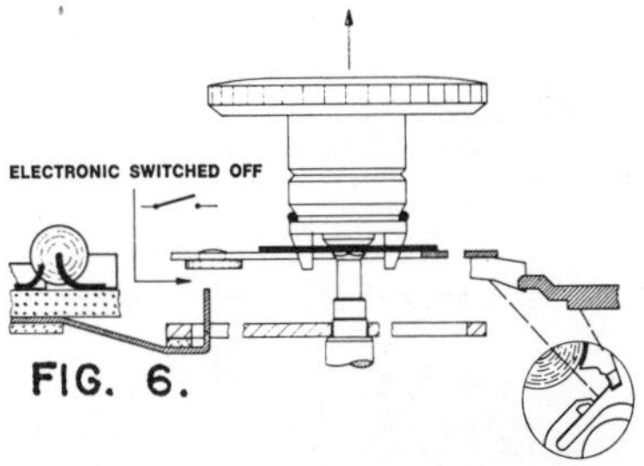

square portion of the set stem Figure 6, and "G" Figure 4. The clutch disc will rest against the bottom of the square portion of the stem. In this position the projection on the setting spring must contact the stopping finger on the balance wheel by the amount shown. When the crown set is pulled into the "set" position, Figure 5, the stopping finger of the balance wheel must be in full contact with the projection on the setting spring. For this adjustment bend the area marked "K". The nose "H" of the stop switch must clear the rivet "J" by at least ½ to 1½ times the thickness of the setting spring. If necessary, adjust this clearance by bending the setting spring in area "L", Figure 4.

To remove the clutch mechanism from the movement, first lift the plastic sleeve from the stem with tweezers, Figure 8.

Next remove the clutch disc from the stem with tweezers. Next the screw "A", Figure

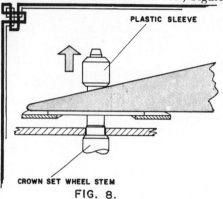

PLASTIC SLEEVE

CROWN SET WHEEL STEM

FIG. 8.

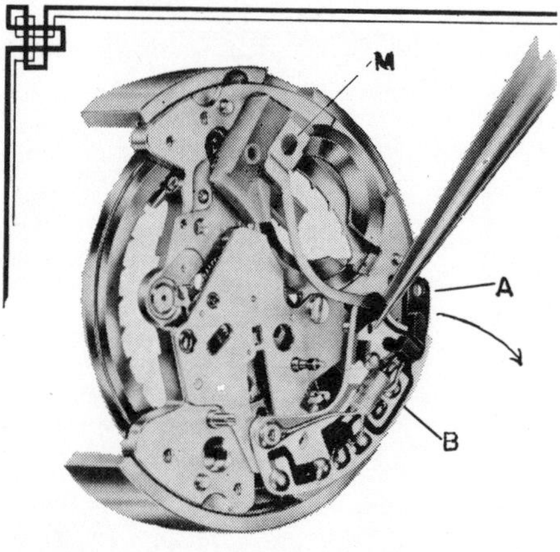

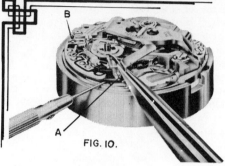

from the stem with tweezers, Figure 8. Next remove the clutch disc from the stem with tweezers. Next the screw "A", Figure

B

A

FIG. 10.

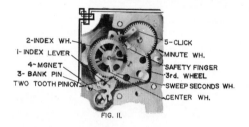

2-INDEX WH.
1-INDEX LEVER
4-MGNET
3-BANK PIN
TWO TOOTH PINION

5-CLICK
MINUTE WH.
SAFETY FINGER
3rd. WHEEL
SWEEP SECONDS WH.
CENTER WH.

FIG. 11.

M

A

B

FIG. 9.

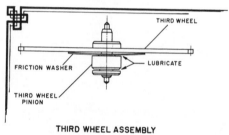

THIRD WHEEL

FRICTION WASHER

LUBRICATE

THIRD WHEEL PINION

THIRD WHEEL ASSEMBLY
FIG. 12.

9, and the setting spring. The electronic circuitry can now be taken off by removing screws "B" and "M" as both these screws are provided with insulating washers which must be repositioned during reassembly, otherwise a short will occur.

The screw at "M" should also be removed. Now lift the circuit base, as shown in the picture Figure 9, and turn it in the direction of the arrow until the stop switch clears the train bridge. Take extra caution that the stop switch is not damaged.

Figure 11, shows the gear train exposed after removal of the train bridge. In action, the gear train functions as follows: The balance wheel when moving counterclock-

wheel 2, forward by one tooth. After it has advanced the index wheel forward by one tooth, the indexing lever comes to rest against the banking pin 3.

The tip of one tooth of the index wheel is attracted and held in position by magnet 4, Figure 11. As the index wheel is magnetically fixed in position, the steel "D" shaped pin on the index lever can not move of its own accord out of its position between the teeth of the index wheel. In Figure 11 when the balance moves clockwise, it moves the index lever to the right. The steel "D" shaped pin will now move the index wheel backward slightly until the pin clears the tooth of the index wheel. The index lever comes to rest against the banking pin and is held by magnetic attraction between the magnet 4 and steel "D" shaped pin. The instant the steel "D" shaped pin clears the tooth of the index wheel, the magnetic attraction retracts the wheel back to its original position where it is set for one tooth advancement during the next counterclockwise rotation of the balance wheel. When the index wheel has thus moved forward three teeth, one tooth of the two toothed pinion fixed to the index wheel engages the sweep seconds wheel and rotates it forward by one tooth. This one tooth rotation of the sweep seconds wheel aided by the click 5, provides the one second jump of the sweep second hand. The safety finger insures that no more than one tooth of the sweep second wheel will index at a time. The click spring must be locked as shown in the illustration. Pre-tension of the click spring should amount to 2 to 2½ times the diameter of the locking pin. The remainder of the gear train functions in the normal manner.

The sweep seconds wheel pinion drives the third wheel. The third wheel pinion, in turn, rotates the center wheel. The center wheel (as usual) carries the minute hand. The teeth of the center wheel mesh with the minute wheel. The staff of the minute wheel projects through to the dial side and carries the minute pinion. The dial train friction is provided by the third wheel assembly, see Figure 12, and a friction washer is interposed between the third wheel pinion and the third wheel.

It is important to carefully lubricate this as indicated after a clean job. The index magnet may be removed to check the train. During removal of the magnet, the index finger must be in position as shown Figure 11. When assembling the hands, it is important that the sweep second wheel assembly be supported at its pivot to avoid damage.

Assembling the electronic circuit position the electronic circuit as shown in Figure 13 above pin "P", push down the stop switch to a level slightly below the nose of the train bridge "R." While holding the stop switch down, move the circuit to its final position over pin "P." This will lock

the switch into position below the nose of the train bridge "R." Be certain that the stop switch insulator which is a part of the circuit board is in its proper position between the nose of the bridge and the stop

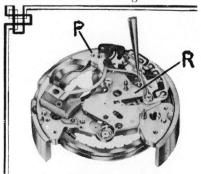

FIG. 13.

switch. (NOTE: the stop switch is insulated from the bridge.)

Use care to avoid damage to the stop switch. Now assemble the setting spring and the screws holding the circuit board. Use the disassembly procedures as a guide for further reassembly. When replacing the movement into its case, pull the crown set out to the set position to facilitate entry of the setting stem into the crown set.

The movement, including the electronic circuit may be cleaned by the usual methods, using normal watch cleaning and rinsing solutions. The balance must be cleaned separately to prevent any damage to its coil. Do not clean the battery with any liquid. If necessary, it may be wiped with a dry cloth only. After cleaning any particles adhering to the magnet should be carefully removed before assembly. A piece of scotch tape rolled to a point will be found useful in removing particles. This should not be done while the movement is assembled as there is danger of severing the lead wires to the balance coil. The other parts of the movement must be free of particles, especially steel or nickel which would be attracted by the magnet. Needless to say, the watch should not be demagnetized. The movement should be re-oiled in the normal manner using only high grade watch oils (factory uses Elgin M. 56 b.).

Under no circumstances should oil or grease containing silicone be used. These points require lubrication: (a) the jewel bearings and pivots of the train wheels and balance; (b) minute wheel and set stem bearing surface; (c) steel "D" shaped pin on index lever (d) the surface of the click which rests against the sweep second wheel; (e) third wheel assembly as indicated Figure 12; and (f) pipe of the crown set wheel so that the lub will seep down to the rubber waterproofing gasket which surrounds the pipe. Never lubricate the connecting point between the stop switch and setting spring.

The best performance from the Timex electronic is achieved if the hairspring does not vibrate between the pin and the key of the regulator. The outside edge of the hairspring should be in light permanent contact with the inside edge of the regulator key. Make sure that both hairsprings have good clearance to all other moving parts, as the balance bridge and upper shunt driving magnet.

Watch Sizes . . . English or American?

IT IS UNIVERSALLY ACCEPTED among researchers that an error repeated often enough and long enough becomes fact. A careful check tends to show that these repeated errors are committed more often by those without a craft than by craftsmen themselves.

When Mr. Eric Bruton came out with "Dictionary of Clocks and Watches" (1962) that paragraph following "Size" hit me squarely between the eyes, it reads: "American system of watch measurement originated by A. L. Dennison, based on thirtieths of an inch. O size is the basis, equalling 35 thirtieths of an inch. 1 size is a thirtieth larger, i.e., 36/30ths, and so on. 1/O size is a thirtieth smaller, i.e. 34/30ths., and so on." end quote.

The measurement here is correct . . . the 'credit' is incorrect; it is neither American nor originated by A. L. Dennison. As an apprentice, I was taught that this system of guaging the movement by thirtieths of an inch was by the "Lancashire" guage, which guage came from the Lancashire district around Liverpool.

It did seem rather odd that an Englishman, Mr. Bruton, would credit an American, Mr. Dennison, with devising a horological 'standard' when the established trend is very definitely the other way around. So, we decided upon a bit of "spade" work. Aaron L. Dennison was born at Freeport, Me., in the year 1812; in 1830 he was apprenticed to a watchmaker, James Carey, at Brunswick, Me. By 1839 he was proprietor of a general watch and jewelry business at Boston, Mass. By 1840 he had invented the "Dennison Standard Mainspring Guage," which was immediately accepted and is in general use to this day.

There is nothing in the record that indicates Dennison originated any sort of watch size guage and, in my judgment, it was the popular acceptance of his mainspring guage that gave rise to the idea. Mr. Dennison went on to become known as the "Father of the American Watch Factory" and after being associated with several watch manufacturing ventures went to England about 1868 to sell one of those factories. While there, he went to Birmingham and started a watch case factory. This factory is active today, "Dennison Watch Case Co., Ltd., 222 Soho Hill, Birmingham." Their Secretary, Mr. H. R. Barnsley, wrote: "We regret from our records we are not able to state that Aaron L. Dennison originated the watch size system of measurement by the thirtieth of an inch."

Working backward from the Bruton volume we come to Brooks Palmer's "The Book of American Clocks"—1950. Page 14 says: There are two systems of measurement of Watch movements—the American

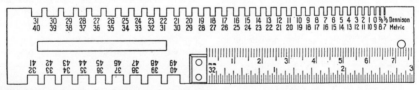

DENNISON & METRIC MAINSPRING GAUGE

and the French or Swiss. Watches made in America are measured by a system devised by Aaron L. Dennison. Zero (O) is the base size and equals 35/30ths., of an American inch."

Mr. Charles Crossman—1856-1930—was a prolific writer on horological matters and in the Jewelers Circular for August 1886 credited Dennison with the watch size guage.

No doubt Crossman had talked with watchmakers who had known Dennison; was familiar with his starting factory production; familiar with his mainspring guage, etc., and they just naturally in their admiration for the genius of this man credited him with watch sizes without bothering to check. Back when this young nation was being founded, in the 1770's there was growing up around Liverpool in the Lancashire district a tremendous watch manufacturing business.

All around in the district—Ormskirk, Prescott, Preston, Chesterfield and Frodsham—there sprang up watchmakers. The Lancashire district became the home of the English raw watch with casemakers and factories in Liverpool. About 1800 Liverpool was a great watch export center and the trade flourished up to about 1870 and the coming of automatic machinery.

With the movements being made out in the district to be cased in Liverpool a 'standard' for movement size became an absolute necessity. A pin-point date for the "Lancashire" size guage and/or its actual originator seems lost in time. We have in the past few years written many letters to the district, also to B. H. Institute, Mr. J. H. F. Wadsworth, Technical Inquiry Officer, British Antiquarian Horological Society. Mr. F. A. Mercer of Thomas Mercer Ltd., et al. All are agreed that the 'system' is known as the Lancashire guage. But, nothing upon the who and when. Britten, Saunier, and Frodsham all designate it as "Lancashire Guage."

Charles Frodsham, in "The Elements of Watch and Clock Making"—1862—had this to say: "I found no small difficulty in giving a value to the old Lancashire movement guage, for, although I conversed upon the subject with some of the oldest men in the

trade, they only treated it as a tool, without regard to any standard measurement whatever. I at length, however, unravelled its meaning. The Lancashire movement guage then is a three-inch rule subdivided duodecimally; a watch movement one inch in diameter is said to be O size, and the second inch is subdivided into thirty equal parts or sizes, so that each size is one-thirtieth of an inch." end quote.

If, in 1862 Mr. Frodsham was discussing the Lancashire size guage with old timers within the trade, it is quite conceivable that their memories went back half a century, fifty years from 1862 takes it back to 1812. This is the year Aaron L. Dennison was born. One final thought—many descriptions of the Lancashire system stress the fact that the movement is measured from the smallest diameter of the back plate and that five-thirtieths of an inch are allowed for the dial size. During this era nearly all movements were 'hinged' into the case and this 'step' in size from the back plate to the dial plate was very necessary for the case-maker to know. The very fact that movements were being made out in the district—Lancashire—and coming into Liverpool to be cased of itself required some sort of 'standard' measurement, and it is quite conceivable that this could have occurred before 1800.

Model 62 Timex Quartz Crystal Movement

A brief glance at her vital statistics—the Timex Model 62 is 12¾ ligne—28.7 mm. or 1.13 inches diameter. It takes Timex type "A" energy cell and the balance wheel operates at 21,600 cycles per hour. The mechanical portion closely resembles their model 40 movement—most readers will be familiar with that electric; therefore servicing it would be about the same. Speaking of servicing, it is well under stood that Timex has authorized service stations in many large cities and have suggested to wearers that they patronize these if and when it is practical. This was accepted by the consumer and the bench watchmaker while the bulk of their production was, let's say $20 and under, retail. With the coming of their electrics at higher prices, owner-wearers tended more to rely upon their watchmaker; my thought is: the quartz will further this trend for when a man plunks down a hundred and a quarter for a watch the chances are very good that he will want to drop in upon his regular repairman for any service, adjustment, etc. Right through this gap, and for the next twelve months, the factory suggests that no servicing be performed in the field—all quartz watches should be returned to the Timex Corporation, P.O. Box 2740, Little Rock, Ark. 72203. The piece will still be in warranty and there will be no charge for this service.

We show three photos of the model 62 —"A" shows the complete watch with only the back of the case removed; "B" is with the insulator ring removed, and "C" is of the sub-strate board after it has been removed. This board carries the quartz crystal and the integrated circuitry board. Fig. 1 is an exploded sketch of the movement while Fig. 2 is the exploded sketch of the entire watch. Both are virtually self-explanatory, having each part designated, etc.

"B"

"C"

"A"

the TIMEX Model 62 Movement (exploded view)

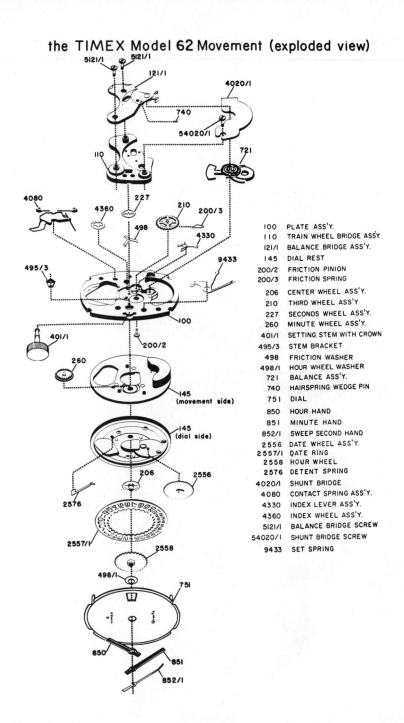

100	PLATE ASS'Y.
110	TRAIN WHEEL BRIDGE ASS'Y.
121/1	BALANCE BRIDGE ASS'Y.
145	DIAL REST
200/2	FRICTION PINION
200/3	FRICTION SPRING
206	CENTER WHEEL ASS'Y.
210	THIRD WHEEL ASS'Y.
227	SECONDS WHEEL ASS'Y.
260	MINUTE WHEEL ASS'Y.
401/1	SETTING STEM WITH CROWN
495/3	STEM BRACKET
498	FRICTION WASHER
498/1	HOUR WHEEL WASHER
721	BALANCE ASS'Y.
740	HAIRSPRING WEDGE PIN
751	DIAL
850	HOUR HAND
851	MINUTE HAND
852/1	SWEEP SECOND HAND
2556	DATE WHEEL ASS'Y.
2557/1	DATE RING
2558	HOUR WHEEL
2576	DETENT SPRING
4020/1	SHUNT BRIDGE
4080	CONTACT SPRING ASS'Y.
4330	INDEX LEVER ASS'Y.
4360	INDEX WHEEL ASS'Y.
5121/1	BALANCE BRIDGE SCREW
54020/1	SHUNT BRIDGE SCREW
9433	SET SPRING

Figure 1.

41

TIMEX QUARTZ WATCH (exploded view)

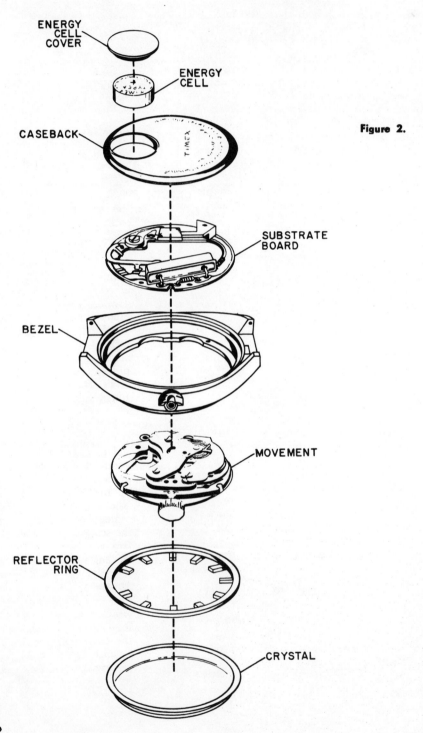

ENERGY CELL COVER

ENERGY CELL

CASEBACK

Figure 2.

SUBSTRATE BOARD

BEZEL

MOVEMENT

REFLECTOR RING

CRYSTAL

That basic principle embodied in the Timex 62 — it's not new — possibly in the first application to a watch worn upon the wrist and goes back to about the turn of this century when Frank-Hope Jones and William H. Shortt came up with their free pendulum, precision regulator in which they utilized a pendulum to do the work of powering the hands along with a second, extremely accurate pendulum which acted as the time standard and made a "slave" of the work pendulum.

Timex 62 has an orthodox balance and hairspring, but this balance is not the time standard, it is merely the motor to perform the work of rotating the hands, moving the date ring, etc., and is the "slave" of the quartz crystal which holds it precisely to six beats per second. Therefore, the time standard of the 62 is that highly accurate crystal vibrating 49,152 cycles per second.

Some 300 transistors in a micro computer system step the cycles down to six per second to hold the balance-motor to a very close time tolerance—the manufacturer says on the order of fifteen seconds per month.

Think that one over—it poses the question as to whether the average bench horologist will ever service it or not? To do so requires SPECIAL electronic equip-which is now available only at the Timex factory. It may or may not be made available to the general repair trade in the future; at this point in time I would doubt it: 1) it would be very expensive, 2) it would require special training to use. Both the crystal and the integrated circuitry appear to be easily detachable; thus it is reasonable to speculate that they along with other parts may be made available in due course.

As with all electric watches that first step in disassembly is to remove the energy cell. The flat circular piece on the back is the cell cover, insert a knife edge under it at the point where it says "Lift Here" and pry the cover off. The case back is brought off in the same manner via a notch located at the energy cell end—a sharp blade and pry up.

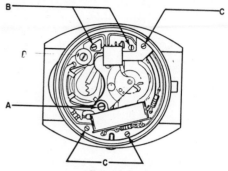

Figure 3.

Photo "A" shows the 62 with case back removed. The regulator—that one on the hairspring you are accustomed to seeing—should not be moved because it has already been positioned at the factory for the best performance. Actual regulation is made with the variable capacitor screw shown at D, Fig. 3.

Clockwise rotation to make the watch go faster and counterclockwise rotation to make it go slower. Turning this screw only a very little should bring the desired time rate; if the watch fails to respond to these movements such would indicate that some electronic changes have occurred in which case it shouuld be returned to the factory for their analysis and correction.

The sub-strate board carrying the quartz and integrated circuit as shown in photo "C" is removed by these four steps: 1) Remove the balance bridge screw A in Fig. 3, and the gold washer under it. 2) remove the two sub-strate board screws B again Fig. 3, very carefully; caution must be exercised here to assure that no damage is done to the legs which support and connect the integrated circuit. 3) remove the three case screws marked C. 4) The sub-strate board is now free of the movement and case and may be lifted out.

Under the sub-strate board you will find a plastic insulator; this is loose and has to be lifted out. Note closely the up side of this insulator as well as its orientation to make sure of correct reassembly. Next, slide the energy cell connector from under the balance bridge—note its position as well as exercise care not to deform the spring.

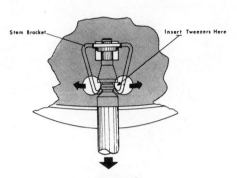

Stem Bracket

Insert Tweezers Here

Figure 4.

This brings us to the stem—see Fig. 4—being electric the sole function of this crown and stem is to stop the movement, set the hands and the date. A new and novel method of stem retention is employed. Stem and set pinion are one piece; it is retained in the movement by a flexible stem bracket—see exploded view Fig. 1 at 401/1—no screws or levers hold it.

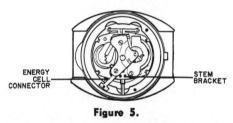

ENERGY
CELL
CONNECTOR

STEM
BRACKET

Figure 5.

To remove pull it to the setting position and continue a slight outward pull while inserting the points of heavy tweezers into one of the two stem removal holes as clearly shown in Fig. 4. That action releases the stem bracket arm on that side; your stem now tilts sidewise. Push the tweezer points into the other hole while pulling outward. When the second bracket has released, stem and its pinion comes out easily.

To reassemble the stem and pinion to the watch, presss the stem firmly into place with a slight rotation motion to make the stem pinion teeth mesh with the minute wheel teeth. The bracket will grasp and secure the stem automatically.

We now have the mechanical portion out of the case and ready for such servicing as may be indicated. We mentioned

before that it is close to "Model 40" — the significant difference being in the balance assembly, item 721 in Fig. 1; the contact spring assembly, item 4080, and the regulator upon the balance bridge assembly, item 121/1.

These are particularly delicate and should be handled with special care to prevent distortion or damage. When this special care feature has been observed, the movement can then be cleaned and/or serviced as per those instructions in the Timex service manual section 40, covering model 40. Section 40 is some 14 pages of illustrated instructions, I would surmise that these instructions are available from the Little Rock office if requested upon your regular business stationery, however, I am not authorized to say so.

Since those cleaning and lube instructions barely make one page I'll jot them down here for good measure.

Quote: "Cleaning the Model 40 Movement. Timex has found, after careful investigation, that the best way to clean the movement is to disassemble the movement only to the point of removing the balance bridge and the balance. The balance should be cleaned separately in a small jar to avoid damage to the coil. The coil is composed of ultra-fine copper wire and should not be handled with tweezers or other sharp instruments.

"Only standard watch cleaning solutions should be used throughout. Particles adhering to the magnet can be removed with Scotch tape.

"Lubricating the Model 40 Movement: the movement should be re-lubricated in the normal manner using high grade watch oils—oil used in factory assembly is Elgin M56b. The balance bearings should be filled half-full before inserting the balance. Other lubricating points are: 1, Impulse pin or fork slot. 2, index lever pivots. 3, index wheel teeth. 4, all wheel pivots. 5, the junction of the center wheel pinion and friction washer. 6, the junction between the minute wheel and dial rest. Apply grease — Hamilton PML type — to the stem where it is held by the stem bracket. DO NOT lubricate contact spring or contact pin on the balance. DO NOT use oil or grease containing siilicone." End quote.

Having cleaned and lubricated the mechanical portion of this movement, we are now ready to reassemble: Orient the movement; insert the stem through the pendant and replace the crystal making sure to position it to insure water resistance. Next, turn your watch over and reassemble as follows:

1) Slide the energy cell connector under the bridge and position as shown in Fig. 5, making sure that the hole in the connector coincides with the hole in the case. 2) Drop in the insulator, positioning it exactly as it came out. 3) place the substrate board on top of the insulator and position so that hole in the energy cell spring is centered around the balance bridge screw, exercising care not to damage the board. Insert and tighten two substrate board screws—"B": in Fig. 3 — again exercising extereme care so as not to deform or damage the leads of the integrated circuit. 4) Insert and tighten the three screws marked "C". 5) remove the balance bridge screw—"A"—center the gold washer on top of the hole in the energy cell spring, and secure with the tightened down bridge screw. 6) position the case back with the tab in the small notch opposite the energy cell end and snap it into place. 7) Replace energy cell and energy cell cover, then set to time and correct date.

Unlike some other Timex electrics, the sweep seconds hand of the "62" does not move by seconds, rather it is advanced six times per second giving the appearance of continuous moving as upon sync. electric clocks.

Quartz crystal accuracy is with us as we see it; this slave adaptation of it needs hold no fear by the bench watchmaker because of its sophisticated electronic circuitry. We predict he will take it "in stride"—make new satisfied clients in this moon walk age of ultra precision timekeeping and that, it will become a vital part in his service business—time will tell.

Watch Has Chain Drive

I have an old watch, which has a chain drive, and not only sets with a key, but also winds with a key.

The back of its has engraved on it the following: M-, Will E. Edwards, Derby, #2310.

Could you give me any information regarding age, and manufacture of the watch?

A.

There are a number of "William Edwards" listed, but only one for Derby — so, he must be our boy.

Williams Edwards, Derby, was actively at work from 1801 ro 1825.

All key wound watches were also "key-set" i.e. no winding stem, no setting stem — it had to be key. Derby — note: it is not Darby — is a sizable town in Derbyshire, about 50 miles north of Birmingham, England. The #2310 was his serial number — actually, it does not mean any more than just that, these old makers followed any method that struck their fancy; add to this the fact that we have no records of their individual systems and you can see how meaningless it is. I've been told that many had a yen to start with a pretty high number; this tended to give the impression that he was a pretty big operator and/or had been in business for many years — perhaps, some of both.

During the period indicated above, a very great percentage of watch work was entirely by hand, however, this does not mean that old Willie sat down and produced every piece one by one with his own fingers as it was done several years before. Blanks and parts were available from "specialists" throughout the country — there were hand makers, dial makers, chain makers, etc. Even blank-pinions were obtainable, the chances are that he assembled semi-finished parts and with the aid of an apprentice or two began to build the complete watches — in all likelihood he obtained his cases from case-makers down in Liverpool.

CLOCK DATA

This clock came in a rather neat, plain, medium-sized mahogany mantel case. Small label on its back read "The Anniversary," while on the porcelain enamel dial was lettered "Year Clock Company, New York." Stamped on the back plate, "Series A" No. 713, Patented October 21, 1891, February 8, 1898, and December 29, 1903, other patents pending. Checking with the Patent Office for copies reveals that the 1891 and 1898 were issued to Sigmund B. Wortmann and the 1903 to Martin Wortmann. Basically, all three may apply as they are primarily devoted to the driving power. However, that of 1903 by Martin Wortmann is almost identical and the only one of the three with a mechanism compact enough for a movement of this size.

In patent No. 748,250, December 29, 1903, Mr. Martin Wortmann says: "One of the objects of the invention is to provide a center wind. That is to say, the winding arbor has the mainspring coiled thereabout and the construction is such that a very short wind in proportion to the length of the spring to be wound is obtained. Another object· of the invention is to provide means to compensate for the unwinding of one end of the spring by winding at a proportionately less speed from the other end so that the spring will not unwind as fast as otherwise would be the case."

Fig. 1 shows the power plant of this clock and illustrates clearly how the above ends are accomplished. The winding arbor has regular 8-day size square and fitted fast thereon is the ratchet wheel; the ratchet click being mounted on the large gear on the right. Inner coil of mainspring, a full inch wide by 12 feet long, hooks on the arbor and the outer end hooks to the barrel. The lesser gear on the left, while smaller than the barrel, is a solid part of it (barrel).

Fig. I

Above the barrel is the second arbor of the train. The wheel and both pinions are fast fixed to it—the smaller pinion on the right is threaded on as the safety pinion center of a watch. It is a safety feature just as in watches—in case of spring breakage, reverse power unscrews it. The barrel diameter is 70.0 mm., that of its lesser gear on the left is 60.5 mm. with 93 teeth. The gear on the winding arbor (right) is 66.0 mm. diameter with 102 teeth. The wheel of the second arbor is 38.0 mm. diameter, 95 teeth. The larger pinion next to it, 18.5 mm. diameter, 27 leaves, while the small pinion (safety) on the right is 12.5 mm. diameter with 18 leaves. It requires a full eighteen turns of the key to wind.

Fig. 2 shows the remainder of the train located in front of the front main plate. The two main plates are 92.0 mm. diameter; a third and smaller plate, 63 mm. diameter, fits above the train and just under the dial. *Fig. 3* is the dial view.

Fig. 2

The largest wheel in *Fig. 2* is the third wheel of the train. The 95-tooth wheel in *Fig. 1* drives this third wheel by meshing with a pinion 5.2 mm. diameter, 12 leaves just under the third wheel. Center (fourth wheel) 15.0 mm. diameter, 80 teeth, pinion 4.0 mm. diameter, 10 leaves. Fifth, 12.5 mm. diameter, 75 teeth, pinion 2.0 mm. diameter, 10 leaves. Sixth, 11.4 mm. diameter, 80 teeth, pinion 1.7 mm. diameter, 10 leaves. Escape wheel, 8.0 mm. diameter, 15

Fig. 3

teeth (club), pinion 1.4 mm. diameter, 8 leaves. This extreme high gearing gives approximately 65,856 revolutions of escape per revolution of the mainspring barrel; cut ex-

pansion balance wheel, flat hairspring, 7 jewels.

GOLDEN HOUR CLOCK

We've already noted an issue or two back the Golden Hour mystery clock. At that time we asked for any instructions or technical data, etc. F. A. Delaney, sales manager for Jefferson Electric Company sends down instructions for replacing the Golden Hour glass.

Fig. 4 is an exploded sketch of this clock. It operates on 110-125 volts, A-C 60 cycle current powered by a Hayden synchronous motor, a unit already familiar to the repairman.

To take the clock apart, first set both hands at 12 o'clock. Unscrew cone numbered (1) at front. Minute hand (2), lock washer (3), flat gold washer (4) and fiber washer (5), will all come forward and off in that order.

Second, the hour hand and counterbalance unit (10) then comes out the back. Take out the flared fiber washer (9) and lay the clock flat, face-down.

Third, remove gold retaining ring (8) by gently prying out with a screwdriver inserted in the small slot at the 12 position.

Fourth, entire glass (7) then comes out with its ring gear attached. Now, take out the three small leaf springs (6) to prevent losing them.

Your job is disassembled now and ready for the new glass. To reassemble is the exact opposite of the above. Begin by making sure that all three leaf springs (6) are in proper position in their sockets then slip in the new glass (7) making sure that the ring gear meshes properly with the main base gear. Snap gold ring (8) into place. Next place flared fiber washer (9) in center hole; now the hour hand and counterbalance assembly (10) go on. Make sure that it is aligned straight up—hour hand pointing exactly to 12 and counter weight straight down to 6. Put the remainder back in reverse order from taking it down, 5, 4, 3, 2, and 1, lining up the minute hand with the hour hand and both to 12 o'clock. Adjust the hands to allow approximately ⅛-inch clearance from glass. To set, turn the minute hand forward (clockwise) to the desired minute, then revolve the counterbalance on the back of the clock until the hour hand points to the desired hour. Caution: Never turn the minute hand backward.

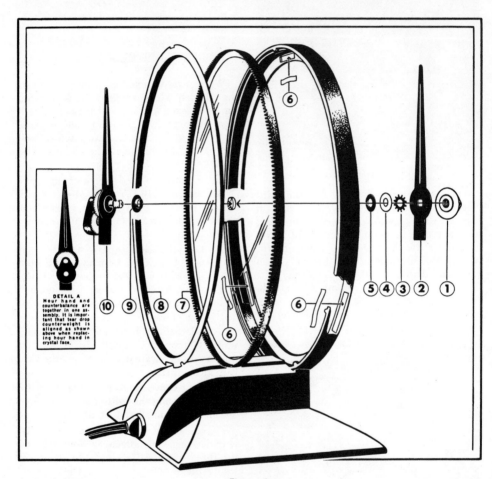

Figure 4

5 SPOKE WHEEL

We have had several discussions on why there are five spokes in a train wheel. As yet we haven't found a good reason why. I would appreciate any information you can supply on this subject.

A. The reason must be structural rather than horological; for a wheel with any number of spokes—or even solid—other conditions being the same, would work. It is quite obvious that weight is a factor, in other words the lightest possible wheel is desired, and likewise, strength is essential. To build a wheel with an even number of spokes will allow it to more easily bend straight across a diameter running between spokes; with an odd number of spokes the straight-across bend would not transverse two spaces. Three isn't enough; seven, too many; thus five.

SETTING HANDS

The question I have in mind is in regard to setting the hands on clocks and watches backwards. I personally feel that with the exception of strike clocks there is no harm in doing this. However, there seems to be a dispute among a group of us watchmakers about setting alarm clocks backward. Some of the fellows contend that it will change the setting of the alarm. I tried setting both the electric and wind types backward and found that it had no effect on the alarm setting. This did not seem to satisfy some of the others as they claimed it did not always work the same. So I would greatly appreciate it if you would settle the question for us.

A.

As a rule it is always better to set alarm clocks forward. I note you say you tried setting them backward and found that it had no effect.

You will get no effect from a slight backward setting, if the time indicated by the hands happens to be a few hours from alarm time. Take the nearest old alarm clock at hand and remove the dial, turn the alarm set forward until it releases, and you will see that little lip directly under the alarm hand has dropped into a small slot allowing the alarm set wheel to raise up and release the alarm hammer. Now, if you grasp the time set and turn the center post *backward* (set the hands backward) you will see that the alarm set wheel also turns backward. The back side of slot is straight, not

"V" cut. Thus as the wheel turns backward it pushes the alarm hand post backward because the little lip can't ride up as it does when the clock is turning forward.

JACQUES MOREL CLOCK

Also enclosed was photo (see illustration) of a clock built by his close friend, M. Jacques Morel, at Isigny-s-Mer, France. It was first exhibited to the public in that city July 14, and is shortly to go to Paris. Much of its outer construction is plywood, and I get the impression of "Snow White and Seven Dwarfs." However, he does not mention it. The over-all dimensions are 2.25 mm. high by 1.20 mm. wide. "The lower part comprises the astronomical works, while the upper part houses the clock work and mechanism for operating the automatons; they all work at noon."

At the top, the acrobat makes 15 revolutions on the parallel bars; every two hours is given by the statesman with his pistol. Two rabbits in front strike the quarters; small rats strike the hours which are repeated by the fawn. At noon, the little character on the right turns the mill while a cuckoo makes 12 calls; at the bottom, the moon, the sun and seven stars representing the seven days of the week parade by Father Time who nods to each one; on the stairs (right) a little dog bearing "No. 1" on his nose, steps up. Another little animal has "No. 2" and other little characters carry other numbers up to 12. The bear on the bicycle with a bell has the bell struck by another bear 12 times; then everything stops until next noon. The Paris hour is given above, while another dial on the right gives the hour in four capitals of the world. In the lower section is a sphere half black and half gold which gives the moon phases. The central dial gives the date, the day and the planet corresponding to the day and the tides in Grandchamp-les-Bains bay (a harbor near his home). On the left are the seasons, the signs of the zodiac and a globe making one revolution every 24 hrs., indicating noon in all parts of the world.

We give you the lay-out of the movement in Figure 5. While he has built a good looking, mahogany grand-

Jacques Morel's Clock

teeth by 63.30 millimeters diameter. The third, 90 teeth by 59.70 millimeters diameter. All pinions are nicely cut, 12 leaves and 8.60 millimeters diameter. Plates 7¼ inches by 10½ inches, clearance between, 49.40 millimeters Graham dead beat escapement is used. (Note the ball bearings on the main and center arbors.) We were especially interested in this project, not so much because it has been discussed before, but rather because Mr. Young, starting from "scratch" made it 100 per cent. He even made up his own cutters. He is using invar for the rod and when the final touches are put to it and installed permanently in the case, he has promised us a record of the "rate."

MEASUREMENTS – ELLIOTT

'The following measurements are exact for an eight-day Elliott, English grandfather chime clock, linticular bob, lead filled, weight six pounds; diameter, 5-15/16 inches; thickness at center 1-⅛; suspension spring, 7/16 wide by ten-thousandths thick; length from hole center to hole center, 1-⅜ inches; overall length (bottom of ball to center top suspension spring hole) 43-⅝ inches."

JAMES FERGUSON

father case for it, we thought our readers might be more interested in the mechanical angle. The main wheel has 144 teeth, and is 97.40 millimeters diameter; the hour wheel, the same, and the center wheel, 96

Back in the mid-1700s, there lived in London an eminent astronomer and mechanician, James Ferguson, (b-1710, d-1776) who made many improvements in the clocks of his day and many inventions along this line. In 1771 he published "Tables and Tracts." In 1775, "Select Mechanical Exercises" and "An Introduction to Electricity." This latter book contains the first English reference for electric clocks. He is probably best known by his "Mechanical Paradox," Henry Abbott, and describes it as "a curious machine made for the purpose of silencing a London watchmaker who did not believe in the doctrine of the Trinity. Major Chamberlain says: "Ferguson's paradox in gear-work will preserve his name as long as civilization continues to use gearing." Possibly his next best known work was a clock made with only "one" wheel.

Fig. 5

Mr. Reum located in an old issue of the British Horological Journal a description of one of Ferguson's astronomical clocks, and proceeded to recreate it. Lest I make some error, I shall quote his description directly from his letter answering my request:

"The pendulum is the standard wood and lead pendulum, weighing about eight pounds. There is only one driving weight, 11 pounds, and it drives the entire mechanism. The winding square was located in the lower left-hand corner, connected to the barrel arbor by a train of four gears; it had to be constructed this way on account of the revolving dials in this clock. I used a Graham dead-beat escapement; the pendulum beats standard time, and the rotation of the sidereal dial of once in 23 hours and 56 minutes is obtained by means of gearing from the center wheel—the same also applies for the moon ball.

"I first made a full size drawing of the gearing, then I enlarged each wheel and meshing pinion to ten times larger in order to make my cutters. Each wheel and pinion had to have a special cutter—I used the module or metric system when making the cutters.

"The dial plate shows the twenty-four hours of the day; each hour is divided into twelve equal parts; thus each small division indicates five minutes of time. Within the division of the

The Reum Clock

hour circle is a flat ring, the face of which is in the same plane of the 24 hour circle. This ring is divided into 29½ equal parts and shows the moon's age from change to change; this ring turns once in 24 hours and has a fleur-de-lis upon it, serving as an hour index to point out the time of the day or night in the 24-hour circle. In the photo, the clock shows 10:09 Central Standard time and the small clock movement above the 24-hour dial shows 11:09 Daylight Saving time. This small dial was added by me as it was not in Ferguson's clock. The motion for this small dial is obtained by two pairs

of small helical gears driven by the center wheel of the main movement.

"Within the moving ring and about three-quarters of an inch below its surface is a flat circular dial on which the months and dates of the year are drawn and within these on the same plate is a circle containing the signs and degrees of the ecliptic, divided in such a manner that each particular day stands over the sign and degree of the sun's place that day. Within this circle, on the same plate, the ecliptic, equinotical and tropic are drawn, and all of the stars of the first, second, third and fourth magnitude that are seen in this latitude according to their respective right ascensions and declinations. This plate turns in 23 hours, 56 minutes and 4 seconds of time, being the length of a sidereal day, and consequently makes 366 revolutions per year.

"The motion work of the clock is such that the sun moves once around in 24 hours, the moon in 24 hours, 50½ minutes, and the stars in 23 hours, 56 minutes and 4 seconds. The sun is carried around upon a wire attached to the fleur-de-lis on the moving ring. The moon is carried by a wire attached to the center of the clock, and also turns upon its axis on that wire by means of two pairs of spiral gears in 29 days, 12 hours, and 45 minutes, so that is shows all of its phases for every day of its age from one new moon to another new moon.

"Upon the clock glass over the dial is drawn an ellipse representing the horizon, all stars within it are visible, and those outside are below the horizon at that time."

We are especially grateful to Mr. Reum for sending down this photo and description—far too great a percentage of the general public, and also too great a percentage of present day horologists have the idea that all horological knowledge, skill and activity can be completely covered by four words: i. e.., "clean, stem, staff and jewel."

Perpetual Calendar Mechanism

By J. E. Coleman

In answer to a question submitted by Samuel Zullo of Union City, New Jersey, concerning the mechanism which controls clocks made with perpetual calendar, J. E. Coleman, Clockwise and Otherwise editor, gives a complete explanation, incorporating material which has not been in publication since 1880.

THE MODERN CLOCK by Ward L. Goodrich has one chapter dealing with perpetual calendar mechanisms. It deals in detail with the Brocot perpetual calendar, a mechanism we sometimes find on foreign grandfather clocks and the Waterbury version of the American perpetual calendar. A thorough study of this chapter is a splendid approach to any serious understanding of this little-understood clock attachment.

This form of calendar mechanism—one compensating for 30 to 31-day months, leap years, etc.,—occupied much of the attention of our Early American clockmakers, Benjamin B. Lewis, Henry B. Horton, Galusha Maranville, James E. Mix, Joseph C. Burritt, Andrew Jackson Gale, and others.

The Waterbury, described by Goodrich, is not met with very often, and of course we see very few by Brocot. Gale's and Maranville's bob up once in a while. Those that the repairman is most often called upon to service are the Ithaca and Seth Thomas—both illustrated here. In basic workings, all are pretty much alike, because they do the same things. One might say that Fords and Chevrolets are alike—they, too, do the same things—but in detail, the various functions may be achieved by quite different mechanical actions.

First off, all your calendar mechanisms are tripped once each 24 hours—at midnight. Ninety-nine per cent do this by having a cam revolving once in 24 hours lift a connecting rod or wire (in case of the Ithaca, two wires) allowing it to drop by gravity at midnight. The drum, or indicator, for the week days is not complicated at all, for the simple reason that Monday follows Sunday, etc., and one forward move per trip is all that is necessary for its continual operation. The day-of-the-month hand has its complication because all months aren't the same; however, these changes are relatively simple when you trace them down. On the end of the month

drum (in the Seth Thomas it is No. 25 mounted on the inside end and on the Ithaca it is mounted on the outside end) is the month wheel. They call this a 12-tooth wheel. In reality, it is of 12 flat surfaces different distances from the center. This distance from center governs whether the day-indicating hand jumps across 31 or stops on it. It follows that the month-wheel is made fast to the month-drum, so the 31-day flat (tooth) is always even with January, etc.

Leap year has its variation taken care of at the February flat (tooth) of course. The depth of this flat is cut to 28 days, thus that depth will actuate the day-of-the-month hand to jump across 29, 30, and 31, landing correctly on 1 when the month drum turns up to March. There is a floating plate riveted to the month-wheel (No. 25) and this plate has attached to it, one leaf or space which will raise the February flat or notch up by just one day, making it a 29-day depth for leap year. This leaf is actuated by a pinion (No. 8) which revolves planetary fashion on a stationary pinion (No. 7). The stationary pinion is attached to the month-drum support. The ratio is 4-to-1; thus the February flat is of 28 days' height during the three revolutions, and on the fourth, the floating plate moves into place, making it of 29 days' height.

A cam on the day-of-the-month hand actuates the month-drum, i. e., each revolution of the month-hand trips the month-drum one notch or tooth forward.

From the "Fashion" clock booklet, we illustrate all the parts of the Seth Thomas perpetual calendar mechanism, and have located the corresponding parts' numbers on our photo of the actual mechanism.

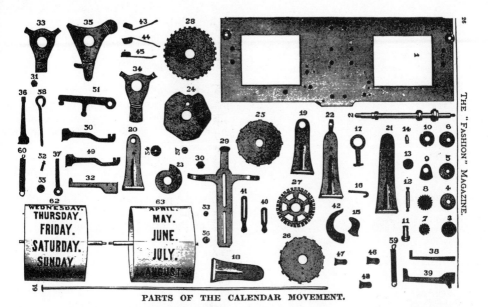

PARTS OF THE CALENDAR MOVEMENT.

Fashion clock booklet illustration.

Seth Thomas movement with parts numbered.

Follow-
ing is the partial list as published with the
"Fashion" photo:

1. Plate
2. Center shaft
3. Disk hub
4. Month-wheel hub
5. Day-wheel hub
6. Center-wheel hub
7. Stationary gear
8. Revolving gear
9. Revolving gear plate
10. Safety ratchet
11. Center-lift hub
12. Center-lift hub stand
13. Slide bushing
14. Connecting loop pin
15. Safety click
16. Steeples for spiral springs
17. Shield
18. Outside roll standard (2 in each movement)
19. Stationary gear standards
20. Front center standard
21. Back center standard
22. Center lift and day roll standard
23. Center shaft cam
24. Disk
25. Month-wheel (12 teeth)
26. Day-wheel (14 teeth, 2 weeks per rev.)
27. Friction center wheel
28. Center wheel (31 teeth)
29. Slide
30. Standard rivets (six in each movement)
31. Revolving gear rivet
32. Center locking spring
33. Month click plate
34. Day click plate
35. Center click plate
36. Detent spring
37. Leap year pawl spring
38. Passing spring
39. Leap year pawl
40. Center lift loop
41. Slide loop (2 in each movement)
42. Friction spring (3 in each movement)
43. Month click spring
44. Day click spring
45. Center click spring
46. Day click
47. Month click
48. Center click
49. Day locking spring
50. Month locking spring
51. Center lift
52. Center lift pin
53. Disk hub screw
54. Connection check nut
55. Slide rivets (2 in each movement)
56. Locking spring and screw (5 in each movement)
57. Standard screw (6 in each movement)
58. Connection loop screw
59. Day and month spiral springs
60. Center spiral spring
61. Connection rod
62. Day roll
63. Month roll

Quoting further from this listing: "Slide
29, which is attached to the connecting
rod 61 by the connection loop screw 59,
is raised once in 24 hours by a cam at the
back of the time movement. When the
slide raises the passing pin on click, plate
35 passes up on the outside of passing
spring 38; also the click on click plate 34
passes up outside of day locking spring 49
when it drops from the cam; the click and
pin pass down inside of their respective
springs, unlocking wheels 26 and 28, when
the clicks cause them to be moved forward

one day: then the spring returns to place
locking them as before.

"The disk 24 governs the length of the
month, assisted by leap year pawl 39 and
shield 17. The pawl follows the surface of
the disk. W'.en on the highest point it allows the shield to pass the point on the opposite side of the pawl from the disk, making 31 days in the month. When resting
on flat places of the disk, the short step
of shield 17 passes under the point of
pawl, unlocking wheel 28, and allowing
locking spring 32 to pass one tooth in the
wheel, making 30 days in that month.
When the pawl rests on the bottom of the
deep cut in the disk it allows the long
step of the shield to pass under the point
of pawl, causing wheel 28 to be carried
along three days before locking again, making 28 days in that month. The revolving
gear plate 9 is a cam and comes before
the deep cut once in four years, and
shortens the distance enough to allow the
middle step of the shield to pass under the
pawl and make 29 days that month, which
is February—Leap Year.

"The month roll changes when the center lift 51 drops off the cam 23 on center
shaft 2, when the click on click plate 33
passes down inside of locking spring 50,
and carrying the month roll forward one
month when it is locked as before.

"The month and day rolls may be turned
forward or backward at any time without
disarranging the calendar, but the day of
the month-hand must not be turned back
after the 28th day, and no farther than the
1st".

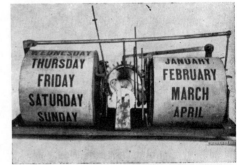

Ithaca Calendar

I've followed calendar mechanisms pretty
closely for many years. One sees very little

about them, and I believe this is the first time the above has been published anywhere since 1880. The little Fashion magazine was put out by the Southern Calendar Clock Company, and one copy was given to each purchaser of their clock.

New Danish Clock 'Eighth Wonder of the World'

The world's most accurate clock, which will gain only four-tenths of a second in 300 years, is nearly ready to be installed in the town hall in Copenhagen. The lifework of a Danish locksmith, Jens Olsen, who died before it was completed, the clock weighs four tons and has over 110,000 different parts.

The clock in Strasbourg cathedral, hitherto regarded as the world's finest, has an inaccuracy of eight seconds in a century.

The Jens Olsen clock contains 12 main sections. The main dial, in the centre, shows the time on a 12-hour face as understood by the man in the street—the time known to navigators and astronomers as the local mean time.

But if the man in the street looks at the other dials, he is likely to find that the question "What is the time?" has more than one answer. If he should not be satisfied with the answer in the man-made division of the day into 24 equal hours (local mean time), Jens Olsen's clock will give it to him in sidereal time—the time as measured by the stars. A day and night measured in sidereal time is slightly shorter than a man-made 24-hour day.

Nor does the clock stop there. Another dial gives the hour in solar time—the time as measured by the sun. The three times are slightly different and the differences, although unimportant in normal usage, are vitally important to navigators plotting their positions by observations of the position of the sun or stars.

The most spectacular section of the clock comes into operation only once a year—at midnight on Dec. 31—and takes slightly more than five minutes to complete its function. The results of this are spread over five dials and a rectangular calendar. They show the days of the week and months against each new date for a whole year, the epact (the age of the moon on Jan. 1), the phases of the moon, the dates of the movable feasts and other facts relating to the movements of the moon and of the earth around the sun.

The operating mechanism takes leap years into account. The mechanism for showing the epact (from which is worked out the date of Easter) also takes into account a correction necessary every 19 years; and if this 19th year happens to be a leap year, the mechanism (run by electricity) takes this also in its stride.

Elsewhere on the clock can be read off the local mean time in nearly every part of the world.

The Olsen clock also shows:

1. The time of sunset and sunrise each day.
2. The date of the month, the name of the day, the name of the month and the year. The mechanism operating this takes leap years into account and includes a wheel which takes 400 years to revolve once around its axis. The fastest rotating wheel takes 10 seconds to complete one revolution and the slowest takes 26,000 years.
3. Positions of the main stars. The mechanism here has to be adjusted every 3,000 years to take accumulating minor corrections into account.
4. The relative positions of the sun, earth and moon.
5. Eclipses of the sun.

The plans for the clock were completed in 1919, but Jens Olsen did not succeed in raising sufficient funds to start work on it until 1944. Many of the parts had to be made by hand.

Danish watch-makers describe the clock as "the eighth wonder of the world."

GRAVITY CLOCK

From the patent office we have obtained copies of the two Davies patents—No. 4,354, issued January 15, 1846, covers a gravity clock—the general idea being to hang a weight-driven type clock by its weight cord and allow the clock's weight to act as its own driving weight; the specifications indicate a non-striker.

Patent No. 4,687 of August 12, 1846, covers only the strike train, and we are sure that this is the strike Mr. Hagans has—quite a unique arrangement and we are sure will interest many of our readers. Fig. (1) is the patent drawing, and following is Mr. Davies' description taken verbatim from the patent:

Description.—The drawings are not made with reference to showing all the working parts of a clock complete; but merely such parts as are necessary to illustrate the new principles as the other parts would only serve to confuse. (See drawing.) Let R be the center of the hour and minute shafts. V the center of the strike wheel. S the center of the lifting shaft. Y the center of the fly wheel shaft. U the center of the gear wheel shaft from the strike wheel to the fly. M, P, the strike wire which plays upon 13 pins in the circumference of the strike wheel. L O the hammer spring. N the wire carrying the hammer which strikes the bell. T K the fly. S G the arm to stop the fly and raise the connecting rod H, J, S, F, (bent wire) the means by which the lifting part is raised by the bent wire R, W. *a, a,* the register. 1', 2', 3', 4' 5' 6', 7' 8' 9' 10' 11' 12' being indentures each one answering for an hour except the indentures marked 5', 6',

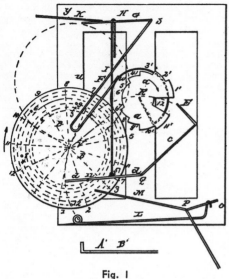

Fig. I

7' which answers for 3 hours, *d d*. C E arms upon a center shaft 2, one leading to the register, the other to pins or stops marked 12, (1.11) (2.10), (3, 9), (4, 8), (57) and 6 upon the strike wheel. The end of the arm *d, d,* made as is represented at A' B' turned toward the wheel and made a little hollowing so as to catch the pins more firmly, 1, 2, 3, 4, 5, 6, 7, 8, 9, 10, 11, 12, 13, being pins against which the strike wire M, P, plays. Now suppose the clock in operation and the center shaft connected in the usual way with the time works. We will also suppose that the hook on the end of the arm *d d* has just left the stop pin 12, and that the end of the arm of the lever C, E, has left the space on the register marked 12, and that the lifting rods and works are all in the position represented in the drawing. The register being firmly attached to the hour socket will of course travel with it, and when the register will have so far progressed that the lift wire S F falls from the bent wire R, W, the arm *d, d,* will fall at the same moment and carry the end E of the lever C, E, onto the division on the register marked 1' and the end of the arm *d d* will fall into such a position as that it will catch a pin in the strike wheel marked (1, 11). The fly when the lift wires drop will be liberated and striking parts commence to move and of course the pin on the opposite side of the strike wheel at 3 will catch the arm M P and cause one blow upon the bell with the hammer. But before another strike pin comes to the arm M P the further progress of the wheel is stopped by the pin (1, 11) catching the end of the lever *d, d,* so that in this position the clock strikes one. Let the works again progress in a short time the bent wire on the center shaft will begin to raise the lifting parts and at the moment the arm *d, d,* is raised from the pin

(1, 11) the wire S, G, comes within range of the stop on the fly wheel and the clock is prevented from striking till the end of the hour when the lifting parts again fall and the end of the arm C, E, falls on the division marked 2 on the register and the end of the lever *d d* into the next outward consecutive circle and the clock will strike two in the same way as before and stop upon the pin marked (2, 10). The same for 3, 4, and 5. It now strikes 6 and 7 upon the same circle that it struck 5 upon and then commences its course back toward the center of the strike wheel striking alternately 8, 9, 10 and 11 upon the same pins and upon the same circles upon which it struck 4, 3, 2, and 1. It strikes 12 in the same way by passing from 11 to 12 on the register and stop pins. There are here described seven pins or stops arranged in six consecutive circles and it is entirely conventional upon which of the circles the pins are placed provided always that the register is made to correspond and that the pins 6 and (7, 5) are on the same circle. The same object can be accomplished with any number of pins or stops on the strike wheel from 7 to 12. In case 12 wire used arranged in 12 consecutive circles upon the strike wheel and placed regularly from in to out or from out to in the register would assume the form of the common snail but of course applied for different objects and to serve different ends. The same end could be accomplished by having a separate wheel upon the strike wheel shaft or arms to run from the strike wheel shaft to hold the stops.

What I claim as new and original and desire to secure by Letters Patent is—

1. Applying to the hour socket of a clock a register made as above described for the purpose of counting off as the hours go around to stops upon the strike wheel or to stops arranged upon the strike wheel shaft.

2. I also claim the application of two arms from a center shaft essentially as above described the end of one of which strikes upon a register as above described guiding the end of the other to stops upon the strike wheel or to stops arranged upon the strike wheel shaft.

3. I also claim the new mode of stopping the striking parts of a clock by means of pins or stops arranged upon the strike wheel or upon stops arranged upon the strike wheel shaft, essentially as above described.

4. I also claim the combination in a clock of the lifting part, the stops arranged as above described, the two arms form a center for the objects above described, and the register made and applied as above described, all together or any two together.

I am sending you a few pictures of some of the jobs we have done. This, we believe, is the answer to many a clockmaker's headache, especially the bi-synchronous Hammond (the $3.98, 20 years ago mantle clock); the French clock without visible pendulum that has been mutilated; one prize photo shows a Waterbury ship's bell movement where the escapement was ruined beyond repair, the strike mainspring barrel cover was ruined, as you can see the repair on it. Now these clocks are a useful modern timepiece with all of the inside aspects of grandma's old clock.

This has been our answer to satisfactory time which makes our customers very happy. The photo showing the dial and case of a 4-jewel Waterbury in a large marble unit with barometer and temperature gauge, now the customer is very happy, as I am, with the Ansonia chime which is mine.

Figure I

From all evidence Mr. Kemp is quite versatile when it comes to applying the synchronous motor to old clocks. In figure

Figure 2

number one, a Telechron motor has been applied to a Seth Thomas 77-B (80-beat regulator) ; in figure number two, an old English grandfather movement has been completely electrified (both time and strike) by driving the time train with a Hansen 600 series motor and the strike train by a Hayden motor.

The third photo is the common garden variety of eight-day American mantle movement with a Telechron motor driving the time train; the strike train was left

Figure 3

intact. It is wound weekly and strikes exactly as if the time train was propelled by its original mainspring.

Personally we've never been able to whip up enthusiasm for substituting a synchronous motor, but on the insistence of the customer, we've done it a few times when we could not talk them into a restoration job. Successful department stores insist that "the customer is always right," but my experience has been that the customer is seldom right.

Why should Mrs. John Doe go to an auction and bid her socks off for some clock simply because it is said to be an "antique," then immediately have it modernized? This sort of doing reminds me of the story of the fellow who wanted to take a plane ride, but keep one foot on the ground. Let's either ride or stand on both feet!

If Mrs. Doe wants an electric clock, she ought to hie down to a reliable jeweler's and buy one. If she wants an antique, she ought to buy same, but keep it so by paying some clockmaker with equipment and ability to restore it to its original mechanical condition. This is just one man's opinion. Friend Kemp seems to be doing a good job of what he attempts—maybe he is making his customers happier than I do mine. After all, we must have those groceries. We'd like to hear from him and from some of our readers on the question: "To Electrify or Not to Electrify?"

How To Read Chronometer Dials

By no means is our memory comparable to that attributed to the elephant, but, it will reach back over a few weeks and we recall that this is the third request for some explanation on reading chronograph dials. This last one asked that we "please publish".

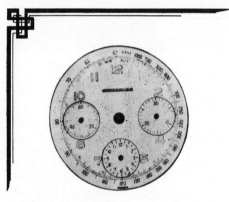

TACHYMETER-TELEMETER DIAL.

Our cut shows an example of a chronograph dial calibrated to show the tachymeter and the telemeter combined. Perhaps the most popular form; there are slight variations but basic principles are the same. The seconds track is divided into 1/5th, second divisions; on either side of it are two additional scales. The outer "tachymeter" scale shows the speed of a vehicle traveling over a measured mile. The sweep hand is started

at the beginning of the measured distance and stopped at the end, thus you read miles per hour at the tip of the stopped hand. It is at this point we encounter some of the variations, i.e. for different measured distances. Such as 1/4th mile or 1/2 mile—this may always be determined from the figure at the starting point; that figure in the illustrated dial is 60 indicating that this scale is for a measured mile. For a measured quarter mile that figure would be 15, and, for a measured half-mile the calibration would indicate 30.

The inner "Telemeter" scale is for showing the approximate distance between an observer and a simultaneous sound and sight occurrence such as a gun fired (when you see the flash) or as a lightning flash and thunder. When the flash is seen the sweep hand is started. When the sound is heard the sweep hand is stopped, the figure under the tip is the distance from the observer. The speed of light is considered instantaneous and the time is based on the speed of sound through air at approximately 1,129 feet per second.

Where one has a practical need for using the "Telemeter" scale he should use a magnifier to read it with. Above all; for accurate timing there is no substitute for practice, a timer is only as good as its operator. The correct use of a chronograph and/or timer is comparable to firing a rifle. The pushpieces have to have a certain amount of 'play'. Just like the rifle the watch trips at a certain point when the finger feels the proper tension. This point is determined by practice with your own watch. For the greatest accuracy the pushpiece should be depressed almost to this critical point so that very little additional motion will cause the watch to stop or start, as the case may be.

With proper operation and practice the error in timing will only be a few hundredths of a second—timers that are not used regularly ought to be kept under cover to protect them from dust laden air, actually, they should be operated about once every week or so to keep the oil fluid and before serious timing it should be allowed to run for two or three hours.

Specifications for a Church Clock at Lyme, Conn. December, 1828.

On the plate (opposite page) is shown the work of a town clock. 1 in. equals the foot (in original drawing). **A** is the plan. **B** a front view. **C** elevation of cams for striking and **D** view of the cam wheel.

Time part .... Fig.	1 is verge wheel	7½ in. diam.	24 teeth
" " .... "	2 pinion	1½ " "	10 "
" " .... "	3 wheel	8½ " "	76 "
" " .... "	4 "	1½ " "	10 "
" " .... "	5 "	9 " "	80 "
" " .... "	6 "	1¾ " "	12 "
" " .... "	7 "	16 " "	120 "
" " .... "	8 "	6 " "	48 "
" " .... "	9 "	6 " "	48 "
" " .... "	10 "	10¾ " "	120 "
" " .... "	66 "	1 " "	10 "
" " .... "	11 "	7¾ " "	96 "
" " .... "	12 cam wheel	9 " "	
" " .... "	13 dial	8 " "	
" " .... "	666 wheel	1¼ " "	8 "
Striking part.......................... Fig.	1 wheel	10¾ in. diam.	120 teeth
" " .... "	2 "	9 " "	80 "
" " .... "	3 "	1¾ " "	12 "
" " .... "	4 "	1½ " "	10 "
" " .... "	5 "	8¾ " "	78 "
" " .... "	6 "	1¾ " "	12 "
" " .... "	7 a tenon on end arbor that takes in teeth of strike and draws it up		
" " .... "	8 fly	7½ in. long and 5½ wide	

Frame 5 feet long, 2 feet 3 inches high. 2 feet wide.

a is shaft that operates hammer—

b finger that connects to wire that leads to hammer 4½ inches long.

c finger that catches pin i in wheel 1 and trips hammer—

d is hollow tube that carries hour hand through which arbor c passes for minute hand.

ff ends of arbors for cord wheels: for which to wind the clock.

g a plate supported by two posts for arbor bearings—

h arm that extends from lever 17, that catches the pin i in the wheel 5 which stops the striking part.

k verge, the arms 5¾ in. long from center to point of pallets. The pallets are 5½ from point to point. Pendulum hangs one inch above the verge at c.

14 is cord barrel, 7½ in. diam., 14½ in. long—

18 is cord barrel, 7½ in. diam., 14½ in. long for striking part,

m is lever that throws the rack back just before striking—

o pin to fetch up against arm which when rack n falls back,

i lever that falls in and stops it when it has struck the number of times.

q is the end of lever 17 made crooked; there is a cam on the shaft of the wheel 666 which when it comes round it catches on the end of **q** and bearing it down raises the arm **h** and slips it by the pin **i** which raises lever **q** and slips the end from the rack **n**. The rack then falls back a certain number of teeth according to the cam. 7 moves the rack one tooth every time it strikes till the end of **h** falls in the notch of the rack with the pin **c** and stops the striking.

d is the cam wheel, 12 cams from 2 ins. long to ¾ in. long and 4½ in. to 1 in. from center.

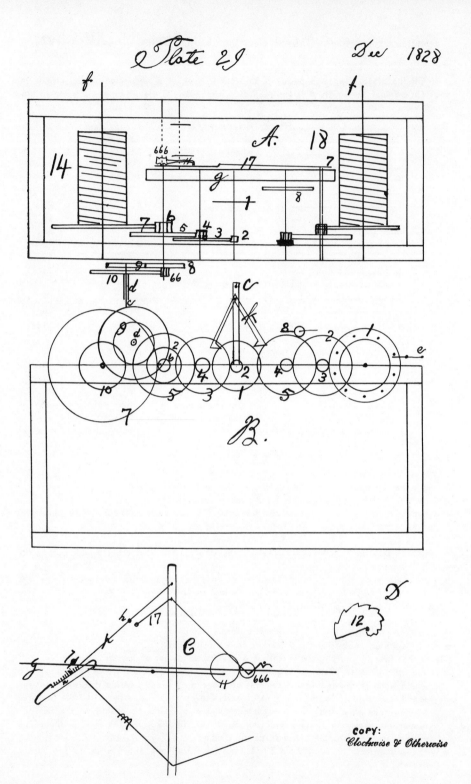

Plate 29

Dec 1828

COPY:
Clockwise & Otherwise

60

Seth Thomas A-400 Westminster Chime

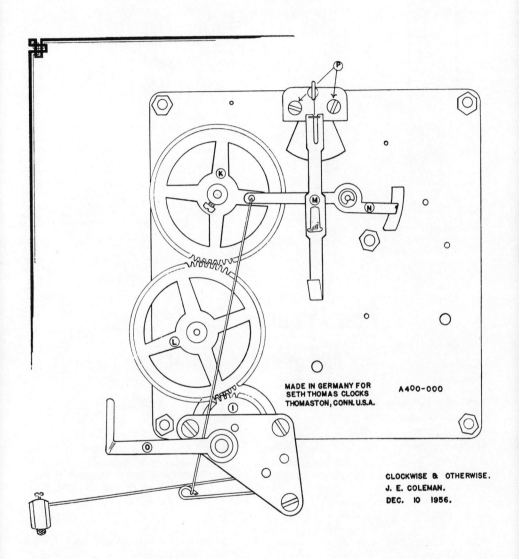

MADE IN GERMANY FOR
SETH THOMAS CLOCKS
THOMASTON, CONN. U.S.A.

A400-000

CLOCKWISE & OTHERWISE.
J. E. COLEMAN.
DEC. 10 1956.

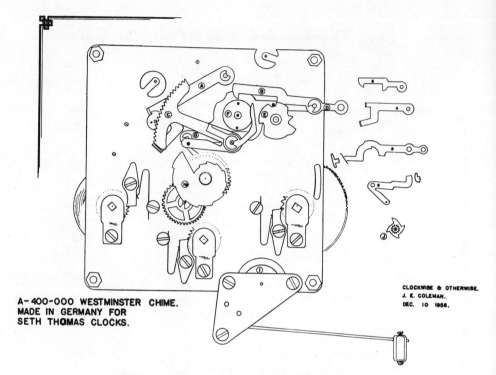

A-400-000 WESTMINSTER CHIME.
MADE IN GERMANY FOR
SETH THOMAS CLOCKS.

CLOCKWISE & OTHERWISE.
J. E. COLEMAN.
DEC. 10 1966.

How the moon disc is driven
and what it indicates

THERE ARE HUNDREDS AND HUNDREDS of fine old clocks in service whose moon work is inoperative and, I suppose, almost as many watch and clockmakers have been driven to all kinds of trouble and loss of time at the bench by these "moon works" failing to operate.

Much of this is occasioned by lack of understanding of how the moon disc is driven, or what it is supposed to indicate — sometimes both. It is sometimes referred to as "the Moon's phases."

This is incorrect, for at no time, excepting full moon, is the white part anywhere near correct shape. This mechanism is intended to show the "moon's age."

We know that the length of a lunation is approximately 29½ days and thus there is a scale marked from 1 to 29½ upon the lower edge of the dial opening. You imagine a line right through the center of the moon extending up to this scale just as the minute hand extends up to the minute-track and that imaginary hand shows you the "age of the moon." True, as the moon disc revolves it may in some respects seem to show the moon's phases, but let's stick to age.

The setting "to time" of such a moon disc is simple: At the new moon (or change) turn the disc with the fingers till the moon is hidden. At other times refer to the almanac for the moon's age. Should you be nine days past the new moon (change) turn the disc until your imaginary hand points to 9.

One can't have half-teeth upon a

wheel (or disc), thus two lunations are placed upon the disc — twice 29½ equals 59 days. If the moon disc is cut with 59 teeth that means that it must be advanced once each 24 hours and there will be, somewhere under the dial, an auxiliary wheel making one revolution per 24 hours in which there is a pin to kick the disc over by one tooth.

To avoid the cost and trouble of making a wheel to revolve once in 24 hours, many moon discs are cut with twice 59, or 118 teeth, and are advanced once each 12 hours by a pin planted in the hour wheel.

We recently had a fine old grandfather clock whose owner said he had had it in two shops and both men told him "some wheels were missing" therefore they could not make the moon-work function. Only the pin in the hour wheel had, through use, loosened and dropped out. Actually, it required less than ten minutes to stake in a new pin.

Sometimes the moon disc will fail to work properly. It will go all right for a time then run off, even stop the clock. To test for this fault hold a rule or straight edge in line with the center of the moon disc and the center of the wheel carrying the kick-over pin. The working faces of the teeth should come on the line of centers. Try each tooth of the moon disc in this way. There should be 59 or 118 teeth, if they are spaced evenly and the jumper spring is properly placed and adjusted to hold each tooth to this "line of centers" there will be no trouble.

If some teeth come before the line of centers and others considerably after it, you may find a spot where the point of a tooth on the moon disc will butt against the pin and fail to operate the disc or even stop the clock. In such case, it may work for several days and then fail to operate.

When one finds a wheel with unevenly spaced teeth, or, teeth failing to line up on the centers, first check the bearing in the moon disc; it should fit "snug"—no wobble or play. Check the wheel carrying the kickover pin for excess play. Sometimes where the teeth are unevenly spaced the trouble can be overcome by shifting the position of the jumper-spring to the closest possible position to the kick-over pin. It can readily be seen that where the jumper spring contacts the moon disc a quarter or half way around from the kick-over pin that all the irregularities in all the teeth in between these two points affect the locked position.

Testing the truth of the teeth in the moon disc in this way while you have the clock down can save much subsequent trouble.

After setting, if you keep the clock running steadily, the moon's age will be shown near enough for 16 months, after which the moon will be found to be about a half-day ahead of her schedule and may be re-set. This is caused by the fact that in this simple mechanism the lunar month is exactly 29½ days, which is over 44 minutes less than its true length. Such a variation is not serious when we consider that the lunar month varies over 12 hours; so, when you keep your moon disc within half a day of the average lunation it is practically as good as nature herself.

This error in your moon mechanism, and the variation in the length of the lunar month sometimes correct each other, but at other times the errors add, so that finally, the best method is to compare the moon age (as shown upon your clock) with the almanac every month or two and when the error exceeds a half day (that's the least you can move the 118) set it.

How to Handle Westclox 'TT-1'

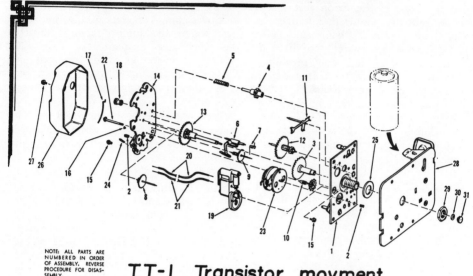

TT-1 Transistor movment
300 beat - 1.5v. - 3 jewel.

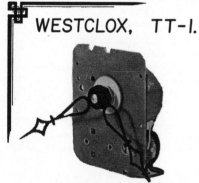

WESTCLOX, TT-1.

1.5-v. TRANSISTOR Movt.

The "TT-1" is the only clock of its type completely manufactured in the U.S. and is, of double interest to the bench horologist; 1, it is coming in Westclox models "Stanton," "Meredith," "Varsity" and "Wakefield"—these you may be called upon to repair. 2, it is also available as a "fit-up" kit from your regular material dealer for converting any clock to battery operation—price $10.95—it is 3¼ inches high by 2½ wide by 1⅛, thick; center mounted comes boxed singly with two pair hands and the regular Westclox 90 day guarantee ("C" battery not included).

We are grateful for Mr. Charles Britten, of the Young-Neal Co., (315 Fourth Ave. N., Nashville 3, Tenn.) calling our attention to this new clock and to Mr. R. M. May, Manager of Trade Repairs up at La Salle, Ill., for supplying data and the blow-up sketch we are using here.

On this blow-up all parts are numbered in the order of assembly; for dis-assembly simply reverse the procedure, beginning with hand-nut No. 31 and working down to No. 1 the front plate. Below is the list of parts set opposite Westclox "Stock Number." Note: that when you need to order a part for the "TT-1" you have to merely locate that part's number on the blow-up chart and precede it with "TT-1-5."

Stock No.	Part Name:
TT-1-501	Front Plate
TT-1-502	Balance Screw
TT-1-503	Hour Wheel
TT-1-504	Set Shaft
TT-1-505	Starter Shaft Spring
TT-1-506	Starter Lever
TT-1-507	Starter Shaft Lever
TT-1-508	Third Wheel
TT-1-509	Fourth Wheel
TT-1-510	Escape Wheel
TT-1-511	Lever
TT-1-512	Motion Wheel
TT-1-513	Minute Wheel
TT-1-514	Back Plate

We've faithfully copied this list according to Westclox' engineers; omitting listing the price in order to lessen details, because all parts are 'comparable' in price with other Westclox parts with which you are already familiar. Two exceptions might be: TT-1-523, the complete balance wheel, it's single-unit price is $1.95 the other, TT-1-519 Bracket Coil Assembly, single-unit price $3.60 (this is the complete electrical system; including transistor & coil). We have a slightly different idea upon a few of the parts as listed and while we have no intent of going counter to their engineers, they are noted, in order listed, because such note may help to clarify things in the mind of the repairer.

First: No. TT-1-511 is listed "lever" when actually it a ratchet-lever, both the listing and its looks have a tendency to be confusing because of its resemblence to an 'orthodox' lever (one that imparts power from the train to the balance). It is truly a ratchet-lever; getting its power from the balance and advancing the ratchet-wheel by one tooth for each stroke of the balance wheel.

By the same token, No. TT-1-510 is listed Escape Wheel, when in reality is a ratchet wheel; being ratcheted forward by the ratchet lever since the power is directed from the balance down.

TT-1-524 Hairspring Wedge. As the movement is now coming off the line, their hairsprings are cemented and there is no wedge. When effecting repairs you can easily dissolve this cement with lacquer thinner; then upon assembling either recement or make use of a wedge.

No. TT-1-512 is listed Motion Wheel—this is many times called 'dividing wheel'

as its main function is to drive the hour wheel at a 1 to 12 ratio from the center post, i.e. divide the minutes & hours. In this operation, it is also engaged by the pinion of set shaft 4 when the back set-knob is pulled out for setting hands from the back. So much for our little 'difference' the fact remains that both the engineers and this column have the same identical goal, that of getting correct data into the hands of the bench repairman.

The TT-1, is a three jeweled movement; fully transistorized and thus creates no radio or TV interference. The balance runs in two "V" type jewels and the back pivot of the ratchet-wheel (TT-1-510) arbor is jeweled to reduce friction at a critical point of wear. It is powered by one (1) "C"-size standard flashlight battery which will operate it for 12 to 14 months. The hairspring is flat and the regulator is standard. These as well as the train itself require no comment as to maintenance and repair.

It is the "reverse" type of clock; that is, the balance-wheel is impelled by electromagnetic force and it, in turn drives the clock ratchetwise; the entire electrical system is contained in part No. TT-1-519; located in the upper right corner of the movement; easily detached by simply removing two screws. The balance-wheel is unusual in that there are two of them; both frictioned upon the one staff, they are spaced 8-mm. apart and each has a small permanent magnet slightly better than 1-mm. thick attached to its inside rim, exactly opposite each other —the clearance between these magnetic blocks is roughly 5-plus mm. Positioned in this space is a little coil, approximately 10-mm. diameter by 3.5-mm. thick. This coil is merely an extention of part TT-1-519, and is automatically positioned when that part is inserted.

When in motion these two magnets passing across the ends of the coil induce within it a small current, sufficient to bias the transistor. This switches the battery current into the coil whereby the balance is then impulsed, it is returned by the hairspring, and, the cycle repeated again as the magnets swing across the coil. The clock beats 300 times per minute and is virtually noiseless.

Located in the bottom side of the lower balance (clock face-plate down) is the impulse or roller pin acting in the ratchet lever

(511) exactly as any roller jewel, save, in this case the roller pin is transmitting the power to the lever instead or receiving the power from the lever. The ears or horns of the fork are a bit longer than to the o.s. diam. of the staff; the staff is flattened just opposite the roller-pin to allow passage when the pin is engaged forming the orthodox safety feature so familiar to all repairmen.

The TT-1, has one feature we've never seen upon a clock of any type before; namely a "motion limiter" or as they call it, a "Damper Control"—this is located between the double balance-wheel, exactly as the little coil and just 180 degrees across from it. It is simply a small block of copper (actual content we don't know). With the vibration of the balance the magnetic field of the two little magnets is brought across this block of copper setting up a magnetic hysteresis and in effect a break or drag upon the balance. This simple little device has been engineered to serve two (2) purposes; 1, it eliminates overbanking conditions. 2, the motion of the balance is held to one turn regardless if the battery is fully charged or not. Mr. May, says: "this alone is assurance of good timekeeping qualities." We must say the movement under observation has done remarkably well for the two weeks we've been running it, also, that such simple tests, like quickly altering its position, etc., that we've been able to devise for checking the "damper" control seem to indicate that it works as intended.

In absolute fairness to my readers I should say, the hysteresis explanation above is purely our own deduction; I regret that neither Westclox engineers nor Mr. May, mentioned it or detailed just what actually establishes the damper's control. One word of caution, installing a battery incorrectly *may* cause damage to the movement. To install a new battery—use a "C" size flashlight battery. Holding your clock in a position so that the battery holder is below the clock movement, install the battery in its clip, so that the contact point in the center of the battery is to the right hand side, as diagrammed on the battery holder plate. Always pass this caution on to your customer.

Semca Clock Co.

We are indebted to Mr. Robert D. Aubrey, Executive Assistant, up at the "Semca Clock Co." (30 Irving Place, N. Y. 3, N.Y.) for some data upon the "Semca" transistor clock. "Semca" brought out this neat little movement about three years ago and just now a few of them are reaching the repair bench; he tells the column that they have been very successful, and, that the quantity of needed repairs have been well below the usual percentages. Fig. 1 is enlarged photo of the escapement. It is manufactured under the Ato patents—the balance is electro-magnetically impelled; transistor switched, and ratchets the train forward via a spiral or worm mounted upon the lower end of the balance-staff; repairmen familar with the old 6-volt Jaeger auto clock will immediately recognize this form.

The balance wheel carries two ferrite elements vibrating freely astride a small solenoid similar to the Westclox TT-1 as described in the March column. Current consumption is of the order of about 120 microamperes per hour. This is low and means that a new battery should perform for about a year and a half. The clock will operate without any time varations under voltages of 1.6 down to .9 of a volt. It is compensated—thermal range from minus 20

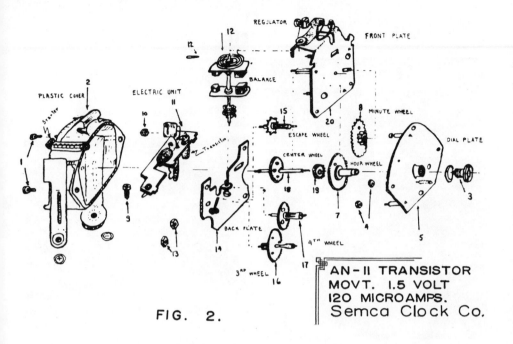

FIG. 2.

**AN-II TRANSISTOR
MOVT. 1.5 VOLT
120 MICROAMPS.
Semca Clock Co.**

to plus 203 degrees F. The Thermic coefficient between 32 and 95 degrees F. is a minus .3 second per 24 hour day.

The gearing portion requires no comment being the same as all clocks—sometimes, in rare instances a jolt or jar at the proper instant can cause it to overbank. To correct, it is suggested that the lower cap-jewel (plainly visible in Fig. 1) be unscrewed to free the lower balance pivot; reposition the spiral ratchet, then reset the jewel back to its original position.

Where the electrical circuit is damaged; replace the whole assembly. This is No. 11 on the schematic, Fig. 2. It comes as a complete unit; is easily inserted and cost the repairman $2.25.

The parts numbered on the schematic sketch, Fig. 2, indicate the order for dissembly. The nomenclature of same are as follows:

1—screws holding plastic cover to dial plate,
2—plastic cover with starter and battery terminals,
3—nut for holding dial and washer,
4—nuts holding movement to dial plate,
5—dial plate,
7—hour wheel,
8—minute wheel,
9—screw holding electrical unit to movement,
10— }
13— } nuts attaching back plate,
11—electrical unit, includes transistor, resistor and bobbin, $2.25
12—balance assembly, includes hair-spring, magnets and ratchet, cost $1.75
14—back plate, lower balance jewel-bearing, tension spring,
15—ratchet (escape) wheel,
16—third wheel,
17—fourth wheel,
18—center wheel,
19—cannon pinion,
20—front plate with regulator assembly and upper balance bearing.

For the sake of brevity, we never detail every price, however, on unusual parts which the repairman may not be familiar with, we try to give it as an aid to making estimates when such a repair comes in.

We've found the AN-11 to be a good timekeeper, rather quiet running, the ratchet (escape) wheel being plastic (nylon?) the average balance swing is about 250 degrees and it responds readily to the regulator. Naturally it has all those advantages obtained by transistor switching, etc. we are grateful to Mr. Aubry and "Semca" for good cooperation.

Spilhaus Clock Construction Explained

12, Mean time of star rise and star set. 13, Current time high or low tide. 14, Current stages of the tides. 15, Mean solar time.

Below the large dial are two four inch dials.

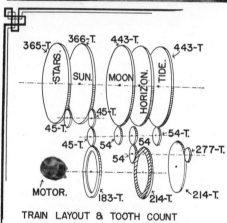

TRAIN LAYOUT & TOOTH COUNT

The dial on the left records local standard time. The right dial, records 24-hour time, and the time in principal cities of the world —the dark half-circle border on the outer circumference indicates that part of the world is in darkness. And, the white radii, indicating the individual cities, remain stationary as the 24 hour ring moves. The various continent land masses are a vivid gold on a blue field and are highly visible.

The clock stands approximately 16 inches high; its base is 11¾ by five inches—to better illustrate the working of this clock here is rough sketch of its cross section:

The five transparent discs, numbered one to five, are of Plexiglass. It will be noted from the train layout sketch that only the horizon disc does not turn. The rotating discs are mounted in Teflon guides for free low friction movement. Running in guides all center mounting is eliminated, thereby leaving the entire disc free of obstruction for viewing through to the next, etc. No. 2, the Sun disc, has additional play in its guides to allow lifting it out of mesh for setting purposes; friction-setting is provided in appropriate manner for the other indicators.

The 'standard' clock is powered by a heavy duty, AC-110-V. 60 cycle synchronous clock motor ("Synchron" by Hansen of Princeton, Ind.) straight through as indicated upon the cross section. The 4-inch World time dial at the right and the 8⅝

The large dial at the top is 8⅝ inches diameter; is in fact literally five dials, transparent and mounted concentrically. From it you get 15 readings: 1, The Horizon and the visable heavens. 2, The sun's position in the sky. 3, The moon's position. 4, Position of the stars. 5, Relative position of the sun, moon and stars. 6, Day of the month and year (s perpetual calendar). 7, Solar time of sun, moon and stars at meridian. 8, Star or sidereal time (for use with astronomical tables). 9, Current phase of the moon. 10, Time of daily sunrise and sunset. 11, Mean time of moon rise and moon set.

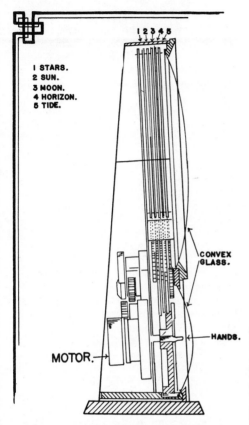

1 STARS.
2 SUN.
3 MOON.
4 HORIZON.
5 TIDE.

CONVEX GLASS.

HANDS.

MOTOR.

CROSS SECTION SPILHAUS CLOCK.

inch dials at the top are driven by the same power via idler gearings of correct toothage for ultimate accurate readings as shown in the train layout.

Repairwise, complicated as it seems, there isn't much indication for 'service' barring a wreck or accident; running in Teflon guides, lubrication in not necessary; the bench repairman is already familiar with the Hansen "Synchron" motor and/or its replacement when necessary. Edmund Scientific Co. will supply needed parts on direct order, when needed. All in all, this is a delightful clock as it is. It will be referred to as the "standard" model; just now getting into real production there hasn't been time for further elaboration, however, a different drive power such as a spring-wound or battery (transistor) power has already been mentioned for use where regulated synchronous current

is not available, such as upon a boat, etc.,— so has interior illumination plus various other additives that always suggest themselves for new pieces.

Need News of Alarm Clocks?

Westclox announces two new numbers: the first is a lighted dial, wall model, sync-electric. Mounts flush; 7⅛th inches diameter; sweep second hand; front hand set. Translucent dial lighted from the inside making it ideal for a night light in kitchen, play room, den or bathroom. Consumer price $7.98.

The second is a key-wound automatic drowse alarm, coming in the format of their old "Hustler," "Fawn," and "Spur" models. The Hustler Drowse is 4½ inches high, radiolite hands and numerals, ivory or pink; at $4.98 The Fawn Drowse is only 3¼ inches high, round, ivory or pink; plain $4.98, luminous $5.98.

SPUR DROWSE

The Spur Drowse, square, is 4⅜th inches across, black or ivory, luminous $5.98.

The sync-electric is equipped with the latest Westclox motor, etc., and needs no technical comment. The drowse feature on the spring wound is different, and a description is in order.

To operate, wind the movement fully (only one mainspring), then set the alarm indicator hand to the desired alarm time.

69

As the hands advance in the clock's normal running, between ten and fifteen minutes prior to the "set for" alarm time, the hour wheel recess becomes coincidental with the alarm indicator wheel cam which allows a drop-off, commencing the drowse alarm ringing cycle. This cycle is but three seconds. It is designed to operate that three seconds ten to fifteen minutes in advance of the set alarm time. Example: if the alarm indicator hand is set for six o'clock, the drowse cycle is performed ten to fifteen minutes before six o'clock.

On the drowse cycle, tripping is only partially accomplished since there is a step on the indicator wheel cam arresting the hour wheel in its new position. The trip soring at this time releases the hammer stop and the alarm system commences rotating the main wheel shaft, on which has been installed a drive pinion. This drive pinion engages a tooth extension of the drowse segment, rotating the segment ramp, thereby depressing again to its engaging with the hammer stop. This is the extent of the drowse cycle. It is now necessary for the time train to advance through ten or fifteen minutes to bring the let-off corner of the drowse step coincidental with the hour wheel recess so the trip cam can fall fully into the recess; this releases the remaining depression of the trip spring, permitting a full run-down of the alarm cycle.

On full run-down, the pinion attempts to drive further the drowse segment, but cannot because only four teeth are provided. This stop preserves spring power for the running of the clock, i.e. prevents the spring from running all the way down. It is at this point that the original adjustment is made.

To adjust for proper functioning: Place the unit in full trip position (point mentioned above) and allow full run-down of the alarm cycle. Adjust the trip spring height so that there is approximately .010" to .012" clearance between the formed down tab and the hammer stop. During the alarm cycle there will be a slight bobbing of the trip spring due to the motion of the segment ramp. This .010" to .012" is from its lowest position with the hammer shaft in ring position.

To verify your adjustment: Wind the unit fully, which removes the segment ramp from its position over the trip spring. Now, rotate the hands (forward) slowly until the drowse trip-off occurs. The unit will ring drowse for approximately three seconds and then stop. At this stopped position, the geared portion of the segment should be about halfway, or centered with the drive pinion. Also, the segment ramp should be positioned with approximately one-half to one-third of the ramp remaining. These additional amounts are sufficient to accommodate extreme variations in component parts. This procedure applies to all Westclox spring-wound drowse alarm clocks.

We are grateful to Mr. R. M. May, manager of Trade Repairs, and all the good folk up at "Westclox" for a "look-see" at these two new models and their good cooperation.

Here is a new thought on the four-I being used upon clock dials instead of IV. Mr. C. A. Osborne, 3 Pardon House, Loughton, Essex, England, writes: "Re your clockwise on page 48 why IIII instead of IV, I have always understood that this goes back to before the clocks had dials when the hours were struck only. Confusion occurred on a Roman strike (on two bells of different notes) between the four and six, so when the dial came along this error being kept in mind, the Roman four was written wrongly. It's all tied up with the Roman strike. The late Mr. Oakes knew a great deal about this particular point. To go on four o'clock with the Roman strike was one note upon each bell, with six o'clock it was the same only the other way around in tone. Eight (one note on one bell and two on the other) eleven (two on the first bell and one on the other) was not so confusing." end quote.

We are grateful to Mr. Osborne for his catching our answer and giving us this new 'slant' upon it. Besides, it is always a pleasure to note how the column is followed abroad. The 'Roman' striking system is not so well known on this side—in fact, I've been racking my 'non-elephantine' memory and can only rake up three (3) in my whole experience, therefore some explanation of it may be in order.

The clock is provided with two bells, one a low tone and the other of higher pitch —to portray the sequence of its striking, we've devised a chart upon which we designate the low tone bell by 'dong' and the high tone bell with 'ding'.

Roman Striking System.

LOW TONE = DONG.   HIGH TONE = DING.

ARABIC	ROMAN	BELL STROKES
1	I	DING.
2	II	DING-DING.
3	III	DING-DING-DING.
4	IIII	DING-DONG.
5	V	DONG.
6	VI	DONG-DING.
7	VII	DONG-DING-DING.
8	VIII	DONG-DING-DING-DING.
9	IX	DING-DONG-DONG.
10	X	DONG-DONG.
11	XI	DONG-DONG-DING.
12	XII	DONG-DONG-DING-DING.

Of the three we've had the opportunity of observing; one was our own repair job, the second was a repair job of a fellow clockmaker who could not make heads or tails of its strike, and, the third is a rather odd number in Jan's modest little collection, made in Sweden, prior to 1791, by A.A.S. Mora. All iron but well made, seconds pendulum. The two bells located over the movement just like English long-case clocks; the smaller bell (ding) being mounted under the larger (dong) bell and almost inside of it. Having actual knowledge of only three Roman strikes does not by any stretch of the imagination make us an expert upon them, and, we are further confused by this Swede number having "Arabic" numerals upon its dial.

Early Railroad Clock Made by E. Howard

How many of you are aware that the "sire" of that clock upon the dash-board of your car was the clock mounted upon the cab of the locomotive, back in the days before trains were run by watches? It is difficult to pin-point the exact time of change from clock to watch operation;

chances are it was sort of a transition covering several years. The fact is the story of the locomotive clock has not been fully researched and written up. If we were to select a pin-point time, it would in all likelihood be the day of "Two Noons"—Sunday, November 18, 1883, when all railway clocks governing operation of trains in the U. S. were set to the (then) new standard time at exactly 12 o'clock noon. Prior to that adoption of a "standard" time, it is conservatively estimated that at least one hundred diffirent local times were used by the railroads of the nation. This change to one standard time caused quite a furor over the country and most newspapers carried long editorials of it. One Indianapolis paper said: "The sun is no longer to boss the job, people — 55,000,000 of them — must eat, sleep and work as well as travel by railroad time. It is a revolt, a rebellion . . . People will have to marry by railroad time, and die by railroad time. Ministers will be required to preach by railroad time—banks will open and close by railroad time.

It may come as a surprise to many of you, that, though generally adopted and put into practical use even by the federal government, states and cities, it was not until some thirty-five years later—March 19, 1918— that it actually became official when Congress passed the "Standard Time Act."

The first passenger railroad in the U. S. was opened to traffic by the B. & O. May 24, 1830—some fourteen miles of it by horse-drawn railcar. It is quite conceivable that this operation could have been without either watch or clock. Mr. Charles Fisher, secretary of Railway and Locomotive Historical Society, Inc., writes me that, "The earliest record I've come across in the matter of a clock in a locomotive cab was around 1850." References to a clock in locomotive specifications are rare; however, there are some. In 1870, eight locomotives were delivered to the Alabama & Chattanooga Railroad by the Taunton Locomotive Works; their specifications read: "black walnut cabs, name of locomotive under glass on cab, cab upholstered and beautifully painted—with a bracket or shelf for a good Seth Thomas clock."

Mr. Fisher has documented one instance where a crew had a certain locomotive and its engineer had his own Seth Thomas clock up to almost the turn of this century. So far as I've been able to determine, only three factories were featuring locomotive clocks, they were: Vernon Clock Co., Fair Haven, Vt.; Seth Thomas, Thomaston, Conn.; and E. Howard & Co., Boston, Mass. Most, if not all the cases were made by other than clock manufacturers—the Crosby Valve & Gage Company, Wrentham, Mass., seems to have gotten the bulk of the business—they were supplying cast-brass cases to match their steam-gage cases, thus the clock and steam-gage "matched". Vermont Clock Co. was carrying locomotive clocks in their catalog as late as 1900.

There is an outside chance you may be called upon to repair one of these "oldies" and an even better chance you may be asked about them since they are being sought by clock collectors. They were well made and thus good timekeepers—unless badly butchered, rebuilding and/or restoring one presents no special problems. Fig. 1, is a

FRONT PLATE   **FIG. 2**

damaskeened. Note: the fifth-wheel (seconds) has individual cock and that the escapement beyond it is detachable. Fig. 3, is back plate view with the movement still

HOWARD LOCOMOTIVE CLOCK.
FIG. I

view of the complete clock—cast-brass case, overall diameter 6½ inches; overall thickness 2⅞ inches; hinged bezel with lock and a glass opening of 4¾ inch. Dial, painted on zinc blank, minute track 4¼ in. diam. with 1¼ in. seconds-bit at the XII.

Fig. 2, is the under-dial view of the front plate, the plates are nickled and highly

BACK PLATE   **FIG. 3**

mounted to the bezel-frame—mainspring barrel is under separate cock and easily removable for inserting a new spring without disturbing the clock. The main spring barrel (wheel) is 1-29/32 in. diam, and has 84 teeth. The mainspring is ½ in. wide by

16/1,000 thick, 56 inches long. The barrel cap is "keyed" in, i.e. key-pin in the barrel so that it can only be inserted one way. The second wheel is 28-7/10 mm. diam. with 70 teeth; its pinion 16-½ mm. diam., ten leaves. The third wheel (center or hour) is 21-3/10 mm. diam. 80 teeth; its pinion 5-7/10 mm. diam. with ten leaves. The fourth wheel is 28-2/10 mm. diam. 75 teeth; its pinion 3 mm. diam. with ten leaves. Fifth wheel (seconds) 15-3/10 mm. diam. with 80 teeth; its pinion 3 mm. diam. with ten leaves. Escape wheel 18-3/10 mm. diam. 15 teeth; its pinion 1-7/10 mm. diam. with eight leaves.

To count this train, we have only to work from the seconds forward: one rev. of the 80 toothed fifth wheel will revolve the escape pinion of eight leaves eight times. Thus eight times the fifteen teeth of the escape wheel=120 teeth; with two-beats per tooth gives 240 beats per minute, or, 240 divided by 60 seconds equals four beats per second—14,400 per hour.

Fig. 4, is an enlarged view of the detachable escapement; the balance is cut, bi-

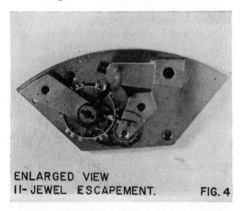

ENLARGED VIEW
II-JEWEL ESCAPEMENT.   FIG. 4

metallic, overall diam. 27-3/10 mm. diam. Flat hairspring, 14 coils—note: the odd way of pinning the hairspring; the stud is held to the top of the escape wheel cock by a screw. Eleven jewels with a rack type regulator, moved from the front of the clock by a small key. Lever is counter-balanced (poised)—as Fig. 2 and Fig. 4 show, the escapement is held to the inside of the back plate by two screws.

The complete movement attaches to the dial frame with four large screws; that frame is mounted to the bezel frame by four

screws—see Fig. 3. The bezel frame fits into the case and is held to it by two large screws outside at the IX and III position.

Though, we've already determined the 'beat' of this clock by calculating from the seconds-hand on out, since we have the complete train count it is a simple step to document the 'whole' count: the third wheel (center) of 80 teeth in one revolution (1 hour) revolves the pinion of the fourth wheel of 10 leaves eight times. That wheel of 75 teeth will in its turn revolve the fifth wheel (seconds) pinion 10 leaves, seven and one half times. Thus, 7½ times 8 equals 60—the correct ratio between hours and minutes 60 to 1. There is a stop-work mounted upon the barrel cap—clearance between plates is ⅝ of an inch—as can be seen this only affects the second, third and fourth wheels. The mainspring barrel is stepped up by a cock and so is the fifth (seconds) wheel, while the whole escapement is stepped down to the approximate proportions of an 18-size watch movement. Plates are positioned by four, large, turned brass pillars, attached both front and back by large screws whose heads are a rich blue, as are all the other screws.

Excepting the escapement, the construction tends toward the heavy side—no effort was made to calibrate the pivots; they are well made and highly polished. Upon the whole, this 'Howard' shows a better 'finish' than comparable locomotive clocks made by Seth Thomas, though I could not say the overall construction is any better. This method of fixing the hairspring stud to the escape-wheel cock was used extensively by Howard on bank vault clocks they were building during this same era. I've never had the opportunity of examining one of the "Vermont" locomotive clocks, but have repaired a number of the Seth Thomas, in fact have one in the "Big Hoss" collection. If this description generates sufficient interest, we might detail it in a future column, when it is indicated that we get out of the 'groove'; might even be lucky enough to 'borrow' a Vermont?

The Seth Thomas Perpetual Calendar

Another parallel—20 or 25 years ago one could go out and pick up the common garden variety of calendar clock for a song &

dance and sing it yourself; one of the most sought after models, the "Fashion" could easily be had from $25 to $40 each. Today the going rate is $200 to $300 per; recently we saw a fine "Fashion" specimen go at an auction for $325. As a repairer, there is one thing you may bank upon, when your customer goes out and pays that kind of money for a clock, he is going to want it to "work" —work as the factory intended it to work.

Two other factors indicate that a detailed description of the Seth Thomas perpetual calendar would benefit a large number of bench repairmen; 1, apparently S. T. never used but one model in all their production including those they manufactured for "The Southern Calendar Clock Co." (Fashion). 2, we can't pin-point a volume wherein Mr. Gould, can locate the info. even our favorite, Ward L. Goodrich's "The Modern Clock" does not illustrate and describe it. Goodrich has a fine chapter—XIX at p. 347—for the next twenty pages, gives much upon calendars but completely omitting the S. T.

First, and perhaps most importnat of all, the bench repairman should not allow the perpetual calendar to "buffalo" him simply because he is not familar with its working— as with any unfamilar mechanism the initial

step is to determine just what the manufacturer intended for it to do, then, proceed to the how it does it. With those two points understood fully, your careful examination plus your mechanical experience will pin-point the malfunction as well as indicate what you should do to correct it.

Our calendar becomes a bit complicated because we have to make it to the "civil year" of even 365 days. Basically a year is one complete revolution of the earth around the sun; actually that revolution requires 365 days, six hours, nine minutes and nine and one-half seconds; this is called the "siderial year". Further, our civil year must have a practical relation to the recurrence of the seasons, so, our practical civil year is begun at the vernal equinoctial point; calculating from here it is called the "tropical" year.

The tropical year comes out some 20 minutes shorter than the siderial year. To best balance out our 365 day "tropical year", we have our twelve months of 30 and 31 days, with a February of 28 days for three years; then every fourth (leap) year we give it 29 days.

This is a brief outline of our calendar in simple terms; there are other inequalities, such as this system not exactly balancing out so we have a "great leap" year every 400 years, etc. but this is not built into the perpetual calender and thus has no place here.

A simple calendar mechanism merely shows the day of the month—nothing more; a perpetual calendar mechanism, the type we are dealing with, is one which indicates the day of the month; the day of the week and the month of the year. It automatically adjusts for the varying number of days per month and is self correcting for the leap year.

Fig. 1 shows a typical Seth Thomas perpetual calendar dial indicating Friday, February the 4th. The day of the week (Friday) shows through a little window on the left; the month (February) through a similar opening on the right while the day of the month (4th) is indicated by a pointer (hand) pivoted at the center of the dial.

Now that we've seen what the perpetual calendar indicates (has to do) let's see how it does it. The clockmaker is regularly dealing with simple mechanical progression and when he runs up against the irregular progression necessary to the operation of a perpetual calendar mechanism he tends to view it with a bit of 'misgiving'. If only he would stop and reflect that we generally obtain irregular progression from regular progression by simple mechanical means; his fears would be abated at once.

The calendar trips every midnight from a simple cam attached at the back of the clock movement turned by a member geared off the dividing wheel to turn once every 24 hours. This cam merely raises a lever, dropping it at the midnight hour; this one simple drop—a regular mechanical progression—operates the calendar mechanism.

This drop, or trip, whichever you choose to call it, operates all three functions of the perpetual calendar.

Taking the items one at a time, we shall first consider the day of the week—upon the left of the mechanism is a little drum, 2¼ inches in diameter by 1⅞ inches wide; around it has been glued a paper strip with 14 days printed upon it—beginning with Monday, running through two weeks and ending with the second Sunday. These are the week days that show through the left window—since week days follow each other in a regular sequence the operation of this drum is by regular mechanical progression—upon the inside end of the drum is located a notched wheel of 14 notches—one for each day, thus when the clock trips the lever at midnight the drop advances the drum by one notch turning the next day up to show through the window.

Next, we'll have a look at the months: this operation is identical with the days of the week—a similar drum—same size, with a paper strip glued around it for the twelve months. On its inside head is a wheel of twelve notches—one for each month; here again we have regular mechanical progression, the printed strip begins with January and ends with December. One trip and the next month shows through the right window.

Because this trip (drop) is called for at the end of the month, it can not be taken from the midnight trip so it has to come from the day of the month-hand arbor.

Located upon this arbor is a small cam whose drop point is set to coincide with the passage of the month-hand from 31 to 1. Also located upon the inside end of the month drum, adjacent to the 12 notched wheel, is a second disc with twelve little flats (faces)—one for each month; this disc positions a small lever; spring loaded to ride against it, in or out, to correspond to the month it represents; i.e. if the month showing through the month window happens to be January, the flat against which the lever rests holds it (lever) out in a position where the locking finger for the day of the month hand is not interrupted thus permitting the day of the month hand to lock upon every one of the 31 notches of its wheel.

We shall come back to this point later—there is still a third pinion located next to the position of the month disc fixed to the frame (no turn)—in the "flat", representing February there is riveted a small disc with one high side. The February flat is cut to the exact height for 28 days; this little disc has attached to it a pinion working into the fixed pinion just mentioned, at a ratio of 4 to 1.

By this arrangement the normal flat for February is presented to the lever for three successive years (28 days) then via the 4 to 1 ratio of the little, disc the high side of it is presented to the lever the fourth year thus making the day of the month hand register 29 before jumping.

The third item of operation is the day of the month hand: this is actuated at each midnight drop by the same action that advances the day of the week—here we have regular mechanical progression for the first 28 days, or, the end of February. Then, the irregular progression has to function. The day of the month hand mounted upon the center arbor has on the back of that arbor a wheel of 31 notches—one notch for each of the 31 days shown upon the dial. On the front of this 31 wheel is positioned a small sector with a flat-face of three steps. This sector is fast upon the center arbor, so positioned that its third step coincides with the 29th notch of the day of the month wheel.

As already pointed out, the spring loaded lever that is positioned from the disc of twelve flats at the end of the month drum has a finger (or tip) which comes in contact with this three-step piece upon the step indicated by the month showing, or, if it be a 31-day month the finger is held back (positioned) so that it does not touch the step piece at all and thus allows the day of the month wheel to operate through each of its 31 notches. This is the action you get with January, March, May, July, August, October and December.

For the months of April, June, September and November, this finger is positioned so that it rides over the first step; as that step holds the finger up, one notch of the day of the month wheel is permitted to escape locking thereby allowing the day of the month hand to pass on over the 31 position and stop upon 1 for the first of the next month.

In this same operation (movement) as the day of the month hand passes the 31 position the little cam upon its arbor allows the spring loaded trip lever resting on it to drop and advance the month drum by one month. The same happens with the 29 day February month—the 4 to 1 ratio disc has turned so that its high side is presented to the in and out spring loaded depthing lever making the finger ride over step two; thus allowing the day of the month hand to pass on over both the 30 and the 31 notches. The following three Februarys when the high side of the disc is revolved out of the February flat, the finger rides up over the three steps and the day of the month hand passed over 29, 30 and 31.

Perhaps a little "detailed", but, all in all, not overly complicated. To avoid some of the details we've purposely avoided, the little ratchets, and, the locking pieces of the week day and month day wheels—these are simple and can be immediately fathomed by just one time tripping the mechanism by hand. The entire action is sturdy and positive—rarely ever has to have attention unless it has met with an accident or fallen into the hands of a "butcher".

To test the S. T. perpetual calendar: a half-dozen drops by hand will show that the weekday drum and the day of the month hand are ratcheting forward correctly. It is not necessary to hand-drop it 365 times to test for the whole year.

The day of the month hand is spring frictioned to the 31 notch wheel and may be manually turned forward (never backward); thus by turning it by hand twelve revolutions you may test it for the whole year.

Note the action of the little 4 to 1 disc; we sometimes encounter calendar mechanisms that have been assembled with this 4 to 1 disc pinion improperly meshed and the high flat does not completely cover the space it is intended to fill. When so assembled, it will not correctly compensate for the leap year.

To correct; set the month drum with February showing through its window, then position the 4 to 1 disc so that it completely fills the low notch; in this position it will register the 29th day. This same feature should also be looked after when you've completed the job.

Ascertain what year, i.e. leap, 1, 2, or 3, after leap year it will be when next February is presented to the window and set the calendar accordingly. Example: let's say you are assembling the clock for delivery to your customer this month (Nov. '66) then, the next time February comes up (Feb. '67) it will be the third year after last leap year, set the calendar so that the 4 to 1 disc is positioned just before filling the notch, then when February 1967 rolls up, the spring loaded position finger will ride in the 28-day notch, clearing the third 28-day month after leap year. When the next February rolls up (Feb. 1968) the 4 to 1 disc will have positioned in the notch and give you the 29-day month.

Many, if not most that come in have been "oiled" despite printed instructions pasted in the case by the manufacturer stating: "Never oil any part of the calendar mechanism." Often this oiling soaks the week and month paper strips rendering them very dark and in some instances unreadable. Fortunately, replacement strips are available from most material suppliers.

Applying new strips is a bit of a time-killer, but, not difficult—first mark the end of the drum to show the beginning point— January on the months and Monday on the days—clean the drum off with an old razor blade; then, go over it with steel-wool to remove any corrosion and glue left. Glue on the new paper strip (we've found McCormick's Iron Glue works well) by aligning the starting word (Monday or January) between the two marks you made on the end of the drum. Note: there is a bit of extra space at the bottom and top of each strip—when you have it smoothed out around the drum these extra bits will lap — with a straight-edge and razor blade cut midway between the two words; this gives a butt joint and when burnished down smooth can hardly be seen. Paper replacements for the calendar dial are also available.

The New Model 77 Baby Ben

DELUXE 77.

22-K. finish. $15.⁰⁰

From Miss Lucy Driscoll, of the Mac Manus, John, & Adams Agency comes the announcement the Baby Ben has been redesigned. It is now being marketed in three new deluxe styles. The new case is oval design; the luxury item of the three is a rich 22K gold finish with a gold color dial and raised luminous numerals and markers. It retails for $15.00. The other two styles will feature silver grained dials, raised numerals, and pierced luminous hands; with polished brass bezel or with antique silver case and polished nickel bezel—both will retail for $9.88.

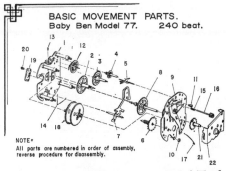

BASIC MOVEMENT PARTS.
Baby Ben Model 77.   240 beat.

NOTE=
All parts are numbered in order of assembly, reverse procedure for disassembly.

From Mr. R. M. May, manager of Trade Repair up at LaSalle, we got the mechanical dope—friend May, sent down couple of clocks and some pointers on the mechanical changes. Basic servicing i.e. cleaning; re-pointing balance staff; installing new mainspring, etc. etc. have not changed, thus suggestions or instructions are not called for here.

Our prime object is to acquaint the bench clockmaker with this new model and the changes made in it. No doubt, these changes were wrought by the good folk up at Westclox, to place an improved clock on the market. It is a distinct pleasure, repairwise, to note most of these changes accrue to the benefit of the bench repairman in that they have made it a bit easier to service the 77.

CLIP SPRING.   NUT.

A.H. & J. PHOTO.

Fig. I.

Use of retaining rings to secure the movement to the back half of the case have been discontinued and the conventional "nut" is now being used—see Fig. 1. The single mainspring to drive both the time and alarm has been retained, but, the single set for both alarm and time goes back to the

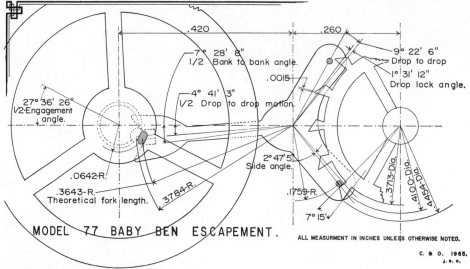

MODEL 77 BABY BEN ESCAPEMENT.

ALL MEASUREMENT IN INCHES UNLESS OTHERWISE NOTED.

C. & O. 1965.
J. O. C.

old method for an individual set for each. The back half of the case fastens to the bezel portion via a clip-spring method which makes for easy opening and closing of the case.

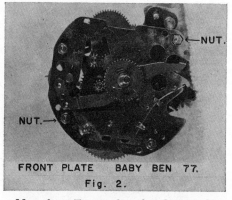

FRONT PLATE BABY BEN 77.
Fig. 2.

Note from Fig. 2, that the alarm indicator hand remains concentric with the hand center. In the exploded sketch all parts are numbered in the order of assembly—note No. 13; the hairspring is again being secured by the old well-liked wedge method instead of by cement.

In the following table, the reference number corresponds to assembly number upon the exploded sketch, it is followed by the correct "Westclox" stock number and the part name:

Ref. No.	Stock No.	Name of Part
1.	Pl. 2395	Back plate (60905)
2.	Wheel 4464	Third wheel (609120)
3.	Wheel 4192	Fourth wheel (60911)
4.	Wheel 4168	Escape wheel, Time (60909)
5.	Lever 2064	Lever (60910)
6.	Wheel 4131	Escape wheel, Alarm (60908)
7.	Hammer 1344	Hammer (60915)
8.	Wheel 4044	Center wheel (60904)
9.	Plate 2469	Front plate (60901)
10.	Nut 2226	Pillar nut (61V interchange)
11.	Screw 2670	Balance screw (61-V interchange)
12.	Wheel 3975	Balance wheel complete (60913)
13.	Wedge 3930	Hairspring wedge (50744)
14.	Spring 3437	Alarm ratchet spring (52426)
15.	Spring 3436	Set shaft spring (52457)
16.	Shaft 3061	Set shaft (60921)
17.	Spring 3435	Switch spring (52454)
18.	Barrel 0123	Barrel complete (60917)
19.	Bridge 0329A	Barrel bridge (52446)
20.	Screw 2730	Bridge screw (50298) (48-H interchange)
21.	Wheel 4249	Hour wheel (60919)
22.	Bridge 0301	Alarm set bridge (60920)

Since the days of Frederic Roskopf (b-1813 d-1889) and Achille Brocot (b-1817 d-1878) the "pin-pallet" and/or pin-lever escapement has been one of the more efficient escapements of inexpensive timepieces.

Westclox engineers have completely redesigned the Baby Ben pin-lever—while the design of an escapement is not directly within the province of the repairman we give it, in detail in the escapement sketch, that he may familiarize himself with it.

The first thing he will note comparing it with the old Baby Ben escapement is that this new improved escapement spans three and one-half teeth whereas, on the old type only two and one-half teeth were spanned. This, you can see creates an entirely different action for a pin-lever escapement, especially on the exit pallet, where on previous escapements there was practically no draw or slide allowing the guard pin to always rub on the safety roller; this improves the timekeeping and running to a great extent, eliminating back roll problems and giving greater action under dry and dirty conditions. This new type is said to have as much draw proportionately as is found in good watches.

The Revere Clock Company No. 100 and No. 300

Lately there have been a number of inquiries upon the "Revere" synchronous Westminster mantel chime clock. The Revere Clock Co. was a division of the Herschede Hall Clock Co., of Cincinnati, Ohio, which a few years ago removed to Starkville, Miss. 39759.

During the 1930's Revere produced a vast number of these clocks and as of this date they are coming to the "144" for service—both Model 100 and Model 300 embodied some unique construction features new to the repairman. It is upon these we propose to comment here. Even one point, neither unique nor new, deserves some mention—the drive motor.

Both movements are powered by a "B" type "Telechron" motor, 1 r.p.m. If you check a catalog listing Telechron rotors you will see some "B" type 1 r.p.m. rotors selling for $3.75 while another portion lists a "B" type rotor for Revere, Herschede, G. E. clocks at $8.95.

Outwardly, both rotors look the same, and some clockmakers have utilized the $3.75 rotor upon the Model 100 and Model 300. Since both rotate at one r.p.m. if the movement is clean and freshly lubricated, the lock will time out in your shop, however, if you will observe closely you can note a sluggishness in the chime and strike operation and while you may get the clock off the repair shelf and into the hands of its owner it will soon develop "trouble" . . . sometimes before your one year guarantee expires.

The $8.75 rotor is much stronger and designed to carry the load of keeping time, chiming, and striking operations. This is one of the first points to be carefully checked when one of these clocks comes to your bench. Because these rotors look exactly alike—outwardly—it is one point easily overlooked. If you will take your jeweler's saw and cut off the potence of the cheaper rotor that goes into the coil you will see only two magnetic wheels there to be activated by the magnetic field. Cut the higher priced rotor and there will be four magnetic wheels—doing this will illustrate the difference in a way you will not forget, etc.

The center-post of both movements revs. at 1 r.p.m. and carries the sweep-seconds hand upon both; this center-wheel also served to drive the chime and strike. Model 100—see Fig. 1—drives both the chime and strike via a most unusual mechanical arrangement which we might term one "train." Model 300 has a chime "train" quite similar to orthodox Westminster construction plus a third "train" to strike the hours. It is in the regular orthodox, rack & snail style.

Both movements embody a "self-corrector" i.e. the hour can only be struck after the clock has completed chiming the fourth quarter—this will be touched on later.

The strike trains and chime trains on these movements operate a bit differently from the usual in that they are NOT under power during their silent periods. There is no positive lock and warn-run action; they simply remain static until the action of the trip places drive wheel "W" in mesh—gear—with center wheel "Y" Fig. 1. When checking Fig. 1, it must be remembered that center wheel "Y" turns clockwise while the locking disc turns counter-clockwise. And that though lifting disc "E" and center wheel "Y" are concentric, Y revolves at 1 r.p.m. while lifting disc revolves 1 r.p.h. The quarter-hour lifting pins are located in disc "E," lettered: A, B, C and D—note that pin "D" is located much nearer the outside rim of the lifting disc; this means that pin "D" lifts the lever higher thus thrusting the shifting lever much further to the right. This is the "self-adjusting" feature.

Fig. 1 shows the position of the chime locking disc at the completion of the third-quarter chime operation—step "O" on the locking disc "N" has a notch in front of it. This step "O" represents the fourth quarter and/or hour chime. When pin "M" on the gear arm "V" is in the depression at the fourth quarter step "O", it requires a longer movement of the lifting lever "F" to disengage pin "M" from the depression than it does to disengage it from steps

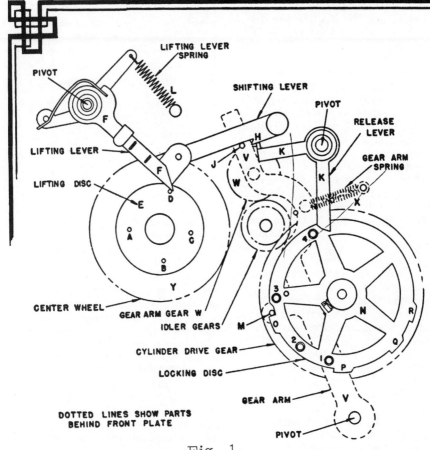

LIFTING LEVER SPRING

PIVOT

SHIFTING LEVER

PIVOT

RELEASE LEVER

GEAR ARM SPRING

LIFTING LEVER

LIFTING DISC

CENTER WHEEL

GEAR ARM GEAR W

IDLER GEARS

CYLINDER DRIVE GEAR

LOCKING DISC

GEAR ARM

PIVOT

DOTTED LINES SHOW PARTS
BEHIND FRONT PLATE

Fig. 1.

"P", "Q", and "R".

Pins "A", "B", and "C" being located nearer the center will not disengage pin "M" when it is in the depression at step "O"; thus pin "D" is the only lifter that will move the shifting lever far enough to the right for hook "H" to drop behind the shift pin "J" to bring the gear arm "V" to the left and place drive wheel "W" in mesh with center wheel "Y" to drive the chime through the fourth quarter.

As has been seen, pins "A", "B", "C", and "D" move the lifting lever "F" to the right, causing the shifting lever hook "H" to drop over the shift pin "J" which is located upon chime gear arm "V". The lift should be far enough to permit a 1/32 inch clearance between the shift pin "J" and the shifting lever hook "H". Each lift pin should be tested; it follows that when

testing pin "D" for this 1/32 clearance, the locking disc "N" should be in the position as shown in Fig. 1.

As the lifting lever "F" drops off one of the pins "A", "B", "C" and "D" on the lifting disc "E", it is pulled back to almost its original position by the small coiled spring "L", and since the shifting lever hook "H" has hooked the shift pin "J" on the gear arm "V", the gear arm "V" is pulled with it toward the left of the movement, thus placing the chime drive wheel "W" in mesh gear with the center wheel "V" which wheel is constantly under power and in motion at 1 r.p.m.

The shifting lever "H" holds onto the shifting pin "J" and holds the gear arm in mesh through the chime operation. Thus shifting lever hook "H" is released by the lever "K", which in turn is activated from the locking disc "N".

The locking disc "N" has four pins designated 1, 2, 3, and 4 around its rim. The appropriate pin raises the lever "K" which releases the shifting lever hook "H" at which point the spring "X" disengages the mesh allowing the clock to stop chiming.

Sometimes, clockmakers encounter difficulty at this point; occasioned when the locking disc "N" is slightly out of adjustment. So long as the chime train is under load spring "X" is not strong enough to separate—disengage—drive wheel "W" from center wheel "Y" to stop the chiming operation and they get an over-run. It is so easy to jump to the conclusion that spring "X" is too weak, which is NOT the cause. Pins 1, 2, 3, and 4 must be synchronized to that point where they trip "K" at the instant the last note of the chime has been sounded. While the chime train is not loaded, i.e. pulling, far less power is required for the disengagement and "X" is sufficiently strong to do the trick. Check and re-check this point before you attempt to increase the strength of "X". Bend the top arm of "K" upwards for a 1/32 inch clearance over pin "J". The locking disc "N" determines the proper quarters on the chimes by the distance between pins 1, 2, 3, and 4.

The locking disc "N" has about its outer rim four steps, lettered "O", "P", "Q", and "R". These steps are to hold the chime gear arm "W" in mesh with the center wheel "Y" after the shifting hook "H" has released and until the chime has been completed. The chime gear arm "V" has another pin "M" that protrudes through the movement plate at the rim of the locking disc "N". When the gear arm "V" is released from the shifting lever hook "H", pin "M" will hit one of the steps "O", "P", "Q", or "R" on the locking disc "N" and then drop off the step thus releasing the gear arm "V". To correctly set the chime cylinder—see Fig. 2—loosen the set screw 5 on the locking disc "N". Insert a piece of wire approximately .056 diameter in the hole shown in locking disc "N", then on through the bushed hole in the movement plate.

This hole is found to the extreme right edge of the movement plate under the rim

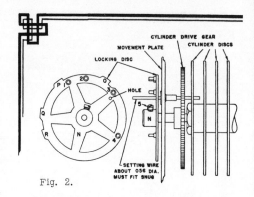

Fig. 2.

of the locking disc "N". Turn the cylinder until a large hole in the cylinder drive gear is found. Push the wire through this hole and further into the small hole found in the first cylinder disc. Keeping this wire in place, tighten set screw 5 on the locking disc and then remove it. Your cylinder will then be set in correct relation with the locking disc and the chimes will be set.

The rack strike system of Model 300 does not call for any special comment other than to point out that it is a "dead" system on which there is no lock and warn run, etc. Like the chime operation described above if the disengage lever is so timed that it drops behind the strike rack while the train is lifting a hammer, it will NOT pull the drive wheel out of mesh until there is no load upon the train and you get an over-strike. Time the disengage lever to drop behind the strike rack at the instant between strokes—that is: while the train is not loaded.

The hour strike upon the Model 100, being entirely different, has to come in for some comment. Refer now to Fig. 3, it shows this strike mechanism at the instant of having struck the fifth blow of five o'clock. The hour control wheel is revolving clockwise and before lift point 6 reaches the hammer to raise it, the pin 8 will have dropped off the rack support lever 3, thereby permitting the coiled spring to pull the twelve toothed rack up and back so that the remaining seven tips do NOT contact the hammer tail, as the hour control wheel continues to rotate to its stop activated by step "R" on the locking disc "N" shown in both Fig. 1 and Fig. 2.

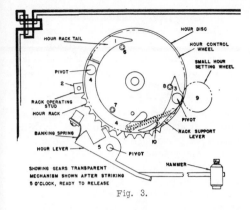

Fig. 3.

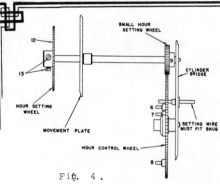

To correctly set up the hour strike, refer to Fig. 4. Turn the hand set knob until the lifting lever "F" just drops off the hour pin "D", Fig. 1, on the lifting disc "E". Loosen the two screws 13 on the

Fig. 4.

As the cylinder is turning and chiming the fourth quarter, the tail of the hour rack 1—Fig. 3—hits the square rack operating stud 2 and the hour rack 4 is moved out from behind the hour disc thereby bringing the teeth on the hour rack 4 into the path of the strike hammer tail. The hour rack 4 is locked in this striking position by the rack support lever 3, when the last note of the fourth quarter chime has been struck, that first tooth of the hour rack 4 will lift the hour hammers lever 5. The two hammers that sound the hour will continue to strike until the correct number of strokes have been made. The instant the last stroke of the hour has been struck, the rack support lever 3 will engage pin 6, 7, or 8 in the hour control wheel and release the hour rack 4 and allow it to fall back into its original position so that the remaining teeth upon the hour rack—on this sketch, 7—cannot engage the strike hammer tail 5. The hour control wheel has three pins numbered 6, 7, and 8 equally spaced and equal distance from the rim. This hour control wheel is driving from the time train one revolution every 36 hours; thus each of the three pins 6, 7 and 8 operates the rack support lever 3 for a period of twelve hours, or through one period of one to twelve hammer strokes. Upon close examination of the action here you will see that the pin 6, 7, or 8 that trips the rack support lever in any particular hour is advanced each hour by the distance of one tooth of the strike rack, thereby allowing the rack support lever to hold the hour rack in striking position for one more tooth each hour.

hour setting wheel 12 thus permitting you to turn the hour control free. Upon the back of the cylinder bridge is a bushed plate hole—insert a short wire very near the diameter of the hole through it and then turn the hour control wheel until this wire can enter a hole in the hour control wheel. While held in position with the wire, tighten the two screws 13 in the hour setting wheel 12 and remove wire. The hour will always be correctly set.

G. E. TORSION BAND

One new clock this month—Mr. D. H. Buddenhagen, manager of the time products division of General Electric Company, has just announced its new torsion-band, battery clock; stating that some eight models are in production ranging in price from $15 to $100.00. Our illustration shows Model 2572, suggested retail price $40.00.

We are grateful to Mr. C. B. Marble of G. E. engineering for supplying a "sample" movement more than two years back and more recently one of the refined movements now going into production. Mr. Buddenhagen's announcement indicated that "Torsion Band" movement clocks go into general distribution during the second half of 1972.

This is truly a "new" clock in that its time standard is entirely different from anything upon today's market. Also, it is truly electric—many battery clocks coming to the repair bench are not electric per se —merely orthodox clocks with a hairspring

and balance for their time standard; spring drive and battery wound. These automatically inherit all the evils and inaccuracies of the balance-hairspring assembly and many have the added objection . . . a noise made by the periodic wind operation. The "torsion band" movement is completely without noise, making it ideal for bedroom operation.

The torsion band method for a time standard is not new to the clock industry; Silas B. Terry, patented one October 5, 1852, No. 9,310; several must have been marketed as some are around this date. Apparently the idea lay dormant 'til the early part of this century when Mr. Henry Warren, as reported in this column for last December, began experimenting with his

violin string type oscillator, etc.

The torsion band movement uses two transistors in an electronic circuit. One transistor drives a small magnet attached to the center of a thin band of nickel steel that has both ends firmly clamped in the movement. This provides a frictionless support for the band. The magnet swings back and forth at a constant frequency of thirty cycles per second, controlled by the torsion band. The magnet passes through a second coil, thus inducing a 30 cycle per second current within that coil, the second transistor steps up or amplifies the 30 cycle per second voltage to drive a small synchronous motor; from that motor on out it is merely a driving of the hand train. With this system the timekeeping element is completely divorced from, and independent of the motor, so that any friction losses and work by the motor do not influence the timekeeping element. By such a method, the timekeeping remains accurate even as the power in the battery decreases.

It is powered from one "D" size, carbon-zinc flashlight battery, and our indications are that it is very conservative with its current supply, as one battery kept the time through fourteen months. It has a unique regulator arrangement in that it is a slotted screw designed to take a dime in the slot; the screw-head is counter sunk so that the dime rides the edge of the sink which is calibrated making any regulation move quite precise.

The movement is center mounted; comes in a moulded case 3½ inches wide by 3⅞ inches high by 1-19/32 deep—the hand set on the back is counter sunk so that it may hang flat against the wall. It also comes sans any back set knob for those clocks with exposed hands. To put the movement into operation: 1) Insert "D" size cell into the case with the positive end toward the small terminal. 2) Allow 20 or 30 seconds for the torsion band to reach operating amplitude; then start the motor by pressing the "start" lever down and releasing quickly. The seconds hand will rotate showing that the clock has started. 3) To set the time: turn the set knob at the back, or for clocks with exposed hands, simply rotate the minute hand. 4) Rate adjustment we have already covered above. 5) Battery replacement is indicated when the clock stops and is difficult to re-start.

At this early stage the factory has not mentioned the exact accuracy to be expected but I'd say well within a minute per month which is very, very good for a piece in this low price range. The mere fact that the time standard of this movement embodies a magnet makes it self evident that it should not be located adjacent to magnetic metals; in fact, the factory suggests a non-magnetic dial and non-magnetic hands, stating that magnetic materials should never be located closer than one inch of the movement capsule. Repairwise, we see very little in this clock for the tender of the "144"—designed with moulded self-lube bearings there just isn't much to go wrong in normal use.

S. MARTI No. 4751.

EARLY CLOCKS

AROUND THE YEAR 1800 clockmaking ceased to be a one man, one clock operation. All over the world the manufacture of clocks took a tremendous forward jump. Shortly before the century's turn, in England there were firms like Osborn of Birmingham and later another, Wilson, of the same city, making a specialty of supplying the clockmaker with iron weights, dial blanks and sub-frames for clocks.

A similar situation existed in the U.S.A. Elisha N. Welch was operating a foundry to cast weights for clocks—his first connection with the clock business. He later became one of the largest producers of Connecticut clocks.

In the year 1806 Eli Terry contracted to manufacture 4,000 movements in three years. A similar upsurge was taking place in France; George Frederic Japy—1748-1812—started a factory at Beaucourt, a small town eleven miles south of Belfort, to manufacture watch ebauches with machine tools in the late 1700s, to be followed by a similar plant at Badrel in 1810 for the production of clock ebauches.

This was followed a little later by S.

MOVEMENT No. 6383.

Marti Cie. Both firms supplied many French casemakers with their movements; today the U.S. clockmaker receives many of these clocks for repair. In contrast to the clockmakers in the U.S. and England, the French casemakers were producing much smaller cases—these small cases by necessity took shorter pendulums and had less space for their swing. This made it necessary for the case people to have a method of quickly determining which movement was adaptable to the case in hand—i.e. the pendulum's length, etc.

Exactly by whom and when is somewhat indefinite; but it became a practice of the movement makers to : 1, stamp the pendulum with the movement serial number: 2, stamp the movement with the pendulum length. Any time you take in a Frenchy for repair and its pendulum number does not match that of the movement you can rest assured that it is NOT the original pendulum; it may be of a size and length for satisfactory running but no less a substitution.

Simply because they are detachable, pendulums are frequently lost—any time you take in a French clock for repair whose pendulum is missing this length stamping comes in handy. Not one clockmaker in a hundred takes the time required to count the time train and calculate the length of a missing pendulum. Either from experience with a similar movement or the space allowed by the case he will hang on a pendulum he thinks a little long and cut it down 'til he has timed the clock. This may necessitate two or three "cuts" but at that it consumes less time than count and calculate—utilizing the French stamp you can hit it the first time. We've photoed a couple of typical French movements, unmarked movement No. 6383 and "S. Marti" No. 4751. Their respective pendulums are shown alongside a ruler for comparison.

That figure slightly above the center of the back plate and to the extreme left is the "serial" number. Those figures at the very bottom indicate pendulum length. Those numerals to the left of the pillar-post indicate the French "Pouce" while the numerals to the right of the post indicate French "lignes" thus for movement No. 6383 the length becomes four pouces and six lignes. A French dictionary defines the puce as "thumb or inch". De Carle defines ligne as 1/12 inch French. Pouce is an ancient French measure and perhaps refers to an inch differing by a few thousandths from today's standard inch; however,

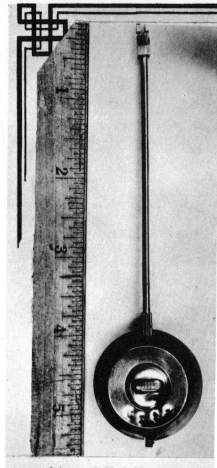

No. 6383.

this measurement is not super-critical because you have the variance of your adjustment of the ball.

Experience in applying this figure indicates that it is to the center of gravity, not the over-all length to the tip. So, four pouces and six lignes becomes four and 6/12 inches, or 4½ inches. Projecting the 4½ inch point upon the ruler across to the pendulum, we see it comes about the top of the regulating nut, or approximately the center of gravity spot. On the No. 4751 it is seen that 4½ inches strikes

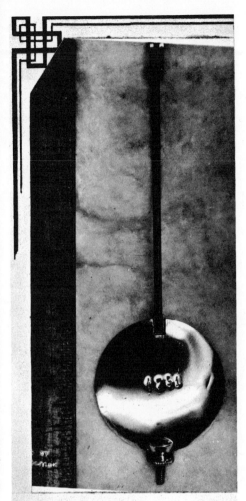

No. 4751.

about the same spot. For all practical purposes you may translate inches and twelfths and have your length in a "jiffy".

QUARTZ CRYSTAL CLOCKS

Two divisions of General Time Corp., "Seth Thomas" and "Westclox" announce the first commercial quartz crystal clocks. By the time this reaches you, you will be able to go into the market place and purchase a quartz clock for as little as $50—that represents a tremendous break-through at least pricewise. We had become accustomed to think of the quartz wrist watch on the order of $900 to $1,250 when one of the major watch manufacturers announced a few months back that it would shortly be marketing one on the order of $300—now comes the $50 clock and the trade is buzzing with rumors that at least two of our major watch manufacturers expect to break the $100 order before 1972. The clock manufacturer is not so hampered sizewise as the watch manufacturer; he can utilize a much larger battery as well as a much larger mechanism thus his price breakthrough is bound to be more rapid; one can easily see even less expensive quartz clocks; even a quartz clock for your car; perhaps a quartz alarm clock for your bed room. The application of a quartz crystal to drive a pair of clock hands is completely comparable to the application of the pendulum. Like a pendulum the quartz possesses an inherent quality of constant vibration—but vastly more accurate than a pendulum. It is for this very reason the quartz is desired over and above the pendulum accuracy. It has been stated—Cowan—that some observatory quartz clocks have run with a calculated accuracy of 0.002 seconds per year.

The principal of the vibrating quartz is NOT new; it is known as "the piezoelectric effect" and was discovered by the Curie brothers in 1880. It was almost 54 years later—November 15, 1925—that Mr. Warren A. Marrison, of the Bell Laboratories, came up with a practical suggestion of controlling a rotating device such as a clock from such a high frequency. Considerable experimenting went on; they built a quartz clock and the whole matter as a full blown clock was rolled out in a paper Mr. Marrison read before the British Horological Institute in 1947.

As late as 1958 Harrison J. Cowan was writing of the quartz-crystal oscillator placing the cost of a crystal at $200. Since that time vast and rapid strides have been made in the production of crystals; in electric circuitry, and miniaturization of same. Every step has effected a considerable price reduction and today we have arrived at the $50—retail price—crystal clock.

I verily believe that if you were to think of the quartz clock as being an assembly of three modules; then thought of them as one dollar each, then for a safety factor doubled it and came up with a six dollar figure for actual manufacturing cost and posed it to a competent engineer, he would not term it absurd, or unreasonable. In fact, he might just say such is within sight.

In Fig. 1, we show a schematic of the "Quartzmatic" movement, we are indebted to the Westclox Div., and it's engineer, Mr. R. H. Preiser for a sample movement which we have been running, observing, and examining for more than a month. It is an excellent runner; keeps very close time, and appears to be a very substantial movement.

The Seth Thomas Div. is cataloging nine models, ranging in price from $65 to $175, and the Westclox Div. ten models priced from $50 to $500.

WESTCLOX QUARTZMATIC "C".

We have chosen to illustrate Westclox Model "C" not because it is the $50 clock but because it will have an especial appeal to the bench horologist as a shop regulator.

It's twelve-inch, full numeral, super legible dial with a sweep seconds hand combined with quartz accuracy makes it an excellent clock for public display in a repair shop.

General Time's crystal clock developement was initiated at La Salle, Ill., by the Westclox Division in the later part of 1968. Every major division of the company participated in a well coordinated development program and contributed substantially to the final design of the product. Their engineers proceeded to carry forward the basic plan of a modular design concept of three separate modules—a quartz electronic module, a synchronous inductor micromotor module, and a precision time-train module, as shown by Fig. 1.

The quartz crystal is mounted in a hermetically sealed capsule protecting it from moisture, changes in atmosphereic pressure, and temperature changes. The micromotor is the synchronous inductor type of the latest in permanent magnet materials. It revolves at 256 rpm in synthetic sapphire jewels. Engineers rate its efficiency at 30% as compared with the less than 1% efficiency of most present sync motors. This accounts for it's ability to swing big hands.

The intergrated circuitry of the electronic module is contained in a small rectangular slip of silicon approximately one-sixteenth of an inch each side along with several fixed capacitors, carbon resistors and a trimmer capacitor, and, the crystal.

This integrated circuitry is known within the electronics world as: "LSI"—initials for Large Scale Integration, and they weren't kidding when they appied the term large scale, for I'm told that this one contains the equivilent of several hundred transistors, etc. All this becomes pretty "heady" stuff for the lowly tender of the "144", including your scribe. So, let's skip the highly technical and see what it does.

Lastly comes the "gear reduction module" —here the bench horologist can plant his feet firmly upon the ground, for it is the old familar time train, calculated to reduce the revs. of the sync motor down to 1-rpm for the sweep seconds hand. Further explanation on this point is not required. One may be practically sure that Mr. Marrison never envisioned a six-dollar quartz timepiece when he delivered his

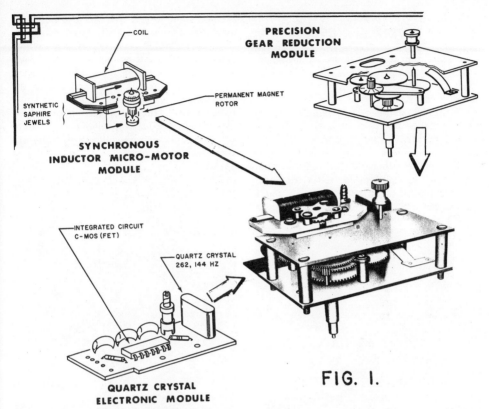

COIL

PRECISION
GEAR REDUCTION
MODULE

SYNTHETIC
SAPHIRE
JEWELS

PERMANENT MAGNET
ROTOR

SYNCHRONOUS
INDUCTOR MICRO-MOTOR
MODULE

INTEGRATED CIRCUIT
C-MOS (FET)

QUARTZ CRYSTAL
262, 144 HZ

FIG. 1.

QUARTZ CRYSTAL
ELECTRONIC MODULE

paper before the British Horologist Institute back in 1947, but his closing statement was no less prophetic for he said: "Whether or not such an 'absolute' clock becomes a reality of its time in the future, the quartz crystal clock, because of its accuracy, compactness, great convenience, and versatility is likely to continue to be a most useful instrument in all precision time measurement." end quote.

QUARTZ MOVEMENT – CQ2000

Last column we mentioned the Staiger "Quartz Movement CQ-2000"—Mr. Rudolph Erenhouse, president of Cosmo Electronics Ltd., 2145 Marion Place, Baldwin, N. Y. 11510, sent down a "sample" movement for that in hand look-see. We are grateful to Mr. Erenhouse for his cooperation.

He writes: "We have the exclusive distributorship in the United States with the understanding that we will sell to the small

FIG. 3.

users from our stock, whereas large users can buy through our efforts as an agent directly through Gebr. Staiger."

If convenient turn back to the column in the May 1970 issue in which we described the "Chronometron Type 1." The CQ-2000 is a twin-sister—it utilized the same permanent magnet and pivoted coil and the principal material used is DuPont's "Delrin." Both movements drive their center-seconds hands ratchetwise; the Type 1 advances by half seconds while the CQ-2000 advances it by seconds steps.

Like the "Quartzmatic"—July column—the CQ-2000 is made up of three modules —a gear train, an electromechanical transducer, and a quartz timed electronic module. Fig. 3.

The time-train is of the simplest possible construction and already familiar to most clockmakers knowledgeable upon a seconds

jumper. The center seconds hand mounts upon the pivot of an arbor carrying a sixty saw or ratchet toothed wheel; said wheel is ratcheted forward by one tooth via a pawl on the electromechanical transducer at each electrical impulse. This center-seconds arbor being geared to the minute hand on a sixty to one ratio, it in turn is geared to the hour hand on a twelve to one ratio.

FIG. 2.

Fig. 2, shows the transducer—top—with the time-train just under it. We would like to have illustrated these two modules with a better photo of our own making, but this "sample" came to us with specific instructions that it be returned thus we hesitated to disassemble it for photo purposes. Fig. 1 shows the complete movement in its plastic shell. It can be noted that the transducer and time train is located between the battery and the quartz capsule. Outside dimensions of this case eighty by seventy-one by twenty-eight mm.

The transducer employs the moving coil system; the pivoted coil mounts within a permanent magnet and when energized the polarity aligns it with the magnet thereby delivering a mechanical thrust to the drive pawl. Herein lies a sort of mechanical paradox; precision timing is maintained by the quartz, yet the ratchet action occurring only once per second is rather "coarse"

FIG. I

—quite a contrast to one of the tuning fork wrist watches in which the ratchet action is extremely fine due both to a very small wheel and a high frequency of the action.

The heart of the CQ-2000 is, naturally, the electronic circuitry—Fig. 3 and Fig. 4—it operates at 1.2 volts and the "C" size cell maintains it well above one year. The crystal is an XY flexure-mode bar resonator, shock mounted between two electrodes in a metal case containing a special atmosphere. Perhaps the easiest rule-of-thumb illustration here is the common thermos bottle—the object of this sealed metal capsule is to insulate the crystal against temperature variations.

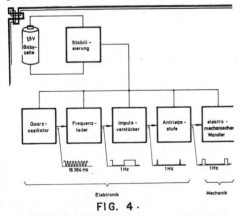

FIG. 4 .

The block sketch—Fig. 4—indicates the functions of the individual modules of the electronic circuitry. The stable frequency of 16,384 Hz generated in the quartz

crystal is divided down to 1 Hz by a fourteen stage binary scaler. The voltage square wave at the output of the scaler is passed to the pulse amplifier which converts it to narrow needle-point pulses. These pulses are processed in the divider stage to make them suitable for driving the transducer. The whole circuit is supplied with a constant voltage of 1.2 V via a stabilizing stage. The power consumption of the electronic circuit is rated at 0.46 Ah pa and that consumed by the transducer coil at 0.84 Ah pa making the overall power consumption 1.3 Ah pa.

The moving coil type transducer is highly efficient producing a torque sufficient to drive hands on a twelve-inch dial. The time train is suspended in a rubber mounting to provide noise suppression. Most of it plus the transducer is precision die cast from DuPont Delrin whose main properties are resistant to corrosion and wear, and it has a high resistance to aging.

The setting is orthodox via a conventional set knob on the back. Also on the back—lower left corner Fig. 1—is a small red slide switch; moving it to the right kills the circuit to the transducer thereby stopping the sweep seconds hand, enabling the operator to set it to the split second.

Again, your C. & O. is in that time bind we often encounter in the race to get you the news first. As of this writing, production costs are still being calculated and thus the price to the trade has not been firmed up. Our guess is, that it will be competitive in the quartz field and we shall bring it to you in a future column.

Basically, the conversion of the stable quartz current to timekeeping via ratchet action is not new. I believe the quartz wrist watches utilize it, but carrying the stable current on down to the one Hz approaches the problem of mechanical action from a slightly different angle, permitting the use of the moving coil which is vastly more powerful than those rapidly vibrating ratchets. One can easily envision tying this movement to a relay to impulse a line once every second and from that line operate a string of slave—jumper—clocks in the home, school, or factory at quartz accuracy. Incidentally, we failed to mention that Staiger says under average room temperature it is accurate to plus or minus five seconds per month. The movement we've been running for approximately forty days appears to be well within that range.

It is a bit early for any prediction as to the impact the quartz clocks are going to make repairwise—frankly, barring accidents, I see very little maintenance indicated. It is a certainty, the orthodox clock plus the antiques will be on the "144" for many, many years to come. Very definitely the quartz is going to shove the clockmaker into an area of greater precision; he will have to watch his shop regulator closer and perhaps rely more upon WWV.

Several months back, WWV changed the format of their broadcast, you now get a voice announcement during the last 7.5 seconds of every minute. Their broadcast emanated from Fort Collins, Colo. on carrier frequencies of 2.5, 5, 10, 15, 20 and 25 MHz. twenty-four hours around the clock. At the time they went to the new format they instituted a telephone service. If your short-wave radio is not working or you have trouble with reception you can have the exact time by dialing (303) 499-7111. They caution that due to instabilities and variable delays of propagation by radio and telephone combined the listener should not expect accuracy of the telephone time signals to be better than thirty milliseconds.

Kundo Clock

KIENINGER AND OBERGFELL manufacturer of Kundo Clocks recently responded to a letter appearing in J. E. Coleman's September 1974 Clockwise and Otherwise column concerned with repair of these timepieces and stated that the clock in question could quite possibly have been a transistor model.

Because of the time element involved — owner of this particular clock supposedly had it for years — it was disputed as to what type of Kundo model Edward Stein, author of the original letter to Mr. Coleman, was in possession of. According to Kieninger and Obergfell, this company was the pioneer in this field as Kundo transistor pendulum models were made prior to 1956, when production of contact clocks was terminated. Although this does not mean absolutely that Mr. Stein's clock was transistor, it is possible that he indeed had one of the earliest of this Kundo line.

Mr. Coleman's assertion that battery must first be changed was quite correct, according to Kundo clock manufacturers. In order to repair a transistor contact clock, however, case type must be ascertained and is of utmost importance when determining what battery to use.

Provided in this response to Mr. Coleman's answer were directions governing different transistor models and visual aids from an accompanying technical notice, designed to help in selection of the right battery for Mr. Stein's clock, should it be a transistor mechanism, or any other repairman struggling to fix such a model.

After removal of old battery, replacement must be correctly poled as explained earlier by Mr. Coleman making sure that terminals or spring plates which maintain direct contact with that battery are cleaned. Bending them slightly will assure good contact.

Figure A shows the first of three models. This particular one requires a mignon cell, leakproof 1.5V battery size AA, called an alkaline type battery, to be fitted into its battery holder. Generally, running for 12 months, this type is locked into the base of the clock.

Figure A

Mono-cell leakproof battery size D fits into battery holder demonstrated in Figure B. This Braunstein battery is expected to last between 12 and 18 months.

Figure B

Circuit mounting, connection wires and solder tags used with the special air-oxygen-element No. 825 is shown in Figure C and this type is designed to last for up to five years. Element itself is not represented on the drawing.

After choosing the right battery, and placing it into its battery holder, Kundo transistor

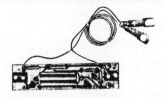

Figure C

model clocks should be placed so that the pendulum points to the center punch of the coil case — pendulum, of course, has been stopped — and pushed slightly to detect whether or not repairs have been performed correctly. If they have been, pendulum oscillation will achieve its full amplitude within a few moments.

However, should pendulum movement stop suddenly, this is a sure sign that circuitry has a defect. If this happens on a newer model which has circuit mounting on the printed circuit located at base of the clock, entire printed circuit must be exchanged against a new one. If it is an older model with circuitry problems, and circuit mounting is not located in base, it will be necessary to dismount the coil and transistor together with coil within coil case.

This information from manufacturer of Kundo clocks was sent to American Horologist and Jeweler as a supplement to Mr. Coleman's advice which was sound, but did not cover completely the possibility of the clock in question being transistor pendulum model. Also, by this contribution to American Horologist and Jeweler, Kieninger and Obergfell hopes to prevent many future problems in identification and restoration of these Kundo clocks.

The Brigg's Rotary
By J. E. Coleman

In any collection of clocks those that always attract attention are the ones that exhibit a mechanical action different from the orthodox pendulum swinging to and fro. I'll place the subject of this article—"The Brigg's Rotary"—at the top for getting attention. If you don't believe me, just put one of these little fellows between your high-priced Terry's, Willard's and Rittenhouse clocks and see over which one John Q. Public, lets out the Ooh's and Ah's!

As for its inventor (at least he was granted two patents), John C. Briggs, of Concord, New Hampshire, very little is known. Letters to Miss Doris King, of the reference department of the Concord Public Library, and to Mr. Otis G. Hammond, of the New Hampshire Historical Society, bring replies. "We have been unable to locate any reference to a clock maker in this vicinity by the name of John C. Briggs." A small advertisement in a Concord daily failed to bring a single reply. The best explanation I've had for this and similar conditions was from Dr. Hugh Grant Rowell, several years ago when he wrote: "It is, as you know, very difficult to trace out these patentees and even some makers. These fellows were seldom of much local consequence and are rarely mentioned in local histories. They failed to advertise much and left few traces."

None of these clocks are marked— neither dial nor plate—with a manufacturer's name, and only the later and smaller one had stamped on the top plate: "Patented August 1855" and below that "July 1856". Perhaps the total absence of markings accounts for the almost total lack of information about them. Some owners persist in calling them "French". Just why, I've never been able to figure out unless it is because they are

JOHN C. BRIGGS ROTARY CLOCK.

Arbor	MR. S.A. RECTOR Wheel Diam.	No.Teeth	Pinion Diam.	No.	REV. CHAS R. BREWER Wheel Diam.	No.Teeth	Pinion Diam.	No.	PROF GEO. B. DAVIS Wheel Diam.	No.Teeth	Pinion Diam.	No.	MR. EDWARD INGRAHAM Wheel Diam.	No.Teeth	Pinion Diam.	No.
MAIN	42.0%	48			42.0%	48			42.0%	48			42.0%	48		
2ND	31.0	36	5.0%	8	31.0	36	5.0%	8	31.0	36	7.8%	8	31.0	36	7.8%	8
3RD	30.0	36	6.0	6	30.0	36	6.0	•6	28.5	36	6.8	6	31.0	36	7.8	8
4TH	29.5	36	6.0	6	29.5	36	6.0	6	25.0	36	5.5	6	25.5	36	5.3	6
5TH	25.5	48	6.0	6	25.5	48	6.0	6	25.0	48	5.3	6	25.5	36	5.5	6
6TH	19.0	48	6.0	8	19.0	48	5.0	8	19.0	48	4.2	8	25.0	48	5.0	8
7TH			4.0	8			4.0	8			3.7	8	19.0	48	4.5	8
8TH	NONE				NONE				NONE						3.6	8
DIAL TRAIN																
CENTER			9.5	10			9.5	10			9.5	10			9.5	10
DIVIDING	25.0%	30	8.5	8	25.0%	30	8.5	8	25.0%	30	7.8	8	25.0%	30	8.4	8
HOUR	23.5	32			23.6	32			26.5	32			26.5	32		
M-SPRING	10% in. wide 50 inches long												5/8 in. wide 9 ft. long			

small and rest under a glass bell jar. The teeth, the lantern pinions, the paper dial as well as its entire construction shouts AMERICAN with a very loud voice. Many, a little more familiar with American clocks, say that they are just another "brain child" of Silas B. Terry. This is a logical conclusion because Silas B. certainly came up with several unusual escapements bordering on the "gadget" class. Nevertheless, it is not correct.

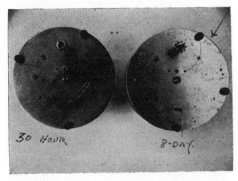

To date it has been impossible to obtain any idea of the number manufactured; all indications are that that number would run fairly large. I personally know of the existence of some 25 or 30. The famous "Believe It or Not!" Robert Ripley, located one on the Isle of Man, which he cartooned Dec. 29th, 1941.

Checking the patent records brought up patent No. 13,451, August 21st, 1855, and No. 15,456, July 15th, 1856. both issued to John C. Briggs, Concord, Merrimack County, New Hampshire. Both photo-copied herewith. Just why he applied for, or, received the second patent is open to question since it is worded practically the same as the first. While no exhaustive study has been made to determine the origin of the "conical" or "rotary" pendulum; I do recall that two or three forms are mentioned by Moinet, in his "Traite d'Horlogerie" (Paris, 1820). Naturally these antedate the 1820 publication date.

We are indebted to Mr. Edward Ingraham, for the manufacturer of

these clocks. He sent down a page from an Asher & Adams Historical Atlas,

Top Plate Removed

ROTARY.

1873 Advertisement

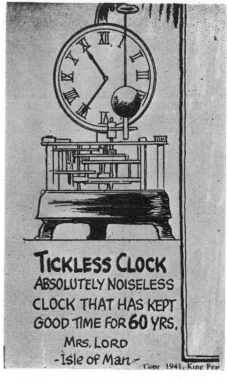

TICKLESS CLOCK
ABSOLUTELY NOISELESS
CLOCK THAT HAS KEPT
GOOD TIME FOR 60 YRS.
MRS. LORD
-Isle of Man-
Copr 1941, King Fea

Cartoon by Robt. Ripley

Close-up Dial Train. Note Coiled Spring for Setting Friction.

published in 1873, showing an E. N. Welck advertisement containing photo of the Welck factory and also a photo of the "Rotary" clock. I quote from the Welck advertisement: "The E. N. Welck Manufacturing Company, make a specialty of rotary clocks and it is claimed that they are the only American manufacturers of reliable clocks having this escapement."

Since the original patent date is 1855 and Welck was advertising them strong in 1873, it is reasonable to assume that the period of manufacture extended over several years—possibly 20 or 25. Close observation of a number of these clocks leads to the conclusion that there was just one model; with a slight variation after they got into quantity production. The chart, Fig. 1, shows a comparison of wheel sizes and train count on four—one from the collection of Mr. Edward Ingram, Bristol, Conn., one from the collection of Mr. S. R. Rector, Winchester, Ky., one from the collection of Rev. Charles R. Brewer, Nashville, Tenn., and one from Prof. George B. Davis, San Antonio, Texas. The Ingraham piece is the only eight-day one

I've seen or heard of—I'm inclined to think it was just an experimental model, altered by hand and never entered into regular production. Fig. 2, shows comparison photo of its top plate and the top plate from the regular 30-hour model. The plates are the same size, and would interchange; thus indicating that someone took a 30-hour model and inserted one arbor between the main and second arbors, making it an eight-arbor train instead of seven— note the cross arcs in the photo where this new arbor was laid out. On this eight-day piece the lower bearings for the seventh and eighth arbors are drilled only half way thru the lower plate, thereby giving the effect of a cap jewel, while on the 30-hour model only the seventh has this cap. Practically the only difference in the first and second versions was: the first had a round pillar-post with the top plate attached by screws. The pendulum cord threaded thru an eye at the end of the curved support and extended

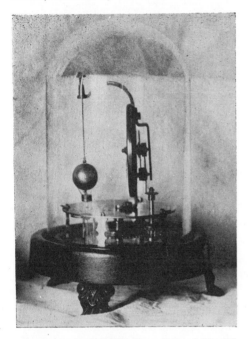

Collection of Dr. Rowell. Note: Stamped Flat Pillars Top Plate Pinned On.

Note: Additional Wheel and Arbor Converting it into an 8-Day.

Front View: From Collection of Mr. Edward Ingraham. Note: Round Pillars. Plate Held on by Screws.

back to the regulating nut located about the center of the curve. The later variation has pillars stamped from flat brass with the top plate held on by pins. The pendulum is suspended directly from its regulating screw placed in the very end of the supporting piece.

The serious student of Horology needn't sneer at this busy little timekeeper for if he will pause a moment to consider, it poses a number of problems that can keep you thinking for quite some time. If gearing happens to be one of your pet lines of interest: here is a piece higher geared than the "year" and 400-day clocks usually encountered, in fact that eight-day model is just about the highest geared piece you've ever heard of: 6x4½x6x6x6x6x6 equals 209,952 revs. per one turn of the main wheel. Makes you want to go back and re-read Jules & Hermann Grossman on gearing and friction, doesn't it? If pendulums are your pet hobby you will immediately jump to the conclusion that so short a pendulum—about 51 m/m.—won't run within five minutes per day right. There is a surprise in store. This little fellow rates well and is capable of keeping right up with its brothers of equal construction and same length pendulum. A conical pendulum is

only by compulsion. It is, actually a controlled to and fro pendulum like any other. If you count this clock, then compare the length of the pendulum on Gourdin's tables, you will note a loss of about 20 per cent over that of a free pendulum. Is this caused by reason of the longer forced arc thru the control mechanism? These and many other problems bob up as you go further into it.

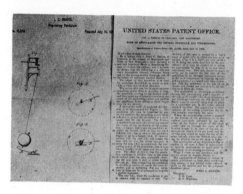

Last, but by no means least, is the winding mechanism. Fig. 3, showing the underside view and large pilot-wheel type winding. This was so constructed that you may stick a finger between the base of the clock and the floor it sits upon and wind it without stopping it or lifting it up. Some clocks have lost this wheel and oddly enough a regular eight-day key will fit the square. A few owners feel that is the way they were wound. Examine one without the wheel and most likely you will find that the arbor has been broken off right where the pin-hole was drilled. If the maker had intended a key wind there would be no occasion for drilling a hole thru the square.

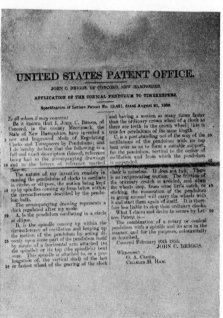

ANSONIA CLOCK

A customer brought us a musical alarm clock marked "ANSONIA" Pat. 1877. This clock is American made, and has but a single spring for both alarm and time. Its unusual feature is the fact that the alarm plays a tune, music-box fashion.

This clock is in fair shape, and could easily be put into running condition. We are interested in the background and history of this timepiece. Can you give us any information?

A.

Ansonia Clock company was incorporated in 1873 at Brooklyn, New York. They made an extensive line of clocks, and cheap nickel watches up to about the time of World War I. Shortly after that, all the factory machinery was sold to the Russian Government, and shipped over there. I believe that clock manufacturing was a part of their first "Five Year" plan.

It is to be assumed that "Ansonia" began manufacturing these clocks (with one spring driving both time and alarm trains) about the time of the patent date—1877. We have a 1907 Ansonia catalog in which they are listed; a much later catalog numbered 501 which is undated, but must be around 1912 or 1914, does not list them.

I feel sure that this clock (with the single spring for both trains) was the first of that particular type made in America. No doubt you have noted that several alarms being made today (Waterbury and Traverlarm, etc.) employ this principal.

GRANDFATHER CLOCK

I have an old "Grandfather's Clock" which my grandfather purchased in 1889. The following history came with the clock: "I send you the short but authentic history of the clock. It has been in the Noyes family four full generations. John Noyes died at 78, his father at 82, his grandfather at 90 and his great grandfather at 68 and that is all that could be ascertained as to its age. The clock came from England to Coventry, Conn., thence to Warner, N. H., and then to Lebanon, N. H."

The clock was made in Birmingham, England. The works are of brass and iron put together with metal pins. There are no screws. The dial is of iron but has no false dial behind it.

There are two features of the clock which puzzle me. One is the method of numbering the hours on the large dial and the seconds on the small one. Mr. Mitman believes this numbering may be due to an error when the dial was repainted, however I do not believe the dial has ever been repainted. The other is a semi-circular opening where the letter

"S" appears every few months. This "S" remains stationary for many weeks then gradually moves and reappears. As yet I have not been able to determine the exact frequency of its appearance.

I wonder if you would be so kind as to

furnish me with a clue as to the age of this clock and to the meaning of the numbering system and the "S"? This clock has been in continual use since it was purchased by my grandfather.

A.

. I am inclined to agree with you that the dial has never been repainted. It looks very much like the original; certainly one with the ability to make such a faithful reproduction would not purposely leave off the cross bars on IX and XI.

We often see dials on which the bar of the X's and the thin sides of the V's are worn off from cleaning, etc. My guess is that this has happened to your dial. Clocks of this type were popular around the early 1800's. Painted dials did not come into general use before 1790. I note that you say the clock was made in "Birmingham", and as the dial has no makers name I am wondering why you think so. Sometimes the iron frame to which the dial is pinned carries the mark of a "Birmingham" founder —in which case it does not mean the movement was made in "Birmingham", many London makers had parts cast in "Birmingham".

The semi-circular opening just under the center post is the calendar. If you will remove the dial you should find a small solid wheel, about three inches in diameter, revolving upon a post made fast to the dial. This wheel should have 62 saw-like teeth. On the hour-pipe there should be a pin or projection that engages this wheel; thus you will see that this projection moves the calendar wheel forward one tooth each time the hour hand passes XII, or twice per day, in 31 days it has revolved the calendar wheel one complete revolution. The only explanation I have for your observing the letter "S" appearing at irregular intervals is what you believe to be an "S" must be an old "3" or "8" and as the wheel is not set on the 30 day month, it naturally does not appear upon the same day of the next month. Directly under the center post— probably in the upper side of this semi-circular opening is a slight projection of a pointer—this points to the day of the month as they are lettered on the calendar wheel. Usually these wheels are lettered only with odd numbers with just a dot for the even days. From your photo I would say the mintue hand is original, but the hour hand has been supplied later.

JEROME & CO.

Recently, while cleaning and rebushing an old eight-day weight clock, we were wondering how we could determine its age. On the inside back of the clock, printed on a badly faded paper, we made out the following: American, Extra Bushed Movement Clocks, Manufactured by J. E. Rome & Co., New Haven, Conn., Eight-Day.

Will appreciate any information you may be able to give us.

A.

The clock you ask about must have been made between 1845 and 1860. I am sure that you have copied the name from the label incorrectly. Instead of "J. E. Rome & Co., New Haven, Conn.," look and see if it isn't "Jerome & Co."

"Chauncey Jerome" was in the clock-making business with various companies —at Plymouth, Bristol and New Haven— from 1816 to 1860. On the 23rd of April, 1845, his Bristol factory burned. From there he moved to New Haven.

Since he retired in 1860, clocks with the New Haven label must fall between 1845 and 1860.

COLUMBUS CLOCK

I am enclosing a photo of a Columbus clock, which has a picture of Columbus on the front, an hour hand only, one weight and the date "Anno 1492." The clock has wooden wheels. Thanking you for any information you can give me as to the date and origin of this beautiful clock.

A.

The photo showed that the clock is definitely a "Standard" Columbus clock—these

were made by the Bostic & Burgess Manufacturing Co., Norwalk, Ohio, about 1892 for the Columbian Exposition.

Writing about the "Columbus" clock, Professor Willis I. Milham said: "The Columbus clock may be called the clock of mystery since there are more stories about who made it, and more uncertainty about its history, than about almost any other clock." Professor Milham, has written a book about it which you will find advertised in the book list of the American Horologist & Jeweler, and for sale by them

E. N. WELCH

Some time ago I repaired a mantel clock. The owner of this clock was wondering about the age of it. The instruction sheet inside the clock had the name R. or P. or F. (the initial was partly gone) N. Welch Mfg. Co., Forestville, Conn., 8-day brass clocks.

A.

In reply to your letter, no doubt you are mistaken about that first letter being either "P" or "R." It should read "E. N. Welch Manufacturing Co., Forestville, Conn." The "E" initial is for "Elisha."

In 1855, Elisha N. Welch bought the property and business of John C. Brown (a well-known clock manufacturer). In 1864, he organized "The E. N. Welch Manufacturing Company," Forestville, Conn. This factory is now "The Sessions Clock Company."

Chauncey Jerome, writing of Mr. Welch (Aug. 15, 1860) had this to say: "The next one in the business to whom I shall allude is E. N. Welch of Bristol, Conn. He is about 50 years of age and has been in many kinds of business. He was deeply interested in the failure of John C. Brown, a few years ago, and succeeded him in the

Works of the E. N. Welch Manufacturing Co., Forestville, Conn.

clock business. He is a leading man in the Baptist Church, and has a great tact for making money; but he says that all he wants of money is to do good with it. He is a Democrat in politics, and never wants an office from his party."

CHAUNCEY JEROME

I have a clock in for repairs and the customer is interested in establishing the clock's age. On the back of the case is a printed paper that says "Brass Clocks, made and sold by Chauncey Jerome, Bristol, Conn."

The clock is a weight driven time and hour strike only. The case is about 2½

feet tall and the time and strike cable go up and out the top of the case over a pulley and down inside the case. The clock has to be wound every day.

A.

Your Chauncey Jerome, with the Bristol label, was made before Jerome moved to New Haven, Conn. in 1845. Now since Jerome "devised" the one-day weight clock about 1837, we may safely conclude that this clock was made between 1837 and 1845.

WELCH "PATTI"

Offered for your consideration is a sketch of a clock that we have in our service department for repair. Only part of the label remains on back of clock, as shown by sketch.

The movement is made up with two separate mainsprings—for each side—and the outer ends of the springs are attached and wind in opposite directions. One end is attached to winding arbor of main wheel, and the other to pinion that extends through plates and main wheel, with square for winding.

I have never seen a clock with this type springs. Can you give me any idea of the maker from part of label shown, as well as the approximate year made?

A.

It just so happens that the clock you sketch and describe is one of my favorites. Thus, we have a little more than the usual data on it, so here goes: (A photo of the label is being forwarded to you to help you finish out the missing parts of yours. These clocks always had the label on outside of the back).

This is the famous "Patti" model made by Welch, Spring & Co., Forestville, Conn., and it first appeared in their 1880 catalog, page 49. The new and different mainspring you mention was patented by Benjamin B. Lewis, No. 249,845, Nov. 22, 1881. You may obtain a copy of this patent by writing the superintendent of the Patent Office and sending 25 cents. It makes good reading, and says in part: "My invention is designed principally for the strike side of a clock movement, although some parts of it are applicable to either side; and the invention consists in the peculiar construction of a double spring. . . ."

Writing of the Patti clock, William K. Sessions, president of the Sessions Clock Co. (successors to Welch) said: "The 1880 catalog describes the Patti clock as having a visible pendulum, but does not show it with a visible escapement, although we believe there were some turned out in this manner." I have never seen or been able to locate a Patti with escapement showing

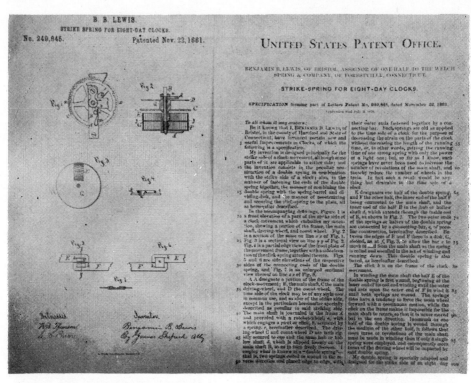

PATENT GRANT TO INVENTOR BENJAMIN B. LEWIS FOR HIS EIGHT-DAY CLOCK STRIKE-SPRING.

AT LEFT ABOVE, PATTI V. P. SPRING MODEL, EIGHT-DAY STRIKE AS ILLUSTRATED IN OLD WELCH, SPRING & CO. CATOLOG. MODEL WAS AVAILABLE IN 18½-INCH HEIGHT, 5-INCH DIAL; AND 10¼, 3-INCH DIAL. AT RIGHT ABOVE, PHOTO VIEW SHOWS THE CLOCK MOVEMENT EMBODYING THE LEWIS INVENTION.

in th dial, and if you or some of our readers have, we would certainly like the data. Of all the Patti models I have examined, the escapement was the same, located just under the dial, on the front plate, all the lift on the face of the escape wheel tooth, the pendulum hung by clevis from the verge pin, and no pendulum spring.

About this time it was a popular custom to name products for famous characters. Mme. Patti being very famous at this period, it was but natural for someone in Welch, Spring & Co. to suggest her name for one of their top models. I have never been able to establish whether or not one of these clocks was presented to the famous singer. It must have been a good seller because there are quite a number of them in service today. My old friend Bill Donnelly told me that in 1884 the B. & O. railroad named a boudoir car "Adelina Patti" and that it was put on a special publicity run between Chicago and Balti-

ADELINA PATTI, THE CELEBRATED 19TH CENTURY BEAUTY AND OPERATIC SINGER WHO HAD A CLOCK NAMED IN HER HONOR. (PHOTO COURTESY OF D. APPLETON-CENTURY CO.)

more. The time was 22 hours and 20 minutes.

Mme. Adelina, renowned high soprano, was born in Madrid in 1843 and was brought to America when only a few years old. She first appeared as a prodigy vocalist and became equally successful in concert and opera. She was married three times; first to Marquis de Caux in 1868, divorced 1885 then married to Signor Nocilini in 1886, and after his death married Baron Cederstrom, 1899. She died in 1919.

CLOCK GLASSES

A number of years ago we were so impressed with the fine craftsmanship of a reproduction of an early American clock glass that we set about to see if there wasn't a story there. Sure enough there was, and as is so often the case this story had for its background two very familiar fundamentals: 1) Craftsmanship passed from father to son (in this case father to daughter), 2) thorough historical knowledge.

Back in the era of early American clock manufacture, William Bennett Fenn (B. July 11, 1813 at Plymouth, Conn., D. March 1890) was making many of the dials and glasses for such famous clockmakers as Seth Thomas, Silas Hoadley, John C. Brown, Atkins Porter & Co., Boardman & Wells, Terry & Andrews, and Hopkins & Fields, all of Connecticut.

Today in her home at Red Stone Hill in Plainville, Conn., Mrs. Mary E. Stephenson, daughter of Mr. Fenn, has been devoting her full time to restoring or reproducing early American clock glasses, many of which were originally made by her father, for more than thirty years. She has a great deal of her father's equipment and many of his original stencils. Some of these stencils were cut about a century ago (Mr. Fenn was working almost exclusively for Seth Thomas, 1840 to about 1863) and she refrains from using them unless it is absolutely necessary. In lots of restorative jobs the original design is completely worn or peeled off and it is necessary to duplicate the piece free hand. In these cases the stencils as well as photos serve well for reference.

Much of the work is done in gold leaf, as was originally used, and many of the designs are so intricate that it is hard to believe they can be restored free hand. Mrs. Stephenson attended Pratt Institute, where she graduated from the fine arts course in 1898. She served as a teacher of art in the public schools before taking up her father's trade. When speaking of her work, she will hasten to explain that it is exactly the reversal of painting on canvas, as her painting is applied on the back side of the glass and must be done "backward." All fine detail is painted on first and the background last.

Mrs. Stephenson is exceptionally well versed on early American clock history and is the proud owner of two of these clocks—a Seth Thomas eight-day calendar clock and a Silas Hoadley clock—both of which her father obtained from the makers during his business connection with them.

A portrait of William Bennett Fenn, 19th Century American Clock dial and glass decorator, and a current study of his daughter, Mrs. Mary E. Stephenson of Plainville, Conn., who is carrying on the highly skilled profession

SHARP GOTHIC

I have an American striker which is printed on the inside: Sharp Gothic, Day Striking, Jerome and Company, Haven Connecticut, U. S. A. Could you approximate its age? I think about 1860. You could probably get a better idea of the movement if I just say that the pallets are mounted on a pin outside the front plate below the escape wheel. I also have a Birge and Fuller wagon spring clock. I understand that it would be about 1844.

A.

Your dates for the Jerome Sharp Gothic are about right. This style of case was invented by Elias Ingraham, who conceived it while on a voyage to Caracas in South America, either in 1840 or 1844. It was not patented; quickly became very popular and was produced in quantities by other manufacturers. Chauncey Jerome moved from Bristol, Connecticut, to New Haven in the winter of 1844. Some time later, date not definite, he was operating under the name Jerome Manufacturing Company when it failed in 1855. Your clock is probably 5 or 10 years older than your 1860 date.

The Birge and Fuller firm was composed of John Birge and Thomas Fuller. As determined from the tax rolls of Bristol, this firm was in business 1844 to 1847. I recently copied one of these labels: "J.

Ives Patent Accelerating Lever Spring, thirty-hour Brass clocks. Made and for sale, wholesale and retail, by Birge and Fuller, Bristol, Connecticut. Patent secured February 24, 1846."

SETH THOMAS

Recently I had a customer bring in a S. Thomas clock, Plymouth, Connecticut. I'd like to know how old this clock is. The frame of the works is pinned together, and it strikes on the hour. The customer said the clock has been in his family for 174 years,

A.

Seth Thomas, son of James and Martha Thomas, was born August 18, 1785, and died January 29, 1859. Thus, you see, he was born only 166 years ago, and couldn't possibly have a clock 174 years old.

About 1808 he was still with Eli Terry, and was later with Silas Hoadley in the firm of Thomas & Hoadley. He started in business for himself, under his own name, about 1813, making wooden clocks.

Movements of the type your sketch indicates, were made following the wood era, or after 1837. The name of the town was changed from Plymouth Hollow to Thomaston in his honor in 1866. The movement in question must have been made between 1837 and 1866. Chances are, it is around 100 years old.

DAVIS & BARBER

Can you supply any information on a clock made by Davis & Barber, Greensboro, Georgia? I'm pretty well convinced that it must be a "contract" job; the movement is wood and resembles the Seth Thomas wooden works more than any I've seen. I've tried to sketch it as best I could.

A.

Replying to your query about "Davis & Barber" Greensboro, Georgia, clock:

Your deductions that it was a "contract" job is exactly correct, further, since it is a wood movement clock, it must be one of their (Davis & Barber) earlier sales; from what I have upon them their principal sales were brass clocks, which naturally followed the wood ones after 1837.

From your sketch I'd say you have the "regular improved Terry" clock (one-day, wood) which we see so many of. So far as I know, nothing has ever been published about this venture and for this reason the entire file might be worth while, this being the second Davis & Barber inquiry received within the past year. First, the reason: Many southern states passed acts taxing clocks, therefore to evade these high taxes many clockmakers of the East located assembly plants in the South. Chauncey Jerome at Richmond, Va., later removing to Hamburg, South Carolina. Case, Dyer, Wadsworth & Co., Augusta, Ga., J. W. McMillian, Greenville, Alabama, Couch, Stowe & Co., Rocksprings, Tenn. and others. It appears that these so called assembly plants were not exactly as we'd use the term today; the movements were already assembled; they were only installed in the cases which came separately and had labels pasted therein with the Southern address at the time and place the movement was installed.

I quote a from a letter received from Mr. Edward Ingraham, April 17th, 1940. "E. C. Brewster commenced the manufacture of clocks in the shop built by Ira Ives, which stood upon the site of Mr. Ingraham's movement shop. He manufactured movements for Messrs. Davis & Barbour, who cased and sold them in the southern market. Mr. Davis, Jerome like, started a factory in Macon, Georgia, buying cases and movements here, and putting them together and selling there, thus avoiding a heavy license and greatly pleasing the inhabitants by having the clocks all made in their state" (from a letter written May 10th, 1872, to the Bristol Press by Milo L. Norton.)

From another letter from Mr. Ingraham, Oct. 25th, 1948, he quotes from page 352 of the History of Bristol, (published in 1907) from the history of Elias Ingraham, as follows: "After working for Mrs. Mitchell (George), for about two years, he commenced work for Chauncey & Lawson Ives, at what is known as the Eureka shop, continuing in their employ until 1836, when he contracted to make cases for Davis & Barbour, who were shipping cases and movements separately to the South, where they were put together, this saving the payment of the heavy state licenses."

There was, about the time of the war between the states, a Davis Clock Co. at Columbus, Miss., and the question is often asked if there was any connection with Davis & Barber. The Mississippi concern was owned and operated by Mr. N. L. Davis, no relation or connection with Josiah Smith Davis. Mr. T. B. Rice, official historian for Greene County, Georgia, has investigated the Davis & Barber story about as thoroughly as it can be done there. What he sends me makes more interesting reading and just about rounds out their history. We'd like to hear from present owners of these clocks; it would be interesting to see how well scattered they are today. Following is the Rice report in full:

JOSIAH SMITH DAVIS was born in Harwinton, Conn., Litchfield County, January 13th, 1802; died in Greensboro, Georgia, February 9th, 1869. He married CLOE BARBER, of the same town and county (date of marriage not known), but she married Josiah S. Davis in Connecticut. She was born October 6th, 1802. Died in Greensboro, Georgia, February 12th, 1860.

Josiah S. Davis' second marriage was to Frances Loyd Park, daughter of Ezekiel E. Park, who came to Greene County Georgia, at an early date; he was a revolutionary soldier. Mrs. Frances Park Davis died July 8th, 1872. There seems to be no record of any children by this marriage.

The following death notice seems to be the only key as to the date Josiah S. Davis came to Greensboro:

DIED

"In Greensboro, Georgia, Feb. 12th, 1860, Mrs. Cloe Davis, wife of Mr. Josiah Davis, in the 58th year of her age. Mrs. Davis was a native of Harwinton, Conn., and removed to Greensboro, Georgia, about 25 years ago."

This seems to fix the approximate date of Josiah Davis' arrival in Greensboro, around the year 1835-1836, which date corresponds also with the records where he bought a home in Greensboro. In the year 1836 the Georgia Railroad had reached Greensboro, and cotton had been crowned king. Greensboro was in the heart of the cotton producing section and planters were "rolling in wealth" to the envy of "Yankeedom." "Yankees poured into Georgia, with a view of outsmarting the "yokels." Clocks, Jim Crow carders and other "Yankee" geegaws were scarce and the fields were "ripe unto the harvest." Josiah S. Davis heard of this Promised Land and like the forty-niners during the California gold rush, he headed for Greensboro, Georgia.

DAVIS & HALL, Merchants
The Green County records show where Josiah S. Davis and Isaac R. Hall formed a partnership and engaged in the mercantile business in Greensboro on May 30th, 1844, and that Josiah Davis had stablished the business some years prior to that date. The partnership agreement is recorded in Green County deed book 0-0, page 138, and was for a period of four years from date. This partnership was renewed on May 30th, 1848. The capital employed was $5,000. Mr. Hall owned the building in which they did business.

First Record of DAVIS & BARBER
Green County deed book N-N, page 128 shows where Davis & Barber loaned to Jesse M. Thornton $275, and as security for said loan they took a bill of sale to a "Yellow man, named Edward, about 22 years of age." This transaction was recorded on October 29th, 1841, and shows that the firm of Davis & Barber was already in business for some years prior to the Davis-Hall partnership.

It is reasonable to suppose that Orville Barber, a nephew of Mrs. Josiah Davis, came to Georgia with his aunt and uncle and that they soon thereafter began assembling clocks and peddling t h e m throughout Georgia and neighboring states, and that these clocks were also sold by "Uncle Josiah's" mercantile establishment.

Other records show where DAVIS & BARBER loaned money to several people and took bills of sale to secure the loans. In other words, this proves that although DAVIS & BARBER were Connecticutt "Yankees" they had no scruples against owning slaves.

Orville Barber Goes Back to Connecticut
Green County deed book P-P, page 197 shows where, on October 20th, 1849, Orville Barber of the town of Harwinton, Litchfield County, Conn., deeded to Josiah S. Davis, of Greensboro, Georgia, certain lands in Cobb, Floyd, Cherokee and other Georgia counties, that belonged to the firm of DAVIS & BARBER, the consideration was $3,000 for Orville Bar-

ber's one-half interest. This seems to indicate that this transaction terminated the firm DAVIS & BARBER, further that the firm had prospered, and had invested a portion of their savings in Georgia lands.

Other records show that: soon after the Confederate States were organized, and the "war clouds" began to gather. Josiah S. Davis deeded his Greensboro home to his nephew, Orville Barber of Harwinton, Conn. Also that after hostilities ceased, said Orville Barber deeded the property back to his uncle. The prevailing opinion of this transaction was that Mr. Davis feared that his property might be confiscated in the event the Confederacy won the war.

When this writer came to Greensboro in September, 1889, there were many people still living who knew Josiah S. Davis personally and the two-room house in which DAVIS & BARBER assembled their clocks was still standing. Edward, the "Yellow" man DAVIS & BARBER had acquired under bill of sale, was still living. It was from these people this writer obtained much first-hand information about the old clock firm.

Leila Harper Wood, an old colored woman whose master lived across the street from the Josiah Davis home and shop, told me many things concerning the Davis family. According to her story Orville Barber had charge of the sales end of the business while his uncle looked after the shop, and the slaves owned by DAVIS & BARBER did the actual work of assembling the clocks. The works were shipped here from Connecticut and after the clocks had been assembled, they, together with other "Yankee" gewgaws such as Jim Crow carders, small articles of tinware, etc., were loaded on wagons that scoured the countryside for customers.

There is no record of Mr. Josiah Davis' activities after the War Between the States, and the presumption is that he lived a retired life up to the time of his death in 1869.

There were several Davis families living in Greensboro and in order to distinguish one from the other, Josiah was referred to as "Old Man Clock Davis."

There are many old DAVIS & BARBER clocks scattered throughout Georgia and adjoining states; many of them are still in running order and keeping good time. If you happen to own an old DAVIS & BARBER clock you may rest assured that it is around one hundred years old. I am reasonably sure that none were made prior to 1937 and none later than 1850.

PETER CLARK Succeeds Davis & Barber

Several years ago an old clock was brought to my office to find out something about its maker, and when he made clocks in Greensboro.

It was similar in design to the Davis & Barber clocks. The label on the inside of the case was identical with that of the Davis clock and read as follows:

Patent Brass Thirty-Hour Clocks. Manufactured by ————? Clark. Greensboro, Georgia., and sold wholesale and retail. Guaranteed to run if well used. Printed by Joseph Hulbut, Hartford, Conn.

By carefully scrutinizing the label, I found that the name, ————? Clark, was pasted over the name of DAVIS & BARBER. In other words, ————? Clark, whose given name was Peter, used whatever supply of labels Davis & Barber had left over. He simply covered their name with his own.

Who was PETER CLARK, and when did he make clocks in Greensboro?

By chance, a Mr. Charles Davis, a retired railroad conductor who lives in Jacksonville, Fla., dropped into my office and after introducing himself, he said:

"I was born in Greensboro, Ga. My father's name was Jacob J. Davis, who was a son of Josiah Davis, the man who made and sold clocks in Greensboro many years ago."

That brought up the subject of the old DAVIS & BARBER clocks so I proceeded to quizz my visitor. I handed him a story that I had written about the old clock firm. After reading it, he said:

"Your article coincides with what my father told me about my grandfather, and the years he spent in Greensboro. I appreciate your preserving the story."

I then asked him about Clark, and when he began making clocks. He said:

"I know very little about PETER CLARK, other than that he was related to my grandfather, and that he is said to have made clocks in Greensboro after my grandfather went out of business, and that he lived with my ancestor."

This put me on Clark's trail, so I proceeded to the courthouse to see if I could find him in the records. I did, and here are the results.

Greene County Deed Book Q-Q, page 181, shows the following:

"On May 12th, 1854, an agreement was entered into between Josiah Davis and Peter Clark whereby Peter Clark deeded three negro women, his live stock and other personal property to Josiah Davis, the consideration being that the aforesaid Josiah Davis was to take care of Peter Clark, both in sickness and in health." The three negro women are described as follows: "Winnie, a negro woman about 45 years old, and Martha, the daughter of said Winnie, who is about 31 years old, and Adeline, the daughter of Martha, about 16 years old."

No mention is made of the clock business, but the above transaction, May 12th, 1854, seems to indicate that he had acquired the clock business prior to that date, and that Clark was in poor health when he deed his property to Davis, with the understanding that Davis was to take care of him during the rest of his life. Same book, same page, Josiah Davis confirmed the above contract with Peter Clark, and the same was recorded. Peter Clark died and was buried by the side of Josiah Davis. Or to be more exact, Clark died first and Davis was buried by his side. Thus did the clock making business end in Greensboro, Georgia.

FRENCH CLOCK

I wish to obtain the historical background on a French clock.

This clock and candelabrum are made from porcelain "Platine" and the works are marked: No. 1017 Paul Miche, Amsterdam, Japy Freres and Company—Cve Med D'Hon—Brocot Propte. The case is elaborately decorated with ormolu.

Any information you could give me would be greatly appreciated.

A.

Since my history is practically confined to "Early American", your question is a bit difficult.

"Platine" is French for "Plates of a watch."

Your piece it seems, is the No. 1017 by Paul Miche, of Amsterdam. Baillie does not list a Paul Miche at all. There is a Stanislas Miche, Paris, 1780, and a Charles Leon Miche, Paris 1785-1789.

Frederic Japy, born 1749, was the first horologist to manufacture watch ebauches by machinery in 1776. He started a factory for clock ebauches at Baderel in 1810, the Japy Freres & Company. He died in 1813.

Achille Brocot was born in Paris in 1817. He was an eminent clockmaker, patented an escapement and devised an adjustable pendulum suspension. He died in 1878.

I take it that this clock was made by Paul Miche at Amsterdam, from ebauche manufactures by Japy Freres Company, which had either the Brocot escapement or regulator (or both) and that at some expositions the ebauche manufacturer had been awarded the "Medal of Honor." All of which does not give us a date. Allowing that Brocot was at least 21 years old before his inventions were made, would bring us up to 1838. It was popular to import clocks of the general type as yours in the 1840's and 1850's. A good guess as to its age would be one hundred years. Sorry I can't give you something more definite.

J.C. BROWN

I have found an old clock which has been in the family a number of years and would like to know its history and when it was made.

Stamped on the plates is J. C. Brown, Forrestville, Connecticut. Pasted instructions on the back of the clock case read: Eight-day brass clocks, Forrestville Manufacturing Company, J. C. Brown, Bristol, Connecticut. It has an eight-day movement with a coil wire spring gong. The clock is about twenty inches high and ten inches wide.

A.

Check the label of your clock again to make sure. Forrestville Manufacturing Company, Bristol, is listed as 1835 to 1839, and Forrestville Clock Manufactory, Bristol, is listed 1839 to 1855. Chances are your clock was made in the 1840's.

J.C. BROWN'S CLOCK MANUFACTY.
Forrestville Conn.

John C. Brown was a colorful and very active character in early American clockmaking. Jerome mentions him on page 85: "A man by the name of J. C. Brown carried on the business in Bristol for a long time and made a good many fine clocks, but finally gave up the business." In the writing of E. N. Welch he said: "He was deeply interested in the failure of J. C. Brown a few years ago and succeeded him in the clock business."

Like many other Connecticut clockmakers, Brown was associated with several concerns at the same time. His activity covers from 1827 to 1855. He was born October 8, 1807 at Coventry, Connecticut, and died in Bristol in 1872. Probably the outstanding feature of his clocks was the Acorn clock, so named from the resemblance of the case to an acorn. At the height of his career he built a very fine home and so far as I know was the only clockmaker to use a photo of his residence on the "tablet" of his clocks. We are running photos of one of these "tablets" and an old cut of the factory.

FUSEE WATCH

Recently I purchased a fusee watch and would like some information on it— maker, date of manufacture, etc.

Sterling silver case with bezel and brass plate inside hinged as penant.

Hand-ground crystal with round indention in center.

Dial pinned to hinge plate has 15 sec. second dial.

Movement also pins to hinge plate. 18¾ L, key wound.

Lower plate, dial side are found the numbers 17 and 7.

Balance bridge engraved, "Patent".

Upper plate engraved, Liverpool, M. Tobias & Co. 8799.

8799 also in back of case.

The movement has a pointed tooth escape wheel, detached lever with the pallet fork geared to the balance instead of the usual roller jewel action. The hairspring and regulator are mounted under

108

the balance wheel and attached to the upper plate.

The balance cock holds only jewels.

So much for history.

The watch came minus a minute wheel. It has a 12 leaf cannon pinion, 42 tooth hour wheel. I tried a 12-40 minute wheel, but the ratio comes out 11.7-1 as near as I can figure.

I worked out a formula which gave me something like 7-12 which would be much too small for the distance from the minute wheel pin to the cannon pinion.

My belief is that the hour wheel may have been changed, too.

A.

M. Tobias & Co., was actively in the watch business at Liverpool, England, 1810 to 1829.

Your type escapement is not exactly a "detached" lever, but is a "rack lever," sometimes called "rack and pinion escapement," first invented by Abbe d'Hautefeuille (B. 1647, D. 1724) in 1722. Later Peter Litherland of Liverpool took out British patent No. 1830 on October 14, 1791.

Under the firm names Peter Litherland, 1790 to 1814, Litherland Whiteside & Co., 1800 to 1816, and Litherland Davies & Co., 1818 to 1837, all of Liverpool, vast numbers of rack lever movements were turned out. Major Chamberlain says: "Many of them came to America, as did others in great quantity under the names of Roskell, Moncas, Tobias, Fisher and others."

Try a minute wheel of 24 teeth and seven leaf pinion. In 12 hours (12 revs.) your cannon pinion of 12 would turn the "minute" wheel of 24, six revs. 6 revs. of the 7 leaf pinion would drive the hour wheel of 42 one rev. or, giving you a ratio between cannon pinion and hour wheel of 12 to 1.

SETH THOMAS

Could you give the dates Seth Thomas made clocks with the label Seth Thomas, Plymouth Hollow, Connecticut? I think it was from 1813 to ?.

A. Seth Thomas was born at Woldott, Connecticut, about 1785, learned the carpenter trade and about 1808 went to work "with" Silas Hoadley and Eli Terry at Plymouth, Connecticut.

This is generally spoken of as the firm of "Terry, Thomas & Hoadley." Details of the partnership have never been made perfectly clear. Mr. Carl Drepperd says: "A partnership of legend if not fact." Here he did "joiner work," that is made cases, and he also "put together" clocks, that is assembled the movement. He continued in this way for the years 1808, 1809 and 1810 when Mr. Terry withdrew and the firm became "Thomas & Hoadley." That partnership lasted about two years. Then Mr. Thomas sold out to Mr. Hoadley and moved to Plymouth Hollow where he began to make clocks upon his own account in the old Heman Clark factory.

It was a success from the word go. By 1853 Mr. Thomas had amassed a fortune and was ready to retire. It ran through "Seth Thomas," "Seth Thomas Sons & Company," "Seth Thomas Company" and "Seth Thomas Clock Company," which company he organized under the joint stock laws of Connecticut in 1853.

Mr. Thomas died January 29, 1859, and that portion of the town where the clock factory was situated was named "Thomaston" in his honor. Thus clocks labeled "Plymouth Hollow" are considered to have been made before 1859.

LIVERPOOL WATCH

I have a watch of considerable age and wish any data available regarding its maker and history. The only history I have is the fact that the watch was worn by Capt. Alexander Richard Maclean (British Army) when he attended the famed funeral of Sir John Moor, who was killed in the battle of Corunna in Spain.

The plate bears what I believe is the maker's name, a place and a number: Gn. Robert — Edinburgh 394.

The dial plate measures 1 7/10 inches, the bottom plate 1½ inches and the balance wheel is 8/10 inches in diameter.

The movement is key wound and the regulator is adjusted by key also. A small dial numbered from 5 to 30 acts as an indicator in moving the regulator. The movement has no jewels and the balance staff is the same diameter throughout except for the hairspring seat. There are actually no pivots as we know them today. The mainspring barrel has no teeth as the power is delivered by chain drive (fusee). The hairspring lies under the balance and has only four coils. The cock is the usual elaborate hand worked pen work type that is common to these old movements. The watch may be very common to collectors but it is the first I have actually seen.

A.

The watch you have is quite common to collectors here. I believe the general type watch you have is referred to as a Liverpool watch because so many of them were labeled from that city. This type of escapement called verge escapement was used in all the earliest watches and according to Major Chamberlain, up to nearly 50 years ago. It was superseded by the Cylinder usually attributed to George Graham, but actually patented by Wm. H. Houghton in 1695.

I believe you are in error in thinking that the pivots are the same size as the body of the staff. These verge staffs usually had very small pivots. Isn't it possible that they have been broken off? Re-examine them closely and look for any indication of the bearings being enlarged and the bridge lowered to make up for the lost length. Like the detent escapement, the verge requires some safety feature to prevent it from allowing the train to fly down and cause great damage. This, together with the key regulator, hairspring under the balance wheel are typical features of Liverpool watches.

ENGLISH WATCH

I have an old English-made key-wind and key-set watch that looks like a verge movement. It has Wm. Rider, London — No. 5550 engraved on it. Can you tell me how old this movement is?

I also have an old key-wind and key-set New Haven watch. I would like to know how old it is

A.

The English-made watch you refer to resembles the verge watch made by Napier & Dunn, Glasgow, Scotland, about 1783. Baillie's list does not give a Wm. Rider of London, at all. However, Wm. Rider, a watchmaker, is listed as being in Liverpool from 1800 to 1803, so again the date indicates the watch was made somewhere around 1800.

SETH THOMAS ALARM

I would like some information on a Seth Thomas alarm 8-day, ½-strike clock. On the dial side the plate is engraved Thomston CT. U.S.A., 5⅞ Patented December 28, 1875. Is that the day and year made? What does 5⅞ mean? Also, where can I get a suspension spring and how can I determine the length and thickness if I have to make one?

A.

The patent date, December 28, 1875, is merely the date upon which the patent office issued the patent and has no connection with the date of manufacture. American movements of this period didn't have the date of manufacture stamped on. I imagine your clock was made near the turn of the century as striking clocks with pendulum and alarm attachment were popular about that time.

I think the 5⅞ indicated the overall dimension of the movement and was used by the factory for casing purposes.

As to the strength, width and length of a suspension spring for your clock, this feature is far from exacting as a little deviation in any or all of the measurements will not affect the satisfactory performance of the clock.

CASE, DYER, WADSWORTH & CO.

Can you tell me in what year clocks were manufactured by Dyer, Wadsworth & Co., Augusta, Georgia? The clock is 33″ high, 17″ wide and 4½″ front-to-rear. It winds with a key with weights on either side. It also has a full length picture of George Washington on the clock door with the name of a New York concern and a firm at 128 Main Street, Hartford, Connecticut. Any information you can give me on this will be appreciated.

A.

I quote from Chauncey Jerome's *American Clockmaking,* (New Haven, Connecticut, 1860) pages 54 and 55: "In 1835, the Southern people were greatly opposed to Yankee pedlars coming into their states, especially the clock pedlars, and the licenses were raised so high by their legislatures that it almost amounted to a prohibition. Their laws were that any goods made in their own states could be sold without license. Therefore, clocks to be more profitable must be made in those states. Chauncey and Noble Jerome started a factory in Richmond, Virginia, making the cases and parts at Bristol, Connecticut, and packing them with dial, glass, etc. We shipped them to Richmond, and took along workmen to put them together. Everyone knew it was a humbug trying to stop the pedlars from coming to their state. We removed from Richmond, to Hamburg, South Carolina, and manufactured in the same way. This was in 1835 and 1836. There was another company doing the same kind of business at Augusta, Georgia, by the name of Case, Dyer, Wadsworth & Company, and Seth Thomas was making the movements and cases for them."

It is noted in your inquiry that you omitted the name Case from the firm name as given by Jerome. Will you check this label again and make sure? All too little is known about this concern and it is quite possible Mr. Case dropped out, however, if he did none of the lists of early American clockmakers indicate it.

BLACK FOREST CLOCK

I have put a clock in running order and would like very much to find out how old it is. The dial says London 1764, but since it is a striker this couldn't be correct, could it?

A.

The mere fact that your clock strikes does not preclude its being made as far back as 1764. Clocks struck even before they had dial or hands—much farther back than 1764. In fact, it might be said that clocks named themselves as one very early French name was *cloche* and the Saxons used *clugga,* and I'm told that both words mean

Mr. Byrd's clock

"to strike a bell."

The decorated, metal dial marked London 1764 in your photo is definitely not the original dial that came with this movement. The movement is from the Black Forest of Germany, and dates back to the early 19th century.

ALDEN A. ATKINS

I am writing to see if you can give me any information concerning age, etc., of a clock of the following description: Made and sold by Alden A. Atkins, Bristol, Connecticut, has two flat weights, 30-hour striking clock and has a crank.

I also have a very nice, walnut, 8-day Kansas mantel clock. The label says it was manufactured by F. Kroeber, 8 Cortland Street, New York. Can you tell me how old this clock is?

Mrs. Wills, a friend of mine who is now 72, thinks the clock is well over 100 years old as it belonged to her grandfather, who traded it for a cow. By so doing he was in very bad with the grandmother who would not speak to him for days. Mrs. Wills estimates it at 125 years.

A.

Alden A. Atkins was making clocks at Bristol, Connecticut from 1837 to 1846.

Drepperd lists F. Kroeber as being active in the Yorkville district of New York City during 1850 to 1880. I'm reasonably sure that this is the Florence Kroeber, New York City, who obtained several patents on minor improvements in clocks in the 1880's and

111

90's and it is my thought that he was active up to the very turn of the century. Mr. Drepperd says: "Casemaker who purchased movements stamped with his name from Seth Thomas, Ingraham, and other Connecticut makers." The Kansas on your label no doubt refers to his style of case as it was customary to designate case types with names (each maker devising his own method and series of names.)

ENGLISH BRACKET CLOCK

I have an English bracket clock which is the same in every detail as No. 211 in Wallace Nutting's clock book, with the exception of the name on the dial. The back plate is elaborately engraved and in the center of the plate are the words: "Wright, watchmaker to the king, London." Can you give me the date of this horologist?

A.

The English list contains some 52 Wrights, the majority of them with a London address. In this case it is fortunate that only one is listed as watchmaker to the king.

Thomas Wright, free of the Clockmakers Company 1770, died in 1792. In 1783 Thomas Wright patented a bimetallic strip for compensating the length of a pendulum to temperature changes. There is a watch and a bracket clock by this maker in Guildhall Museum.

GEORGE MARSH

. I would appreciate any information you can give me on the following described clock: It is a weight-driven, 1-day, hour and one-half hour strike, and was made and sold by George Marsh.

A.

Moore's Old Clock Book lists George Marsh as being active at Winstead, Connecticut about 1820. Carl Drepperd's list gives George Marsh, Bristol, Connecticut, 1820 to 1830; Walcottville, 1830's. Marsh isn't mentioned in Chauncey Jerome's history.

THOMAS EARNSHAW

Can you give me information on a man named Thomas Earnshaw, born in Ashton, Underlyne, England? I have been led to believe that he was a very important figure

in the watchmaking profession at one time.

A.

The first Thomas Earnshaw was born February 4, 1749, died in 1829. At the age of 59 (1808) he published a volume of some 314 pages which he titled, "Longitude, An Appeal To The Public." This is a very rare book but if you can manage to locate a copy, I promise you it will be some of the spiciest reading you will run across in horological history because he set to paper just what he thought of his enemies in no uncertain terms.

He was succeeded by his son, Thomas, and that firm was taken over by Thomas III. He is best known to the horological trade as originator of the spring detent. However, he was a top-flight mechanic in every branch of the trade. It is related that once a jewel maker advertised his tools for making watch jewels for $500.00, but was asking an additional $500.00 for permission to even look at the tools, explaining that to view the tools would give away the secrets of jewel making. Earnshaw, being a poor journeyman watchmaker with a family to support, was unable to even see the tools. This incident fired his ambition anew and he set to work and in a few months devised a method of making and jeweling watches with tools so simple their cost was about four pounds. Some of the very fine old John Brockbank ruby cylinder watches you may sometime run across will have its ruby cylinder made by Thomas Earnshaw.

D. J. GALE

I have an 8-day calendar strike clock for repair. It was patented by D. J. Gales and manufactured by E. N. Welch Manufacturing Company, Forrestville, Connecticut. The clock movement is in good condition The calendar movement has the Gales patent, April 21, 1885, stamped on the back plate. At one place on the calendar movement it looks as though someone has cut away part of the lifting arm. I will attempt to draw a rough sketch of the calendar movement, hoping you can tell from it what parts are missing.

A.

Daniel Jackson Gale was born December 24, 1830 at Waitsfield, Vermont, the son of Richard and Lucy Cummings Gale. When a young man, Gale moved to Sheboygan,

Fig. 1

diaries. I hope that in some manner these may be made available for prolonged and serious study because from it a completely new light might be thrown upon early American clockmaking as well as establishing many dates, etc. Example: "August 2, 1887, Mr. Welch died at 12:10 this noon. All the shop shut down this P. M." That was E. N. Welch, head of the E. N. Welch Clock Company. Other notations at random: "April 12, 1871, commenced work for Messrs. Welch, Spring & Company, manufacturers of best clocks, Bristol, Connecticut. Wages $2.25 per day." "February 28, 1872, Milo Norton called in the evening to note my calendar clock for publication (probably the Bristol *Press*)." "June 30, 1853, some of my poetry appeared in print for the first time." "February 1, 1886, opened my new shop in Forrestville to repair shoes, sewing machines, clocks, etc." The days following he was busy in the new shop, here is one day as noted in March. "March 10, 1886,

Wisconsin where he opened a shoe repair shop. While there, he developed and patented a calendar attachment for clocks. He came East to find market for his invention, settling in Bristol, Connecticut. He died at the age of 71 in Bristol, June 17, 1901.

This last paragraph is more than most lists give. The truth is, a whole book could be written about this man — a poet, mechanic, shoemaker, farmer, musician and all-around solid citizen. He left a most complete diary of day-to-day happenings covering forty-two of his seventy years. It has been my good fortune to receive from his great-grandson, a few excerpts from these

Fig. 3

work today: Watch—take up hairspring, 10c; Sheldon, clean sewing machine, 40c; Steam fitter, half-sole and heels, $1.10; Woodruff, close rip boys shoe, 5c; harness job, 10c; total, $1.75.

Many times he notes that he worked 'til 3 o'clock in the morning on his inventions. On other occasions we find that he awakened about 3 o'clock to begin this work. At other spots mention is made that this work was done on his own time, etc. This entry is typical of the calendar clock struggle:

Fig. 2

Fig. 4

"October 3, 1868. The idea has come to me today how I can make a perpetual calendar clock. The hand for the day of the month to go around once a month and skipping over all the short months from 30 days and from the 28th or 29th of February, making it perpetual setting itself for all the long or short months and leap year besides the day of the week, months and week of the year and changes of the moon. One can see any day in the year just how many days since it did change and how many days before it will change again. I have now been studying about this some seven years and have finally accomplished what to me has always been a mystery."

In all, Mr. Gale was granted five patents: four U. S. and one Canadian. His first calendar patent was No. 96,792, November 16, 1869. The second was February 14, 1871. The third was the Canadian patent April 13, 1874. The fourth was No. 316,254, April 21, 1885, all covering calendar mechanisms. The fifth, No. 402,917, May 7, 1889, covered a strike train. The drawing for the Canadian patent was made by two ladies, Misses Annie and Elizabeth Robertson of Colborne, Ontario.

Fig. 5

Fig. 1 is a photo of Mr. Gale lifted from a group, made by his son Herbert, July 4, 1885. Under that date in his diary he records: "Herbert and Lola, Howard and Ella, with baby and Eunice Perry and Henry Whitman were here to dinner. The table was set out in the grape arbor; then after dinner, Herbert takes group pictures of us all at once with his new drop-shutter lens and the camera he made himself."

The American Clock Company, 501 Broadway, New York, New York was the sales agency (this firm represented many Bristol mfgrs.) for the Gale new calendar clock, manufactured by Welch, Spring & Company. One of his memos indicates that they sold 140 clocks in 1876, 154 in 1877 and 104 in 1878, a total of 398 clocks. Labels were printed on a fairly stiff cardboard often tacked to back of the case. *Fig. 2* shows the back mechanism and *Fig. 3* the dial side of

114

the calendar you are inquiring about, the one made under the April 21, 1885 patent.

Under the date of August 23, 1875, he records: "Three of the Gale 24-inch calendars, new, start for California." As best I've been able to determine, the 24-inch clocks were made under the February 14, 1871 patent. *Fig. 4* shows one of these clocks owned by Dr. E. A. Burger of Detroit. This same clock was made with a 12-inch dial. *Fig. 5*, is from an E. N. Welch Company catalog of the 1880's.

As I said before, it is truly hoped that Mr. Gale's descendants may some day see fit to make his complete recordings available for prolonged study, not only for the complete story of Daniel Jackson Gale, but also for whatever related clock history there is indicated there. It is quite evident that some rivalry developed concerning the Benjamin B. Lewis calendar clock. Then he (Gale) kept such detailed memos of salary raises, the great fire, death of prominent clock men, and other activities related to clockmaking of his day, it amounts to a veritable gold mine of information.

I trust this bit of history will interest you as well as add additional pleasure to the ownership of this clock.

ANSONIA CLOCK

Would you be so kind as to give me whatever information you can concerning the following described clock?

This clock has a very ornate porcelain case; 10¾-inches high, 8 inches across the widest part and 4 inches deep. The face on the sides of the case appear to be some kind of Viking god with flowing mustache and whiskers. Also, there appears to be a Fleur-De-Lis design at the top and bottom front of the case and on the back the word "Chemung" is impressed near the bottom. The gong post is mounted on a block of wood supported by four platforms cast in porcelain with holes for bolts. The wood is so old that it crumbles when removed. The gong is a spiral of flat steel wire and the works were made by the Ansonia Clock Works and has a patent date of 1882. All the gears and wheels appear to be made of brass and the two springs are of flat spring steel. The gong operates only on the hour

and half-hour. The clock keeps fairly accurate time, if regularly wound. The raised surfaces around the outer edges of the front of the case are colored in a sort of red-pink and the sides are banded with a gold stripe. The flower design on all the flat surfaces of the case appear to be of the daisy; the coloring was or is not very bright in this respect. The case is not chipped or broken but close examination shows the porcelain to appear to be cracking or checking.

I am wondering about the possible history of the clock. It is not for sale but it would be interesting to us to know more about it if such information is available.

A.

You have a splendid and very accurate description of what I usually call the run-of-the-mill Ansonia china case clock.

The Ansonia Clock Company, Ansonia, Connecticut was active from about 1855 to 1914. Many of the china case clocks we see today belong to the late 1890's and early 1900's. I've checked one of their 1907 catalogues and the china case line was quite heavy with them about then but do not locate the exact design you describe.

They imported these china cases from Germany and I suspect did not exercise too much control over the minute details of design. The 1907 line ranged from $9 to $125 each. All of them had the striking gong mounted on a wooden board (sounding) which also served as the bottom of the case, fitted in as you describe. Actually, there wasn't a very great difference in the mechanical construction of the movement.

The cheaper numbers have brass, lightweight bezels, paper glue-on dials with common verge between the plates. The better movements were made after the Brocot escapement pattern, jeweled pallets, visibly working through the dial, heavy gold plated bezels, bevel plate glasses, mainsprings in barrels and such other mechanical refinements including fine fired porcelain dials. These better movements went into the "middling" line and the higher priced line. The highest priced line was cased in hand-painted cases, signed by the artist. Shortly after World War I, the old Ansonia machinery was sold to the U. S. S. R. and I believe went into their first five-year plan.

VERMONT CLOCK CO.

Would it be possible for you to give some information on the history of the Vermont Clock Company of Fair Haven, Vermont?

I have seen only one example and the makers certainly had some original ideas as to how a mantel clock should be made.

A.

It seems that the Vermont Clock Company entirely escaped the compilers of clock lists. Carl Drepperd lists the Vermont Clock Company of Fair Haven, Vermont, n.d., meaning no date or no data.

H. W. Maynard of Fair Haven, tells us he remembers that it was about 1895 that the clock factory was in operation. It lasted about five years and made three types of clocks—one a mantel clock something like Seth Thomas, glass enclosed; an office clock with wood frame (case) and a very unique wall clock called the "Crusader" with weights. He further says: "They employed about 250 men, finally failed."

JAPY FRERES

A lady customer of mine has a clock which she would like information concerning the maker, date of same, etc. The markings on the clock are 111XXX, Japy Freres.

A.

The type French clock indicated was imported in goodly numbers in the 1830's, 40's and 50's. Many of them can be seen in use and in repair shops today. Most were wood cases and columns; some few in marble or alabaster.

Frederic Japy, Beaucourt, (born 1749, died 1813), was the first to manufacture watch ebauches by machine tools in 1776. He founded the watch factory of Japy Freres and designed its machines. In 1810, he started a factory for clock ebauches at Baderel. Many French makers bought ebauche from this firm. Some added their own stamp and name, doubtless, some did not. I am reasonably sure that the firm was continued after Mr. Japy died but at the moment can't determine exactly.

FASHION CLOCK

I am trying to obtain some parts for a calendar clock made by Seth Thomas Clock Company for Southern Calendar Clock Company, patented December 8, 1875. The parts needed are, escape wheel, verge, feather springs and pendulum bob.

A.

The "Fashion" clock, made by the Southern Calendar Clock Company, St. Louis, Missouri, has an escape wheel entirely different from those used in the calendars sold by Seth Thomas, and also the model that was later marketed from Columbus, Mississippi.

In the early 1880's, Culver Brothers built a large foundry at St. Louis and began manufacturing stoves. This stove manufacturing business grew rapidly and soon absorbed all their time and interest. They ceased to operate the Southern Calendar Clock Company in September, 1899. Material of the escape wheel type has long since disappeared from all available markets. You will have to obtain one from an old movement or have one made.

JEROME & DARROW

I am interested in ascertaining the approximate age of a desk or shelf clock that has come into my possession. The clock was manufactured by Jerome and Darrow of Connecticut. The works of the clock are made of wood.

A.

Carl Drepperd lists Jerome and Darrow, Bristol, Connecticut, 1824 to 1833. Further down his list we find: Jerome and Darrow firm name when spelled Jeromes instead of Jerome and Darrow, indicates that the two Jeromes, Chauncey and Noble, were in the firm. This listing gives no date.

Frankly, I haven't been able to exactly figure out what, if any, difference there might be in dates for Jerome and Darrow, and Jeromes and Darrow.

I quote from page 49, Chauncey Jerome's book (1860): "In the fall of 1824, I formed a company with my brother, Noble Jerome, and Elijah Darrow, for the manufacturing of clocks, and began making a movement that required a case about six inches or eight inches longer than the Terry patent. We did very well at this for a year or two, during which time I invented the Bronze Looking Glass Clock."

In a paper titled "Sketch of the Clock-making Business" written by Hiram Camp, March 1893, we find the following: ". . . there was a number of other makers at work in the town of Bristol, where Mr. Jerome was, who about this time (1824) formed a co-partnership. The stockholders were Chauncey Jerome, Elijah Darrow, and Noble Jerome. Chauncey Jerome was a joiner, Mr. Darrow was adept in bronzing and ornamenting glass, and Noble Jerome had served an apprenticeship at the movement making business." Mr. Camp was Chauncey Jerome's superintendent at Bristol and later at New Haven. The Jerome and Darrow firm was succeeded by C. & N. Jerome 1834 to 1839. Neither the Jerome book or the Camp paper makes any distinction between Jeromes and Darrow and Jerome and Darrow.

BIRGE, MALLROY

I have an 8-day Birge-Mallroy clock made in Bristol, Connecticut. The movement is of brass and has weights. Can you tell me something about this clock and when it was manufactured?

A.

From 1834 to 1858, John Birge was the leading figure in a number of clock companies. Various lists differ in the dates given and Mrs. N. Hudson Moore in the "Old Clock Book" omits the Birge and Fuller firm entirely.

The tax rolls of Bristol, the official public record, show them to be:

1834—Birge, Case and Company
1835 and 1836—Birge, Gilbert and Company
1837—Birge and Gilbert
1838 to 1843—Birge, Mallroy and Company
1844 to 1847—Birge and Fuller
1848—John Birge and Company
1849 to 1858—Birge, Peck and Company

This would place your clock between 1838 and 1843. John Birge was born in

Torrington, Connecticut in 1775, where he was apprenticed to a carpenter. About 1810 he moved to Bristol, Connecticut where he established a wagon manufacturing business. No doubt he was the maker of the wagons used by the Connecticut clock manufacturers and peddlers. In all likelihood the very clock you have was brought south in one of his wagons.

In addition to that contact, clockmaking and clock selling was taking on something of the nature of a boom and Bristol was the center. Mr. Birge was soon making clock cases on contract—from this it was but a short step into the clock business. It is said that he had other clock interests than the seven firms listed above and he is generally spoken of as being the "principal backer and moving spirit" in his firms. He was a soldier in the war of 1812; became one of Bristol's leading citizens, holding several public offices. He retired about 1856 and died February 5, 1858.

His partner in your firm was Ranson Mallroy.

SAMUEL TERRY

In regard to the clocks made by Eli Terry & Sons, I have a clock made by Samuel Terry, Bristol, Connecticut. I can't say when it was made, but it has wooden plates and wheels and has a repair listed back in 1831 by Lewis W. Linds in Putman County, Georgia. I would like to know about how old it is and would like to know the age of this as an antique. I notice it was made before the fall of 1824 when the Jerome Brothers formed a company with Elijah Darrow.

A.

You do not copy label or give definite description of your Samuel Terry wood clock. He was a brother of Eli Terry and they marketed clocks under a partnership label, "Eli & Samuel Terry," from about 1824 to 1827.

If your clock bears a "Samuel Terry" label, it is my thought that it was made after 1827, for prior to his partnership with his brother, Eli, he (Samuel) did work for many clockmakers and I doubt if any completed clocks include his name.

Miss Josephine Terry, a great-grand-daughter of Mr. Samuel Terry, has kindly supplied the writer with many bits of information; however, I haven't had the time or opportunity to go over his complete records, therefore my data is far from complete. In 1819 Samuel Terry was working for Eli Terry and boarding in Plymouth with Henry Terry. In 1823, we find him putting together wood clocks for Eli, Jr. and Henry Terry. On the 15th of April that year he billed them with 402 clocks, $201.00. On December 12th he billed Chauncey Jerome with a punch press and dies, $100.00; and a little later he billed Luther Goodale for $222.20 for making 202 cases at $1.10 each.

Mr. Terry was born January 24, 1774 and died May 4, 1853.

SETH THOMAS DATES

Could you give the dates Seth Thomas made clocks with the label Seth Thomas, Plymouth Hollow, Connecticut? I think it was from 1813 to ?.

A.

Seth Thomas was born at Woldott, Connecticut, about 1785, learned the carpenter trade and about 1808 went to work "with" Silas Hoadley and Eli Terry at Plymouth, Connecticut.

This is generally spoken of as the firm of "Terry, Thomas & Hoadley." Details of the partnership have never been made perfectly clear. Mr. Carl Drepperd says: "A partnership of legend if not fact." Here he did "joiner work," that is made cases, and he also "put together" clocks, that is assembled the movement. He continued in this way for the years 1808, 1809 and 1810 when Mr. Terry withdrew and the firm became "Thomas & Hoadley." That partnership lasted about two years. Then Mr. Thomas sold out to Mr. Hoadley and moved to Plymouth Hollow where he began to make clocks upon his own account in the old Heman Clark factory.

It was a success from the word go. By 1853 Mr. Thomas had amassed a fortune and was ready to retire. It ran through "Seth Thomas," "Seth Thomas Sons & Company," "Seth Thomas Company" and "Seth Thomas Clock Company," which company he organized under the joint stock laws of Connecticut in 1853.

Mr. Thomas died January 29, 1859, and that portion of the town where the clock factory was situated was named "Thomaston" in his honor. Thus clocks labeled "Plymouth Hollow" are considered to have been made before 1859.

R. & I. ATKINS

I have in my possesion a clock which has been in our family for an undetermined number of years. It was manufactured by R. and I. Atkins at Bristol, Connecticut. The works are made up entirely of wooden gears, with the exception of the escapement wheel which is brass. It also has only four brass bushings—these are on the main wind-up wheels. The clock is driven by lead weights.

I would like to determine the approximate date that this clock was manufactured, and whether it has any value as an antique.

A.

R. & I. Atkins were in business at Bristol, Connecticut, 1833 to 1837. "Rolin" and "Irenus" Atkins, brothers.

Irenus Atkins was one of the leading Baptist preachers of that community and kept up much of his church work during the time he was promoting clockmaking. We first hear of the Atkins brothers when they went into partnership with their brother-in-law, George Mitchell (Mitchell married Mary (Polly) Atkins about 1830). The firm of Mitchell & Atkins bought the old Baptist church building in Bristol and moved it to a location on a nearby brook to have access to water power and there began to build clocks. This partnership was short lived for we next find Irenus Atkins, about 1832, forming a company with Anson Downs, known as "Atkins & Downs". A year or so later the Atkins brothers got together and formed the firm named on your clock. This was a successful venture lasting to the big depression of 1837 which put an end to all wood clockmaking.

Not much is recorded of Irenus Atkins until he formed the company of "I. Atkins & Company" with his nephew, George R. Atkins, 1847. This firm produced clocks up to 1857. In 1850 they obtained from Joseph Ives exclusive rights to manufacture his famous "wagon spring" clock. The "Atkins Clock Company" was formed in 1859 with Irenus Atkins as President. It failed in 1879 and was taken over by "Barnes Brothers Clock Company" in 1880, in which Irenus Atkins was a stockholder. Mr. Atkins died in 1882.

I'm reasonably sure all "original" wood movement clocks are considered antiques.

FIRST CUCKOO CLOCK

I would like to know where the idea originated, the inventor and any other interesting facts concerning it. I have an old German one about 90 years old, and I have been curious about it. I have looked in all of the reference books at the library but cannot find out what I want. It just shows the mechanism of the clock. This information would be most appreciated as the clock I have is always brought to school for the children to see and hear, and I would like to know the history or story behind it when they ask me such questions.

A.

Franz Anton Ketterer, of Schonwald, a village in the Black Forest of Germany, is credited with making the first Cuckoo clock. Born 1676, died 1756, the date of his first clock is usually placed at 1730. This clockmaker is also credited with being one of the first to start clockmaking in the Schwarzwald.

Simon Dilger was another instrumental in starting the industry in the Schwarzwald at Scholenback in 1720. Another was Matthaus Hummel at Waldau and later at Glashutte, active from about 1740 to 1780. He is mentioned as being among the first to make cuckoo clocks.

I fear we cannot supply "the story behind it," which after all, would impress the children far more than cold historical dates. However, we may be of some assistance in furnishing a lead. Along about this period in world history there was a great wave of building "Automata." I'm

sure you are familiar with the little singing birds and believe they antedate the cuckoo clock. It is but a short step to combine a simple singing bird with a clock.

J.C. BROWN

I would like some information. I have an old 8-day weight clock. The inscription in the back reads "Forestville Manufacturing Company, J. C. Brown, Bristol, Conn., U.S.A."

The name J. C. Brown is monogrammed on the dial and stamped on the movement. I have repaired clocks for 25 years and this is the first clock of this make I have ever seen.

A.

John C. Brown was one of the big operators in Early American clockmaking. It just doesn't seem possible that you have handled clocks as long as you have and not run across one before now.

According to tax records, The Forestville Manufacturing Company, Bristol, Conn., was in business 1849 to 1853. About 1832, Mr. Brown bought the interest of William Bartholomew and Elias Ingraham, and formed the firm of Bartholomew, Brown & Co. In addition to these two, he was the leading figure in Hills, Brown & Co., J. C. Brown & Co., Forrestville Hardware & Clock Co., and the Bristol Clock Case Co. He was born in 1807 in Coventry, Connecticut, died in 1872 in Nyack, New York and was buried in Brooklyn.

So far as this writer knows, Brown was the only one of the Connecticut clockmakers who used a picture of his residence and sometimes his portrait on some of his clock tablets.

JENNINGS BROTHERS

I have a clock which I would like some information on. The back of the case is engraved: "The Jennings Brothers Mfg. Co., Bridgeport, Conn., U.S.A." The dial is enameled on both sides and the numerals are fancy Arabic. Sweep second hand has its own dial directly below the center opening (cannon pinion). The dial is numbered from 10 to 60, but the dial has marks in-

dicating 1 to 60. The dial is 2⅛ inches in diameter. The bezel is two piece.

The clock has a 24-hour movement, but runs 30 hours, losing time the last hour and a half. There is only one spring in barrel without cover.

The case is cast lead on four legs and is very ornamental. Height, 7⅜ inches; width (at widest point), 3½ inches. Case is copper plated and over that is bronze plating.

A.

According to our information, this firm was first organized in 1890 under the name of "The American Jewelry Co.," for the purpose of manufacturing silverware, hardware specialties and novelties. Mr. Erwin M. Jennings was president, and Mr. Edward A. Jennings, treasurer.

In 1892 the name was changed to "Jennings Brothers Mfg. Co.," officers remaining as above, save for Mr. Henry A. Jennings being treasurer until 1927. In that year, he (Henry A.) became president and Mr. Erwin S. Jennings was secretary. In 1928, Erwin S. Jennings became president, Edward A. Jennings, treasurer, and Menta Oviatt, secretary.

Erwin S. Jennings is the son of Henry A. Jennings. Both Erwin M. and Henry A. died in 1937. This firm is still operating under the name of Jennings Brothers Mfg. Co. Present officers are listed as directors; however, we have no date of incorporation.

All cases (and we think this is what J. B. Mfg. Co. made) made of soft metal are first copper plated, then the final plate, silver, nickel, gold, etc., is applied to the copper. There are a number of reasons for this, the principal ones being that these soft metals take copper better and therefore a better final finish is obtained using less of the more expensive metal. We've seen a number of these small clocks, novelty cases, with the trade mark "J.B.C." and recall that most looked very much like movements made by Waterbury.

GEORGE MARSH

I should be greatly interested in obtaining information concerning a clock made by George Marsh of Bristol, Connecticut. It was supposed to have been purchased in 1833, but I am not certain that it was new at that time. Would you be able to tell me more about it? It is a mantel clock with wooden works.

A.

George Marsh is listed at Bristol, Connecticut, 1828 to 1830, and at Walcottville in the 1830's. Chances are that when this clock was purchased in 1833 it was new.

BIRGE, PECK & CO.

A customer of mine has a mantel clock that stands about three feet high. It was made by the Birge, Peck & Company in Bristol Connecticut, is an extra 8-day rolling pinion, steel pivot brass clock. We could find no date on it.

Would you please tell me when it was made and any other information you might come across?

A.

Birge, Peck & Company is listed as being in business from about 1849 to 1859; it was John Birge, Ambrose Peck, Samuel Taylor and William R. Richards. We believe he was christened Jonathan, but he is generally listed as John, and there is no question about him being one of the most colorful of the Connecticut clockmakers. He was the principal and moving spirit in about eight firms beside marketing clocks under his own name.

Birge & Hale about 1823; Birge & Ives 1832 and 1833; Birge, Case & Company 1833 and 1834; Birge & Fuller 1844-1848; Birge & Gilbert Company 1834-1837; Birge & Tuttle; Birge, Malroy & Company 1838-1843; Birge, Peck & Company 1849-1850.

Stray Bits of Timepiece History

By J. E. COLEMAN

Samuel Emerson Root

SAMUEL EMERSON ROOT was born in Broadalbin in Fulton County, New York, October 12, 1820. He married Jane Minerva Henderson, Bristol, Connecticut, November 5, 1845, and died in Bristol, April 7, 1896.

This name is to be found in most lists, but it is never mentioned that it can also be found on clocks. Neither are you told that when you drive in for gasoline, in all probability the device counting the gallons from the pump was manufactured by The Veeder-Root Corporation, Bristol and Hartford, Connecticut, founded by Mr. C. J. Root, son of S. E. and, therefore, directly traceable to the original Root factory. The accompanying photograph of the factory was made by a Mr. Moulthrop in 1865, and was obtained for the writer by Mrs. A. S. Brackett, granddaughter of Mr. S. E. Root, from Mr. George E. Moulthrop, who made it from the original plate made by his father.

Patent No. 92644, dated July 13, 1869, is titled: "Improvement in deadbeat verge for clocks" and was issued to Noah Pomeroy. In that patent we have this wording: "To make a better article of the common clock, without increasing its price, is the object of my invention." He goes on to say: "The ordinary deadbeat verge is so expensive as to prevent its general use on cheap clocks." The method of manufacturing the new type verge is then described, closing thus: "The cheapest of these old-style deadbeat verges cost six cents each, and the other parts of the clock are generally made for a corresponding price. The cost of my improved verge cannot exceed two cents each; therefore I produce a good deadbeat timer for about one-third the usual cost. I do not claim the common recoil verge, which has only two pallets, both of which are shaped by file, although the body of the verge is swaged. Neither do I claim the application of a deadbeat verge to a cheap clock, unless the verge is constructed as described.

Editor's Note: Here is another in Mr. Coleman's series of short timepiece stories. He will welcome similar stories provided they have never before been published and they can be documented. Proper credit will always be given for leads.

But what I claim as new, and desire to secure by letter patent, is: a deadbeat verge, substantially constructed as described, and for the purpose specified." (Signed, Noah Pomeroy. Witnesses: George W. Atkins, Charles A. Roper.)

The only patent we've been able to locate issued direct to Mr. S. E. Root is No. 23950, May 10, 1859. Reissued August 3, 1875, covering a clock dial and sash. Mr. Truman S. Safford, member of a New York legal firm and son-in-law of Mrs. Brackett, furnished us a transcript of the suit, Root vs. E. N. Welch, U. S. Circuit Court, District of Connecticut, which makes very interesting reading—entirely too long for "Stray Bits." It was decided February 13, 1880. Mr. Safford writes: "I do not know

Samuel Emerson Root

of any other patents issued to Mr. Root. It is quite possible his experience with this one made him doubt the value of patents. As appears from the decision, he was led to surrender the invention by disclaimer by being confronted with the facts of a supposedly prior sale of the Terry Manufacturing Company which later was proven to be one of his own early models."

Mr. Edward Ingraham, quoting from a letter by Milo L. Norton, of July 26, 1872, says: "In 1855 Mr. Root commenced making eight-day, half-hour striking and marine clocks, and purchased the Elijah Manross machinery." From "The Historical, Statistical and Industrial Rerview" (1884), which he says was apparently written to please clients and only recognized those who made some form of contribution. he quotes the following: "Manufacturers of clocks and toy movements, etc., S. Emerson Root & Company carry on one of the most important industries that so materially enhanced the prosperity of Bristol. In 1835 Mr. S. Emerson Root came to Bristol and in 1845, in a small way, began to manufacture clock dials, which in that day were painted on zinc and enameled, the process consuming several weeks. By a peculiar process, invented and patented by Mr. Root, this is now done in 24 hours. For 21 years Mr. Root enjoyed the fruits of his fertile brain, but after sundry renewals, his patent expired, and his process is now used by manufacturers without payment of royalty. But in the meantime, Mr. Root had so perfected his works that it has been found that a successful competition could not be carried on, and clockmakers often buy their dials from him."

Mr. Root's mother died when he was seven, his father when he was eight, and he was brought to Bristol to live with uncles and aunts, Mr. and Mrs. Chauncey Ives (Sabrina Ives) and Mr. and Mrs. Joel Root (Piera Ives). Mr. S. E. Root's mother, Philoteta Ives, was a sister of the famous Ives brothers. How could anyone so closely tied to the Ives brothers be anything but a clockmaker? Mrs. Brackett had a difficult time explaining the correct relationship to me until she wrote: "The seemingly complicated relationship be-

Employees gathered around the original Root factory.

Left above, 30-hour alarm movement, stamped S. E. Root, Bristol, in a clock from Mr. Edward Ingraham's collection. Right above, 8-day calendar clock stamped S. E. Root, Bristol, Connecticut, from the Charles R. Brewer collection, stamped patented July 13, 1869. Below, a reproduction of Patent No. 23,950 issued to S. E. Root on May 10, 1859, and reissued on August 3, 1875.

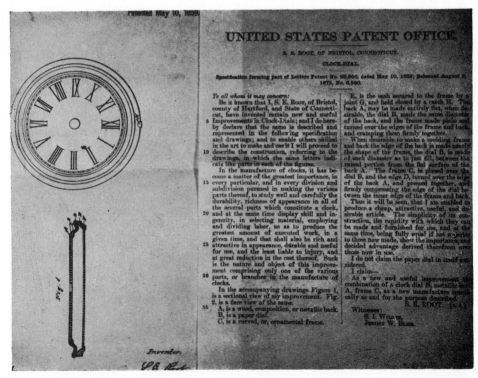

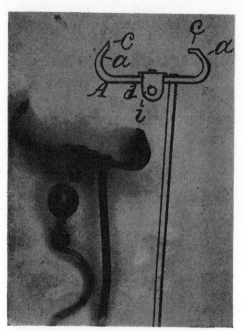

Actual verge from Brewer's S. E. Root clock shown with a drawing of the Pomeroy patent.

comes simpler by saying that two Root brothers and their sister married two Ives sisters and their brother."

S. E. Root was a life-long member of the Congregational Church and well known for honest, upright dealings with his fellow man. He was outwardly somewhat stern; his granddaughter mentions this but says inwardly he was very tender and kind. Mr. W. K. Sessions also remembers this for he tells me that the Root home (Christian Science Church since 1931) was located on the corner and next to his home. He remembers well a time when Mr. Root "chased two of us youngsters out of his yard with a buggy whip because we had the temerity to cross his property for a short cut."

Let's peep between the lines so to speak and close. 1. Note Pomeroy's effort to reduce the cost of making a verge. 2. Note that the stop works were stamped out of the front plate, obviously to save brass. 3. Note that Mr. Root not only reduced the time and cost of dials considerably, but also his method of production, to the extent it defied competition. That is something to make our present-day efficiency experts sit up and take notice

JAPY FRERES

Recently I had a customer bring in a clock found by him in an old attic. I would like some information concerning it if you have any.

The clock case is of the type usually found on a mantel, only this clock has a pendulum that fits inside the case entirely enclosed. The case has for some reason been completely lined with cement, possibly to reduce vibration. The case has a glass dial cover and a glass rear door.

The works are very well made, entirely machined, with a good finish. It has two mainsprings, one of which operates the striking mechanism.

On the back plate there is an emblem, apparently stamped, of a Victoria Cross with a crown on top. This emblem has the following around it in a circular manner: Japy Freres & C., G Med D. Honn, Exp. 1885. In the center of the cross there is a man's head, placed in a circle.

The dial is enameled with Roman numerals.

A.

The clock you describe is French, and since it was awarded the Medal of Honor at the 1885 Exposition, can't be over 65 years old.

Georges Frederic Japy, Born May 22, 1749, died 1812, was the founder of the firm Japy Freres. His company was the first to manufacture watch ebauches by machine tools. About 1810 he started a clock factory at Baderel for making clock ebauches.

The "Etablissements Japy Freres" is still **very active to this day.** Their address is 6, Rue Marignan, Paris 8. It is a firm very much like our own General Electric Company whose clock making efforts are only a very small part of present production.

You describe a typical French clock of about 1900 and the statement that the case is lined with cement leads me to think that the case is made of marble or stone. Such cement lining was to hold the case together and reinforce it rather than to reduce vibration.

FRENCH CLOCK

I am enclosing some photos of an old clock which I have come into possession of. I would like to know some history of it and whether or not it should be considered an antique.

A.

Evidently your clock is French. We've seen a number of this type of unmarked French pieces and think is can safely be said that they are antique.

In the late 1700's and early 1800's the French were making some wonderful clocks in gilt cases, some in ultra-fine cases, made by noted sculptors and also signed by them. These were of heavy solid brass and they were liberal with the gold. Naturally, there followed the imitations.

From the photos, I'd say the front portion of your case was made from some composition metal (principally lead), the back portion a thin sheet metal, and the whole fire-gilded in the most economical way. Most of these pieces sat on a black, grooved wooden base and were covered by a glass dome. This is why you have neither front glass over the hands or a back door to the case.

I'm sure you've noted that the pendulum is to be suspended by a silk cord which, tied in one hole of the support bracket, hangs in a loop for hooking the pendulum, extends up through the other hole of the bracket and reels up on the thumb-screw to the left to shorten and lengthen the pendulum for regulation. We've done quite a bit of checking (recently) and haven't come up with any definite idea of the period during which the silk suspension was in use.

JEROMES & DARROW

I have been advised by a local jeweler that you can furnish me with information regarding a clock manufactured by Jeromes & Darrow.

This clock is of the pillar type, hanging wall model, mahogany veneered finish, and from the information I have been able to obtain from library books, it was manufactured during the years from 1822 to 1837.

I am particularly interested in obtaining a picture of the design that was painted on the pillars. It was in gold paint but has faded out beyond recognition. The bottom is of frosted glass and has a decal in each corner, similar to a daisy.

It states on the instructions that this was a brass-bushed clock, but I have been unable to obtain any information on clocks with bushings of this kind, made during this period.

I would appreciate any information that you can forward to me in regard to the above.

A.

No doubt you have noted the spelling on your label is "Jeromes." This indicates that the two Jeromes, Chauncey and Noble, were in the firm. The third member was Elijah Darrow. The following quotation is taken from Chauncey Jerome's book, "American Clockmaking" (1860):

"In the fall of 1824, I formed a company with my brother, Noble Jerome, and Elijah Darrow for the manufacturing of clocks. . . . The business increased very rapidly between 1827 and 1837. During these ten years Jeromes & Darrow made

125

more than any other company."

Palmer's list indicates that the firm of C. & N. Jerome succeeded the Jeromes & Darrow firm, and dates it from tax records, 1834 to 1839; this is not to be considered as conflicting, since the various firms of clockmakers of this date very often overlapped.

This firm made both brass and wood movement clocks, and while you do not specifically state that yours is wood, I'm pretty sure that it is, for the term "brass-bushed" was used in labels found in wood clocks where the pivots were set in brass bearing. Some makers, especially Silas Hoadley, made wood clocks with bone bearings; his labels read, "With the improvement of ivory bushings . . ."

The writer has been mainly concerned with the mechanical and historical angles, paying very little attention to case decorations, and therefore, cannot supply the design for the pillars. I would suggest that you pay a visit to the museums and antique dealers of your city, where you should be able to locate a clock of similar size and style to yours.

ANSONIA CLOCK CO.

I am enclosing two pictures of a clock, hoping that you might be able to give me a few facts about it. This clock had been the property of my parents who bought it around 1895 or 1900.

I was told that it was one of a pair of clocks that had been made expressly for a centennial or exposition of some kind, and I was also told that John Wanamaker of Philadelphia (founder of the department store), had purchased the mate to it.

The clock is a white, non-magnetic metal that is darkened on the surface with age. It is quite heavy. The base is 23 inches wide, with an over-all height of 21 inches. On the back of the works are these facts: "Ansonia Clock Co. Pat. June A 14-81. Pat. June 18, 1882, New York, U. S. A."

Any information you can supply me on this clock will be greatly appreciated.

A.

The story of "only two," one for an exposition and another specially for some celebrity has a sort of standard or stock

ring to it—we've heard it before.

This identical clock is catalogued in Ansonia's 1907 catalogue, page 135, as follows: "Don Cesar and Don Juan, height 20½ inches, width 25½ inches, finished in gilt or Japanese bronze. List, each, $42.50. Fitted with eight-day, half-hour gong striking movement, beveled glass, porcelain dial, 5½ inches, Arabic or Roman visible escapement. Finished in Barbedienne or Surian bronze, add 10 per cent, list additional."

The square with "A" in the center, which you sketch was the Ansonia trademark. We've seen quite a number of this model (15 or 20) and believe that it was popular and marketed over a period of years around the turn of the century.

JAPY FRERES

I have a gold column plate glass-encased key-wind mercury pendulum French clock on which there is a metal seal (sketch enclosed) bearing the words, "Japy Freres et Ci, Med. D'Honheur." Below the seal is the inscription, "Made in France" and the serial number, 13613 52. I am interested in knowing when the clock was manufactured, whether the company exists today and whether or not there is any historical value.

A.

The makers of your clock are still in operation; however, like our General Electric, they have grown to be literally a group of distinct industries, with factories scattered about France. In 1939 their head office was transferred from Beaucourt to Paris. You may address them: Establissements Japy Freres, 6 Rue de Marignan, Paris 8, France. M. Albert Japy is "le directeur general."

Frederic Japy, after having studied watch and clockmaking in Switzerland, settled at Beaucourt, a little town in the principality of Montbeliard, in 1776. His clockwork factory grew and expanded rapidly; at the dawn of the 19th century other new branches of industry were added. To meet these expansions, a company was founded in 1854 "in partnership and shares," named Japy Freres & Cie. In addition to clock works, screws, lock work, kitchen and domestic hardware, pumps and electrical motors were gradually added; typewriters were added in 1910. In 1950 the clock factory at Beaucourt (their first establishment) employed 260 producers and 90 cooperators, and was averaging 35,000 alarm clocks, 3,000 desk clocks, plus 6,000 wall or shelf clocks per month.

Baillie records that Frederic Japy was the first to manufacture watch ebauches by machine tools in 1776, and that he started a factory for clock ebauches in 1810.

The metal seal you sketch simply denotes that the company has been awarded a Medal of Honor. I'm pretty sure the figure, 13613, is the serial number, and am sorry we have no way of approximating the clock's age from it. The figure, 52, set apart, denotes pendulum length (see Otherwise in this issue). Unless a clock is especially manufactured for an occasion or a celebrity, its historical value would accrue through association, etc. Naturally we have no way of determining that.

TERRY CLOCK

Could you help me with the maker of my antique clock? It has a patent date of May 10, 1859. The outside case is metal and the back is wood. The alarm sets by turning a disc behind the hands. It has a pendulum which is attached directly to the verge. I am enclosing a photograph of the clock.

A.

While your clock in question bears a patent date of May 10, 1859, it is my thought that it may be some 20 years younger. We've seen two or three of these little alarms so like your picture (pendulum fast to the verge arbor, crooked to miss the center post, small ball, regulates by turning entire ball, etc.) that we believe yours was also made by the Terry Clock Company, Pittsfield, Massachusetts.

This Terry Clock Company was organized at Pittsfield in 1880 by George Bliss and the sons of Silas B. Terry. It was reorganized in 1884 as Russell & Jones Clock Company.

CONTRACT CLOCK

The customer claims it is about 300 years old.

The case is all made of metal. On the anchor is the word, "Rancoulct" or "Rancoulet." On the face of the dial, by the numeral 6, is "Frankfurt a/M & G Hinrichs." There is a number on the back plate, 1274, also a round emblem with a star in the center, with the following wording, "AD. Mougin—Deux Medalles."

This clock has a strike mechanism; time and strike springs are enclosed in a barrel. It has a verge escapement. The escape wheel has very fine pointed teeth. It seems to be in fine condition except for the fact that it is very dirty.

A.

Yours is another "Contract" clock. Sorry that we can't give you something more definite on it. We've lately begun to work on that angle, and hope in the near future to obtain something of a general picture of the French clock industry.

From general appearance in the small photo, it looks French. Rancoulet might be the "sculptor," "designer" or "maker" of

of

the case; however, the lettering on the anchor seems a bit large for a signature.

The dial markings could be that of a German jeweler who sold it. There are two Frankfurts—Frankfurt-am-Oder, located 47 miles southeast of Berlin in Brandenburg, population 75,000 in 1940. Frankfurt-am-Main is in Hesse-Nassau, and its **population in 1940 was 546,000.** The plate marking merely means that the movement has won two awards or medals.

Three hundred years would take you back to 1650. Clockmaking was pretty crude then, certainly not the fine machine work you see in this clock. Chances are that it would press it to go back beyond 1850.

H. J. DAVIS

I have for repair a clock which the customer would like to have some information on, if possible. The movement is brass, 5¼ by 3 9/16 inches. Stamped on the movement is "H. J. Davies, New York, 6½." There are two papers in the back of the clock case, not inside, which read:

"Notice—This clock is fitted with a superior movement, with polished springs, stop work, and an improved attachment which admits of the hands being turned backwards without injury to the clock."

The other paper reads, "Established 1858. Leo - 8-day striking. Manufactured by H. J. Davies, N. Y., successor to G. A. Jones."

The case is mahogany, and the front opens as the door. I would like to know about how old the clock is.

A.

Mr. Books Palmer lists an H. J. Davis at 5 Courtland Street, New York City, no dates. Note that he spells it D-a-v-i-s, while you list it D-a-v-i-e-s. He also lists a George A. Jones & Co., at Bristol, Connecticut, and 6 Cortland Street, New York City This firm is in the tax records for 1870 and the directory for 1872.

It is my guess that your labels are purely for a "contract" clock. In the 1880's, and even past 1900, it was quite popular for a merchandising organization to buy clocks

on contract and place their labels upon them.

The G. A. Jones Company bought out Wilfred H. Nettleton of Bristol, Connecticut, about 1870. Nettleton operated from about 1850 to 1870; this fact could account for that line, "Established in 1858." Since Davis or Davies took over Jones after 1872, your clock is certainly this side of that date. From its general style as per your sketch, I'd say maybe ten or twenty years. We've checked some old Waterbury and Ansonia catalogues and none have a Leo model. One Ansonia catalogue for 1907 carries two models, "King" and "Parsian," quite similar in size and style.

ENGLISH VERGE MOVEMENT

I have an old English verge-movement with fusee of which I am attempting to find out the age. The following information is from observation of the watch: "J.T. or I.J. Clarke, London" on barrel plate or bridge; number 8640 on train bridge; balance cock elaborately engraved; key-wound and key-set; hall-marks include lion's body facing left in shield, old English letter "M" in shield, tiger's head facing front in shield. Letters "JB" over "WW" are stamped along with hall-marks.

A.

The lion in the shield, facing left, was the standard silver mark for London. You should locate the quality figure somewhere near it, such as .425, or some other figure to designate sterling.

Our hall-mark book is not specific on the point of distinguishing between Gothic and Old English lettering; in fact, the letter would appear to be a sort of combination of both. The letter series preceding and also that following is so different that I feel there can be no mistake. The "M" I have in mind was for 1848-49.

What you call a tiger's head, I think they referred to as a leopard's head. It was the office or location mark for London, and prior to 1823, was crowned—thus a gold case hall-marked at London for 1848-49. The letters were the maker's trademark, for which we have no record. Baillie's list only extends up to 1825, and we can't look to it for a name listing.

FRENCH CLOCKS

We are still trying on those French clocks. Mr. R. Marti, of Establissements S. Marti, 22 Rue General Leclerc, Mountbeliard, France, sends over a very nice letter, and says the firm of S. Marti was founded in 1835 to manufacture movements for clocks. He does not say anything about the markings on the very earliest movements, but does give this table:

Movements stamped: "S. Marti & Cie. —Medaille de Bronze, 1867 to 1889.

Movements stamped: "S. Marti & Cie. —Medaille d'Argent, 1889 to 1900.

Movements stamped: "S. Marti—Medaille d'Or, 1900 to 1931.

Movements stamped: "S. Marti—Grand Prix Paris, 1931, later than 1931.

The clocks with the stamps, Medaille de Bronze and Medaille d'Argent are not repairable, the plant being destroyed.

It may come as a surprise to some of our readers who have asked about the old Marti clocks, to learn that they are producing movements today; descriptions were included of four movements, one 15-day, two 8-day and one 30-hour. Also, one "Marine" clock center seconds hand for bulk-head mounting, jeweled movement, "a precision of up to less than ten seconds a week."

E. N. WELCH MFG. CO.

I have an 8-day clock that has the inscription, "E. N. Welch, Mfg. Co." That is all there is on it—no numbers at all. The top part of the movement is held together with two pins. The lower part has two screws which screw into the post that holds the loop end of the mainspring.

Could you tell me anything about how old this clock is,

A.

Elisha N. Welch was born at Chatham, Connecticut, February 7, 1809, and died at Forestville, Connecticut, August 2, 1887. He was one of the largest clock producers during the latter half of the 19th century.

Early in his life he ran a foundry to cast clock weights, and in about 1850, he began to acquire clock factories, first the John C. Brown clock interest in 1855, then the F. R. Otis Company and the E. & C. H. Manross clock factories in 1856. About 1868, Soloman C. Spring, who had previously acquired the Birge and Peck factory, came into the organization, and it was known as Welch, Spring & Co.; apparently Mr. Welch had consolidated his clock factories in 1864 under the name, E. N. Welch Mfg. Co. The Welch, Spring & Co. activities were carried on in the old Manross factory building in Forestville until 1884, when it too was merged with the E. N. Welch Mfg. Co.

The business continued successfully up to Mr. Welch's death, but within ten years (1897) it was in receivership. It was reorganized in 1903 as The Sessions Clock Co., a firm which is active to this date.

TERRY CLOCK

Among some old furniture which came from my grandmother's home, I have found a plain 1-day clock made by the Terry Clock Company of Waterbury, Connecticut. In the clock there is no date of manufacture shown. It does not have a suspension spring and rod, but it does have a round pendulum ball attached to the verge. I am wondering if you can give me any ideas as to the age of this clock.

A.

We are familiar with the little clock you describe, but have never seen one with the Waterbury, Connecticut, address.

· Wallace Nutting lists a Terry Clock Company at Pittsfield, Massachusetts. It was active from 1880 to 1888, when it was reorganized and named the Russell & Jones Clock Company. Nutting does not list a Terry Clock Company at Waterbury in his "Clock Book."

Brooks Palmer, in "The Book of American Clocks," carries a Terry Clock Company, Waterbury, Connecticut, no date, and says that possibly such a firm existed. He also lists the Terry Clock Company of Pittsfield, Massachusetts, as above, and another Terry Clock Company at Winstead, Connecticut. The latter was organized in 1852 by the sons of Silas B. Terry, who headed the firm till 1876, when the sons moved to Pittsfield.

This little movement with the pendulum very light and attached directly to the verge arbor was patented by F. A. Lane of New Haven, Connecticut, January 25, 1881, No. 237,128.

E. KROBER CLOCK

A customer brought in a pendulum clock (8-day) and asked for an estimate of its age. I would appreciate it very much if you can help me out. The name stamped on the movement is, "E. Krober Clock Co., New York. Pat. Oct. 9, 1894."

A.

We've been interested in this clock concern for a number of years. In the absence of absolute proof that F. Krober actually made or was directly connected with a factory actually making clocks, we have to conclude that he was a seller of clocks—a merchant.

Mr. Wesley Hallett went down to the New York library last year and copied all the Krober data he could find in the city directory. Florence Krober was first listed in the 1865-66 directory (Trow's) at 25 John Street. His residence was at 171 Elm Street.

Since the clock in question has the October 9, 1894 patent date, it must have been made after that date. F. Krober & Co. was dissolved in 1904; at that time Florence Krober was listed as "manager" and his residence was given as 207 West 107th Street. The same listing continued through 1911. One might be fairly safe in placing your clock between 1894 and 1904; however, there might have been considerable stock on hand or on order which Mr. Krober could have sold off from his residence between 1905 and 1911.

Patent dates on clocks of this period, and earlier, many times prove very unreliable. We've seen several Krober clocks so marked (see illustration) but have never

Krober Clock

been able to locate a patent of that particular date, or one specifically covering an attachment exactly like the one in this photo. I would like to know if your clock checks in every detail with it.

We have in the file seven patent copies as issued to Florence Krober, as follows:

October 6, 1874, No. 155,656; claim: improvement in strike; name: F. Krober, Hoboken, New Jersey.

July 31, 1877, No. 103,663; claim: calendar clock dials; name: F. Krober, Hoboken, New Jersey.

June 1, 1880, No. 228,202; claim: alarm clock; name: F. Krober, New York, New York.

October 3, 1893, No. 506,050; claim: coating clock cases; name: F. Krober, New York, New York.

September 25, 1894, No. 526,399; claim: beat adjustor; name: F. Krober, New York City.

August 18, 1896, No. 28,799; claim: trade-mark, "Eclipse"; name: F. Krober, New York City.

February 9, 1897, No. 576,587; claim: pendulum clamp; name: F. Krober, New York City.

The attachment illustrated and marked "Oct. 9, 1894" more nearly resembles the 1897, No. 576,587. According to the patent drawing, the ring just above the pendulum ball swinging over a rod is there, but instead of a similar ring at the bottom of the ball there is a spring and clamp arrangement for fastening the ball when the clock is being moved.

The movement in the photo closely resembles Ansonia construction, and came from a China case. Many Krober clocks were cased in china and cast iron, a line followed quite a bit by Ansonia. Thus we conclude that Florence Krober must have contracted with Ansonia Clock Company to build clocks embodying his patents.

We've only seen one Krober calendar clock and think it was built by Welch. He must have had quite a merchandising organization and contracted with several manufacturers over the period of his operation. The above list of patents is given as the best we've been able to catalogue over a period of years, and as yet, I am not prepared to say that it is absolutely complete. The entire Florence Krober history is far from complete, and we would especially appreciate hearing from any reader who may have photos or data relating to it.

HISTORY - HISTORY

Can you give me any information on the following timepieces: a silver watch marked "T. W. Benson, 58 & 60 Ludgate Hill, London, to H. R. H. the Prince of Wales and H. I. M., the Emperor of Russia, No. 33966? It is fusee driven with a compensated balance.

Also, a watch, double cased, marked, "Robert Murray Lauder, No. 11500." It is fusee driven and has a crown escapement, solid balance wheel with a balance protector perforated and engraved with a standing lion or dog.

The recent issues of A. H. & J. outlining the history of certain American watch manufacturers were most interesting. Could it be that there was another New England Watch Company" in Boston, Massachusetts, prior to 1880? Can you give me some information on a watch so marked, No. 23018? It is key-wind and set with hairspring stud bracket attached to the train frame. The lever, which is actually a verge, is slotted endwise to accommodate the jewels, and that is attached

to the fork-banking bar in the usual manner.

Was there ever a clock manufacturer in Reading, Pennsylvania, by the name of Lovell Manufacturing Company who made a calendar clock, probably for stores or offices of the time? Perhaps they were case makers. The movement pillars are riveted to the back frame, but they are pinned to the front frame, showing some antiquity. The calendar arrangement is under the dial, with the date hand from the center to the extreme outside edge of the paper dial, which is pasted on zinc. It is a striking clock with a heavy wire gong.

Would you say that the first 30-hour steeple clocks made by the New Haven Clock Company predated those set on a base, say around 1850-60?

How can the maker of a 400-day clock be identified? This clock frame measures a little better than 3½ x 2½ inches, and has a porcelain dial. The front frame is screwed to the pillars, but the back frame is pinned to them. The movement is set up on two pillars attached to a wood base covered with brass bezels with black plush velvet. The weight is a brass cylinder, further weighted with brass discs attached by a screw underneath. There are two small regulating cylinders with steel adjusting screws on top of the weight. In order to preserve this clock in the original, would a copper or steel torque spring be used? Just how old can a 400-day clock be?

A.

Baillie's list only comes up to 1825, and we believe your Benson piece to have been made since that date. Also, will you check the piece again to see if it isn't "J. W. Benson" instead of "T. W."?

The Lauder piece could come within Baillie, but he only lists two, John and James. Slip us the correct name of the Benson and give us a "rain-check" on these two pieces.

Haven't you heard the cliche that anything can happen about watches, and usually does? There could have been a New England Watch Company at Boston prior to 1880; however, we have nothing to indicate such a company existed. I suggest that you write to Mr. Ernest A. Cramer, 4400 Teesdale Street, Philadelphia 36, Pennsylvania, describe this piece and ask his opinion. He might like to examine it, but don't send the actual watch until he gives you the "green light" on shipment.

None of the general lists, such as Mr. Brooks Palmer's, contains a listing of the Lovell Clock Company at Reading, Pennsylvania. We have nothing for Reading. Palmer lists a Lovell & Company at Philadelphia, about 1880; a Lovell Manufacturing Company, Ltd., at Erie, Pennsylvania, from an 1893 advertisement (for an alarm clock). Then there is a Lovell & Smith from a Philadelphia directory, 1841 to 1843. Apparently this became the Lovell & Company of 1880 at Philadelphia. Your guess that this concern was a dealer or case manufacturer strikes me as being right. Such points of construction such as pinning on the front plate are not too reliable for determining the age of a piece because customs and methods died out very slowly rather than came to any abrupt stop. While you may look on that feature as indicating antiquity, the paper dial applied to zinc is looked-upon as not being too old.

The "Steeple" or "Sharp Gothic" as it was called by its originator, Mr. Elias Ingraham, did not have what we think you call a "base," i. e., a lower section with a separate door. The New Haven Clock Company was organized in 1853; steeple clocks with and without the lower sections had been popular before this date —therefore, it would be difficult to tell what the first New Haven models were— maybe some of our readers will comment.

The German version of the 400-day clock dates from about 1880, and was first manufactured in Freiberg in Silesia by A. Willmann & Company. It soon became popular and other firms there began making them. Wender & Metzgar in Frankfort-on-Main about 1890, Wilhelm Koehler in Fuerth in 1904, Gustave Becker in Freiburg in 1904, Phil Hauck of Munich and Gebruder Junghaus of Schramburg, about 1906.

The replacement of the suspension spring in our thinking would not enter

into the preservation of the piece "as in the original." The best available springs are neither copper, bronze or steel, but a special alloy called "Horolovar,"

S. B. TERRY

I am desirous of a little information regarding a marine clock by S. B. Terry (Brooks Palmer, page 292). A photostat, same size, is being sent to you. My question is, were many clocks of this type made, and are same scarce today?

A.

S. B. Terry torsion pendulum clocks are pretty rare. It is this writer's opinion that not many of these little torsion pendulum clocks were ever made; however, we've seen this movement in both wall and shelf cases.

Aaron D. Crane of Caldwell, New Jersey, patented a torsion pendulum clock as early as 1829, and is probably the first American clockmaker to use this principle, though it was known in Europe previous to that date. Terry deviated from the usual construction by clamping both ends of his

Fig. 1

suspension spring, and mounting the pendulum or balance in the middle, and so far as I know, was the only man to do so.

Silar Burnham Terry was born in Plymouth, Connecticut, February 1, 1807, and died at Winstead, Connecticut, on May 20, 1875. He was the fifth child of Eli Terry, Sr., and Eunice Warner Terry.

If the question were raised as to which of the Terry's clock men was the all-round mechanic, I'd have to vote in favor of Silas B. I do not mean to detract from

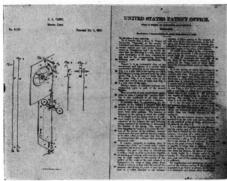

Fig. 2

his illustrious father or any of the others. Their success attests to their ability. Silas, most certainly, covered a much wider field—he built more different kinds of escapements, and was the only Terry clockmaker to label himself as a "horologist." His use of the term, "horologist" leads me to believe that possibly he may have read more horological books than the others, and his various forms of escapements tend to substantiate this thought. Proceeding along that line, I've tried for the last 20 years to obtain some definite information on his books, tools, etc.—with very little success.

Your clock was covered by his patent No. 9,130 issued October 5, 1852, witnessed by O. D. Munn and E. C. Polhamus. Perhaps his greatest contribution to the clockmaking industry was a method of tempering coiled steel springs.

E. N. WELCH

I would appreciate any information you can give me as to the age of a pendulum-strike wall clock bearing the name, "E. N. Welch Mfg. Co., Forestville, Conn."

A.

Elisha N. Welch was one of the largest clock producers in Connecticut during the latter half of the 19th century. He was born February 7, 1809, and died August 2, 1887.

He first operated a factory for casting clock weights, later acquiring various clock factories. About 1864, he consolidated his clock companies under the firm name of The E. N. Welch Manufacturing Company. This firm operated successfully and on a rather large scale till Mr. Welch's death in 1887. It went into receivership in 1897, and was reorganized as the Sessions Clock Company in 1903.

This 33-year period, 1864 to 1897 is as close as your description dates this clock.

SMITH & GOODRICH

I have an old clock which was made by Smith & Goodrich, Bristol, Connecticut. I would like to know the approximate age of the clock.

It is an 8-day clock and does not strike. The verge is on the left side of the escape wheel rather than underneath. It is not a large clock, probably 14 inches tall.

A.

Smith & Goodrich of Bristol are listed on the tax records from 1847 to 1852. The firm was Chauncey Goodrich and Samuel C. Smith; it did an extensive business, and reported about 1850 to be making 15,000 clocks per year. At one time they had four factories in Bristol (one on East Main Street, one on Brook Street, and two on Stafford Avenue) and a branch in Philadelphia.

Chauncey Goodrich was at work as early as 1828, and in 1832 and 1833, was in the firm of Ingraham & Goodrich, making clock cases. Later he was with the John C. Brown organization, then into your firm, as above. After 1852, he was in the clock business alone. Mr. Smith was also with John C. Brown (Bristol) prior to 1847.

BENJAMIN GRAY

I recently repaired an old grandfather clock and the owner would like to know when it was made. I guessed it to be more than 100 years old, and possibly as much as 200 years old. It is a weight-driven, seconds beat, recoil escapement. The strike train strikes the hours only, on a cast brass bell about 4 inches in diameter, mounted on top of the works.

There is a calendar arrangement which shows the days of the month through an opening in the dial. It is a ring about 8 inches in diameter, mounted concentrically with the dial center. It has the numbers 1 to 31 equally spaced around it, and is advanced one space each night by a pawl driven by a wheel at half the hour wheel speed.

The plates and wheels are brass. All arbors are individually forged with the pinions integral.

I am sending you a pencil rubbing of the name plate on the dial. (Benj. Gray— Just. Vulliamy, London.) Can you identify the makers and tell me when it was made?

Also, I have a weight-driven wall clock. It is an 80-beat regulator type clock, with a dead beat escapement, and is an excellent timekeeper. Its error seems to be not more than a minute a month. The dial bears a star within a circle, marked 1817, New Haven, 1853.

Am I correct in assuming that this clock was made by the New Haven Clock Company in 1853?

A.

You must have had a very fine old English clock. I certainly would have liked to have seen it while you had it down. Your second guess was better than the first—it was made between 1743 and 1762.

Benjamin Gray (1676-1764, London) was first in business in Pall Mall. In 1727 he moved to St. James Street and later returned to Pall Mall. He was clockmaker to King George II from 1744.

Justin Vulliamy came to London from Switzerland around 1730, married Gray's daughter and became a partner of his father-in-law in 1743. The Gray & Vulliamy firm was located in Pall Mall and lasted until 1762. Both men were exceptional mechanics, making both watches and clocks of the finest order. Neither seems to have written any special papers or books dealing with horology, as they are not listed in Baillie's "Clocks & Watches." Vulliamy's son, Benjamin (evidently named for his grandfather) became clockmaker to King George III.

The date, 1853, in the New Haven trademark of the second clock mentioned does not necessarily mean that your clock was made in that year. The figure "1853" was incorporated in the trademark because it was the date that firm was organized. The capital stock was $20,000. Governor English subscribed $5,000 for himself, and Mr. H. M. Welch and Mr. Hiram Camp,

$5,000. The other $10,000 was taken by the workmen. Mr. Camp was president and Mr. James E. English, secretary-treasurer.

New Haven was advertising this type of wall regulator as late as 1917, and I suspect your clock was made at least since the turn of the century (1900).

JEROME & CO.

I have an old clock just recently brought back from Sweden (although made in this country) for repair, and the owner would like to know how old this clock is and its history.

The clock is weight driven and strikes on the hour only. The cords go from the main wheel drum up to the top of the clock over small pulleys, and then down. The plates are 4 11/16" high, 3 11/16" wide and 1 11/16" deep or thick, from front to back. The pendulum rod is 11⅛" long. I am sending you a facsimile of the large label inside of the clock. Any information you can give me regarding this clock will be greatly appreciated.

A.

At one time, Chauncey Jerome (born June 10, 1793, died April 20, 1868) was the largest American exporter of clocks, and it isn't too unusual to run across one that has found its way back to the U.S.A.

Mr. Jerome was one of the most colorful characters in the clockmaking business, being in and out of several firms from about 1824 to about 1860. He at one time maintained two large factories in Bristol with an additional assembly plant at New Haven. The Bristol plants were destroyed by fire in 1845. Since your clock is labeled "Jerome & Company. New Haven, Connecticut" and in 1850 there was a reorganization that changed the name to "Jerome Manufacturing Company," I'd guess that between the 1845 fire and the reorganization, 1850 would be about the right date for it.

Mr. Jerome wrote "American Clockmaking," a 144-page history, largely personal, in 1860. Chances are your local library has a copy. I can recommend it—both you and your customer will enjoy it.

Stray Bits of Timepiece History

=James M. Bottom=

By J. E. COLEMAN

THE first turning we ever did was upon a dinky little brass lathe marked (branded) simply "J. M. Bottom, New York. 3 9 5." At that time it was referred to as a "wax lathe," for the very simple reason it did not take chucks—the head or revolving member protruded through the front support and whatever was to be turned was cemented to it with lathe cement or wax.

I often wondered about J. M. Bottom. The lathe wasn't listed in any of the available catalogues then, and I recall when I first got a copy of Henry G. Abbott's "American Watchmaker & Jeweler, An Encyclopedia for the Horologist and Jeweler," the disappointment at finding neither the lathe nor its maker mentioned.

That disappointment did not exactly cause a search to be instituted, but from that day to this, a weather eye has been kept out for the name—J. M. Bottom. Bottom's lathe cement or black wax was listed in material catalogs as late as 1929, but nary a word about the man or lathe was to be found. Mr. S. M. Risdon (Waltham Watch Company) recently unearthed a typed, bound volume titled "Complete History of Watch & Clockmaking in America," by Charles S. Crossman, which he loaned to us. Portions of it may have been published in The American Jeweler in the 1880s and 1890s—this is yet to be verified, but that is getting away from the lathe story. Imagine our very great satisfaction at finding a paragraph devoted to Mr. Bottom! That paragraph follows:

"James M. Bottom was born in Connecticut and came to New York City in 1842, and formed a partnership with Mr. A. B. Van Cott, who carried on the jewelry business in Grand Street. He was one of the finest and quickest workmen ever known to the trade. Later he moved to Nassau Street, and while there invented and patented in 1850, what was known as the 'Bottom Lathe,' using foot power instead of the old-fashioned bow. This was quite an innovation for that day, as previous to that all work had been done upon a bow lathe. He had them made for him and sold them quite extensively. He also made the escapement of watches a special study; he claimed that no watch could be made to run correctly with a soft hairspring, and to him must be largely credited the introduction of what is now long been known as 'tempered hairsprings.' He went to making them as a business and was the first and for some time the only maker of tempered hairsprings in this country. His process he kept a strict secret, not even allowing his apprentices to learn the art. Mr. William Wales, at that time an apprentice of his, related that at one time being taken seriously ill, and fearing he would not recover, put all the tools he used for that purpose in a rubber bag with some brick and sank it in the North River.

"Mr. Wales learned something of his process, however, and says at first he wound the hairspring wire in a box with a piece of light, soft mainspring to make the distance between the coils. He could only temper one at a time in this way, but afterwards adopted the plan of tempering three at a time as is now done. He experimented with oil and quicksilver to temper it, but found oil gave the most satisfactory results. His hairsprings made him famous. He made them for some of the American companies and for the watch material trade.

The Bottom Lathe

"Of his personal characteristics it may be said of him, he was eccentric in many things and a man of very positive nature;

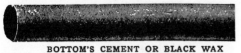

he never married. He died in 1879, after a somewhat lingering illness."

Thus we learn James M. Bottom was the first watchmaker in the U. S. to do watch turning by foot power and also the first U. S. watchmaker to make tempered hairsprings.

MARSH, GILBERT & CO.

I have an old wooden geared clock which is now rivaling our electric clocks for operating accuracy. It is a mantel clock about 36 inches high. The case is mahogany with crotch mahogany veneer used in some parts. A printed label pasted on the inside back of the case is something like the following, and in addition, has a column of operating instructions on each side: "8-day clocks, with the improvements of ivory bushing, manufactured and sold by Marsh, Gilbert & Company, Farmington, Connecticut."

The signature of the original owner and the date are written on this label. "Mary A. Downer, November 8, 1832."

The face is a solid piece of wood about 5/16 inches thick and the original pencil layout marks of the draftsman still show on the entire white surface. The minute divisions are somewhat irregular in size. My grandfather inscribed several items on the back of the face. He was a clockmaker and died at the age of 89 in 1913. He states, "This clock belonged to Dr. Downer of Preston, Connecticut. I bought it of Louis Ackley, great grandson of Dr. Downer, price, $2.00, in 1885. The case is a modification of the pillar scroll-top case invented by Chauncey Jerome in 1825. The clock was probably made in or a little before 1832, possibly from two to four years earlier. Twelve pound weights when wound up, made the clock top-heavy and the cord was too liable

to break. X. A. Welton changed the 12-pound weights for 6 and 7 pounds. With these, it will run 4 days and 12 hours. This change was made in 1885."

I have been informed that you have information available about such old clocks and would be very appreciative if you would send me some. My information came from a man in Pasadena who repairs clocks.

The clock had a 37-year vacation from the time of my grandfather's death until it came into my possession. It cost me $30.00 to have the case restored to its original beauty—quite a bit for a $2.00 clock, but it would take a lot of money to get the clock now.

A.

The date written on the label of your clock could very well be the date of its purchase, for Marsh, Gilbert & Company were in business from 1830 to 1835, first as William L. Gilbert and George Marsh. Mr. William Lewis Gilbert (1806-1890) was first a school teacher before going into partnership with his brother-in-law, George Marsh.

Afterwards Gilbert and Company was in Birge, Gilbert and Company, 1835-37, then in Jerome, Gilbert, Grant & Company, 1839-40; then to Winstead, Connecticut about 1841, with Lucius Clarke, as Clarke, Gilbert & Company. This firm became William L. Gilbert & Company about 1850; the Gilbert Manufacturing Company from 1866 to 1871; from 1871 to 1934, the William L. Gilbert Clock Company; and from 1934 to this date, the William L. Gilbert Corporation.

I think your grandfather was in error when he attributed the origin of the pillar-and-scroll style case to Chauncey Jerome. Credit for it is generally given to Eli Terry. Now it was Jerome who came up with the idea that the pillar (post) could be split in half and placed with the flat side against the case, giving quite a pleasing appearance, and at the same time enabling him to produce that case with one instead of two posts. Now if your case is one of those with half a post on either side, that was truly Jerome's invention and is also a modification, after a fashion of the Terry idea. Possibly that is the real meaning your grandfather had in mind when he wrote upon the dial.

Now we go to the weights. Your latter figure of six or seven pounds sounds nearer correct for an 8-day wood movement, and I seriously doubt that the 12-pounders removed in 1885 were the original weights, unless the fall was compounded. This may explain your 4-day and 12-hour run, for many of the early 8-day wood clocks did have a double fall. That is, the cord came from the drum up over a pulley in the top of the case, down under the pulley on the weight, and back to tie in the top of the case. Examine your case closely. See if there is a hole in the top halfway between the pulley and the outside edge of the top board where the cord was tied if the fall was double.

You can readily see that with the double fall, twice as much cord is reeled off the drum, and thus twice the length of run, and that twice the weight would be required.

FRENCH CLOCK

I am sending you a picture I took of what I would call a steam boiler clock. I had to make the bezel, as it was missing. Also, I had to make a key, as the clock mainspring arbor was rounded so the original key wouldn't work, and the arbor had to be squared up.

The governor will run by winding a movement in back of the barometer. There is a thermometer to the left of the barometer. The movement is a cylinder. There is no name on the clock anywhere. Could you tell me who made the clock

A.

Shortly before the turn of the century, animated or "motion" novelty clocks were quite popular in France, and they were made in great numbers. Many mechanical ideas were carried out, such as the merry-go-round, etc. Possibly the steam engine was the most popular and we suspect it could have been because the makers were able to use an aneroid barometer to imitate the steam gauge, and a thermometer to imitate the water glass gauge.

We've seen many of these, and although some were vertical like yours, and some were horizontal like the one in Clock Manor Museum in Denver, all stuck pretty near to the same general build, i. e., the engine ran or the governor turned by winding a separate mechanism and having the thermometer, barometer, and clock. Most have cheap cylinder movements and are unmarked.

Naturally we cannot date or give you the maker of an unmarked piece like this. It is my guess that they were probably gotten up by some novelty manufacturer

who would not be listed in any of the horological books, and further, that he bought his clock movements from any manufacturer who could deliver at the time they were wanted.

AGES

I am sending you a description of three old clocks that have fallen into my possession. I am anxious to verify their ages and value. Please tell me how I may obtain this information.

The first clock bears the name of Dyer, Wadsworth and Company, Augusta, Georgia. All mechanism is wood.

The second clock is brass, made by Seth engraved, "H. H. Taylor," and barrel Thomas at Plymouth Hollow, Connecticut. The third clock is brass, made and sold by Chauncey Jerome of Bristol, Connecticut.

A.

In reply to your first question concerning the Dyer, Wadsworth & Company label, wood-movement clock, the most authoritative answer would be a quote from "History of the American Clock Business," by Chauncey Jerome, the only Early American clockmaker to write and publish a book covering Early American clockmaking. It was published at New Haven in 1860. The quotation, from page 54 of the book, follows:

"In 1835 the Southern people were greatly opposed to Yankee pedlars coming into their states, especially the clock pedlars, and the licenses were raised so high by legislatures that it amounted almost to a prohibition. Their laws were that any goods made in their own state could be sold without license. Therefore, clocks to be profitable, must be made in those states.

"Chauncey Jerome and Noble Jerome started a factory in Richmond, Virginia, making the cases and parts at Bristol, Connecticut, and packing them with the dials and glasses, etc. We shipped them to Richmond and took along workmen to put them together. The people were highly pleased with the idea of having clocks made in their state. The old planters would tell the pedlars they meant to go to Richmond and see the wonderful machinery there must be to produce such articles, and no doubt would have thought the tools we had there were sufficient to make a clock. We carried on this kind of business for two or three years and did very well at it, though it was unpleasant. Everyone knew it was all a humbug trying to stop pedlars from coming to their states.

"We removed from Richmond to Hamburg, South Carolina, and manufactured in the same way. This was in 1835 and 1836. There was another company doing the same kind of business in Augusta, Georgia, by the name of Case, Dyer, Wadsworth & Co., and Seth Thomas was making cases and movements for them."

The No. 2 clock, by Seth Thomas, because it was made of brass, must have been made after 1837, and before 1859, when Plymouth Hollow was re-named "Thomaston."

The No. 3 was made by the writer of the volume mentioned. We can only date it after the wood-clock period ended in 1837 and before 1846 when Mr. Jerome moved to New Haven, Connecticut.

HENRY MARC

I have received a clock for repair, and the owner wishes to know its approximate age, the maker of the movement, the maker of the case, and any other information that might be helpful.

Here is the information the owner gave me: The clock has been in his family about 175 years, and was obtained in —France (city unknown) and brought to this country about 1898. The movement is $3\frac{1}{8}$ inches in diameter. Both plates are brass, $\frac{1}{8}$ inches thick, and the depth is $1\frac{3}{4}$ inches. It has a solid steel verge in the escapement, is spring-wound, 8-day, and strikes the hour and half-hour on a bell. Both springs are in closed barrels.

Markings on the back of the movement are "13-5, Hy Marc, Paris, 23717," plus a repair marking, I believe, "D-20-1-20-1, 1057." On the bezel is stamped, "B B, 717". The dial is enamelled, with Roman numerals. The name on the bottom of the dial is as follows, "2, Hry/A, M a r c, Paris." Also written on the back of the dial is, "717, Aeburge, Y 7," and as I understand, the above is actually "G F".

The case and candle arbors to go with the unit are as follows: Center piece, 13 inches long; over-all height, 15 inches; depth, $3\frac{3}{4}$ inches. Complete case and arbors are of cast brass.

Mounted on top of the case is the figure of a young man with a bow in his right hand and a bird (appearance of a quail) in the left hand. The boy's height is $5\frac{1}{2}$ inches and this is included in the over-all height of 15 inches. Sitting along side of the boy is a dog, whose size is $1\frac{1}{4}$ by 2 inches. Measuring $4\frac{1}{4}$ inches up from *the bottom on each side of the case are two white marble stones, polished on one side and rough on the other. The stones are 1¾ by 3 by ¼ inches. On the left stone, the marking, "G A X" is scratched in, and written is, "OE-2₀." On the right stone, the marking, "X G A" is scratched, and written is "O²-26." On the inside of the back, in black crayon, is writing which I interpreted as "Moices & Cemberg". I am also sending you a few pictures of this clock.*

A.

Your clock is approximately 150 years old. Its movement was made by Henry Marc of Paris. He was actively making clocks there around 1800.

Very little is given in the Marc listing, and we do not know whether he made his cases or not. I rather suspect he might have supplied the movement, complete with dial and hands, to some manufacturer specializing in such elaborate structures as this case, with its corresponding candlesticks. During this period, and even a bit later, these mantel sets (clock case with two matching pieces—statues or candle holders for either end of the mantel) were quite popular.

ATKINS CLOCK CO.

I wonder if you could tell me something about a wall clock made by the Atkins Clock Company of Bristol, Connecticut. This clock is a 30-day clock with equalizing springs. The cord winds up on two fusee drums (with key, of course).

Any information concerning this type of clock—when made, etc., (and might I add, why?) would be greatly appreciated.

A.

The Atkins Clock Company was organized to carry on the business of the Atkins Clock Manufacturing Company. This firm lasted some 20 years—from 1859 to 1879.

About 1850, the firm of Atkins, Whiting & Co. was formed. Joseph Ives sold them rights to the use of his rolling pinion and 30-day wagon-spring clocks, etc. About 1855, this firm was succeeded by the Atkins Clock Manufacturing Company, and was later taken over by the first-mentioned firm—the name that is upon your clock label.

The "why" is a good question. We think the clock was prompted from two angles (1) accuracy and (2) a special type for banking houses, etc.

Your letter does not indicate the size of this piece, but it is our guess that the same is altogether too large for even a large living room. Better business houses, banks, etc., created a demand for a large wall regulator about that era. These firms, Atkins, Whiting & Co., Atkins Clock Manufacturing Company and the Atkins Clock Company made and marketed a wide variety of clocks catering to the current demand at the time.

Winding once in 30 days not only enters the accuracy angle (disturbed once instead of four times a month) but many fine offices have very high ceilings and it was the custom to place these regulators well above the floor to be well in view. That posed the problem of climbing up to wind them—again, once instead of four times per month.

SETH THOMAS CLOCK

I have received an old clock for repair and the customer wants to know the age of it, or the approximate age. It is a large rosewood 8-day, weight, Seth Thomas clock, and the movement carries the number "18" on it. The clock itself is illustrated on page 119 of "American Clocks and Clockmakers" by Carl Drepperd, on the upper right-hand corner of the page, and is exactly as illustrated, with the same dimensions as those given under the illustration. It is supposed to be a picture from the Seth Thomas catalogue of 1876, but the book states that Seth Thomas bought the factory from Heman Clark at Plymouth Hollow in 1813. As this movement carries the number 18, I am wondering if this may not be one of the earliest Seth Thomas models, and approximately 140 years old.

A.

This type of clock was very popular in the 1870s and 1880s. The Drepperd data is very accurate. We think that the "18" you noted refers to the pendulum length, and know that these movements were never serially numbered. Thus it is not No. 18.

The shop Heman Clark sold to Seth Thomas in 1813, was the same shop Clark bought from Eli Terry in 1807. You must remember that the shelf or mantel clock did not enter the American industry before about 1816, possibly not in noticeable quantities before 1820.

Shortly after Terry invented his shelf clock in 1814, Seth Thomas purchased from Terry the right to make the new "patented" clock. This was a wooden-movement clock. The chances are that practically all of Thomas' production was wood up to about 1837.

Check the label in your clock. If the town name on the label is Plymouth Hollow, it would indicate that the clock was made before 1859, the year the town name was changed to Thomaston. We believe your label will read "Thomaston," thus definitely indicating it was made since 1859.

Old French firm still in business

Your column is enjoyed very much and is most educational, especially for us who only get occasional clock work and must rely on your skill for our experience.

My request is for historical information on a French clock that was recently taken in for repair. It is a round movement, 3¼ inches in diameter, 8-day, hour strike, in an alabaster case that stands 14 inches high without top ornament. The movement is stamped in the center bottom, Medaille de Bronze, L. Marti et Cie., with No. 5905 and a 6 below. The top of the regulator is marked L. BROCOT Bte. S.G.D.G.

The movement is in excellent condition and only needs minor repairs to the striking mechanism, and a good cleaning.

Any historical information along with the approximate age and the quantity made would be appreciated

A.

It is good to know you enjoy our column. We always hope, but only actually know when readers drop a line and say so.

Chances are it will come as a surprise to learn that the manufacturers of your clock are still in business. I quote, verbatim, a paragraph from a letter by the present head of the firm, a few years back —Mr. R. Marti:

"The firm 'Est. S. Marti,' one among the most old firms in the country, was founded in 1835 about, for the make of movements of clocks. Very numerous rewards were got in various exhibitions, in France and in foreign parts, beginning by an 'honorable' mention in the exhibition of 1839 in Paris, and, more lately, 'Grand Prix' in the International Colonial exhibition of 1931."

It is not practical to pin-point dates of manufacture from the serial numbers, however, various periods are quite definite from the award indicated—in your case the Bronze Medal. The stamp "S. Marti & Cie—Medalle de Bronze" was used from 1867 to 1889. The lettering you note below the regulator indicates that they were using the Brocot patented regulator.

Achille Brocot Paris, b-1817, was himself a very prominent horologist. He devised the visable escapement with the half-round jewel-pins and the adjustable pendulum suspension both of which bear his name (see two-part article by Rawlings & Coleman, American Horologist and Jeweler, December, 1955, and January, 1956).

Boardman Was Big Clock Manufacturer

I finally located and acquired a wooden works clock. Please send me as much information as you can concerning the clock and its maker The label states, Improved Clocks manufactured and sold by Chauncy Boardman, Bristol, Conn. In the bottom corner of the label is the printers name, P. Canfield, Hartford. The entire instruction label is legible.

I'm not looking for an appraisal but would appreciate any information you can give me as to the comparative rarity, age, quality, etc., of Mr. Boardman's clocks.

A.

Chauncey Boardman clocks are not ultra rare, however those with wooden movements aren't so plentiful as the many brass works made after 1837.

Born 1789, Chauncey Boardman died in 1857. For forty years — approximately 1810 to 1850 — he was one of the leading Connecticut clock manufacturers. He began making hang-up wood movements with Butler Dunbar, about 1811 and is listed upon the tax rolls of Bristol, for that year. The firm was Boardman & Dunbar.

He was in partnership with Col. Joseph A. Wells, under Boardman & Wells, Bristol, 1832 to 1843. The tax rolls for 1832 also show him in Boardman & Smith (Samuel B.) for 1832. Both firms were producing 30-hour and 8-day wood movements until 1837. After that, brass movements. One of the largest manufacturers of that period, he was operating as many as four factories at one time. He was one of the early makers of spring driven clocks—received patent No. 4,914 Jan. 7, 1847, for a reversed fusee. In 1844 the firm divided, each continuing to make clocks under his own name; failed in 1850 and Dr. Charles F. Foote, his son-in-law, acquired assets. Since the short pendulum (shelf) wood clock came into general use about 1816 and manufacture of wood movements ceased with the depression and rolling of brass in 1837, you can safely date your clock between 1816 and 1837.

ILLINOIS WATCH CO.

The Illinois Springfield Watch Company was conceived in the mind of one J. C. Adams whom several historians have dubbed "The Great Starter" because he was instrumental in starting more watch factories than any other one man. He succeeded in interesting the Springfield Board of Trade to the extent that a new company was formed in January of 1869; a capital of $100,000 was set and John T. Stewart named President; W. B. Miller, secretary, with Mr. Stuart, W. B. Miller, John Williams, John W. Bunn, George Black and George Passgeld named to the Board of Directors.

Mr. Adams returned to his home town of Elgin, and secured trained mechanics for the new plant; he signed up Mr. John K. Bigelow, for plant superintendent; Otis Hoyt, as foreman of the train room; C. E. Manson, for foreman of the escapement room; D. G. Currier for model-making and finishing; George White to be the pattern-maker, with John Nickerson as jeweler. Thus Springfield Watch Company got its start with men of proven ability and experience, something not all starting factories had enjoyed. Work upon a new building was commenced in May of 1870; January 1872, just 21 months later, their first movements hit the market.

Those watchmakers familiar with Illinois movements will recognize some of the model names from among the organizers. Perhaps one of those best known is the "Bunn Special" a sixteen size, three-quarter plate, made in two grades, 21 and 23 jewel, adjusted to six positions, etc. It was named for Jacob Bunn, a son of John W.

Very early in it's history, the corporate name was changed to Illinois Watch Company. By 1927 it had produced some five million movements when the plant was taken over by the Hamilton Watch Company, of Lancaster, Pa.

One of the most colorful characters ever to be associated with the manufacture of watches at Springfield was George F. Johnson, Mr. Johnson, was a practicing dentist when he went to work for the Rockford Watch Company at Rockford, Ill., in 1874 at the age of 24. That first Rockford connection was of short duration and for the next 27 years Mr. Johnson did quite a bit

of moving about. Among other things, he attended the Northern College of Optometry at Chicago where he earned the degree of O.D.—Doctor of Optometry. For a short spell he practiced optometry and watch-making—repair—in Canton, Ohio, and he did a stint in the Elgin Watch Factory. In 1885 we find him in Aurora, Ill. at the old Aurora Watch factory; in 1891 to the U.S. Watch Company, Waltham, Mass. Thence in Jan. 1892 to Dueber-Hampton Watch Co., Canton Ohio—in 1901 back to Springfield, Ill. This stop was very short for he went back to Rockford to become Plant Superintendent. In 1904 he accepted the spot as Factory Superintendent at Illinois—Springfield. Here he remained, even after Illinois was closed down in 1928, as director of the Astronomical Observatory; which post he held 'til his death March 16, 1931.

In the early 1950's it was my good fortune to correspond with Miss Julia E. Johnson of Springfield, a daughter, and Mr. Edwin R. Johnson, of Centralia, Ill., a son. I am indebted to them for much personal and detailed history upon their father. Miss Johnson supplied the photo.

About 1911 Mr. Johnson outlined a plan to build an astronomical observatory to the then President of Illinois, Mr. Jacob Bunn. It was promptly approved and Bunn & Johnson launched a "project" that just has to be termed purely Public Relations, plus one that must have been ultra expensive if looked at from the angle of direct advertising. Just what it did for the sale of Illinois watches as well as whether or not it entered into some of Illinois financial problems has yet to be answered. The Bunn-Johnson "plan" resulted in what was described as a beautiful, completely equipped astronomical observatory, including a radio broadcasting station. Among other things, Mr. Johnson was a licensed radio operator.

He was named director of the Observatory in addition to his position as plant superintendent. He resigned as active superintendent about 1919 and was made consulting superintendent, still holding the spot of director of the Observatory.

This brings us to the question, what portion of this elaborate observatory was of direct use to the manufacture of watch movements and what portion was Public Relations? For the purpose of having correct time in the factory, we might assign about 5%—we must remember that several factories were doing quite well with their master clock by checking against Western Union time as checked daily by the Naval Observatory. Only one other watch factory, Waltham, had its own observatory; it was somewhat upon the smallish side and was operated in conjunction with the Allegheny Observatory, Pittsburgh, which supplied a time-check by telegraph. This leaves 95% that has to be chalked-up to Public Relations.

We can NOT consider the use of the big Equatorial telescope which was designed by Mr. Johnson and built in the watch factory shops, with the exception of optics, as being a part of any precision

time determination. This instrument with its free movement in every direction is not practical for that purpose. Sidereal time is determined by a transit instrument; said transit is firmly bolted down to concrete piers solidly anchored in the earth and adjusted so that its lateral motion is nil— as near as humanly possible. It must not deviate the ten-thousandth part of an inch. A Frenchman named Pettitidier, at Gertner Scientific Laboratories, Chicago, ground the lenses for the big Equatorial; it was also Gertner who supplied Dunn & Johnson with a transit instrument, a chronograph, and two fine astronomical clocks, one a Riefler.

While Illinois was the second factory to set up an observatory, it was the first to broadcast the time, to be followed in this endeavor by South Bend Watch Factory and lastly Elgin Watch Factory.

Elgin began broadcasting accurate time in 1927 via its station KS2XAT or 4797.5 Kc. It had a fine little observatory with ONLY a transit; no Equatorial scope. When the Elgin operation was phased out several years ago, the observatory was presented to the Public School System of Elgin.

While the new observatory building was being erected and the equatorial scope was being built in the company shops, a tent was erected on the grounds wherein the mechanics and carpenters were building the revolving dome for the telescope room. Expensewise, this again brings us to that difference between the use of a transit and an equatorial telescope. For the transit, only a stationary window is required whereas a powered, revolving dome is required to accommodate the equatorial, etc.

The building of this observatory, equip-ing it with the finest instruments available, plus the radio broadcasting station must have been a pretty expensive undertaking. Staffing it and making it available at all hours was still another expense. The American Ephermis published by the U.S. Naval Observatory for 1921 listed some 256 observatories of the world, placing Illinois as No. 205. In that same year Radio News —a trade publication out of New York City—ran a feature article on Illinois station 9ZS, stating "This concern is probably the first in the country, if not in the world, to actually transmit time signals regularly."

Bunn, Johnson et al must have enjoyed this type of publicity—P. R.—and they were so proud of their observatory they took advertisements in trade journals announcing it. The accompanying reproduction is from the Keystone for March 15, 1914.

When Illinois Watch Company closed down in 1929, it was acquired by the Hamilton Watch Company of Lancaster, Pa. The watch portion along with some partially finished movements were transferred to Lancaster; the grounds and buildings were sold to the Sangamo Electric Company, and a little later the observatory was sold to Bradley University, at Peoria, Ill.

Besides their department of horology Bradley also offered a course in astronomy and planned to re-erect the observatory on ground adjacent to the university. The dome on the telescope room, its track, the big scope, the transit, the chronograph, and the two clocks were shipped to Peoria. The horological school took over the two clocks and the rest was stored—several plans to erect an observatory failed to materialize and when the ground passed to the U.S. Government for the Regional National Laboratory, the scheme was dropped. One clock (which?) along with the transit, equatorial, the chronograph and the dome were given to the Peoria Academy of Sciences.

During the long storage period which included several shifts, the transit lost all its optics and gathered considerable rust— the Academy having no use for the carcass did not take it and it was junked. The Academy erected a fine observatory at the Northmoor Golf Course in Peoria which

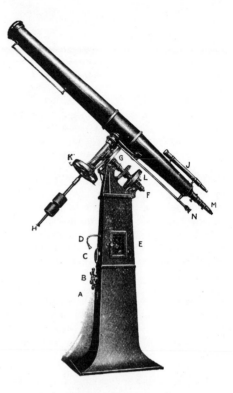

Equatorial Telescope
Illinois Watch Company's
Astronomical Observatory
Springfield, Illinois

This telescope was designed by Mr. George F. Johnson, superintendent of the watch factory, and all its parts, with the exception of the lenses, were made in the workshops of the company.

It is conceded a marvel of accuracy and is said to be one of the finest instruments of its kind. It has an 8½ inch lens with a focal length of twelve feet.

was opened in the summer of 1955 and the old dome and scope are rendering yeoman service today.

CLOCK WEIGHTS

When the making of clocks in the Connecticut Valley first began in the 1700's, both lead and cast-iron were scarce and expensive. In true Yankee fashion pioneer clockmakers met their weight problem—clock, that is—head-on. To power their 30-hour, long-case, wood clocks they simply hung on a tin cylinder with wooden heads, filled with sand or stones. A simple, cheap and satisfactory solution until Terry came up with the shelf clock about 1815, and the greatly reduced weight fall brought on weight problems. It was quite evident that a space on the order of thirty inches occupied by a ten inch long weight would have a fall of only twenty inches. The weight had to be shorter and at the same time smaller. By that date the metal industry was greatly improved; small foundries were operating and they quickly met the demand of clockmakers with small, cast-iron weights. Like "Topsy" this branch of the clockmaking industry just "grew up"—the drive force (gravity) required for these thirty hour wood movements was not critical; about the only specification for a weight was it's diameter. It had to be small enough to run freely in the space alloted within the clock case and thus the whole weight production effort resulted in more or less of a hit-and-miss affair; no specific standards were needed or set.

Back around the turn of this century if a clockmaker required a weight, he either cast one himself from scrap lead, or there was a small foundry near by where they would utilize the weight he had for a pattern and cast him a weight at the next pouring. Today, those small foundrys are gone; clock owners want their clock weights as near duplicates as possible causing the cast-iron weight to be revived so to speak.

As to how the problem was handled sans any standard is left to your imagination. Perhaps when the early clockmakers ordered a batch of weights it was like the little girl with a bad stutter who could not say vinegar—she just passed the container over to the storekeeper and said: "smell the jug and give me a quart." When Stuart M. Young, clockmaker of Box 1151, Huntsville, Alabama 35807, decided to go into the weight casting business he also decided to do something about a "standard", 1, to enable the repairman to order weights intelligently, 2, allow him to supply a weight as near original as practical—he came up with this chart:

SIZE →	1	2	3	4
A - IN.	$1\frac{11}{16}$	$1\frac{3}{4}$	$1\frac{15}{16}$	2
B -	$2\frac{15}{16}$	$3\frac{3}{8}$	3	$3\frac{5}{16}$
C -	$2\frac{1}{8}$	$2\frac{5}{16}$	$3\frac{1}{8}$	$3\frac{1}{2}$
WIGHT #	$2\frac{1}{4}$	$2\frac{3}{4}$	$3\frac{1}{8}$	$3\frac{1}{2}$

So far as we can determine, this is the first time an attempt has been made at standardization; Mr. Young is offering to repair trade, weights of cast-iron with recessed lifting eyes as per this chart at $2.15 each or $3.95 per pair.

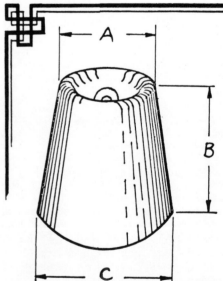

From the practical point, the repairman wishes to supply the heaviest weight the case will accommodate; its critical figure being the "C" measure—largest diameter—he can quickly measure that distance from the back of his dial to the back of the case and thereby determine the largest "C" measurement he can use.

BIRGE, PECK & CO.

I have a clock movement for repair made and sold by Birge, Peck and Company, Bristol, Conn. The movement measures 9 x 6 inches, has eight-day weight, train is in the back, the name on the engine is "The Breeze," although the clock itself has no name. I would appreciate any information on this clock.

A.

Birge, Peck and Company were active 1849 to 1858, and the heads of the firm were John Birge and Ambrose Peck. John Birge, born in Torrington, Conn. in 1785, died at Bristol, Conn., June 6th, 1862, was one of the most colorful characters in the early American clock industry. He was taught the trade of cabinetmaker, fought in the war of 1812, and was a successful wagon builder 1820 and 1821.

With the rapidly booming clock business of about that date, practically every cabinetmaker, and most of the available lumber were pressed into making clock cases, and it was only natural that Mr. Birge was swept in. Tradition has it that he went to New York City about 1830, and was the moving spirit in releasing Joseph Ives, the clockmaker who had been imprisoned there for debt. Somewhere in this transaction, he obtained certain rights to various Ives patents for a reported price of $10,000.00.

Mr. Birge headed up several clock concerns—the history of his business activities would closely parallel that of the clock industry for that same period. The principal firms were:

Birge and Tuttle	1823
Birge and Hale	1823
Birge and Ives	1832-1833
Birge, Case and Company	1833-1834
Birge and Gilbert	1837
Birge, Gilbert and Company	1834-1837
Birge and Fuller	1844-1848
Birge, Mallory and Company	1838-1843
Birge, Peck and Company	1849-1858

Birge retired from the firm in 1855 to farm, farming being his special interest all his life. This firm was later merged with J. C. Brown and following several succeeding firms is now the Sessions Clock Company.

The locomotive "Breeze" was a favorite with them and used quite a lot. Birge and Fuller had used a steam locomotive on some of their labels; this one was named "Puffin Betsy."

E. TERRY

I write to you for information about old clocks, especially those invented by Eli Terry. I have a clock of my great-grandfather's which was bought in 1840 or before, and is still running.

It has all wooden wheels, except the one the pendulum swings on, which is brass. It was invented by Eli Terry, but I can find no date of manufacture. I would appreciate it if you could tell me where to find this information.

A.

Eli Terry, Sr., the oldest child of Samuel and Hulda (Burnham) Terry, was born at East Windsor (now South Windsor), Connecticut, April 13, 1772, and died at Terryville, Connecticut, February 24, 1852.

Following are the approximate dates of his prinicpal firms: 1792 to 1793—Eli Terry, East Windsor, Connecticut, 8-day brass movements, tall cases; 1794—Eli Terry, Northbury, both brass and wooden movements for tall cases; 1807 to 1808—Eli Terry, Greystone (a part of Plymouth); 1809 to 1810—Terry, Thomas and Hoadley; 1810 to 1818—Eli Terry, Plymouth; 1818 to 1824—E. Terry and Sons, Plymouth; 1824 to 1827—Eli and Samuel Terry, Plymouth; 1824 to 1833—E. Terry and Son, Plymouth; 1833 to 1852—Eli Terry, Plymouth.

You do not describe your clock—long case or shelf, etc., and neither give complete wording of the label. There were many clocks made whose label bore the line, "Invented by Eli Terry." Some makers (especially Seth Thomas) purchased the right to manufacture, but far more pirated both the mechanical design, and in some way contrived to work the name "Eli Terry" on to their labels. The manufacture of wooden movement clocks ceased abruptly with the great panic of 1837. It is quite possible your grandfather bought the clock new in the 1830's.

LUMAN WATSON

I was called upon to service a clock which had a wooden clock movement, and had been in the customer's family since the year 1811. Would like to know who manufactured this movement—the name on the dial is L. Watson, Cincinnati, Ohio.

A.

Luman Watson was born at Harwinton, Connecticut, October 10, 1790, and he died November 28, 1834, at his home at the head of Race Street, Cincinnati, Ohio. Whether Watson was apprenticed to a clockmaker is not known, but the fact remains that he grew up in Lichfield County in the heart of the wood clock industry.

Miss Annie Hodge Lockett, in a paper entitled, "Luman Watson, Clockmaker, Poet in Gadgets" for the Philosophical Society of Ohio, says: "In 1809 Ezra Read, of the Cincinnati firm of Read & Watson, was selling clocks in the Mad River, Ohio, country."

The firm of Read & Watson was dissolved about 1817, thus your clock marked "L. Watson" must have been made after that date, and we have to date it between 1817 and 1834. A Cincinnati directory for 1819 lists Watson as an ivory and wood clockmaker located on 7th between Main and Sycamore Streets, producing clocks valued at $30,000.00 (annually) and employing 14 hands, the machinery being driven by horsepower. The U. S. census of manufacturers for 1822 lists Hamilton County, Ohio, wooden clocks manufactured at $15,000.00, and that the industry employed 10 men and women at annual wages of $6,000.00. An 1834 directory lists Watson's factory as employing 25 hands, and using steam power.

Mr. Watson was a church man, a Mason, and very active in the civic life of his community; was a charter member of the Mechanics' Institute, serving as its treasurer from 1829 to 1830, and one of the organizers of the Cincinnati Chamber of Commerce.

Miss Lockett closed her paper with this sentence, "Watson gave generously to the life of his time, and we are still benefiting from his contributions, though his death occurred at the early age of forty-four."

GUSTAV BECKER

Can you give any information about a German clock manufacturer of about fifty years ago by the following name: Gustav Becker. Any information would be appreciated.

A.

Gustav Becker of Frieburg, Germany, was born 1819 and died 1885, and had a sizeable clock factory with a large output of clocks and regulators.

This factory began to produce 400-day clocks about 1904, and were producing them twenty years later (1924). Somewhere along the line the Junghans Clock Company (Schramberg, Germany) seems to have taken over, the date is a little indefinite—we are not sure whether before or after World War II. Through my section of the U.S.A. we see several of the Becker 400-days, and a few Becker chimes.

Some of the latter are a fair quality movement—complete three train Westminster chimes in the orthodox manner, several of the two train type with the chime drum shifting back and allowing that train to strike the hour also.

EARDLEY NORTON

A few years ago in Munich, Germany, I purchased an old, interesting looking gold watch from an antique shop. I would like to sell the watch now and thought perhaps you could give me an idea of its value. A jeweler looked at it and suggested I send you the following information about the watch: Engraved on the inside back is "Eardley Norton, London, 172," the same is engraved on the plates, it is a key wind, key set, key adjustment with alarm, chain wind, and enclosed escapement.

The case is gold with the following engraved on the outside of the back: "Geschenk Alexanders 1, Kaisers von Russland an seinen damaligen Pagen den Cadetten Carl v. Witzleben am 23. November 1805." (Translation: "Gift of Alexander 1, Kaiser of Russia, to his page of that time, Cadet Carl von Witzleben, on November 23, 1805.")

A.

Eardley Norton, St. John Street, London, is listed 1762 to 1794 and is referred to as a maker of repute of watches and complex clocks. In 1771 he patented a striking mechanism for clocks and repeating watches. Examples of his work are to be found in many museums; there was a fine organ clock in the Palace museum at Peking, a clock in the National Museum at Stockholm, another in the Virginia Museum, a marine chronometer in the Ilbert collection, and there is an astronomical clock by him in Buckingham Palace.

An encyclopedia gives Alexander I as 1777 to 1825, and as per the engraving the presentation was made the 23rd of November, 1805. A piece made by Norton could have easily been used as a gift some eleven years after his death, however, the accuracy of the inscription would not hinge on that one fact.

WM. L. GILBERT CLOCK CO.

Recently I bought several old clocks from a long established jewelry store and some of them had been on the shelf in the back room since the twenties. One of these clocks is an 8-day striking pendulum clock with "Patd June 3, 1879. Wm. L. Gilbert Clock Company, Winsted, Connecticut, U.S.A." on the lower part of the front plate. On the upper left hand corner of the front plate near the arbor which would carry the fan fly is "Patd. Feb. 26, 1884."

Instead of the fan fly in this clock, there are two flat springs fastened to the arbor just past the pinion and extending parallel with the arbor into a shallow barrel fastened to the inside of the front plate. On the end of each of these springs is a lead weight shaped to fit the contour of the barrel. Each weight has a pad and as the arbor gains momentum these weights extend outwards until the pads come in contact with the wall of the barrel. This, of course, regulates the speed of the striking train and it does a very nice job of it.

I wrote the William L. Gilbert Clock Company, giving a description of it and had a nice letter from the service man-ager. Sorry I cannot read the signature, but here is what he said:

Gentlemen:

This will acknowledge your letter of April 10, and although the writer has been connected with Gilbert for some 35 years, I do not recall having seen a pendulum movement constructed such as the one you describe. All the 8-day pendulum movements manufactured between 1915 until they were discontinued around 1940 had the fan type construction which covered the speed of the strike.

It could be that the movement is a model which someone may have developed, but apparently it was never used to any great extent in production. Sorry that I cannot give you more definite information concerning it.

A.

We are quite familiar with the type construction you indicate for controlling the speed of the strike train, having noted one several years back and obtained a copy of the patent. That patent is No. 294,262, issued to George B. Owen, county of Litchfield and state of Connecticut (Winstead), and was filed April 24, 1883 and granted February 26, 1884. It was witnessed by Frank D. Hallet and Henry B. Able; there was no model and no assignment.

It is indeed difficult for one to say definitely how many of Gilbert's clocks made use of Mr. Owen's "Improvement in speed regulation for the strike mechanism." I think I'd be perfectly safe in saying that I've averaged seeing better than one per year over a period of years, know the location of two right here in town and have one on the repair bench right now (a third). They most certainly went far beyond the model stage. You may obtain a copy of this patent from the U. S. Patent Office for 25c by noting the serial number and date above.

Your question is so truly a case in point that I'm tempted to digress for a moment —might even call your attention to the Otherwise column in the April issue. I believe that your letter must have come from S. A. Ransom—he has been Gilbert's service manager for a number of years. We've always found both him and the Gilbert organization very cooperative. Despite their sincere desire to cooperate, there are many, many points, types of construction, dates, etc., which the factories simply do not have any record of, and therefore, cannot supply.

TERHUNE & EDWARDS

I have an old clock with the front 16x10, cast-iron, two figures, one on each side, holding bibles in their hands. The clock was made by Terhune & Edwards, 98 Courtland Street, New York.

The mainwheel (time) is worn out, and I am wondering if the clock has enough antique value to warrant trying to repair. It looks like a regular St. Thomas or New Haven movement, and I would appreciate it if you could tell me the approximate age of this clock.

A.

It was first Terhune & Edwards at 50 Courtland Street, then Terhune & Edwards at 48 Courtland Street about 1860. 18 Courtland Street according to an 1872 directory. They were either case-makers or merchants, most likely both, and are known to have used Chauncey Jerome movements in a lot of their clocks.

Now as to antique value—this we never comment on, at least not in dollar figures. Practically all American clocks made before 1900 are in demand to one degree or another, and there are some special demands for iron front clocks as a type, etc.

R. ROSKELL

I have in my possession a silver cased pocket watch made in Liverpool, England by R. Roskell, and has the number 3282 on the movement and case.

I would like all possible information

A.

Robert Roskell is listed at Liverpool and London 1798 to 1830. Roskell, like Joseph Johnson, and the Tobias family also of Liverpool, was a very active exporter of watches. It is known that he made use of many of Litherland's rack and lever escapements, also that he sold both cylinder and regular lever watches. In all likelihood he was a watchmaker in his own right, but the chances are that when his business reached the active exporting stage, he was buying all his movements on the then very active Ormskirk market.

The serial number is practically meaningless since they were most likely of some maker rather than his own. We have photos in the file of one of his regular levers numbered 27020, and another of a thin cylinder type, No. 16442—this latter piece, though elaborately engraved with his name and 'Liverpool,' looks very Swiss, and I doubt that either the movement or the case was made in England.

Robert Roskell is generally referred to as a celebrated watchmaker—we have a clipping from the Liverpool Mercury for February 2, 1883, which reads as follows: "The late Dr. Richard Roskell, bishop of Adera, formerly for nearly 22 years Roman Catholic Bishop of Nottingham, whose death has just been announced, was born in Liverpool on August 16, 1817, and was the son of Robert Roskell, the celebrated watchmaker."

ELI TERRY

I have in my shop for repair an upright mantel clock about 30" high which has all wooden works (except for the escape wheel). Both the owner and myself would like to know how old it is. It has a date on it where it has been repaired 1863, but I will give you all the information I have.

Invented by Eli Terry, made and sold at Terrysville, Connecticut, by Eli Terry, Jr. Of course, this is a weight clock.

A.

Eli Terry, Jr. was the second of **nine** children born to Eli Terry, Sr. (1799-1841). He is listed as building 6 arbor, 8-day wood clocks from 1834 to 1837 with labels very similar to the one you indicate. You do not state whether this clock is one or eight-day and the 30 inch height seems rather short for an 8-day.

Terry, Jr. was apprenticed to his father and was later with him in the firm of Eli Terry & Sons, and went into business for himself about 1825. If your clock is a one-day, it would fall between 1825 and 1834.

SKELETON CLOCK

I am sending you a photo of a clock which has been in our family for a great many years, in fact, it was handed down from grandfather who had it many years also. Can you give me any information regarding the maker, which I presume is A. E. Fowle whose name is on the front; the date is 1828.

The clock is in excellent shape and a very good timekeeper; it is mounted on a marble base and it strikes just once each hour. Any information you are able to give me will be greatly appreciated.

"Skeleton" Clock

A.

You show an excellent example of the "Skeleton" clock which was very popular in England over a period of years. Donald de Carle in his "Watchmakers and Clockmakers Encyclopedic Dictionary" uses a cut along these very same lines with his definition: "Skeleton Clock—a movement having the plates cut away or pierced so as to render the train, etc., visible."

Many were single train such as yours, with a lift on the center-post which raised the hammer and let it fall for just the one stroke at the hour, some had two trains and conventional hour striking arrangement, while a few were three train and chimed each quarter.

We do not locate any record of A. E. Fowle, Westerham, however, Baillie does list a Humphrey Fowle, Westerham, as having made a watch about 1769. One might speculate that "A. E." could have

been his son, further, that this son only made a very few pieces and therefore, did not get listed. It would seem pretty certain that if Humphrey Fowle (son or no son) had made enough "fuss" to attract attention at all, Mr. Baillie would have him listed.

KROBER CLOCK CO.

I have a clock manufactured by the Krober Clock Company, and would appreciate any information you can give me.

A.

There is still something of a question as to whether or not Mr. Florence Krober ever actually made clocks. If he did, the facts are clear that he was much more of a merchant than a clockmaker, since it is very evident that by far the greater portion of clocks bearing his mark were made on contract for him.

We know that some clocks bearing the F. Krober Clock Company brand were manufactured by Seth Thomas, utlizing the old No. 89 movement and we've seen a number of his clocks with his pendulum clamping attachment, which movements were made by Ansonia.

At present we have on loan from Wesley Hallett (for study and photos) a horse race timer of rather cheap construction and definitely on the large side, being as large as the old model Big Ben alarm clock. One would imagine that the well-dressed devotee of the horses wearing one of these on a strap (probably hung from his neck) would look a bit clumsy.

Mr. Hallett, Box 192, Flushing, New York, a prominent member of the National Association of Watch & Clock Collectors, probably has more information on Krober than any other collector. He has furnished our files with the listings in the New York City directories from 1865-66 (first listing) to 1904-05 when F. Krober & Company of 45 Maiden Lane was dissolved.

From Krober clocks that have passed over our bench we have obtained seven patent dates and secured copies as follows:

October 6, 1874, No. 155,656, an improvement in strike train.

July 31, 1877, No. 103, 663, calendar clock dials.

June 1, 1880, No. 228,202, animated alarm clock.

October 3, 1893, No. 506,050, method of coating clock cases.

September 25, 1894, No. 526,399, put-in-beat adjuster.

August 18, 1896, No. 28,799, trademark "Eclipse".

February 9, 1897, No. 576,587, pendulum clamp.

E. N. Welch, clockmaker of Forrestville, Connecticut, supplied Krober with clocks and we believe possibly all his calendar clocks. Shortly before the turn of the century, one of the most popular selling calendar clocks in the U. S. was one called "Fashion" with that word in large gold-leaf letters across the central portion of the glass. Its popularity caused other makers to offer clocks of similar construction with large gold lettering on the glass, and the "Eclipse" was one of them.

If you have a convenient photo of your clock we might be able to identify the actual maker.

Early U. S. clock resemblance

I know that you are well up on the early clockmakers and having several old pieces in my possession, I would appreciate knowing a little more about some of the makers. Eli Terry, Eli Terry & Sons, Seth Thomas, Chauncey Jerome, Welsh, J. C. Brown, and Waterbury are among the most important. I would like to know if they had an association with each other, as some movements seem to be exact duplicates of others.

Did Seth Thomas and Terry work together or apprentice with one or the other? Was Chauncey Jerome associated with Thomas or Welch? I would appreciate hearing from you

A.

First, we should take the over-all picture; all of these gentlemen lived in what we of today would consider a small community. Besides being in the same line of endeavor, practically all of them were church-going men and a great many belonged to the same lodge, thus you can see that they were thrown pretty close together.

Eli Terry, Sr., Seth Thomas and Silas Hoadley were in a partnership at one time about 1809 at Greystone (now Plymouth), Connecticut. After something like a year or more, Mr. Terry withdrew, leaving the firm Thomas & Hoadley, until Mr. Thomas sold out to Hoadley about 1813. In the fall of 1816, Chauncey Jerome went to work for Eli Terry making clock cases.

Over and above such associations as mentioned above as a probable cause of clock movements looking alike, you must remember that there was much barter and trading in clock movements. For example, in his "History of the American Clock Business," Jerome writes that in 1821 he sold his home to Mr. Terry for "one hundred wood clock movements with dials, table glass and weights." Then he went over to Bristol to see George Mitchell and bought from him a house with barn and 17 acres of land for 214 movements.

Mr. Jerome said, "I finished up the hundred parts which I got from Mr. Terry, exchanged cases with him for more, obtained some credit and in this way made out the quantity for Mitchell." Now here we have movements by Terry, cases by Jerome and I'm pretty sure that many, if not most, of those clocks bore the name of Mitchell. One might say a George Mitchell clock resembled the Terry movement when it is not a resemblance at all, but an actual Terry movement.

Mr. Elisha N. Welch first operated a foundry to cast clock weights before he purchased the entire J. C. Brown clock industry about 1850. One would naturally expect that Welch continued to make clocks with the Brown machinery and thus of a necessity turned out movements looking like those under the Brown label.

Re: your direct question. "Was Jerome associated with Thomas?" Insofar as I can determine, he never was. However, there is good reason for a resemblance between the Thomas and Jerome movements.

I again quote from the Jerome history, page 103: "He (Thomas) sent his foreman over to Bristol where I was then carrying on business to get patterns of movements and cases and take all the advantage he could of my experience, labors and improvements.

"I allowed my foreman to spend more than two days with his, giving him all the knowledge and insight we could of the business, knowing what his object was." This was about 1840.

You mentioned Waterbury clocks and again I quote from Jerome: "The Benedict and Burnham Company, now making clocks in the city of Waterbury under the name of the Waterbury Clock Company, is composed of a large number of the finest citizens of that place. My brother, Noble Jerome, who is an excellent mechanic, and as good a brass clockmaker as can be found, is now making movements for this company."

This was about 1860, so you can readily see why some Waterbury movements resemble Chauncey Jerome movements—both were made by Noble.

S. Marti clocks

I am desirous of obtaining information relative to a French-made clock I have in my possession. This clock seems to be very old and has the name "S. Marti & Company" and the number "2419" stenciled on the back of the mechanism. It is in a case about 20 inches wide, 10 inches high and 10 inches deep. The case is made of a black heavy material that could be onyx and is about 50 pounds in weight.

I wish to know the date it was made and the kind of material the case was made of and, if possible, the number of clocks of this type manufactured. Any information will be highly appreciated.

A.

The firm of S. Marti, 22 Rue General Leclerc, Mountbeliard, France, now in business at that address, was founded in 1835 to manufacture clock movements. There is no key to the serial numbering, thus your No. 2419 does not convey any information.

Along with the trade mark stamping, there should be some other wording. Those stamped "Medaille d' Bronze" were made between 1867 and 1889; "Medaille d'Argent" were made between 1889 and 1900; "Medaille d'Or" were made between 1900 and 1931. Those movements made after 1931 were stamped "Grand Prix, Paris."

Any guess as to the number of this type manufactured would be impossible. You see they (Marti) were manufacturing movements to be sold to case makers, and these certainly must have been turned out in great numbers as we see many of them. We've been told that those black cases are a fine Italian marble. True onyx is of the agate family.

Robson and Snow clock data

I am writing you with the hope that you will be able to give me some background on two clock makers.

First, Will Snow, bearing No. 465 on the dial, oak case, 30-hour movement, flat bonnet, square brass dial, Roman numerals, Arabic seconds, raised time ring, date dial, no chimes.

Second, movement and dial by Michael Robson, County Durham, presumably English, Scotch or Irish. Brass works, brass bands, eight-day movement, hand-painted dial with moon.

Any information you can give me regarding the above will be greatly appreciated

A.

Michael Robson: Chester-le-Street 1803 to 1812, Chester-le-Street was a small town six miles north of Durham, in County Durham.

Will Snow: Baillie lists three "William Snows." The first William Snow was at Otley about 1710 with notation "check with William Snow below." Second William Snow was at Padside in 1763. Third William Snow at Otley in 1780. Otley is nine miles northwest of Leeds, in Yorkshire. There is no further data from which to check. Though 70 years apart, it is possible that the first and third are the same man, or the third the son of the first.

The number 465 on your Snow dial has no particular meaning since we have neither a record of the method he numbered his clocks by nor any assurance that he began with number one. If the old boy was making clocks over a 70-year period, he could have easily reached No. 465. Had he made one per month, he would have reached No. 850. Evidently neither Robson or Snow did anything oustanding—at least nothing is recorded.

Ansonia models

It is a "Queen Elizabeth" made by the Ansonia Clock Co., and, according to a label on the back of the clock, was named the prize model at the Paris Exposition in 1878. The clock measures 36 inches tall in an oak case.

I have another five-foot Ansonia that I believe is called a grandmother clock.

A.

Your "Queen Elizabeth" model, Ansonia clock, was made about the turn of the century, and therefore is about 50 years old. It is listed in a 1907 Ansonia catalog as follows:

Queen Elizabeth, dark wood or oak.

Eight-day time........................list $11.00

Eight-day, half-hour gong strike 12.40

Calendar, 40 cents list additional, packed singly and strapped in package of three.

Dial eight inches—37 inches high.

About the same period, Ansonia was making and marketing a line of floor clocks which they called "Mission" and "Cottage Hall" clocks. These ranged in height from 60 inches to 72 inches. Their regular grandfather clocks ran from 93 inches to 104 inches. We suspect the 60-inch clock you refer to as a "grandmother" may be one of their "Cottage Hall" clocks.

Imperial electric clock

My problem is an Imperial electric strike clock that I took in for repair. It is electrically wound with a platform escapement. The clock is in good shape except for the coil. I have tried unsuccessfully for some time now to find a new coil or have one wound.

A.

We doubt that a coil (from stock) is available for your Imperial, jeweled escapement clock. These were made from 1929 through 1933.

A couple of years back, Mr. Fowler gave us this brief history of the Imperial: "The Imperial electric clock was originated and started by the brothers Feraud—Frank, Joseph and August. The first patent was No. 920,124, issued to Frank H. Feraud of Granite City, Illinois, May 4, 1909. It was a battery wound, weight driven clock, and an exceptionally accurate one. There are thousands of them in service today.

"These clocks were of the wall type, usually housed in large cases, and were first manufactured by the Feraud brothers at Granite City. Later the factory was moved to St. Louis, and the assets of the Sempire Clock Company were purchased and combined with those of Imperial. However, the Sempire line was discontinued.

"In order to obtain additional capital, some people in Kimswich, Missouri, were interested, and shortly thereafter, the factory was moved to that city. They operated there only a short time, as the need for more capital arose. At this time some people from St. Louis became interested in the business, and a program evolved to build a factory and a town around the factory. Accordingly the factory was built and a town founded at Imperial, Missouri, which is about 30 miles south of St. Louis.

"The town prospered, but the factory did not. (Imperial, Missouri, is in the news and on the maps.) Sometime prior to the founding of this town, the Feraud brothers sold their interest in the Imperial Clock Company. After the factory was built, and the town founded, the company was again in financial trouble, and the St. Louis backers, in order to protect their investment, moved the assets to St. Louis, and established a factory on Rutger Street, just east of Grand Avenue, in a building which I understand was leased.

"This brings the history up to the time of the first World War. For a time the manufacture of clocks was discontinued, and war orders were secured that kept the factory operating during the war. For some reason, this operation was not profitable, and after the war additional capital was needed. A man named George A. Abell invested in the company and became its manager. The company continued to be operated until 1920, when it became insolvent, and Mr. Abell was appointed trustee.

"At that time, the writer, then 26, purchased the assets of the Imperial Clock Co. and organized a new company under the laws of Illinois, moving the assets to a factory building at Collinsville, Illinois. They operated there for one year, and then in 1922 moved to Highland, Illinois, and have operated there ever since that time.

"They discontinued the manufacture of the battery operated clocks in about 1928. In the meantime, the writer invented an electrically wound clock (still a pendulum clock) prior to the time when synchronous clocks became popular and upset most of the clock factories.

"About 1929, the writer resorted to a marine escapement with 11 jewels, which was quite popular for a time. The escapements were purchased from the Tavannes Watch Company of Switzerland. Later, because of high duty, they were purchased from the Waltham Watch Company and the Illinois Watch Company. However, the synchronous motor was making greater inroads, and about 1933, they commenced to manufacture clocks with synchronous movements. The motors were purchased from the Hansen Mfg. Company of Princeton, Indiana, and the movements were fabricated entirely in their own plant under their own patents.

"Over a period of years, the writer developed and patented a strike mechanism and a Westminster chime mechanism. They began manufacturing these clocks about 1940. Orders from the War Production Board stopped clock manufacturing entirely during World War II. Immediately after the war, Mr. C. J. Hug and his son, J. C. Hug, became interested in the manufacture of the Westminster chime, and the hour and half-hour synchronous clocks were again manufactured. The name of the company was changed to C. J. Hug, Inc., but the trade name of the clock continues under the name "Imperial."

"The movements is the most simple of construction, and the smallest of its type being manufactured. This enables us to install them in small cases of exceptional design, and they are meeting with constant trade approval."

Patent list

I collect old clocks and repair them, and would like to know if you have available listing of the different patent dates, and numbers of the American Clock manufacturers of the past, as I would like to order the different drawings from the patent office.

A.

In a panel discussion, or public forum, one of the tricks of the trade employed is to say to the questioner "You have a good question there," then proceed to do a bit of hedging and shadow boxing to cover up the lack of an adequate answer.

You do have a good question, and we do not have the full answer. Actually, if we listed all the clock patents, it would probably fill several whole issues.

About 15 or 17 years ago, we started a study of the patent situation as to clocks. The original plan was to divide it into blocks of 25 or 50 years, etc., and we published a chronological list of all the clock patents issued during the first 50 years of the Patent Offices—1790 to 1840. We made a start on the next 25-year block —1840 to 1865, and to be quite frank, it isn't finished yet.

Only 66 clock patents were issued during those first 50 years. We believe that today there is much more interest along this line and we have prepared this list for you.

I have two suggestions. Write Mr. Mark F. Massey, 752 Silver Springs Avenue, Silver Springs, Md. Mr. Masey, in addition to being a good mechanic, is an enthusiastic collector, and an authority on clock patents. He probably has done more research and investigating along that particular line than anyone. Secondly, you might try your local library. There you should find index volumes by the year as issued by the government printing office. A brief study will acquaint you with the method of listing. Originally, timepieces —watches and clocks—were in section VII, but this varied over the years, as you will see.

We understand from Mr. Massey, that the first numbered patent for a clock was dated July 1, 1836, and that of the unnumbered patents, no copies are available, the Patent Office can furnish photostats at 30 cents per page on all except five:

December 22, 1814, B. E. Freymouth, alarm clock.

July 3, 1832, Wilson, alarm clock.
May 13, 1834, H. Twiss, clock.
May 13, 1834, H. Twiss, clock.
May 23, 1836, J. S. Ives, clock spring.

If any of our readers have one of these five, or know of the whereabouts of one, it would be a great favor to clock lovers and to the Patent Office if they would send them in so that photostat copies could be made to complete the record.

If you go about your patent studies in a systematic way, keep some duplicate records that you can share with us. I suspect Mr. Massey may have something to say on this.

A word of caution, and I'll close an answer that has already grown lengthy. First, don't get your hopes very high over patent copies. Second, study the patent index carefully before you order, to make sure that it is what you wish. Note the difference between "mechanical patents" and "Process patents" and "design patents."

Clock Patents Arranged Chronologically from 1790 to 1840

DATE	INVENTION	PATENTEE	RESIDENCE
1793, Jan.	30—Pendulum for clocks	Robert Leslie, Philadelphia, Pa.	
1793, Jan.	30—Pendulum, double	Robert Leslie, Philadelphia, Pa.	
1793, Jan.	30—Pendulum, double	Robert Leslie, Philadelphia, Pa.	
1797, Nov.	17—Clocks	Eli Terry, Connecticut	
1800, Mar.	8—Timepiece, silent	Simeon Jocelin, Connecticut	
1802, Feb.	8—Timepiece	Simon Willard, Massachusetts	
1803, Mar.	21—Timepiece	David F. Lanney, New York	
1806, Jan.	22—Balance pendulum	Goodwin & Gains, Baltimore, Md.	
1809, July	7—Clocks, astronomical	Thomas Newall, Sheffield, Mass.	
1809, July	7—Balance, pendulum	Samuel Goodwin	
1809, Oct.	13—Wheels, cast for clocks	Lemuel J. Kilborne, Pennsylvania	
1809, Oct.	12—Clocks, strike, parts	Lemuel J. Kilborne, Pennsylvania	
1809, June	24—Clocks, time and strike	Ira Ives, Bristol, Conn.	
1810, Jan.	15—Timekeeper, marine	Isaac Gill, Charleston, S. C.	
1812, Feb.	24—Pinions	Ira Ives, Bristol, Conn.	
1814, Aug.	22—Wooden wheels for clocks	Asa Hopkins, Litchfield, Conn.	
1814, Aug.	22—Wire pointing for clocks	Anson Sperry, Waterbury, Conn.	
1814, Aug.	22—Wheels, teeth and pinions	Curtis & Bradley, Cairo, N. Y.	
1814, Aug.	22—Plates, boring	Joel Curtis, Cairo, N. Y.	
1814, Aug.	22—Pinions	Bronson & Curtis, Cairo, N. Y.	
1814, Aug.	22—Clocks, wooden	James Harrison, Boston, Mass.	
1816, June	12—Clocks, wooden	Eli Terry, Litchfield, Conn.	
1816, July	12—Clocks	Lemuel Curtis, Concord, Mass.	
1819, Dec.	8—Clocks	Simon Willard, Boston, Mass.	
1820, Sept.	13—Clocks	James Henry, Maysville, Ky.	
1821, Oct.	25—Clocks	Buritt & Burdick, Ithaca, N. Y.	
1822, May	26—Wooden wheel clocks	Eli Terry, Plymouth, Conn.	
1822, Mar.	21—Clock cases	John Ives, Bristol, Conn.	
1825, May	18— 30-hour wooden clocks	Eli Terry, Plymouth, Conn.	
1825, Sept.	9—30-hour wooden clocks	Eli Terry, Plymouth, Conn.	
1825, May	5—Clocks, astronomical	Henry Miller, E. Hanover, Pa.	
1826, July	5— 30-hour wooden clocks	Eli Terry, Plymouth, Conn.	

1826, Mar.	4—30-hour wooden clocks	Eli Terry, Plymouth, Conn.
1826, Mar.	4—30-hour wooden clocks	Eli Terry, Plymouth, Conn.
1827, Dec.	6—Clocks	Harrison J. Dyer, New York
1829, Mar.	18—Clocks	Aaron D. Crane, Caldwell, N. J.
1829, Dec.	5—Clocks, self moving	Richard Ward, Waterbury, Conn.
1830, Oct.	1—Glass wheels for clocks	John P. Blakewell, Pittsburgh, Pa.
1830, Nov.	3—Springs, spiral, for clocks	Silas B. Terry, Plymouth, Conn.
1830, Nov.	20—Clocks	Jacob D. Custer, Norristown, Pa.
1830, Oct.	1—Clocks	Abija Gould, Henrietta, N. Y.
1830, Mar.	2—Clocks	James Bogardus, Henrietta, N. Y.
1831, June	13—Clocks, wooden	Orasmus R. Fyler, Chelsea, Vt.
1832, Nov.	27—Clocks	James S. Seger, New York
1832, May	18—Clocks, strike part	James Bogardus, New York
1832, April	7—Clocks, strike part	George Parker, Ithaca, N. Y.
1832, June	22—Clocks	Rufus Porter, Billerica, N. Y.
1833, May	22—Clocks	James S. Seger, New York
1833, April	12—Pinions, rolling	Joseph Ives, Hartford County
1833, April	12—Clocks, strike part	Joseph Ives, Hartford County
1833, Sept.	6—Escapement	Orsamus R. Fyler, Bradford, Vt.
1833, April	26—Clocks	Blydenburg & Beebe, New York
1834, May	13—Clocks and timepieces	Hiram Twiss, Meriden, Conn.
1834, May	13—Pendulum, balance	Hiram Twiss, Meriden, Conn.
1835, May	22—Clocks and timepieces	William Pardee, Albany, N. Y.
1835, Sept.	13—Clocks, air propelled	Andrew Morse, Jr., Bloomfield, Me.
1835, Dec.	30—Escapements	James Fulton, Shelby County, Ky.
1836, Feb.	20—Timepieces	William Pardie, Poughkeepsie, N. Y.
1836, May	23—Springs for clocks	James S. Ives, Bristol, Conn.
1836, July	1—Clocks	Joseph Ives, Bristol, Conn.
1838, May	4—Springs for clocks	Joseph Ives, New York City
1839, June	27—Clock, strike part	Noble Jerome, Bristol, Conn.
1840, April	30—Duplex escapement	C. Edw. Jacot, Baltimore, Md.
1840, Sept.	10—Alarm	Benjamin Knight, Statesville, R. I.
1841, Feb.	10—Clocks	Aaron D. Crane, Newark, N. J.

(Antedated: December, 1840.)

Marti clock

Can you please give me some information on the following clock? The approximate measurements of the case are 16 inches wide, nine inches high, eight inches deep. Case is made of some kind of ebony black stone, and I would guess it weighed about 50 pounds.

The following is inscribed on the back plate: on bezel—4509 EB; then 4-6, and in a circle on the plate, "Medaille de Bronze, L. Marti et Cie."

A.

Since the number 4509 appears both on your bezel and on the clock plate, we take it to be the serial number. The 4-6 is probably the pendulum's length. However, you do not indicate where and how it is located.

Generally, this figure is located on the outside of the back plate, down near the bottom. One figure is usually on the left of a pillar post and the last figure on the right. If this is true in your clock, it would indicate that the proper pendulum should be four "pouces" and six lignes long.

One "pouce" equals 28 mm. and one ligne equals 2.26 mm. Thus, four pouces or 108 mm. plus six lignes or 13.5 mm. total length, 121.5 mm.

Establishments S. Marti, at 22 Rue General Leclerc, Montbelaird, France, is in business today. It was founded in 1835 to manufacture movements for clock cases. Those movements marked "Medaille de Bronze" as yours is, were made between 1867 and 1889.

"Medal of Honor" clock Is a Japy Freres model

I am in possession of a very heavy marble clock with brass legs and trimmings, and would appreciate some information about it. There is no name on the dial and the dial seems to be also made of marble.

In the back, when I unscrewed the bell, there was a little stamp that I have reproduced as closely as possible for you. The numbers on the bottom of the movement are 1397 and 64. The first four are close together and the second two are separate. On the outside ring where there is a glass covering the rear as well as the front of the movement, is the number H 1397.

A.

"Establissements Japy Freres" celebrated their two-hundredth anniversary back in 1949, being established in 1749.

The trade-mark you sketch merely indicated that movement of this type won a "Medal of Honor" in the year 1855. No doubt it was used upon back plates of similar movements over a period of years as that was the custom.

A good guess would be that your clock was made in the late 1870's or 1880's.

You do not show a sketch of the back plate and the location of the numbering indicated. There should be, right at the bottom of the back plate, numbers upon both sides of the pillar-post coming through the center. That number upon the left side is "pouces" and that number upon the right side is "lignes."

One pouce equals 27 mm. and 1 ligne equals 2.26 mm. Example: upon the left of the pillar-post 8, and on the right 4. Eight pouces would be 16 mm. and 4 lignes would be 8.92 mm. or for all practical purposes 9 mm. Added to the 216 giving a total of 225 mm. Just about 9 inches. We have found that this rule generally works out for a practical beginning; further, that this measurement means from the hook at the top of the rod (not to include the suspension spring) to the reg. nut which in most French balls is in the center of the ball.

Notes on Noah Pomeroy

This is a calendar clock made by N. Pomeroy. Under the maker's name is "Bristol C.T." and the date, July 18, 1869.

Any information you can give me about this clock will be greatly appreciated.

A.

Noah Pomeroy was active in Bristol, Conn., producing both eight-day and 30-hour clocks from about 1847 to 1878 when he sold his business to Hiram C. Thompson.

He was in Pomeroy & Robins, 1847. Organized Noah Pomeroy & Co., about 1849, then it was Pomeroy & Parker from 1853 to 1857. He was successful under his own name from 1857 to 1878.

He is mentioned by only one line in Chauncey Jerome's "American Clock Business For the Past Sixty Years" (1860), page 105, i.e. "Noah Pomeroy of Bristol, is also engaged in making pendulum movements for other parties."

It is unusual for an early Connecticut clock to be dated . . . was the July 18, 1869, written in the label? If printed, did it represent a patent date? At any rate it is probably accurate enough to take for date of its manufacture . . . certainly not after 1878.

How old is this Seth Thomas?

A customer brought in a Seth Thomas clock for repair and would like to know how old the piece is. It is a very small 24-hour with winding arbor at 3 o'clock. The case measures nine inches high by seven inches wide.

I was much surprised when repairing to find it has a brass mainspring. Were many of this type of spring used? It doesn't seem very practical although it is still serving its purpose well enough.

A.

It is a bit difficult to pinpoint dates for brass clock spring production.

Elisha C. Brewster of Bristol, Conn., was the developer of the brass clock spring.

Such springs are found in his clocks and later in Brewster & Ingrahams clocks.

E. C. Brewster (1791-1880) traveled through the south as a "Yankee Clock Peddler" for Thomas Barnes, Jr. & Co. About 1833 he bought the Charles Kirke clock factory which was operated until about 1855. Palmer dates Brewster & Ingrahams, 1844 to 1852.

In 1946 Mr. Fuller F. Barnes wrote: "Ten Generations of the Barnes Family," which volume is probably the most authentic record of spring making existing. Quoting from page 138, "Brewster's development of the brass clock spring took a stride forward when on May 23, 1836, his foreman, Joseph A. Ives, took out a patent on a brass spring. He sold this patent to Mr. Brewster. Brass springs produced under this patent were made for many years, possibly as late as 1862."

On May 4, 1838, Joseph Ives took out a patent on steel springs. That steel springs gradually supplanted the brass is evident but it is hard to arrive at any practical idea of the proportion of brass to steel for the various years of their overlapping period. For "round" figures, we might move Mr. Brewster's date of entering business back from 1833 to 1830, and likewise move Mr. Fuller Barnes' 1862 end date back to 1860, then take 1830 to 1860 as the "brass spring" period.

Elisha Manross (1792-1856) was quite a user of brass springs, and we encounter brass springs occasionally in other makes. No doubt the Brewster establishment supplied brass springs to other clockmakers, including Seth Thomas (your clock).

Another quote from Mr. Barnes: "They (referring to E. C. Brewster, Joseph S. Ives and Col. E. L. Dunbar) had to discover the method of tempering clock springs made of brass. Stranger still, after a hundred years we today do not know the method they used to put sufficient temper into brass to make a coiled mainspring. It was not an easy process, as the brilliant Terry family of Plymouth discovered. They experimented in this line but their brass springs had a tendency to granulate and break. On the other hand, brass clock springs produced by Brewster & Ingrahams were warranted not to fail."

You say that the spring in question is "serving its purpose well enough over the years." . . . I've met with a number of brass springs and can't recall ever having seen a broken one.

Do you sense a similarity between brass clock springs and the "non-break" watch mainspring of today? It's quite possible that we had "non-break" springs in clocks before they did in watches, isn't it?

Facts about Frodsham

The chronometer in question is the conventional type — gimbal mounted, brass bound box, etc., retired from sea duty and although apparently rather old and a little scarred from use, it still maintains a small and beautiful rate. The dial is silvered, with black Roman numerals, and inscriptions bearing the maker's name, address and the number of the instrument as follows:

CHARLES FRODSHAM
7th Pavement   Finsbury Squ
LONDON   No. 1754
With the exception of the number, the information above is repeated on the ivory plate on the outside of the box.

A.

From Britten's we learn that Charles Frodsham was the son, and also the apprentice, of William James Frodsham. That Charles was born 1810, died 1871. His mother, Alice Harrison Frodsham, was the granddaughter of the famous chronometer maker, John Harrison.

A skillful and successful watchmaker, 7 Finsbury Pavement, 1842, he afterwards succeeded John R. Arnold at 84 Strand. He wrote many papers on technical subjects; served as vice president of the (British) Horological Institute; was admitted to Clockmakers Company, 1845; master, 1855-1862.

Mr. Frodsham devised a code for dating his watches using his name. Evidently this marking was used after he moved to the Arnold shop at 84 Strand, and we are not sure whether it was used on chronometers or not. Major Chamberlain had four chronometers marked "J. R. Arnold-Chas. Frodsham" ranging from No. 7265 to No.

12373, which he referred to as "Frodsham's earlier piece." After dropping the Arnold name Mr. Frodsham prefixed a zero to his chronometer numbering.

This fits in with your No. 1754 with the 7 Finsbury Pavement address, i.e., a number below those used after taking over Arnold.

A typical "Dutch Hood" clock

I would be pleased if you could examine at your convenience, the enclosed photographs of an antique one-day strike clock which runs with one weight.

This clock is in first-class working order and my customer is anxious to learn as much about it as possible.

A.

Your photos show a typical "Dutch Hood" or "Friesland" clock.

Britten says, "Friesland clocks which did not appear until the early 18th century, were probably in origin only a cheaper form of Zaandam clock. The movement is of lantern form with iron plates at top and bottom connected by boldly turned corner posts. As with the Zaandam clocks, the wheels are pivoted in three parallel brass plates. Friesland clocks are never signed and practically never dated."

The arrangement whereby "one" weight drives two separate trains is known as the "Huygens Fall" for its originator, the celebrated Dutch horologist Christian Huygens, B-1629, D-1695.

This type of clock with but slight variations was made throughout the whole of the 19th century. The main points that mark them are: the typical painted dial, the break arch hood, the hollow wall case containing the pendulum, the brass canister weights, etc. An odd thing about them is that most beat 66 or 72 times per minute.

This is a "turn-of-the-century" Waterbury clock

Recently I overhauled a clock and the customer would like a little history on it. I thought of you right away—if anyone can tell me I know you can.

This clock stands about 6 feet high; it has 2x2's at each corner, and it is all open except for the movement, which is all enclosed. The face and hands are all open.

There is no number but the name "Waterbury Clock Co., Waterbury, Conn.," is stamped on it. The clock has two weights, each about five pounds. The pendulum is 36 inches long. The weights are on a ladder type brass chain, and both weights and pendulum are exposed to the open.

The gong is the spring type and is hit by one hammer, which strikes the hour and the half-hour. The count wheel is loose on its pivots and is turned by a pin of the next wheel. This movement is similar to the Gilbert clock movement.

A.

The type clock you describe was being manufactured around the turn of the Century and in the early 1900's.

This clock (or one matching your description) is listed upon page 88 of their 1902 catalog. This clock came with plain, square, dial at $68. Its height was 88 inches; width, 22¼ inches. With arched dial containing moon-phase the price was $88.

Manufacture of this type movement ceased somewhere around World War I. None is listed in the No. 175 Waterbury catalog for 1923. I distinctly recall that movements of that type were available in 1920-21; whether they were produced in those years or were carried over from pre-war production stock, we cannot determine.

Many generations of Websters were clockmakers in England

I thought you might be able to give me some information on a very interesting clock I have been working on. The clock belongs to one of our good doctors here.

The doctor would like to know when this clock was made. It is a mantel clock 21 inches tall, wood case, with glass on four sides. Very well engraved on the back of the movement is the name "Wm. Webster, Exchange Alley, London" and on the bottom of the dial appears the name "Webster-London." The movement is chain driven with the springs in a barrel (strikes the hour only) with the escape wheel on the top of the plate, and the verge engages the wheel on either side. The owner was told that the clock was made in 1765, but I would like to find out for sure, if possible.

The clock is in good running condition as I have cleaned it and made a small repair on one of the spring barrels.

A.

We find three "William Websters" listed. The first William Webster was free of the Clockmakers Company in 1710, i.e., upon his own; he was a Warden of C. C. and died in office in 1734. His place of business is given as "Exchange Alley," no number.

There is some question about his apprenticeship. From the books of C. C., he seems to have been apprenticed to one John Barnett. In Baillie's list, it says: "apprenticed to, and journeyman with, Thomas Tompion."

In the volume "Thomas Tompion, His Life & Work" it says that: "William Webster, who had at one time been Tompion's apprentice and journeyman, inserted a similar advertisement in several of the newspapers." The ad referred to, ran in the ENGLISHMAN, Nov. 21-24, 1713; MERCATOR OF COMMERCE REVIEWED, Nov. 21-24, 1713; in the POST BOY on the same dates; and, in the LONDON GAZETTE, Nov. 24-26, 1713. That advertisement read: "On the 20th instant Mr. Tompion noted for making all sorts of the best clocks and watches, departed this life. This is to certify all persons whatever quality or distinction, that William Webster, at the 'Dyal and Three Crowns' in Exchange Alley, London, served his apprenticeship and lived as a journeyman a considerable time with the said Mr. Tompion, and by his industry and care is fully aquainted with the secrets of the said art."

His son, William Webster, is listed as being at No. 26 Change Alley; was apprenticed in 1727, master of C. C., 1755, Livery 1766, and is referred to as an eminent maker of bracket clocks.

The third William Webster was a son of and apprenticed to William Webster. Apprenticed 1756, free of C. C., 1763, his address is simply London. Since all the lists give both the "Exchange Alley" and "Change Alley" addresses, one must conclude that they are not one and the same. And, since your clock says "Exchange Alley," it looks as if we'll have to give it to the first William. Many generations of Websters are listed as early as 1675. Taking the Webster list as a whole, one notes a number of women—there was a Sarah, 1688, Anne and Mary, sisters of George, 1698, and a Margaret about 1711.

Who was Thomas F. Cooper?

A customer has asked me about on old watch he owns, and I would appreciate any information you can give about it for him. It is a hunting model, approximately 18 size, key wind and set, with this inscription inside "Straight Line Cooper, Full Jeweled, Hands . . . No. 24070, Thomas F. Cooper, London." Centering the inscription is an "X" inscribed in a square, and both inside a circle. The watch has a lever escapement and is in running condition.

A.

Thomas Frederick Cooper was a watchmaker of repute, active in London about 1820-1840. He is recorded as being a supplier to the American market. We have no data upon his serial numbering system and thus cannot pinpoint the year from the serial number you give.

No doubt you have already noted that

this watch has its escape arbor, lever arbor and balance staff in a straight line and/or have seen English watches wherein the escape wheel is set to one side with the pallets parallel with the lever rather than right-angled to it. Mr. Cooper was calling attention to his type construction by calling it "straight line Cooper."

Chime is nest of bells, set horizontally

I have taken in an old English fusee chime clock and am curious to know something of its age and history. The movement plates are 7½x8 inches, and the time, strike, and chime are each run by a separate fusee. The chime consists of a nest of eight bells set horizontally, one inside the other, on top of the clock movement. What appears to be the original dial, 12 inches in diameter, is attached to the front plate with the usual four legs pinned in the back. This dial has been drilled and four legs of a 14-inch dial pinned to it. There are no marks or name of any kind on the movement or on the 12-inch dial.

On the 14-inch dial under the 12 is the name "Roskell, 1661." Under the keyhole is the word "Liverpool."

My customer, the owner of the clock, thinks that the number "1661" on the dial is the date when the clock was made. This, I doubt very much. Do you know anything about such a clock and is it uncommon? Any information will be greatly appreciated.

A.

Since there is a fair number of English fusee, cup-bell chime clocks of the type you describe around, I would not say it is uncommon or rare. They date, roughly, around 1800—give or take a few years.

About this same period, Liverpool was a great export center for all types of timepieces. Many dealers bought pieces wherever they could obtain them; some were sold "nameless" and others carried the dealer's name, etc. During this same period, the Roskell family was very active —over here we see many more "Roskell"

watches than clocks.

Robert Roskell was active from about 1798 to 1830 and used both a London and a Liverpool address. Baillie says he was in the firm of "O'Neil & Roskell, Liverpool" prior to 1798.

John Roskell is listed as a watchmaker at Liverpool, 1805-1821. Robert & John Roskell were in a partnership at Liverpool, 1805-1821. Robert & Son, was an active firm at the same date, and Nicholas Roskell is listed as a watchmaker in 1825.

That completes the entire "Roskell" listing, save for Robert's London connection and/or address, all of it was in Liverpool and covering the same period. It is quite possible that one of them either made or sold this clock, and having need for a larger dial than the clock already had, just put his own over the old one as you say. Upon the other hand, it is just as likely the clock was made and sold by others, the Roskell dial having been applied later by some repairman, etc.

Of one thing you can be sure: the "1661" does not denote the year in which the clock was made. Clocks of this type were not made that early—the number must be either Roskell's model number or serial number.

AMERICAN WATCH CO.

I have an old 18-S American Watch Co., watch with the serial "157414." Can you tell me when the movement was manufactured? I presume it was a product of the American Waltham factory.

A.

It was the American Watch Co., from February, 1859-1885. They absorbed the Nashua Watch Co., in April of 1862. The factory was rebuilt and enlarged 1878-1883. It became the American Waltham Watch Co., in 1885, then in 1906 the Waltham Watch Co.

According to a listing put out by Waltham in 1954, serial numbers 150501 to 158800 were an 18-S, model 57, 11-jewel, three-quarter plate with steel escape wheel marked both "P. S. Bartlett," and "Wm.

160

Ellery," and used "A" type material.

Approximating your watch's age from the serial number is far from definite as per the above mentioned listing, Waltham started with 1,000,000 in 1870. Another listing places Waltham at 2900 in 1858. If you roughly apportion it, 16 years were required to reach the 1 million mark; allowing for the slow beginning you could call your 150,000 the same as one-fourth of that 16-year production, or place it around 1861 (1857 plus 4).

Amsterdam movement proves complicated

I have in my possession an old pocket watch which I inherited from an old clock-maker friend in Amsterdam, Holland. He acquired this movement, minus the case, about 68 years ago.

Never having seen a duplication of such a movement (and I have handled many old watches) I wish to know if this movement is valuable. Of the hundreds of old movements that I have repaired and sold, I have never found one so complicated as this one.

From the following description, I hope you can inform me as to the date of manufacture, etc.:

Plates are made to swing and set in a one-piece case with removable bezel. Plates and wheels are of brass. The levers, springs and cannon are steel. The movement is chain-driven with mainspring in barrel. The dial is white porcelain (perfect) with black Roman numerals as well as with 5 to 60 for minutes. The movement was manufactured by Joseph Martineau, A.S., London 1476 (on back plate) cover of alarms. The watch has two alarms; the hammers are controlled by an independent 12-tooth semi-circular gear and the other by a double 3-tooth gear. It has two hammers. The number 1476 is imprinted on all parts for assembly. Inscribed in bell housing is "B. Ples, Jr., 60 1/29." The movement is in perfect condition, but requires a chain.

A.

Joseph Martineau is listed in London, 1744-1794, first at Orange Street, and later

St. Martins Court. Major Chamberlain says: "There was another Joseph Martineau, 1850-1870."

Baillie's list, from which the first reference was taken, indicates that Martineau was a maker of repeater watches, and lists examples as being in the Metropolitan Museum in New York City and the Museum of Dresden. Also other examples of his watches were in the Ilbert and Chamberlain collections.

The latter reference was to the first Chamberlain collection. This column reported that collection stolen from Michigan State University (East Lansing) the week end of June 29-30, later recovered. The catalog of that collection lists No. 93 as a verge in silver pair case; Martineau, probably 1760. Perhaps a letter to the Metropolitan would bring you a description of their watch for comparison with yours.

I am inclined to feel you may be a bit confused when calling your piece an "alarm" watch, and rather think it is a "repeater" because the 12-tooth semi-circular gear must be for striking the hours. And, the 3-tooth one for the quarters; also, the two hammers indicate a repeater.

Thwaites is a familiar name since 1740

We have in our shop for repair, a very interesting old clock. It is a verge escapement, and on the back plate (5 inches wide — 7 inches deep), it has "John Thwaites, Londres, No. 3020" in an oval shield, and is a fuzee.

On the front plate there is also the name "Thwaites" and at bottom of this plate, "020." Would you be kind enough, please, to give us any information that you can?

A.

Thwaites is a familiar name in English clockmaking, extending over a good many years. We believe the present firm of Thwaites & Reed, Ltd., now of 15 Bowling Green Lane, London E. C. 1, was established about 1740.

Ainsworth Thwaites, London, started

clockmaking about 1735. His son, Benjamin, started about 1762, and another son, John (maker of your clock) about 1772. John was active to about 1820—he made the clock for St. Paul's Chapel, New York.

We have no data upon John Thwaites system of serial numbering and therefore cannot pinpoint the year your No. 3020 was made.

Information on handmade Ansonia

We would like to have some information, if possible, on this clock

The owner gives this following information: Ansonia Clock Company had it handmade for World's Fair in 1893. It is 10 feet, 11 inches tall and about 30 inches wide; mercury pendulum, hand carved case with gold inlay.

A.

Beyond those facts you have already set down in your letter, there is not much we can tell you about this Ansonia clock. As you probably know, Ansonia practically ceased production during World War I; there was a slight revival which lasted to about 1922 when manufacturing ceased completely. About 1930 the machinery was sold to the Russian government and shipped over there.

Even if the factory was in operation today, I doubt that any record could be found upon this clock. It was a custom of many manufacturers to have a special display-piece made up for big expositions. The chances are that Ansonia may have constructed the case in their own plant since they were at that time building and selling grandfather clocks. On the other hand, the plant was not regularly producing precision astronomical regulators and it would seem reasonable that it would have been more economical to farm out the movement to some specialist rather than engineer and construct it themselves in their factory. Check the lower edge of the front plate for name or marks; these "specialist contractors" often so marked their pieces.

Ansonia's exhibit at the World's Columbian Exposition, Chicago, 1893, must have been a "bang." I recall seeing a photo of that exhibit in one of the books devoted to the exhibition many years ago. I checked one of our local libraries to see if I could locate something . . . no luck. Supposedly there was a complete history of the World's Columbian Exposition, edited by Russell Johnson and published in four volumes in 1897. It was duly catalogued, but when we went to look for it, volumes 2, 3 and 4 were missing. Vol. 1 was devoted to the preliminary planning, financing and erection of the buildings thus none of the exhibits were shown or illustrated.

Check with your local library, here is hoping you'll have better luck than I did today. There is another large library here but it is several miles across town; at the first opportunity I shall check there and if something can be located I shall write you the details.

Large and expensive clocks like this do not usually change hands very often, and when they do there is usually some record or passing of pertinent facts. Individual history upon a special piece can sometimes be traced back up the line through successive owners.

Some facts on a Waterbury Regulator, No. 70

We have a Waterbury clock, Model Regulator No. 70, oak case stands 6 ft., 10 in., base to top and is designed to either stand on floor or hang on wall. The clock is 20 inches wide, 8 inches deep, with 12-inch, white enamel dial with 1½-inch rim.

The clock is weight - powered and cable wound; 8-days run. It has mercury compensated pendulum with nearly a quart of mercury in two glass tubes. Each arc of the pendulum swing, one way, constitutes one second. This is a regular clock with very fine pendulum adjustment and does keep very good time. It has no striking or chime mechanism.

We would like to know the approximate age, the original price,

A.

"Regulator No. 70" we've located in Waterbury's catalog for 1902. It is described thus:

"Regulator No. 70, 8-day, weight time, brass weight. Finely finished movement of best quality encased in iron box, deadbeat escapement, sweep second, retaining power; 12-in. porcelain dial; height 82 in., width 26 in., with compensating mercurial pendulum, oak—$135.50, mahogany—$143.50.

It is practically impossible to pinpoint the very year of manufacture, and, for general purposes, one can assume that models might have a 10-year run, so let's place yours 1895-1905. Perhaps you note that the catalog width is 26½ inches while you give 20 inches — cases were made up in lots and varied slightly, again, precise case width measurement depends u p o n where you take it. I believe the catalog used the very widest, perhaps taken from the mold-trimming.

GILBERT CLOCK HISTORY

We have for overhaul an old brass-movement clock, 30-hour model. Repair markings show "1812 - $1.00" and "December, 1818." The manufacturer's printed instructions are still in good condition, and show that the clock was made by the Gilbert Manufacturing Company, Winsted, Connecticut, manufacturers of spring-wound 30-hour and 8-day brass clocks.

Can you please tell us during what period this company was in existence, and approximately when this clock might have been made?

A.

In a great many instances, markings that appear to be those of a repairman cannot be trusted—based upon my own experience, I'd say less than 50 per cent, and I'd like to compare notes on this point with other experienced repairmen.

William Lewis Gilbert was just six years old in 1812. He was born in the year 1806. We find him first in the clock business, after having taught school, at the age of 22, when the firm of Gilbert, Marsh & Company was formed. George Marsh was his brother-in-law.

Gilbert was with John Birge in the firm of Birge, Gilbert & Company at Bristol from 1835 to 1837, then in the firm of Jerome, Gilbert, Grant & Company in 1839 and 1840. He moved to Winsted, Connecticut, in 1841, where with Ezra Baldwin and Lucius Clarke, he organized Clarke, Gilbert & Company. This firm became the Wm. L. Gilbert Company about 1850. In 1866 it was changed to the Gilbert Manufacturing Company, and in 1871, to the William L. Gilbert Clock Company. This name was retained up to 1934 when it became the William L. Gilbert Corporation.

From this, we must conclude that your clock, made by the Gilbert Manufacturing Company, was made between 1866 and 1871.

S.T. RAILROAD CLOCK

I have recently acquired a very old Seth Thomas clock. In trying to trace its history your name was suggested to me. This clock was in a Pennsylvania Railroad station here in Foxburg for at least 10 years. The number on the works of the clock is 77B. It is a weight clock and still keeps perfect time. There is a number on the dial which I believe to be a number for identification for the railroad. However I'll give it to you just in case it may mean something to you. It is 5445 in large black letters.

I'd like very much to know the age of this clock.

A.

According to old Seth Thomas catalogues, I'd say the No. 77-B movement came out in 1917 as it is first listed in catalogue No. 735, for 1917-1918.

Catalogue No. 707, for 1915-1916 does not list the 77-B movement at all.

Railroads used a great number of Seth Thomas, 80-beat regulators; in most instances they were serviced at a central point and it was about as much the rule as the exception for movements to be switched about, thus, your case could easily have seen service in the Foxburg station for years before 1917.

No. 77-B movement is illustrated, exact size, page 36, Catalogue No. 735, and described thus: "New Keystone s h a p e movement. Heavy polished plates. Graham dead-beat escapement. Maintaining power. Grooved barrel with a new special click, which makes it easy to unwind cord from the barrel without injury to click spring. The dial wheels are outside the plates, making a more perfect bearing for the center post than in the old pattern. Fitted in regulators Nos. 1, 2, and 4, on page 37. Iron bracket with suspension spring fastened to same. Movement is secured to bracket with four long screws between the plates so it can be removed easily and the screws cannot be lost or mislaid. A very strong and durable movement."

I recall well the No. 77 movement. It fitted onto the iron frame that was secured to the back of the case over posts and was held to the frame with pins. Its plates were rectangular, not keystone shape and the hour pipe pivoted in the front plate just as the common eight-day mantel clock—gave some trouble by the looseness of the doubled bearing.

163

ENGLISH TALL CLOCK

I have a problem child for you. It is a tall clock of the standard garden variety, probably English. The dial is 12x12 with an arch, all painted, with a scene of a hunter, two dogs and a pheasant in the arch part, at each corner of the dial proper is a group of wild flowers with the predominate colors blue and brown. I am telling you all this because it looks old enough to be original. It has a second hand and a calendar disc showing thru the dial below the center (seconds hand is above the center). The winding arbors are two and one half inches on center and one half inch below the hand center.

On the back of the dial and cast in before painting the name W''kes with the word BIRM under it. The bottoms of the second and third letters are missing and it looks as though from a broken die rather than wear on the parts bearing the print. I am printing this on a separate sheet and sending rubbings. It appears the same way on the back of the dial, on the calendar wheel. On the square plate which connects to the movement by three pinnd feet the initial S. thus appears before the W''KES but in this case the hole for the foot is drilled through the missing letters.

There is nothing on any other part of the clock case or movement to identify it. It is an hour strike only, no ½. rack and snail, Pend. is sec. beat, wire with a brass front 4 inch lead bob. Sec. hand is an extension of the esc. wheel arbor.

A.

The stamping you see upon the back of your dial, and, on the sub-frame is that of the "supplier" of those parts. We believe it to be: "S. Wilkes, Birmingham."

The movement you describe is typical English of the late 1700's and early 1800's.

Birmingham was, as you know, quite an iron manufacturing center. Naturally there grew up there some firms who made a business of casting dial blanks and sub-frames to furnish to the clockmaking trade, along with this went some dial painting. Many clockmakers purchased these parts from Birmingham. We see a number of "stamps" like the one you describe; perhaps the names most often seen over here are Wilson, or Osborne. Sometimes "Wilson & Osborne". They were first mentioned as partners in the Birmingham Gazette for Sept. 28th, 1772. The partnership was dissolved in 1777 after which both continued to make dials and sub-frames independently. Osborne died in 1780 and his wife and son carried the business forward until 1815. Wilson continued to produce until his death April

3rd, 1809. While we do not have detailed history upon "S. Wilkes" I feel sure that his was a similar operation; that the maker of your clock bought the dial and frame from Wilkes. Your own examination shows that Wilkes stamped the sub-frame with his stamp, then, when it got to the hands of the maker of the movement he found it necessary to locate a dial foot right where it was stamped.

Patti Mainspring

I have run into a clock with two springs coiled side by side on the arbor. They are separated by a flat disk, all enclosed in a sort of going barrel. What is the purpose of the two springs, and how are they held together? I have been afraid to tear down the going train for fear of more trouble. Have tried by myself several times.

A.

This spring arrangement is known to the trade as the "Patti" because it was used in the famous "Patti" model parlor clock, manufactured by Welch Spring & Co., Forestville, Conn., 1868 to 1884. (Elisha N. Welch, b.-Feb. 7th, 1908 d.- Aug. 2nd, 1887, and, Solomon Crosby Spring, b.-1826 d.-1906).

It was named for the famous 19th century beauty and operatic singer, Mme. Adelina Patti, and first appeared in the Welch-Spring catalog, page 49, for 1880. (If you have, or have access to a file of A. H. & J. the Patti clock was written up with photos in "C. & O." for May 1948).

This unusual application of double mainspring was patented by Benjamin B. Lewis, (b.-Oct. 30th, 1818 d.-May 5th, 1890,) No. 249,845 issued July 31, 1879. Mr. Lewis is far better known to the clock trade for his many patents on calendar mechanisms for clocks.

All too little is known about either Mr. Welch, or Mr. Lewis. Our Early American clockmakers spent almost none of their time keeping detailed journals or writing for future clockmakers — very often we must deduce vital facts solely from their clocks. I quote from Mr. Lewis' obituary, published in one of the local papers, May 8th, 1890: "Mr. Lewis was a very intellectual man, and always a great reader, being especially fond of poetry. . . . In appearance Mr. Lewis was quite distinguished looking having a noticeable wide and high forehead plainly showing his remarkable powers of thought." End quote.

In this particular instance, deductions can be a bit easier because Welch (and Lewis) were the only ones to use this double spring as well as the only clockmakers to use an escapement with all or a good portion of the "lift" across the face of the escape tooth. We must remember that the "clock" was practically handed to the Connecticut makers complete and "full blown" from both England and the continent, but, he was no less knowledgeable about its errors and problems. He well knew that the clock's train was mathematically accurate; that errors in timekeeping lay solely in the pendulum, and, that by building little shelf clocks with very short pendulums he could not reduce those errors by having the pendulum stroke a lesser number of times. Thus a reasonable deduction is: he (the clockmaker) endeavored to solve that problem by driving his short pendulum with more "even" power. This is definitely what Mr. Lewis endeavored to do with his double spring.

Perhaps you have noted that your "Patti" springs are 5/16ths in. wide by .013 thick, by 72 inches long; giving you the equivalent of a spring 12 feet long. With 12 feet of driving spring at his disposal, designer Lewis was able to build a train with a much lower gear ratio simply because he could revolve the main wheel so many more times.

It is noted that you call it a going barrel — in its ultimate action it is, as the winding arbor remains still but the barrel portion is not attached to the main wheel, I believe this is generally known as a "floating barrel." You need not be afraid to take the springs out; they are relatively easy to reassemble. The main-wheel floats and rides free on the front half of the winding arbor. The two springs coil in opposite directions, their outside ends coupled together by a brass clip. The brass disc placed between the two springs has a slot cut into its side to enable this clip to move in and out as the spring is wound and unwinds. The hub on the main-wheel has a hook like any winding arbor and hooks into the inner end of the front

spring. The back half of the winding arbor also has a hook catching the inner end of the back spring; thus, when the winding arbor is turned, it winds the back spring. It (the back spring) in turn winds the front spring by its outside end pulling the outside end of the front spring and just as with a going barrel the spring is pulling the main-wheel forward all during the wind operation.

What ever was B. B. Lewis' reasoning, or, how he arrived at such a spring arrangement, the chances are we shall never know. That his conclusions and resultant spring are perfectly sound is attested by the fact modern engineers agree with it 100%.

In an article on mainsprings, by Sir James Swinburne, in the British Horological Journal for January 1950, he described the "Patti" spring to a-"T", referring to a book by Dr. J. A. Van den Broek, titled "Elastic Energy Theory" (John Wiley & Sons, Inc. 1931). I later got a paper titled "Spiral Springs, A New Theory Regarding Their Stress, Strain, and Energy Function" delivered by Dr. Van den Broek, before a meeting of The American Society of Mechanical Engineers, and, learned that he was Professor of Engineering Mechanics at the University of Michigan. I wrote him about the Lewis patent and the Welch-Spring application. He was surprised to learn that his theory (independently arrived at) had already been applied commercially, etc.

This incident is merely another one pointing up the need for thoroughly documenting all the activities of our early clockmakers; to this writer it is no mystery that Dr. Van den Broek was not aware of the Lewis spring. Scientists, engineers, etc., going into our libraries to do research, can only make use of what is there. If it has not been committed to paper, how can it be there?

That no other maker used this spring was probably due to Lewis' patent; Welch-Spring did use it in one or two other models which were not sold in great numbers like the "Patti." Its use was extensive enough for it to be catalogued in the material catalogues of that era; it is illustrated in the 1899 Purdy material catalog, page

581: "No. 45 Patti clock springs, pair 30c, doz. pair $3.50."

We like to think of Lewis' long spring (double) drive as another substantial piece of direct evidence; pointing up the fact that the early American clockmaker was a better trained horologist, well grounded in basic mechanical principals, than he is usually given credit for.

Back in the year 1835, Judge Thomas Chandler Haliburton published a series of articles in the Nova Scotian, titled "The Clockmaker" or "The Sayings and Doings of Sam Slick of Slickville." Judge Haliburton is credited by no lesser an authority than Artemus Ward as the founder of the American School of humor. Be that as it may, in so doing, he hung the "Sam Slick" image about the neck of the American clockmaker in the era when American clockmaking was in the transition period of going from wood movements to all brass, and there it remains to this good day.

If my memory serves accurately; Sam practiced the art of clockmaking by virtue of his knowledge "of saft sodder and human natre." In line with accurate reporting, I might add that we at the repair bench today often see evidence that the Sam Slick's of the 1960's operate upon the "saft sodder" principle.

By and large, the Early American clockmaker was a serious mechanic; he was pretty well versed upon mechanical principles as well as being well grounded in horological theory. It is quite true he can't claim such "break-through" inventions as the lever escapement; jewels, dead-beat escapement, etc. One of the great things he gave to the horological world was mass production. Farm folk and people in the lower income brackets in America could own practical timekeepers long before their counterparts in other nations could. It is paradoxical that this fact should seemingly enhance the "Sam Slick" money-grubbing, flim-flam image rather than accord to him the credit due to a mnaufacturer trying to give the consumer a better product, at a better price.

FRENCH PROVINCIAL

Am sending the enclosed photos in hopes you may be able to identify the clock and give us some idea when and where it was made. Have tried to show the detail of escapement and strike rods.

A.
The clock you show by your excellent photos is the type generally called "French Provincial" over here. In France, I believe they are called 'Comtoise' clocks— my French is poor and this apparently is a tricky word—perhaps a fair translation would be country clocks. Roughly, their production spans the first 2/3rds., of the 1800's.

Many of them — perhaps upwards of 50% we see are unmarked as is yours; those that are marked are quite difficult to pin-point because the name is either that of a small clockmaker, or, the merchant-seller. This was occasioned by: 1. 'brand' or names carried very little weight; especially if it was unknown. 2. it was generally a 'contract' operation, i.e. the clockmaker (or merchant) bought the movement from some of the factories in the mountains of French Jurs.

All follow pretty closely the same mechanical pattern; they have the. vertical-drop strike-rack and repeat the stroke in about a minute. The time-train being located on the IX side, under one strip-plate. The strike-train on the III side under its strip-plate. The motion-train in the center with it's own strip-plate. The off center verge being connected to the center hung pendulum via a pitman-rod.

They came in two styles; grandfather (or floor) clocks, weight driven, and, wall clocks spring driven. In most wall models, the movements are slightly smaller; quite a bit thinner but still identical in construction even to the decoration upon the counterbalance of the strike lift piece. Main-spring are in barrels. There are a good many of them in circulation; most collectors have one or two, practically all clock museums have examples, Clock Manor has three wall models and four floor models. I happen to have one of each, in the little granddaughter's collection.

Jerome Clock Company Began In 1838

Could you give me any information on a Jerome clock (New Haven), 30 hour weight movement, brass, iron weights, brass cable, hour strike only, 25-¾ inches high case, long pendulum rod, crankwind. I got this clock from Minneapolis, Minn. for repairs. This clock is as good as a new one. I think it is about 120 or 125 years old.

A.

This type of clock is plentiful in the East and South of the U.S. Jerome is credited with originating it. Jerome conceived the idea for a 30-hour, brass clock in the fall of 1837, at Richmond, Va. Upon returning to Bristol, he went over this "new" idea with his brother Noble, and they went into production that year— 1838.

Up to the great depression of 1837, the principal clock production was wood movements—some brass clocks were made, but it seems they were always 8-day. It seems rather odd that no one thought of producing a one-day brass clock before.

In his book "American Clock Making for the Past Sixty Years" (1860, Roberts Book Company has re-print #B-570, $4.95 plus 15c post), he says: "What I originated that night on my bed in Richmond has given work to thousands of men yearly for more than twenty years, built up the largest manufactories in New England, and put more than a million dollars in the pockets of the brass makers."

Your clock has the "New Haven" label. In the winter of 1844 Jerome opened a new plant in New Haven for making his clock cases. In April of 1845 one of his Bristol movement factories burned down and the greater portion of his movement manufacturing was transferred to New Haven, about June. According to the Palmer list, the Jerome Clock Co. of New Haven would date from about 1845 to 1855.

"Rack and Pinion" Was Invented in 1722

My hobby is collecting antique key-winding watches. I recently purchased one with which I am unfamiliar, and I would appreciate any information you could give me concerning the period it was made, the reputation of the maker, etc.

The watch is a fusee type. The case is 18K gold and is marked T. H. 15298. The face is very ornate applied gold. The hands are set with the key. The watchmaker's name, which is engraved on the movement, is either Sutherland Davies or Litherland Davies. I cannot be sure whether it is an L or S in the first name because it is engraved over a jewel. "Patent 15298" and "Liverpool" are also engraved on the movement. The movement is hinged and swings out of the case.

A.

"Litherland, Davies & Co., Liverpool" was active from 1818 to 1837. This dates your watch.

Under the firm names: "Peter Litherland," 1790-1814, "Litherland, Whitesides & Co.," 1800-1816, and "Litherland, Davies & Co.," 1818-1837, a great number of "rack-lever" watches were made, and many of them found their way to America.

Peter Litherland, of Liverpool, was granted patent No. 1830 for a rack-lever escapement, October 14th, 1791. And, patent No. 1889 was granted him the following year for a rack-lever that beats seconds.

Your letter reads as though you might think it was made under patent No. 15298—above is the only patent record we have upon Litherland, and, since that same number appears in the case, it is clear that 1598 is the serial number.

You have a very interesting bit of mechanical construction, if yours is a rack-lever. It was sometimes called "rack and pinion." The first form of it was invented by "Abbe d'Hautefeuille" in 1722. In brief, a pinion is fitted upon the balance-staff, and the end of the lever is a segment of a toothed wheel meshing into this pinion; thus as the power of the train kicks the lever back and forth, the toothed segment rolls the pinion giving motion to the balance-wheel. It is readily seen that the "rack and pinion" is in mesh at all times, so the lever is never free.

It was about 1759 that Thomas Mudge (1715-1794) constructed the first "free" or detached lever escapement. Christian Huygens (1629-1695) came up with a sort of rack and pinion escapement. However, d'Hautefeuille, Huygens, et al. failed to make this form of construction popular, and it remained for Litherland to turn the trick. In this era, Liverpool became a great export (for watches) center — several makers made rack-levers under the 1791 patent of Litherland's. One or two members of the Tobias family, Roskell, Moncas, Fisher, and others, sent a great number to the U.S. Apparently, the London makers did not take to the racklever; very few have been seen with a London address, and they appear to have been made of Liverpool ebauches.

Ithaca Calendar Clock
Can Be Repaired

I have a clock that I have taken to three or four jewelers, and they were afraid to work on it. The clock is called a calendar clock and was made by the Ithaca Clock Co. The marking on the clock is H. B. HORTONS, PATENTS APRIL 18, 1865 & AUGUST 28, 1866. The clock just stopped running.

A.

Thank you for your query — but — it is not clear what you wish: 1. history, or 2. where to get the clock put in order. So a pointer upon both.

History: Mr. James W. Gibbs, prominent member of the National Watch & Clock Collectors Association, published, in January of 1960, an 80-page book titled "The Life and Death of the Ithaca Calendar Clock Company." We believe this was published privately for distribution to the membership of the Association, but also believe that you might obtain a copy from: Adams Brown Co., Horological Literature, Epping, N. H. From the 80 pages indicated above, you can see that we could not give much of its history in a letter; above that: it was founded in 1865 and that the final winding up of its affairs covered half a decade, 1915 to 1920. And, that the first calendar clock in America to be operated by the clock mechanism was invented in Ithaca.

Repair: Any competent clockmaker can make the necessary repairs;

Information Lacking
On Sessions Clock Co.

Please forward any information on this clock: "Eight day, half hour strike, cathedral gong. Turn back. The Sessions Clock Co. Successors to the E. N. Welch Mfg. Co., Forestville, Conn. U. S. A." "Ruby."
All of this is written on paper and pasted inside of the back panel. The clock has a black lacquer cabinet with round ornate dial and pillars on each side marbleized in green and white and a handle on each side panel.

A.

The model name "Ruby" would instantly identify your clock if we could check a catalog listing it. I regret to have to report that our "Sessions" file is rather lacking, and spotted.

It goes back to a 1912 factory catalog, i.e. one issued by the factory and listing the complete line for that year. There is no "Ruby." A check of catalogs for 1917 and 1924 also fails to reveal a "Ruby."

The Sessions Clock Company was organized in 1903, as your label states: successors to the E. N. Welch Clock Co. The 1912 catalog does indicate that they were that year making mantel clocks in black lacquer, celluloid columns with metal end ornaments like handles, etc. That catalog makes no mention of their succeeding Welch — it is my "guess" that since they were approximately 10 years old and manufacturing a great number of clocks, they were well enough established to drop the Welch connection. And, still guessing, that: the Ruby model carrying the Welch mention was made between 1903 and 1912.

Manchester Is Common Clock

I recently purchased a clocck which bears the Sessions label. According to this label, the clock is a "Manchester 300, eight day, one half hour strike, cathedral gong."
This clock stands about fourteen inches high, is made of a medium brown grained wood, and has a white ceramic face. It is decorated with what appears to be a wood inlay of a contrasting color. A repair date found on the inside of the clock is 1918.
I was told by Mr. Searles that you might be able to give me some information about this clock. For example, when was it made, what was the original cost, what kind of wood is it made of, and what is the inlay? Is there any historical significance attached to this particular model?

A.

Your "Manchester" dates 1912.

It is listed in the factory catalog, page 14, as follows: MANCHESTER, solid mahogany case, inlaid with colored woods. Convex glass. 5-inch cream tinted porcelain dial. 8-day cathedral bell, half-hour strike on cup bell. 13¾ in high, 8¾ in. wide. Price $14.00.

Krober Clocks Date to 1865

I have a clock that I would very much like to learn the who and when about. There's no patented name or date on either side of the works. I am sending you a part of the dial with letters of a company (I suppose) on it. I believe the dial is originally the one that the clock had first. I may be mistaken though. Would it be possible to get parts for same?

The frame is a round wood top and plain. To take off the front the hands must come off first. The back and all are in one piece. Height is 9 inches and the base is 7¼ inches across. The clock strikes only on the hour.

A.

The "trademark" you enclosed — "F. K. C. Co." was of the Florence Krober Clock Company.

Florence Krober first appears in the N.Y.C. directory for 1865/66 at 25 John Street (residence 171 Elm St.). The last city directory entry: "F. Krober Clock Co., 45 Maiden Lane, dissolved." Mr. Krober died May 16th, 1911.

The whole of the Krober history is somewhat difficult to piece together — the New York Times ran a brief death notice, May 17, 1911 — it stated that he was 70. That would spot his birth year as 1841; thus, the first directory listing would have come at 24. That he was quite an "operator" is attested by the fact that so many Krober clocks are around at this late date.

From his first patent Oct. 6th, 1874 til his last, Feb. 9th, 1897 — he was granted nine patents. It is generally agreed that he did not have a factory manufacturing 'complete' clocks; that he contracted for movements, principally from Seth Thomas but bought from most of the big producers. Most of his patents were for little improvements, such as his beat adjuster, improvement in strike trains, pendulum clamp, etc. Naturally, his clocks had his improvements, and it is thought that he 'traded' rights to some of them to the factories in part payment upon his movement contracts. Judging from your description, yours must date about the turn of the century. Material (repair parts) naturally are not to be had. The trademark is returned as you might like to trim it out and glue it to the new paper dial.

Dents Famous In Clockmaking

My questions concern two grandfather clocks. First, I'd like to know, if possible, some historic information, value, etc. of a Dent, London clock, on dial is "1746." Height is about seven feet, strikes on hour and half hours; weight and chain powered. This clock, it seems from the drive, had told the numerical date and month but the movement now has no mechanisms for this. How can I determine if the present movement is the original one? If so, where can I get parts to restore the clock to the original calendar operation? If the movement is not the original, how would I go about restoring the clock to the original condition, i.e., who supplies such movements? Also, the two lead weights are not the same weight. I find that a few more pounds for the strike side keeps it going. Therefore, I liked to get a weight to replace the lighter one. Where can I get this old type weight? Second, I would like to identify a clock which is 80" tall, about 40 years old with a ¼ hour strike and symbols and strike hammers markings inside the case on a metal plate. Also is there an approximate value which you place on this clock? What other information do you have available concerning it? Lastly, could you refer me to book(s) which have photographs and/or information of these clocks, particularly the first clock mentioned.

A.

Dent has been a famous name of London clockmakers since about 1674. It runs through upwards of a dozen, right down to the present day. Perhaps the most famous would be Edward John Dent, b-1790 d-1853, who made the famous "Big Ben" (Westminster). However, it was completed by Frederick, his step-son.

Determining whether or not a movement is the original depends on many factors and certainly an "in hand" close examination of both the movement and the case.

Unless you are quite familiar with calendar operation, it could be that there is no mechanism missing. Many calendar devices were simply driven by a mere pin located in the hour wheel or a wheel geared to turn only once in 24 hours. Often, owners feel that a lot of wheels, levers, etc., are missing because they do not know how these old English calendars worked.

Perhaps the best chance for a very positive answer to all your Dent questions would be to secure good photographs (at least three—case, movement and close-up dial) and send them along to "E. Dent & Co., 41 Pall Mall, London S.W. 1, England" with your inquiry. Enclose an International Reply (two if you wish prints retd.) coupon.

Your second movement is German, made by Junghans. This firm UhrenFabriken Gebruder Junghans A. S. of Scramberg, (Wurttemberg) Germany, celebrated their 100th anniversary last year, there is nothing in your information that would indicate any dating; it could well be one of many imported right after World War I, when there was quite a revival of those clocks.

British Tenacity Brings Reward

William George Schoof (1830-1901) with the sale of just one of his "Five-Tooth" chronometers to the British Admiralty obtained that coveted right to say: "Chronometer Maker to the Admiralty."

In our meager little horological library is a small, flex-cover booklet, 4¾" x 7½", sixteen pages, titled "Improvements in Clocks and Marine Chronometers," by W. G. Schoof, Chronometer Maker to the Admiralty, 1898. This unusual little volume deals with first, a one wheel clock with an odd type of gravity escapement. He suggests that this wheel have 3,600 teeth and the clock have a six-seconds pendulum. Only the last two pages, 15-16 are devoted to the five tooth chronometer. Many years ago I wrote Malcolm Gardner (London) to inquire about Schoof. His reply came: "You asked about Schoof. The three sources of information, apart from his own pamphlet on his lever escapement are his biography in the Horological Journal for August of 1901, Gould and Chamberlain. There is also his will which shows little of horological interest apart from a gift or two."

This very absence of something upon this British Horologist was enough to spur me on to some effort for more. Mr. Gardner and I correspond quite a bit. Mr. Gardner remembered seeing Schoof coming to Lloyd Square to play chess with his father. This was first-hand information and thus qualified Schoof for a future "Stray Bits." But rather it qualified me, for in the very beginning we stipulated that all "Stray Bits" would have to contain some first-hand information and that not hitherto published.

If one could make a depth study of this character, I think he would find that it would range in direct proportion to his mechanical thinking, from a wheel of 3,600 teeth down to one with a mere five teeth. A highly respected personality in Clerkenwell for nearly a half century, Schoof spent many of those years "battling" just about the whole of the British horological profes-

WM. G. SCHOOF

sion. Mr. Gardner remembers him as always dressing well and wearing a hard high hat. He had a great passion for chess and regularly visited the Vienna Cafe on New Oxford Street called the home of evening coffee and chess.

Our file of the British Horological Journal for the School period has some gaps, but from those yearly volumes we have been able to examine, it is clear that Mr. Schoof supplied and caused to be supplied a great deal of copy. Typical is Vol. XXVII (1884) in which Schoof's own comment and those replies he provoked runs to about eighteen items. After he invented his five-tooth escapement and hit the horological press with his claim that he had increased the efficiency of his chronometer by some 66⅔%, the Journal apparently called upon some of the leading men of the profession for their opinion. Both Edmund Beckett and T. D. Wright in some of their letters saw fit to remind the Journal of this request.

In his letter which occupied a full page in the April, 1885, issue, Beckett starts by saying: "At your request and on behalf of some members of the Council, I have done my best to understand Mr. Schoof's trigonometrical proof, etc." In June the famous Thos. D. Wright wrote: "I only wrote my opinion of Mr. Schoof's escapement and

Mr. Herrmann's trigonometry to back it at your request, and I am not concerned to argue with either of them." Every one of these letters seemed to bring a long reply from Schoof, sometimes extending into three pages. He replied to Wright in the July issue with two pages, starting thus: "I should have left the further discussion on the five-tooth resilient escapement to the judgment of the intelligent reader of the Horological Journal had it not been for your correspondent Mr. Thomas D. Wright's emphatic remarks," and thus launched into another long defense of his theory.

Beckett was severe upon Schoof from the beginning; Wright was more tolerant, however, toward the last he was answering like this: "I am afraid that any attempts to convince Mr. Schoof of his incorrect reasoning will be fruitless. His last contribution is a mass of mistakes."

Schoof entered chronometers in the Greenwich trials beginning in 1883 and continued til his win in 1896 when his No. 6059 was purchased by the Admiralty, thus enabling William George Schoof to style himself "Chronometer-maker to the Admiralty." I'm practically sure that he must have used that coveted line in his advertising, however, it so happens that my volumes for that period are from the library of M. Ditisheim who carefully deleted all the ads before having his journals bound.

1887 SCHOOF TRADE JOURNAL AD.

In his ads previous to the acceptance of No. 6059, Mr. Schoof always ran a little sketch of his escapement at the right side and on the left his pet theory: "The extent of vibration is as the square root of the work done. Work done equals the positive minus the negative quantities. The negative quantities are directly, and the positive inversely proportionate to the number of teeth in the escape wheel."

While Schoof was battling the trade and entering pieces in the Greenwich trials every year he was also seeking other competition. Some pieces were sent to the Geneva trials, and he sent at least one to the Yale Observatory in New Haven, Conn. Another Schoof resilient escapement piece was submitted to the Yale trials by a watchmaker from Syracuse, N. Y., named George E. Wilkins. Yale's rate sheet shows that it was awarded a Class I certificate. After much effort we have never been able to get a line upon Mr. Wilkins. It so happened that Schoof's chronometers had been coming out way down near the bottom of the list at Greenwich. His No. 6059 did not do much better than upon previous years, but a little. He had persuaded his good friend Robert Gardner, who was one of the top finishers of that day, to adjust and time it, then, instead of the Admiralty purchasing 25 or 30 instruments as they generally did, in 1896 they bought some 55. Thus Mr. Schoof's tenacity to buck the line year after year finally "paid off." The "trade," at least a portion of it, looked upon his victory as a hollow one, but I am sure that it gladdened his heart no little.

Discussing Schoof with the late W. J. Gazeley, he felt Schoof was badly treated by members of the profession, comparing him to Sully in that he kept flogging the same horse after it was unsatisfactory. Mr. Gazeley, who was close to the Curzon family knew that Mr. Charles Curzon made the escapements to Schoof's design. His son William Curzon said his father thought very highly of Schoof.

Lieutenant-Commander Gould in his "Marine Chronometer" called Schoof's math second-hand and rather agricultural and Major Chamberlain repeated it. Malcolm Gardner felt Gould's remarks were rather cruel. It was my good fortune to discuss this with the late George Garbe and he pointed out that Gould also said: "The teeth are of the resilient pattern introduced by J. F. Cole." This is incorrect. The teeth are not resilient, rather it is the lever banking that is resilient. He also felt that the center distance of six to ten (6 portions lever center to escape center—10 portions lever center to balance center) "downgrades his escapement immediately to low efficiency." Mr. Gazeley said: "In both the five

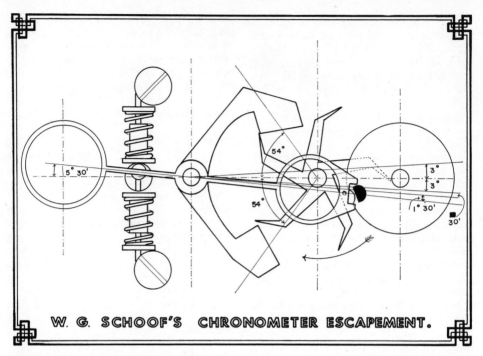

W. G. SCHOOF'S CHRONOMETER ESCAPEMENT.

tooth and later the ten tooth wheel, he forgot the most important factor, that is the balance arc." One might conclude that Mr. Schoof was so concerned with construction and mechanical problems that he failed to give full attention to "motion." His original gravity escapement clock now in the South Kensington museum, the arc of the pendulum's swing is about one-half degree. One writer reports that to one standing relatively close to it at first he has difficulty determining whether or not the clock is going.

Despite Gould's criticism of Schoof's math, his general description of the man is at least charitable for he called him "a man of the Harrison types, a trained watchmaker and a clever business man, but a rule-of-thumb mechanic." That he was a good business man is attested to by the fact his estate was some $25,000—quite a sum at the turn of the century. While he sold only one chronometer to the Admiralty, he owned some interest in a North of England shipping company and his sister's husband was a sea captain. These connections enabled him to sell all the chronometers he could make.

Apparently they gave a "reasonable" service but we must recall that these ships were in the Baltic trade and their chronometers were never subjected to the heat of the tropics. Some reports have it that Schoof willed Robert Gardner one of his five-tooth chronometers and a pocket chronometer by John Arnold. Malcolm Gardner says this is an error. He did will the Arnold silver pocket chronometer which he had treasured most of his life, but, there was no other chronometer. He had promised to send over a copy of Schoof's will but passed away before getting around to it. In one of his last letters he said: "You say that Schoof bucked his critics, he did even better. My father who had been a stern critic became a firm and staunch friend. My father did not make friends easily nor could he abide fools. Thus I think there was more to Schoof than either Chamberlain or Gould would admit."

Perhaps William George Schoof did fail to establish the superiority of the lever over the detent, or, even its equal performance to the detent, but he certainly kept British horology upon its toes for more than two decades and I'll wager that many a tender of the "144" had a better conception of escapements when the hassle ended.

Davis & Barber, Greenesborough, Ga.

OF THE FOUR STANDARD volumes carrying a listing of American clockmakers and firms, only one of them lists Davis & Barber, it gives no dates and places them at Bristol, and states "Ingraham made cases for them. Shipped south movements and cases to avoid tax."

Via an extended tendon of the "144"— that square foot in the center of the watchmaker's bench—we've encountered a number of Davis & Barber clocks and have heard of several others; one in Kansas City, another in Denver, and still a third on the west coast. Some were the conventional one-day wood movements and some were weight driven eight-day brass movements. Their labels read: "Improved brass bushed clocks, manufactured by Davis & Barber, Greensboro, Ga." and were printed by Joseph Hulbut of Hartford, Conn. Josiah Smith Davis was born at Harwinton in Litchfield county, Conn., January 13th, 1802. He died in Greensboro, Ga., February 9th, 1869. He married Cloe Barber of Harwinton. This date we've been unable to determine but it was before his move to Georgia.

Greensboro is the county seat of Greene county located about half-way between Atlanta and Augusta. It was named for General Nathenial Greene and originally spelled Greenesborough, but with time the spelling was changed to Greensboro. The Davis & Barber clock labels carried it Greensborough.

In its early history, Greene county recorded among its notables two teachers, William H. Seward and Louisa M. Alcott. Miss Alcott taught at the Greenesborough Female College, a fact she never mentioned in any of her writings.

In the year 1836, the Georgia Railroad reached Greensboro, about the same time came Josiah Smith Davis from Connecticut with his wife, Cloe, and her nephew, Orville Barber. Davis & Barber were well established by 1844 when Davis took on a partner in his mercantile business. This partner was Isaac R. Hall, the owner of the building in which it was located. This partnership agreement is recorded in Greene County deed book O-O, page 138, May 30th, 1844. It was for a period of four years from date and was renewed May 30th, 1848. The original capital was $5,000. It is indicated that Davis & Barber immediately began to assemble clocks upon their arrival in Georgia, and when a sufficient number had been assembled and tested, they were loaded onto a horse drawn wagon and peddled about the countryside. The first record located touching upon the firm was in deed book N-N, page 218, recorded October 29th, 1841. It indicated that Davis & Barber had been in business some years and showed that they loaned to a Jesse M. Thornton $275, taking as security a bill-of-sale to a "yellow man named Edward about 22 years old."

In deed book P-P, page 197, under the date of October 20th, 1849, it is learned that Orville Barber, of Harwinton, Conn., Litchfield County, deeded to Josiah Smith Davis, of Greensboro, Ga., certain lands in Cobb, Floyd, and Cherokee counties that belonged to Davis & Barber. The consideration was $3,000. This was the dissolution of the Davis & Barber operation and indicates that Orville Barber had already returned to Connecticut.

Thus, were we listing Davis & Barber it would be 1836-1849. T. B. Rice, who was the Official County Historian for many years, came to Greensboro in September of 1889. He knew one Leila Harper Wood, a former slave whose master had lived across the street from Josiah Davis' home and shop which was different from the Hall Building where the mercantile business was carried on. She told him much about the Davis family, that Orville Barber took over the sales or peddling end of the clock business while his uncle remained in the shop to assemble them. That, most of the manual work was done by slaves, including "Edward the yellow man."

Several years back, discussing Davis & Barber with Ed Ingraham, he wrote, quoting a letter by Milo L. Norton to the Bristol

Press, September 20th, 1872, about his grandfather Elias Ingraham, "After remaining with George Mitchell about two years, Mr. Ingraham commenced with C. & L. C. Ives, in the present 'Eureka' shop, and made cases for Ives till about 1836. At that time he commenced making cases for Davis & Barber, who were putting them together there (Ga.) thus avoiding heavy state licenses."

Lately, I have grown to give less and less credit to the tax avoidance angle. In our files is a photostat of the hand-written Tennessee Clock Tax Act dated January 5th, 1830, and in part, it states: "Any person or persons wishing to peddle in the article of clocks shall apply to the clerk of each county in which he wishes to sell the same, whose duty it shall be to issue to said applicant a license authorizing him to sell said article for the term of twelve months provided said applicant pays to said clerk the sum of twenty-five dollars and the sum of seventy-five cents fees of office."

There is absolutely nothing in this act that, of itself, exempts locally manufactured clocks. I have spent some hours in central Tennessee in an effort to find a record of where a local county court clerk issued a clock peddler's license. I've spent two whole days in the Georgia Department of Archives and History searching through the journals of the Georgia House from 1820 to 1835 and found no mention of a clock tax. It is not likely that such an act was passed prior to 1820 since the clock "boom" was yet to come. Now, it may have been after 1835 and it may be that my search was not thorough enough, but right now I doubt that the state of Georgia had a special act taxing clock peddlers, and, if it did, again would locally produced items be exempt?

Communication in the 1820s and 1830s was exceedingly slow by today's standards. "Due process" was even slower. One has only to read "Sam Slick" or "Hawkers and Walkers in Early America" to know that a shrewd Yankee peddler could slip in, make some sales, and get out before being caught.

"Brand" names had not become a substantial part of merchandising. Today, we just automatically associate Colt with the six gun, Campbell with pork & beans, and Stetson with good hats. Those clockmaker names we revere today were not known throughout the southern countryside in that era. The Georgia farmer did not know Seth Thomas or Eli Terry, but he did know Davis & Barber with the big store at Greensboro. Their guarantee really meant something.

A similar assembly operation was carried on near me. We occasionally see wood-movement clocks labeled "Couch & Stowe, Rock Springs, Tenn." Couch & Stowe were proprietors of a big general store, long established and well known, and their label meant something. The "local" label may, or may not have been a tax incentive, that remains to be researched further. The "Madison Avenue" value of the local label can't be denied and I'm quite sure that it was used to the limit. What became of the Davis & Barber operation when Orville Barber went back to Connecticut? It was carried on by Peter Clark. There are clocks in North Georgia with old D. & B. labels and Peter Clark's name pasted over.

Factual data upon Peter Clark is exceedingly hard to come by. Mr. Charles Davis, a grandson of Josiah, only remembers that Clark was a relative and lived with him. Refering back to Greene County deed book Q-Q, page 18 we find the following: "An agreement was entered into between Josiah Davis and Peter Clark, whereby Peter Clark deeded three negro women, his livestock, and other personal property to Josiah Davis, the consideration being that the aforesaid Josiah Davis was to take care of said Peter Clark both in sickness and in health." The date of this agreement is unclear for on the same page in the same book Davis confirmed the above contract and the same day which was May 12th, 1854, duly recorded that Peter Clark died. Continuing our effort at listing we would place those clocks with the Peter Clark labels 1850 to 1854.

Soon after the Confederate states were organized, Josiah Davis, deeded his Georgia property to Orville Barber, then after the war was over Barber deeded the property back to Davis. This, apparently is the last record involving Davis. It is presumed that he led a retired life until his death on February 9th, 1869.

174

CONSTANT GIRARD-PERREGAUX

Every bench clockmaker has given much thought to his shop regulator, but not one of you has been thinking in terms of the nanosecond accuracy. That is the NEW feature of this article—it is telling you that not only will you have it in your shop, but it will be available in every household . . . possibly in 1972.

Nineteen seventy two will see the entry of one of the old established Swiss watch manufacturers entering the clock field — Girard-Perregaux S.A. of La Chaux-de-Fonds.

They date the founding of the establishment back to 1791 when Bautte & Cie. was founded. Your scribe became interested in Girard-Perregaux work some forty years back when shown several original pieces of this maker by the late Major Paul Chamberlain—among them was a very small, approximately 'O' size, American 'tourbillon' with a detent (chronometer) escapement; the smallest ever built up to that time. It retained this place for some 75 years. Shortly after 1880 Girard-Perregaux planned and executed three of these movements. At that time one was in a London Museum;

one was owned by Mr. Jean V. Degoumois, of Neuchatel, and the third was in the Chamberlain collection. When one considers this construction, i.e. that the "carriage" contains the balance-wheel, the escape-wheel, and the detent along with the hairspring plus the bascule return spring, and the regulator plus a safety feature to prevent over-bank, all to turn once per minute and small enough to fit into an 'O' size movement, it taxes the imagination just about as much as that billionth of a second.

Constant Girard was born in La Chaux-de-Fonds in 1825. When through school, he spent several years in La Sange where he served his watchmaking apprenticeship; in 1845 he began work in Geneva for the old established firm of Bautte & Cie.; in 1854 he married the youngest daughter of Henri Perregaux, one of the leading watchmakers of Le Locle, combining his family name with hers as was the custom, if desired, in that part of Switzerland; thus he became Constant Girard-Perregaux.

CONSTANT GIRARD-PERREGAUX.
B. 1825. D. 1906.

G-P Tourbillon Carriage (enlarged).

He moved back to La Chaux-de-Fonds and entered into business for himself. About 1870 Henri Perregaux Jr., who had succeeded to his father's business, sold it and came with his brother-in-law. In 1878 Mr. C. Girard-Perregaux took his eldest son, Constant Girard-Gallet, into partnership.

175

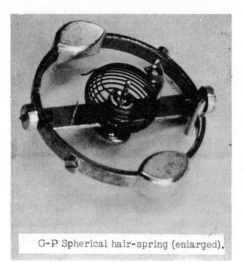

G-P Spherical hair-spring (enlarged).

In 1906 "Girard-Perregaux & Cie." bought the former "J. F. Bautte & Cie." firm of Geneva, with its complete stock and tools, and thus the present organization is the combining of "Henri Perregaux," "Girard-Perregaux" and "Bautte & Cie." They have always been known for their "precision pieces.

CONSTANT GIRARD-GALLET.

B. 1856.   D. 1945.

Reporting upon the La Chaux-de-Fonds exhibition of 1881 for the October issue of the British Horological Journal, Mr. Robert Gardner—English chronometermaker and father of the late Malcolm Gardner—said:

"The best exhibit of watches was undoubtedly that of the house of Girard-Perregaux, Chaux-de-Fonds. I was told this house manufactures principally for the South American market. They make a specialty of the Tourbillon escapement . . . . . . when in action it is certainly a most beautiful piece of mechanism, but as regards utility it would be difficult to show the benefits to be gained by its use, although this house has time and again taken first rank at Neuchatel with its Turbillon watches." end quote.

I am indebted to Mr. Constant Girard-Gallet for his photo, that of his father, and much history of this fine old firm. We were corresponding just before W.W. II; I was photographing some fine old pieces in detail and sending them along for his comments. That war brought on censorship and a point, I think in the Bahamas, was established where at first they turned back the photos letting the letter portion go through; later all the letters were returned. Mr. Girard-Gallet passed away in 1945 and we never resumed the research.

In February, Girard-Perregaux will announce a quartz wrist watch, to retail upon the order of $265.00, $350.00 with a slightly higher price for the 18-K gold cases. Some time this year they have plans for announcing three clocks. A quartz desk clock with calendar, a quartz digital clock with a readout to the tenth seconds already given the model HD-171, plus a third clock—perhaps more accurately a clock system upon their drawing board which is a quartz Master Clock that can monitor dozens of slave clocks, time recorders, acoustic signals etc. to an accuracy of one ten-thousandth of a second and will be designated Model H.M.-201. This is still in their planning and engineering stage; prices have not yet been firmed up.

Has Whiting Clock

I have acquired an old one day weight clock with wooden works, except escapement wheel and verge. It has a large face and is fancy painted. The case is dark and has post designs on each side, with flower looking designs painted on each side. It was made by Riley Whiting, Winchester, Conn.

Could you give me the history of this clock? How old is it? All that is in the clock is "Modern Day Clocks" by Riley Whiting.

A.

Riley Whiting is known to have been at work as early as 1807. He was first with the Hoadleys, Luther and Samuel, making long-case, wooden clocks. Dr. Amos Avery, past president National Association of Watch & Clock Collectors, has a clock labeled "Hoadley & Whiting, Winchester, Conn."

Whiting was in the clock business along in 1813 and when the shelf or short pendulum wood clocks came in about 1820, he began making that kind. Many of his clocks are running to this day. He died in 1835, at Winstead, Conn. His death caused a flourishing Winstead clock business to stop for some time.

About 1840, Lucius Clarke and William Gilbert took over and revived the Whiting clock manufacturing business, operating as Clark, Gilbert & Co. It later became a joint stock company, the William L. Gilbert Clock Co. They occupied a brick building built by Riley Whiting in 1825. It burned in 1871 and all the company records were lost in that fire. It later became the present Wm. L. Gilbert Corp.

Your letter indicates a shelf clock; this would date it between 1820 and Whiting's death in 1835.

Clock Is German

I picked up a wall clock. It is 45 inches long, 8-day, weight driven strike. The name of Gustave Becke, 107583, Friedsburg, is on it. I was wondering about how old it is and if it is German or Swiss.

A.

Your clock is definitely German.

Gustave Becker, born 1819, died 1885, established a factory at Freiburg, a town 33 miles west-southwest of Breslau; perhaps the territory is best known as The Black Forrest? His factory grew to pretty large production and operated long after his death; I'm sure up to World War I. In the early 1900's many of his clocks, practically all types, were being sold in the U.S.; he was one of the early producers of the "400-day" clock.

The movement serial number — 107,583 — is no help in dating your piece since no date listings for their serial numbers have ever been published. These watt clocks with 80-beat pendulums were being sold in the U.S. in great numbers around 1910 and 1912; chances are, yours may be one of them.

SETH THOMAS BANJO

Quite some time ago, I overhauled a Seth Thomas double spring Banjo.

At the time of overhaul, it did not appear too offbeat to me, but since talking to many of my jeweler friends, none seem familiar with this clock.

The case was of mahogany, about four feet long. The wood was not veneer and the cabinetry was of very good quality. The movement was of solid brass plate, about seven inches by four inches wide. To look at the clock in the case gave the appearance it was a striking clock, but both main springs wind time.

The center arbor is mounted offset or below the center of the face plate. Below the center arbor is a short post on which two identical wheels are placed on top of each other. To these there is attached a short coil spring. This allows one to turn the two wheels counter to each other, thereby creating friction to the center arbor. The pendulum is suspended on a mounting block fastened to the back of the clock case. It has a slot cut in it to accommodate the crutch of the verge.

The clock was very difficult to put in beat; since the escape wheel, pallet, etc., were in very good shape I was puzzled to find one side of the beat, the impulse side, sounding odd. The assumed tick-tock harmony used to set in beat was off and I never was able to get this odd noise eliminated.

The clock is also very sensitive to regulate, as the pendulum is 24 inches long and the only means is by a screw at the bottom. It runs for 60 days on one winding.

This movement had no marks on it except ST in a circle, embossed on the front plate. The dial had Seth Thomas written on it.

Realizing how vague my information is, I would appreciate it if you could tell me something about this type of clock, when it was manufactured, the approximate age, and where it was made.

A.

Thank you for yours. Without something a little more definite, there isn't much we can tell you about the Seth Thomas. It was made at Thomaston, Conn., that much is for sure, because they have never constructed pendulum clocks anywhere other than at Thomaston.

Sixty days with one winding is not at all familiar. During the 1880's and 1890's, Seth Thomas made a number of "regulators," some of them upon the general lines of the banjo type, dual-spring powered, to go for 30 days, for banks, counting houses and public offices. I'm wondering if the clock in question isn't one of them. Perhaps it was originally equipped with "stopworks" which some negligent repairman has left off.

The double wheel spring together with little coil spring is an arrangement that eliminates play or lost motion in the hour hand. As to regulation, it was only in the rarest instances that any other arrangement than the nut at the bottom of the pendulum was used.

In all likelihood, Morris Tobias was a member of that famous timepiece family. Baille lists "Morris Tobias, London, Wapping, 1794-1840;" then "Morris & Levitt, London, Wapping and Minories, 1817 to 1824." Again, "Morris & Co., London, Wapping, 1802 to 1808." This sort of pin-points the Minories address to 1817-1824.

A Brief Note on the Maximus

Several inquiries have prompted a brief research into the production of the Waltham "Maximus"model watch. Two features of this little search point up that this model is possibly better known to watch collectors than to today's bench horologists and that almost no mention of material for the Maximus appears in old material catalogs.

It was about 6:00 a.m. on the morning of May 8, 1939, when it was my happy privilege to accompany the late Jacob Freistadter, then Factory Superintendent of Waltham, for his morning walk during which he indulged in one of his little hobbies, that of pausing before jewelry store windows and counting the number of Waltham watches upon display. In his conversation Mr. Freistadter made two statements which I well recall.—1. That it was the intent of Waltham to produce the finest pocket timepiece to ever be mass-produced in their "Maximus" model. 2. That they had backlogged material for same for all time to come. A check less than 30 days ago reveals that much Maximus material is available this date. The first step in our research was naturally to "Serial Numbers With Description of Waltham Watch Movements, a 114-page, 11 by 8½ inch book put out by Waltham in September of 1954, listing all serial numbers from 1 through 33,820,900. This search revealed 99 entries for the Maximus models, showing that the first Maximus was No. 7,-157,001, the first of a lot of 1,000 movements to come through the factory about 1896—a twelve size, 21-jewel model 94, pendant set, hunting style. The last was No. 25,798,000, a ten size, Maximus A. 23 jewel open face style.

By subtracting the initial serial number from the last of each of these 99 listings it was determined that some 27,552 Maximus movements were produced in this nineteen year period. Nowhere in this official listing is "Premier Maximus" mentioned though it has appeared in Waltham advertising and catalogs. It had always been my understanding that the Maximus models were produced in three qualities named "Premier Maximus", "Riverside Maximus" and "Maximus"—23-jewel, 21-jewel and 19-jewel in that order. This listing reveals that some 900 movements in their jewel series, 10-ligne and opera, were designated Maximus and had but 17-jewels. These came through about 1910. The late Walter Prindel, a long time factory employee, told me that Mr. I. E. Boudrer, general manager, directed that all Maximus movements on hand be sold for $100 each, shortly before World War II.

Some old-timers say that the top Maximus, I presume the Premier Maximus, was 25-jeweled—that is not mentioned in this official listing and neither have we been able to locate one in a catalog. One unusual point in this listing is No. 16,000,000. It came through the factory as a "special".

—just one. Wherever no. sixteen million is today, it's proud owner certainly possesses a "collector's item".

Sometime, in the not too distant future, we may tabulate these 99 listings of the Maximus; run a break-down upon the various sizes, jewels etc.; tack on any additional vital info that turns up and publish an article on these pages if suffcient interest happens to be indicated.

Queen of Holland Receives
'Garbe No. 14' Precision Regulator

IN 1955 HER MAJESTY Juliane, Queen of the Netherlands, requested G e o r g e Garbe, the then professor of Horological Engineering at the Christian Huygens School in Rotterdam, to construct a precision regulator for the exhibition shortly to be held. Result: the "Garbe No. 14"—a precision, seconds beat regulator, equipped with his own "constant torque escapement" and a type "J" Riefler precision pendulum all housed within a "Garbe" air-pressure compensation jar.

GEORGE GARBE   1908 - 1969.

Upon coming to the U.S. in 1957 he brought it with him. Last September it was announced that the Garbe family has presented this outstanding timepiece to Her Majesty the Queen of Netherlands, in his memory. It will go on permanent exhibition at the Utrecht Museum of Horology at Rotterdam.

For the past 12 years the Garbe family resided at Waterbury, Conn., where he was employed by the U.S. Time Corporation as engineer and draftsman. In announcing the sad news of his sudden death last summer, the German Society of Chronometry said: "This branch of advance chronometry loses with the death of this member a remarkable craftsman and theoretician who possessed an unsual amount of knowledge in this specialized field. Born in Dessau, Germany, in 1908, George Garbe, received his first training from his watchmaker father; then completed the well known courses at the Glaschutte Watchmaking School."

After the war, he joined the French Government Air-Navigation Department, thence from there to Hamburg, West Germany, where he established himself as a chronometer maker, specializing in precision chronometers and watches. From there he went to the Christian Huygens school and to America. During his tenure at Christian Huygens school he constructed No. 14. He was a master designer and mathematician and was such a perfectionist that his many escapement designs, based upon his own recalculations are of perfect executions and great scientific value.

He was an active member of the New England Chapter of the National Watch and Clock Collectors Association. He and Mrs. Garbe were familar figures at their meetings.

FAUTH & CO., REGULATORS & CHRONOMETERS

SCATTERED ABOUT THIS NATION there are upwards of half-a-hundred fine astronomical regulators, and perhaps an equal number of astronomical chronographs . . . all marked "Fauth & Co., Washington, D.C." Search as you may, you will not find this firm upon any of the American Clockmaker listings. Because it has not heretofore been published and because we were able to obtain some "source" facts, the story qualifies for one in the "Stray Bits" series.

"Fauth & Co." was founded in 1874, at No. 59-B Street, later moving to 132-134 Maryland Ave., 'til it closed in 1905.

Factually, "Fauth & Co." was George Nicholas Saegmuller, born in Germany Feb. 12, 1847, died Feb. 12, 1934 upon his 87th birthday. Factually, "Fauth & Co." was a firm producing scientific instruments, which may account for its failing to appear upon any listing. Palmer in his TAC lists "Sagsmuller, George N., Rochester, N. Y. ca. 1875. Made clocks. Famous designer of scientific instruments, as transits and levels; was for a time in partnership with Bausch & Lomb." There is no indication of any connection with Fauth & Co., the spelling includes an "s" and the time off by some thirty years since Mr. Saegmuller did not go to Rochester 'til 1905. He is exactly correct stating that Mr. Saegmuller was a famous designer of scientific instruments. That he built upwards of a hundred timepieces—the Chronagraph is a time piece—including at least one regular six foot wall clock, now owned by a granddaughter, Mrs. John Fielding Burns; certainly qualifies him for a spot upon maker listings.

Mr. Saegmuller arrived in New York, aboard the SS City of Cork about the middle of June, 1870, and immediately went to work for a Mr. Werner in a shop specializing in the building of "models" for patents, etc. This connection was short lived; he met a Mr. William Wurdemann, who had an instrument shop in Washington, D.C. with a large contract with the Coast and Geodetic Surveys.

When the Wurdemann contract was completed, Mr. Wurdemann planned to return with his family to Germany; this practically meant the closing of the Wurdemann shop. Mr. Saegmuller was offered the position of Chief Mechanician & Custodian of Instruments for the coast surveys at a salary of $1,600.00 per year, which he accepted. He and Camill Fauth, another employee of Wurdemann's shop who in the meantime had become his brother-in-law, tried to buy the Wurdemann business but found his price out of reason. Mr. Saegmuller and Mr. Fauth discussed it with a mutual friend, one Henry Lockwood, who came up with the suggestion of a new firm and offered to put up $2,000 as his share in the partnership. He further agreed to put up a building upon a lot he owned at the corner of B street and First Street S.W.

The partnership was perfected orally. No papers were signed; Lockwood was to do the bookkeeping, answer mail, etc.; Fauth was to manage the shop, and Saegmuller was to make all the drawings and designs and otherwise assist in the business while keeping his government position. Because they hoped to obtain government contracts, it was thought better that the name Saegmuller should not appear in the firm's name and thus it was named "Fauth & Co."

Lockwood put up the building; the basement and first floor were occupied by the shop; Fauth had his dwelling on the second floor, and Saegmuller had a room on the third floor.

Work was immediately commenced. Their first project was making instruments for display at the Philadelphia Centennial to be held in 1876. This exhibit was to include an Equatorial telescope, an engineering transit of the highest order, and a chronograph designed by Saegmuller, said by him to be superior to anything then in use by the surveys at that time.

Lest the modern watchmaker become confused, some brief remarks upon this "chronograph" are in order. Like the term, chronometer, the term chronograph has changed over the years; he quite probably conceives a chronograph to be a wrist watch with a start, stop and fly-back seconds register. The astronomical chronograph truly

CHRONOGRAPH.

lived up to its name as derived from chronos meaning time and graph meaning to write or record, for it actually writes the time. Our short research indicated that as of this period in time only three firms in the U.S. were producing astronomical chronographs—The John A. Brashear Co. Ltd., Allegheny, Pa., The Warner & Swasey Co., of Cleveland, Ohio, and Fauth & Co., of Washington, D.C.

There was a mechanical problem involved when driving a graphsheet to write the time; an orthodox (ticking) clock would of necessity move that sheet forward by "jerks" each time the clock ticked while it was desired to move the sheet at a steady rate. To obtain this steady drive a conical pendulum device was used, patterned after the steam engine governor, or "Watts Regulator." Saegmuller was not the originator of this device; it came over from England— I believe Cooke & Sons—but he did a great deal to perfect it. Of it, he said: "I would often run a chronograph sheet across the entire cylinder, which required 2½ hours, when the seconds breaks would show a perfect straight line, not differing 1/100th of a second from beginning to end."

The Fauth catalogue for 1883 describes their perfected chronograph thus: "Cut No. 33 represents our style of chronograph, which for compactness and regularity of action, cannot be surpassed. It is noiseless in action, and the governor regulates the speed so perfectly that the seconds line is perfectly straight.

The cylinder is 14 inches long and 7 inches diameter, and runs about 2½ hours, with three feet fall and a weight of about

eighteen pounds. Saegmuller's maintaining power, however, allows winding up without affecting the rate.

"The clock work is strong enough to drive three or four cylinders, which can be readily attached. By pushing a button the speed of the cylinder is doubled, which is very convenient in exchanging clock signals in longitude work. Price $350.00. Each additional cylinder with frame, carriage slide, and magnet, $150.00. Chronograph paper for the above, per 100 sheets, $1.50." end quote.

So much for the chronograph—while not a clock or watch it has its definite niche in horology.

Mr. and Mrs. Fauth returned to Germany for reasons of Mr. Fauth's health in 1887, and Mr. Saegmuller bought his interests in the firm—having previously bought out Lockwood. The 1894 catalogue shows the name: "G. N. Saegmuller, successor of Fauth & Co." The 1898 catalogue has it: Fauth & Co., Geo. N. Saegmuller, Prop."

In the fall of 1903 Mr. Edward Bausch, of Bausch & Lomb Co., visited Mr. Saegmuller in Washington; their talks led to a suggestion of a merger. On a later visit these plans were perfected, again without any formal or signed papers.

Saegmuller had been appointed a "judge" for the St. Louis Exposition, and his firm had several government contracts to complete. It was agreed that he would move the entire operation to Rochester, N. Y., when both were completed. In the spring of 1905 Fauth & Co. made the move; a companion firm was formed, "Bausch—Lomb & Saegmuller." Exactly when this was phased into the present "Bausch & Lomb Co." is not available. In February of this year one of their directors wrote: "I'm sorry, but a check of several informed sources in the company fails to reveal anything about Fauth & Co."

There is an exhibit at the Smithsonian, a Fauth four-legged gravity, astronomical regulator. They also show a Fauth chronograph ca. 1885 from the Smithsonian Astrophysical Observatory.

Capt. John R. Hankey at the U.S. Naval Observatory has checked their old hand written inventories for 1887, 1897, and 1926. No Fauth & Co. clocks appear.

"Joseph Barborka"

IT WAS DURING THE Omaha UHAA Convention two years ago that James Hamilton, chairman of UHAA Technical Board, and the writer discovered upon an unusual tower clock in the Omaha Post Office, a simple little brass casting with raised lettering "J. Barborka, Mfgr., Iowa City, Iowa."

At Sioux City, this past April, Jim and I were to again see a duplicate of that little name plate upon a similar tower clock in the City Hall.

At first sight, the name "Barborka" did not ring a bell with either of us but such was no occasion for concern as we'd only have to "look him up" or consult some "listing." It turned out that, that name could not be located anywhere—the search then took on the "needle in the haystack" air and the only thing left was simply search everything pertaining to or connected with tower clocks, and hope. Finally, it turned up among bids submitted upon a tower clock for the U. S. Customs House, at Memphis, Tenn., in July of 1899—"Western Tower Clock Manufactory, Joseph Barborka, Proprietor."

First inquiries to Iowa City (usual sources), as is many times the case, proved disappointing—it was sheer luck when we contacted Dr. Carl L. Gillies, an enthusiastic clock collector of Iowa City, who was successful in interviewing some people who knew and remember Joseph Barborka, and obtaining a photograph from IOOF Lodge No. 6, which Mr. Barborka one time served as treasurer. While Dr. Gillies was working in Iowa City, we located a number of Barborka clocks—No. 9 is in the Post Office, at Carson City, Nev., installed about 1890. Another was installed in the Louisville, Ky., Post Office in 1899 and still another in the Post Office at St. Joseph, Mo. Mr. Floyd E. Robinson, watchmaker and clock collector par excellence of Rock Island, Ill., came up with Barborka tower clock No. 17 (non strike), which was originally built for the Rock Island Railroad about 1903.

Then we learned from Mr. J. E. Reizenstein, of the Iowa City Press-Citizen, that Mr. Barborka installed three clocks in Iowa City; a large, 3-train chime clock in the tower of St. Mary's Catholic church, one in the City Hall and another upon Dostal's Brewery (now dismantled). Mr. Reizenstein remembers Mr. Barborka well, and says: "Among his specific achievements in the field of curio-construction are a clock that ran a year with a single winding and a watch mounted in a No. 12 ring with the same number of pieces in any watch of ordinary type. I saw the watch, it was seven-eighths of an inch in diameter and the depth was one-fourth inch." Apparently, the year-clock was a mantel clock and it is believed that he constructed other mantel clocks. The Robinson clock carries the same cast brass (raised letter) plate as do the Omaha and Sioux City clocks; the No. 17 being painted upon the main frame—if the two clocks examined were ever numbered we presume it was in like manner and that it has either been worn off or painted over.

JOSEPH BARBORKA
1839 – 1921

No. 17 has a one seconds pendulum, wood rod and Graham dead-beat escapement; its escape wheel resembles very closely those we usually see on Ansonia mantel clocks with Brocot visible escapement, i.e., the back side of the tooth is undercut up next the tooth tip.

Both the Omaha and Sioux City clocks are equipped with gravity escapements, but not true to the Denison type—instead of the three or six legs as used in the Denison, they have an escape wheel of the size generally found in tower clocks of comparable size with dead-beat escapement. Again the teeth are cut on the back at the tip . . . 15 teeth to the wheel, thus with their two-seconds pendulum, the escape arbor makes one revolution per minute. The Sioux City clock has a seconds hand mounted on pivot of escape arbor just as with usual English grandfather clock.

Both clocks have "Harrison" gridiron compensation the full length of their two-second rods; five iron and four brass rods; roughly about one-half inch diameter; cylindrical type ball, weight 350 pounds. Gridiron pendulums upon American tower clocks are unusual, as most relied upon well seasoned wood rods.

Mr. Barborka was born in Bohemia, Sept. 2, 1839—came to the United States in 1874, settling in Chicago; two years later he removed to Iowa City, where he died Nov. 30, 1921. Mr. Robinson visited the Iowa City cemetery and tells me that he located the following upon his tombstone:

"Narozen — 2 — Srpna 1839
Zemril — 30 — List 1921"

Upon arrival in Iowa City, he opened a jewelry store at No. 21 Dubuque Street; in addition to the regular line of watches, clocks and silver, he stocked organs and pianos. He married Lydia Dusanek of Bohemia, June 15, 1863. To this union were born six children, Augusta V., Thomas, Rosa, Minnie, Joseph and Bertie. Minnie was taught engraving and did that work for the store—after Mr. Barborka's death "Gusta" (Augusta) took over care of the local tower clocks.

In Bohemia, father Barborka, a blacksmith, wanted Joseph to learn the trade and felt that a 15-year-old lad would do better to learn to make good nails by hand than just hanging around a jewelry store, which he felt would never lead to more than just a tinkering idler. One night he heard a ticking and knowing that there had never been a clock in his house started to investigate. Upon locating a clever little wooden clock made by his son, he consented to the boy being apprenticed to a jeweler in Prague.

Possibly the installation nearest and dearest to his heart was the big 3-train chime clock in St. Mary's church, and the 17-bell carillon. One bell was used by the clock to strike the hour, and, four were utilized for the chime. The combined weight of the bells is given as 20,000 pounds. Mr. Barborka hung the bells in the highest part of the tower in an irregular manner above and below each other. What appears to be carelessness is born of reason for he placed each bell where it would give the best tone in relation to the others.

Far down in the lower part of the steeple he located a piano-like box with plow handles for keys—each key being connected with its bell by rope, and music could be played in the keys of C and G. There was a music rack above the keyboard giving somewhat the resemblance of an organ with large stops. The cost of the clock was $1,750. The church owned two bells and fifteen were ordered from H. Stuckstade & Co., of St. Louis, Mo., at a cost of $3,591.95.

In later years he told friends that one of his greatest pleasures was to be up in the tower Sunday morning as the carillon was played and to feel the quiver of the great bells as they boomed so near him and watch his fellow citizens stream into the nearby churches.

Fig. 1 is an outside view of the Sioux City clock. Fig. 2 is a close-up of the time train, showing escape-

FIG. 1.

FIG. 2.

ment and top of gridiron pendulum; also nut for fine regulation at top of suspension and safety device to prevent the pendulum from dropping in case of breakage of suspension spring. Also the brass name plate.

Evidently the architect when designing this tower did not take into consideration the installation of a clock for he located a stairway right in the center of it. This made it necessary to locate the movement to one side, and in order to avoid these stairs, Barborka had to drive the dial on that side with an offset angle—see Fig. 3. Additional gearing entailed allows for some "slack" in this pair of hands.

Sometime in the fall of 1900, the supervising architect at Washington invited bids upon a tower clock for the Custom House and Post Office at Sioux City, Iowa. In response thereto, Western Tower Clock Manufactory wrote, Sept. 1, 1900: "Mr. James Knox Taylor, Supervising Architect, Washington, D. C. Dear Sir: Enclosed please find drawing, specification and proposal for a tower clock for the U. S Court House, Post Office and Cus-

HANDS

FIG. 3.

tom House at Sioux City, Iowa. Also certified check for sixty-nine dollars ($69) which is 5 percent of bid. Yours Very Respectfully. (s) Jos. Barborka."

Either the drawing was returned to Barborka, or it has been lost for it is no longer in the files. We reproduce here the specifications in his own handwriting. They read: "Specification of clock machinery and dials for U. S. Court House, Post Office and Custom House, Sioux City, Iowa.

Clock—

Clock machinery will be composed of a heavy cast iron frame, main wheel 18 inches, all wheels to be made of gun metal—pinions and shafts of cast steel—gravity escapement — compensating pendulum—pendulum 14 ft. Pendulum ball 350 lbs.

Frame work for clock—

The whole machinery including the pendulum to be enclosed in a substantial dustproof wooden house clear, thoroughly seasoned, dressed, matched and beaded pin, 4/7 in. thick. All the above to be placed on the sixth floor in position with dials.

Dials—

Four twelve-foot dials made of crimped galvanized iron in sections, same to be painted black—hands made of galvanized iron gilded—figures and minutes gilded. Small door for placing hands from inside, made waterproof and invisible, in dials."

Bids were opened at 2 p.m., Sept. 6, in Washington, D. C., by J. K. Taylor, in the presence of P. S. Glanton, Chief Executive Officer, and J. Avant Pleut, Chief Computer. Barborka was the only bidder, $1,380, with four months for completion (usually there were three or four bidders; Barborka lost the Memphis job to Nels Johnson).

On Sept. 13, 1900, Mr. Barborka wrote: "Mr. T. A. Vanderlip, Assistant Secretary, Treasury Department, Washington, D. C. Sir: Your letter of acceptance dated Sept. 11, came to hand and contents noted. I shall now proceed with the work according to contract. Thanking you for this order, I am, Very Respectfully Yours, (s) Jos. Barborka."

The clock was made, installed and set going—date we can't locate, but in June of 1901, Mr. J. H. Bottom, custodian of the building, appointed one of Sioux City's leading jewelers, Mr. Will H. Beck, as inspector to examine the clock and we find the following letter dated June 12: "Hon. J. H. Bottom, Custodian U.S.C.H., P.O. & C.H., Sioux City, Iowa. My Dear Sir: I have carefully inspected the tower clock recently made for the U.S. Government Building and beg to report that it is complete and in good working order. I am,

Very Respectfully Yours, (s) Will H. Beck."

On even date—June 12, 1901: "Hon. Secretary of the Treasury, Washington, D. C. Sir: I have the honor to enclose herewith the report of the inspector appointed by me under letter of authority dated May 24, 1901. To my personal knowledge the inspector made three trips up in the tower to look over the work and in view of the fact that the clock has kept very accurate time since installed, I recommend that the clock and striking attachment be accepted and payment of same be made. I enclose certified vouchers, Respectfully, (s) J. H. Bottom, Custodian."

The only remaining bit of data in the files is a letter dated Aug. 15, 1901: "Hon. Secretary of the Treasury, Washington, D. C. Sir: Replying to Department letter "S" dated Aug. 9, 1901, I have the honor to enclose herewith vouchers of Joseph Barborka, $55.15, in payment of repairs on tower clock. In regard to the date of liability I am at a loss to determine that fact. The breakage of the clock occurred about the 20th of June and the date of the repairs was July 20. I leave date open on vouchers for you to determine. Very Respectfully, (s) David Anderson, Acting Custodian."

We can only conjecture that this $55.15 repair charge covered an "accident" because the clock was still less than a year old and certainly within the guarantee period. Closing, it is interesting to note that when inviting bids, the Government did not make or set "specifications" to be met by the bidder. It seems from a number of installations during the 1880's and the 1890's that the bidder rather detailed what he had to offer. In 1900 there were several active manufacturers' especially Nels Johnson of Manistee, Mich.; Howard Clock Co., of Boston, and Seth Thomas, Thomaston, Conn. Competition was generally keen both as to price and time required to complete the job. Why only Barborka submitted a bid for the Sioux City job is any one's guess, unless the Easterners felt he had them beat by reason of transportation cost.

Clock Winding Mechanisms Vary

The Boston Clock Company was another venture of one Joseph Eastman, first at Fairhaven, Vermont as The Vermont Clock Company, thence to Boston as The Boston Clock Company, it was taken over by the present Chelsea Clock Company in 1897.

There are quite a few Vermont and Boston clocks about and most old timers who have serviced one will certainly remember it from its winding mechanism — one of the most unique to be found upon any American clock. The Eastman movements were all 'three-deckers' — that is: there is a third plate between the front and back, the strike train being located between one division and the time train between the other; thus constructed so that either train could be serviced without disturbing the other.

We encounter a number of American clocks built this way, but only the Eastman clocks have both mainspring barrels mounted upon one single arbor where you fit key to the winding square; turn one direction to wind one spring, then turn in the opposite direction to wind the other spring. This works fine for the owner winding the clock once each week, but for the repairman who wishes to let the power off it presents quite a problem since as he places his let-down key to release one spring it will be winding the other as it turns, etc. In addition to the unique construction enabling the wind from one single arbor, each barrel is located under a separate bridge so that either may be removed without disturbing the other, or, dismantling either train.

In discussing this construction several years ago with Mr. Walter Mutz, of Chelsea Clock Co., he wrote: "which to my mind was the invention of the devil, namely having two barrels in a straight line and one winding key—".

We discovered upon one movement a patent date of December 28th, 1880 — according to Eckhardt's list this would be patent No. 236,017 issued to J. H. Gerry. This branches off as the gate-way to another entirely new horological research; who was James H. Gerry, of Somerville, Mass.? Very little has been published upon him yet he is mentioned a jillion times in just about everything one picks up for this era. He was granted a round dozen horological patents in the decade 1880 to 1890 and is perhaps best known for his gravity escapement which was used upon a precision astronomical regulator built by both Seth Thomas and The Self Winding Clock Company.

The price list acompanying this catalogue is interesting; the top clock listed is at $133.50 — rather steep for an American, mantel clock that merely struck the hours and halves; however, it came in an Onyx case. The top Marble case listed for $70.00 — it is presumed that both cases were equipped with the same movement. A difference of $63.50 for Onyx above marble has to indicate their regard for the former.

THERE ARE DOZENS OF WAYS of winding a clock—here are some of them.

Last column, we commented upon that unusual winding method utilized by the Boston Clock Co., temporarily ascribing it as a brainchild of one James H. Gerry, but promising to check it out. Knowing that Gerry was a prolific inventor, having obtained a dozen or more horological patents between 1880 and 1900, we had accepted a statement in the Bulletin of the National Watch & Clock Collectors Association for April 1966 by the late William Drost, that it was Gerry's patent.

Mr. Drost, said—quote: "The single arbor when minipulated clockwise and counterclockwise winds both mainsprings. The patent for this feature was obtained by J. H. Gerry, while in Newark, N.J."

Actual patent copies from the U.S. Patent office prove differently. That patent titled: "Winding Attachment for Clocks" is serial number 235,017, dated Dec. 28th, 1880 issued to James H. Gerry, of Newark, N.J., and assigned to the "Harvard Clock Co.," of Boston, Mass. The name of the Harvard Clock Co. was changed to the Boston Clock Co., May 29th, 1884.

The Harvard Clock Co., was first organized Oct. 11th, 1880 with Samuel S. Campbell, president, Charles M. Campbell, treasurer, along with James H. Gerry and Joseph H. Eastman. That patent covering the 'single' arbor to wind both springs, referred to by Mr. Drost is: No. 343,947, titled "Clock Winding Mechanism" dated June 15th, 1886, issued to Abraham Craig and Joseph H. Eastman, of Boston, Mass., and assigned to The Boston Clock Co., of the same place. Both Mr. Gerry and Mr. Eastman were quite colorful characters and our craft would be the better if we had more detailed information upon their activities. Eastman was a prime mover in a number of clock

manufacturing ventures, the Vermont Clock Co., the Boston Clock Co., and The Eastman Clock Co. In 1868 James H. Gerry was Superintendent of the Springfield Watch Co. in Massachusetts where he had patented a stem wind system. From Springfield he went to Boston with E. Howard; on up through 1890 we meet him at almost every turn of the road with a new patent in his hand. For a time he was in Brooklyn, N.Y. with the Self Winding Clock Co., where he patented a number of electrical set devices, etc., and a couple of patents covering the gravity escapement. The highest precision Astronomical Regulator — and highest priced — Seth Thomas ever built was equipped with the Gerry gravity escapement. One time Superintendent of the United States Watch Co., we later find him as Superintendent of the Hampden Watch Co., at Springfield, Mass.

There can be no confusion between these two patents; that one to Gerry is applicable to only ONE spring and in his specs Gerry states: "This invention relates more particularly to traveling or companion clocks . . ." The two views Mr. Drost shows of his "Boston" clock indicate that it is a traveling and/or carriage type clock, yet the back view clearly reads the patent date of December 28th, 1880; that of the Gerry, patent No. 236-017. Clearly, this error must be credited to the factory for so stamping the movement. The clock is a striker, thus has to have two springs, and just as clearly that single winding arbor indicates that it is wound by the Craig-Eastman method — patent No. 343,947.

The problem created for the clockmaker in this single arbor wind method is in letting the springs down for disassembly. If one of these movements comes to the bench with a broken spring, there is no problem since all one has to do is put on the let-down key and allow the remaining spring to un-wind, but, since in most instances it comes with both springs completely wound to the hilt, you have to relieve one spring before the other can be let down. This may be done by tying back the strike lock; setting it aside and allowing the strike spring to strike down; or, the platform escapement may be removed to allow the time spring to run down — this method can be hazardous and thus should be followed with caution; one — make sure that all pivots are well oiled; two — with a finger to the last arbor break the speed of the run-down to prevent cutting off a pivot, etc.

Some old sage has said that to every action there is an equal reaction, etc.; this really shines here. While Brother Eastman made it easy for

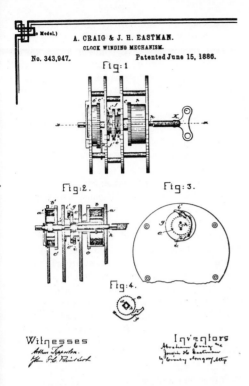

(No Model.)

A. CRAIG & J. H. EASTMAN.
CLOCK WINDING MECHANISM.
No. 343,947.   Patented June 15, 1886.

Fig:1

Fig:2.   Fig:3.

Fig:4.

Witnesses   Inventors

the clock's owner to wind his piece by merely rocking the key back and forth, he made it equally hard for the repairman to let the power down.

The general public, even clockmakers themselves give very little attention to methods of winding a timepiece; but, once you start looking some quite interesting things crop out. One might say that the clock was handed to the American Colonies "Full Blown;" therefore any contributions of the American clockmaker to the craft had of necessity to be "improvements." I like to feel that there are countless numbers of such 'improvements' that bespeak the skill and ingenuity of the U.S. horologist.

No doubt the earliest clocks were weight driven, exactly how wound is beclouded — maybe a pull wind and maybe via being reeled up on a drum. Certainly Christiaan Huygens — b. 1629 d. 1695 — was using a 'pull' wind with his endless rope method. The Black Forest Germany clockmakers may have been utilizing that pull wind via a chain or cord over a toothed or spiked pulley such as comes on the modern Cuckoo clock before the Parmales — Ebenezer Parmale 1690-1777, et al, Seth Youngs 1711-1761, the Cheneys and Gideon Roberts 1748-1813, began using the double-cord pull

wind method whereby a second cord is wound on to the drum as the drive weight descends. This is an ingenious way for the wind and I like to think it originated in the U.S. because I can't find any record of its being used abroad before that era.

We are told that necessity is the mother of invention and I like to think that those Connecticut Yankees may have devised this method because of the lack of metal — lacking metal for the wind-post square they had to resort to wood for the wind. The system is simple, cheap and above all, very efficient.

One of the cleverest winding devices and/or methods ever devised by a clockmaker just has to go to Benjamin B. Lewis for that spring used by Welch-Spring & Co., in their celebrated "Patti" movement.

Right here we run into another of those little 'quirks' one often encounters in these researches. It is almost universal with present-day clockmakers to associate the "Spring" in this firm as a clock spring; it is NOT; in 1868, Mr. Elisha N. Welch — b.-Feb. 7th, 1809 d.-Aug. 2nd, 1887 — formed a partnership with one Solomon Crosby Spring, 1826-1906, to be known as Welch-Spring & Co., which operated successfully until Spring sold his interest to Welch in 1883.

Benjamin Bennett Lewis was born October 30th, 1818 in Athens, N.Y. At the age of nine he was left an orphan; and after a short experience as a clerk in a N.Y.C store, he went to sea and worked his way up to the position of a commander. In 1840 he moved to Huron, Ohio, where he engaged in the drug business, also dealing in jewelry, watches and clocks. While in Huron, he obtained his first patent upon a calendar mechanism. In all, he was granted four (4) patents: No. 34,341 Feb. 4th, 1862; No. 43,214 June 21st, 1864; No. 85,456 Dec. 29th, 1868; and No. 249,536 Nov. 15th, 1881.

I am indebted to The Clock & Watch Museum, Mr. Chris H. Bailey, for this bit of biographical data and the added fact that he died May 5th, 1890 and is buried in the West Cemetery, in Bristol. Lewis is well known in our craft for his perpetual calendar mechanisms, but, few know that he devised the "Patti" spring arrangement.

Patent No. 249,845 "Strike Spring for Eight-day Clocks" was granted Nov. 22nd, 1881, at which time he was a resident of Bristol. He left Huron, seeking a manufacturer of his calendar — date not clear — to join Welch, Spring & Co., where he occupied the position of 'foreman' for several years. That he was an accomplished and efficient mechanical engineer

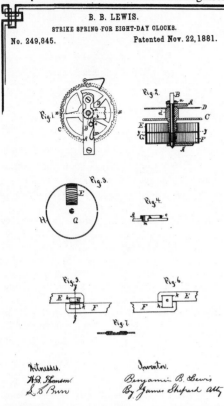

B. B. LEWIS.
STRIKE SPRING FOR EIGHT-DAY CLOCKS.
No. 249,845.   Patented Nov. 22, 1881.

Witnesses.   Inventor.
H.B. Thomson   Benjamin B. Lewis
L. S Burr   By James Shepard atty

is attested by the very simplicity of his calendar. Here he designed a mechanism complicated enough to register day, date, and month, as well as compensate for the different lengths of the months, plus automatic correction for leap years, to a mere four (4) wheels, all concentric — the smallest calendar mechanism then obtainable.

This spring patent goes on to state: "Designed principally for the strike side of a clock movement, although some parts of it are applicable to either side." Upon the "Patti" model, it is utilized on both the strike and time trains. Again, his fine mechanical abilities are exhibited; exact details are exceptionally hard to come by, but it seems clear that Mr. Lewis was faced with the problem of designing a spring of sufficient LENGTH to drive a clock for the full eight-days yet contained in a very small box or barrel for use with a movement much smaller than the conventional eight-day movement. Evidently, he was well aware of the "rule" of spring area being one-third arbor, one-third space, and one-third spring. Then how in this world was he going to maintain his space-area, or even reduce it, and yet come up with a workable, practical spring? Simple; if you can't expand upon the area, how about two areas? And, that is exactly what he did — set one half of the required spring back along the front half. If you can't expand the diameter why not double the thickness?

This quite efficient spring is a bit misunderstood by some tenders of the "144" — many want to call it a double spring. It is NOT; a single spring has only two attaching points — a hole in either end; this one has just that. What he has done is coil one half the spring RIGHT and the other half LEFT, and by a connecting bar in the middle sets one half along side the other. One clockmaker actually confused it with the Craig-Eastman wind method and wrote in to say that he could only wind his Patti one direction and asking how to wind that other spring, etc.?

When you consider this as a single spring, which it is, the winding becomes simple. True, it has two inner coils; one hooked over (to) the winding arbor and the other to the main drive wheel. As you crank up the spring via one inner coil, as it winds up the connecting bar pulls in the other half and this winds it, and, the whole spring, up — turning in just one direction.

Way, way back — August of 1946 to pinpoint the date; we did a short 'bit' upon the Briggs Rotary Clock — a net little 'novelty' timepiece, non-strike, that sat under a small glass bell jar; pointing out that for each turn of its main wheel it revolved the escape arbor 209,952 times which gearingwise placed it alongside the 400-day clock. Years later when compiling his "400-Day Clock Repair Guide" this came to the attention of Mr. Charles Terwilliger, as he successfully launched the 'Guide' — now in its umpteenth printing — and established the Horolovar Company, Box 400-A, Bronxville, N.Y. 10708. Interest in this little clock was shelved until he formed The Clock Trade Enterprises Co., for the reproduction of Early American novelty clocks. First came the "Flying Pendulum" or "Ignatz" model; then, the "Dickory Dock Mouse Clock" and the "Plato" clock — all well known to us tenders of the "144" this date.

Couple of years ago he pulled down the "Briggs Rotary" idea and wrote us re: reproducing it. This month he wrote to say that contract had been firmed up, the re-tooling completed, and they are about ready to go into production. He hopes to see delivery start in July.

As of this moment it is a bit early for a practical figure, but he thinks that the retail price may be upon the order of $135.00. Like his other reproductions, this one will be accompanied with a booklet detailing its history, etc., attesting that it is a 'facsimile' reproduction.

The 'rotary' pendulum is perhaps of French origin; leastways the French produced a goodly number of them over quite a period of years. Louis Moinet, b.-1758 d.-1853, an outstanding apprentice of the celebrated Abraham-Louis Breguet and his secretary from 1791, published a two-volume treatise, "Nouveau Traite d'Horlogerie" at Paris, in 1848, in which three or four applications of the circular or rotary pendulum is delineated. In 1873 E. N. Welch Mfg. Co. was advertising the Briggs rotary thus: "The E. N. Welch Manufacturing Company, make a specialty of rotary clocks and it is claimed that they are the only American manufacturers of reliable clocks having this escapement."

This claim probably held true up to about the turn of the century when Florence Kroeber, began marketing a "rotary." This clock was patented by Gilbert H. Blakesley No. 205,037 and had a worm or screw type escape similar to the then current music boxes. It has upon several occasions been suggested that as Kroeber obtained most of his clocks by contract, that Blakesley supplied his rotary. With the aid of Mr. Ed Ingraham, we researched this point; he — Mr. Ingraham — discussed it with friends who knew Blaksley, one, a Mr. Edward Dunbar, in his mid-90s who once worked for Blaksley. All agreed that Blaksley NEVER manufactured any clocks.

Walter H. Durfree, Providence, R.I.

I hope that from the information I can give you and from the enclosed photographs of a clock movement, that you might be able to identify the country where the movement was made and its approximate age.

It is a grandfather clock with eight chime tubes and a strike tube, and a two position chime drum with "Chime on Eight Bells" in one position and "Westminster Chimes" in the other position.

I am sorry I did not take accurate measurements of the plates when I had the movement out of the case, but to the best of my recollection they were about ten inches wide, eight inches high, ¼

inch thick, and beautifully finished. The chime drum is about seven inches long.

I could locate no identifying names or numbers on the movement and the only other names I could locate in the clock were "Tiffany & Co. New York" on the face of the dial, and "Walter R. Durfree Providence, R.I." printed on the back of the moving Moon Phase part of the dial and imprinted into the metal at the top of each chime tube.

All screws on the dial and in the movement are metric thread, and the only place I have ever seen a snail that functions the way the one on this clock does, was on old French travel clocks, all of which would seem to indicate the movement was imported and cased by Walter H. Durfree for Tiffany & Co.

In photograph number two, is there something missing from the screw clamps on the ends of the hammer lift rods? If not, what is the purpose of the holes in the ends of the clamps and how is the cord held in the clamp?

In photograph number three I found what appeared to be the cut off ends of silk cord between the two parts of the chime drum framework held by the screws indicated by the red ink circles. Where did the cord fit into the assembly and what was its function?

A.

So far as we can determine, only a brief listing by Brooks Palmer in BAC plus a brief resume by Mr. Hamilton Pease, published in 1968 is all the coverage the Durfree operation has had. Palmer also lists Andrew D. Wilson, of Providence, R.I. as active about 1890 to 1920 — but — does not mention any connection with Durfree. Mr. Pease records that Mr. Wilson made, in his own shop, 'replica' Simon Willard movements for Mr. Durfree. And, closes his monograph with: "Elisha C. died this year (1968) and the two generation business ceased abruptly with lamentably little left in print of its owners or their affairs."

This writer was introduced — via mail — to Mr. Walter Durfree, in January of 1932 by the late Wallace Nutting. In Nutting's "The Clock Book," Garden City Publishing Co., 1924, we sensed several mechanical questions left unanswered and sought further clarification from Mr. Nutting, in reply, he wrote: "My expert opinion on the works of a clock is valueless. I pretend to have some knowledge on styles and construction and period, but nothing further. In other words it is the cases and not the works that have received my attention." end quote. He went on to say that

Walter H. Durfree, 1857-1939

he was acquainted intimately with the best clock man in America, and relied upon him and his nephew for technical assistance, etc.; the end result was some very good correspondence with Mr. Durfree, and when he decided to curtail repair activities in his shop in 1932 restricting it to only grandfather clocks, we bought from him a large box of shelf, mantel and wall clock parts.

By reason of that correspondence and the purchase of the residue of clock material and parts we have always felt a sort of 'closeness' to the Durfree operation — any yen to document the Durfree operation did not come until we retired from the bench — we wrote Mr. Elisha C. Durfree, asking his assistance. That request brought a warm and cordial reply in the latter part of 1967 in which he said: "It will take me some time to get together the data which you request. However, as soon as I get the opportunity, I will be glad to do the best I can." Mr. Elisha C. Durfree passed away February 5, 1968 before he had time to complete that promise, thus, we 'go-to-bat' with very little factual data at hand.

Walter H. Durfree was born March 23, 1857 and died August 4, 1939 — he started buying, selling and repairing clocks about 1878 at 295 High Street, which is now Westminster, with a Mr. Dexter C. Cheever, about whom very little is known save at the time he was advertising as a watch and clockmaker. Neither of the Palmer lists include Cheever and he is not to be found

upon any listing at hand; even Nutting does not list him. The Durfree factory moved to 151 Pond Street about 1885 where it remained for some 35 years until it again moved to 270 Washington Street in 1920 — it was at Pond Street that most of the clocks were produced — it remained at 270 Washington Street until Mr. Elisha C. closed it out in 1962.

While at Pond Street, nephew Elisha C. joined the operation, date unknown but one would judge about his 'majority' — born in 1890 he would have been 21 in 1911 and thus we'd take that year as being a reasonable conclusion — nowhere have we any indication of the number of men employed — factorywise the number must have been relatively small. The nephew relates that at the height of the operation, clocks were commenced in batches of 100 — Mr. Durfree's main thought was to produce the "Rolls-Royce" of grandfather clocks and he succeeded to the point he numbered the leading retail jewelry stores of the U.S. as clients: Bailey, Banks & Biddle; James E. Caldwell & Co., Tilden & Thurber, Tiffany, et al. Our photo of a typical Durfree g-f. clock is not the clock mentioned by Mr. Stevens. Mr. Stevens included an excellent color photo of his movement which regretfully we cannot use here — this clock is 97 inches tall; 27 inches wide; movement No. 141, apparently by Waltham, eight tubular chimes with leaded glass door, etc. Mr. Pease thinks he utilized mainly Waltham construction in these g-f clocks though it is evident that he did use a few imports. The Waltham Clock Company operation ceased operation in 1924; perhaps Mr. Durfree then had to turn to foreign made movements — this writer has seen only two Durfree g-f. clocks with movements showing foreign construction — neither were so marked but their general build closely resembled "Elliott" work. Mr. Durfree made many trips to England and was having his tubular chimes manufactured there.

His cases were built upon contract — during that era Waltham was contracting cases from the Herschede Hall Clock Company at Cincinnati — one might speculate that this was also a source Durfree utilized.

After Mr. Elisha C. closed the operation at 270 Washington Street in 1962, he removed the residue to his home in Cranston, R.I. where he carried forward a repair service; made a few clocks — in 1967 he wrote: "I do not think that I have made over 100 clocks in my life." Thus ends the Durfree operation with his death February 5, 1968.

Mr. Stevens included an excellent color photo of the movement in the clock of his question

Typical Durfree clock

I have a French mantle clock that has a small round movement, 3½ inches, that is encased in a bronze case having bronze figurines, a boy and girl looking at a bird's nest against an arbor background. The whole is mounted on an oval wood base that probably at one time was covered by a glass dome. On the movement is stamped, within a small circle, Medaille de Bronze, L. Marti et Ce. The number 993 is stamped both on the movement and the case.

Could you tell me the probable age of the clock and whether such type clocks are scarce or plentiful?

Any information you can give me will be greatly appreciated.

A.

"Establissements S. Marti" of 22 Rue General Leclere, Mountbeliard, France, is active to this date. It was first founded in 1835 to manufacture movements for clocks. A short while back, we had a letter from Mr. R. Marti, the present Director of the company in which he gave us this table:

Movement stamped "S. Marti & Cie. Medaille de Bronze 1867 to 1889.

Those stamped S. Marti & Cie. Medaille d' Argent, 1889 to 1900.

Those stamped "S. Marti & Cie. Medaille d'Or, 1900 to 1931.

Wants Information on
Silas Hoadley Clock

Can you furnish information as to age of an old clock I recently repaired.

The only description I can give is that it is a movement made of wood. On the label inside the clock is the following: "CLOCKS arranged and manufactured by Silas Hoadley, Plymouth, Conn." On the edge of the door is the No. 484.

A.

Silas Hoadley, born 1786, died 1870, was one of the more colorful of the early Connecticut clockmakers, in that he did quite a bit of experimenting; producing some clocks that were a bit different from the usual run-of-the-mill.

Since your clock is wood, it dates behind 1837, the year wood-clock production almost abruptly ceased. You do not indicate whether your clock is long-case or shelf. If long case, possibly being 1825. If shelf, then between 1816 and 1837.

Mr. Hoadley was in the firm of Terry, Thomas & Hoadley about 1809 making long-case, wood movements at Greystone. Shortly thereafter, Eli Terry pulled out of the firm leaving Thomas and Hoadley to operate until Seth Thomas pulled out in 1813. Operated upon his own name until retirement in 1848 when he rented his factory to a knife company. He died at Plymouth at the age of 84.

which I regret we can't use as our reproductions are black and white. Pinpoint answers to his final two questions are difficult — in all probability the two holes he mentions were used for holding the chime tube frame to the packing case for shipment. Chime tubes were generally suspended in cord loops from nubs or pins in the frame — the silk cords he mentions may have been the effort of some repairer to hang the tubes, etc. This would have to be determined from an in-hand examination; from the movement photo I'd say that it is definitely "Waltham" and therefore pre-dates their closing in 1924.

Iron Case is Palermo

George's Watch Shop of San Diego, Calif., suggested I write to you to see if you can tell the approximate age of our clock.

It has an iron case with brass mechanism. On the face is stamped FK in a circle.

On the back door are the numbers 2882. The back plate has 2K 15 stamped on it. On the right side is 10 and on the left side is 2K11. On the bottom, the word "Palermo."

The height is 11½ inches. The length at the bottom is 12¾ inches. The width at the bottom is 5¼ inches, and at the top, 3½ inches.

It is black iron, and has scroll work stamped in it all around the front.

A.

The "F.K." in the dial of your clock is for "Florence Kroeber," first listed in the New York directory for 1865-66 at 25 John Street, and lastly in the 1912 directory at 151 West 80th St.

The iron case, black enameled, came in during the 1880's and ran up into the first decade of this century. The "Palermo" is the style or catalog name for that particular design of clock.

Most, if not all, of Kroeber's clocks were bought by him from other clock factories. Ansonia Clock Co. being one of the larger makers of that era sold many clocks to him. On page 40 of the 1904 catalog they list a "Palermo," enameled iron, and give the height as 10⅝ths inches high. This could easily be your clock. A couple of little ornamental gilt feet could give it the additional inch, and again the size could vary some over several years of production. It is listed at $10.00 regular, with beveled glass and visible escapement $12.25 with a dial 5½ inches in diameter.

Mr. Kroeber was quite active in the clock business. He was granted some 15 or 16 patents, some mechanical and some for case design. So far as this writer knows, no complete history of his activity has been published to date. Mr. C. Wesley Hallett, director, the Clock Museum, Newport, N. H., has a number of Kroeber timepieces in his museum and is very much interested in Kroeber history.

"Wag on the Wall" History

I have just purchased an 8-day clock with two weights; it strikes once at each half hour, strikes the hour and then two minutes after the hour it strikes the hour again. It's shell brass front and pendulum is also shell brass; both pendulum and front have numerous flowers in color. It's a perfect picture of what is called "Wag on the Wall,". The name on the dial is "Lebigot A St. Hilaire Du Harcouet." Would you please, if possible, tell me something about this clock and its age. The movement is in a square metal box with the shell brass sticking way beyond it. The pendulum must be at least three feet long and ten to fifteen inches wide at one point. If you need a picture I would be happy to take one and send to you.

A.

You describe a typical French "provincial" clock; their production dates, roughly within the first two-thirds of the 1800's.

They came in two types; grandfather or floor clocks, weight driven, and wall clocks, spring driven with much shorter pendulums.

They are fairly plentiful over here; perhaps 50 percent or better are 'unmarked' while those that do have a name and town within the dial are just as unidentifiable because that name is of some obscure maker who never got listed, or as in most cases it is that of the merchant-seller for which no list has ever been compiled.

These clocks had a special appeal to the country home for most would have only the one clock; repeating the hour about one minute after first striking enabled members of the household in another room out of sight of it, to get an 'accurate' count. Another appeal was the feature you refer to as "wag on-the-wall," a term originated in Scotland; the clock came as a complete unit and could be either used upon a wall-bracket or installed in brackets in a case when the new owner got around to building or buying a case. Still another appeal was the separate mounting of the trains; I'm sure that you've already noted that you can take out either the time or strike train without disturbing the other train in the least. These movements are always marked by that, and their own peculiar rack strike system wherein the rack falls vertically straight down. The time train being to the left IX side, in order to have the pendulum hang from the center, it is connected with a short pitman-rod to the verge wire. Upon the whole, they are excellent timekeepers and because of their rugged construction require very little service.

Clock History

I have in the shop a grandfather clock. The owner's father has, for years, referred to it as a Chippendale style GFC. There are no markings of any kind. It has a beautifully decorated face and moon dial.

The works are in a very interesting open box. Metal top and bottom, with a post 5/16" x 3/8" x 8½" at each corner and in the exact center. All 5 posts are bradded through the top and bottom plates. The gears and other works are arranged in 3 sets of steel posts 3/16" thick by 5/8" x 8½ split at the bottom and fitting into holes in the bottom plate — threaded into the top of the post and secured with screws through the top plate. The pivot holes have brass bushings.

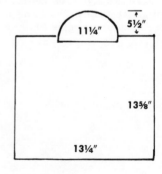

The weights are wound up with a key. Weights weigh 13 pounds each. From the front — the right posts have the strike train. At the bottom, the barrel, No. 1, is the star wheel at back to cause the hammer to strike on an interesting coiled wire gong on a metal rod stand fastened to a cross member — wood — back of the works. The gear No. 2 activates a counting device, which is flat and has teeth like a saw, and which moves up and down inside of the front post. This counting device has a bent wire which makes contact with the snail on the front of the big wheel controlling the hands — located in front of and attached to the front of the center post. This gear No. 2 also has a pin wheel on the back end. The pin lifts an intriguing device which activates the strike. It has an arm on each end and a counter-balance which extends out 1¾" from the center of the staff and outside of the plates. The staff extends through a notch in the front of the post to allow the front arm to contact the hour and half-hour pins on a gear in back of the hand control gear. The back arm releases the warning. Gear No. 3 works off No. 2 and runs the fan, No. 4.

There is a second counter-balanced mechanism located at the top and on the side toward the center of the works on the time train posts, which has an arm about 2" long with a 1/2" brass ball on the end extending from the center of the staff over the escape wheel. The staff has an arm on each end. At the back, the

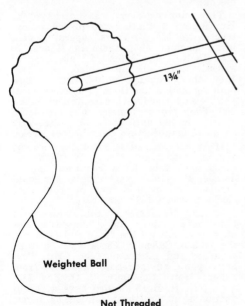

1¾"

Weighted Ball

Not Threaded

arm is activated by the first mentioned counter-balance and sets up the warning. The front arm counts the strike. For me, a fascinating device.

The center posts contain the escape wheel and the verge — with the gears controlling the hands, snail, hour and half-hour pins attached to the front of the front post. There is a hole through the back post to allow the verge wire to pass through to fit in a slot in the long — 39" plus or minus — pendulum bar, which hangs from a brass plate attached with 2 screws on top of the top plate. The bob is heavy. The left posts have the time train. At the bottom of the barrel, No. 1 wheel has an extension through the front plate with two gears to run the hour hand and minute hand, etc., No. 2 gear powers the escape wheel.

Incidentally, no second hand.

A coiled wire around the hour pipe activates the moon dial — 2 teeth per day.

Can you help with who may have made the clock? What year?

A.

Good to hear from you again — you give a very good description of a French Morbier movement — sometimes referred to as French Provincial .

As with any unmarked or otherwise unidentified movement it is exceedingly difficult to assign a maker or pinpoint a date. This general type of construction comes from the mountain provinces of the Jura, the name Morbier is from a little village of that name in the Haut-Jura, about 275 miles south and east of Paris and only about 35 miles across the border to Geneva, Switzerland.

Most movements we see in the U.S. have anchor escapements and roughly date from about 1860 to 1915. Not all, but by far most, of these clocks strike the hour at the hour, then 60 to 90 seconds later repeat the stroke.

I have been told that these clocks were built for the rural folk who could not afford the fine Paris clocks, or a clock for every room and that this repeating the hour strike adapted it to a one clock home, i.e. when in another room and the clock was heard to strike you could simply wait a minute and get with it to be sure what was struck.

I note that you say: "wound with a key" and hasten to add that no weight driven clock should be wound with a key — it should be a crank thus a continuous pull and no jerk like when grasping a new hold on the key. Check back in your Bulletin for April '72, whole No. 157, and see the article, Morbier Clocks, by A. Seymour. Also Tardy's, La Pendule Francaise, Vol. 3, has a splendid chapter and a lot of fine photos. If you don't have it, I feel sure that our NAWCC library has one for loan. So far as I know, these are the only clocks with the vertical rack strike; i.e. a rack that falls straight down rather than one revolving upon a pivot. I have two of these — one g-f movement with calendar concentric with the hands, and a wall model quite like Fig. 14 of Seymour's paper. This clock was given to me by the late Col. Luke Lea, who liberated it from a German Officer's Club in Hannonville, France, in 1917. Col. Lea is the man who almost captured the Kaiser in December of 1918 — see Saturday Evening Post for October 23, 1937 — and created an international incident.

Waterbury Has
Duplex Escapement

Perhaps you can help me identify and date approximately a pocket watch which I believe is 16s. A photo is enclosed to help in identification.

Please note especially the escape wheel with alternating teeth slanted down for escaping on balance; also imprint of N.E.W. Co. I'm assuming National Elgin Watch Co. Is this right? Also note the intricate cut out of plate over plate on the train side or double plate watch case movement and dial side in original make or shape.

I have been a watchmaker for 29 years, but have never experienced such a make or escapement.

A.

Your very good photo which I am returning shows a skeleton Waterbury. Several are around; some were even placed in little carriage type clock cases. What is more surprising is that you have never met up with a 'duplex' escapement before.

"N.E.W. Co." stands for "New England Watch Co."

The Waterbury Watch Co. was organized at Waterbury in 1878, and changed to New England Watch Co. in 1898. Apparently, both companies were a part and parcel of the Waterbury Clock Co., whatever division if any is not at all clear. Material catalogues of the 1890's show these watches as products of the New England Watch Co., while upon the very same page they say, "Always give name of movement and series letter when ordering material." The monogram W.W. Co., and Waterbury, appear on some movements."

Each model was given a series letter. Some had the word "series" and some just the letter. A few models went by name and letter, such as "Columbian" Series H; "Trump" series I; and "Americus" series J, etc. Writing of Waterbury about 1886, Charles Crossman said, "The first series, viz.: A, B, and C, all have open dials, exposing the movement, while series B and C have some closed dials." He makes no mention

of a skeletonized movement. I have an 1896 watch material catalogue which begins with series E and ends with W; there seem to be no U and V. However, we are reasonable that there must have been, including some named models, more than 26 variations.

This is the concern that first manufactured the celebrated "Ingersoll" dollar watch; in November of 1914 it was sold by court order to Robert H. Ingersoll & Bro. upon a bid of $76,000.

Ithaca Grandfather Clocks

I have two, tall grandfather clocks run by springs. On the face is the name Ithaca. I just wonder if you could give me any history as to when they were made and where? If you can, I would like very much to hear from you. These clocks are 7 feet tall.

A.

The Ithaca Calendar Clock Co. was founded upon a patent issued to Mr. J. H. Hawes, in 1853. Their growth and/or formation was a sort of contractural operation. About a year after Hawes' patent, two other men, a Mr. W. H. Atkins and a Mr. Joseph C. Burritt, made some improvements upon the Hawes mechanism.

This improved form was purchased by Huntington & Platts, who placed a contract with "Mix Brothers," operators of a large machine shop there in Ithaca, to manufacture it. Dates of this gradual growth aren't all pin-pointed. In April, 1866 the company moved into a new building and a month later a stock company was formed with a capital of $100,-000. They produced many calendar clocks and it was not until about 1898 that they began to manufacture Grandfather clocks.

If Ithaca was slow a-borning, it was equally slow dying. Mr. J. W. Gibbs records that this death required half a decade, 1915-1920. Accordingly, we could bracket the manufacture of your g-f clocks between 1898 and 1915.

In 1960, Mr. James W. Gibbs researched the Ithaca history and produced an 80-page book entitled the "Life and Death of the Ithaca Calendar Clock Co.," a very accurate and interesting document. Perhaps you can purchase a copy from Adams-Brown Company, P. O. Box 349, Exter, N. H. Brown's also have a reproduction of an old Ithaca catalog, 34 pages, 4 x 8½ inches, for $1.75.

EVOLUTION -ELECTRIC CLOCKS

Clockmaking in the U.S. over the years has followed a definite pattern of cycles; the first was that "round" of long case, wood movement clocks, that extended from the very beginning up to about 1814 when Eli Terry started production of the short pendulum, wood movement. This second cycle ran its course in about 23 years to the great depression of 1837 and the rolling of sheet brass.

Cycle No. 3, would be Chauncey Jerome's thirty hour, weight driven, brass movement which enjoyed a much longer run up to near the turn of the century. These cycles overlap each other making it difficult to assign any definite cut off dates.

Following that came the so called kitchen clock and the golden oak era—roughly the turn of the century up to World War I. The business boom following that war brought on a variety of mantel clocks and a general upswing in clock production with many, many styles and models.

Architectural styles were changing, houses were smaller and with lower ceilings, and the long case clock was upon the wane, not to be revived until after World War II. Overlapping that cycle came the synchronous clock, though a sync self-starting motor had been perfected as early as about 1916 its general use in the lowly mantel clock had to await the regulation of the a.c. current supplied our homes. This came about in the very late 1920s and remains with us this date.

Here we have another big overlap— several years back, there began the "second" cycle of the battery powered clock—still with us. The first cycle of the battery clock came in at the turn of the century; it gave us the "Tiffany Never-Wind" by George Steele Tiffany, the "Warren" by Henry E. Warren and the "No-Key Clock" first manufactured by the Mountain States Electric Company at Wheeling, W. Va., and later at Mount Vernon, Ohio. It was followed by the "Poole" made at Ithaca, N.Y., and later in Weedsport, N.Y., under the name of "Barr."

These four battery clocks are quite similar in general construction—all short pendulum and most coming under a glass bell jar, thus comprising a distinct "cycle." Their builders faced two major problems: 1, poor batteries, 2, contacts that burned, gathered dirt, and failed.

Tiffany approached the problem via the torsion pendulum; stroking much slower he had less contacts and also less battery drain.

Poole was along the same lines; it utilized the "Matthaus Hipp" (b.-1813 d.-1893) hit and miss contact system, whereby the pendulum swings free for some 25 or 30 strokes; then when the arc of motion falls off, a butterfly tail pivot engages a V crotch upon the pendulum tripping the contact, etc.

Mr. Warren made no effort to reduce the number of contacts; he used a repulsion method making his pendulum ball of a permanent magnet and swinging it across a coil. Said coil polarized to repel the pendulum upon its backward swing. He attacked the contact difficulty head on, devising a completely new method—a small glass tube has two wires extending inside; a small globule of mercury is inserted and the air exhausted; when this tube is tilted, the mercury flows to the wires thereby

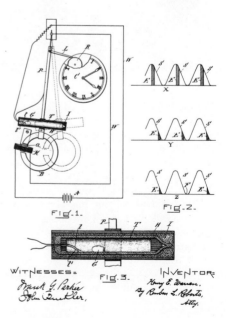

H. E. WARREN.
ELECTRIC APPARATUS FOR DRIVING CLOCKS OR SIMILAR MECHANISM.
APPLICATION FILED JULY 27, 1910.

1,144,973.

Patented June 29, 1915.
2 SHEETS—SHEET 1.

Fig-1.   Fig-2.

Fig-3.

WITNESSES:
Frank G. Parker
John Denkler,

INVENTOR:
Henry E. Warren.
By Barton L. Roberts,
Atty.

closing the contact; tilted the other direction the mercury flows away opening the circuit again.

Here lies a most interesting little side story and one that is very little known. Several horological patented items have cropped up in other later construction, like the "Bendix Drive" which is the principle of the old watch safety pinion. That patent had passed into the Public Domain and its inventor reaped no profits from the automobile industry. The Warren patent No. 1,144,973 was active when the silent-mercury switch came in and it has been reported that he realized more from it, by far, than from the sale of those clocks using the mercury contact. See Fig. 3 page one of the patent copy.

FIG. 2.

HENRY ELLIS WARREN.

Henry Ellis Warren was born in Boston, Mass., May 21, 1872—graduated from M.I.T. in 1894 with the degree of B.S. In 1907 he moved to Ashland, Mass., and began investigating the construction of electrically operated clocks. In 1912 the "Warren Clock Company" was organized to manufacture and sell an ingenious battery powered clock—Fig. 1. This operation was begun in a small outbuilding, then removed to a barn on his farm. Fig. 2 is a 1917 view of this building at which time he had eight employees. By 1924 they had moved into their first factory building, at which time 25 employees were reported.

FIG. I.

Returns upon this manufacturing operation were satisfactory, but Mr. Warren was not satisfied with the clock. Despite the perfected "contact," it had its eccentricities and still depended upon a somewhat unreliable battery.

Mr. Warren was already experimenting with his sync motor—as early as 1916 he had developed a self-starting sync motor that could carry the load of a gear train plus a pair of clock hands. Once perfected, this clock pointed up the inaccuracies of the current as then being generated so Mr. Warren turned his attention to that problem. He devised a master clock for generating plants. This clock had a large dial

196

with two hands, one black and one gold; each center mounted and making one rev. every five minutes. The black hand was driven by an accurate, seconds beating pendulum and the gold hand driven by a "Telechron" motor.

The two hands are started off together, and so long as the frequency remains "on time" they stay together; if the frequency is slow, the gold hand falls behind; if faster than "time" it moves ahead of the black. The generating station operator watches this clock and adjusts his turbine governors regulating the frequency so as to keep the black and gold hands in line. When doing this, he automatically causes all other sync clocks plugged into the system to keep correct time. To this extent, the sync clock upon your mantel or the wall of your shop gets corrected several times per day. Keep in mind that here we are speaking of "household" time for the lack of a better description—a good household time it is, but far, far from precision accuracy. It is so inaccurate that while the manufacturer of your watch rate recorder drives it with a sync motor, he CANNOT feed the raw 60-c current from the mains into it. He first takes this current and re-cycles it by a quartz crystal or a tuning fork to obtain the required precision to rate a watch in a couple of minutes.

Mr. Warren demonstrated his master clock at the L street Boston Edison Company October 23, 1916. Generating plants accepted it readily—some even advertised that they were regulating their current so that the consumer could have correct time back in the late 1920s.

This was NOT the whole truth—the prime reason for closely regulated current was to enable the efficient coupling of several generators into the same system. Having perfected his sync motor and the system for current regulation, Mr. Warren had to name his motor. He chose "Telechron," a combining of two Greek words, Teles and Chronos, interpreting it to mean "Time From A Distance." Not a great deal has been recorded upon his early experiments and efforts; only a few of the tenders of the "144" even know that his first production was a pendulum clock, still fewer know

of another time device he originated, the violin string clock, or vibrating-wire frequency standards built by the Lombard Governor Corporation of Ashland, Mass., of which he became president. This device —clock—is not generally known to our craft. They were not produced in great quantity, and their users take care of their own maintenance. In a paper by John S. Hall and Arthur A. Hoag, of the U.S. Naval Observatory, and published in Sky & Telescope for Nov., 1956, we are told that the "brains of the console are two vibrating-wire frequency standards. Developed by Henry E. Warren, President of the Lombard Governor Corporation, and inventor of the Telechron clock." This is at the Flagstaff station observatory. Same paper also states that similar frequency standards are used by the great Palomar and Lick observatories.

Lest you get the feeling that our rambling is going far afield and that we've completely lost the old "144," let me say that within a year, you are going to be seeing a clock constructed along these violin string principles. One of our major clock manufacturers has been experimenting with it since 1968—your "C. & O." has been running one of the experimental models for almost two years. Just as soon as they take the wraps off, we shall detail and illustrate it for you.

Mr. Warren is often called "Father of Electric Time" by reason of his "Telechron" alternating current synchronous motor and the "Warren" master clock. It would be more accurate to say that he was the father of synchronous time—time from a distance, "Telechron." There is no desire to get into semantics and certainly no intent to detract in the very least from his great accomplishments—we've had "some" electric time from the days of that great hassle between Alexander Bain and Dr. Wheatstone; the first Bain patent dates from 1841, 31 years before Mr. Warren was born.

The first U.S. patent I've been able to locate was No. 11723 to Alex Hall, of Loydsville, Ohio, titled "Improvement in Electric Clocks" and dated Sept. 26, 1856 —some sixteen years prior to Mr. Warren's birth. It was my good fortune to have corresponded with Mr. Warren when we were both members of the Boston Clock

Club. Being a great one for accuracy, I verily believe he would have approved my insertion of the word "synchronous" before time in a title he so richly earned.

If one desires to "ramble" through electric time, it is interesting to speculate just how it came from Edinburg all the way out to Ohio in just sixteen years, communications being as slow as they were 125 years ago? For practical purposes the 16 years just indicated could be trimmed to about ten—some time had to elapse between the time Hall filed and was granted his patent; add to that he must have spent some time experimenting, etc.

The first paragraph of his patent reads. "Be it known that I, Alexander Hall, of Loydsville, in the county of Belmont and state of Ohio, have invented certain new and useful improvements in electric clocks." This indicates that he was familiar with electric clocks (electric time) and any way you care to look at it, for that period in time Alex Hall was pretty close upon the heels of Alex Bain.

Presently the trade is into two overlapping cycles, the long case clock is being sold more today than ever before; we are seeing new battery clocks almost monthly, and we are just entering a third cycle, that of the quartz crystal clock. This column has mentioned the quartz so often during this year the reader could easily conclude that ole "C. & O." is "teched-in-the-head" quartzwise. My sole defense is: we have to call the shots as we see them. A recent issue of Electronic News carried the notice that Motorola, at their Schumberg, Ill., communications division, is apparently taking a close look at the expanding market for watches, clocks, and timers. That they will soon be grinding out volume production of half-inch quartz crystal oscillators for them must be accepted as a true indicator of things to come.

What is very much desired at this point in time are some equally good "indicators" of the impact of the quartz construction upon the "144." Despite its radical construction—viewed from the old time view point—no instrument—watch, clock, or machinery—is going to operate day in and day out without some degree of maintenance; the questions are: 1, how often?, 2, how much? We can be sure that the level of accidents will remain the same; broken glasses, bent hands, etc. Whether the manufacturer will or can make available parts and modules remains to be seen. Much has been said over the past decade about built-in-obsolescence and even more about the general attitude of manufacturers toward the service industry. 1971 is a far cry from the days when big manufacturers like Elgin and Waltham kept "missionaries" in the field to assist repairmen with their problems; I'd bet you that there are many tenders of the "144" who never saw a factory "missionary"—perhaps many who never heard of one.

What Is Age of Lantern Clock?

I have in for repairs a French Lantern Clock, 18" high. It has the same movement as in Practical Clock Repairing by De-Carle, page 161. I would like to know how old it is, and if this movement is the original one. As you can see, the brackets are of stainless steel and there is a piece of 12 gauge electric wire around the rear dial. These markings are on the back plate.
ETIENNE MAXANT
BREVETE
PARIS
10139
4 11

A.

Tardy records Etienne Maxant as being active on the Rue de Saintonge, Paris, 1880 to 1905. Brevete is French for patented, the 10139 is his serial number and the 4 on the left of the pillar post with 11 on the right indicates the correct pendulum length.

This same number should show on your pendulum ball. The 4 indicates four "pouce" and the 11 eleven lignes — old French measurement terms.

To say whether or not this movement is the original is exceptionally difficult. The chances are it is in most instances it is a bit difficult for a clockmaker to implant a completely different movement without some indication that the alteration was made.

SPRINGS

MAINSPRINGS

I would appreciate any information you might be able to supply concerning mainsprings for 8-day striking clocks. Is there any known way to get the length, width and strength?

A.

To hand you a simple rule whereby you may quickly and easily determine the proper mainspring is just about out of the question. Fortunately, the common garden variety of 8-day mantel striking clock does not work to a very close tolerance and this wide latitude enables most repairmen to run somewhat by "rule-of-thumb".

We've checked a few old catalogs and give you a partial list herewith. However, it is easily noted that once they are listed they do not take on a pattern. Further proof that specific rules are evasive.

One can always get a fair idea of width from the clock, even though every vestige of the old spring is missing. By counting the train and for mainspring length purposes, you will need only to count from the main wheel up to the hand-center to determine the number of revolutions required of the main wheel to drive it 8 days. With your spring in the clock, take the letdown key and let it out to about where you think it ought to be when run down. Count the number of coils, wind fully up and count coils again, subtracting the first count from the last will give you the number of revolutions that spring will drive the clock. Since you have already determined this figure, you know instantly whether or not the spring is long enough.

After all, "rule-of-thumb" isn't the poorest method on earth, especially where one doesn't have a better one. Most clocks within the category you designate are equipped with recoil escapements. If you put a spring too strong in a recoil escapement clock, the extra power transmitted to the pallets will cause the pendulum to take a shorter arc

and therefore gain time. Where the pendulum is short and light, this effect will be even greater than on a clock with a long heavy pendulum. Experience and practice are a great aid in determining whether or not the spring may be on the weak side. Close observation of the escapement action, arc of pendulum swing, and sound are good indicators. All 8-day mantel clocks repaired should be run at least one full 8 days before delivery; two weeks would not hurt. Any job you may have doubt about should be carefully checked and observed twice a day—upon opening shop in the morning, and at closing time, noting closely pendulum motion, sound of tick, etc.

I'm not sure whether or not this practice prevails in our clock factories today, but in years past they used to check all mainsprings for power and to see that they uncoil evenly. Those that passed this test were labeled No. 1 and used in the time side. The others were marked seconds and placed in the strike train. Goodrich says: "A rough mainspring will lose one-third of its power from coil friction."

STEEL USED IN MAINSPRINGS

What is the S.A.E. number of the steel used for mainsprings of clocks? Is it 1095?

Describe heat treatment. Give temperature and oil or water quench. What hardness is usually acquired by hardening? Approximate Rockwell number.

What drawing or stress relieving procedure and temperatures are used?

A.

The great majority of all clock spring steel is S.A.E. 1095.

Normally it is supplied in a pre-tempered state and would not require any heat treating.

Standard Clock Spring Steel has a Rockwell hardness of C-47/51.

In the factory spring steel is hardened and tempered continuously in long coils, then the metal is heated in a lead bath and quenched in oil at 1,400 degrees. It then feeds through a second lead bath and is drawn to approximately 750 degrees to obtain the proper hardness (Rock. C 47/51). This hardness seems to be pretty well standard with most makers.

The metal is then wound up on a reel, is brightly polished and is again heated in lead to obtain color which may run from a light straw to dark blue, depending on the customer's requirements. The matter of color, of course, has nothing to do with the hardness of the metal and is simply used as a matter of finish.

As a general rule, it is not necessary to do any drawing for stress relief after the spring has been formed. If it is necessary to stress relief a spring there is no general procedure. Competent spring makers determine this by experimenting.

LeCOULTRE MAINSPRINGS

If you repair small traveling alarm clocks, probably you have had one of these little clocks come in from which the entire mainspring had been removed. Many of these are made by "LeCoultre." Mr. M. Friedman, of their material department (Longines-Wittnauer Watch Company, 580 Fifth Avenue, New York 19, New York) has supplied the following chart giving the correct measurements (metric) for LeCoultre clock mainsprings:

SAFETY KEY
I would like to know if there is a safety key for winding clocks. I have a customer who received a very bad cut and bruises on his hand when the mainspring broke while he was winding same. Has there ever been such a key on the market?

A.
I have never heard of a "safety" key being on the market. The kick-back when a mainspring or ratchet breaks can be pretty nasty, and I know just what you have in mind

You might be thinking of the "safety center pinion" as found in some watches; we think this threaded arrangement in a clock key would not work. Suppose you have a clock on which the time and strike sides wind in opposite directions? Even should both wind to the right (clockwise) your key would have right threads of necessity, and when the spring breaks or the ratchet lets go, the kick would be to the left (counter clockwise) just tightening the threaded portion of the key instead of unscrewing, as the safety pinion does.

Why not provide your customer with one of the wooden handle "let-down" keys? The winding operation could be performed by gripping the round wood handle in the full palm; then in case of accident, there would be no broken nails or skinned knuckles.

MODEL:	WIDTH:	STRENGTH:	LENGTH:
9/10Ro 428	110/100	8½-8¼	290,
90L 460	136/100	5¾-6,	230,
90LM 490	136/100	5¾-6,	230,
11LSC	105	10¼-10½.	345.
11LO 438	105	10-10¼,	345,
12½L 449-450	128	12½-12¾,	420,
12A 476	110	8¾-9,	250
17UOC C. 429	98	18½-18¾,	420,
10ROL C. 480	1.29	.09	....
12″ R.C. 489 time	1.14	.10	380,
″ ″ alarm	1.95	.07	400.

Manufacturer		Width in inches	Thick. mm.	Length, inches	End.
Seth Thomas	164 Sonora	1	.59	115	loop
Seth Thomas	86 Ventura	3/4	.64	115	loop
Seth Thomas	86	3/4	.47	96	loop
Seth Thomas	85	3/4	.46	105	loop
Seth Thomas	89 strike	3/4	.39	96	loop
Seth Thomas	O.S. No. 48	3/4	.35	80	loop
Seth Thomas	41	11/16	.39	96	loop
Seth Thomas	110	1/2	.40	60	loop
Seth Thomas	119	1	.66	115	hole
Seth Thomas	113-A Chime	1	.45	96	hole
Seth Thomas	143	5/8	.55	96	hole
Sessions	Westminster	3/4	.49	96	loop
Sessions	Verdi Strike	11/16	.39	96	loop
Sessions	30-hour	5/16	.27	30	loop
Ansonia	30-day	3/4	.36	96	loop
Ansonia	Light-weight	3/4	.30	72	loop
Ansonia	Visible escapement	5/8	.37	96	loop
Ansonia	Simplex	5/8	.30	78	loop
Ansonia	Regular 8-day	1	.44	96	hole
Ansonia	Marquise	3/4	.35	72	hole
Ansonia	8-day strike	11/16	.39	96	hole
Waterbury	Mantel strike	3/4	.37	96	loop
Waterbury	Hanging strike	3/4	.37	96	loop
Waterbury	Strike (round movt.)	3/4	.30	54	loop
Waterbury	1-day	5/8	.33	56	loop
Waterbury	8-day, lever	1	.45	96	hole
Waterbury	Chime	1	.42	96	hole
Waterbury	Ships Bell	3/4	.28	54	hole
Waterbury	Small mantel	7/16	.31	54	hole
New Haven	Petite	9/16	.38	80	loop
New Haven	Theta Chime	7/8	.34	68	hole
New Haven	12-day Glass reg.	3/4	.39	72	hole
New Haven	Chime Strike	3/4	.37	90	hole
New Haven	1-day, lever	5/8	.36	60	hole

Manufacturer		Width in inches	Thick, inches	Length, feet	End.
Gilbert	No. 30 mov.	1/2	.013	5'	hole
Gilbert	8-day	5/16	.011	6'	loop
Gilbert	4582 time mov.	7/16	.018	5'	loop
Ingraham	8-day	3/4	.018	8'6"	loop

CLOCK MAINSPRING WINDER

I have a heavy brass winder with a crank that ratchets both ways. If I wind the spring on the winder, holding the barrel in my left hand, how can I unhook the outer end of the spring from the barrel?

In winding it back, should the outer end be hooked in the barrel held in the hand, and then wound in with the winder? Or if I wind the spring on the winder and slip the barrel over same, how can I be sure the outer end will hook on the barrel?

You also advocate straightening out springs for cleaning. How many coils should be left at the center to avoid stretching the spring too much?

A.

Your first question has to do with removing the spring from its barrel, or more specifically, how to release it from the barrel hook after compressing (winding) it out of the barrel.

1. Release or turn loose of the winder crank with your right hand and slip a "clip" or "restraining ring" over the spring.

2. Continue to hold the barrel in your left hand, and with the thumb of the right hand, trip your click on the winder, gradually allowing the spring to expand by turning the crank back.

Either or both of these methods relieves all tension and frees your right hand to assist in unhooking from the barrel. And either may be reversed to replace the spring in the barrel.

Yes, I do advocate straightening the spring for cleaning. The last two coils next to the winding arbor need not be straightened. Rub briskly the entire length of the stretched portion with fine steel wool, then sponge the spring off with a clean rag saturated in some cleaner like gasoline or benzine. Lastly, give it a good wiping with a clean, dry cloth, working this cloth through those last two coils with a piece of peg wood. Replace in the barrel with a winder and lubricate with Moebius mainspring lubricant.

SUSPENSION SPRING

I have a German striking clock that had a string for a suspension spring. What kind of cord string or catgut is best for replacing it?

What do you do to the stationary balance screw bearing in Westclox? Can I grind it out some way so that the balance will take a nicer motion?

A.

We suspect the clock in question to be French instead of German — have never seen a German clock with a silk suspension. Silk is the ideal replacement; I don't think gut would work because it stiffens with age, and usually these silk suspended pendulums include a method of winding the cord over a small arbor for shortening or lengthening the pendulum (regulating) and it is too small to be adaptable to gut.

The cone-bearing screws are entirely too hard for an efficient or quick grinding operation to remove pits and rust. Replacement bearing screws for the Westclox line come very reasonable, and your regular material house can get them for you if they do not stock them. Many of them are interchangeable and it isn't necessary to carry a very large stock.

When replacing bearing screws, always chuck the balance in your lathe, and with fine oil stone slip, touch up the pivots, being careful to maintain the original angle. Any Westclox so treated should give you a motion equal to the new ones.

WATERBURY CLOCK

I currently have for repair a Waterbury clock with ship's wheel in front that is used for winding. It's an 8-day, jeweled clock with a 3-inch dial and a pin-lever escapement.

What would the beat-per-minute be in vibrating a new spring for a clock of this kind?

A.

The beat (number of strokes the balance makes per hour or minute) is predetermined by the designer of a timepiece when he plans the gearing. It was for years held to a fairly rigid standard by watch manufacturers, but small balance-wheel clocks were of varied design and gearing, and came out with just about every figure imaginable. It isn't possible to determine the beat of the piece in question from your size and description.

If you will count the train of this clock carefully, the correct beat of its balance can be easily determined. Count the teeth of the center (hour) wheel and divide that number by the number of leaves of the pinion it drives (next arbor) through the train.

To illustrate, let us say a clock has (beginning with the hour wheel) center, third, fourth and escape wheels, and that each wheel has 50 teeth (save the escape) and that each pinion has five leaves, and the escape wheel has 15 teeth.

Now the center of 50 will turn the third pinion of 5 ten times. The third wheel of 50 will turn the fourth pinion of 5 ten times, and the fourth wheel of 50 will turn the escape pinion of 5 ten times. So 10x10x10 equals 1,000; that is, the escape arbor will make 1,000 revolutions while the center wheel is making one (one hour).

When the escape wheel of 15 teeth is revolved 1,000 times, we have 15,000 escape teeth passing a given point, but you have two points (receiving pallet and let-off pallet), so we multiply the 15,000 by 2, and get 30,000 beats per hour.

By so counting your clock, the correct beat is determined.

MAINSPRING WINDER

We use it on all jobs, but by no means consider it an easy risk-free operation, especially with large mainsprings and their barrels or mainspring boxes.

We received instructions with winder to wind mainspring into barrel or mainspring box with winder as follows: Hook center of spring with winder, placing a few coils in the barrel, pressing gently at an angle against spring and winding the spring. It goes in very nicely, but I tried this method at least one-half dozen times over a period of time, each time feeling guilty.

I checked same by winding and com-pressing spring into retaining ring, releasing and removing, and found they are a little distorted—not bad at all, however, considering some I have seen. Maybe we are still doing something wrong. Your suggestions would be appreciated. Our treatment of barrels and mainspring boxes after the clock has been disassembled is to remove cap, if it has one, and fully wind mainspring up in the barrel, and put retaining ring or clip around the mainspring while in barrel.

We find the clips that come on mainsprings are usually too thick for the remaining space, and other ones we make up often are too weak. If the clip doesn't spring too much, one can unhook spring from barrel. Remove clip by winding up mainspring in winder, releasing tension on clip and removing. Then stretch out mainspring, except for a couple of coils, clean and lubricate, repeating process in reverse. Sometimes the clip is not strong enough, since a clean, oiled mainspring has more power.

To eliminate clip failures, your suggestions concerning type of construction and type of material used would be greatly appreciated. We also experience difficulty in shaping the inner coil of mainsprings, also in removing arbors, especially in barrels and mainspring box types. Suggestions would be greatly appreciated.

In several years of our inquiry with wholesalers and distributors on detailed operation of Bergeon clock mainspring winder, it has brought no results. They have offered to send me one for inspection and trial, but can't answer a simple question such as, "Can one remove mainspring from barrel with tool?" Their reply is, "We don't know if it can be done." We are interested in correct procedure.

I understand they are introducing another new model Bergeon clock mainspring winder. What is your opinion of the winder? We have found other Bergeon tools to be of quality, but fully realize that proper use of any tool is essential to its life and its productive efficiency.

A.

It is also a pleasure to have your attitude toward mainsprings expressed for the very simple reason that from experience we are convinced that many, if not most clock-makers, pay too little attention to the "powerhouse." Glad to see that you have a genuine desire to see that it is properly handled.

We can heartily agree with you on the Bergeon line of tools and are familiar with the mainspring winder they marketed a few years back. Didn't know that a new one was out or coming out—will check at once. My thought is that it is just as important to exercise care and do it with a winder when removing a spring from box or a barrel as it is when replacing it. Whether or not there is an "easy, risk-free" method, we are not sure. It might depend somewhat on your definition of easy and risk-free. Leastways, we've never seen a method that would fit a strict interpretation of it.

The very first thing I do to a mainspring winder is to remove or disconnect its ratchet because I never have use for same. The instructions you received with the winder you mentioned are essentially correct. However, I never place a few coils in the barrel when winding a spring in, for I find that a turn and a half is enough. All that is necessary is just to keep the wound portion of spring from catching on the outside end of the spring or barrel hook—the additional half-turn does the trick.

It is true that one causes a very slight twist or angle bend near the outside coil, but this is of no consequence, and we have it on very good authority that this very same procedure is an established shop practice by a chronometer manufacturer. We know that their chronometers are hanging up some very, very good rates. It certainly should be okay on the "garden variety" of clock.

When the spring is taken out of the barrel with winder, you simply permit it to unwind by either backing the crank backwards or allowing the barrel to spin in your left hand, whichever is the easier. This leaves the spring perfectly free for cleaning, and right here, let me say I like your method of stretching out the spring for a thorough cleaning. Do you ever try rubbing it down with very fine steel wool? Now when you use the above method for rewinding the clip, time

and trouble connected with it is again eliminated.

We know of one clockmaker who keeps a supply of heavy, soft wire (large) on hand, and before removing a spring, he will cut off a length, bend it in a loop horseshoe-wise and lay it handy. Then he winds the spring out of its barrel, latches the crank by the ratchet and, while still holding the barrel with the left hand, puts the wire loop over the spring and gives it a securing twist.

The barrel is unhooked, the spring taken from the winder and, grasping it with the left hand, he untwists the wire, permitting the spring to expand free for cleaning. The replacing operation of his is exactly the reverse; the spring is wound to a circle slightly smaller than the barrel, while the outside end is hooked to a fixture on the winder, the wire hook applied, it is removed from the winder and then inserted in its barrel.

All this to me is simply so much lost motion, when I can do the operation in half his time and know that my method is just as good. Sometimes his hook on the barrel fails to catch, while by this method it never fails.

Insufficent Mainspring Power

I do clock work for both my own shop and the trade. I have been having a lot of trouble with Seth Thomas (later models) chime clocks. After cleaning and properly oiling both the movement and springs, I don't seem to get enough power from the springs to run eight days.

Sometimes it is on the time side and again on the chime springs. Are others having this trouble? I put in new springs and they don't hold up for long on some jobs. The springs I have been purchasing (ST) seem to straighten out much easier than other eight-day springs I use, as if they did not have the proper temper.

I will be very grateful for any information you can give me on this matter.

A.

We haven't noticed any particular trouble with S. T. mainsprings themselves.

The No. 124 Westminster chime, the No. 120 series as well as several other of the late models have their springs either in a "box" or barrel. These movements are not over powered as is the case with earlier movements with their springs in the "open."

You will note that both the 120 and the 124 have their springs mounted under a separate and removable bridge. This bridge or plate "laps" or fits on top of the plate proper, and to hold it level there is placed on the two lower posts of the 124, and the single lower posts of the 120, a spacer or washer the exact thickness of the plate. We see lots of these movements come in where this spacer has been lost. Thus when the bridge is screwed down it is at an angle and usually binding on the winding arbor. In many instances, this alone will cause the clock to stop after three or four days' run.

Again we've observed many of these springs twisted in by hand. When removed from the box or barrel, they stand up like the spiral spring from an old mattress.

1. Always check to see that the spacer is there and that the arbor can turn freely.
2. Use a winder when replacing the spring. Many repairmen just don't realize they are choking a lot of driving power out of the spring when they "cone" them.
3. Use a lubricant of proper consistency (Moebius or K-V Medium). Light oil is pressed from between the coils when the spring is wound tight, and thus fails to lubricate.

Drawing Clockspring Temper

I sometimes find a clock part that I cannot obtain from material houses and would like to make it by hand. Frequently it is a spring of some type that I could make from an old clock mainspring. How-ever, I have never found a satisfactory way to anneal clock mainsprings so that they can be shaped easily — particularly right angle bends. Is there any special secret to drawing the temper on a clock spring?

A.

There is no special secret to drawing the temper in clock springs. Possibly you are doing one of two things: 1. not heating the metal hot enough. 2. letting it cool too quickly. It could be that you are doing both.

Suggest that you use a charcoal block, lay the steel on it and heat slowly to bright red. The charcoal will glow red also. Set it aside and allow to cool while still on the block. This slows down the cooling and leaves your metal workable, whereas if you heat your metal holding it with tweezers air can cool it too quickly. As some unthinkingly do, you lay it on a cold anvil or other piece of metal and that will hasten the cooling process and thereby restore some of the temper.

What size mainspring?

Will appreciate it if you will advise correct size of loop-end mainsprings to fit a Wm. J. Gilbert 1910 8-day time and strike mantel clock. The original has been replaced and I have no sample.

A.

We do not readily pin-point your movement by the 1910 designation, however the common Gilbert 8-day, striking mantel clock, taking a "free" (loop-end) mainspring can just about be pinned down to two sizes: ¾ inch wide by .017 inch thick by 10 feet long; ¾ inch wide by .018 thick by 8 feet long.

It is at once evident that both models make identically the same number of hour-revolutions for their 8-day run. By counting the train you determine the number of revolutions of the main (drive) wheel required to run it a week; from that an indication of whether the eight foot or ten foot spring is required.

Changing Mainsprings In 8-Day Striking Clocks

I am havivng a hard time trying to figure out some way to change mainsprings in eight day striking clocks such as the Seth Thomas and Ingraham.

I know the springs have to be clamped off but I haven't found anything so far small enough to slip between the spring and the side of the frame.

A.

There is no necessity for working an 8-day spring "ring" (clamp) between the spring and frame sides.

Perhaps your thinking is being influenced by watch mainsprings you see come in clamps made of rather thin metal.

The ring that comes clamping your 8-day springs as you purchase them from your material dealer, serves this purpose very practically. It, you will recall, is NOT a complete ring; is made of quite heavy round stock, and has opening resembling a horse shoe.

We like to take the spring as it comes from the wholesale house, remove it from the clamp (or ring) for the purpose of cleaning it thoroughly; then, with mainspring winder, coil the spring back into the clamp Assemble the clock; wind the spring up, tight, and ease the ring off via the opening. In many instances (most) your spring will NOT coil down to a lesser diameter than the opening; meaning that the ring can not be pulled directly out the side, however, the wound-up diameter of the spring is so much less than that of the ring you may easily remove the ring by revolving it bringing one end out beyond the frame.

BRASS MAINSPRINGS

Speaking of the "antiques" we occasionally get a question about the brass mainspring; if my memory is correct, this factual forum of friendly informality has not commented upon it. Many clockmakers upon their first encounter with the brass spring immediately conclude that it is "set" and proceed to substitute a modern steel spring. This is definitely a "No-No." First, it can be classed as a major alteration definitely destroying a large portion of the movement's antiquity. Second, despite the fact that when compared to the steel spring the brass appears to be "set", nine times out of ten it still retains enough power to drive the movement satisfactorily.

The developer of the brass spring was Elisha C. Brewester—b.-1791 d.-1880—Bristol's first spring maker. It is known that he was working upon it prior to 1832. Brewester's foreman, Joseph S. Ives, took out a patent on brass springs May 23, 1836, which patent he sold to Brewester. Many clocks made by Brewester, Elisha Manross, and Brewester & Ingrahams, were equipped with brass springs. A few other makers used a few. Brewester & Ingrahams labeled them: "Warranted not to fail." Mr. Fuller F. Barnes in his, "Ten Generations of the Barnes Family," when mentioning the brass spring quotes from "The Trader & Canadian Jeweler" issue of April 1944 as saying: "Certainly they have not failed yet."

Our experience bears this out—of all those we have serviced, we were able to pass them back to the owner performing satisfactorily. One that I've kept up with from its first servicing approximately forty years ago is still operating with the original brass spring. Not all, but most, brass spring powered movements have their springs operating in a "box." The difference between a box and a barrel is: the box does not turn and the spring drives the movement from its inner coil, whereas with the barrel the outer end turns the barrel and drives the clock.

When cleaning a clock with brass spring in a box, you should treat it as with the barrel; that is the spring is removed and re-inserted with a proper winder. Always be very careful not to kink or cone it. The spring can be straightened out across any flat surface all save about four inner coils; wiped clean with a soft cloth saturated with white gasoline, benzine, or alcohol, and carefully inspected for any crack or appearance of break. If any rough spots are noted, smooth them with very fine steel wool and hand-burnish with a jewel burnisher.

The origin of the brass spring is in doubt; some feel that they originated in Holland many years before Brewester, but no positive proof has come to light.

Mr. Barnes says: "If Bristol spring pioneers had knowledge of the fact—Holland originated—it was of no practical value. They had to discover the method of tempering clock springs made of brass."

Brass springs made under the Ives 1836 patent were produced up to about 1862.

The Barnes family have dominated the spring making in America for nearly two centuries, and Mr. Barnes, easily qualifies as an expert on the art, so it is astounding to have him say: "Stranger still, after a hundred years (1946) we today do not know the method they used to put sufficient temper into brass to make a coiled mainspring."

This "bit" of history points up the fact you should use the original brass spring if at all practical. Your customer may, or may not know these facts. If you pass them along to him you will not only enhance his appreciation for his clock, but his regard for you as a knowledgeable clockmaker. Most antique clock movements you handle with steel springs are vastly over powered—this is not true of those with brass springs.

They have sufficient power but not much to spare; therefore you MUST see that the movement is in the best of order. Check closely the pendulum suspension spring—most have been replaced with one overly strong. There is not much of a chance you can use one that is too weak; remember that some of the finest French clocks suspended their pendulums with a silk cord; also that the French seem to get by with much less drive power. Pay special attention to the escapement; see that the pallet surface is not pitted and that it is correctly set for depth. It is my considered judgment that any good clockmaker can make the brass springs work satisfactorily. These clocks are not astronomical regulators. At best, they can only deliver a fair degree of "household" time—say an error of three or four minutes per week.

WATCH MAINSPRING LENGTH

Some ninety days back one of our Canadian readers fired in a question upon the calculation of the length of a watch mainspring. Said he had been given the formula

$$\frac{pi\ (A^2\ minus\ b^2)}{8\ X\ thickness}\ equals\ length.$$

Where the thickness of the spring is known; the barrel must revolve eight turns and a is the inside radius of the barrel; b the outside radius of the winding arbor.

This is not a valid formula for the answer sought, simply because that answer has to be in terms of linear distance and/or length and nowhere in the formula is linear distance inserted. That answer is merely the area of the plain ring within the barrel in which the spring operates.

From rules given in just about every horological treatise, we know 1) that the proper spring should occupy one half of this space; 2) that the number of coils when down subtracted from the number of coils when fully wound gives the number of turns that spring will deliver to the barrel. Even with the known thickness of the spring the problem is far too complex to be reduced to any two plus two equals four arithmetic. In an effort to do just that, we have corresponded with a number of knowledgeable horologists with varying degrees of success. Perhaps the best practical answer came from The Watchmakers of Switzerland Info Center; they get by the ultra-complications by resorting to a table —we quote verbatim: "Calculation of the Mainspring. Today, it is very easy for a watchmaker to order a mainspring according to the trademark and caliber reference number of the movement.

"Because of this method of ordering, watchmakers do receive the correct mainspring replacements from their material distributors. However, if the watchmaker is concerned with an old timepiece, an unidentified movement, or if he wants to check to see if the mainspring is correct for the particular watch being serviced, this is the method to use: A watch is supposed to run for a minimum of twenty-four hours; therefore, the mainspring should be calculated for a theoretical run of thirty-six to forty hours. This is the basis upon which mainspring calculations should be made.

The number of teeth of the barrel and of the center pinion are counted. Let us assume, for example, 84 to 12: the ratio 84/12 equals seven. This means that one barrel rotation corresponds to seven hours run. Six rotations corresponds to forty-two hours, etc. . . .

Number of Development Rotations	(e) Thickness of the Spring	(L) Length of the Spring
5	0.0249	53.085
5¼	0.0241	55.607
5½	0.0239	56.088
5¾	0.0235	57,361
6	0.0231	58.791
6¼	0.0227	60.133
6½	0.0225	61.619
6¾	0.0219	62.648
7	0.0215	64.260
7½	0.0209	66.800
8	0.0203	69.400
9	0.0192	74.200
10	0.0182	79.100
11	0.0173	83.800
12	0.0165	88.400

This table is calculated for a barrel inner radius equal to 1 mm. and gives the sizes corresponding to the maximum development. It is sufficient to multiply these figures by the barrel's inner radius in order to obtain the desired values of the spring. This table gives the ideal theoretical sizes; that is to say for a spring where the coils leave no space between each other without taking into account the space occupied by the hook, by the brace and also by the portion of the spring attached to the barrel arbor.

That is the reason why in the calculations made, you add one rotation for the number of rotations up to six and one and one-half rotations above six.

Example:

Wrist Watch: 70 teeth in barrel, 10 leaves in center pinion. Inside diameter of the barrel, 5.20 mm; radius 2.60 mm; Void barrel space, 0.95. The ratio of the number of teeth being 70/10 equals seven we admit 5 development turns. The theoretical duration of the run is 5 X 7 equals 35 hours. The dimensions are by calculation upon five plus one equals six turns.

Thickness of the spring (e) equals 0.0231 X 2.60 equals 0.06 mm.

Length of the spring, (L) equals 58.791 X 2.60 equals 153 mm.

Height of the spring, (h) 0.95 minus 0.05 equals 0.90 mm.

Remarks:

The height of the spring is calculated by measuring the void space inside the barrel and deducting for the safety of the small movement .05 mm, for the large movement .10 mm. and for clocks 1.0 mm." End of quote.

Thus we see that he goes to the table, and at six turns gets the figure of 58.791 for the length factor and multiplies it by the radius of the barrel, which in the example is 2.60 mm. and comes up with a spring 153 mm. long.

Another of our regulars chides us for having said in the past that Goodrich's "The Modern Clock" contains ALL the answers and sends in this problem:

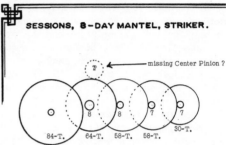

SESSIONS, 8—DAY MANTEL, STRIKER.

He has an eight-day, American mantel clock with a missing center pinion. His problem is: how many leaves should this pinion have? While his sketch is factual, it is not a problem capable of being worked for the very simple reason it is incomplete. The desired answer must be in terms of "time." All center pinions revolve once per hour, and nowhere in the info supplied is that time factor.

We answered by pointing this out to him and asked that he give us the 'beat' or the length of the pendulum. Back comes the reply entire pendulum and rod missing. We suggest that he mount the movement in the case and from the general case dimensions approximate a practical pendulum length—you guessed it, his third letter said: "no case either."

All this presents an impasse because sans a time factor there is no solution.

Right here lies a point that seems to confuse many bench repairmen—it is the auxiliary driven center, most train calculations are based upon the center being an integral member of the time train—when it is, we automatically know that it revolves once per hour and the time factor becomes a part of the problem, enabling one to calculate wheels, pinions, and even the theoretical length of the pendulum.

Just when and by whom the auxiliary center drive was introduced into clock work appears to be lost in antiquity—it was quite early in the game, the so-called Thirteenth Century clock with its foliot escapement had its dial train auxiliary driven. The Germans used it early for we see it in many Black Forest clocks with wood plates. The Dutch used it, and it was occasionally used by the French. Perhaps the English stuck closer to the inside the train method than any, for it is rarely seen in an English clock.

At any rate the practice was quite well established long before clockmaking came to America. While the U.S. clockmaker did not originate the idea, he most certainly made the most universal use of it during the heyday of American clockmaking—that would be the era between the turn of this century and World War One, I verily believe that fully 95% of all mantel clocks had their centers auxiliary driven. Prior to Eli Terry's short pendulum clocks beginning about 1816 very few short pendulum clocks were produced here. Our early long case clocks and even the shorter pendulums of the Willards had their centers within the train. Somewhere about 1790 Connecticut clockmakers began driving their centers auxiliary in their long case wooden movements.

Terry carried the system into his shelf clocks and when the industry went all brass about 1837 it was retained. Utilizing the auxiliary center drive; that is, driving it from a wheel of the train as opposed to having it frictioned to an arbor within the train gave the manufacturer a very wide range of pendulum lengths from the same train—in other words he did not have to cut an entire new train every time he wanted to use a different length pendulum. It enabled him to adapt a train to many different pendulum lengths for a wide variety of case styles and sizes. Good though it was for the manufacture and marketing of many clocks, this little "monster" raises his ugly head today to plague the bench repairman: 1) it produced a blue jillion different beats and fractional beats and is one of the reasons it is impractical to rate mantel clocks upon today's rate recorders; 2) it plagues the repairman when he has to calculate a lost wheel or the pendulum's length, etc., as evidenced by this man's question.

We MUST establish the time factor before we can arrive at a practical center-pinion replacement and have suggested that he place this movement into its original case, or the case in which it will be housed and determine therefrom a practical pendulum length. Because it is difficult to estimate the center of gravity in any pendulum assembly, it is more accurate to go for the 'beat" count. Put the clock going and count the beats for exactly sixty seconds.

One other avenue is open—perhaps a bit more accurate—would be to clamp a pointer to the clock frame extending across the second wheel; mark the wheel even with the pointer then run the clock for exactly one hour, timing it to the second from the sweep-seconds hand of an accurate regulator. Then make a second mark and count the number of teeth upon the second wheel between these two marks; this will give the number of teeth the missing center pinion should have to be turned exactly one rev. in one hour's run, q.e.d.

Any time you repair clocks you are going to have problems; let's hope that all of them are not basket cases, sans center pinion, sans pendulum, and sans a case. Without "problems" C. & O. just might not be here —after all, that is one of our main purposes, to lend an assist—we may not have the ready answer, Goodrich may not have it, as stated, but we will do our very best to research it, trim it down to manageable proportions—maybe inserting the proper "factor" and get the answer into the mails same day received.

Selecting a Mainspring

Can you tell me how to select a new mainspring for a clock when the spring is missing from the barrel?

A.

The basic rule is: have the winding arbor occupy one-third of the space in the barrel; the empty space, one-third; and, the spring occupy the remaining third.

For most timepieces coming to the repair bench, the old 'rule of thumb' method is practical. It is: with the spring in and lying against the wall of the barrel, measured across the coils, it should equal one-eighth the diameter of the barrel.

Another of the old rule-of-thumb methods is carefully mark a scratch in the bottom of your barrel with the spring lying against the wall. Then wind it fully up and see if the outside coil comes to your scratch mark. You can see that this is a test of the other basic rule: i.e., since the arbor must occupy one-third the space, the open space be one-third, and the spring one-third, the volume which the spring occupies when it is down would be no greater and no less than the volume of the empty space around the arbor on to which it is to be wound, so that the outermost coil when fully wound will occupy the same place which the innermost occupies when it is down.

Now, you always easily ascertain two points about a spring to go into a barrel: 1st, you get the width from the depth of the barrel, and 2nd, by counting the train you know how many revolutions the barrel must make to drive the piece the required time, 30 hours, or 8-day. A mainspring in the act of uncoiling in its barrel always gives a number of turns equal to the difference between the number of coils in the up and down position. For instance, if you have 17 coils with the spring lying against the barrel wall—down—and 25 coils when wound tight on the arbor, it will require eight turns in uncoiling, the difference between 25 and 17.

Letting Mainsprings Down

Could you please tell me the correct way to leave the mainsprings down and dissemble a Boston ½ hour strike with a single winding arbor?

A.

You can let the mainsprings down on the "Boston" clock with your regular hand-let-down-key. As you have already discovered, it is a tricky operation.

Study closely this unusual mechanical arrangements. You have two springs, wind and strike, riding upon one wind post. Turn it right and you wind one spring; left and wind the other, thus if you relieve the pawl on one spring and allow the let-down-key turn to "unwind" that spring, it will be winding the other spring unless you have first "detached" if from that other spring.

Observe that the winding arbor (the hub within the barrel) carries two pawls: one to engage the wind-post when it is revolved in the direction to wind that spring; the other, to retain the spring as it is wound. Now, that pawl that retains the spring can't be released unless you are prepared to take the wound-up pressure against your let-down key, but, you can release that pawl that connects the wind arbor to the post. So disconnected then the other spring can be let down without winding again the first spring.

Once you have one spring down, trip both pawls upon that arbor and go to the other spring, re-engage the pawl acted upon the wind-post, then proceed to let that spring down in the usual manner. This unique type of single wind for two springs has baffled many workmen. The one fortunate feature is that it poses no problem when re-assembling the clock. Assemble the clock in the usual way with all four pawls in place under their respective springs, and, wind.

Vibrating Hairsprings

Some of my column readers have chided us with the fact that such is not fully covered in my favorite treatise Ward L. Goodrich's "The Modern Clock." It is a fact that most clock repair manuals fail to detail the vibrating of a clock balance spring, Gazeley's "Watch and Clockmaking and Repairing" does lay out the old time method for 'vibrating' a new balance spring for watches. De Carle's "Practical Clock Repairing" — T. R. Robinson's "Modern Clocks, Their Repair & Maintenance" as well as Goodrich give this particular point short shrift. "Precison Time Measures" by Charles Higganbotham, and, "Modern Methods In Horology" by Grant Hood delineate well the old system applying same to watches. It follows, or should, that the basic relation of a hairspring action to a balance wheel is the same for both watch and clock.

Perhaps, the writers of our clock treatises calculate one should have certain basic principals tucked away in their minds before taking up clock repairing.

Dr. Robert Hooke, London, B-1635, D-1703, is generally credited with inventing the hairspring; he did not publish his invention, but, we get from his diary his famous maxim: "Ut Tensio sic vis." — As is the tension, so is the power — this prinicpal — law — constitutes the chief value of the hairspring as a governor for a balance wheel.

There are two methods of fitting a new hairspring, one, is called 'vibrating' this is the selection of a spring of the proper strength; two, is known as the weighting method, in this, the weight of the balance wheel is adjusted to a given hairspring.

When I was serving my apprenticeship, the shop had quite a stock of hairsprings for clocks. There were two varieties, one without the collet which my mentor called 'blank hairspring' the other came collected; they occupied two drawers in the material cabinet. Needless to say, my first experience was with the 'blank' springs. I never knew whether it was because the blanks came cheaper, or, to give me some experience in pinning the inner terminal — one did NOT ask questions, you simply did what you were told to do. I ruined a number of springs, but it was good experience and the skill attained always stood me well in hand.

2574

Figure 1

Fig. 1, shows a "Hairspring Vibrating Tool" carried in material catalogues as late as 1925 — at that date, it sold for $1.75. One careful look at this cut and the clockmaker can easily make his own; the main standard is adjustable up and down, the lateral rod can be moved in or out, and the end piece is merely a little clip in which to pinch outer end of the hairspring under trial. The first requirement in the vibrating operation is to ascertain the beat of the balance — you have to know what you want the balance to beat; this involves counting the train. Many later balance timepieces were more or less 'standardized' to beat 14,400 per hour or quarter seconds, but, counting some of these oldies brings forth some pretty weird numbers. They were equiped with some pretty large and heavy balance wheels; one correspondent wrote to say his looked like a "space station" — right here is where that seventh mile sets in, they require a strong hairspring; plus one of very large diameter. One correspondent relates that he succeeded in 'making' one of these hairsprings from a very small mainspring intended for a ladies' wrist watch, etc. On this, I've had no experience — off hand it would seem that such would be very short in length.

Back to train count — let's take an old Welch, Spring & Co., Octagon Lever which has a minute wheel of sixty, a third arbor with 48 and a pinion of eight; a fourth arbor of forty and a pinion of eight; escape arbor of 21 and pinion six, thus:

$$\frac{60 \times 48 \times 40 \times 21 \times 2}{8 \times 8 \times 6}$$ equals 12,600 beats per hour, and 210 beats per minute — the figure we must work to. Assuming that the clockmaker has constructed his "vibrating" tool he selects a hairspring which in his better judgment approximates the original, and, one of as near the original diameter judging from the location of the reg pins from the balance-staff center, and proceeds to try — vibrate — it. Pin the spring to the collet or if colleted stake it on; catch the spring near its outer end in the clip and adjust the height of the tool until the lower end of the staff rests very lightly upon the crystal of an open-faced watch so that the seconds hand can be easily watched as the vibrations are counted. Set the balance in motion with the feola or a camels hair brush and as it vibrates it will generate an up and down motion giving off a sound as the staff pivot taps the crystal. It is readily seen that as the balance vibrates, it taps the crystal of the watch every other stroke; therefore, since we are seeking 210 strokes, we shall wish to get a count of one hundred and five. The first try or two can be counted for thirty seconds then as you get nearer to the point the count may be extended to the full minute, 60 seconds. Once you have reached an accuracy you feel is 'practical' mark the spot at which the hairspring is clamped in the clip; with the regulator lever set center, this point should ride between the reg pins when the spring is pinned to the stud.

This procedure is NOT complicated though it usually is a time killer. There is some latitude; if the new spring happens to be of a different diameter it may be necessary to re-locate the reg pins to conform to the new diameter; another latitude is; if a spring is very slightly weak a wee bit of weight may be removed from the wheel, etc. It can be done, others do it, why not you?

My thought is, the reluctance of trade shops and material houses refusing to vibrate these old clock springs is: the clockmaker fails to give the 'beat' when sending an old wheel in; or, that calls for further correspondence thereby adding to the cost. Lastly there just isn't enough demand for such jobs to pay them to cater to such. The fact remains that the restoration on of these oldies falls within the better paying bracket, owners be they collectors or no, wish their pieces to keep time and anytime you succeed in delivering a job that perhaps has been turned down a couple of times, you have enhanced your image as a competent clockmaker to your clientele which not only gets you more jobs, but, better prices for the same. Herein is an open request to: tenders of the "144", material supply houses or even manufacturers who may read these feeble remarks to send that card upon any sources for large, heavy hairsprings — we need 'em for the files. Pehaps, slightly upon the rough side, these early slow-beat lever movements will run if given half a chance. The one biggest problem being their hairsprings and we sincerely hope that the above has at the very least partically aided in solving that problem.

Jerome, Welch, Kirk and others produced these in no small quantities over a long period of years — generally catalogued as 'Marine' timepieces, other than being balance-wheel controlled as opposed to the pendulum, there is no other resemblence to the 'ship's' and/or marine chronometer. Many were engineered to beat quarters — 14,400 per hour — but running upon an unusual figure like the 12,600 here is not at all unusual. Very little has been recorded upon the engineering of those pieces and that particular angle is exceedingly hard to research. Why beat quarter second? Perhaps because the English watch as introduced in America beat quarters. Recently discussing an old watch with a young watchmaker, I pointed out that it was a 'slow train' watch and he promptly asked what I meant by that. Many early American watches beat quarters, then they were stepped up to fifths (18,000) — exact date like other transistions is hard to pinpoint — I'd guess that maybe Waltham pioneered them along with their watchmaking machinery, etc. About that time and for many years after, those beating fifths were referred to as 'fast train' watches. Fifths were 'standard' for many years and it was only in recent years that a number of faster beats was introduced; evidenced by those scales upon your rate — recorders. It seems odd that while today's horologist is aware of various beats, those terms 'slow train' and 'fast grain' have faded out, as regards fifths and quarters.

That our early designers and engineers relied solely upon the seconds beat pendulum for their timing operations and experiments could easily be one explanation for it is a short step from the second to the half and still a shorter one to the fourth. Thus 'beating' a balance to the quarter when using the 'royal' — seconds — pendulum easily came out even. Ending up with an odd beat could be attributed to: a miscalculation in train count; deliberately, so to accomodate a given pinion.

That we've multipled words dealing with a very basic subject is self-evident, the over-all intent is to say: don't back away from these jobs which can bring you a better rate return per hour than the common run of bench clock repairing.

Westminster Clock Has Two Mainsprings

We have in our shop a Sessions eight day Westminster chime clock with two main springs instead of the usual three. The clock was given to us because another clock repairman could not make it keep time, and neither can we.

We cleaned the clock which didn't help, then we reversed the main springs, that didn't do any good either. Then we put in new springs on both sides which were supposed to be the correct size, ¾ inch x 108 inch.

The clock gains about 15 minutes the first two days after winding, then holds steady for two days then loses 15 minutes the next two or three days. Also it strikes fast at first then slows down and stops in about seven days.

Do you think the springs are the wrong size? If so, what size should we use.

A.

This writer takes a pretty dim view of your reversing the mainsprings. Let's look at it this way — if your spring had "set" crystalized, or whatever happens, to the extent that you have to reverse it, at the very best, your effort is quite temporary and after a winding or two it is right back where you started.

You failed to give the thickness of your springs. The spring usually used is .018 inch thick.

The time side first. Once the mainspring is right, check all your pivots and bearings — make sure no cut or scored pivots and that the bearings fit correctly. Next check your suspension spring, it should be pretty weak — these clocks originally came with a suspension spring about twice as long as the average one. Read Goodrich's chapter, beginning page 81, on suspension springs.

Now, to the strike train. Again, the mainspring must be correct. Noticably slowing down of the strokes as the clock runs on towards the end of its weekly run indicates excessive friction. Besides checking the pivots and bearings of the strike train; check the lantern pinions; especially that one driven by the main wheel, they show a tendency to wear excessively and often have to be rebuilt.

How to Mesh Teeth of a Geneva Stop

I am sure you can explain to me a quick and easy way to properly mesh the teeth of the two wheels of a Geneva Stop.

After trial and error I finally get them in the correct relation to each other, so the spring is almost fully wound at the stop, and the clock will run for eight days.

Many clockmakers have the idea that 'stop-work' is solely to prevent over winding. This is a carry-over from the old fusee clock wherein the stop-work merely stopped your wind at its end. Truly to prevent over wind.

The basic idea of the Geneva type stop is to permit you to use the center turns of your drive spring; eliminating the tight-up turn and weak last turn, thereby gaining a more constant drive force.

On your better grade clocks with going barrels, you can easily determine how many turns the spring will make by winding and counting them. Now, determine the number of turns the stop-work allows — subtract from total turns and get the number of over turns — divide by two.

Let's say the total turns are twelve — that, your stop allows eight turns. 8 from 12 equals four over turns; 4 divided by 2 equals two turns you desire outside of either stop.

Wind the clock all the way UP; let off two turns and place the stop on at the stop-lock position. Determining the turns given by the free-spring, those not in a barrel, is not as positive since it depends somewhat upon your judgment of the down position — the basic principal is the same.

Clock Appears to Have Dual Springs

At present, I have a Welch Spring Company clock in for repair. It is a Patti V.P. and has two springs in each spring barrel wound in a different direction. When winding you go so far, then the spring band revolves and it unwinds. I have heard about being able to wind in both directions, but the winding will not reverse. Frankly, I do not know what to do with my problem, so I am seeking your assistance.

What is wrong? What is the solution? I hope I have given you enough information: I don't know anything else that I could tell you.

A.

Whoa! Let's back-up and take a long, hard look at your problem: 1) you do NOT have a 'double' spring; 2) you do NOT have a barrel; 3) it can NOT wind both ways.

The ONLY wind system that winds both ways is the "Gerry" system as found on the Vermont Clock Company and Boston Clock Company clocks. It has two springs mounted upon the same arbor — see my Otherwise for February 1974.

The true barrel is that one attached to the main wheel and turns as the spring unwinds (delivers power) — several Early American clocks and some recent one such as the Seth Thomas #124 chime have their springs in a 'box' which is fast to the back plate. Others have their springs in a box not attached to any place—this is called a 'floating box' — your "Patti" spring is in a floating box.

The spring system as used upon the Patti was devised and patented by Benjamin B. Lewis, No. 249,845 November 22, 1881 — better known to clockmakers as the inventor of the Lewis Calendar mechanism, perhaps the simplest perpetual calendar device ever built.

Every 'simple' mainspring has two ends. One drives the clock; the other it is wound by — note that your Patti spring has just two ends; thus it is NOT a double spring. One end hooks to the main wheel to do the driving; the other hooks to the winding arbor

for winding. This is a most unusual arrangement. One half of this spring is wound clockwise and the other half winds counterclockwise. It is joined at its middle by an offset clamp enabling the spring to be inserted into its box with each half side by side; thus when one half is wound clockwise, it also winds the counterclockwise half by the pull at the outer end of that half. Result: the whole spring is wound by one direction of the winding key.

At this point a good question is why? Notice that your Patti movement is rather small for an eight-day striking clock. The designer (Lewis) was faced with the problem of using a small barrel or box. By his ingenius arrangement of placing each half of that spring side by side he was able to come up with a box just half the diameter of what it would have been in the orthodox construction.

Springs Keep Breaking

About two years ago I took an 8-day Gingerbread clock for cleaning and a new strike spring. I ordered ¼ dozen springs from my supply house and did the job. About six weeks later the clock came back with a broken spring. The next one lasted about the same length of time so to solve the problem I removed a spring from an old movement and no more problem. I have used new springs of that size and type since then and all have broken within six months. After the first clock came back. I reordered springs from another supply house as I thought it might be faulty springs and had same trouble. As you can see I have about run out of old movements to strip for springs.

I clean and oil each new spring before putting it in the clock and wind it up and let it down several times, but still have the problem. I don't have this trouble with watch or other clock springs such as 400-day clocks, 1-day clocks, etc.

A.

Sorry, but I do not have the pat answer to your spring problem — in fact, I very seriously doubt there is one.

Despite all our progress in metallurgy, there is a great deal to be known about tempering steel. It stands to reason that a manufacturer can and does come up with a bad batch of springs once in a while.

Before installing a new main-spring, you should stretch it out — not the three last coils — clean it thoroughly and inspect it. Look for any cracks — run your thumb nail down each edge and feel for a crack. This sometimes shows up a spring that will break after a few windings, etc. Always check broken springs and note where they break. Sometimes an inner hook that is too long will cause a break where the spring bends over it. Some old timers used to check for magnetism. Frankly, I don't see how a new spring might become magnetized and neither do I understand why such would cause breakage. Many old timers were wont to couple spring breakage with severe electrical storms; after a severe electrical disturbance, my old mentor would say: "Watch out for some broken springs"—sure enough within the next few days we would get a broken spring or two, watch. I never considered it a true test. Some could very well have been coincidence.

Perhaps you did the right thing obtaining the next

order of springs from a different supplier, but again I can't envision you hitting two bad batches in a row. Springs should be handled very carefully — never allow one to be kinked. We are told that most breakage comes from crystalization. Then, the question becomes: what makes them crystalize? I'm sure that you have parted springs and steel wire by rapidly bending at one place. It is said that this action crystalizes the metal at that point thus causing the metal to part—the why, I can't explain.

A Bit About Fusee Movements

Any information pertaining to the Fusee movement, would be greatly appreciated. I am also interested in knowing how long it runs on winding, history of Fusee merchandise and any other pertinent information.

A.

Your query just about covers everything pertaining to the fusee; an adequate answer is both difficult and much too long for a letter. Most any volume you get upon general horology will have a chapter or two upon it. Most libraries have copies of "Time & Timekeepers" by Willis Milham, and "Horology" by Eric Haswell, its a pretty sure thing that you will locate one or both in the Troy library. Both have interesting, illustrated chapters dealing with the fusee.

The exact origin of the fusee is lost in antiquity; for a long while it was credited to one Jacob Zech, of Prague and dated about the year 1525, however, it is now proven, beyond question that the fusee was in use some 75 or 100 years earlier than that.

The first mechanical escapement was the 'verge'; it was in general use for some 300 years; as you know, the verge has a tremendous recoil in addition to its other faults. This made those timepieces gain rapidly when the spring was wound up and loose quite a bit as it neared the run down position.

The first attempt to remedy the unequal pull power of the mainspring between its up and down position was the 'Stackfreed'. It consisted of a strong curved spring and a cam, when the spring was up and at its greatest force the curved spring had to be raised from a depression in the cam; later as the spring went down and weakened the cam turned to where the curved spring was falling into the depression and was supplying a little additional power to the mainspring. This form of 'equalization' of the mainspring's power lasted only a few years and was succeeded by the fusee.

Basically, the fusee is a coned shaped pulley upon which is wound a gut cord or chain the other end being wound around the outside of the barrel containing the mainspring. The central arbor of that barrel is 'fixed' i.e. it does NOT turn. One end of the mainspring is hooked to this central arbor while the outside end is hooked to the inside of the barrel. The fusee or cone shaped pulley is fixed to the main wheel for driving the timepiece; the mainspring is wound by turning the fusee, as it reels the cord from the barrel the mainspring is wound.

The cord begins at the base or larger diameter of the cone, this larger diameter gives more leverage and and/or a greater pull, when the spring is near unwound, as the cord is reeled on to the cone and diameter grows less and less as the pull power of the spring grows greater from the tighter wind—the cone diameters; size of the barrel; strength of the mainspring, etc. are all correctly calculated to accurately give the mainspring a constant or equal pull power at any and all stages of its

winding.

Your question: How long does it run? They are calculated for and made to whatever type of timepiece it is applied; one-day, eight-day and 30-day as the case may be.

When the detached lever escapement came in, this uniform pull of the mainspring was not so necessary; refinements in mainspring making had come along as well as the going barrel and the fusee was abandoned in pocket watches. English makers continued using it long after Swiss, French and American makers gave it up.

We do not see it today except upon the marine chronometer; perhaps, one of your local jewelers keeps a marine chronometer in his window; if you can catch him at winding time some morning, ask for a look-see.

SUSPENSION SPRING

We get many questions which are not answerable per se — we are often asked to supply the formula or method of calculating the length and strength or the suspension spring — that is something that can not be calculated. "Springwise" the suspension does not enter into the timekeeping function of the clock movement, thus there is nothing to calculate. That statement always brings some argument, something I like, for the very moment a clockmaker starts to argue I know I have him thinking. Many serious bench men have noted a change in the time a piece delivers after they have made some alteration to the suspension spring. They jump to the conclusion that the spring change caused the altered time when in fact that change in delivered time was caused from altering the length of the pendulum. Consider the lowly cuckoo clock—its pendulum is "clivis" supported. Many fine French clocks utilized a silk cord — the Bulle battery clock has its pendulum suspended by a silk ribbon. Some very fine astronomical regulators had their pendulums supported upon a knife-edge agate bearing. In all four instances there is absolutely no suspension spring action — positive proof that a suspension spring is NOT necessary to either continuity of run or rate of time delivered. The prime function of the suspension spring is to support the pendulum assembly — rod and ball — nothing more. Giving it a little width deters the ball from waltzing and wobbling.

If you are interested in proving this to yourself, allow me to suggest a little serious experiment. Take any clock that you know its approximate rate — this is not a seconds splitting matter — and carefully count the beat of the pendulum for exactly sixty seconds using a large dial sync clock with sweep-second hand or a stop watch. Make three separate counts: add and divide by three. Next, alter the sus-

214

pension spring in any way you choose, within reason, longer, wider or stiffer. After the spring change, re-count the beat of the pendulum and adjust it until you get the same original beat. Put the clock upon a 24-hour run and you will get the same as the original rate before you altered the spring, thereby proving that altering the suspension spring does not alter the time rate, etc.

MAINSPRING STRENGTH

A third question we often get is for a method of calculating the strength of a main-spring. If in a barrel, there may be some aids that might assist in a close approximation, but with the American, loop-end, free spring it borders very closely upon the incalculable. To maintain the continuity of run, your main-spring merely has to deliver enough power to restore that force lost at each stroke of the pendulum; perhaps just a wee bit more to take the train over any rough spots. It is scientifically possible to determine what this energy loss is for a given pendulum, but determining what a spring of a given width and thickness can and will deliver to the pendulum through the thrust of the crutch, embodies many variables which include the type of escapement, length of the crutch wire where the force is applied to the pendulum, loss via friction in the various members of the train, gear ratio, etc. Therefore, when a clockmaker writes in, saying, "I have an eight-day American clock — how do I figure the strength of the main-spring?" we can NOT give him a "pat" rule because one does not exist. As President Lincoln said about the length of a man's legs, "they should be long enough to reach the ground," we might say the spring should be strong enough to drive the movement and be of more help to the inquirer than suggesting some very long and complicated computation involving a dozen variables.

We often hear certain features of any craft are perfected through actual experience, etc. Perhaps the three discussed above fall in that category — daily observing clocks in action noting the bend of the suspension spring, hefting the pendulum ball for its weight, or listening to the escape tooth drop on to the pallet gives one a feeling for what is practical and right — that gut instinct that is the final perfection of any craft.

PENDULUMS

I would appreciate any information you can give me on the following question: What causes the weights of a grandfather clock to vibrate about the same as the pendulum, and in a short time will stop the clock? This motion only happens when the weights are at the same level as the pendulum; at this time the clock is three-quarters run down. The clock is mounted on our clock frame which is made of wood, and sits on a concrete floor and is as solid as we can make it without being anchored to the floor. We put cardboard around the frame to keep out the air, but it did not work. I hope this description is enough.

A.

Recently I had a German-made, tall case clock for overhauling. The clock had a reputation for stopping. After performing the usual cleaning and oiling operations and some minor repairs, I set the clock to running.

I found after about five days, when the weights were just in front of the pendulum bob, the weights would start to swing, and after a period of time, the clock would either stop or have a very poor motion.

When the ·weights were higher or lower than the pendulum bob, they didn't swing and the clock's motion was good, as there was no vibration of the case.

The clock has a wooden second pendulum, large brass bob, swinging behind the weights and supported from the clock's rear plate in a conventional manner. It had the usual three weights, each supported on a single strand of brass chain, and were wound up like a cuckoo clock, not by a key.

My theory is that when the bob and weights were opposite each other, the gravitational pull of the masses caused all to assume a swinging motion, and the clock not being able to swing all these heavy weights would stop.

I remedied matters by placing a sort of shelf in the trunk of the clock which held the weights steady at the proper time.

When two clockmakers have identically the same problem there is no good reason why we can't make one answer cover both, hence this "double" letter. While located in entirely different communities and writing at different times, it is not unusual that you both have the same problem. In fact, what you have both discovered is sooner or later encountered by every repairman who handles many clocks. Some recognize it—others do not.

"Sympathetic vibration," i.e., the effort of the weight to swing in sympathy with the pendulum is the thing both of you have encountered. A quick check on a couple of volumes does not reveal anything indexed under "sympathetic vibration," so we will take it the rough and ready way.

I know that you have heard the story of the cat crossing a bridge and making it vibrate more than a horse. The horse weighed many hundred times more than the cat, why should the lesser weight cause the greater vibration? Simply because the cat's steps were nearer "in step" (sympathy) with each vibration of the structure. Also, as a youngster you have propelled yourself in the common swing by "pumping." Just a little additional urge by your own muscles shifting the center of gravity at the proper instant, not only enabled you to keep the swing in motion, but you could increase the arc of swing at will, (this is beside the point, but that was probably your very first step towards a keen sense of timing). Sir Isaac Newton presented three laws of motion in his celebrated "Principia," published in 1686. The third law was: "To every action there is an equal and opposite reaction."

Mr. King states that his weights go single, and Mr. Barley does not specify, but chances are his weights go single too. Sympathetic vibration is encountered in single fall clocks much more often than compounded weights, because the single suspension point makes of the weight a pendulum more easily influenced than one suspended at two points. When the weight in its descent, reaches the point where it, as a pendulum is approximately the same length as the pendulum, the reaction of the pendulum swinging tends to set the weights in motion — a sort of sympathetic swing.

To just what extent this action goes depends upon how well the clock is set up, how heavy it is and many other factors. In many instances it will progress—just as you pumped yourself in the swing—until the clock is stopped. Once the motion is set up it absorbs energy from the pendulum and when it draws off enough of the impulse energy, the pendulum stops from the lack of sufficient power to drive it; in rare cases the weight (or weights) will vibrate enough to bump the pendulum and stop it.

Mr. King's method of preventing the weights vibrating in sympathy with his pendulum no doubt is successful. It can usually be remedied by bracing the case to the wall, tightening the movement to the seat board, bracing the seat board in the case, etc.

We would especially like to hear from you both; first, as to whether the foregoing information is clear; and second, how successfully you succeeded in overcoming the trouble.

LEVELING CLOCKS

Do you know of any device or mechanism for a pendulum clock, particularly the table or mantel models, whereby the clock can be set in place, and irrespective of whether it is in a level position, this mechanism will automatically adjust the pendulum and escapement into proper synchronization? In other words, as you know, it is the usual requirement that when a pendulum clock is set up it must of necessity be leveled up and this is frequently accomplished by placing strips of cardboard, wood blocks, etc., under one side of the cabinet to get the pendulum and escapement working or ticking in correct synchronization or, otherwise, the clock will not run at all or soon stop. I have never seen such a mechanism or heard of any having been invented, and thought perhaps if any ever has been made that you would know about it.

It has been my experience the average owner of such clocks is not sufficiently familiar with how to get these clocks correctly

synchronized to keep them running without trouble and I have had to go frequently to the owner's house to adjust the clock to the proper position before it would keep going and it is my belief this one type of trouble can be responsible in a large measure in causing clocks of this kind to become less popular than they should be. Actually, such clocks, when put in correct running order, are more reliable, run longer, and keep better time than almost any other kind of clock.

I also have observed that comparatively few repair men seem to be versed well enough in adjusting the pallets to the escape wheel in correct relationship, usually moving the pallets entirely too far toward the wheel, resulting in making it necessary for the pendulum to perform a very wide arc if the escapement is to keep working, and due to insufficient driving power to overcome the increased pull of gravity by this large arc of the pendulum, the clock stops intermittently after being put into motion. There is no reason at all when one of these clocks has been correctly adjusted, synchronized, cleaned and oiled, that it should not run for as long as 15 to 20 years without further attention, as many of them of course, do.

A.

The problem of setting the pendulum clock in beat has plagued the repairman ever since Christian Huygens first applied it to clocks.

It is reasonable to suppose that many clock makers have endeavored to eliminate this problem just as about every other problem has been attacked down through the years. Evidently none have proven too successful else we'd find them in use today. Not too much is known about the fight to lick this difficulty but I can cite a few outstanding American examples.

One William Hart, Maysville, Wisconsin, was granted patent No. 33990 on December 24, 1861. Quoting the fifth paragraph: "It also consists in so applying the stud from which the above mentioned slotted pendulum is suspended in combination with crankpin or eccentric wrist as to make the said stud self-adjusting for the purpose of bringing the pendulum always in beat, thereby enabling the most inexperienced person to set up a pendulum clock without difficulty."

Patent No. 163868 was granted to Vitalis Himmer of New York City, June 1, 1875. In his application he states: "This invention has for its object so to construct a pendulum clock that the same will be in proper running condition even if not suspended or supported in the exact vertical position for which it may have been constructed." Himmer's invention looks pretty good on paper. He simply introduced a friction joint in the crutch-wire of the ordinary recoil escapement American clock verge; then attached to it a tail-wire to work between two banking pins in the plate. Evidently, it wasn't so hot, for despite its ease of adaptability to most clocks being made about that time, I've never run across a working example.

Patent No. 526399 was issued to Florence Kroeber (gentleman or lady?) of New York City, September 25, 1894, titled: "Apparatus for adjusting the beat of pendulum clocks." The patent's third paragraph states: "The primary use of the invention is to enable mantel clocks to be started and maintained in proper beat if placed on a mantel which is not level or considerably out of plumb." This was a device with screw-adjustment whereby the entire movement could be shifted in its case very much like the "in-beat" screws found on high-grade grandfather clocks and regulators. Florence Kroeber was granted several other patents, most of which were aimed at pendulum problems.

No. 576587 issued on February 9, 1897, was an elaborate clamping device, that: "Has for its object to produce a device which will lift and support the pendulum, taking the weight of same off the pendulum-rod and tension-spring, so that the clock may be transported with the pendulum in place."

Another Kroeber patent pendulum is sometimes on Ansonia movements in China cases. You've probably seen it; two small rings, one above the pendulum ball and one below about half-inch opening; two straight brass wires anchored to back plate one through each ring.

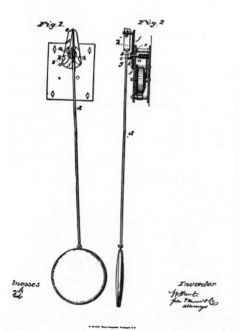

W. HART.

Clock Escapement.

33,990.

Patented Dec. 24, 1861.

UNITED STATES PATENT OFFICE.

WILLIAM HART, OF MAYVILLE, WISCONSIN.

IMPROVEMENT IN CLOCK-ESCAPEMENTS.

Specification forming part of Letters Patent No. 33,990, dated December 24, 1861.

To all whom it may concern:

Be it known that I, WILLIAM HART, of Mayville, in the county of Dodge and State of Wisconsin, have invented a new and Improved Pendulum-Escapement for Clocks; and I do hereby declare that the following is a full, clear, and exact description of the same, reference being had to the accompanying drawings, forming part of this specification, in which—

Figure 1 is a back view of the escapement, and Fig. 2 a side view of the same.

Similar letters of reference indicate corresponding parts in both figures.

This invention consists in an escapement composed of a simple crank or eccentric wrist-pin, which derives a revolving motion by its attachment to the ordinary escape-wheel spindle, or to any suitable rotating spindle geared with the clock-movement, and which works within a slot in the pendulum-rod, as hereinafter explained, such escapement dispensing with the escape-wheel and the verge and its appendages, and being cheaper, more durable, less likely to get out of order, and requiring less power to run it than the verge and wheel-escapement.

It also consists in so applying the stud from which the above-mentioned slotted pendulum is suspended, in combination with the crank-pin or eccentric-wrist, as to make the said stud self-adjusting, for the purpose of bringing the pendulum always in beat, thereby enabling the most inexperienced person to set up a pendulum clock without difficulty.

To enable others skilled in the art to make and use my invention, I will proceed to describe its construction and operation.

a is the spindle which commonly carries the escape-wheel, deriving motion in the usual manner.

b is a disk secured fast upon the end of said spindle, for the purpose of carrying the crank-pin or eccentric-wrist *c*, which may be made of steel or ruby, and is fast in the said disk at a distance from the axis of the spindle *a*.

d is the pendulum-rod, and 3 the slot in the said rod for the reception of the crank-pin *c*.

e is the stud from which the pendulum-rod is suspended in the usual manner. This stud is arranged above the spindle *a*, where it is

fast in the upper part of a plate *f*, which is fitted to oscillate upon a fixed hub *g*, which surrounds and is concentric with the spindle *a*, said hub being fast to the back plate A of the clock-frame.

h is a forked spring slipping into a groove in the hub *g* for the purpose of confining the plate *f* thereon, and holding the small hub *i*, that is provided on the back of the said plate, against the plate A, and thereby producing sufficient friction on the said plate to prevent it from oscillating too easily, the said plate being only desired to move when the position of the clock is changed, and the stud *e* being intended to remain stationary while the clock is in operation.

The operation is as follows: The crank-pin, revolving with the spindle *a*, is brought into contact first with one and then with the other side of the slot 3 in the pendulum-rod, and detained until permitted to escape by the movement of the pendulum being reversed, giving impulse to the pendulum at each detention. In Fig. 1 the pendulum is represented as just completing its stroke to the right and having allowed the pin *c*, which revolves in the direction of the arrow shown upon the disk, to escape from the right side of the slot 3 and fall against the left side thereof, where it is detained until the pendulum commences to swing to the left, when its revolution proceeds slowly until the pendulum has moved far enough to permit it to escape and pass quickly over to the right side of the slot, where it is detained until the pendulum moves to the right again, when it moves slowly with the pendulum until allowed to escape and fall again against the left side of the slot. In case of the clock getting accidentally put out of level, the weight of the pendulum-rod brings the plate *f* to an upright position—that is to say, with the stud *e* vertically above the spindle *a*—and so makes the stud *e* self-adjusting. The arrangement of the stud in this plate allows the clock to be placed in any position in which the stud *e* and spindle *a* are nearly horizontal, for the weight of the pendulum, if the latter is started with sufficient force to move the stud, will always bring the stud to the proper position, and the pendulum will bring itself into

Shown here is a print of the William Hart patent No. 33990.

WEIGHT vs. TIME KEEPING

Several of us are concerned over the problem whether the weight of the pendulum on a clock makes any difference in the timekeeping of the clock. I say that it doesn't, but others say it does. From what I have read and experienced, the weight does not have any direct bearing on the rate of the timepiece. This applies to pendulum clocks only. I would very much appreciate your view on the question.

A.

You have a good one. Hot discussions on this subject will go on as long as man can hang on a heavier ball, make the clock go slower, and thereby prove to himself that by adding a little weight he causes a pendulum of the same length to beat slower.

I'm reminded of the watchmaker who once experimented with the principle of a high-grade railroad watch, accurately timed at sea level, running at a different rate in higher altitude and rarified air. He carefully timed a good watch upon his bench for several days, and then suspended it for several days more from a window sill of his shop (shop was on second floor). He came up with the same time, and his careful observation proved to himself that altitude and air pressure made absolutely no difference.

If your friends who claim that adding weight makes the clock go slower have a good regulator handy (the Seth Thomas No. 2, eighty-beat, is good or any similar piece with a large heavy ball), just place a fifty-cent piece at the top of the ball, calling their attention to the fact that you are increasing the weight of the pendulum by the weight of a half-dollar and ask them to honestly time it for a few days and watch it gain. It is usually easy to gently wedge a coin between the top of the ball and the rod.

Continuing this same experiment, you may place the coin at the bottom of the ball and watch the clock lose time. In the true theoretical pendulum all the mass (weight) lies in one given point at the very end. In actual everyday practice a portion of the mass (weight) of the entire pendulum lies in the rod, etc. Thus the center of gravity is somewhere above the lower, or tip end. Practical application of the pendulum to the clock has proven that the length is *from the center of gravity to the point of suspension.*

Back to the coin experiment: Take the pendulum from a regulator and place it on a knife-edge, moving it back and forth until you get it balanced. Mark this point because this has determined the practical center of gravity. Place your coin at the top of the ball and you will find that to balance it, it will have to be moved down a bit—mark this point, that is, the center of gravity with the weight of the coin added. It can easily be seen that the distance from the point of suspension is *less.* In practical work you have *shortened* the length of the pendulum by the difference between the two marks you made when you balanced the pendulum twice, yet the ball and regulator nut have not been moved.

Now, for a practical application: If you have in the shop a good regulator that is a bit sensitive to turning the regulator nut, place at the top and bottom of the ball (the farther apart the better—should be about equal distance above and below the center of gravity) two small cups. Time the piece as close as possible with the regulator nut, then if you note a gaining rate after a few days place a shot in the bottom cup. If it should show a losing rate place a shot in the top cup. You will soon discover that you can get a micro-fine regulation by the addition of shot in the proper cup.

SESSIONS CLOCK

I have a Sessions 2-spring standard strike clock, pendulum movement. When I wind it up the first day it gains 2 minutes and on the 7th day it slows down enough to be on time. Can you tell me why the long pendulum motions (arcs) are faster than the short arcs? I know very little about isochronal adjustment for pendulum clocks. Could you give me the answer?

A.

The theory that pendulums of equal length beat in equal arcs in equal time applies to the true, free theoretical pendulum. The moment you harness your pendulum it ceases to be a free pendulum; too, the practical pendulum has some mass in its rod and here you have gotten another step further from the theoretical law.

Thus the very best we can hope for is to make our practical pendulums approximate isochronism. This is best accomplished by holding the arc of motion to the smallest practical point. Ever note upon some fine jeweler's regulator or astronomical clock how very small the arc of swing is?

To oscillate through all arcs in the same time, that is, to be isochronal—the pendulum bob should move in a cycloidal path. Christian Huygens (1629-1690), the celebrated Dutch mathmetician, demonstrated about the year 1665 that the arcs described by a pendulum were not truly isochronal unless the path was that of a cycloid instead of a circle. He endeavored to make correction by placing cycloidal cheeks at the point of suspension. However, in practical work it was not satisfactory and such practice was quickly discarded.

In your particular case you have a clock with a recoil escapement and mainspring driven, and here is where the greater part of your error sets in—the escapement itself. When your clock is wound up the great power on the escape wheel speeds up the pendulum during the transmission of the impulse, thus tending to shorten the period of oscillation. After the delivery of impulse is completed on one pallet, a tooth of the escape wheel strikes the opposite pallet and is forced to recoil against the power of the spring. This recoiling brings the pendulum to a stop much sooner than if it were swinging freely, thus shortning the period of oscillation still more. It is apparent that the greater the power on the escape wheel, the shorter the period of oscillation of the pendulum will be. Such error is inherent in the construction of your clock and I'd say that it isn't practical to try to eliminate it.

NEW HAVEN CLOCK

I have a New Haven weight clock with just the train and plates as the weights, pendulum and suspension spring are missing. Could you give me the weights of these and the length of the suspension spring? The main wheel has 78 teeth, the second has 78 teeth and the escape wheel has 42.

A.

Evidently you refer to one of the 1-day, weight-driven New Haven mantel clocks, because it would seem that the time train has only three wheels. However, you did not include the pinion count and for this reason we cannot accurately determine your required pendulum length.

Usually on this type of clock the center post is auxiliary driven. The figure you want is: the number of times it ticks or beats per

hour. From this you can calculate the correct pendulum length. It is noted that your main wheel has 78 teeth and I think you will find that the main wheel drives the second pinion and the center post. Count the center post drive pinion, second pinion and third staff pinion. To revolve the minute hand (center post) through one exact hour, the main wheel will have to move forward the exact number of teeth you find in the center pinion. This number divided by the number of staffs in the second pinion will give you the number of revolutions the second staff will make during one hour. Divide the number of leaves in the third pinion into the 78 teeth of your second pinion and this will give you the number of revolutions the third wheel makes per one revolution of the second. Multiply that figure by the number of revolutions the second wheel makes per hour and you have the number of revolutions the escape wheel makes in one hour. Multiply this by the number of teeth in your escape wheel and again by two because each tooth delivers two impulses; one to the receiving pallet and one to the releasing pallet. This final figure is the number of times your clock must beat in one hour to revolve the center post exactly one revolution or one hour on the dial.

The time of vibrations of pendulums are in direct ratio to the square roots of their lengths; thus, by using the royal pendulum you may determine the length of a required pendulum squaring the number of beats per minute required into the constant 141,120.0. Example: Suppose the pendulum you require must beat 120 times per minute. Square 120 and you get 14,400; divide into 141,120 and you get 9.8 inches. It might help you to remember the constant if we went into details on it. We know that a royal pendulum is 32.9 inches long; square the number of beats per minute, 60, and get 3,600 times 39.2 inches equals 141,120.0, our constant. Bear in mind that at all times you are using beats per *minute* and *inches,* therefore, you must use the number of beats required per minute and your result is in inches.

Another example: Suppose the pendulum you require must beat 90 times per minute; 90 squared equals 8,100 divided into 141,120 equals 17.42 inches.

It might also be well to point out that this

is not the over-all length of your pendulum. The practical clock pendulum is always longer than the theoretical pendulum because you have some mass in the rod. Imagine that you have your proper pendulum balanced across a knife edge; this balancing point will always be above the center of the ball because you have the weight of the rod added to that of the ball. Should the rod contain considerable mass it could even be above the top edge of the ball. The figure you obtain by the above method is from the point of suspension to the center of gravity. With a little practical experience you should easily be able to cut a pendulum wire within the scope of the regulating nut.

Weights for these clocks were usually around 3½ pounds. Originals were cast iron and on the rough side. This makes it easier for you as a finished weight is not required. Obtain a common cardboard mailing tube of a diameter just small enough to work freely in your case. Cut it about 3½ inches long (one for each weight), brace them upright over a boxtop or any convenient container holding about an inch layer of casting sand (jewelers), insert in the sand little wire loops (can be cut from wire coat hanger) about ½-inch and extending upward in your form about half-way. Place 3¾ pounds of scrap lead (allowing ¼ for dross) in any convenient container and allow to melt on a hot plate, pour it in your form and you have the weight. Allow to cool and peel off the cardboard form. If you care to spend the time you can dress them up a bit with a file and give a coat of chrome or gilt paint.

JOHN THOMPSON

I have a grandmothers clock which was shipped to the U. S. from England. The name of the maker on the dial is John Thompson, London. It has no striking arrangements. The shipping firm did not deliver a pendulum and I have to replace it. Can you tell me how long such a pendulum should be? The escape wheel has 30 teeth and has about 60-64 beats per minute.

A.

Sixty-four beat clocks are quite rare. It's almost a certainty that your clock is sixty times per minute, seconds, or as the English

clockmakers used to call it, a "Royal" pendulum.

To beat seconds, a pendulum should be 39.14 inches from point of suspension to center of oscillation. With the average simple pendulum where the weight contained in the rod is only a very small fraction of the total weight of the complete pendulum, the center of oscillation and the center of gravity (point where you might balance the whole across a knife blade) is very close together and may be considered the same for working purposes since the adjusting threads will more than take up for the difference.

CALCULATING TRAIN

There are several questions I would like to have answered as I have been unable to find the answer in books.

(1) When figuring a watch train, I figure wheels times escape wheel times two, over pinion leaving out the center pinion. How do you figure a clock with regular train and with 5 wheels?

(2) If a pendulum is lost, how would you know what weight and length to put on and where do you measure from and to? Is any part of suspension spring or rod counted? How long should suspension spring be and what is best to make one of? I had plenty on hand but all were too short —had to make the rod longer.

(3) When finding the center of oscillation, would you put the pendulum at the bottom of the rod to balance across a knife or how would you go about that? It is my understanding that weight added to or taken away from the pendulum above the center of oscillation will slow down or speed up the time. Is that true?

A.

(1) Calculating a clock train is exactly the same as with a watch and the number of wheels in the train does not matter. You take the center post (1 revolution per hour) as your base, and by counting the teeth of the wheels and leaves of the pinions you determine how many revolutions of the escape wheel are required to turn the center post exactly one revolution or one hour. The number of revolutions of your escape

wheel times the number of teeth in that wheel, times two, because each tooth must tick or beat one time for each of the two pallets, will give the correct number of ticks or beats per hour.

(2) The figure obtained as above, will give you the proper length of the required pendulum. The time of the vibrations of pendulums is in direct ratio to their lengths and the number of vibrations made in any given time are in the inverse ratio of the square roots of their lengths; thus we can determine this rule and calculate the correct length for any desired pendulum.

Multiply the number of vibrations made in a minute by the seconds (60 beat) pendulum by itself, which is squaring it. Multiply this by the known length of the seconds pendulum, 39.2 and divide this last product by the square of the number of vibrations per minute of the pendulum required and the quotient will give you the

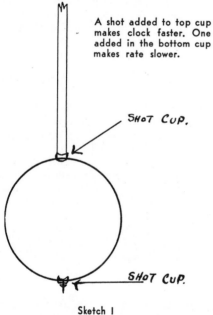

A shot added to top cup makes clock faster. One added in the bottom cup makes rate slower.

SHOT CUP.

SHOT CUP.

Sketch I

length in inches and decimal parts of the required pendulum.

Example: Let us say you have counted the train of a clock with missing pendulum. You found that the escape arbor has to turn 90 revolutions per hour. Reduce to minutes by dividing by 60 and you get 1.5 revolutions per minute. The escape wheel has

30 teeth; 30 times 1.5 equals 45 teeth that have to pass a given point to drive the clock one minute. Two beats per tooth equals 90 beats per minute; thus, you require a pendulum that will beat 90 times per minute—90 squared equals 8,100; 8,100 divided into the constant 141,120 equals 17.42.

I hope that I've made this clear, rather than run any risk I shall repeat: The constant we obtained from the rule as set forth above, inasmuch as the royal or seconds pendulum is the base and always squaring its 60 beats and multiplying by its length 39.2 inches always gives us 141,120; we simply use that figure as a constant.

Another example: Suppose you require a pendulum to beat half-seconds, 120 times per minute. Square 120 and we get 14,400. Divide 14,400 into 141,120 equals 9.8 inches, the correct length for a pendulum to beat half-seconds.

(3) In the theoretical pendulum, the center of gravity and the center of oscillation are one and the same point, but we cannot have a pendulum of pure theory on a practical clock since the practical pendulum

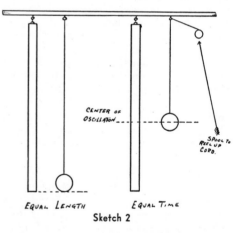

CENTER OF OSCILLATION

SPOOL TO REEL UP CORD.

EQUAL LENGTH   EQUAL TIME

Sketch 2

requires a substantial rod to support it, spreading the weight out over some space rather than having it all concentrated in one point. No doubt you've noticed the big gridiron pendulums on popular jewelers regulators; further, that these range from 56 to 60 inches long—over all. Whereas, there may be hanging near it a smaller wall regulator with a light wood rod and lead bob some 42 to 45 inches long—over all, and both will be beating seconds.

Since these two pendulums beat the same —60 times per minute—their centers of oscillation must be the same. From the point of suspension to the center of oscillation on each would be 39.2 inches. The effective length of a pendulum is that which governs its time of vibration. It is called the theoretical length. Measured from the point of suspension down the pendulum, the lower end is called the center of oscillation. This is the length always given in tables. The center of gravity of a pendulum is found at that point at which the pendulum can be balanced horizontally on a knife-edge.

In all pendulums where the greater percentage of the weight is in the ball, the center of oscillation and the center of gravity are so near the same point they need not be considered separately because the clock has sufficient latitude in the regulating threads to bring it to time.

In the last part of this question you are exactly correct. One favorite method of regulating clocks used in repair shops is by adding shot; never taking one out. See *Sketch 1.*

In closing, I'd like to suggest that you conduct a little experiment yourself. Obtain a lead ball any convenient size, a piece of heavy wood (oak, etc.) about one inch square and three feet long with a small nail or eye-screw. Suspend the wood by a silk thread then suspend the lead ball through an eye-screw and adjust to the same length as the wood rod. Start both to swinging and note the difference in time. Shorten the silk cord (regulate), suspending the lead ball until the two pendulums will beat the same, now note the difference in length. See *Sketch 2.*

PENDULUM MOTION

A perfectly pivoted (frictionless) pendulum, mounted in a vacuum and set in motion would continue to swing forever through its full arc without the application of any force.

From this it can readily be seen that the only force necessary to keep a pendulum in motion would be just enough to over-

Fig. 1

come friction; further, since there is absolutely no relation between the weight of a pendulum and its period of swing it develops that (within reasonable limits), the "weight of the pendulum ball" does not matter. All of which puts us right back where we were a few issues back—to the "rule of thumb."

While on the subject of pendulums, let's clear up another question—for quite

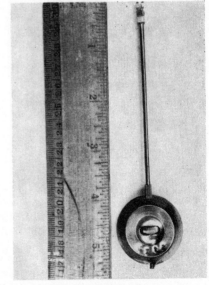

Fig. 2

some time we've heard conflicting stories about the pendulum's length being stamped on the back plate of French clocks, and the method of calculating that length from the numerals so stamped; we asked our French friend, M. Lassaug, for the real "low down." He explains it thus: Note in photos, Figure 1 and Figure 3, the numbers on the left and about the center (vertically) are the factory serial numbers. This number will always be found, or at least the last three digits on the original pendulum, see Figure 2 and Figure 4. Now, at the very bottom you will see "4" on the left of the pillar post and "6" on the right on the No. 6383, and "1" on the right No. 4751. This is an old French system of expressing the pendulum length in "pouce" and "ligne"; for example, the left cipher is four "pouce" (on the No. 4751), and the right cipher is one "ligne."

One pouce equals 27 millimeters; one ligne equals 2.26 millimeters; one inch equals 25.4 millimeters. So if we measure our pendulum in inches we shall have to

Fig. 3

multiply 4 pouces by 27 and one ligne by 2.26, giving a total of 110.26 millimeters.

Thus, 110.26 millimeters divided by 25.4 millimeters equals 4.33 inches.

For practical purposes this actually means from the point where the suspension spring flexes through the regulator chops

to the center of gravity, or, where the pendulum and its rod would balance upon a knife edge.

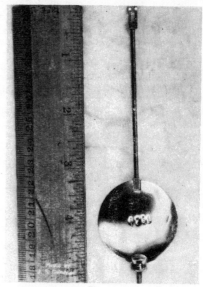

Fig. 4

SMALL PENDULUM

Recently I bought a small 7-day French clock with a very light pendule about 2½ inches long. The pendule is attached directly to the pallet arbor. without crutch and without suspension spring. It keeps fair time up to about the fifth day, after which it gradually gains about 20 minutes during the last two days.

Is there any means to make it keep correct time up to the last day?

A.

In the little French clock you describe, you have a "shining example" of about what the proper suspension spring can do towards isochronal correction. I fear there isn't much we can suggest, because both the shortness (2½ inches) of your pendulum and its being attached directly to the pallet arbor serve to increase your trouble.

As a first suggestion, I'd see that the movement is perfectly clean and perfectly lubricated. Then try a little lighter spring (also longer). If in a barrel, a thinner, lighter spring will give you more turns, say enough to run nine days; then when you follow the routine of winding it weekly, you will not be using those last two days when your spring is weakest.

It would be of some help if you could suspend the pendulum by a spring (proper, of course) and fit a crutch to the pallet arbor. No clock with a 2½-inch pendulum is going to keep railroad time (U. S. term for very accurate) but if you could effect both of the above changes, it would eliminate 17 or 18 of those 20 minutes.

WOBBLING PENDULUM

We have a Waterbury "regulator" clock in for repair in which a new suspension spring and rod have been fitted. When running, the pendulum doesn't travel back and forth in a straight line—that is to say, it has two actions, one back and forth from side to side, and also a twisting action.

This clock has been here for over a year, and the customer hasn't called in to see about it, but we can get in touch with him whenever the clock performs to our satisfaction. I've taken the pendulum out of this and hung it in a vise and tinkered away on it for an aggregate of a few hours, but with no success.

A.

The condition you describe is generally called a "wobbling pendulum" or a "waltzing pendulum". It can be the result of several causes, or a combination of them.

To catalogue a few, there are (1) Suspension spring bent or kinked; (2) a spring of unequal thickness; (3) pallet staff not at right angles to the crutch; (4) when the slot from which it hangs is not parallel—pinching, either front or back will cause it to waltz; (5) where the suspension spring is made of two members and one is a trifle shorter than the other; (6) if suspension spring is made up by having a brass clamp or chock riveted to it, the rivets may have been swelled by excessive hammering, making the equivalent of a kink; (7) in some instances where the pendulum hangs from the back of the clock case and the movement is not installed "square" to that case back.

For cases 1, 2, 5, and 6, make a new spring. Cases 3, 4, and 7 can be easily checked and corrected. It is presumed, of course, that there is no loose play between the pendulum rod and the pendulum ball. The ball must fit the rod by friction, or spring tension, to eliminate any wobble at that point.

SETH THOMAS ADJUSTMENT

A customer brought a Seth Thomas 8-day wind, mantel clock to me for repair. When the clock was examined it was determined that a general cleaning and adjusting was in order. The clock runs fine, but gains ½ hour a day. I added weight to the pendulum and it still gains 20 minutes a day. The adjustment is down to the last, and I cannot lower the pendulum any more. Now I find out a cat knocked the clock off the mantel onto the floor.

How can I slow down the clock? Is there anything I overlooked?

A.

You do not state the model of the Seth Thomas 8-day mantel clock. However, practically all of them have the conventional wire pendulum rod. Chances are, someone before you has replaced the original rod with one too short, or has shortened the original rod.

The weight of the pendulum ball does not vary the time on your clock, unless by adding the weight you have lowered the center of gravity, and thus made the pendulum longer. See the reply to Mr. Odenath in this Clockwise column.

The above supposes that the movement is in order and no wheels substituted. We often run into trouble like yours, i. e., a clock that apparently can't be made to run slow enough. Seth Thomas, especially, made quite a number of 8-day movements with but a very slight difference in the time train to adapt them to different cases. Some of the differences were only in an escape wheel with different number of teeth. Others changed the train count slightly for the same purpose. Now sometimes a clockmaker gets a repair job with a damaged train wheel, extracts the same wheel (second, third or fourth, etc.) from a movement identical in plate contour, etc., to the movement being repaired as a replacement. It works and the repairman is sure it is correct, without counting too match both the wheel teeth and pinion leaves.

If you are sure that this movement is in its original case, and by that you will know that it once had ample pendulum room, set the regulator in the center and cut a new pendulum rod as long as the case will permit (that is allowing the pendulum ball to swing clear about one-eighth inch above the case floor), time the clock, and if it is still fast, you can look for train alteration. If it runs just a little slow, possibly the regulator will take care of the error; if it runs very slow, allow the regulator to remain in the center and shorten the rod a little.

MISSING WEIGHTS

This one is an old 8-day wooden case weight clock and made by Birge, Peck & Company, Bristol, Connecticut, with "Extra 8-day rolling pinion, steel pivots, brass clock" printed on the fancy paper back, along with a lot of instructions to set up the clock and for its care.

The weights are missing, also the pendulum rod and pendulum. Do you have any information about when this clock was made? Also, how long the pendulum rod should be, and the size and weight of the pendulum.

A.

The operation of the firm of Birge, Peck & Company covers the ten-year period from 1849 to 1859. It was John Birge (1785-1862) and Ambrose Peck. Mr. Birge retired from the firm in 1855 to continue farming. This company was later merged with the John C. Brown clock organization, and after several other changes, became what is now the Sessions Clock Company.

Mr. Raymond S. Behrle, 4142 Deyo Avenue, Congress Park, Illinois, makes a specialty of clock weights and is in position to supply you with this item. Most material houses carry the standard "fisheye" pendulum ball, complete with its bob in two sizes, one and eight-day. You will find their 8-day size suitable for this clock. Material houses also stock wire pendulum rods with pendulum spring either attached or rolled on one end. I believe the maximum length they come in

is about 22 inches.

Practically all clockmakers never bother to count the clock's time train and calculate the proper pendulum length. Rather, they just apply one of these wires as long as the case will permit, screw the pendulum ball all the way up and proceed to time the clock by six or twelve-hour intervals, cutting off small lengths of the pendulum wire rod until the clock is slightly fast in rate, then regulate it by letting the ball down.

You can count the clock time train from the center or hour post up to the escape wheel, determining the number of revolutions the escape wheel makes per hour. Multiply this figure by twice the number of teeth in the escape wheel and you get the number of beats per hour. Divide by 60, and get the number of beats per minute.

Reid gives the following rule: "The times of vibrations of pendulums are in the direct ratio of the square roots of their lengths, and the number of vibrations made in a given time are in inverse ratio of the square roots of their lengths."

Thus, you would multiply the vibrations made in a minute by the seconds pendulum (60) by itself, which is squaring it, and this being multiplied by the standard length of 39.2 inches. This last product is divided by the square of the number of vibrations per minute of the desired pendulum, and the quotient will be the length of that pendulum in inches.

Since all pendulum lengths are determined from the standard or Royal pendulum, we may just square the 60 beats and multiply by 39.2, getting 141,120.0 and retain that figure for future use. Then all we have to do is square the number of vibrations desired and divide into that figure. For example, let us say that after you have counted your Birge & Peck clock and find that it beats a hundred times per minute, you will want a pendulum that beats that number of times. Square your 100 and you get 1,000; divide into 141,-120.0, and you get 14.112 inches long.

Another example: Say you desire a pendulum to beat 80 times per minute; 80 times 80 equals 6,400; divide into 141,120.0 and get 22.05 inches.

SYMPATHETIC VIBRATION

The clock is a standard three-weight Herschede grandfather clock with Westminster chime. The clock keeps perfect time until the three weights hang exactly in front of the pendulum. Then it stops. We have checked for vibration which might cause the weights to rub the pendulum, but this does not happen.

The weights themselves do not vibrate, nor does the pendulum. The teeth on the gears are all sharp and perfect. Frankly, we're stuck. Could you help us?

A.

We assume that your clock is in perfect order, and further, that you have observed no bumping or touching of the weights or pendulum, and have not noted any perceptible swing of the weights when they reach the approximate length of the pendulum.

We think your difficulty is "sympathetic vibration." Clockmakers encountered this condition very early—just how far back, we've never made any special check. We do recall that it was observed by John Ellicott, London, (1706-1772) and that Thomas Reid, Edinburgh (1746-1831) mentions it in his treatise published in 1826. And you have probably experimented with two similar stringed instruments by placing one in one room and the other in another room, striking a certain string, and then going to the other instrument and finding the same string set in motion. Well, all this has a bearing on your problem.

We've seen aggravated cases of sympathetic vibration overcome by simply setting the grandfather clock firmly on the floor instead of on a carpet, by bracing the case to the wall, and by shifting the movement on the seat-board, etc.

What is happening is that when your weights descend to a certain point, they start to vibrate in sympathy with the pendulum. This sympathetic vibration either bucks (opposes) the vibration of the pendulum, or by its motion, absorbs the power that rightfully should propel the pendulum. It does not have to be of a magnitude readily noticeable to the eye.

Quoting from page 378 of Reid's treatise: "It has been observed that when two clocks are set a-going on the same shelf, they will disturb each other, and that the pendulum of one will stop that of the other, and that the pendulum which was stopped will, after a while, resume its vibration, and in turn, stop that of the other clock."

In your clock, the stopped pendulum is the weight (or weights), and while the basic principle is the same, the condition differs materially because the weight is descending as long as the clock is running, and thus is a pendulum of varying length.

Often such a condition as you describe is due to the seat-board. They are slotted —usually in three places to permit reeling off the cable, drilled to permit the tying of the outer end of the cable, and sometimes under-cut in the back for the pendulum to swing. This weakens the board in the center, and then when the weight of the movement, weights and pendulum are placed upon its center with the case supports at either end, there can easily be a tendency for the weakened board to vibrate up and down under certain conditions. We recall cases of sympathetic vibration being satisfactorily remedied by bracing the seat-board.

Such bracing depends upon the ideas of the clockmaker and construction of the clock. If the end supports can be lowered, another seat-board cut exactly as the original can be glued and screwed fast to the underside of the original, thus rendering it much stiffer.

Shelf brackets or angle irons can be placed at the ends of the seat-board, just under it, and when screwed fast to the side of the case and to the underside of the seat-board, can eliminate vibration.

I recall one job wherein the clockmaker overcame this condition by making a cherry post about one inch square and three inches long. This post was placed under the seat-board very near the center, left and right, and just between the weights and the pendulum, fore and aft. A small wood screw from the top held it in place, and a wire, evidently from a coathanger, was anchored in the seat-board support on the right (III o'clock side), up right close to where the seat-board rests, then brought across the clock under the lower end of the cherry post and anchored in the left side (IX o'clock) of the seat-board supporting member up very near its top. In this wire he had placed a small turn-buckle. This can be a neat job and you can readily see it is an approved, sound system of bracing.

Sympathetic vibration can be difficult to cope with, and rather mean to set down on paper. We hope that we've given you enough to lick your problem and to satisfy the customer. This problem isn't met with too often, and when it is, the clockmaker invariably says, "It wasn't that way before—why now?" The answer would be as long as the first—possible seasoning of the wood, loosening of the case, etc.

TIME KEEPING RATE

I have an 8-day pendulum clock with Westminster chimes made by KC Company of Germany. Can you tell me how close its rate of timekeeping should be? How should the rate vary from full wind until the last day?

A.

No doubt you have noticed that jeweler's regulators and most every other clock that makes any pretense towards accurate time-keeping, has: 1. a relatively long pendulum, 2. no strike train. The first is for the reason the longer the pendulum the slower it strikes and fewer pendulum errors accumulate per hour; the second, the lift and unlocking for strike (and chime) places an additional load upon the mechanism. A better way to put it might be it varies the load.

It's pretty certain that you have a short pendulum and we know that the chime must be tripped every fifteen minutes. I do not know of any particular figure set up that I might quote — one has to be governed pretty largely by the above-mentioned factors plus the general construction of the clock. For my own purposes I aim at from two to four minutes tolerance per week — a poorly made piece with short pendulum and extra loaded

every quarter hour is doing pretty well to come out within three or four minutes at the end of a full week's run. One of better construction and a long mainspring can be counted on to do much better, and some of these clocks have springs of sufficient length to drive them nine to eleven days, thus when wound every seventh day they never get down to the real weak end.

Some are wont to express astonishment at the four minute error. In the week's run there are ten thousand and eighty minutes, thus the fraction 4 over 10,080 or one part in each 2,520. At least to say it's accurate to better than one part on 2,500 doesn't sound so bad.

How To Construct An Exhibit To Demonstrate Pendulum Law

Is there a simple model that I can make in order to mount two small pendulums on suspension springs and show that they will swing together even though one pendulum is swinging farther than the other?

Is there another model I can make to show that a small pendulum and a large pendulum will swing out at the same speed if their center of gravity is the same? Possibly by my questions you can tell that

I am not too informed as to the scientific explanation of the pendulum theories, but I am interested in making up these two models, so if you can help me, I surely would appreciate it.

A.

By all means do some experimenting with pendulums, also whenever the occasion arises where it is convenient, perform one or two of the experiments for some interested customer. Incidents of this type will serve to make your customer remember you four or five years hence when again his clock needs servicing. One serious handicap the clockmaker has to buck is that of doing a good job, yet because it lasts four, five or six years, the customer forgets who did it. A satisfactory repair is expected, thus something more is required than just that to so fix the repairman in the customer's memory that he won't forget.

Down to the "meat" of your question. Frankly, I don't have the how-to-do-it answer in minute detail, but a few suggestions may help you attain the desired results. First, you indicate small pendulums' best results are obtained by longer pendulums, not that the actual end results are any different, but the period of swing of the longer pendulum being longer will enable you to make a better demonstration. I'd say the "royal," or seconds pendulum, 39.14 inches, would be the best.

Over the years practically every length pendulum imaginable has been tried, and old tower clocks may be found with pendulums thirty to forty feet long. Many modern tower clocks are equipped with two-seconds pendulums (13-plus feet). In his experiment to demonstrate the motion of the earth, M. Foucault hung a pendulum in the Pantheon, 160 feet long. Possibly the longest was that used by M. Mascarat suspended from the Eiffel tower, 377 feet long.

First, your anchorage or point of fastening must be the most solid possible— a heavy beam of the building, an iron support securely bolted to a brick wall, etc. Any light support such as a wooden frame you might make up, even though it feels pretty steady, will allow one pendulum to influence the other and defeat the purpose of your demonstration.

There is no limit to the many experiments or demonstrations you can work up —they will suggest themselves as you work along. Buy or cast some lead balls, say one of one pound, one of two pounds, and a third of five pounds; in fact you will find use for these in equal pairs. Drill a very small hole clear through each and suspend with good cord (fishing line is excellent), run the cord through and wedge it tight by driving a needle in the bottom. It is well to allow the needle to extend down a good half-inch below and outside the ball. This affords a point for holding and releasing your balls.

It isn't always necessary to have both balls adjustable—just have one and adjust it to the other. However, you may have a take-up on both if you care to make the additional suspension. A good one is made up by taking the worm-drive tuning key from an old guitar; a solid support for it may be soldered (soft) up with heavy brass strips. From your old watch junk, select a plate with good smooth jewel whose hole is a good fit for the fishline suspension and solder this old plate just under the tuning key. With the lead ball fastened to the lower end, thread the cord through the jewel hole and fasten to the arbor just as the string of the guitar was originally and reel up several turns. Now you have a convenient micrometer adjustment. Turning the key a quarter-turn either lengthens or shortens the pendulum the very slightest bit since by its screw or worm gearing, the arbor is scarcely moved. It is needless to add that one ought to permit the pendulums to hang for a day or two in order that the fishline will attain its maximum stretch.

Hang two of your pendulums and vary the adjustable one until you have them beating together (in step). After all, this is the only way two pendulums can be determined to be of the same length, i. e., when they beat in the same time.

Now you are ready to demonstrate the law as determined by Galileo: "Pendulums of equal length swing in unequal arcs in equal time." Take any light piece of wood, common advertising yardstick is excellent, tack to it two cross pieces, say one on the end and one eight inches back. Catch the needle of one pendulum behind one block and that of the other behind the second block, and draw the pendulums aside until the one held by the end block is eight inches from center or zero point. This puts the other pendulum 16 inches from the zero point. Hold steady until all is at perfect rest, then a quick downward motion of your stick releases both pendulums at exactly the same instant. You will observe one pendulum covering twice the distance as the other, yet doing it in identically the same time.

As you work your way into and through various experiments, refinements and improvements will suggest themselves. Take another yardstick; remove the numerals with your hand motor or a burr or a little sanding disc in your lathe, mark or paint the center (18th inch) zero (0), and beginning with one number each way from center. Mount this under the pendulums with the zero mark accurately centered under the rest or dead point. The yardstick on which you have tacked the little cross blocks for holding the pendulums back may have its other end nailed to a heavy block of wood (about 8 x 8 inches, 1 foot long). This can be pulled back holding the pendulums to start an experiment, then when all weight is completely at rest, a quick stroke downward will spring it down and out of the way, then you may pull it aside in plenty of time to be out of the way before the balls return.

You may use a ball of 5 lbs. along with one of 1 or 2 lbs. to clearly demonstrate that it is the length, and not the weight of the ball that determines the time or period of each stroke.

The longer the pendulum, the longer you can have its arc of swing, thereby making more evident or magnifying the points you wish to stress. The law holds good regardless of length, but the very short ones stroke over a very little distance, and do it so much faster it can be difficult for you to point it out to the untrained eye.

Rules for Calculating Lengths of Pendulums

I am told that you would have the formula for figuring the length of a pendulum of a clock. Is there any difference with respect to dead beat? I would greatly appreciate it if you would tell me the formula as I've been asking and reading a lot, and as yet have had no results.

A.

The type and/or kind of escapement does not enter into your problem at all; a pendulum of a given length will make the same number of beats per minute regardless of whether it be driven by recoil, dead beat, La Pute or Brocot escapement. Probably the very best article you can get on the clock pendulum is found in chapter III of Dr. Arthur Rawlings' "The Science of Clocks and Watches" (2nd edition, A.H.&J. Book Department, $5.00 plus 10c

postage). In it he covers the pendulum pretty thoroughly in just 40 pages.

Having first learned from Reid's "Treatise on Clock and Watchmaking," I continue using Reid's method from force of habit, I guess. The following is a quotation from Reid: "The lengths of two pendulums are reciprocally to one another as the squares of the numbers of the vibrations made in the same time. If then the number of vibrations that a pendulum makes in a given time is known, and the length of the pendulum, we can deduce the length of any other pendulum if the number of vibrations which it must give in a certain time is known; and reciprocally the length of a pendulum being given, we can find the number of vibrations it must make in a certain time."

To calculate the length of a pendulum when you have given the number of vibrations, multiply the number of vibrations made in a minute by the royal, or seconds pendulum (60) by itself which is squaring it, and this being multiplied by the royal's length of 39.2 inches, and the last product divided by the square of the number of vibrations, by the pendulum whose length you seek, the quotient will be the length of that pendulum in inches and decimal parts of an inch.

Let's say you have a pendulum beating or vibrating half-seconds, that is 120 times per minute, and you wish to calculate how long it will be: Square the 120

$$
\begin{array}{r}
120 \\
120 \\
\hline
2400 \\
120 \\
\hline
14400
\end{array}
$$

Square the 60 beat known length.

$$
\begin{array}{r}
60 \\
60 \\
\hline
3600
\end{array}
$$

Now, the square of the desired pendulum 14,400 is to the known length 39.2 inches as the square of the known length 3,600 is to?

14,440: 39.2: 3600: ?

$$
\begin{array}{r}
39.2 \\
3600 \\
\hline
235200 \\
1176 \\
\hline
1411200 \\
\end{array}
$$

$$
\begin{array}{r}
14400)\ 141120.0\ (9.8 \\
129600 \\
22520 \\
.0 \\
\hline
115200 \\
\hline
\end{array}
$$

Thus a pendulum to beat 120 times per minute would be 9.8 inches. Note when working this way you always have the 60 squared of the vibrations of the royal pendulum times the 39.2, the length of the royal pendulum, so there is always that 141,120.0.

Just keep and remember it, and the problem becomes very simple. Let's say you have just cleaned an 8-day mantel clock and have counted its train; it must beat 140 times per minute. Merely square the 140 and divide into 141,120.0:

$$
\begin{array}{r}
140 \\
140 \\
\hline
5600 \\
140 \\
\hline
19600 \\
\end{array}
$$

$$
\begin{array}{r}
19600\ )141120.0(\ 7.2 \\
137200 \\
\hline
3920 \\
.0 \\
\hline
39200 \quad 7.2\ \text{inches} \\
\end{array}
$$

When your problem is the other way around, i. e., you know how long the pendulum is, and wish to know how many times it will beat, you have only to divide the known length into 141,120.0 and take the square root of the quotient. Say you have measured a very long pendulum and found it to be 156.8 inches and wish to know what it beats:

$$
\begin{array}{r}
156.8\ )141120.0(\ 900 \\
14112 \\
\hline
0 \\
\end{array}
$$

$900(30 \qquad$ Thirty times, or two seconds

Now this came out very well simply because we already knew the correct length of the two seconds pendulum as used on tower clocks. The point is: if you were totally unaware of the 13 feet (156 in.) .8 in., you would not so measure it. Further, the active or horological length of a pendulum is *not* the over-all, but from the point of suspension to the center of gravity. Neither of these points being so definitely fixed as to permit easy measurement to the last tenth of an inch.

Practical clock pendulums are suspended by a suspension spring—the flexing of that spring brings the suspension point a little lower than the actual bottom edge of the top chock, or what would be the ⌐oint if we were considering the ideal theoretical pendulum on a drawing. Again, since the center of gravity would fall where the complete pendulum would balance if laid across a knife-edge, we have to judge or estimate it. Don't be discouraged when problems do not work out to the final tenth of an inch. To save the poor clockmaker's hide is the regulating nut at the bottom of the pendulum, and in many instances, still another device at the top for varying the point of suspension. Thus, if you have missed your calculation by a few tenths, just remember that by the regulating nut you can still vary the length by many tenths of an inch.

A little practice and one becomes pretty adept at estimating the center of gravity —familiarity with the method, use of it for a little while, and you can cut a pendulum rod that will come well within the regulating adjustment of most clocks at the very first try. We posed this problem of calculating the pendulum's length in last month's column (April).

In regular shop practice, the repairman should use this and similar calculations that are time savers. We've never known just why men persist in cutting pendulums "by guess and by gosh," and having to do it two to four times—sometimes cutting too short and having to supply another rod when it cuts production down like it does. In its final analysis, all the repairman has to sell is jobs, and the shorter the time consumed on the job, the more jobs he can turn out.

T.V.-Magnetized Pendulum?

A customer of ours has a key-wind pendulum clock. The clock will run all right until he puts it on his television set. It will then stop after two hours or less.

We put a compass on top of the television and it has a magnetized field. The pendulum was magnetized. Would the field be great enough to stop the clock? If so, how could this be corrected?

A.

This is a new one—we've never met it before!

There is a tremendous magnetic field when you get very near some TV sets. About the time of World War I, lots of eight-day American pendulum clocks came with "iron" pendulum balls and I can readily see that to set one of these clocks within a strong magnetic field it would soon stop, due to the magnetic forces acting on the ball.

Naturally, any magnetic force acts on every steel or iron part of the clock. I seriously doubt if its action on the spring, pendulum wire, etc., would be great enough to cause stoppage.

Check this clock and see if it has an iron pendulum ball. If it has, substitute one of lead and try it. You might go so far as to substitute an aluminum wire for its regular pendulum wire and a brass suspension spring for the present steel one. The column would especially like to hear from you again—just what you did and the results.

I'm reminded of a question-and-answer department I used to read in a farm journal as a boy. One farmer wrote in for a remedy for getting rid of wild onions, and got the reply "move off and leave them." After all, you could persuade your customer to locate the clock in some other part of the room.

This is an Ansonia clock

This clock stands 30 inches high and is of a cast material, either lead or pewter. The casting job is beautiful.

The movement has lantern pinions and a standard anchor escapement with steel verge, highly polished. The counter weight in the verge keeps the clock in motion once the four suspension springs get the clock in motion.

The clock ran four hours slow daily when I got it. I found that lengthening the center shaft by means of a screw in the center of the pendulum made the clock run faster, as did adding weight to the ball. I finally changed the four suspension springs and made them weaker by about .05 mm.

This did the trick. It now keeps excellent time.

A.

The clock you indicate was manufactured by the Ansonia Clock Co., around the turn of the century, therefore, for round figures, it is 50 years old.

It is illustrated and listed on page 35 of their catalog for 1907 as follows: "Fortuna Ball Swing, fitted with eight-day time movement, dial 4½ inches. Figures finished in Art Nouveau, Barbedienne or Syrian Bronze, etc. Ball finished in blue or red enamel, also Barbedienne or Verde Bronze. Height, 30 inches. List, each $55."

Regarding your difficulty in regulating, you have run up against a thing which has confused lots of men not completely familiar with the "compound" pendulum. If you will observe the marking and reg nut just under the suspension block you will find that to turn the reg nut towards the letter "F" to make the clock run faster, that it will lengthen your pendulum . . . just the reverse of a single pendulum.

Look at it this way, you have a great deal of weight above the point of suspension; suppose that you screwed the pendulum weight (lower) up until it exactly balanced that weight above the suspension point, then you would have a "poised" balance wheel and no pendulum at all, and unlike the poised balance wheel of a watch, no hairspring to bring it back to center position.

Possibly your weakening your suspension spring did do much towards bringing the clock to time; after all, your compound pendulum is not isochronal by a long shot and allowing it to make longer strokes it just required more time in which to make them. In case you would like to go into this further, I'd recommend Chapter II, "The Pendulum" in "Science of Clocks and Watches" (second edition) by Dr. A. H. Rawlings. There is probably a copy in your local library .

Rate of one to two seconds per month is very good

I would like to ask a question today regarding Invar pendulums for precision regulators. I made a new Invar rod for my Seth Thomas regulator using the old bob, also made a new suspension spring out of Invar. The result in timekeeping was quite different than with the old wooden rod. I now have the regulator keeping time within one or two seconds per month, tested over a period of 18 months.

Now I am wondering if this pendulum could be improved by installing an all-Invar bob? In my pendulum I suspended the old bob from the center and used a one-inch brass tube as compensator. All the rest of the rod, including the suspension spring and the rating nut is Invar. What is your opinion as to the use of Invar for the bob also?

Do you know of anyone who has ever experimented with it? I am surprised that a scientist like Rawlings does not in his book refer to an all-Invar pendulum. That makes me think it is probably not desirable, but what are the reasons?

A.

First off if you have your regulator taking a steady and reliable rate of one to two seconds per month—DON'T TOUCH IT. How much better can you expect?

Your conclusion that an all-Invar pendulum is not desirable, is exactly correct. It boils down to simply this: one cannot get a substance (metal or wood) that is not affected in some degree by change of temperature, so you take Invar because it is affected the least. Since there is to be some expanding and contracting, the very best you can hope for is to "compensate" for it and here again, one does not reach absolute perfection. Of necessity your rod must have a much greater length than your bob. Don't you see that if you use a 39.14-inch rod, and your bob was of the exact same composition, it too, would have to be 39.14 inches in order that it expand upward from the reg nut by the same amount the rod expands downward?

Prof. David Robertson, in his splendid paper "The Theory of Pendulums and Escapements" says: "The right length of compensator is not that which will keep the center of gravity of the bob at a constant level, but that which will cause an error equal and opposite to the sum of all the other errors, including the expansion of the rod down to the top of the compensator."

Our initial sentence above was not intended as a wisecrack, it is simply that if you have your regulator under that good control you are doing extra well. Your reference to Invar for a rod, etc., deals solely with the temperature side of errors. There is the question of barometric errors. Real high precision pendulums are run within a glass jar from which much of the air has been exhausted and the pressure within that jar is held constant. The air surrounding your pendulum affects its rate (1) a reduction of effective weight by its buoyancy, (2) air friction as the pendulum swings to and fro.

Frankly, the writer has no actual, in-hand, experience to speak of with ultra-high precision pendulums. It is my understanding that these pendulums are made of a special Invar stock; each bar after proper aging, etc., is subjected to laboratory tests to ascertain to a high degree, its individual coefficient of expansion; that equal care and precision goes into the entire construction of the complete pendulum assembly, and that after all this, it is hung as mentioned, in a fixed or constant pressure jar.

Don't think for a moment it stops here; despite all the precision and care exercised up to this point, the pendulum (with its container) is mounted upon a "solid" post or support, one well anchored in the earth and insulated from the building so that any building vibrations are not transmitted to it. And as a further precaution to off-set temperature changes the clock vault or room is automatically maintained at a pretty-near-fixed temperature. This vault or clockroom is not entered except when absolutely necessary. All observations, regulation and management of the clock can be accomplished by remote control by the man in charge looking through the double glass in the door or special window.

Let's go back to your present error of one or two seconds per month and take the high figure of two seconds. In a 30-day month you have 720 hours—3,600 seconds per hour gives about 2,592,000 seconds. For practical purposes, call it $2\frac{1}{2}$ million. Then 2 over $2\frac{1}{2}$ million equals an error of one part in $1\frac{3}{4}$ million—a high degree of accuracy, and that's why we said "Don't Touch It."

Concerning French clock pendulums

I have a French clock for repair. It has no name on the movement. On the dial it says "Thomaa. A Paria."

This clock has a half-hour striking movement. My trouble is that the customer has lost the pendulum. I made a temporary one and it runs several hours slow per day. The type I made is a very light one and hangs on a thread. I checked the mainsprings; they were too narrow and set. I changed them to the proper size and it still runs slow. In my estimation, the pendulum should be approximately 11 inches long.

A.

The French system for marking the correct pendulum length on the back of the back-plate was to place a figure at the very bottom of the plate; this figure is often divided by the hole for the bottom pillar-post. The digits upon your left are "pouces" and upon the right of the hole are "lignes."

One pouce equals 27 mm., one ligne equals 2.26 mm. Thus if you were to see upon a French clock a "4" upon the left, and a "1" on the right you would have 4 pouces or 108 mm. and 1 ligne or 2.26 mm. The pendulum should be $110\frac{1}{2}$ mm. from point of suspension to the center of gravity.

As I write there is before me a little French, silk-suspended, clock. On its back plate to the left is the one figure "5," this indicates that the pendulum should be 135 mm. long.

This pendulum ball is roughly the size and thickness of a 25-cent piece, and a hole in its center about 3 mm. in diameter. Measuring from the point of suspension down, 135 mm. comes within this hole.

Basically, altering the driving force on a pendulum clock (changing springs) does not change the rate of running. To change that rate, first make sure the clock is in order, then do it by changing the length of the pendulum. IF your clock has not been altered, that is, pinions or wheels changed, and if your center friction is NOT slipping, then the ONLY thing that will make it run slow is a pendulum too long.

Should it be one of those made before they started the system of stamping pendulum length on the plate you can always "count" your train. Begin with the center or minute post, divide the number of teeth in the wheel by the leaves of the pinion it drives on up to the escape wheel, thus you will determine the number of revolutions the escape wheel makes per hour. Multiply that number of revolutions by the number of teeth in the escape wheel, then multiply by 2 because each tooth makes two ticks. This last figure is the number of ticks or beats per hour. Divide by 60 for the beats per minute.

To find the length of a pendulum that beats "X" times per minute, square "X" and divide into 141,120. Let us say you need a pendulum that will beat 140 times per minute—square the 140 and you get 19,600. Divide 19,600 into 141,120 and you will get 7.2, seven and two-tenths inches.

234

Conical Pendulum Clock
Needs Replacement Parts

This clock is in my shop now and before proceeding too far on repairs I need information. Looks like some parts are missing and I see no way to control the train or no way to regulate it. I would like to know what type of escapement this is. This movement is the same as any run of the mill eight day movement, time side and hour strike. Until we get to the escapement. There is no verge or pendulum. Instead of working on a verge the escape wheel drives a small worn gear attached to a small rod. This rod rotates and extends up and almost through a hole located in the top of the case housing, and there it ends. Standing on top of the case is a statue of a woman with one upraised arm and she is holding a hook in her hand which is directly over the hole in the case where the rod ends.

Perhaps you can see from my drawings what type of clock this is and help me by sending me a sketch of what is missing and how to control and regulate it.

A.

I hope that we can help you restore your Florence Kroeber, Noiseless Rotary. Another term or name applied to this type is conical pendulum clock. We can not give you specific measurements, weight, etc., only a general description of how it works. Fortunately in this instance, those missing parts you require are not complicated, and they can be most easily made. It is just going to take a bit of cut and try upon your part till you have it to time.

From the hook being held by your statue was suspended via a silk cord a little ball. On the vertical rod extending upward from the escapement was a simple crank with a slot in it. In the bottom of the ball was a wire; this wire works in the slot of the crank. Start the ball swinging in a circular motion and the crank as it is driven by its worm gear will keep it whirling. The wire must fit the slot perfectly free; as the clock speeds up, centrifugal force causes the ball to swing in a larger circle and thus slower, or as it slows down in a smaller circle and so faster.

Originally, the crank was made just like a seconds hand, i.e. it had a split pipe for a friction fit upon the drive shaft — you can readily see that this fit must be rather tight. Regulation is attained by lengthening or shortening the pendulum. Perhaps you can discover in the back of the lady's hand where some method of reeling in or letting out the silk cord was located. As a starter I'm going to suggest

that you might take the brass lead-filled ball from an old 400-day clock, it should be near the correct weight (can be lightened by reducing lead), it is about the right size and will look well. A medium size needle in the bottom will serve as a smooth pin to work in the slot. That should do it.

Over the years I've seen but one of these Kroeber Rotaries and heard of only two others. Evidently they weren't made in great numbers.

Adjusting the Compound Pendulum

We talked the formula-type problem over with a local friend, knowledgeable within the printing industry and he suggested that one way to solve it is by small cuts. So, we've inked-in the formulas from the Prasil paper that follows:

Text books do not give the formula for this complex form of pendulum. They all give the familiar formula for the period of the simple pendulum, where 1 equals length of pendulum from suspension to center of bob in cm. and g equals accleration of gravity, 981 cm/sec², which sheds no light on problem.

$$T. = \pi \sqrt{\frac{L.}{G.}}$$

However, if we back up a step and obtain the more fundamental relation from which equation 1 is derived, we can derive a formula which gives the period of the pendulum in question.

The basic relation is given by A. L. Rawlings in Chapter III of his book, "The Science of Clocks and Watches."

It is:

$$T. = \pi \sqrt{\frac{\text{MOMENT OF INERTIA}}{\text{RESTORING COEFFICIENT.}}}$$

This formula applies to any system having an oscillating rotary motion. The moment of inertia of the simple pendulum about its point of suspension is ml^2, where m is the mass of the pendulum bob. The restoring coefficient, or the amount of pull necessary to displace the pendulum per unit angle from its rest position is mg1. Substituting these in equation (2) yields equation (1) for the simple pendulum.

The equation for the metronome pendulum is obtained almost as easily. The pendulum is illustrated in Figure 1.

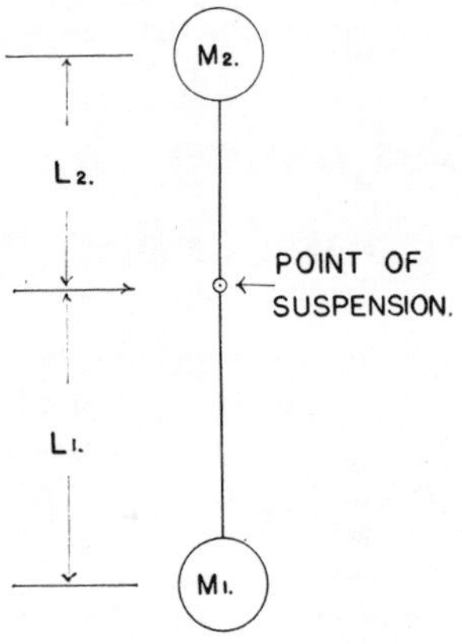

Fig. I.

Its moment of inertia about the point of suspension is the sum of the moments of inertia of each section about the suspension or

$$M_1 \; L_1^2 + M_2 \; L_2^2.$$

The restoring coefficient, however, is the difference of that for the two ends, for while the bottom mass, m, resists the displacement, as in a simple pendulum, the top mass, m^2, aids the displacement force by trying to tip the pendulum from its rest position. Thus, the restoring coefficient is $m_1 l_1 g$ minus $m_2 l_2 g$.

Substituting these in equation (2) gives the equation for time of swing of the double pendulum,

$$T = \pi \; \sqrt{\frac{M_1 \; L_1^2 + M_2 \; L_2^2}{G \; (M_1 \; L_1 - M_2 \; L_2)}}$$

If m, and m_2 are equal, the formula reduces to a simple form,

$$T = \pi \; \sqrt{\frac{L_1^2 + L_2^2}{G \; (L_1 - L_2)}}$$

These equations may not convey much meaning. It may be instructive to look at a tabulation of values of 1 and m required to produce a seconds pendulum. These are given in Table I.

TABLE I.
Lengths required to give a seconds compound pendulum.

Length. L_1	length. L_2	mass. M_1	mass. M_2	time. T
99.4 CM.	0 CM.	M	0	I SEC.
75	16.0	M	M	I
50	20.5	M	M	I
25	16.1	M	M	I
75	29.0	M	1/2 M	I
50	36.3	M	1/2 M	I
25	29.0	M	1/2 M	I
75	8.5	M	2M	I
50	11.2	M	2M	I
25	8.6	M	2M	I

A.P./J.E.C.

The five second pendulum, like that of any other beat, can be obtained by an infinite number of combinations of 1, l_2, m, and m_2. The ratio of m, and m_2 must be chosen, a length for 1 selected, and the appropriate value of l_2 determined. It may be easiest to try several values of l_2 in the equation until it come out to be close to the desired value.

Assuming m, and m_2 are equal, and 1 is 10 cm. l_2 must be 9.9 cm. Thus, it is apparent that small pendulums for long times are more easily brought to time by an adjustment than by computation and painstaking construction. It is also evident that this adjustment is very critical.

Focault Pendulum Makes Fine Show Piece

Our college here has built a new science building and I am trying to get them to install a Focault pendulum.

All the height they can come up with is 12 feet. Is this enough? If so, could you tell me how it should be built? I have only a vague idea of how to do it and would appreciate any help you can give me.

Appreciate your question, the Focault pendulum is an item in which I've been very much interested for a good many years. At the outset, I must remind you that we are endeavoring to cover a tremendous lot of territory in one letter; of necessity, much of it has to be references.

Dr. Atlantis Sudbury (816 Mines Ave., Montebello, Calif.) whom I consider one of the top authorities upon the Focault pendulum, tells me that one can be made to demonstrate the rotation of the earth, as short as seven (7) feet long. It is noted that you say your limit is 12 feet — it is my hope that you can "fudge" on this quite a bit — it is desirable to have the ball swing within a pit (if wire breaks, no damage) thus if you can cut into the floor you might add, say three feet. Perhaps there is a chance; if it is a first floor location, single story, to go into the attic section for the actual suspension point and gain another 3 to 5 feet bringing your "drop" to the order of 20 feet or more.

When building a Foucault pendulum, you are limited by only two things, 1, money. 2, labor. One may be set up in a short time for a dozen or so dollars — upon the other side, you can easily pour 2,000 or 3,000 dollars into it plus many, many hours of labor.

One of the first decisions to be made, is: whether it is to be driven, or a free-swinger. To "drive" one is something quite different from maintaining a clock's pendulum in motion. The drive power must be applied in a manner that will NOT affect the direction of swing; i.e. the pendulum must be left perfectly free to remain in the original plane in which it was started. Here is where goodly portion of cost lies. In his original experiment, Prof. Foucault utilized a "drop" of better than 200 feet — he had no method of "drive" and thus it was to his interest to use the longest possible suspension so that his pendulum would swing a longer number of hours.

Naturally, any Foucault installation is of necessity a "show piece" — here again, you can pour in money to your heart's content. As you know, such a pendulum set up at the North Pole would complete the 360 degree circle in a sidereal or star day (23 hrs. 56 min. 4.09 sec.) while at the equator it would show no deviation at all. The time required for the Foucault to complete the circle at points in between can easily be determined by dividing 24 hours by the sine of the latitude; most installations have some sort of a "dial" located directly beneath the pendulum calibrated in accordance with that calculation; such a dial and calibration can be simple markings upon a circle drawn upon the floor, or, as elaborate as you

choose. Perhaps the most expensive ones are those made of terrazzo embodying elaborate maps or design.

At a very little expense one can make a very effective dial. Simply choose a map — that of the Northern hemisphere with N. pole at its center — a portion of the U. S. with your location at its center, or, a section of your state (counties) with your town in the exact center; photograph it with a 35-mm. color film so you get it back as a slide, from a substantial piece of linoleum cut the desired size (4, 6, 8, 10 or 12 feet diam.) circle, paint a suitable border and divide it in accordance with calculation you have made for your latitude. (In my case, I had luck — Nashville figures out 40 hours and 40 minutes, very near — so I divided my border into 40 divisions.) By projecting the slide upon the circle inside the border, you can paint the map easily. Correctly locate upon the border, N. E. S. and W. (paint or cut-out brass letters) place it so that when the pendulum is at rest it is directly over your city, the N. correctly to true north and you'll have a presentable as well as impressive "dial."

There is no end to the work one may lavish upon such a project — being a "show piece" it needs either a lecturer, or, some "explanation" nearby — such an explainer is limited only by your imagination — you can secure at the five and dime store, a metal globe about ten inches in diameter — with your jewelers' saw, cut at the equator, mount the northern half over a sync clock motor on which you have reversed the motion (earth turns from West to East) to counterclockwise and you have the world turning 1-rpm. Build a display of Masonite or plywood; mount your turning world center of base, etc. Through the back-board extend a stiff wire to carry a little pendulum to swing right over the pole, this pendulum can either be actuated by a clock movement, or, one of those little battery driven display things you have salvaged; hidden behind the back board. Result, you have a spinning world and a simulated Foucault pendulum swinging over the pole. Various and sundry data, explanation, etc. Through the back-board extend a stiff and mounted either side of the little pendulum, on the back board. Such will add greatly to the display.

Write: California Academy of Sciences, Golden Gate Park, San Francisco, Calif. and ask for their booklet No. 10, "Our Spinning Earth," another to Springfield Museum of Science, Springfield, Mass., asking for their leaflet "The Focault Pendulum." 50c to Scientific American (415 Madison Ave., N. Y. 17, N. Y.) will bring a copy of their June 1958 (vol. 198 No. 6) issue containing Mr. C. L. Stong's article "How To Make A Pendulum That

Will Demonstrate The Rotation Of The Earth." Another half-buck to Sky & Telescope (Harvard College Observatory, Cambridge 38, Mass.) will bring their Jan. 1960 (Vol. 19, No. 3) with a splendid article "A Foucault Pendulum." We hope this will serve as a starter; if you have other questions don't hesitate to fire them in, and, by all means keep up posted upon your project, would especially appreciate photo plus detailed description when completed, for the file.

CALCULATING PENDULUMS

Whether it is a lost pendulum, adapting a movement to another case, or, just a simple repair job, the length of the pendulum is always of vital concern to the bench clockmaker. Scarcely a month goes by that C. & O. does not receive some inquiry upon the length of the pendulum. This established trend was highlighted this month by two long distance phone calls, one from Florida and one from Ohio. Both were related to pendulum length.

Within every mechanical action there is a "gap" between pure theory and the practical. That "gap" between the pendulum in theory and the pendulum hung to your clock may not be as wide as some, but, it is none the less confusing. This perplexity is heightened within the thinking of the clockmaker every time he applies a ruler to his "practical" pendulum and comes up with figures that do not match the pendulum of theory. To understand these discrepancies he must first understand the theory and then the practical application of that theory. The pendulum of theory has its suspension at a very fixed point, for example, at its very top extremity and all its weight at the very bottom end. It is self evident that you do not have either of these requirements met in your practical pendulum.

Unless you have one of those rare Frenchies whose pendulum is suspended by a silk thread, you do not have a definite suspension point. On those pendulums suspended via a small, thin spring, the actual "point" of suspension is where that spring bends. This bend is not abrupt, rather it is a gradual curve, so, where upon this

curve does one place his ruler to begin that measurement? This is why a stiffer suspension spring will show a faster rate. Being stiffer, it bends further down from the anchor point, in practical effect making a shorter pendulum. To make an accurate ruler measurement you also have to have a terminal point. This one is even more elusive because it is impossible to have all your pendulum weight concentrated in one point. There is some weight all the way up the ball. Add to this that weight constituted within the rod and your total weight goes further up. That point of extremity is considered to be at the center of gravity, where, if the ball plus the rod were laid across a knife-edge it would balance. Not only does the clockmaker not know where to lay his ruler to begin his measurement, he does not know exactly where that measurement ends. It is exceedingly difficult to make any ruler measurement where both the beginning point and the ending point are nebulous.

Once these basics are fully understood you have only to couple them with a little practical experience, and, you come up with a sort of rule-of-thumb operation which will stand you well in hand for practical clock work. Count the train of any clock to ascertain the number of required beats per minute; locate that number on the right-hand column of the chart, follow that line across 'til it intersects the pendulum curve; then follow that line down to the inch scale at the bottom and you have the theoretical length of the pendulum. For example, let us say your clock beats 120 to the minute—this brings you across to 9.8 inches—measure its pendulum and compare that measurement to the 9.8. Your measurement will be a bit longer. Note this difference and you begin to build up this rule-of-thumb understanding. It is hardly necessary to add that these measurements do not have to be micronometer accurate as you always have considerable lee-way via your regulator, raising and lowering the ball.

Where the entire pendulum has been lost, it is necessary to know the beat of the clock when determining the length of the required pendulum. Making the train count is not overly difficult, one is not concerned with the first or great wheel (sometimes the 2nd wheel) only from the center post to the escape wheel. We know that the center-post turns one revolution per hour. Count from the center to the escape and determine the number of revs the escape wheel makes, then multiply that figure by the number of teeth in the escape wheel and double that because each escape tooth makes two beats (one entering and one leaving the verge). This gives the number of beats per hour. Divide by sixty to reduce it to minutes (this is already computed on the chart, right hand column).

The rule for finding the length of a pendulum, for a given number of vibrations is given by Reid as: "Multiply the number of vibrations made in a minute by the royal or seconds pendulum, (viz 60) by itself which is squaring it, this being multiplied by the standard length of 39.2 inches, and the last product divided by the square of the number of vibrations given in a minute by the pendulum whose length is required, the quotient will be the length of the pendulum in inches and decimal parts of an inch." Since 60 squared times 39.2 gives 141,120 you might just remember that figure and not have to make the calculation again and again.

As an example lets say you have counted a train and find that you require a pendulum to beat 120 times per minute. Square your 120 and get 14,400. Divide that into the 141,120 and you come up with 9.8 inches. Supposing 140 vibrations per minute are required square it to get 19,600 and divide into 141,121 and get 7.2 inches. Easy.

Clockmakers sometimes become confused because the center (hour post) is auxiliary driven. Many, if not most American shelf clocks have their centers auxiliary driven. Right here lies the reason for it. By driving the center outside of the time, the factory is able to adapt the same movement to a wide number of pendulum lengths, just as when the center is an integral part of the time train, you begin with it. Say the center (hour) is driven by the second wheel, when you count the number of

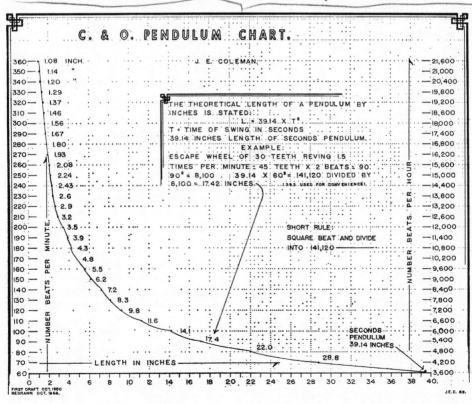

C. & O. PENDULUM CHART.

J. E. COLEMAN

THE THEORETICAL LENGTH OF A PENDULUM BY INCHES IS STATED:
L = 39.14 X T²
T = TIME OF SWING IN SECONDS
39.14 INCHES LENGTH OF SECONDS PENDULUM.
EXAMPLE:
ESCAPE WHEEL OF 30 TEETH REVING 1.5 TIMES PER MINUTE = 45 TEETH X 2 BEATS = 90.
90² = 8,100 . 39.14 X 60² = 141,120 DIVIDED BY 8,100 = 17.42 INCHES.   1382 USED FOR CONVENIENCE.

SHORT RULE:
SQUARE BEAT AND DIVIDE
INTO 141,120

SECONDS PENDULUM 39.14 INCHES

LENGTH IN INCHES

FIRST DRAFT OCT. 1950
REDRAWN OCT. 1969.   J.E.C. 69.

teeth in the hour-post drive wheel you have determined the number of teeth in the second wheel required to turn it one rev. (hour), then this very same number of teeth will have passed through that pinion on the next wheel of the time train. Carry your calculation forward from there to determine the number of revs. the escape wheel makes per hour. This brings you right back to the original calculation—— times the number of teeth in the escape wheel, times 2 for the beats per hour, divided by 60 for the number of beats per minute. This calculation, in some instances may bring forth a rather odd figure occasioned by the auxiliary drive like 143. Don't permit this to baffle you, remember, the latitude in raising or lowering the ball via its bottom nut can easily make up for the difference of three to five beats per minute. Our chart is made up by tens per minute with five graduations between, thus each of the fine lines represents two beats—it's close enough to calculate to the nearest five. The precise value in inches long for the seconds (Royal) pendulum is given as 39.1416, however, for convenience we have used the figure of 39.2 inches and for all practical work this is plenty close.

The Compound Pendulum

For a starter, we might look for a definition of the compound pendulum. Donald deCarle, in his "Watch & Clock Cyclopedia" does not give one under compound, rather, under pendulum he states: "A compound pendulum appertains to those used in clocks especially when designed to obtain compensatory effect. To some degree every physical pendulum may be said to be a compound pendulum."

Dr. A. L. Rawlings,—"The Science of Clocks & Watches"—in his chapter three titled "The Pendulum" is equally skittish upon the compound pendulum, but, in describing the ideal simple pendulum—all mass at the extreme end—does say: "These conditions are never fulfilled in practice so we must extend our investigation to deal with the real pendulum, otherwise known as the compound pendulum."

HUNTER BALL SWING
Or with the Fisher Figure.
Eight-Day Time.
Dial, 4½ inches.   Height, 25 inches.
Finished in New Art or Syrian Bronze. . . . . List, each, $32.00
Ball finished in Blue Enamel.
FIG-1.

With all due respect for these two outstanding authorities, neither of them have dealt with or defined the compound pendulum we deal with here and as most clockmakers this date think of as being a pendulum with a goodly portion of its mass or weight ABOVE the point of suspension. Claudius Saunier in his big treatise is a bit more explicit upon this point though his comments are confined to barely one page, in which he concludes by saying: "This device can not be employed in high class horology, at least not as a reliable regulator, but Maelzel made a very interesting application of it in the metronome, an instrument for beating time for music."

Indeed the metronome is a shining example of this 'compound' pendulum we are speaking of—in it, we have a pendulum approximately ten inches in over-all length, beating the same seconds as the Royal simple pendulum of 39-plus inches. When handling swing clocks, the clockmaker should always remember the metronome where he raises the weight for a SLOWER beat.

Our favorite authority—Ward L. Goodrich, "The Modern Clock"—is equally as skittish upon pendulums with a goodly portion of their mass above the point of suspension. At any rate the bench clockmaker will do well to restudy his chapter II titled, "The Natural Laws Governing Pendulums." I can accurately report to you that we've had more difficulty putting the points covered in this "Otherwise" over than almost any other point of horological construction. Perhaps Saunier did not forsee a day when clocks would be mass produced along the metronome principle, and since Goodrich, his book, dated 1905, may not have seen such a clock, he too omitted it. Certainly deCarle and Dr. Rawlings can not have that excuse.

One questioner who was sure his Ansonia swinger had its "S" & "F" markings reversed, refused our explanation and fired back a lengthy letter to point out that upon the metronome moving the weight up to go slower was the equivalent of lowering the ball weight on the simple pendulum, because that direction is away from the suspension point. In other words he is arguing that the pendulum was just inverted, etc.

This is incorrect reasoning—while it is quite true that going from the lower ball to the top ball or clock, you cross the suspension point as he pointed out, you have NOT reversed gravity—up is still up. Such will lead us into a semantic field, i.e. that very thin line dividing mechanical laws from natural physical laws. So long as you have a pendulum, be it compound or simple, that pendulum remains governed by the natural laws of gravity. When elevating the weight, either below the suspension point or above it, you are elevating the center of gravity and as has already been stated, raising the center of gravity on a 'compound' pendulum makes it beat SLOWER.

When and if the center of gravity may be raised to coincide with the point of suspension your compound pendulum ceases to be a pendulum and becomes a balance wheel—no longer controlled by gravity, but is then governed by the mechanical laws and requires a hair-spring to bring it back, etc.

The exact origin a hair-spring clock is a bit beclouded in history; most likely in France. They were quite popular around the turn of this century—the French made many; apparently only Ansonia made them—Fig. 1. —their 1904 catalogue listed some six models all from 25 to 30 inches in height, priced from $32.00 to $43.00 each. Their style names were derived from the statue supporting them such as "Diana," "Juno," etc.

The first model—only a few made—the top or clock portion was drum shaped like an alarm clock; in later models it was a spherical shape and called "Ball Swing." This sphere was some 4½ inches in diameter. All were suspended via a very unusual crisscross spring arrangement which we shall comment upon at a later date.

Those produced by Junghans were a bit smaller, perhaps ten inches or a foot in height. Some were supported by little statues of ladies and some were held aloft by an elephant with extended trunk. This particular type of clock was not the most satisfactory timepiece since it had to be stopped to wind it, and, if placed where wind current struck it, could be stopped. Since World War II, Shatz brought out a wall model—see A. H. & J. Nov. 1963—called the Queen Anne; it was battery powered thus avoiding the stop to wind problem, and though a consistant runner it is not a precision timepiece.

From our correspondence we are forced to the conclusion that these swing models are giving the tender of the "144" considerable problems. The many letters pointing out that the "S" & "F" markings are incorrect clearly indicates that those principles governing this compound pendulum are not understood—that he is not aware that these pendulums regulate UPWARD to go slower. Oft-times these swingers come to your bench after some clockmaker or tinkerer, who did not understand them, had completely upset the original balance by altering that weight within the lower ball. We encountered one job out of balance because the little "bow-knot" decoration upon the top was missing, something the previous repairman did not know or take into account.

Once you have the clock in order—cleaned, bushed, correctly lubricated and in-beat; set the reg. nut at the center of its travel and time it out. If the error proves to be beyond the scope of the reg. nut then look for weight alterations. First in the top ball; if weight has been added here, remove it—we've seen gobs of soft solder used inside the ball. Then if it will not regulate, look to the lower ball; should the timing show a 'gain' rate you will wish to raise the center of gravity to make it run slower—decreasing the weight in the lower ball does the trick.

Not all cases of Ansonia Swing Clocks coming to the repair bench with their original balance disrupted are occasioned by tinkering with that weight contained in the lower ball. There is atop the big ball a little decorative sort of head-board in the form of a bow knot with flowing ends; these can be broken and lost and neither the new owner nor his repairer knows that it should be there. This bit constitutes considerable weight and must be replaced—either by a similar decoration, most desirable in restoration, or by including an equal amount of weight inside the top ball, at the very top.

Once you have adjusted that weight in the lower ball (or top) till the movement times out within the travel of the reg. nut, you have restored the original balance. Some workmen try to alter the run rate via the suspension springs; this method is incorrect—you just might note some slight change in rate, but same will be because you have altered the bend point thus raising or lowering the point of the center of gravity and it will NOT be enough. That problem is not encountered upon the Junghans or the Schatz as both are pivoted upon points and have no suspension spring.

Upon the Ansonia the suspension spring device is a bit stronger than one might find upon a simple pendulum because it swings against the whole wieght of the clock, etc.; you should lean to the weaker side, remembering that the pivoted type has no spring at all.

How to Correct
Pendulum Suspension

I have enjoyed restoring old clocks for some years now with some success, as a hobby.

A few years ago I cleaned and refinished a weight operated clock made by Waterbury Clock Company, which besides the name stamped on the movement is marked 13 in. and the patent date Sept. 22, 1874. Perhaps you can get an idea of the type of movement. The pendulum suspension is the type that is rolled down a thin section so it is one piece.

My problem is what type of pendulum bob was used, since the one I substituted while the clock runs O.K. and keeps time, does not swing in a plane but wobbles somewhat as an arc.

From the above description is it possible for you to advise how to make the pendulum swing in straight motion in a plane.

A.

Within a reasonable scope, the actual weight of your pendulum ball is not critical. Since the ball you are now using shows that it would be satisfactory keep it.

The sole cause of waltz or wobble of your pendulum is: the suspension spring — not the ball. In some way this pendulum is unevenly suspended;

spring has been kinked? is it hung at an angle? Or, your spring may be thicker on one edge than the other — these rolled springs sometimes are.

First, I'd suggest a "new" suspension spring and wire — preferably the two-piece, where the spring portion is made from regular spring steel. Second, use a very weak spring, fact is, it can't be too weak — some of the best timekeepers in short pendulum clocks have utilized a silk thread. Third, make sure that the slit in the post holding the top of the spring is "square" i.e. at right angles to the swing of the pendulum.

The Conical Pendulum

There are four general types of pendulums: 1) the simple pendulum, acting in a vertical plane; 2) the compound pendulum — including the inverted compound as encountered in the Metronome — also acting in the vertical plane, 3) the tortion pendulum as in the 400-day clock; operating in the horizontal plane, and 4) the conical pendulum also operating in the horizontal plane. All four types are influenced by centrifugal force; however, types one and two move over such a short arc, this force is for all practical purposes quite negligible. Not so with numbers three and four operating in the horizontal — the 400-day revolves over an arc of some 360 to 450 degrees — one to one and a quarter turns — centrifugal force from those arcs is a great influence as evidenced by the movement of the weight outward from the center to make the clock run at a slower rate.

The conical pendulum can be said to operate through a 360 degree arc; add to this the fact that its swing is a continuous circle and it is easily seen that the centrifugal force is quite a factor.

Van Nostrand's "Scientific Encyclopedia" defines centrifugal force: "A manifestation of the inertia of a body moving in a curved path, the effect being that of a force directed radially toward the convex side of the curve." T. D. Wright, in "Technical Horology" defines the conical pendulum thus: "A conical pendulum usually consists of a straight rod with a spherical bob. The bob describes a circle in a horizontal plane. The rod during one revolution, traces out the surfaces of a cone, hence its name." Claudius Saunier, attributes the application of the conical pendulum to M. Wagner, saying: "The ingenious instrument of which the first specimen was exhibited by M. Wagner at Paris gives good results." That must be Jean Wagner, born 1800, died 1875, a maker of many improvements in turret clocks and various instruments. Its actual inventor as well as the date remains in some doubt; it may well have been Wagner? It appears that the French were the first to apply it to a clock. There are no indications that the English used it to any degree. U.S. clockmakers took it up about 1855 — in later years the Japanese manufactured a few; info here is hard to come by.

Patent No. 13,451 August 21, 1885 and No. 15,456 July 15, 1856 were issued to John C. Briggs, Concord — Merrimack County — New Hampshire.

The Briggs Rotary and/or conical was manufactured by the E. N. Welck Co., initial date uncertain. Welch was advertising it in the late 70's. The period of manufacture has been variously estimated at 20 to 25 years — it is definite this was the only mass production of this type. In the August, 1946 issue of this journal, we illustrated and described it. One other conical was U.S. produced for Florence Kroeber, under patent No. 205,037 issued to Gilbert H.

Figure 1

Blakesley, June 18, 1878 — thought by some to have been manufactured by Wm. L. Gilbert for Kroeber — there are precious few examples existent, leading to the thought that only a very

few were ever made. The Blakesley version employs a worm drive like the fan-fly in the music box to attain its high gearing. One model was housed under a glass bell jar, much as the Briggs, while another model closely followed the French pattern having a regular mantel clock with a statuette of a lady on top of it holding the pendulum, etc.

Fig. 1 shows a popular French model. Fig. 2 shows the movement to be made from ebauche as supplied the trade by Japy, Marti, et al by simply applying a contrate wheel to drive a pinion as in the platform escapement of the carriage clock. Most treatises seem to completely ignore the conical pendulum. T. D. Wright has a short paragraph; Saunier has only a brief paragraph; Dr. Rawlings, whose long suite was the pendulum, does not mention it. Moniet, in his "Traite d'Horlogrie" has a 'bit' upon it — his publication date is 1820. This date does not completely jibe with Saunier attributing the conical pendulum to Wagner of Paris, because in the year 1820, Wagner would have been

Figure 2

only twenty years old, and, it is a certainty that whatever Moniet has was based upon a few years before his publication date. Reid in his famous treatise, 1826, devotes much space to the pendulum without mention of the conical version.

The mathematical formula given for the simple pendulum, No. one, is: T equals Pi on to the square root of length over gravity — where T denotes time and G acceleration due to gravity. This gives the time of a single vibration, i.e. a complete swing in one direction;

clockmakers generally stick by this method because one swing represents one beat or tooth of the escape wheel. Physicists and engineers tend to utilize a complete swing and return of the pendulum; that is, from the high point upon the right over to the left and back to that high point which is often confusing to the clockmaker. Since the conical pendulum is continuously upon the move, its period and/or time must be calculated upon the complete 360 degree circle; this necessitates a slightly different formula which Wright gives as: T equals 2 Pi on to the square root of H over G. H represents the height of the cone the pendulum is describing at any instant; again G is gravity. From this we see that the time required for a conical pendulum to make one complete revolution is equal to the time of a double vibration, a swing in each direction, of the simple pendulum. From the earliest days of the foliot right down to the 1974 solid state quartz timepiece, accuracy has been attained via interruption, stop; perhaps the conical pendulum is the only timepiece with a continuous motion. Fig. 3 illustrates an original Briggs conical by Welch, by no manner or means an instrument of high precision, yet it provides an accuracy well within the definition of "household" timekeeping. Let's look at how this accuracy is attained from continuous motion; protruding from the ball is a pin which rides in a loop similar to the small end of the Gem paper clip thereby enabling the ball to swing outward as it is urged by

centrifugal force; this outward — upward — swing is opposed by the pull of gravity until the one force balances the other thereby holding the rotation to a remarkably steady rate. It is evident that should we apply more thrust to the ball, it would swing further out cutting a larger circle and require longer to make the circuit and register a slower time; Wright records this feature thus: "It [conical pendulum] is not such a good timekeeper as a vibrating pendulum controlled by an escapement, as any variation in the energy supplied to it will affect its rate."

Saunier completely overlooks any error from variations of the drive force and has this to say: "— but it is influenced by one source of error which we proceed to indicate. When a conical pendulum is employed, the differences are not more than fractions of seconds. These differences are due to the fact that it is almost impossible to ensure that the bob shall describe perfect circles. It can only describe ellipses that approximate very closely to circles."

In actual operation the problem of applying a constant drive force is not as great as it first appears to be; the gear ratio of this clock is the highest to be encountered in any eight-day timepiece — approximately 96,000 to one — designed as an eight-day piece its spring is of sufficient length to actually drive it approximately ten days; though called eight-day, the

Figure 3   Figure 4

intent is to wind it once per week; therefore, at the expiration of a seven-day run, the torque in the main-spring has not diminished greatly. If we designate the torque when fully wound as "X" and that at the end of the seventh day as "Y", then that difference in drive force is X minus Y — spread out over seven days and further reduced by the gear ratio it would appear that only one/ninety six thousandth of X minus Y is active at the point of application to the pendulum ball.

By sheer coincidence while we were in the midst of this bit of investigation, the postman handed in "facsimile reproduction" No. 3 of the Briggs Rotary, sent in by The Horolovar Co., Box 400-A, Bronxsville, N.Y. 10708. Back when Horolovar packaged their 400-day suspension springs in soda straws; we called it the neatest bit of package engineering we'd seen; now that bit will have to take second billing, because the packaging — styrofoam, I think — for shipping this clock is a bit of engineering to admire. Because of it, ours arrived

Figure 5

in excellent condition — see Fig. 4. To obtain the required high ratio this has to be an eight arbor train with the following count:

Main arbor,	40 teeth,	no pinion,
2nd.,	40	10 leaves,
3rd.,	64	12
4th.,	60	10
5th.,	60	10
6th.,	55	8
7th.,	60	11
8th.,	no wheel,	12

Fig. 5 illustrates a movement disassembled. It is said that beauty lies within the eye of the beholder — the popularity of the lowly 400-day clock is well established by the thousands that have been sold; by no stretch of

the imagination can they be called beautiful. Therefore their appeal has to lie because its pendulum operates in the horizontal. The little "Briggs Reproduction" also operates in the horizontal; it is truly a thing of beauty, and the little pendulum whirling makes it an "eye catcher" — the retail price: $150.00. In addition to the "400-Day Clock Repair Guide," Horolovar has reproduced the Flying Pendulum Clock, the Mouse Clock, the Plato clock, the Anno 1492 clock, and now the Briggs Rotary.

SYMPATHETIC VIBRATION

WHAT ABOUT SYMPATHETIC vibration? Toward the end of my apprenticeship I was afforded the high opportunity of visiting an observatory; one of the high spots was naturally the clock room, located in the basement below ground level — virtually a room within a room. The clock room and/or vault was a relatively small room in the center; perhaps twelve feet square; the door to which was located across one corner with a double glass for insulation purposes which afforded a view of the three clocks therein. One clock was located in the corner opposite this door directly facing the door; the clock in the corner to the left faced the center of the room while that in the right corner set at an odd angle but quite visible through the door. It was explained that each clock was anchored upon a steel reinforced concrete pillar which extended some twenty feet further into the earth; that there was a one inch space between the pillar and the floor to prevent any vibrations of the building being transmitted to the clock and that this inch space was caulked with felt again for insulation purposes. Our guide was the astronomer-in-charge. The odd angle of the right hand clock struck me as being a bit unusual simply because it did not face the center of the vault as did the other two clocks. I inquired as to the why and was told that they could not permit two pendulums to swing in the same plane. This answer did not mean very much to an eager lad desperately trying to grasp everything possible pertaining to our craft. So, one more question, why? That answer was simply 'sympathetic vibration.' This was well before the days of Dale Carnegie, but it was self-evident that our astronomer guide was not interested in making friends or meeting people; he droned on with his set lecture plainly resentful of any interruption by questions. We came away with a determined desire to investigate 'symphathetic vibration.'

A quick check into those authorities at hand, Grant Hood, Ward L. Goodrich and Charles Higganbotham afforded no help. All our friends of authority were definitely watch orientated and, hence, no help.

It has been mentioned here more than once that this 'furious forum' is largely orientated by those questions and letters we receive to the extent that it takes on the appearance of a poll — professional poll takers operate via predetermined questions, etc. It has been suggested that by so slanting the questions and applying certain 'yard-sticks' when evaluating them, the end result may be slanted. As we do not field questions, we can not operate in that manner, however, we do have the option of applying any type of 'yard stick' we may choose. That can be the number of replies received; the length of them or the enthusiasm indicated in their content — upon all three counts, that squib in the December clockwise delineating the Compound Pendulum scores above any column in the last couple of years — one tender of the "144" phoned from out of Kansas to say thanks as he was just about to turn back a swinger to the customer because every effort to bring it to time failed.

Casting about for the 'why' it was easy to come up with the fact that so very little is to be found in our literature upon the compound pendulum — if we utilize that thinking as our 'yard stick' then it would indicate that an "Otherwise" dealing with a subject that has received little or no coverage would be sure to 'ring-the-bell', and, that brings us to symphathetic vibration.

Search as we might, the complete answer to sympathetic vibration was elusive; even Claudius Saunier, who is supposed to have all the answers, did not have it. The fact is, we met the problem, head on, and did not recognize it. A grandfather clock persisted in stopping after about a 3½ day run for no apparent reason. Being reasonably sure that the movement was in good order, the first thing looked for was a crossed cable on the drum — nay, it was spooled perfectly. Determined to locate the trouble, the movement was pulled down twice and each time gone over very carefully, checking the depthing, looking for bent or worn teeth, etc. It ran well on the rack in the shop but when installed in the case in the home stopped after about three days. In desperation I sought the help of an old German

clockmaker, and explained the problem in detail. The first question he asked was: Does the case stand upon a heavy carpet? Answer, yes. "Does the clock set diagonal across the corner?" Answer, yes. He then told me that "your pendulum is 'wiggling' the case—this makes the weights swing and when they get down to the pendulum ball they bump it and that stops your clock. To correct this, you take a little board about an inch and a half wide by ½ inch thick, cut it the length to fit the back of the case and rest against each wall—screw it to the case and move the case back till about one-third of the pressure upon the back feet is supported by that board." These instructions were followed and the clock performed satisfactorily.

The word sympathy was not used and I did not make the connection until after I'd met the problem a couple of more times and secured a copy of Thomas Reid's treatise, "Clock and Watchmaking, Theoretical and Practical," Carey & Lea, Philadelphia, 1832; in it there was chapter XIX titled: "Sympathy or Mutual Action of the Pendulums of Clocks." As the Reid treatise has not been available for many years and there aren't many around, it may be well to quote verbatim a major portion of that chapter—quote:

"It is now nearly a century since it was known, nay, it is much longer, for this was known even to Huyghens, and has been observed by many since his time, that when two clocks are set a-going on the same shelf, they will disturb each other; — that the pendulum of one will stop that of the other; and that the pendulum which was stopped will, after a while, resume its vibrations, and in its turn stop that of the other clock, as was observed by the late Mr. John Ellicott — that would be John Ellicott, F.R.S. b. 1706 — d. 1772.

"When two clocks are placed near one another whose cases are very slightly fixed, or when they stand on the thin boards of a floor, it has been long known that they will affect a little the motions of each other's pendulum." Mr. Ellicott observed that two clocks resting against the same rail, which agree to a second for several days, varied 1'36" in 24 hours when separated. The slower having a longer pendulum, set the other in motion in 16⅓rd. minutes, and stopped itself in 36⅔rds. minutes. It never could have been supposed, however, that when very strong fixtures were made, it was possible for anything of this kind to take place. About ten years ago, in a room where astronomical clocks were placed under trial, two strong deal planks were firmly nailed to a tolerably stout birch wall or partition, the ends of the planks being jambed between the adjoining partitions. The planks were six feet long by six inches broad and 1⅝ths. inches thick. One of them was placed behind the suspension, and the other behind the balls of the pendulums. The pendulums were suspended on strong massive cocks, partly of brass and partly of iron, which, with the backs of the cases — one of which was very hard oak — firmly screwed to the upper plank, the middle of the cases to the lower one, the bottoms being free and independent of the floor. Two clocks, whose pendulums were nearly of equal length and weight, and whose suspensions were distant from each other about two feet, keep so unaccountably close together for the greater part of twelve months, as to become a matter of considerable surprise. When cold weather commenced in November, they made a small deviation from one another for a few days, and then resumed the same uniformity which they had before.

"An account of this was published in Mr. Tilloch's Philosophical Magazine, where the observations of M. de Luc — that would be J. A. de Luc, F.R.S. ca. ca. 1815 — which seem to have been a very near approach to the cause, were inserted by way of a reply. The pendulum which was in one of the clocks was a Ward's kind. On its being taken away, a gridiron was put in its place: but this which was longer than Wards, the clock could never be brought to time as before.

"Their arcs of vibration continually varied, and no satisfactory going could be obtained from them, although we were all aware that they were competent to have given a very different performance. The gridiron pendulum clock was one of the best possible in its execution, and had one of the best recoiling escapements we have ever seen or made. The clock was taken from its case, to have an escapement of a different kind put to it. In the meanwhile, the pendulum being left hanging in its place, was observed to be in motion, which was first imputed to some shaking of the house. On being stopped, it got again in motion, and upon observing it narrowly, it was found to be in such a direction as any shaking of the house could produce, swinging quite in time with the pendulum of the going clock, the two pendulums mutually receding and approaching each other. The cure was instantly obvious; and after the upper plank was sawed through between the two clocks, the pendulum became in a little while dead and still. The arc in which it vibrated was about twelve minutes of a degree on each side of the point of rest, which was nearly about the

greatest extent of vibration in the arch of the two pendulums. It would be impossible to make two clocks go closely together, in any other situation than the one that has been mentioned.

"After the plank was cut through, the going clock was observed to be losing nearly at the rate of a second and a half per day; and if the clock which kept so long in unison with it had been tried under the same circumstances, it is probable that the rate would have been found to be fast. The rate they had for a period of eight or nine months or more, when they went closely together, did not exceed two tenths of a second fast a-day, and this may have been a mean of the natural rate of each pendulum, if it may be so expressed; that is, suppose one clock was going slow 1.5 seconds per day, the other fast 1.7, there will be two tenths of a second left for the acceleration of both, which seems to be the only way of explaining this phenomenon." end quote.

This has been rather a long quote — in fact, virtually lifting out the major portion of that chapter XIX, since then I've met sympathetic vibration a number of times in floor clocks. With that thought in mind it was always easily corrected — when the weight (s) of a g-f clock decend to the point equal to the length of the pendulum they tend to vibrate in sympathy with the pendulum — they do NOT swing to the extent that the pendulum is bumped as my German friend suspected; but, energy impulsing the pendulum is absorbed and/or diverted to the weight thus robbing the pendulum of its full input and the clock actually stops for LACK of power.

Rarely ever is sympathetic vibration met with in a shelf clock — in all my experience have I met with it but twice; once on an eight-day, wood movement clock and once in an OG, brass, 30-hour movement. The same may be due to the short stroke of the pendulum; the light-weight weight of the ball in proportion to the movement mass, and/or the more rapid decent of the weight — that is yet to be determined.

It is, indeed, infurating to have a clock which you have carefully overhauled stop for a reason that is NOT immediately detectible. The problem of sympathetic vibration does not plague the watchmaker but that does not mean that it can not apply; I've seen 16-size pocket watches hung upon the regulating rack balanced so that the ticking of the balance vibrated the whole watch — the watch will register the most eratic rate, and, in some instances stop via having its power absorbed by that vibration or swing.

Another question we often get is for a method of calculating the weight for the pendulum ball. That is another of the incalculables — there is no way. A ball can be so light as to be unwieldy and thus deliver an erratic rate, or it can be so heavy the clock can't maintain it — anywhere in between is okay. This also can be easily proven by careful experimentation; the point is to keep and/or maintain the exact same length pendulum. As indicated above, we utilize the ''beat'' as our measurement of length — any time you can have two pendulums beating the same, they are of the SAME theoretical length. Again take a clock you know its rate, gain or loss, for 24 hours; carefully count and record the beat; take off the ball and substitute one weighing twice as much; count the beat, three times for accuracy; and adjust until you have the self-same beat. Now you have the same as the original length. Put the clock on a 24-hour test and you will come up with the SAME rate, thereby proving that doubling the weight of the ball does NOT alter the rate. These two experiments will prove to you in a way you won't soon forget: 1) that you can't make the suspension spring too weak; 2) that as long as you have a reliable continuity of run, the pendulum ball is NOT too heavy. Certainly neither item is super critical.

CLEANING

Can a spring-wound clock, not taken apart, be cleaned in soap and water and rinsed in clear water? Will a rinse then in high-test gasoline remove all the water and prevent rusting of springs and steel parts of the clock?

What are the largest round polishing broaches made and where can I buy them?

A.

Let's take the b r o a c h question first. Broaches, both cutting and round, are usually measured by Stubb's gauge, with the number indicating the largest portion of the broach.

No. 1 is the largest, being roughly 5½ mm. in diameter. Those larger than No. 1 are designated by letters and run up to F. Write any of the material houses advertising in *A. H. & J.* for a supply.

Under no condition would we tolerate cleaning clock movements without taking them down. Further, I wouldn't recommend cleaning the mainsprings after they have been removed by any method that included water.

I've heard of even boiling complete movements in various solutions, including soap and water, and am prepared to say from experience that such methods do not clean. To be sure, some part of dirt, grit and dried oil can be removed but far from all of it. That which remains retains some part of whatever chemical is used, plus some of the various rinses, all to be ground into the fresh oil applied at the first few revolutions of the pivots. The very fact that the workman does not disassemble the piece indicates that the movement gets nothing more than the dunking. It is rare indeed when we see a clock brought in for servicing that doesn't need something more than mere cleaning. In my book, the customer who gets back a clock whose movement has only been dunked and oiled, gets back a clock in much worse condition than when he first brought it in. One

can no more clean a clock without disassembling it than he can clean (bathe) his feet without first removing his shoes and stockings.

LACQUERED PLATES

Most of the finer clocks have a lacquer coating on the plates to keep them bright and shining. This is all well and good; I like the idea. The trouble comes in when I clean the clock. The clock comes out very clean, but the lacquer is now dull, and one clock peeled. I lay the blame on the cleaner and rinse. Therefore, this letter. What kind of cleaner and rinse should I use on these lacquered plates? Should the plates be brushed with the solutions? If so, what kind of brush?

My present method is to brush each part in L & R Extra Fine watch cleaner, then in a rinse of L & R No. 3 rinse, then in white gas for the final rinse. I dry the parts under a 200W spot light with a fan blowing air across the set-up. The method seems to be efficient except for the lacquer.

Your information will be greatly appreciated by me.

A.

About nine out of every ten lacquered plate jobs should have all lacquer completely removed, and then new lacquer applied after the plates have been cleaned— and I have my doubts about that tenth job. On rare occasions, one may get a clock very nearly new on which the lacquer is clear and perfect.

Once the clockmaker has decided to retain and preserve the original lacquer on the plate, he should not clean by any caustic method or rinse in alcohol. They can be immersed in *white* gasoline, brushed with a very soft brush, and wiped dry with a soft, clean cloth. Go extra heavy on the peg-wood.

We prefer to always remove all lacquer;

this does not present any additional problem if using the ammonia-acetone-oleic cleaning solution, hot. It strips the old lacquer nicely and leaves the plate bright. Plates are then first rinsed in warm water and later in alcohol, dried with a soft, clean cloth or a gentle blast of warmed air, or both. A thorough pegging is always in order.

For a long time, re-lacquering plates posed quite a problem for the repairman. Applying lacquer with a brush was always a laborious task, and the resulting job was never quite satisfactory. Dipping requires, and also wastes, lots of lacquer. Came the spray-gun, which does an excellent job, but it is expensive, takes up a lot of shop space, and kills lots of time cleaning the gun.

HIGH SPEED RUST

Since I often get several at once, is there anything in which a watch or clock could be immersed—until I can get at it—which will prevent the rapid rusting? I find that even when I have received a watch immediately after immersion, corrosion sets in before I can get it completely apart. In some cases I have apparently cleaned everything up in good order, only to have a come-back a few weeks later rusted beyond hope. Would immersion in fresh water to dissolve out the salt be of any use?

A.

Rust is quite a problem in any language, and since you stress the summer tourist trade, I feel you have watches in mind, rather than clocks.

Have you tried L & R rust remover? Many workmen use common kerosene with fair results; some employ a soft brass scratch brush following the kerosene soaking. However, such a brush does not remove rust pits if the work has reached that stage. Where pits have eaten into the steel, the metal will have to be turned or ground to a new surface—if originally polished, you will have to re-polish in the usual manner.

About ninety-seven out of one hundred hairsprings with rust should have new

hairsprings vibrated on; however, we have seen some cleaned and used with good results. One such method is by boiling in oil and then plunging in alcohol. Take any convenient container—a small tin material box will do—it can either be held with pliers, or you can twist a wire handle on it, put in a light oil such as Nye's Lathe Oil, at least ¼ inch deep; place the hairspring in it, observing the stud so that you can catch it quickly with tweezers. Hold over an alcohol lamp and boil for about 20 seconds; quickly plunge the spring into alcohol. The object for speed here is not to allow the spring to cool; you should hear a distinct "hiss" when the spring hits the alcohol—this is what knocks the rust loose. One may take the spring through this process two or three times. Carefully handled, it will not draw the temper. There is some probability that your oil may catch fire, and a small piece of flat tin should be provided near at hand; just set your cup down and place the tin flat on it to extinguish any blaze. If immediately put out, this will not damage the spring at all. We have seen this method worked many times, and have in mind right now a couple of railroad watches that had such rust removing treatment some five or six years back. They are still in service and showing good rate.

Flat steel parts, such as winding wheels, setting parts, etc., can be worked over on a fine oil stone and polished on a boxwood lap with diamantine or rouge and oil. Oil stone powder and oil used with the small dental brushes either in your lathe or a hand motor works quite well for the uneven surfaces.

REMOVE RUST

My difficulty is rust in every conceivable form—clockwork and watchwork. I need information on any formulas you may have to remove or prevent rust from tiny steel parts. I've used acids to remove rust, but it returns, and at times, more so.

I have some sodium cyanide here to mix, but am in doubt as to its use. Please send information regarding the use and mixing of this solution in jewelry cleaning. Mainly, I want a good rust remover and preventive in my workshop.

Cyanide is not a rust remover, only a de-oxidizer; for all practical purposes, sodium cyanide and potassium cyanide are about the same, except that the latter is much stronger. Most shops use jewelers' sodium cyanide which comes in one-pound tin cans—egg-shaped balls. For a good strong solution, one "egg" is dissolved in one quart of distilled (or boiled) water. Most of these cans have printed directions on their label.

If you are having trouble with rust on your tools, it may be from your hands.

Just a word of caution—it is noted that you mention "acid." A clockmaker should never use any type of acid on or near the workbench. Tools should even be kept out of reach of the fumes of acid, regardless of how slight they are. If some job involving the use of acid or caustics in any form has to be done in the back room, it is well to not wear the same apron to the workbench, and to always wash the hands thoroughly. Make every effort to prevent fumes or traces of acid being carried to the bench.

CLEANING MAINSPRINGS

When we clean a common 8-day clock with hour and half-hour strike, we proceed by putting a tension on the mainspring and inserting around it a ring similar in manner to the mainspring that comes to us from the manufacturer. We then release the mainspring into this ring. In most cases we also release the click spring. We then disassemble the clock, clean, and at the time, only partially clean the mainspring. Then we assemble the clock and create sufficient tension on the mainspring to remove this ring we first put on.

Next, with the aid of a second person, while one holds the movement carefully, the other one pulls out the mainspring and cleans it in the manner you described, except we finish up by using a soft, freshly oiled cloth with which to rub down the mainspring. Then we re-connect the click spring and wind up the clock. Our experience in this method has brought wonderful results.

We experienced great difficulty with clocks which have barrels, especially the ones with very small diameter barrels and very wide mainsprings. I would greatly appreciate more detail in removing and replacing cleaning and oiling of clock mainsprings of the barrel variety.

A.

Goodrich says, "Three quarters of the trouble with French clocks is in the spring box—mainsprings too weak, gummy or set, stop works not properly adjusted, or left off by some numbskull". This writer thinks the same applies to the common 8-day clock with free mainsprings, even though far more of them are without any stop works at all.

The principal difficulty that I see with your procedure is that you require a second man or helper. Certainly your shop must excell those who make no pretense of cleaning the spring at all.

With the type of clock you mention, we do not use the "clip" or restraining ring until after the spring has been cleaned. With an Olsen let-down key (a key with a large, round wooden hand-hold) placed over the arbor we release the click and let the spring down; the clock is taken apart and the spring removed while cleaning the plates and train. On a metal pin placed in a bracket fast to the wall for this purpose, we place the loop end of the spring, then stretch it out its full length, save for the last two coils. Into the edge of a table some four feet long and placed about seven feet from the wall bracket there has been drilled a series of holes about 4 inches apart, thus when the spring is stretched out in line along its edge, you can locate a hole very near the two coils you leave, and secure it with a wooden dowel pin. Clean and polish the spring from end to end with fine steel wool, finally finishing off by wiping with a rag saturated in benzine or gasoline. Dry by wiping with a fresh, clean, soft cloth. The last two uncoiled coils may be thoroughly wiped with the gasoline-soaked cloth and dried with the drying cloths by fishing them around with a piece of peg wood. Wind with the mainspring winder and place on a convenitnt size "clip". After the rest of the job is completed, replace the springs in the regular way and lubricate with Moebius spring lubricant.

You will find the mainspring and its treatment mentioned in most repair books, but we know of no work devoted entirely to this subject. Fifty cents to the Superintendent of Documents, U. S. Printing Office, Washington 25, D. C., will bring you a copy of the U.S.N. Chronometer Manual, No. 8SS-2270, which contains a couple of paragraphs, one on removing the spring from the barrel and the other on replacing it. Both are well illustrated.

Rancid oil or a poor lubricant is many times the cause of "come-backs". Clockmakers sometimes buy a large bottle of oil, then let it stand uncorked in bright sunlight or too near a heating unit in winter time. We were pleased to note that the navy and Hamilton recommend a glass hypo syringe for mainspring lubricating, because we've been using one for a dozen or fifteen years.

Your respect for mainsprings is well founded. I know just what you mean— this is being typed with one finger (usually two) because the strike spring of a 113 Seth Thomas chime clipped off about 50 per cent of the nail of the forefinger of the left hand two days ago. The mainspring is the powerhouse of the timepiece, and unless it functions properly the entire mechanism cannot.

BRASS POLISH

I operate a watch ana clock repair department and I am seeking a formula by which I can restore the original bright finish to the brass parts on clocks. By this, I mean the bezel of the clock and other exposed parts of the clock case. I realize this is a delicate job without damaging the clock dial. Is there not a paste that I can make myself, that you just spread on and when dry, wipe off, leaving the parts shining like new?

If you have a formula for polishing brass that I can use without damaging the clock dial, I will be grateful to you for the information.

Also, I would like to know the procedure of removing mercury from finger rings. Is it necessary to remove the stones from the ring and then reset them?

A.

We would not suggest making up a paste or brass polish because there are a number of such on the market already compounded. Dupont puts out a metal polish for chrome and brass which is a thin paste—it is an excellent brass cleaner.

It is noted that you mention bezels. Many of the modern bezels, especially some used by Seth Thomas and others, are not brass-finished. Rather, they are made of brass and the finish has been applied in a form of lacquer containing a gold coloring. Any effort to polish these results in removing the lacquer finish and exposing the brass base. In cases where this lacquer coloring has deteriorated by reason of age or efforts to polish, very often the bezel will look much better if it is entirely removed and the bezel brightpolished and then lacquered with a clear lacquer.

As an all-round brass c l e a n e r and brightener, you may make up a solution as follows: 1 ounce of oleic acid, 2 ounces of acetone, 4 ounces of strong ammonia, and 8 ounces of distilled or boiled water. Use reasonably hot in a non-metallic container, enamelled or pyrex. Of course, the desired quantity can be made by doubling or quadrupling the above measurements. Do not use household ammonia, and never permit your solution to reach the boiling point, because that would evaporate the ammonia and acetone, upsetting the proportions of the solution. After cleaning a bezel or other brass in this hot solution, rinse immediately, for if permitted to dry, the ammonia will oxidize the article.

As a rule, most clock dials (metal) are coated with a clear lacquer, making any effort to clean or polish a rather ticklish job. Many have the lettering p r i n t e d thereon, and removing the lacquer also removes the numerals. Drive the hinge pin out and handle the bezel separately from the dial. Where it is desired to clean and polish the reflector rim, first remove it from the dial.

In answer to your second question, mercury may be readily removed from gold by heating the gold to a trifle above 600 degrees F. The mercury will dissipate in vapor, as its boiling point is 675 degrees F. As to removing the stone, you will have to rely upon your judgment on that particular job. Where there is but a very little mercury only on the side opposite the stone, it (the stone) might be wrapped in wet tissue and held in tweezers while heat is applied to the mercury by needle-point flame. Where mercury is near the stone, or where there is the slightest doubt in your mind about the heat damaging the stone, it would be best to remove it.

'Cleaning' Term Can Deceive Customer as to Involvement

IT HAS LONG been our thinking that the bench horologist, when taking in work, should never stress the word 'cleaning'. In fact, he should use it just as little as possible for the very simple reason that it fails to convey to the customer either what is actually done or what is required in knowledge, skill and equipment to do it. At best, your customer relates it to 'laundry' or any other simple 'cleaning' operation and thus concludes it should be done quickly and at a small fee.

I've even seen watchmakers treat it in that light. They explain that the movement must be disassembled; pivots and jewels inspected, etc., and add: "While it's down, we'll clean it". Such terms as general overhaul or completely overhaul coupled with a brief description of the work it involves serves to steer away from the connotation that it is a quick and easy job. The coming of the cleaning machine did not help this situation—many horologists have their machine on or near the bench and freely discuss it's use. Again, to the average housewife, watch cleaning denotes no more than loading her automatic washer.

By the same token, the use of the term cleaning' and 'cleaning machine' within the trade in catalogues and by material houses is quite correct and proper. The practical bench horologist knows from ex-

perience exactly what it—cleaning—involves. Watch cleaning, as it is practiced today, has come a long, long way. Like a lot of other features common in today's watchmaking, such as friction jewels, self-winders and shock resistant jewels, the cleaning machine is not new. Like those features, it was just slow being adopted. This date in the electronic age it is difficult to locate a watchmaker that has even heard of the old chalk method.

My local jobber tells me that at least one manufacturer of watchmakers' benches still builds them with the chalk box. In my apprenticeship days there were no cleaning solutions—every watchmaker made his own —generally by his own "secret" formula— the common ingredient in most of them was tincture of green soap. Grain alcohol was used for a rinse (the Volstead Act knocked that out) and they were dried in warm box-wood saw dust.

Ninety-five years is as far back as we've been able to trace the watch cleaning machine. A Mr. W. W. Thompson, of Smithville, Georgia (Georgia readers take note) is mentioned in The American Horological Journal for April 1872, in a column titled "New Inventions". The paragraph is very short and leaves much to be desired. Quote: "Cleaning watches and clocks: This is accomplished by immersing them in pure naptha or other volatile liquid of similar nature, and twirling them about so that all parts may be exposed to it's action; then dried in air a little heated".

Repeated efforts failed to bring anything upon Mr. Thompson, and a search of patent records did not show where he applied for a patent on his 'invention'.

Next, we found that a Du Quoin, Ill. watchmakers, Mr. J. J. Higgins, patented a watch cleaning machine February 4, 1903, and advertised it in the trade journals of that year (see Fig. 1.). Mr. Higgins launched into the manufacturing of his new machine and endeavored to market it. The trade refused to accept it and he gave up after a couple of years. He died in 1914. When we were first researching it back in 1952, the Higgins Jewelry store was still active in Du Quoin. They had very little info., no machine and could not determine the retail price of it.

The Higgins Watch=Cleaning Machine.

Pat'd Feb. 4, 1903.

Saves watches, saves time,
Makes money, makes reputation.

J. J. HIGGINS,
Du Quoin, Ill.

FIG. I.

The third step in cleaning machine history is short in both years and miles—over to Mr. Elmer F. Knowles, Battle Creek, Mich. He invented and filed for a patent on a watch cleaning machine in January of 1906. Patent No.861.990 was granted

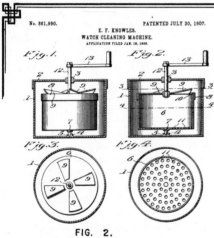

No. 861,990.   PATENTED JULY 30, 1907.

E. F. KNOWLES.
WATCH CLEANING MACHINE.
APPLICATION FILED JAN. 16, 1906.

FIG. 2.

July 30, 1907. We had some correspondence with Mr. Knowles in the summer of 1954—a quote: "The writer the inventor of the above has made several improvements since I obtained the patent. It works fine and does a much better job than the hand method of the time. It requires very little skill. Did not manufacture same on a commercial basis as I had other business that required my time. Owing to it being so simple it could be made at small expense. (s) Elmer F. Knowles, Inventor."

Figure 2 shows the patent drawing—very interesting since the Knowles basket so closely resembles those in use today.

For approximately a quarter century after Mr. Higgins ceased making his machine the watch cleaning machine lay dormant, I think, largely because the trade was not ready to accept it. In the very late 1920's there were two machines on the market in very limited quantities. One was hand operated. In March of 1930 L. & R. Manufacturing Co. sold their first cleaning machine; Zenith Mfg. & Chemical Co. followed with their first cleaning machine in 1942. L. & R.'s first completely automatic hit the market in 1950. Zenith offered their first ultrasonic in 1954 (they still do not manufacture an automatic). By 1956, L. & R. had developed both their completely self-contained ultrasonic cleaning systems and the L. & R. 204 ultrasonic unit which became a part of their "Vari-Matic ultrasonic system. This is the one with top-mounted transducer and the independent cycle control.

With the adoption of the 'machine' methods came many improvements in chemicals. Today's watchmaker has a wide choice of ready-made cleaning solutions and rinses. Just a few months back, L. & R. announced a new clock cleaning concentrate. Latest in the chemical line comes from Mr. B. G. Couch, Groves, Texas 77619—"Elma-Tulon-Automatic", a combination of a rinse—Tulon—and a filter tank. As reported last column, he sent a sample outfit. We've observed it's operation for some 40 days. Apparently, it will be quite satisfactory.

He tells us that Tulon was introduced six years ago and that with the filter-tank a watchmaker ought to cut his rinse expenditure by 50%, have no danger of fire, no oil troubles and no spots on plates. Figure 3 shows the "Tulon-Autmatic" and Fig. 4 is a schematic of its assembly. The complete Tulon-Automatic sells for $25; comprises the tank, one filter cartridge, a one-litre can of Tulon rinse for priming the filter and a 2½ litre can for supply.

The plan is: you set the tank up, insert the filter and pour in the one litre can. Fill your last rinse jar from the supply can, then first thing each morning when you open shop, pour the rinse you used the day before into the tank and draw out a new filtered supply from the tap thus starting every day with a fresh, purified rinsing solution. He tells us that a filter is good for

The Elma Tulon-Automatic

FIG. 3.

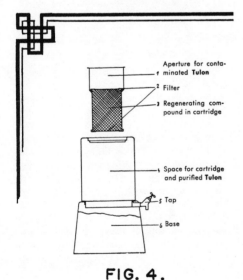

- 1 Aperture for contaminated **Tulon**
- 2 Filter
- 3 Regenerating compound in cartridge
- 4 Space for cartridge and purified **Tulon**
- 5 Tap
- 6 Base

FIG. 4.

about 500 filterings; i.e. 500 working days. A new filter costs $5 and Tulon rinse is $2.50 per litre.

The time under observation has been rather short for a 'test' of this type; one would like to see how well the oil stands up after 6, 12 or 15 months. One significant thing was observed—not a single hairspring came from the dryer with coils 'stuck' together, whereas under the old system, one would occasionally see that.

Besides the "Tulon" rinse and the tank, there is included a little glass vial or tube with simple instructions for a practical test of the purity of the rinse being used. Their lab reports that "Tulon", after being filtered, contains less than six milligrams of impurities per 100-cc as against the purest benzine obtainable on the market having 5-10 times that amount of impurity.

Cleaning Clocks

L ET'S TALK CLOCK CLEANING. My better judgment—and that is: a 50/50 blend of my woman's intuition and my sixth sense—tells me this Otherwise should be initiated with a disclaimer, so here it is: The opinions and statements set forth herein are solely those of the writer; they were not concurred in by any member of our staff and do not necessarily reflect the thinking of the managing editor or the publisher of this journal.

Any discussion of this subject—Cleaning Clocks—in depth necessarily takes me way out upon a limb, so if some of our readers come along and saw it off, I fully expect to go down alone.

In all likelihood "cleaning" is perhaps the oldest subject within our craft. One would think that it has been adequately covered time and time again in the past and thus ask why bring it up now?

Our answer is a valid one; our craft is constantly changing; new methods, new chemicals, and new procedures are being advanced year by year. A second reason, correspondence indicates that there is considerable confusion within the craft upon this very old point; therefore a fresh look at it as of September 1972 is very much in order.

To begin, I am and have always been bitterly opposed to the use of that term "cleaning." One, the term is indefinite; it can and does cover everything from the "Pawn Shop Swing" to a thorough overhaul job. Two, to say "clean" immediately reflects in the thinking of your customer along the line of leaving a suit at the dry cleaners, automatically generating a thought upon the order of $1.50 and thus, when you say to a customer: "Your clock needs cleaning," you have not told him anything "specific" and at the very same time lowrated your service fee in his thoughts.

The term "cleaning" is too well grounded in our craft to be knocked out with one fell stroke; that fact need not deter us from backing off and taking a good long, hard look at its use as well as the results of that use. Every clockmaker knows that a good 99-44/100% of those clocks coming to his bench for service are brought because the clock fails to perform—in most cases stopped and that the movement reached that point long after it should have been cleaned. What seems to be needed is a valid definition for "cleaning." We have had numerous letters asking: "What is Clean?" And many others detailing the exact procedure followed; then asking whether or not that particular type or method was acceptable. These are questions that are difficult to answer with a simple yes or no.

The average dictionary will give you about twenty definitions for the word clean —perhaps the most applicable for our purpose is found along toward the last on the list. It says: "to perform or to undergo a process of cleaning."

Let's latch on to that one because whatever the clockmaker does with a clean job, he carries it through some sort of process. That process could run the whole gamut from merely dunking the movement in white gasoline—the pawn shop swing—to the old-time hand method of completely disassembling the movement; hand cleaning each and every part; thoroughly inspecting every bearing and pivot; carefully and correctly reassembling and properly oiling with a good clock oil.

It can NOT be said that there is anything wrong with the latter per se because it has been proven over many, many years. The ONLY objection that can be raised is that of time; it is certainly the slowest of all methods, meaning that the clockmaker who follows it turns out the fewest number of jobs per day. In other words, his dollar production for an eight hour day has to be the least. Assuming that he may be a relatively slow workman, then, for his eight hour day he may do one job in the a.m. and a second in the afternoon—two per day. If he should follow the dunk route, he may well perform it in an hour and thereby attain eight jobs in his day . . . thus making his dollar production four to one over the old timer, providing both have approximately the same price.

Chances are very good this will not hold true. The "swinger" will immediately see that he can clip the price by 50% and still beat the old timer out two to one— he will in turn lower his prices to attract more business and we are into a price war. This whole line of thinking as reasonable as it may be leads to a pretty nebulous state. If the old timer has arrived at his fee based upon a fair salary plus cost of doing business, taxes, etc., then the swinger using his figure is gypping his customers simply because a four times reasonable salary has to be a gyp figure. Any clockmaker worthy of his salt ought to know he can not build a solid business by any gyp method; be it a gyp in price or a gyp in services rendered.

This column has had many, many letters dealing with every phase of cleaning. Some outline their individual system and ask if it is acceptable; others boast of certain "short-cuts" and praise their success; still others plainly asked for a correct process. If there was one theme common to a large majority of the correspondence received over about a three-year period, it is definitely doubt and uncertainty. Even some men, praising their own process as highly successful, evidenced some doubt with it by asking if there is a better process. The nebulous nature before mentioned becomes more evident as we investigate various processes.

Before we can begin to evaluate any method we must have some sort of a "yard-stick" to use as a measure—as indicated by my disclaimer, the yard-stick I shall use has to be my concept of how a clock movement should be cleaned. For a starter, I do NOT hold with any process in which the movement is treated while fully assembled. Here it is emphasized that the same applies only to clocks—not watches. Many watchmakers are cleaning watches without complete disassembly, utilizing the ultrasonic tank and a rinse impregnated with a lubricant; how successful is still open to question. There are two marked differences between the processing of a clock movement and a watch movement while they are in the assembled state: 1) practically all watches have easily removed mainspring barrels; 2) the watch can be taken through the spin-dry process. That, the clockmaker cannot do with his clock movement, but even if he did have some mechanical facility whereby the movement could be given a high speed spin, I do not believe it would work.

My process calls for completely disassembly of the clock; string each train upon a brass wire loop thence to a good cleaning solution and the hand-brush method, or to the ultrasonic tank. There is no question about it, cavitation by the ultrasonic method is the best scrubber to date. After the scrubbing portion, trains and plates are carried to running hot water for a rinse, next to alcohol to drive the water off and into warm boxwood sawdust to dry.

Remove each spring from its barrel with a good mainspring winder; stretch out the spring and wipe it clean with a soft cloth. If the spring is extra gummy the cloth may be saturated with white gasoline or benzine; any rust spots or rough places should be whetted smooth with fine steel wool; the spring should be carefully inspected for any cracks or signs of breakage before replacing it into the barrel again with the winder; lubricate with a good mainspring grease before replacing the barrel cap.

From a long experience I know this process is completely satisfactory.

Some clockmakers are adverse to stretching the spring out, they feel that to do this is conducive to breakage. One old timer insisted upon that point and we conducted an experiment over a two-year period; we were each doing about a thousand clocks per year and thus that test easily covered some four thousand movements or better. At the end of that test I had one less broken spring come-backs than he did. I am convinced that the stretching out of a spring—not the two last inner coils—is NOT conducive to breakage and equally as convinced that it is the only method whereby you can pass a clock back to the customer as near like it left the factory as it is possible for a mechanic to make it.

Once in awhile you will discover a spring cracked a fourth or a half through; this definitely calls for a new spring. It may be the reason I had less breakage come-backs in the above test—every time you prevent a come-back it is money in your till.

Never, I repeat never, place a mainspring in a cyanide solution or a cleaning solution that has any cyanide content. It has been very definitely proved that cyanide causes crystalization and breakage.

Each plate should have its bearing holes thoroughly pegged out; each should be checked for wear. If slight, it may be closed with a French closing hole punch; if the wear is excessive, the hole should be bushed. Every pivot ought to be inspected for wear and roughness; if any is detected, polish it and burnish while it is yet in the lathe. When correctly assembled and adjusted you can be assured that the clock is in good order and will not be back in your shop before your guarantee period expires.

Question: is anything short of that a real cleaning? In this vast correspondence several wild schemes were suggested; ranging all the way from soaking the complete movement—assembled—in some detergent over-night, to the use of the ultrasonic tank again completely assembled and using the lube impregnated rinse. Several report "grand success" with the latter process. This brings us right back to the nebulous side of this discussion; if we take this man's statement at face value, we must have his definition of what is "grand success." Upon what does he base it?

The sole fact that he was able to turn out the job in about one-eighth the usual time is NOT enough—what will these movements so treated look like two or five years hence? Will they perform satisfactorily and thereby build you a good solid clock repair business? I seriously doubt it. You can never convince me that a mainspring has been cleaned and lubricated while it remains in the barrel with the cap on—it just does not make sense.

One writer relates that he gets a number of German movements where the barrels are removable via extracting the wind arbor; thus he can place the movement into the ultrasonic tank etc., that he hand cleans the spring out of the barrel and lubricates it before placing on the cap. That, is one step nearer our process in that it correctly takes care of the spring portion of a clean job but not the drying feature. He tells that he sets the assembled movement upon a wire mesh screen and blows it dry with a hair drier. It is difficult to say positively that such method is completely satisfactory for the item of lubrication is still to be dealt with. If the lube impregnated rinse was proportioned as used for watches with the spin dry method whereby much of the rinse is slung off, will it not leave too much lube upon the clock movement with the drip dry? Of those relying upon the "dunk" method—completely assembled barrel and all—none have been following it more than a year or so, and about 50% of them say they have not noted come-backs upon their repair record. Here is a feature that needs to be stressed; every clockmaker should keep a "complete" record. Every job ought to be recorded in enough detail to tell him exactly what was done and how. Every time a clock comes back, whether or not its return is within the guarantee period, it should be closely examined and noted upon the record. How better can a clockmaker learn how his work holds up than from his record? No ifs & ands about it, any process deemed completely satisfactory just has to be one that stands the test of time. One can LEARN from his repair record and don't forget that what you learn there is 100% applicable to your very own work.

Surely the first step in determining a process and/or procedure, would be to determine in your own thinking exactly what you sell your customer in a "cleaning" job; i.e. set for yourself a definition for "clean." Walk into a super market; pick up a package and it will be plainly marked as to content and net weight. Your problem when setting up your process is by far not as simple as that, yet it must be comparable because you must have determined what you propose to deliver in your package. That is the corner post from which you survey the lot; from there forward you can begin to definitely work out a process that will deliver to your customer that service which meets your "standard"—next and by no means the least, you begin to seek ways, means, and methods whereby you can attain your standard in the shortest possible time without lowering the quality of your work.

As a trained clockmaker you are selling your skill, augmented by your equipment and experience—the label on your package is "time" not "net contents x ounces." When you come to the "144" in the morning, you have just eight hours to sell. Make no mistake about it, it is up to you to make every one of those hours count in the cash-register for all you can with an honest job at an honest price.

Ultrasonic Machines Clean

A couple of years ago you had an article about ultrasonic clock cleaning machines, that you took a clock to someone to have cleaned, and that it was the cleanest clock you ever saw cleaned.

Are you using ultrasonic machines to clean clocks? And if so, what make and also would like some idea of cost of the same.

We use an L&R tank which connects to our ultrasonic watch cleaning machine, but we do not think this has enough power for cleaning clocks.

We like the Horologist & Jeweler and think it is the best publication out. Self-addressed and stamped envelope is enclosed for your reply.

A.

You are correct that the very small ultrasonic machines simply can't agitate the quantity of liquid required for clock work, and I still say that it really cleans, clean.

Now, cleaning is somewhat like the great Edward Howard said of his watches; someone might make one as good, but it would not keep any better time.

You can clean a clock by hand and get it clean — it was being done long before ultrasonic agitation was discovered. But, you will consume a lot of time doing it; brushing, pegging out the bearings and re-pegging, etc. This brings us to the main virtue of the ultrasonic; you can do a top-notch job so much quicker. The time you save is money to the shop because you can do an additional job.

Rather than trying to go into pinpoint details about "makes," "sizes," etc., I'm going to suggest that you contact your regular material house. Just tell him that you are ready to buy an ultrasonic cleaner for clocks. He in all likelihood has been serving you for years and certainly hopes to continue to enjoy your business. Go over your individual needs with him and let him make suggestions, give you literature upon various outfits, select what you and he think will serve your purpose.

Chances are, he will let you test-try it for a week or 10 days. It's a cinch he wants you satisfied and I don't know a better way to do it. In that length of time, you will know from experience whether or not it answers, or that you want larger and heavier equipment. In the end, you will know just exactly what you are getting and what it will do; he will know that the equipment he is selling you is going to be satisfactory.

ULTRASONICS
An outstanding aid to clock cleaning

NEVER HAVE I APPROACHED a subject, so new, so large, and so confusing, with so little—90 days' actual experience, plus a concentrated effort covering about four years to amass some facts and data upon it.

The experience comes from daily use of a "Sonogen" generator, model AP-10-B coupled to a T-24 tank, cleaning the general run of clocks just as they come in over the counter.

This equipment is manufactured by the Branson Ultrasonic Corporation, at 37 Brown House Road, Stamford, Conn., and retails for $475 (fob). The generator (right) weighs in at 21 pounds, stands 12 inches high by 8 x 10 inches, and is housed in an aluminum case with grey finish and a recessed front panel for switches, control knob and meter. It operates from the regular wall outlet, 115 volts, 60 cycles; delivers a high frequency output of an average 50 watts; peak on pulses of 200 watts and is tunable from about 36 to 40 Kc/secs. The T-24 tank with transducer attached at its base, is 4¼ x 7 x 8 inches; has a capacity of one-half gallon of cleaning fluid.

It was selected because a half gallon is a maximum for the AB-10-B generator and we felt that a rectangular tank is better suited to clock cleaning than a cylindrical tank. It is made of stainless steel—welded — with the barium-titanate type transducer hermetically sealed into the base in such a manner as to efficiently transmit vibrations into the cleaning fluid.

Two tanks may be driven alternately, or, two or more driven simultaneously, provided the effective cleaning area in use at any one time does not exceed 24 square inches. If larger tanks and more area are required a larger generator would have to be used. Branson manufactures generators from the AP-10-B size (24 square inches) up to ones that can handle five square feet of transducer area, the next in size being the AP-25-B (with T-52 tank, $740, f.o.b.) designed to power a two-gallon tank.

Fig. 2, shows the complete strike and time trains from an average eight-day, mantel, striking clock strung upon one

Fig. 2

Fig. 3

wire loop being held above the tank. Fig. 3, is a similar photo showing the two p l a t e s strung.

The T-24 tank is amply large for most clock cleaning as can be seen, thus it is not necessary to buy larger and m o r e expensive units for the general run of clock cleaning.

We have encountered a tremendous interest in ultrasonic c l e a n i n g; l o n g distance phone c a l l s, telegrams and many letters attest this interest throughout the entire trade—here we hope to cover a few basic points, but especially d e s i r e to be accurate, factual and practical about it; that is one reason for the choosing of the title "Ultrasonics—An Aid," for that is just what it is, an aid. Further it must be pointed out that the prime application under discussion is to clocks—not watches, and, when the word "clean" is used, it means just that—clean—and has no referance to, or includes, that "factory shine" the horologist so often includes in his conception of cleanliness.

In all likelihood the "factory shine" conception· originated many, many years ago when the watchmaker stood practically at the top of the precision ladder— no small factor in the formation of that conception was the fact he (the watchmaker) had plenty of time to waste upon the "shine." Today, we have other industries and manufacturers producing small mechanisms and precision machines of an order equivalent to fine clocks, yes, even railroad watches in accuracy, which do not require that ultra-shine of new production to say nothing of repaired pieces.

Depending upon the brightening agent in your solution; its age, etc., you will take from the ultrasonic tank a clock with slight traces of tarnish left, but with the clock clean—cleaner than it has ever been,

and that slight amount of tarnish here and there will not affect either its timekeeping ability or the time it will remain in service before the next cleaning is required.

It is high time the horologist slightly revised his conception of "clean"—the customer isn't going to look inside to judge the shine; he did not even do that when he bought the piece (watch or clock) new. Several of the leaders of our industry share this view despite a reluctance to be directly quoted upon it.

One of the first questions asked by horologists upon seeing ultrasonic cleaning demonstrated, is: "Why no whirling basket?" This is: 1, because the conventional cleaning machine has established the whirling basket idea; 2, a lack of understanding ultrasonic action.

Note the sketch. You take electric current direct from your wall plug at 60 cycles per second, feed it into the generator which converts it to a frequency much higher (the Sonogen alternates at about 40,000 cycles), this high frequency energy is then fed into the transducer which converts it into mechanical energy at the same cycle rate— with the T-24 tank the transduced is made of barium titanate—a ceramic material with the property of changing its shape synchronously when an alternate current is applied to it, thus it converts the electrical energy to mechanical energy, vibrating the cleaning solution 40,000 times per second.

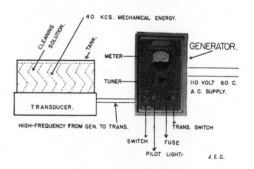

Such rapid agitation of the cleaning liquid sets up a condition called "cavitation," the rapid formation and collapse of millions of tiny bubbles within the fluid and especially at fluid/metal inner surfaces, exerting a gentle yet thorough scrubbing action that literally blasts loose the soil and dirt. This action is sometimes called cold boiling. It occurs upon all surfaces in contact with solution, even deep in blind holes when penetrated by the cleaning fluid. It can readily be seen that a whirling basket would be of no advantage whatsoever.

The second question — invariably — is that of "disassembly." Very early in the game we were told that a perfect job (cleaning that is) could be had with the piece completely assembled. Well, this is only partly correct and that "partly" will stand for a lot of "explaining."

Figs. 5 and 6 show eight movements that have been cleaned with the aid of ultrasonics with only a partial disassembly and I'm prepared to state (and prove if I could show you) that they are just as clean as anyone ever cleaned such a clock, regardless of the method used or the time spent upon doing it. Each was immersed in cleaning solution ultrasonically agitated for from 60 to 90 seconds.

On Fig. 5 top row, left, is a Gale

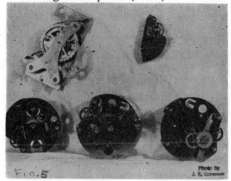

Fig. 5

calendar mechanism; these are supposed to work dry but you scarcely ever get one that some bright chap hasn't liberally anointed it with oil—the plate is pinned on and they are pesky little things to take down for cleaning—it is a distinct advantage to be able to get a good job without that trouble. Next is the time-train from one of the popular Seth Thomas little eight-day desk clocks. On the bottom row, left, is a "Travalarm," then two "Baby Bens." Fig. 6 shows three "Big Ben" movements.

Fig. 6

Note: that all of these have their mainspring barrels removed—you CANNOT clean a mainspring in its barrel by any method, I don't care what anyone says. Neither can you clean those mainsprings which work free (no barrel). First, it will bunch up to one side and you don't clean between the coils where pressed together; furthermore you can't rinse and dry it either.

The "Westclox" type movements in these photos all have the conventional lantern pinions; especially that used in the S. T. is a very small type—ultrasonics gets in there and does a good job, they come out free from foreign matter and clean.

These, and similar little clocks (many little imported desk models with removable barrels) can be cleaned without taking them down. Making this direct statement, we are influenced by two factors: 1, they are not timepieces of the higher order; 2, the remuneration from such jobs does not warrant Patek-Philippe style treatment.

It is a further observation that with the little imported, jeweled clocks, their cap-jewels should be removed before cleaning. Some were tried with the caps on . . . in less than 50 percent of them was the cleaning passable . . . many still retained traces of moisture. Considering that speed was the second object in these tests (cleanliness was first) one had best remove the caps before cleaning.

About the next question would be "cleaning solution." No doubt, a great deal depends upon this — many factors enter, depending upon the equipment being used, i.e. Kc/sec. rate; size of container and type of work to be cleaned, etc. We'd rather not get too far into these details right at this point. A number of solutions were tried out including two sent down by Mr. Hightower with the equipment, prephlorethylene and the old Daniel's solution (1 ounce oleic acid, 2 ounces acetone, 4 ounces stronger ammonia and 8 ounces distilled water). The latter was found quite satisfactory and I'm reasonably sure that it will continue to be used. At the beginning there was the question of whether or not cavitation would dissipate the ammonia content at too rapid a rate—a rough test was devised via the use of Nessler's reagent and it was soon learned that the Daniel's solution stands up almost as long when cleaning with the aid of ultrasonic vibrations as it does with the old hand method. We are still of the opinion that it (Daniel's) is a very good, efficient and economical clock cleaning solution.

The one movement that the clockmaker might desire to clean without disassembly above most others would be the No. 124 Seth Thomas, Westminster Chime. It meets the requirement of "removable mainspring barrels" and with the chime drum removed from the back, easily goes into the T-24 tank. Several were tried and not one came out which we were willing to "let by"—they present a tremendous drying problem; I still prefer to dismantle; string upon wire loops; rinse under hot water, then alcohol and dry in sawdust— since only 60 to 90 seconds in the ultrasonic agitated solution is all that is required one may still dismantle in the old manner and save a wee bit of time.

Beyond the questions of no whirling basket, disassembly, and type of solution, upon which we've merely touched, comes a myriad of others—price, rate of vibration, size, etc. As of today's market, one may purchase equipment from $270 to $1,200 and the equipment varies as much as do the prices. One manufacturer advocates 20 kc. while another says 1,000 kc. with all points in between. Writing upon metal cleaning with ultrasonics, Mr. T. J. Kearney, chief engineer for Detrex Chemical Industries, Inc., a large firm whose entire range of operation in the ultrasonic field is confined to cleaning, says: "Regardless of frequency, ultrasonic equipment must be operated at energy levels well above the threshold of cavitation; in fact, work that can be cleaned at the minimum level for maintaining cavitation usually can be cleaned by other, more simple cleaning methods."

This points up power—your equipment must be powerful enough to do the job at hand—power is not directly related to rate of vibration; that is: a generator may be tuned to 40 Kc/secs. and deliver one or 400 watts of energy to the transducer. We feel that all manufacturers ought to state the watt-power output of their generators in no uncertain terms. Some give an "average" watt-output and add the strength of peak on pulses—again we meet the confusion. One authority writes: "The unit operating at 400 kc. would not be pulsed, in other words, it would be 500 watts continuous input. Our experience has shown that pulsing is of no value on cleaning."

So many variables enter into these statements, i.e., what is said of a generator operating on X-frequency at Y-watts, coupled to a certain transducer to pulsate a tank containing eight ounces of cleaning fluid might mean something entirely different as related to another generator operating on A-frequency at B-watts, pulling another type transducer pulsing a half gallon of cleaning solution of different density; that we shall have to rely upon trained electronic engineers for their detailed explanation and a break-down to easily applied comparisons.

When buying a car, one of your first questions is: "How many horses under that hood?"—we feel such is equally applicable when purchasing ultrasonic equipment. Some horologists who only wish to clean small watches may do so with a small or weak unit—other shops handling watches, clocks and jewelry may desire a unit large enough and strong enough to handle a larger tank for all three.

We've corresponded with practical benchmen over many months and believe our conclusions are supported by their actual experiences. Mr. Charles Fischer of Detroit, writes: "You are correct in that my particular unit is the Sonogen, AP-10-B. I have found this to be the more efficient of several I have conducted extensive tests with. We have employed the unit daily for one year now and thus far have had no breakdown whatsoever. I have working with me, my son, who does the regular run of repairs, and a girl. She handles the regular run of alarm clocks and travel clocks. The unit we use is therefore kept going through most of the day." This is just one example. Another said: "I have tried out about a dozen types, representing almost as many different manufacturers. The one you are now using, Branson's, is about as good a unit as you can get for clock work."

In conclusion, may I repeat, do not hesitate to request data and information from the manufacturer on any equipment you may be considering for purchase—even to asking specific questions about your own particular needs. Do not expect miracles of your new equipment on the first use; chances are it will do all the manufacturer claims it will, but, you will have to "learn" just as with your lathe or rate recorder. Don't be afraid of it, but, above all read closely the instructions furnished with it, then re-read them and make sure that you follow them to the letter.

A suggestion we've followed: mark your jobs in the usual way, then somewhere close to it place a small "u" to indicate that it was ultrasonically cleaned—you will want to have a close look when these come back, months or years later.

Today's economic conditions are such that we must equip ourselves to do better work and do it faster. Ultrasonics is an aid toward this end. I am certain that as you gain experience with this new aid and perfect a method and procedure of using it to its fullest, even though it may not remove every last trace of tarnish, every time, it will still produce better results than any previous method and produce them quicker.

Is Dismantling Necessary for Ultrasonic Cleaning?

Would like your expert opinion on two questions:
1. I've been dismantling clocks completely for ultrasonic cleaning. Some manufacturers claim this is unnecessary. Would sure save time in those cases where rebushing isn't needed. What do you think?
2. I've seen everything from graphite to mineral oil to vasoline dissolved in benzine recommended for lubing clock mainsprings. What do you recommend?

A. 1. Always disassemble a clock movement to clean it, whether ultrasonically or the old hand methods. I regret that some have advocated cleaning without disassembly — that old dog just won't hunt — it is strictly a gimic to sell the ultrasonic tank, etc.

The ultrasonic route is excellent; no doubt about that. But, it simply can NOT clean a spring while that spring is still coiled in the barrel. You can't inspect for scored pivots plus half dozen other things. Cleaner and rinse will seep into your barrel and is not dried out. Such procedure reminds me of trying to wash your feet with your sox still on.

2. The best mainspring lub is, Keystone's KV medium. Available from Emery Brittenham, 8737 Santa Fe Drive, Denver, CO 80221. Half-pint, plastic bottles cost $2.50 postpaid.

Test it between your thumb and fore-finger. Note how it strings out. This shows you how that it does not squeeze out when the spring is fully wound, the besseting trouble with a lighter lub — when wound it squeezes out leaving practically a dry spring and can not fully relieve friction.

LUBRICATION

WHICH GREASE TO USE

I would like to get some information about different types of oiling for electric and manual winding clocks. My problem seems to be in keeping the oil in the spinner type of clock such as the self-starting Sessions. After I clean the clock in naphtha and have it thoroughly dried, I apply regular clock oil to the spinner. I check the spinner after letting it run for 24 hours and find there is very little oil if any. I realize there may be some sort of "well" inside but after re-oiling the spinner and checking it again I find the spinner just about dry.

I have also tried to use a mixture of clock oil and vaseline or some other thicker lubricant but this doesn't work either.

I would also like to know if it is harmful or helpful to use a mixture of vaseline and clock oil on both the time mainspring and the strike mainspring of an eight-day clock?

A.

In reply to your electric clock lubricating question, I should like to quote from a letter recently received from the service manager of the Sessions Clock Company: "From a stand point of economy it would, in reality, be cheaper for the average repairman to purchase a new motor from either one of our authorized service stations or from the factory rather than attempt to repair the old motors."

Synchronous electric clocks are late comers to the repair bench and practically no data has been released by the manufacturers for the repairman. In fact, practically all of them advocate installing a new unit and frown upon any attempt at repairs whatsoever.

This writer cannot agree 100% with the manufacturers policy because I've seen a lot of electric clocks in which there must have been months and months of good operating service and needed only lubrication and simple adjustments. However, just as I feel that their attitude is due to the newness of the electric clock, I could be in error in my own view point for the same reason.

Now I have run into a problem on clock repairing, and that is that I cannot find a suitable grease for 8-day mainsprings. My material house recommended Electrolube, but it did not seem to be suitable for the job. I have used light engine oil, but find that also unsatisfactory. What do you recommend, and where can it be purchased? I will appreciate any assistance you can give me.

A.

To lubricate all your small clock mainsprings, plus French clocks and all small and medium-size springs in barrels, use Moebius mainspring grease, obtainable from your regular material house. For free (no barrel) springs in 8-day clocks, extra heavy springs in barrels, time recorders, etc., get K-V Medium grease. It comes in one-pound tins, put up by Keystone of Pittsburgs. Most machine supply companies stock it. While labeled "grease," it pours, and has been used successfully by repairmen for years.

LUBRICATING WOOD MOVEMENTS

I wonder if you could tell me the type of lubricant to use in wooden clock works? I have received a number of ideas, one of which is to dissolve beeswax and use it in liquid form. However, no one seems to be able to tell me what to use as a solvent. This problem has caused me a lot of trouble.

A.

It is my understanding that the "old timers" did NOT use a lubricant on the wood parts. They suggested, and used, a good clock oil on the metal parts. That is: the pallets since they are acted upon by the brass escape wheel and the crotch wire where it contacts the metal pendulum rod. Some of the later wood movements had brass bushings for the winding arbors. Since these arbors turn as the clock runs down and it is metal against metal I'd suggest good oil there. Where the movement is clean and in good order I believe you will find they run well without further lubrication. If you have some bad or worn teeth and pinions (wood working upon wood) and feel some aid is desirable, never use oil or wax. Try a little powdered (dry) graphite.

Proper Way to Oil Clocks

What is the proper way to oil clocks? Should the escape wheel be oiled? Recently I had an alarm clock which was running fine when it was delivered. In about two days it stopped. I then cleaned all the oil from the escapement and polished the impulse faces of the wheel. That seemed to correct the trouble, but again in about two days, it was back. This time I again oiled the escapement with bracelet watch oil and that set it to running fine again.

This clock is being used in a room where the temperature drops down below freezing frequently. I'm using a French clock oil guaranteed not to be affected by extreme heat or cold. Incidentally, I was suspecting the oil as being the cause of the trouble, and each time before letting the clock go, I put it in the freezing compartment of our refrigerator to test it, and I could not see any noticeable difference in the balance action.

A.

Your question, "Should the escape wheel be oiled?" we presume to mean,

"Does one oil the faces of the escape teeth?" The answer is yes. Most alarm clocks are overpowered to the extent we hardly think that either a heavy oil or an oil made thick by low temperature upon the escape wheel teeth would stop the clock. If the increased viscosity caused by low temperature stops your alarm clock, it would most likely be in the mainspring —or a combination of the mainspring and train bearings.

Now, since you are using a low temperature lubricant, I suspect the oil did not cause the stoppage at all. One of the chief points to watch closely when oiling any timepiece is not to over-oil; that is, do not use too much oil. As to oiling the impulse faces of escape wheel teeth, bracelet watch oil would be a little light for all except the very small jeweled Swiss alarms. Whether you use a dip or fountain oiler, just touch as lightly as possible about every fourth tooth impulse surface, as some of it will be retained by the pallet and then re-deposited upon the next dry impulse surface.

Many repairmen pay too little attention to the escapement of the common alarm clock, and put them up with excessive balance arbor end shake. I've never been able to figure out why, because the cone bearings are screwed in and this one feature is easy to adjust.

The common cone bearing alarm, properly cleaned and correctly lubricated, but with excessive balance and end shake, often ticks along two or three days before the balance slides all the way in on one bearing, allowing the other to flop about at each tick until the guard-pin (if it has one) will wedge against the table and stop it. And if there is no guard-pin, the dropping down of the balance allows the roller-pin to strike against the side of the fork with a similar jamming effect.

With any alarm giving trouble, every action of the escapement should be checked. Many have pin pallets which sometimes become loose in their setting. Particular attention should be given the balance pivots and their cone bearings. Where balance pivots are worn blunt and off-center, they should either be replaced or chucked in your lathe and new pivots ground and polished. Check the cone bearings. With clocks having long service, you often find worn "pockets" in the cone bearings. These call for new cones, or at least turning the worn pockets to the top side.

Oiling Clocks

Recently the question has arisen between another member and myself concerning oiling of clock movements, his argument being a clock should not be oiled anywhere since it causes dust and grit to collect on pivots and holes to wear much faster. Of course, I know there are certain places a clock should not be oiled, but everything I have read tells me to oil the pivots with just enough oil so as not to run out.

I would greatly value your opinion on this matter, as both of us consider your word as gospel.

A.

To have you gentlemen say you take our word as 'gospel' is flattering, to say the least. In answer to your question, "to oil, or not to oil," I can give you the words of a horologist whose words I myself consider 'gospel.'

The great Abraham Louis Breguet, 1747-1823, once told his Emperor Napoleon, "Give me the perfect oil and I'll give you a perfect watch."

Would it help you fellows any if we substituted the word 'lubricate' for oil? The prime purpose for lubricating is to reduce friction, and a lubricant is indicated anywhere you have friction, all other factors being equal.

Old Breguet would have himself a ball if he could come back and make use of some of our fine oils, silicones and special greases today. People are continually going off the deep end with funny theories about oiling. Watch your friend closely, I'll bet he allows the filling station operator sell him a quart of motor oil every time he pulls in for gas. Ask him why he doesn't run his car dry?

It is quite true that fine timepieces, watches, marine chronometers, etc., will show a better and more consistant rate when put up 'dry' — for a very short time. Pretty soon, bare metal sliding upon bare metal begins to cut and score, both the pivot and bearing; if run too long dry, a lot of damage is done. For the long and practical haul, oil as you say, just enough that it does not run out.

Several years ago when Admiral Byrd went to the South Pole, he reported his chronometers had a very, very close rate. Yet, it was so cold there his kerosene froze, etc. We wondered about what kind of oil was used, checked, and learned that they were put up dry. Since WW-2 we've had special silicone lubs that easily withstand extreme low temperatures. Lubrication engineers have made and are making great forward strides in this field. All say: 'other factors being equal,' oil it.

CLOCK BUILDING & REBUILDING

GRAVITY CLOCK

I would like some detailed information about a gravity clock mentioned in the AMERICAN HOROLOGIST & JEWELER, *February, 1948, in regard to construction of hands and number of movements required, also method of attaching same to glass dial.*

I would appreciate your suggestions as to how I can make such a clock.

A. first, there are two movements, one for each hand; second, the hands revolve freely on a pin firmly planted in the glass dial. One method is to drill the glass and fit to the hole a threaded brass stud. Fit to this stud a highly polished steel pin of sufficient length to accommodate the hour and minute hands with a small hole drilled in the free end to pin the hands on with. Place the threaded stud in the hole and screw on a hex-nut—two—on either side of the glass to hold it firmly. When the hands are placed on and pinned on, they must be free to revolve with gravity as the movement shifts the weight.

Gravity Clock. This is a large glass clock dial, with a stud fixed in the center on which revolve two hands, without any visible power to operate them. Hung in a jeweler's window so that it can be inspected from both sides without anyone discovering its source of power, it forms a great attraction to the curious and so becomes a durable and valuable advertisement. Take a plate of glass two feet square and lay out and guild a clock dial upon it, avoiding all ornament in order to give the observer as little to see and as much to guess as possible. Cement, drill or otherwise fasten a stud in the center of the dial, projecting from the rear so as to give facility for adjustment and certain exhibitions, which will be mentioned later. This stud must be perfectly hard and finely polished in order to reduce the friction which is

considerable. The hands should be made of cedar, perfectly dry pine, or some other extremely light wood, left about half an inch thick so that they can be nicely counterbalanced with lead and will appear to the observer to be merely wooden hands. The circular extremities at the inner end of the hands are hollowed out to receive two watch movements and the boxes are closed with a cover fitting closely enough so that it can not be perceived by ordinary inspection. Each side of the two hands is perfectly jeweled with large English fusee jewels, so as to revolve on the stud with as little friction as possible. The two watch movements must be regulated to run as closely together as possible and to keep exact time.

Two half circles of lead are attached to the movements in such a way that their rotation in the hollow ends of the hands will change the center of gravity of the hands, and so cause them to rotate on the stud of the dial.

The lead half-circle of the minute hand is attached to the minute arbor of its movement and that of the hour hand to the hour pipe on its movement. If the wooden hands are nicely gilded, it will add to the deception as the ends for the movements may then be made of tin and much smaller and more symmetrical.

When finished, the clock is hung in the window, suspended by chains from holes bored in the corners. We will suppose that you have the clock finished and running nicely, and that the time shown is 2:20; take hold of the hands, bring them together and send them twirling around the dial. When they stop they will show the correct time, say 2:21. Suppose the hands show 9:45 or 2:45—bring both hands to 12:00 or 6:00, when released they will immediately assume the correct position. Take off the minute hand and lay it on the bench for five or six minutes—put it on again and give it a twirl and it will stop at the correct time. Various other tricks will suggest themselves for the astonishment and mystification of the jeweler's patrons, and considerable benefit will come from the interest of an excited town.

Thus, Henry G. Abbott described this type of gravity clock back in '93. It must have become quite popular as we see one ever so often today. In fact, some concern must have built them in quantity for they were advertised in a few of the catalogs of that day. Purdy's catalog of 1899 illustrated one. The dial was a wire frame, metal Arabic numerals and turned upon the pin freely as did the hands. The figure 6 being weighted so that after a whirl it would come to rest with the 12 up. The whole clock sat on a metal fork-like frame and presented a splendid appearance. Its watch movements were six-size, seven-jewel Elgin. One of these is now in the Clock Manor museum in Denver.

To Mr. Abbott's description I might add one pointer that would be of help to the builder: When you are ready to counterbalance your hands, remove their half circular weights and with a light rubber band bind them directly over the center post. This balances the entire weight correctly but with the center of gravity at the center post spot. Now, when the weight is placed on correctly (as a hand), the center of gravity is off just by that much, causing the hand to assume a position with the weight (hand) acting as a plumb bob. Your weight (hand) is shifted by the running of the movement. The minute hand one revolution per hour and the hour hand one revolution per twelve hours; thus, since gravity always makes it swing straight down, the shifting motion is thereby transmitted to the hands and they go around in time.

GRAVITY CLOCKS

This old timer, who is now retired and able to gratify his love of old clocks to the fullest, is building a rolling or gravity clock. As you know, all wheels and springs are removed up to the center wheel, which as a weight attached to same, in my experiments on the clock it took two hours to roll down a board three feet long, based

upon that. The board would have to be about 35 feet long which, of course, is out of the question. It looks to me as if I shall have to interpose another wheel after the center wheel. If you have any suggestions I shall be delighted to receive them.

A.

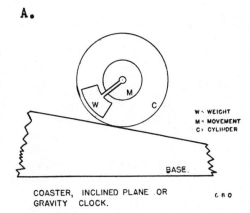

COASTER, INCLINED PLANE OR GRAVITY CLOCK.

J.E.C.'s Sketch

Placing another wheel in the train of your proposed gravity, inclined plane or coaster clock will definitely slow the roll of the cylinder (case) down; i. e., it will make less revolutions per hour and therefore travel a shorter distance in a 24-hour run.

Let's first decide on the approximate length you wish your base to be, then gear the clock accordingly. For example, say forty (40) inches long—if we allow one (1) inch for a stop on each end, the active length of your inclined plane will be thirty-eight (38) inches. If you have your cylinder revolve once per twelve (12) hours, it will have one-half of the 38 inches to do it in, or nineteen (19) inches. Nineteen inches divided by 3.14 would give you a cylinder of approximately six (6) inches' diameter. In other words, a one-day clock of this type whose cylinder turns once per twelve (12) hours, which cylinder is six (6) inches outside diameter will travel (roll down) approximately 38 inches in 24 hours.

Evidently your present clock revolves once per hour; staying with the above example of six inches diameter cylinder, the clock would have to roll or travel 38 feet instead of 38 inches to run 24 hours.

TRAIN PROBLEMS

For a long time I have wanted to build an 8-day, key wind wooden movement grandfather clock, and on building the movement, I find it is running far too fast—10 minutes an hour too fast.

I would appreciate it a great deal if you would show me where I made my mistake in the gear train, and what changes to make to slow it up. I am sending you a picture of my gear train; I would also like to half the pendulum about 38" to 42" in length.

A.

Train problems are relatively simple, but despite that fact they can often be most vexing. Your train as indicated by your sketch is geared way too low, and would require a much longer pendulum to bring it to time.

Let's simplify the problem as much as possible: first, you desire a "Royal" or seconds pendulum, second, we know that the active length of a seconds pendulum is 39.14 inches (active length is from point of suspension to center of gravity— if you had your pendulum off and laid it across a knife blade where it balanced, that would be the center of gravity, thus seconds pendulums are often 42 to 45 inches in over-all length depending on the weight of the rod in proportion to that of the ball).

Now, the reason for a 30-tooth escape wheel in a seconds beating clock is for a seconds hand, i.e., each tooth causes two beats or ticks—2 x 30 equals 60 seconds, or one complete revolution of the escape wheel arbor every sixty beats. The center post, or center arbor (on which is mounted the minute hand) must revolve once per hour, thus the ratio between the center and escape arbors will of necessity have to be 60 to one since we have sixty minutes in the hour.

In the sketch of your clock you show only one wheel between the center wheel and the escape wheel, so your problem is to make that center wheel turn the escape wheel 60 revolutions every time it (center) turns one. Here it is evident that the center pinion and the main wheel have no direct concern in this problem of timing. Take a close look at your drawing—the third wheel already drives the escape 6 to 1 (the 48 teeth will revolve the 8 leaf escape pinion six times) thus the center will have to drive the third 10 times in order that the third will drive the escape 60 times.

Therefore, any ten to one ratio between the center and third will give you the correct train. Inasmuch as you already have an 8 leaf pinion on the third arbor, why not make the center wheel with 80 teeth?

Proof: $\dfrac{80 \times 48 \times 30 \times 2}{8 \times 8} = \dfrac{230,400}{64} = 3,600$

beats per hour; 3,600 beats divided by 60 minutes equals 60 beats per minute. This was figuring the clock to the pendulum.

Repairmen often have to figure the pendulum to the clock when clocks come in minus a pendulum. Here you calculate the train (from the one rev. per hour of center post to escape wheel), take the number of times the escape wheel turns times its teeth times 2 (2 beats per tooth) and you have the required number of beats to make the clock turn exactly one hour (one rev. of the center). See the example on the chart I am sending to you.

This clockmaster knew he wanted a pendulum to beat 90 times per minute; he squared the time 90 x 90, squared the length of the seconds pendulum 39.2 inches, divided the 8,100 into 141.120 inches and got 14.42 inches.

GRAVITY CLOCK DATA

I would like some information about a gravity clock mentioned in Abbott's "American Watchmaker and Jeweler," page 183. The clock has two matched watch movements hidden in the hands and has no apparent source of power. I would appreciate advice as to how to make this clock or any suggestion as to where I could get more information.

A.

The description of the gravity clock on pages 183 and 184 of Abbott's "Watchmaker and Jeweler" pretty well covers the working of this type of clock, but it contains no detailed instructions. Possibly we can assist you a bit.

First you will have to decide upon your dial. It should be either skeleton wire, plate glass or plastic, since any opaque dial deprives the clock of its principal feature—mystery. The hands can be skeleton wire construction, or sawed from a thin sheet-metal. Aluminum is good because of its lightness. Each hand is exactly the same, with two exceptions: first, the hour hand is proportionately shorter; second, the lead weight of the minute hand fits upon the cannon pinion of its movement while the corresponding lead weight of the hour hand fits upon the hour-pipe of the hour wheel of its movement.

Some people use 10½ ligne wrist-watch movements and they are all right if the dial isn't too large. I like about a 15-inch dial and use 6-size movements. These are mounted, two upon each hand (the one near the tip is just a dummy, for symmetry) and the movement is mounted in the back box. Secure the boxes to the back side of the hands, or, if wire hands (skeleton) half through, with the lid or opening next to the dial. Then the movement mounts face plate UP. This is necessary, as the "gravity"-operated hand takes on a reversed motion from the movement.

The most important thing is poising the hands. After you have constructed the hands and selected and mounted the movements, and made the lead weights (they should be approximately one quarter the circumference of the box and about the same curve in order to allow you to use the smallest box possible), don't attempt to poise the hand with the weight in its proper position (like a hand) but drill a small hole about its center and set it upon the center-post. Thus you poise your hand with this weight at the center of the movement; now, when you place on properly (like a hand) the balance (or center of gravity for the back end) has been shifted by the length of the weight arm and by the amount of the weight itself. So, as the movement turns,

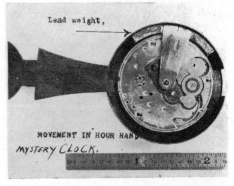

Lead weight,

MOVEMENT IN HOUR HAND

MYSTERY CLOCK.

or tries to turn, the weight, by force of gravity it continues to remain as a plumb bob, pointing straight down, and the entire hand shifts around at the same ratio or speed of the movement—one revolution per hour for the minute hand and one revolution per 12 hours for the hour hand.

This type of clock is not too difficult to build, and does not require very much time, either. The builder is always rewarded with the fun of mystifying his friends and hearing their guesses as to what operates it.

REGULATOR CLOCK

I am building a regulator, using a pendulum made of a wooden rod with a lead bob. I am following instructions found in "The Modern Clock" by Goodrich, 1905 edition. My clock beats ½-seconds, the pendulum being 24" long with a piece of lead pipe 7"x1" diameter supported at bottom with adjusting screw, etc., and top support is a .004"x1/2" spring 1" long.

I have this clock running nicely and am wondering if the temperature compensation will be satisfactory where the room temperature varies from 60 degrees to possibly 100 degrees Fahrenheit. I am using a lead weight of approximately six pounds to drive my clock using a pulley at the weight to get longer running time per winding. I also have a power maintaining spring in the drive wheel so when winding it will not lose time.

I am wondering if I installed friction plate jewels on the pallet and escape arbors if this would improve timekeeping ability. Would plate jewels be O.K.? Can you advise me where I can get a dial made up with seconds bit above center wheel?

What effect does a heavier pendulum have on timekeeping, say a 15-lb. instead of a 5-lb.?

A. Since you are following instructions as given by Goodrich, I fear that it is practically impossible for this column to improve or add to what you have already found in that volume—I consider it to be the very best.

If you haven't too much metal to expand or c o n t r a c t with temperature changes, your clock should perform satisfactorily at room temperatures. This feature can be eliminated by hanging your metal from its center—in this manner you have as much expansion (or contraction) above the center as below. In fact it isn't the exact center but rather the center of gravity. *See accompanying sketch.*

As to jeweling, by all means jewel the pallet and escape wheel pivots—friction jewels are fine. Some may not make a great deal of difference over and above well-fitted and polished brass bearings for a short trial, but for continuous year-in and year-out running jewel bearings make for superior timekeeping.

Cylindrical lead bob. 1-3/4" x 6".	Drill smaller hole all the way through center axis of cylinder. Insert pendulum rod and balance upon knife edge to locate center of gravity. Since drilling of larger hole from bottom will remove some weight, reg. nut should be located slightly above point where balanced. Regulating Nut.

Consult the pages of *American Horologist & Jeweler* for a dial maker; you will find this service advertised there.

Your last question is a complicated one. Up to a certain point adding weight to a pendulum ball you are making should make for better timekeeping. Mr. E. Howard held to this theory when building his fine astronomical regulators. Some of his mercury pendulums were four-jar affairs, weighing as much as 30 pounds. These clocks were sometimes driven with (believe it or not) a seven-ounce weight. Since you are using a 120-beat pendulum **(1/2-seconds)** your problem is slightly different from the "royal" (seconds) pendulum as you will have a greater arc of swing. Your present bob is 1x7, therefore weighs a little less than five pounds—try a bob 1¾x6 which would weigh about 11 pounds after being drilled. We'd be very much interested to receive photos of your clock, especially the movement together with some description of the problems you encountered while building it, and approximately the hours work required.

CORRECT WHEEL CENTERS

I am interested in building up a pendulum clock from an assortment of wheels and pinions. My problem is this: How can I figure the correct distance between centers of wheel and pinion having only outside diameter of wheel and pinion, and number of teeth?

A.

Yours is another of those questions that just has to be answered by "rule of thumb."

We all know that the center distance is the radius of the pitch circle of the pinion, plus the radius of the pitch circle of the wheel, but when one has wheels and pinions already made up, actually taking the caliper in hand and accurately determining just where the pitch circle cuts across the teeth is quite a problem.

Fortunately for you, in building a clock with wheels from your assortment, you will not be working to extremely close tolerances. It is noted that you are taking a course in watch repairing. Are you familiar with the depthing tool? It is possibly the most practical solution to your problem. You will need a clock depthing tool; they are exactly like the watch depthing tool, only much larger.

Make up your plates and fit them on their pillars; then make your arbors and mount the pinions and wheels thereon; naturally you have a pretty accurate idea of the train lay-out, so plant (that is, drill and fit) the center to the plates just where you wish the center post to come, and work each way from your center. Take the center (working toward the escapement now) and the wheel it is supposed to drive and mount them in your clock depthing tool. With left-hand finger, revolve the center wheel to the right (the direction it will run), and with a finger of the other hand acting as a load or brake on the driven arbor. With a good loupe, carefully observe the action of the wheels' teeth in and out of the driven pinion; with the adjusting screw on the side of the depthing tool, alter the center distance until you observe that point where you have the minimum of *slide.*

In other words, under simulated working conditions you are observing the tooth action and are able to adjust it at will until you have the best working point. Once you have determined this point, it is easily transferred to the plate by the points on the back end of the depthing tool runners. Place one of these runner-points in the center and use the tool as a compass to scribe an arc on the plate; the bearing hole for the arbor next above the center can be located anywhere in this scribed arc.

Discard the center, move the arbor it drives to the left side of the depthing tool and insert in the right side the arbor it is meant to drive. Again determine the center distance in the same manner for those two members and transfer the measurement in the same way to the plate; thus you work your way up the train to the escape wheel step-by-step, and are ready to return to the center and work your way down to the main or drive wheel.

Questions on a calendar clock

I want to make a calendar clock out of a clock that I have and I want to know what wheels I need for the calendar date hand and where I can obtain them. I have an old Seth Thomas 12-inch dial that I'd like to convert into a calendar clock. I have been trying for a long time to pick up a calendar clock with this size dial but so far have not been able to do so.

A.

It is presumed that you wish to construct a simple American type calendar which indicates the day of the month only, with the series of numbers from 1 to 31 arranged concentrically with the time dial.

This should be comparatively easy, if the center post of your clock extends far enough in front of the dial to allow the added calendar hand to travel under the hour hand.

Your local materials house can supply a paper dial of the desired outside diameter with the month numerals 1 to 31 printed just outside the hour circle, also a red calendar hand of correct length. All you

will need to make are: a short pipe to ride loosely over the hour pipe; a wheel of 31 teeth, ratchet or wolf type teeth and two wheels with conventional teeth, one with twice the number of teeth as the other.

The 31-toothed wheel is attached fast to the new pipe. The smaller of the other wheels is made fast to the hour pipe barely clear of the front plate and the 31-tooth wheel with its pipe will ride up against it. The third wheel is mounted loosely upon a stud planted at any convenient spot on the front plate so that it meshes properly with that wheel attached to the hour pipe. On the outside face of this wheel you plant a pin that will engage the 31-tooth wheel just deep enough to kick it forward exactly one tooth.

Now you can see that the wheel fastened to the hour pipe will turn the wheel on the stud once every 24 hours as the ratio is 2-to-1 and that the pin on it will kick over your calendar (31-tooth) wheel once every 24 hours. At any convenient point around the calendar wheel, mount a little spring on the front plate to act ratchet-wise against the edge of the calendar wheel and hold it in place from one date change to the other.

Chances are you can select from your stock of old wheels two with a ratio of 1-to-2; mount them as above and you can then determine the proper diameter of the calendar wheel. This, you can lay out with a compass on a piece of brass and saw out with a jeweler's saw. All of it ought to be fairly easy and you will get a lot of fun doing it.

This is quite a problem

Would it be possible to change a 30-hour Seth Thomas weight clock into a spring wound that would run from four to eight days with one winding?

Would the springs, 3/4 inch by 8 inches, taken from a Seth Thomas mantel clock be powerful enough to run the movement to keep fairly good time?

A.

Converting the 1-day, weight driven clock to an 8-day, spring drive presents quite a problem due to the very low gear ratio of the clock.

The second portion of your question. To keep fairly good time does not enter into the problem for once you have sufficent power to drive the clock, the time feature is under control of its pendulum; therefore, would keep the same time when regulated as it did when driven by the weight.

In the 1-day weight clocks the gear ratio varies with the different makes, and even within different models of the same make. Generally the ratio between the main wheel and the center-post (hour) ranges all the way for two revolutions (two hours) of the center per turn of the main wheel to $2\frac{1}{2}$ revolutions per turn of the main. As an average for your clock, let's say that the main wheel in one revolution will drive the center through two hours and 15 minutes. Now there are 168 hours in a seven-day week; to complete that your main wheel would have to turn up about 75 revolutions; in other words, to substitute a spring and make that spring drive the clock seven days, it will have to deliver 75 turns to the main wheel arbor. Roughly, the same problem exists upon the strike side, and 75 spring turns get a bit unwieldy.

We've seen one such attempt where the clockmaker endeavored to work upon the plan of the old E. N. Welch, Patti model, which if you are familiar with it, utilizes two mainsprings that have their outer ends fixed together; winding from one inner coil and driving from the other. This requires a tremendous amount of alteration and work, and ends up with the clock going about four and one-half days. Incidentally, the $\frac{3}{4}$ inch spring you suggest would deliver too much power when fully wound; $\frac{3}{8}$ inch would be nearer correct.

Why not drive your clock electrically, and eliminate winding completely? Any time you convert a weight drive to a spring drive, you have destroyed just as much of the clock's originality as when you use synchronous motors, thus that 100 percent restoration as desired by collectors, etc., must not enter into your problem. All too many clockmakers are unfamiliar with electrifying the strike train and fail to recommend "electric" conversion because they think the strike is lost. Actually it is about as easy (if not easier) to apply a

sync to the strike train as to the time train.

I'm sure that you are familiar with pulling out the entire time train and making a sync clock drive the center-post 1-r.p.h., or adapting a sync motor to the escape arbor (or some arbor in the train above the center) and have the clock deliver correct time.

On the strike train, you simply pull out the main wheel and discard it . . . adapt a sync motor to the fan-fly arbor . . . either direct, or via a gear, depending upon the desired speed . . . and you have it. The lock will hold the motor still until it is released upon the hour by the center-lift, the self-starting motor will immediately take over; complete the strike according to the count-finger and be again locked when the count-finger drops into the low lock notch.

We do not know of any catalog "of old clock repairs." Aside from mainsprings, pendulum balls and pendulum rods (wire) practically no material for clocks manufactured before World War II is available.

Orthodox pendulum is best

I have recently become interested in clockmaking and have several ideas which I intend to try out along the line of electronically driven pendulums for a free slave clock system.

However, my ignorance in many matters of clock design is appalling, and therefore I would like you to answer a question for me.

A seconds pendulum is desirable but rather large. Is there any fundamental objection to the use of a small counterbalanced pendulum such as is used in a metronome to obtain a seconds beat, but with an overall length of less than 10 inches? Have any clocks been made using this type of pendulum?

A.

The reason for the long pendulum in the first place is accuracy. A clock's train is mathematically correct (accurate). Its error lies in the pendulum, and the pendulum error automatically adds up with each beat or stroke, so that a clock beating quarter seconds adds up four errors every second; 14,400 of them every hour.

For example, let us say you are considering a tower clock whose 156.8 inch pendulum beats every two seconds, you'd have only 1,800 added errors every hour.

It is possible to design and build a seconds beating clock with a "compound" pendulum such as those used in metronomes — BUT — you will introduce greater inaccuracies than those possesed by a well built short pendulum. The resultant clock would be a very poor timekeeper.

The common metronome is never used for a long period so the accumulative error never reaches large proportions. Were you to couple hands on to it to register time and endeavor to run it for a week it would be found to be way off. If you have in mind some "novelty" or something to be set in motion for just 15 or 20 minutes, perhaps such a compound pendulum would prove satisfactory, but, if a practical timekeeper for long periods of running is desired, better stick to the orthodox, simple pendulum.

The Simple American Calendar Work

For several months we've been asked a number of times about calendar mechanisms. Now comes a query from a clockmaker who wishes to add a calendar work to a movement. First, he wishes to know whether or not the 'average' repairman without special wheel cutting equipment can do it. Then, comes the how. It is immediately evident that an answer to his questions will at the same time cover most of the repair problems, so, let's have a go at it.

The simple American calendar is just that—it simply advances a calendar hand forward by one day each midnight. It does not show the days of the week, nor the months. Calendar works are divided into three separate divisions: 1, the simple calendar; 2, simple calendar with month and week-day attachment; and, 3, the perpetual calendar mechanism. This is the most complicated of all and is called perpetual because it automatically compensates for the 30 and 31 day months; it even compensates for leap years of 366 days.

It is self-evident that converting the regular progression of the running movement into irregular progression of the perpetual calendar register brings in some complications, and we are not about to suggest that the average workman without wheel cutting equipment, etc., can start and build one from scratch. We do say that he can easily build, or, repair the 'simple' calendar and this "Otherwise" shall address only number one—the simple calendar.

The simple calendar work of the American clock is located wholly without the plates—on the front of the front plate and just underneath the dial. This makes it very easy to remove, or to loosen a part, and thus many clocks with the simple calendar are brought to the repairman not working. Its owner wishes it restored, and this has brought in a good many questions. Our point here is to fully acquaint the clockmaker with details of this construction. Once he understands it, effecting a satisfactory restoration comes easy.

Fig. 1 conveys the general idea—the days of the month are indicated upon a scale of numbers from 1 to 31 arranged concentrically with the dial, just outside of the minute track; the current day (6th) is indicated by a hand, generally of a different color (most often, red) carried on a pipe outside the pipe of the hour hand on the center arbor. The calendar hand is advanced by one day each night at midnight; since the slowest turning member of the clock's movement is the hour pipe which makes two revolutions each 24-hour day, the problem is to construct the minimum amount of gearing to give one revolution in twenty-four hours. Since the dial train of most American clocks is located between the plates, the front of

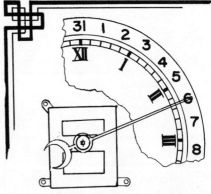

FIG. 1

the front plate is left in the clear—a pinion is simply frictioned on the hour pipe out front; this pinion is geared into a wheel having twice its number of teeth. It then revolves once to each two revolutions of that hour pipe; a second pipe to take the calendar hand rides free over the hour pipe, and attached to this pipe is a saw-toothed wheel of 31 teeth. A pin located near the hub of the kick-wheel, kicks the calendar wheel over by one tooth at each revolution, making the calendar hand indicate the next day, in our case from the 6th, over to the 7th. Due to its very slow turning, this 'kick' operation requires the better part of an hour and the time hands are so set as to make it take place midnight to 1 a. m.

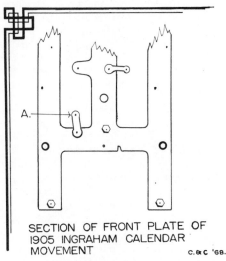

FIG. 2.

Fig. 2 shows a section of the front plate of a 1905 Ingraham calendar movement. "A" indicates the post at the end of an arm that carries the kick wheel. Solely for its general information, we give count and sizes of the Ingraham construction. The pinion frictioned on to the hour pipe is 16 m/m. diameter and has 18 teeth, is four m/m. thick. The kick wheel is 30 m/m. diameter with 36 teeth. Its kick pins is six m/m. long. The calendar wheel is 34 m/m. diameter with 31 teeth—center distance between kick wheel and center-post is 24 m/m. Length of the arm on which the kick wheel is mounted, 18 m/m. Length of the retaining spring 49 m/m. So much for the Ingraham figures—the thing that makes the construction, from scratch, so easy is: these measurements are neither fixed or critical. The builder is hedged in by only two points: 1, it must be located concentric with the center post; 2, the calendar wheel must have 31 teeth. Every other measure-

ment, size, etc., can be varied to suit the material at hand and/or the builder's fancy. Sans wheel cutting equipment; he can select a wheel from a discarded movement for his kick wheel—one of 30 or 40 teeth is suggested because they would give a pinion of 15 or 20 teeth. The drive pinion frictioned to the hour pipe will have to be made, the hard way, with jeweler's saw and file; both 15 and 20 can be marked from the 60 index holes in your watchmaker's lathe. Pinions of odd teeth would pose a problem.

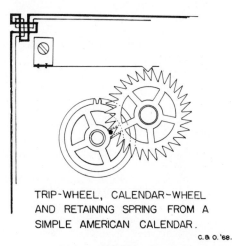

FIG. 3.

Fig. 3 shows the general lay-out and the relative position of the retaining spring. This spring may be of thin steel or spring brass, it terminates in a "V" which the spring tension holds between the teeth of the calendar wheel thereby retaining the calendar hand upon the correct date until kicked to the next day. It must be so positioned as to hold the calendar wheel so that the kick pin will come in just under a tooth —the pin kicks (revolves) the calendar wheel 'clockwise' until the tip of a tooth has passed under the "V", at this point the "V" pressure kicks the hand over to the 'rest' point and holds it there 'til the next kick (day). The distance the kick pin is located from the center of the kick wheel depends upon the diameter of the calendar wheel, but can be located easily by trial and error.

The arm carrying the kick wheel should be riveted to the front plate about half way between the center line and the left-hand edge—see Fig. 2,—the length of it depends somewhat upon the diameter of the kick wheel (roughly, about half the diam. of the wheel). It is self-evident; this being an arm permits correct depthing of the kick wheel into the center drive pinion. The pin upon which the kick wheel turns should be mounted in the arm before it is riveted to the plate in order that a hole can be drilled through its outer end to take a taper-pin for securing the wheel. Laying out the calender wheel of 31 teeth can be a bit troublesome with an ordinary protractor, etc. On a hard piece of stiff white paper, scribe a circle whose radius is two and 17/32nds inches diameter. If your measurements are careful and accurate, it should give you a circle whose circumference is 15 inches. Set a pair of dividers at exactly one-half inch and walk it around this circle, it should come out even and thus divide the circle by 31. Center your wheel blank on this circle and lay off your 31 teeth. Should you not have a suitable scribe for marking brass, one can quickly be made with an old style steel phonograph needle held in a small pin-vice. Cut teeth with a fine jeweler's saw; only two cuts per tooth are required—touch up with a fine file and you have a practical wheel without any special equipment or wheel cutting experience.

The center drive pinion may be the regular cut of thick (approximately 5/32nds) brass, or an open-end lantern pinion. We've seen both work satisfactorily. Of necessity, the open-ended lantern takes up more space and sometimes is not practical where the center post may be a little short. Turn up the blank the determined diameter; drill and broach its center hole for frictioning on the hour pipe. Let's say a kick wheel of 30 teeth has been chosen, then the drive pinion must have 15. Re-chuck the blank, set the "T" rest level with the exact center and use it as a mark-gauge. Every fourth hole in your lathe pulley will give the 15 spacing. Drill the 15 holes about 45/1,000ths, and stake in stubbs steel wire. Let it extend through about a scant 4 m/m., making sure that every wire is driven in tight. When finished the open end as well as the back may be stoned off smooth. Stake on to the hour pipe with the open end down; this gives the hub end up for the calendar wheel to ride

against.

The last member of your calendar mechanism should be the retaining spring. Cut a suitable piece of brass or steel, about nine m/m. wide by 25 m/m. long and bend at right angle about 10 m/m. from one end. Drill the short end of this "L" approximately center to take a screw—see Fig. 3—then two small holes near the front edge of the long end for riveting the spring. Drill and tap a hole in the left-hand side of the front frame about level with the top of the calendar wheel to take this "L". The spring may be of either steel or spring brass; approximately six m/m. wide, crimp a "V" in the end of a size to comfortable fit between the teeth of the calendar wheel as shown by Fig. 3, adjust its length so that it will position the calendar wheel teeth so that the kick pin will engage a tooth just as it enters on its counter-clockwise revolution, mark the two holes, drill and rivet spring to the "L". Thus, the repairing of, or the building of, a complete simple calendar mechanism neither poses any problems for the man a bit short upon equipment, nor entails an excessive amount of work.

Calendar clocks coming to the repair bench, not working, most often have their kick wheel missing. It isn't always easy to find a wheel of the right diameter and the right number of teeth (twice the number of the drive pinion) upon an old movement but as we said at the beginning nearly all measurements are NOT critical—a wheel cut by jeweler's saw and filed up works beautifully—one may take an old wheel of slightly larger diameter, turn or grind the teeth off and re-cut to the desired number of teeth and avoid the time and trouble of spoking-out, etc. We repeat that once understood, the simple calendar should pose no problems.

Of late, the calendar clock has grown in popularity. Two numbers are especially in demand—the Ithaca "Parlor" and Southern Calendar Clock Company's "Fashion". In a later column we shall try to cover their calendar mechanisms; both are perpetual.

ONE DAY TO EIGHT DAY

I have a Gilbert, one-day, spring wind, banjo type clock that I would like to convert a little. The dial is 5½ inches in diameter and the thickness from the back side of dial to inside of back plate measures 1½ inches.

My customer would like to have an eight-day, spring wind movement put into this case, to eliminate winding every day.

I would also like to know what changes, if any, would have to be made to make this work.

This clock is not a pendulum type.

A.

Converting or rebuilding the little Gilbert, one-day movement you describe, into an eight-day movement is highly impractical.

Since it is to avoid winding your customer desires, why not install an electric movement?

If there is an objection to the electric, and spring wind is definitely desired, it will be quicker, cheaper and easier for you to locate an eight-day movement (in some current clock) and install it in your banjo case.

CONVERTING CLOCKS

I have a Seth Thomas 8-day wall clock, Model No. 77-B, with a 40-tooth escape wheel that I want to convert to a seconds-beat master clock for use in my watch shop. Will you please tell me what to do, and how to do the job?

A.

Your 77-B Seth Thomas is an 80-beat, meaning that the pendulum beats eighty times per minute. Each tooth produces two beats, thus the seconds hand of your clock is mounted on the escape wheel arbor and when the pendulum has performed 80 beats the escape wheel of 40 teeth has made one complete revolution.

The result you desire is for that clock to beat 60 times per minute, or beat seconds.

An escape wheel of 30 teeth will give your seconds hand one complete revolution with each 60 beats of the pendulum.

Now the length of a pendulum beating seconds is just about 39.14 inches, meaning you will not only require a new pendulum, but if your clock is in its original case, it will have to be made longer to accommodate the longer pendulum. I do not have a drawing of the 77-B 80-beat escapement before me, but believe you should also have a new verge to correctly match the new 30-tooth wheel.

If you desire to do the job yourself, you will have to learn to draw and cut an escape wheel, draw and make a verge, match and adjust the escapement, make a new pendulum and lengthen (or make a new) case.

GRANDFATHER CLOCK

I have recently acquired a Seth Thomas clock movement with "77A" stamped on the plate. This movement is driven by a weight of approximately 5 pounds and has a 24-inch pendulum. I am constructing what I term a modern grandfather's clock, the dimensions of which will be 6 feet high, 16 inches wide and 12 inches deep. My plan is to convert the above movement to fit this case and at some future date, purchase a different movement for chime strike.

Question 1: Are the dimensions above sufficient to allow for a complete chime weight actuated, pendulum clock?

Question 2: I desire a 48-inch pendulum for the above Seth Thomas movement. My plans are to remove the lead from the present pendulum weight. Is there an established formula for determining pendulum weight and length?

Question 3: Is there a formula for determining the required weight to run the movement?

A.

Apparently you should have ample space to install a chime movement, with seconds pendulum at a later date as you plan.

As we recall, the Seth Thomas No. 77 movement is mounted upon an iron bracket which bracket also has a pendulum suspension post. This should make it easy to mount the movement in your case upon a temporary board the proper distance back of the dial.

The No. 77 came in a series of "regulators", some beating 72 times per minute, and some beating 80 times per minute. It is noted you say a 48-inch pendulum is desired for the No. 77 movement; by this, I'm sure you wish your clock to beat 60 times per minute or seconds.

There is a *very definite* formula for determining the length of any desired pendulum. "L equals 39.1416 times 'time' squared. Where 'time' equals time of swing in seconds, 39.1416 inches equals length of pendulum beating seconds."

I like the rule, as given by Reid, which is virtually the same thing, but probably easier to handle. For practical purposes one may use the figures 39.2 inches as the length of a seconds pendulum. Reid says: "Multiply the number of vibrations made in a minute by the standard or seconds pendulum (60) by itself which is squaring it, and this being multiplied by the standard length, 39.2 inches, and the last product divided by the square of the number of vibrations given in a minute by the pendulum whose length is required, the quotient will be the length of that pendulum in inches and decimal parts of an inch".

Now if we use this method we shall always have 60 squared multiplied by 39.2, which gives the figure 141,120.0, and it will not be necessary to do that each time —just retain that number. Suppose you require a pendulum to beat 80 times per minute. Simply square your 80 and get 6,400. Divide that into 141,120.0, and you will get 22.05 inches.

This is the pendulum of theory which presupposes that the entire weight rests, or is contained in one point. Unfortunately, the actual practical pendulum has quite a bit of its weight or mass in the rod, and for working purposes, one will find that these calculations amount to a pretty close approximation. Suppose you have a complete pendulum and balance it upon a knife edge that will give you the center of gravity (vertically). That point the theoretical length extends down from the point of suspension or center of oscillation. We find that the center of oscillation is always a little below the center of gravity. In other words, you can have a pendulum for your movement whose over-all length is the 48 inches you specify, yet its theoretical length will be 39.2 to beat seconds.

There is no hard and fast rule for practically working out the weight of the pendulum ball. One of the fundamental laws of the pendulum is that the time of swing depends *only* on the length and not at all upon the weight. Hence, as far as time is concerned, one may use a ball of any weight. If a pendulum could be suspended in such a way as to eliminate all friction, then encased in a perfect vacuum and started swinging, it would continue to swing forever.

Practically the same goes for the answer to your third question. A practical method of determining the required weight for a movement in hand is to provide a can or container that may be hung in place of the weight; one whose diameter is small enough to permit the pendulum to swing without bumping it. Fill it with bits of metal or small stones until the clock will escape (tick—having first started the pendulum). Run it and by this test it may be determined just about what is required to carry the load. Weigh the result and add about 10 per cent for a safety factor; then you may proceed to cast the permanent weight.

Since you are converting the Seth Thomas No. 77, I don't think you have any problem at all with either the driving weight or weight of the pendulum ball. You will find that the present weight and ball will both work very satisfactorily. You will need a new escape wheel and a new Graham dead beat verge to match it. If the movement is an 80-beat, it has 40 teeth in its escape wheel. To make it keep correct time with the pendulum beating 60, you will have to have an escape wheel of 30 teeth.

CONVERT 8 DAY MOVEMENT TO SHIP'S BELL STRIKER

If you were called upon to convert a common eight-day mantel striking clock to a Ship's Bell striker, what would your reply be? Or if you just happened to want to make one of these old clocks strike Ship's Bell time, how would you go about it?

Mr. C. L. Ham, clockmaker of 5133 North Concord Street, Portland, Oregon, has solved the problem rather neatly, and in the true cooperative spirit, wishing to share it with fellow clockmakers, sent along sketches and the movement. His letter did not state whether he did it for a customer or just for "the heck of it"— he does point out that before starting the problem he imposed two restrictions upon the solution: (1) no special material, (2) no special tools—just what may conveniently be had in any clock repair shop.

You will immediately recognize from the photo (See page 52) that he chose an eightday Ingraham, hour and half-hour strike—a cabinet clock quite popular 12 to 20 years ago; however, his method can be easily adapted to almost every American eight-day movement with a few slight variations.

Starting with a 16-leaf pinion, 7/16-inch diameter from a manual-wind Westinghouse electric range clock, and a 12-leaf pinion 3/8 inches in diameter from a $1.65 Westclox, he built a plain frame structure of strip brass, two upright members being spaced 5/8 inches apart by pillar post from an old clock movement, said posts being riveted through the cross piece (see sketch) to the back strip. The front strip is held in place by original nuts.

In the center of this framework he drills a bearing hole for its one and only moving arbor; upon that arbor is mounted a brass disc over-all 2⅛ inches in diameter, cut from 1/16-inch brass plate stock. (See Fig. 3, of sketch.) Pivot upon the back side of the arbor extends through the back strip the right distance to take the 16-leaf pinion.

The 12-leaf pinion is staked friction tight upon the second arbor of the strike train, 1/32-inch below the shoulder to give ample clearance above the back clock plate. The frame assembly is riveted to the back plate, upon the outside (back side) as indicated in Fig. 1, in position to make the 16-leaf pinion properly mesh with the 12-leaf pinion staked on the second strike train arbor.

Now, the Ingraham count wheel is actuated forward by two pins extending out of the third strike train arbor pinion, thus you will see that a 60-tooth count wheel being driven forward two teeth per revolution of the third arbor pinion will be advanced 20 teeth per one complete revolution of the hammer lift-pin disc you have just attached (60 teeth in second strike wheel driving 8-leaf third arbor pinion).

The hammer lift-pin disc is inscribed with a circle 2 inches in diameter; this circle is divided and drilled to take 20 pins (steel) as shown in the outside view in Fig. 3; pins are ground or cut to 7/32-inch long both above and below (inside and outside) cut or ground off flush with the brass disc pins as indicated on the inside sketch at 1-bell, 3-bells, 5-bells, and 7-bells.

Secure a 60-tooth wheel of proper diameter to work as the count wheel and cut as indicated in Fig. 4. Since 20 teeth of this count wheel are actuated forward by one revolution of the hammer lift-pin disc, and this disc is already constructed to give the correct ship's bells from one through eight, we shall get three eight-bell watches (20 into 60 equals 3) per revolution of the count wheel.

Two hammers are constructed and fitted to brass collars that work over the frame pillar post. If, as in Mr. Ham's case, it is desired to mount the bell above the case, these hammers work upon the top pillar, and each has a small coiled spring to make it strike the bell from inside. Should it be desirable to mount the bell or gong within the case, the hammers may go upon the bottom pillar-post and fall by gravity. The hammer-tail pieces are made with 1/16-inch difference in length to make the hammers strike "true pairs."

We've condensed Mr. Ham's sketches slightly, and made this suggestion (which he has approved): "Upon other movements—i. e., different strike train ratios— it would be quite practical to enlarge the hammer liftpin disc by approximately an eighth of an inch (2 2/8-inch diameter), still retain the pin circle at two inches, and use the outer edge of it as the count wheel, cutting the lock-slots as indicated

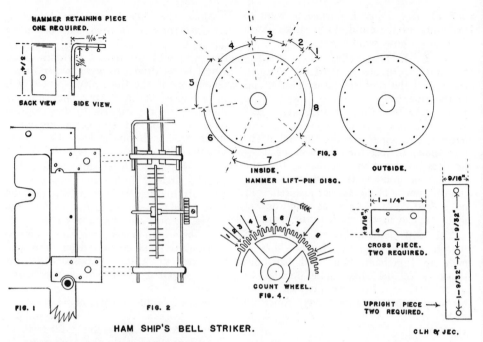

HAM SHIP'S BELL STRIKER.

HAMMER RETAINING PIECE ONE REQUIRED.

BACK VIEW   SIDE VIEW.

FIG. I   FIG. 2

FIG. 3

INSIDE.
HAMMER LIFT-PIN DISC.

OUTSIDE.

COUNT WHEEL.
FIG. 4.

CROSS PIECE.
TWO REQUIRED.

UPRIGHT PIECE →
TWO REQUIRED.

CLH & JEC.

in the inside sketch in Fig. 3.

Ham's Ship's Bell Clock

"The original count wheel of the movement would be discarded, the count finger cut off at the arbor, then the arbor would have to be drilled as near the back pivot as practical and the new count finger, to work upon the edge of the hammer lift-pin disc, inserted in this new hole and brought out the back plate—not a very difficult bit of improvising."

BUILD SHIP'S BELL STRIKER

WHETHER OR NOT this fitful forum has generated some interest in the ship's bell striker, or the several mentions of it here over the past few months have merely fanned the spark of interest into a flame is beside the point. There is sufficient evidence that considerable interest exists at this very moment and even though you as a repairman may not have the slightest desire to build one, the perusal of a few brief pointers upon such a conversion will serve to better fix this strike system in your thinking, and thus make your next ships bell striker servicing job easier and faster.

A lot of "do-it-yourself-kits" have hit the market, and, a number of "how-to-do-it" squibs have been published, but not that first one on the ships bell striker. Why? That answer has to lie with a tricky bit of engineering required to make the movement truly simulate the method time is struck on shipboard; that is, by stroking the bell in "pairs"—one to eight bells in four hour cycles.

If it were not for the "pairs" system, one could take any striking movement, if the count-wheel type, and simply cut a new count-wheel range same one to eight then repeat the cycle. Or, if rack and snail system merely cut a new snail one to eight and revolve it once per four hours.

Exactly who, where, and when this little breakthrough was first made is not easy to research. The first our meager efforts have been able to spade up is a patent issued to one H. H. Ham Jr., of Portsmouth, N.H., No. 215,057, May 6, 1879. His "system" was picked up by the Elisha

FIG. I.
CONVERTED SHIP'S BELL STRIKER.

N. Welch Co., of Bristol, Conn., which, at this stage, appears to be the first American manufacturer of a ships bell striker. Mr. Ham solved the problem by locating hammer lift pins in pairs utilizing one hammer and as his patent states, either count-wheel or rack and snail system.

This writer has never made an in-hand-examination or seen an E. N. Welch movement—one would be welcomed as a vital link in this little research chain.

Other horologists contrived a dual- hammer method of portraying the double strokes also employing both the count-wheel and rack and snail methods. It is an odd

coincidence that another Ham, Mr. C. L. Ham, of Portland, Ore., some twenty-three years after the original Ham, devised the conversion suggested here.

The matter of building a clock movement; either from scratch, or as a modification—conversion—of an already existing movement by the tender of the "144" has over the years brought forth just about every conceivable comment. Some feel that many such instructions dwell too long upon small details leaving nothing to the imagination of the would be builder; others complain that most such instructions are not explicit enough. Still others say: "Why build a clock unless it has something out of the ordinary to reccommend it to your friends, etc?" Still others point out that many "build-it" instructions require equipment not generally possesed by the average bench clockmaker. Having heard these over and over again, we shall try to fulfill all of them. These "pointers" shall be brief enough to satisfy those who object to the nitty-gritty details; the resultant movement does in fact do something out of the ordinary, and we shall keep in mind the absence of special or additional equipment.

The fact is, this conversion can be built with only your lathe and the usual hand tools. All lathe heads have the "60" division thus you can step-off the lift-pin disc and the count wheel with it. You may go the count-wheel route or utilize the rack and snail system, the latter involves more work because the snail has to be revolved once every four hours.

Fig. 2 indicates the method of cutting a count-wheel of 60. It is readily seen that twenty teeth will count off the bells for the four hour cycle. Twenty into sixty and you end up with a count-wheel of three sections.

Let's analyze the ships bell method further. Adding the hammer strokes one through eight we get a total of 36 strokes; since these 36 strokes are performed in eight steps, four for the hour and another four for the halves, and they must follow the "pairs" pattern at each half-hour—odd stroke—we in effect have a half-of-a-pair.

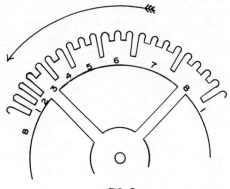

FIG. 2.
COUNT WHEEL.

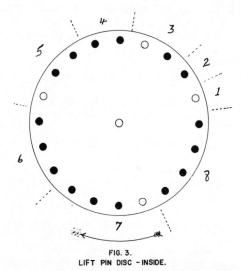

FIG. 3.
LIFT PIN DISC - INSIDE.

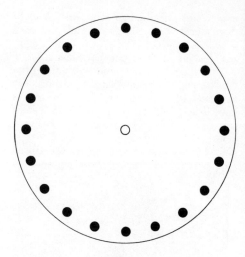

FIG. 4.
LIFT PIN DISC - OUTSIDE.

Utilizing two hammers located upon either side of a disc containing the lift pins, one hammer having its lift-tail slightly shorter than the other to accomplish the double stroke effect, one hammer would make twenty strokes while the other would make only sixteen, so four pins are outlined from the inside as shown by Fig. 3. 20 plus 16, total 36.

Cut a disc of heavy brass approximately 2⅛ inches diameter; inscribe a circle two inches diameter; chuck in your lathe; set the T rest level with the center and use it to scribe by. Step every third hole in the lathe-head and mark the twenty divisions; drill and insert twenty pins, then cut four pins on the inside as indicated by Fig. 3. Locating this lift-pin disc, either inside the strike train or upon the back of the movement is left entirely to the builder. It has to be driven at a ratio of 10 to 1 or 20 to 1 of the fourth arbor of the strike train. If 10 to 1 then the lock-plate on the fourth arbor must have two locks 180 degrees apart. If 20 to 1, then only one lock notch in the plate. Either method gives you a lock—stop—at every 20th pin of the lift disc—here you have full control of the whole strike operation—a ships bell striker completed, one that is "different" and will afford you a great deal of pleasure.

We have not covered the count-wheel because a suitable wheel of 60 is easily located in any shop—same can easily be re-cut using the existing teeth—it can be friction steady as in the old Seth Thomas one-day weight, etc., allowing the fourth arbor to advance—kick—it forward via a pin, or two of them if the lock plate is double.

How to adjust movement for longer pendulum

Other than changing the escape wheel just what is involved to change a short pendulum mantel clock to one using a longer pendulum like a kitchen clock, for instance.

I have several old but good short pendulum movements such as Gilbert, Waterbury, Ingraham. The Gilbert has escape wheel gear count of 30 with pinion of 7 leaves. Ingraham has 48-7.

I want to design and make my own cases for those movements and use pendulums of say maybe six to nine or ten inches. Is this possible?

A.

It is quite possible to operate a clock movement with a longer pendulum by altering the time-train. Further, I'm sure that you will enjoy working the "problem" once you've mastered basic principles.

Now, you give us 30 teeth and seven leaves for your Gilbert; 48 teeth and seven leaves in the pinion for the Ingraham. This is not enough information—one has to know the time-train from the center-post on up through the escape wheel; so let's forget your figures and try and describe how it may be done for any clock movement.

The one "fixed" member in every clock is the center-post (hour-post), i.e. it must make just one complete revolution each hour (60 minutes) and it is from this fixed point we must work.

To "count" the train, you begin with the center; some centers are idle driven others are a wheel of the train, in either case the principle is the same. By carefully counting its teeth and pinion leaves you determine how many teeth in the escape wheel must pass a fixed point when the center post is revolved through a full 360 degree circle.

Example: let's say that you find that 3,600 escape wheel teeth must pass a point for the minute hand to travel through one full hour. Divide by 60 minutes in that hour and you have 60 teeth passing in one minute—we know that each tooth causes two strokes; one on the entering pallet and again one on the let-off pallet, therefore two times 60 equals 120. This means for the clock to keep time (revolve the minute hand one turn) its pendulum must stroke or tick 120 times per minute.

The rule for finding the length of a pendulum for a given number of vibrations must be worked from the standard or "Royal" pendulum, which we know beats seconds (60 times) and for all practical purposes is 39.2 inches long. It calls for squaring the beat; multiplying by the length and dividing by the square of the desired pendulum.

Since 60 beats times 60 multiplied by 39.2 gives the figure of 141,120 we may just sort of forget the formal rule and instead just use that figure (141,120) and merely divide it by the square of the "given number" of beats, thus.

The required pendulum as per the example was 120. Square 120 and get 14,400. Divide that into 141,120 and it gives 9.8 inches, the length of a pendulum which will make 120 vibrations in one minute.

Let us say you have built your case and know approximately how long you wish the pendulum to be, but you do not know how many times that pendulum will beat (tick).

Rule: "Divide the constant number, 141,120 by the length you desire. The square root extracted from the quotient will be the number of vibrations in a minute."

If the desired length be 9.8 inches, divide that into 141,120 and get 14,400. Extract the square root and get 120 beats.

Specifically your problem is adapting a movement to some desired length pendulum. When you've ascertained as above how many times that pendulum will vibrate then you know how many escape teeth you have to drive past a fixed point to make the clock come to time. This is purely a "gearing" problem as you'll readily see. We shall stay with the example already used—120 beats per. min. Take your Gilbert clock with 30 teeth in its escape wheel. With each tooth making two beats, one revolution of it will produce 30 teeth times two or 60 beats. You require 120, therefore that escape wheel would have to make two revolutions per minute.

Looking at it another way: if your escape wheel must make two revs. in one minute it will have to make 60 times that or 120 revs. per hour. Thus, the escape arbor (staff) must be geared through the train at the ratio of 120 to one of the center post. Here is quite evident the why of the 30 teeth and 7 leaves of the pinion being insufficient as mentioned in paragraph two.

One other point. In all these pendulum problems the "length is from the point of suspension to the center of gravity of the pendulum, so don't allow it to confuse you when you may be thinking of the overall length. One bright spot in the picture is that you will be using an adjustable pendulum-ball with some latitude to screw it up or down, so if in calculating you have a small fraction it may be ignored because you can bring the clock to time by raising or lowering the ball. Back to the example; if it were missed by a pretty good margin, say 5 beats per minute, and actually required 125 beats instead of 120 the correct length would be 9.03 inches instead of 9.8.

GENERAL
REPAIR

BLINKING EYE

I have recently acquired an old Blinking Eye clock such as illustrated in the American Clock and Clockmaker Book on page 139 top left: The Continental.

Like other collectors or repairmen I will have to come to you for help. The movements are plainly stamped on the front plate "C. Jerome."

There are some parts missing which is quite a puzzle to me. The rod that operates the blinking eyes is missing and also there is no indication as to from what part of the movement this rod operates.

Could you give me this information? Also the size and weight of the rod with a drawing if possible. I might also need a hairspring as the old one is rusty.

A.

On practically all these "Blinking Eye" clocks, the eyes are operated with a very small wire, not a rod. In some the eyes rolled from left to right. Others sort of bat up and down. No doubt you can determine from the way the eyes are wired in, which way they blinked.

Now, examine the lever close. The movement usually mounts in such a position that the lever and balance wheel are on top—nearest the eyes; on some part of the lever, generally in the arm of the uppermost pallet, you should find a small hole. Try turning an "eye" in the end of a very small, stiff wire and inserting it thru this hole very much in the manner that the bellows lift wires operate in Cuckoo clocks, extend the wire upwards to the clock-eye mechanism and see if some method of operation isn't quite apparent.

You will note that the lever is counterbalanced, this is an effort to off-set the additional weight of the eye-operating wire and will at once suggest to you why that wire should be as light as possible.

Fitting a hairspring is the same old story, and in this case will have to border

upon the "cut & try." The old spring should give some indication of general strength, number of coils, etc. (in these old clocks they used fewer coils than today) ; one should be obtainable from your regular material house.

ANSONIA SWINGER

I am enclosing a photo of a Ansonia clock I picked up some time ago.

This clock appears to be a pendulum for another clock. The case measures about 4¼" in diameter, overall length is around 19". This movement is not of a very good grade. Inside of the case there is a small pendulum about 2½" long, but when this is moving the clock runs fast like an 8-day with the pendulum removed. So I was wondering if Clockwise would have an answer to this as there is no opening at the bottom of the case for an addition to this clock and there doesn't seem to be anything missing.

A.

No, your clock is not the pendulum from another clock. It is a type of swinging clock so-called because the entire clock acts as its own pendulum. I think this particular type originated in · France. Ansonia was building several variations of it around the turn of the century for we find more than a dozen styles illustrated in their 1907 catalog.

Apparently your clock has its suspension spring lost.

By looking with your loupe you can determine that the pin or arm from the ornament held by the statuettes is "original" but the repairman simply made a hook from an old wire coat hanger and looped it over. Actually these clocks were all hung with the upper case (right under VI) just as close to the pin or arm as possible and not touch.

CALENDAR CLOCK

Enclosed are two different views of a B. B. Lewis Calendar clock.

View No. 1 shows the clock, the upper dial is stamped E. INGRAHAM CALENDAR CLOCK, and the lower dial with PAT. 1876.

To me, it appears that a star type wheel and a rod or shaft are missing, as there is no means of causing the day hand and calendar portion of the clock to operate.

View No. 2 shows the inside of the clock. A wheel seems to be missing from mechanism A at point No. 2. This wheel should operate the star wheel B and also the calendar mechanism controlled by a lever at C point No. 1.

A.

Before attempting to answer the questions in your recent letter, I want to thank you for the photos and the details you set forth. They were most complete and therefore made it easier for us to definitely place your particular problem and to help you.

You should find that the pinion driven friction-tight over the hour-pipe, just in front of the front plate, is 16 m/m in diameter and has 18 leaves. Check this carefully and if it is correct there should be a post, riveted fast to the front plate, just 24 m/m (on centers) from the hour post.

Evidently, the only part lost from your assembly is a wheel that fitted over this post and is driven by the pinion on the hour-pipe. This wheel is 29.5 m/m in diameter and has 36 teeth. As your hour-pipe revolves twice per 24 hours this wheel revolves once per day. It operates the day of the week hand in the clock dial and the calendar mechanism in the lower dial as follows: Set into this wheel (which is cut from one solid piece of brass) about 12.5 m/m from the center is a small steel pin. By trial and error, cut this pin long enough to barely miss the clock dial when the top door is closed. By its one rev. per day it engages the brass star wheel one time,, thereby moving the day of the week hand forward one day—at mid-night.

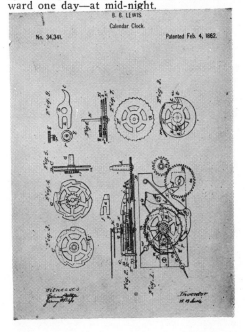

On this same pin, drive a small brass washer fitted friction-tight down against the wheel. The washer should be about the same thickness as the clock plates. Make

285

another washer and drive it on, leaving about one-sixteenth inch or more space between it and the first washer. In this space, between the two washers, hang a small wire with an "eye" turned up in your round nose pliers (wire about the size of the pendulum wire). Close the calendar door and from the back determine just where this wire reaches the calendar lever. Turn a stirrup in the wire at the proper point, and your job is completed. This stirrup with each rev. of the wheel will have an up and down travel of 25 m/m just the right amount to operate the calendar. Be sure that the stirrup is large enough and properly placed so that the calendar trip lever will enter each time the lower door is opened or closed. This will all come to you easily enough as you work out the job. While the back is off and you are fitting the calendar trip wire you may find it advisable to place one or two wire staples in the wood member between the doors to hold it in place and serve as a guide.

We would appreciate a line from you letting us know if the above works out satisfactorily. Should you discover that your pinion on the hour-pipe is more than 16 m/m in diameter, or that it has a different number of leaves—the above principal holds just the same—just alter the measurements to fit your case.

WAGON SPRING

I am repairing a 30-day wagon spring wall clock. Certain links in the chain are missing. While these can be made by hand, it is a slow process. I know that the blanks are made, but have been unable to locate the maker. Could you supply this information? If so, I would certainly appreciate it.

A.

We seriously doubt that links of the exact same size which could be included within your 30-day wagon spring clock chain you have are made today. You might locate a chain very near that originally used and put on a whole new one.

This type chain is known to the trade as "cable chain."

They formerly manufactured this type in a number of sizes.

At the moment we are overhauling one of these 30 day wagon spring movements and since only a couple of links are required, plan to make them. You do not outline your method of making links—I hope it is not tracing or marking each link upon a sheet of metal and sawing

them out with jewelers saw, then drilling. I take a bar of Stubbs steel, nearest in size and shape to the required link, shape an inch or more (required) of it to the exact size and shape of the link, drill, then with jewelers saw cut (like slicing) at the desired thickness, each cut makes one side for link already drilled.

PUNCH ARTIST

Now for Question No. 1: Recently one of your readers mentioned "punch artists" with disgust. Just what did he refer to? I have always understood that a bushing closed with a punch and broached out in the round was okay. I have seen clocks 75 years old with closed bushings still going strong.

I, of course, understand that a bushing which is too far gone must be replaced with a new one, but I am puzzled by the reference to "punch artists." Please enlighten me.

Question No. 2: There is one clock-maker whom you have not mentioned in your column, and I would appreciate any information you may provide regarding Elisha Manross, Bristol, Connecticut. The clock is a spring-wound brass clock in a steeple mantel case. It strikes hourly and runs 30 hours. The glass has a picture of Melrose Abbey painted on it.

Question No. 3: You already have mentioned F. Kroeber of New York, and I have his approximate dates. My question is regarding the regulator pendulum found on one of the Kroeber clocks. It is a Jacots regulator, with which you are probably familiar, and my question is as to whether or not these regulators were standard equipment on Kroeber clocks, or were they a patented regulator which could be bought and applied to any clock?

Question No. 4: Is it possible to determine the exact date or year in which a clock was made by a firm which was in business for 20 or 30 years, and if so, how is it done?

A.

There is a slight technicality involved in your No. 1 question, since the "closing-hole punch" is a "punch." Your interpretation was quite correct, however, when we refer to a "punch artist," it usually means that some joker has used a pointed punch, not a regular closing-hole punch, to crowd the metal in by pinking it forward as many times as he can haphazardly space it around the bearing hole—certainly a botch job if there ever was one. Hole closing with orthodox centering punches (made for that purpose) is quite all right if accurately and properly done on holes that are slightly worn; one must exercise good judgment—always inserting a new bushing when the hole is worn to excess, or enough to raise a question as to the original center.

In answer to Question No. 2, Elishe Manross was working as early as 1813. At that time he was making wooden clock parts for Chauncey Boardman, and he also made parts for Ortons & Preston and Boardman & Wells. He bought the Laporte Hubbell shop from Joseph Iver, and later built a factory near the center of Forrestville, Connecticut (about 1845). It failed in 1854, and sold out to E. N. Welch (now the Sessions Clock Company). He was in the firm of Manross & Wilcox about 1841, and in Manross, Pritchard & Co. from 1841 to 1844. He was possibly the first clockmaker in America to manufacture jeweled movements; he and his son, Newton S., devised methods and perfected machinery for making garnet jewels.

Replying to Question No. 3, we are indebted to Mr. Wesley Hallett of New York City, a serious student of American history, for the best available listing of dates on F. Kroeber. Searching files in the New York City library, he first located Kroeber, 1865-66, at 25 John Street (Residence 171 Elm Street). The final listing was: 1912, F. Kroeber, manager, 151 West 80th Street. I have in the files a half dozen patent copies of patents issued to Kroeber. The first was in 1877 and the last in 1894, but no copies cover a regulator similar to the Brocot. Have you any indication that he patented the regulator in question? Dates? I recall seeing at least two (slightly different) regulators on Kroeber clocks that would fit your description; however, neither gave any indi-

cation of patent dates, else we'd have copies in the file (if available).

I seriously doubt that Mr. Kroeber ever actually manufactured any clock movements. I have seen several in china cases belonging to the 1890's period that were quite definitely Ansonia, even though the back plate was stamped, "Kroeber." I think he had movements manufactured on contract, using his own patented attachments. Chances are, the regulator you refer to was never sold separately, but he might have licensed some of his manufacturers to use it on their clocks—either way, they would be factory applied.

And for Question No. 4, the answer is definitely *no*. When it comes to pinning a clock down to a definite year, one has a mighty hard job—even when you have a series of the firm's catalogues. Models ran over a period of years; sometimes a case of definite style and size may run five, or even ten and fifteen years.

ANSONIA MAINSPRING

We have on the bench an Ansonia regulator wall clock, with 12-inch dial. The over-all size of the clock is approximately 16 inches by 31 inches, and the label in the case reads, "Ansonia Clock Company, New York, Factory Brooklyn."

The clock has been run very little in its lifetime because both the time and strike springs "cock over" and cut into both the side plates of the clock, as well as the great wheels. The bearings are naturally very little worn because the clock has not been used. We have tried tying back the springs with wire, etc., to no avail—they still "cut in" and the clock stops.

A.

If and when one finds mainsprings "cocking over", biting into the clock frame or main-wheel, it is usually caused by an over-sized arbor hook, arbor hook too long, anchor post out of line, or worn bearings.

See that your arbor hook is barely long enough for a "positive" hook, that the post to which your spring is anchored is upright (that is, square with the movement frame) and that your winding arbor is upright and fits its bearings correctly. Put in *new* mainsprings. Once aligned, most

American springs working free in the frame this way give very little trouble.

REFINISHING BRASS PLATES

I have a Seth Thomas "French clock" bought about 1902. The case is made of brass, and I judge solid brass, holding the four glass panels. About half the entire brass surfaces are badly corroded.

Would you give me a step-by-step procedure for returning the brass surfaces to their original gold-like appearance?

I notice you suggest reshaping a clock spring. Mr. Samelius is against reshaping a watch spring. This comment is with no thought of putting you at swords' point with Mr. Samelius, but is stimulated by the same inquiring interest that has advanced me well beyond the average watchmaker. I work for the best interests of the individual watch, not for the seeming profits in "hit and run" watch repairing.

Perhaps the answer to the springs is in the difference in their thicknesses. The watch spring may be too susceptible to even a slight crimp, causing the spring to break in operation, while the clock spring is of so much greater thickness that it would satisfactorily resist crimping. Is this the right analysis?

A.

The basic thought back of finishing any corroded metal surface is to restore that surface to its original smoothness. When you commence to clean your case you will discover that the corroding process has pitted the metal. First you are going to have to establish a new flat and smooth surface. Obviously the pits (low spots) cannot be raised; therefore the high places will have to be leveled down to the lowest spot.

The shape and size of the piece to be handled, plus the depth of the corroded places, vary a great deal, yet they largely govern the method of doing the job.

Roughly, it's a grinding-honing-polishing operation—many small flat surfaces can be handled with a file followed by very fine India stone, and then to the polishing head with your croecus and rouge. On larger and heavier pieces, some type of "sanding belt" or powered grinder must be used.

It has been our experience that on jobs of this kind, it is both cheaper in the long run and more satisfactory to "farm it out" to a plating concern. We have no file on such shops in Bridgeport, but feel sure that you have them. The Cincinnati Plating & Repair Company, S. W. corner Thirteenth and Broadway, Cincinnati 10, Ohio, makes a specialty of refinishing such metal clock cases.

I appreciate your paragraph on mainsprings, but at the moment am not ready to advocate the same method for handling both watch springs and 8-day clock springs. Besides the great difference in size and length, I'm sure you have also noted the difference in temper and metal texture. The clock spring is wound once per week and the watch spring once per day—perhaps this would also enter into it.

METRONOME PENDULUM

No. 1: I have a metronome of which I am sending a sketch. The pendulum or weight that sets the speed swings to the right side too much. I realize this does not interfere with the time interval, as there is a mechanism inside that controls this. I have adjusted the adjusting screws inside, but to no avail — the weight still swings to the right side more than to the left. I have set it on a level place and also tilted it to the right and then it would be fine, but we want to have this setting right. Hope you can help me.

Problem No. 2: I love to repair clocks, alarms, etc., but on one I have now the alarm setting hand keeps moving when I turn the hour and minute hands clockwise. This is the only trouble I have with alarm clocks.

A.

No. 1: Your metronome problem is identical with that of any pendulum clock that is out of beat, save that in this instance the pendulum is inverted and attached directly to the verge arbor rather than being supported independently. We believe that you will find both the pendulum and the verge staked friction tight upon the arbor, and that one or the other, through use or abuse, has been shifted just a wee bit. The adjusting screws you refer to on your drawing are to line up the escapement rather than put it in beat. When properly aligned, your verge arbor should be in the same plane as the escape wheel.

Grasp the verge arbor with strong pliers or a hand vise and shift the pendulum slightly to the left; set the metronome on a level bench and listen to determine whether or not you have moved it far enough. With the mechanism in line and sitting level, it should be in beat and the pendulum should swing approximately the same on either side.

No. 2: The alarm setting is held in place by friction: when this friction wears light, or the tripping from use wears a notch at the point it jumps off, the alarm indicator hand is carried forward by the movement of the clock hands. On most alarms, the friction is on the back plate right under the setting knob. Either a nut screws down to increase the friction or a brass collar is staked on. In the first instance, hold the arbor between the plates by pliers and turn down this friction nut. In the latter case, remove the setting knob, select a punch that will fit over the arbor, and with the front (hand) end of the arbor supported upon the anvil, stake the collar down tighter. In some cases where the clock has seen long service and a notch has worn at the jump-off point, it will be necessary to file it out. After the filing, be sure to burnish the inclined plane so that the trip can ride out smoothly.

BROKEN RACK

I have an Ansonia clock made on the order of French clocks in glass cases, and it has rack-and-snail type strike. The part that holds the rack as it is lifted up is broken, and I can see no marks as to where to put the new piece.

Is there some way I could get a correct sketch of it, one showing how the whole setup should look? Or could I obtain a new piece to put in? What do you suggest?

A.

Ansonia ceased production just about the time of World War I, and in the 1920s the machinery was sold to Russia. There is no Ansonia material to be had now.

You say the pivot that holds (retains) the strike rack is broken. This we call the "retaining pin." It is a half-round brass pin about 2 mm. in diameter set into the lock-lever extending some 7.5 mm. above it (long). Strike questions are always "ticklish" and we'd best review the complete strike operation of this clock to make sure you get the required information. In Figures 1, 2 and 3 (see page 58), the lettering refers to the same parts. Figure 1 represents the back view of the back plate. Figure 2 shows the inside view the back plate, and Figure 3 is a skeletonized sketch omitting the plate. Holes for the pillar post are marked "X." "Z" is the time mainspring winding arbor and "Y" is the strike mainspring winding arbor. "A" is the lift lever, "B" the lock lever; "C" is the rack, and "D," the snail.

In the lock or rest position a pin is inserted in the strike (fourth wheel) back side, extending toward the back plate and resting securely against the end of the lock lever B. When the strike lift-pin (two mounted upon the center post, one for half and one for hour) raises the lift lever A, this in turn raises the lock lever B, thereby permitting the pin of the fourth strike wheel to slide under the end of the lock lever and travel about 170 degrees to lock on the top arm of the lift lever A. This is termed the "warn" operation, and takes place three to four minutes before the striking point.

This fourth wheel pin remains locked on lift lever A until the minute hand reaches the strike point (hour or half) when the lower arm of the lift lever drops off the strike lift pin, thereby lowering the upper lift lever arm and releasing the fourth wheel, permitting the strike train to run. During the warn operation, when the lock lever B was raised, the retaining pin in it also was raised; this allowed the rack to fall upon the snail if an hour strike, or against the No. 1 tooth of the rack if it is half-hour strike.

The back pivot of the third strike arbor extends through the back plate and has mounted upon it a 7-mm. disc in which are set three pins; this is the gathering pallet. As the strike train runs, this gathering pallet turns counter-clockwise, each

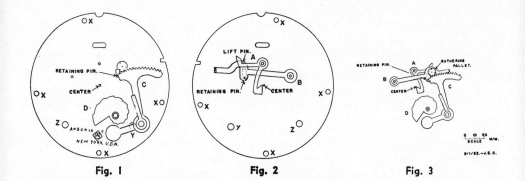

Fig. 1   **Fig. 2**   **Fig. 3**

pin gathering up one tooth of the rack. Three pins are mounted upon the third strike wheel to actuate the hammer tailpiece. Thus, as each pin of the gathering pallet ratchets up a tooth of the rack, the clock strikes one stroke.

The striking operation continues until the retaining pin drops off the end of the rack. This allows the lock lever B to fall to its original position where its end engages the pin in the fourth wheel, locking the strike train in the rest (original) position. It remains here for the next 30 minutes, then the lift and warn go through the same cycle again.

When setting up the Ansonia strike train, place the third wheel in position with the hammer tail positively clearing (dropping off) a lift pin. Set in the fourth wheel with the lock pin against the bent end of the lock lever B (rest lock position) and place the gathering pallet on its pivot so that both pins next to the rack clear it. This point must always be closely checked because if, the gathering pallet is not set to clear the rack, then when the lock lever B is raised, the rack will be prevented from falling to the snail D, and your clock will only make one stroke.

As I said above, strike questions are ticklish. We trust this will solve your problem, but

Repairing an Ansonia "Jim-Jam"

I am repairing an Ansonia "Jim-Jam" clock, and would like to ask for a little information.

This is a statue of one of the goddesses, I believe, who is holding the clock in her hand. The clock is a round ball, shaped like the world, with a long pendulum. The clock swings back and forth in the hand of the statue, with the aid of a suspension spring.

Inasmuch as I have no sample of these springs or how they are connected, I would like to know if you would have a diagram or something, showing how and where the springs are connected.

A.

The Ansonia swinging clock you refer to used a most unusual suspension arrangement consisting, actually, of four springs —two crossed at either end of the block.

This type of clock was first devised by a Frenchman, M. Guilmetin, about 1867. So far as we have been able to determine, he is the originator of this peculiar suspension. Ansonia made a great many of them in the "Gay 90's" and early 1900's.

STICKING HANDS

I have two clocks that stop once in a while. The hands seem rigid and then all of a sudden they let go, and the clock might run for weeks, or only a few days. One of the clocks is a grandfather Herschede and the other is an old-time Seth Thomas weight clock. The grandfather clock ran for weeks in my store and did not act up until delivered, but I ran it with the dial off, and I wonder if it could be that the trouble arises only when the dial is on, and what I should look for.

A.

Both your questions are most difficult—in fact, about the best I can do is a bit of guessing. After you have gone over a movement, I know that you caught any features evident and corrected them. On top of that, you indicate that the hands on both clocks pass through several 12-hour periods before hanging.

Let's "guess" at the grandfather clock first: Most of these Herschede clocks have a moon phase that is operated by a pin in the hour wheel. Have you checked that feature to make sure that the moon disc works freely, and that the pin actuating it matches in between the teeth properly? Sometimes the clockmaker will devote much attention to the time train pivots, etc., and completely overlook the dividing wheel (sometimes incorrectly called the intermediate wheel). It is that wheel and pinion driven by the minute pinion and driving the hour wheel, i.e., dividing the hours and minutes. In many of these grandfather clocks, the dividing wheel operated under a bridge or cock with a pivot hole in the plate and the top pivot hole in the cock. These holes can become worn, and the cock can be bent or twisted to one side, permitting a "hand bind" under certain conditions—check for this. Failure to strike, especially on a rack strike (Herschede's are rack) can cause the hands to bind when the snail tried to raise a rack which was not raised by the striking operation. Always check the strike train.

Your Seth Thomas weight piece has much less to cause the hands to bind

though it may be just as hard to locate. In these clocks, too, it is well to look to the dividing wheel. They have a rather mean arrangement whereby the hour pipe passed through the bearing in the front plate. Of course the minute arbor passes through the hour pipe, making a sort of bearing within a bearing. Now when the hole in the front plate wears, and a little extra load is thrown on the minute arbor, like lifting to strike, the hour wheel can be pushed aside into the worn spot and cause a hand bind. Check this front bearing and also both dividing wheel pivots.

I suggest that you might wire up the strike trip so that lifting it is eliminated; remove the verge to permit the train to run down freely, and then substitute for the regular weight, a weight just barely heavy enough to keep the train in motion. Observe closely through s e v e r a l run-downs. Obviously, this test is carried out with both hands on—often this method will show up a bind.

WEDGED RACK & SNAIL

I have a problem with a Gilbert quarter-hour strike mantel clock. It is the rack and snail type. After running two to three weeks, the rack and snail become wedged together at 12 o'clock on the cam, which stops the clock. I have tried many ways to correct this, but "no soap". Would you please give me an indication as to what my trouble is?

I also have a Hammond electric mantel clock (bichronous, type B-2). This clock runs very fast. It has a sort of damper or governor on the back. The clock was worked on before it was brought into my store. Therefore, I don't know if there is anything missing from the damper or not, this being the first of this type I've come in contact with. I feel quite sure all wheels are in the clock.

Could you give me any help on this problem?

A.

In almost every instance where the snail comes against the count-finger before the clock has completed the striking operation that lifts the count-finger out of the way, the clock stops. Sometimes the center friction is light and merely the hands stop moving while the clock moves on.

In those instances where such a condition does not interfere with the normal operation of the piece, either the long side of the snail or the count-finger (sometimes both) have been curved in such a way as to make the forward going of the snail raise the count-finger up and out of the way.

A condition where the snail can jam against the count-finger should not exist at all. Where it does, one of two things have happened . . . either the twelve stroke was not completed, thereby lifting the count-finger clear, or the warn-run trips a bit early, say ten or nine minutes before the strike point, and when the count-finger drops, it is so close to the high side of the snail, the forward motion of the snail through these ten or nine minutes is enough to cause the jamming. This latter condition can usually be remedied by setting the snail back (counterclockwise) just one tooth of the hour wheel in the dividing pinion.

This jamming point exists twice a day, noon and midnight, 14 times per week. You say it happens to the clock in question at the end of two or three weeks' running. Therefore, we must conclude that it is because the clock failed to complete the striking operation and lift the count-finger out of the way. Possibly your customer fails to wind up the strike side fully. Possibly he may have some system of counting the turns he gives the key. Let us say that he is winding the strike side 90 per cent by some such method, thus he loses about 10 per cent per week and at the end of the third week, he would get his clock wound only about 70 per cent, and it will stop striking before the end of the week. Regardless of at what hour the strike may cease, it would not be noticeable in this jamming feature until 12 o'clock is reached.

The governor of your Hammond B-2 bichronous clock does not play a part in the clock's timekeeping until the current goes off. During normal operation by the regular 60-cycle current, the speed at which the clock runs (keeps time) is regulated (controlled) by the cycles or alternations just as in any synchronous clock.

Now, when the current goes off, the spring-driven train takes over and propels the governor. Since this spring driving force is not always regulated, it is here the governor must exercise its function of governing or regulating the clock.

You will observe upon one end of this governor a small weight held by a flat spring whose tension is adjustable by a small screw. As the governor turns in normal operation, this little weight is held in place by the tension of its spring, but as soon as it speeds up a bit, the centrifugal pull increases, pulling it outside its normal trajectory, where it comes in contact with a "spring latch".

At the factory, the tension of this weight spring is adjusted upon the basis of the 60-cycle current; thus we shall take 60 revolutions of the governor as a basis to illustrate its adjustment. The spring tension is set up so that the weight will not swing out at 60 revolutions, nor at speeds of 61, 62, 63 and 64, but will come into play at 65. When it strikes the latch there is an instantaneous transfer of energy and the governor is knocked back down to 55 revolutions, a speed which is as much below normal as it was revolving when it struck above normal.

Since the governor does not operate while the clock runs synchronously, should it be gaining during the synchronous or current run, that gain cannot be traced to the governor.

It has been some 20 or 21 years since the bichronous movement was produced. With this much operation you are sure to find quite a bit of wear within the motor proper. We believe that you will find that both the synchronous motor pinion and the pinion driving the governor are of a construction unusual to most clock work, i.e., those pinions are hollow and have inserted at each end, fiber disc bearings. As they come at the point of highest revolutions, they are the points of greatest wear. Usually a good cleaning, plus a replacement of these bearings makes the clock good for more years of service.

The main bearings of the trains are a phenol product, vacuum impregnated with a mineral oil at the factory. Therefore, do not soak the plates in any cleaning solution

. . . a good job of wiping and pegging is sufficient. When assembling, use only a mineral oil, and sparingly at that.

400 DAY CLOCK BEATS

I have for repair a Kieninger & Obergfell 400-day spring-wound clock. How many beats a minute is this clock supposed to get? Is it eight or nine times a minute? What is the standard amount of beats a 400-day clock is supposed to have every minute?

A.

All the German 400-day clocks beat eight-to-the-minute, and thus your Kieninger & Obergfell beats eight times per sixty seconds. Sometimes repairmen count or beat in a suspension spring at the right eight beats per minute, and then upon observing that the clock is considerably off time, jump to the conclusion that possibly it might be seven or nine.

Naturally, when counting in a new suspension spring, much depends on the accuracy of the count. Even a poor count generally brings one within the scope of the regulator (always do it with the regulator set in the center) but with practice and care, using a two-minute count of 16, you hit it pretty close.

If, after an accurate count, your clock shows an error beyond the regulator, look for this error elsewhere. A losing time from the hands may indicate loose center friction—a gaining time could indicate escapement "loping" (several teeth at a stroke).

SANGAMO CLOCK REPAIR

About a month ago I took in a mantel clock for repairs, mostly cleaning. This clock was put out by Sangamo Company, with a 7-jewel Illinois escapement. It is an electrically wound clock and runs by a spring which will run for about 30 hours with electricity off. After cleaning the clock, I checked it for about a week and then turned it back to the owner. The clock kept excellent time. After the owner had the clock for several days, he came back and told me that it would gain as much as ten minutes per day. I asked him to return the clock to me and I would re-check it. He brought the clock back

the next morning, and in his presence, I plugged the clock in on the line and set it. He came back for several mornings to check the clock and each morning that he came in the clock was right on time.

He then took the clock back home and ran it for several days, and the clock would do the same thing—gain about ten minutes per day. The current is the same as here at the store, or at least it should be, but it doesn't seem to me that it would have any effect on the timekeeping, since the current doesn't do anything but wind the clock.

Can you give me some help on this? It has me puzzled. I have never had this experience before.

A.

Your question, as put, almost defies any explanation at all. You are correct in stating that the current (electric) merely winds the mainspring which drives the train and balance. Thus it is the balance and hairspring which regulate the clock, and the current has no connection with the rate at all.

We must presume that each and every part of the train and escapement is in order since the job has recently passed over your bench. Further, as the current merely winds the clock and this winding will be virtually the same by your shop current or the owner's home current, it is most difficult to even guess what quirk can take place to make the clock take a gaining rate at the owner's home.

First, reexamine the balance pivots and balance jewels. There is always the remote possibility of a rough pivot or a cracked jewel. The same might be in that end so that when you have the clock at your shop it is slightly tilted in the off direction, i.e., the principal weight is thrown to the good pivot or good jewel and the clock takes a fair rate, while in the hands of the owner, it is tilted in the other direction, bringing the rough parts into principal action, cutting down the motion and thereby producing a gaining rate.

Second, re-check the brake. There is upon these clocks a special brake, with leather face, which stops the winding motor when the mainspring is completely wound, but before it is overwound. It is possible that the stop adjustment upon this brake is not properly set and the clock continues to wind until the mainspring itself stops the motor, owing to the spring's pull becoming greater than the motor's strength. Now if you happen to be located in a building where the supply line is overloaded and your outlets are delivering a weak current with the above mentioned condition, the clock will not wind as hard (tight) as when the clock might be plugged into some residential circuit delivering full voltage. If this is the condition, then the extra winding could be causing the gain. I'm told that while 110-volts is the standard, many building outlets actually deliver from 102 to 106 volts, while some residential areas may register 112 or 113 volts.

Our experience with the Sangamo type you have has proven that much trouble arises from the brakes and brake adjustment. We have found many of these clocks to be without the single little ballbearing that originally goes at the end of the brake wheel. Many workmen are not familiar with the clock, take it down, and the little ball drops out. They do not know that it is supposed to go there; they never knew when they lost it, and therefore the clock goes up without it.

Study the entire brake mechanism closely. It consists of a threaded member upon the winding arbor. As the spring is wound, this threaded member screws inward. There is a yoke working under its outside flange which is pivoted to a pillar block on the opposite side of the plate. Back near the pivot point in the yoke arm is a leather-faced shoe, and when your spring is wound, pulling down the yoke arm, this applies the shoe to a solid brass wheel of the winding train. The opposite pivot to the brake shoe is the one running upon the single ball. The ball is at the end of the pivot just like a cap jewel.

The brake shoe itself is adjustable as its stem is threaded through the yoke arm. It may be screwed down to apply the stopping friction sooner, or screwed up so that the braking friction is applied later or nearer the end of the winding operation. Prior to setting the shoe, the winding arbor must be correctly set in the barrel. This operation is very similar to

the setting of the old Geneva stop works; that is, the threaded member must be screwed fully up (out) when the spring is at rest against the outside of its barrel. Its threading has been calculated correctly so that when the spring is wound it is screwed all the way down (in).

The brake shoe should be adjusted so that the clock is not overwound. Like the stop works, the brake should stop in about one complete turn from the very end (last).

Here is a tip: If the ball that acts as a thrust bearing under the brake wheel is missing, you can find a fair substitute in any cheap ball pen filler.

GUSTAV BECKER ESCAPEMENT

It is a pendulum movement from a grandfather type clock. I am also having trouble with a pendulum Westminster chime movement made by a "Gustav Becker" of Germany, and try as I might I have been unable to get proper depthing of the verge. The front plate has an adjustable bushing, but if I adjust to get a good pendulum oscillation, the receiving pallet gets hung up on an escape wheel tooth (not the same tooth each time). If I lessen the depthing, the pallets receive such a slight impulse that it is very difficult to keep it going, and I might also mention that the pallets are adjustable if it will give you a clue.

A.

As we recall, Gustav Becker used the same type movable pallets with off-center button for center distance adjustment between escape wheel and pallet arbor as they used in their 400-Day clocks. On the whole, these weren't of the highest order of accuracy. Often when we get one of these old clocks, the escape teeth are worn at their tips or have been "topped" by a former repairman. You state that the receiving pallet hangs on a tooth and that it isn't the same tooth each time; this might indicate that there is excess play in either the escape pivots, the pallet arbor pivots or both. As a starter make sure that the pivots fit just as snug as possible, and still be free to act, that all escape teeth are straight and of even length. This is a dead beat escapement and there is no advantage in having the escape tooth drop deep on the locking surface.

When the rceiving pallet hangs or touches the back of a tooth it indicates that the let-off pallet is set too deep, and you can see that the sooner the let-off pallet permits the escape wheel to turn forward, the sooner the tooth passing under the receiving pallet travels forward out of the way of the receiving pallet. You state that when you lessen the depth of the pallets they receive such a slight impulse it is very difficult to keep the clock going. This is an error because the entire impulse is across the face (or end) of the pallet, and you do not lessen or increase the impulse by changing depth. Chances are that when you set the depthing shallow you permit the escape tooth to drop on the impulse surface instead of on the locking (side) surface. Each tooth should just barely lock, i. e. drop on to the locking side of the pallet far enough above the corner to be positive. When setting an escapement, remember: drawing out the receiving pallet deepens the lock on both pallets, yet it deepens the lock more on the let-off pallet than on the receiving. Drawing out the let-off pallet has the opposite effect, deeping it more on the receiving than on the let-off pallet.

If you can spare the time to this job, and sometimes we simply have to do it on those that make so much trouble, I'd suggest that you get a copy of Ward L. Goodrich's "Modern Clock" and read especially chapter VIII "The Graham Dead Beat Escapement" and then following instructions for drawing it. Copy this escapement (Becker, that is), the escape wheel size, number of teeth, teeth included in the pallet span, etc., about four or six times actual size as per Goodrich's instructions, then I'm sure you will be able to correctly set up the escapement the very first try.

CALCULATING TRAIN

Trouble again. I got in a mantel clock, and after cleaning and starting, it would run fast. It had only a five-inch pendulum; I calculated the train, but it having an idler center threw me off in my figures.

$$\frac{60 \times 40 \times 40 \times 31}{8 \quad 7 \quad 8} \div 140904 =$$

pendulum length. Idler center 26?

I set the clock movement in an old grandmother case and put on an old wooden pendulum stick with a four-inch round pendulum. The clock is keeping time, but swings a 15⅜ inch pendulum to center of pendulum. This clock couldn't have been made for a short pendulum, could it? My customer said it used to run good years ago—escapement and all seem to be original, depthing good, etc.

Please give me the rule for calculating a train with an idler center. I have enclosed a rough sketch of the clock train. How heavy an Invar rod should one use to swing a 25- or 30-pound seconds pendulum, also the width, strength of suspension spring and length? Where can I obtain an Invar rod?

A.

Your method of counting the train is correct—that is for the second wheel of 60, and what you get is the proper beat if the second arbor were the center or hour post. One glance at the sketch and you will see that the second wheel does not turn once per hour, but only enough to drive the idle-center one revolution. Since your hour-center has twenty-six teeth, the second wheel of the train must turn exactly 26 of its 60 teeth in exactly 60 minutes (one hour).

The twenty-six teeth of the second wheel required to revolve the hands through one hour will at the same time turn the third pinion of eight (8) three and one fourth (3¼) turns. Now, 3¼ turns of the third wheel of forty (40) will put 130 teeth through the fourth pinion of seven (7), and revolve the fourth wheel of forty (40) eighteen and four-sevenths (18 4/7) times. 18 4/7 turns of the fourth wheel of 40 puts 743 6/7th teeth through the escape pinion. For practical purposes the six-sevenths being almost one, we'll call it 744. Now, 744 teeth will revolve the eight-leaf escape pinion ninety-three (93) revolutions. 93×31 teeth equals 2,883, times two beats per tooth equals 5,766 beats per hour. Divide by 60 minutes and get ninety-six and one-tenth (96 1/10th). Because on the other fraction we added, we can throw away this time and for practical purposes call it 96 beats per minute. Invariably these idle drive centers come up with fractions—remember, the nearer it is to the escape pinion the less it matters, and always you have the regulator nut at the bottom of the ball for the final regulation.

If this calculation be correct, then you require a pendulum that will beat ninety-six times per minute. Reid's rule for finding the length is: "Multiply the number of vibrations made in a minute by the standard or seconds pendulum (60) by itself which is squaring it, and this being multiplied by the standard length of 39.2 inches and this last product divided by the square of the number of vibrations by the pendulum whose length is required. The quotient will be the length of the pendulum in inches and decimal parts of an inch."

60x60 equals 3600 times 39.2 equals 141120.
96x96 equals 9216 divided into 141120.0 equals 10.9 inches.

As to size (diameter) of Invar rod, and width, length and strength of suspension spring, you have a very, very wide latitude to work within. The pendulum of pure theory has no weight in the rod, and no suspension spring at all. Thus you wish to use the smallest rod practical. Many of the grandfather (seconds pendulum) clocks we have to repair have entirely too much metal (weight) in the rod, and a suspension that is on the stiff side.

A suspension for a rather heavy pendulum-ball is better divided, that is, two springs like those found in French clocks. The general rule for a seconds pendulum of average weight is about .60 inch. That is, total width—this is made up of two springs each .15 inch wide with the space between them .30 inch. Total length about

1.5 inches. Make clamps of brass about 3/8-inch long—this will leave some 6/8-inch for the active spring portion. Make sure that your clamps are riveted tight so that no bend takes place beyond the edge of the clamps. Likewise see that the clamps fit very snug into the clock support and the pendulum rod end. Any movement or bending of the spring in the clamp or of the clamp in its fittings will upset a close rate.

Once you have your clock in operation you may make this test for its isochronism adjustment. By varying the weight or driving force observe whether or not the pendulum makes the long arcs and the short arcs in the same time. If the short arcs prove to be the slower, make your suspension a trifle thinner very near its bottom end. If the short arcs are fastest, reduce the spring near the top clamp. Care must be exercised when reducing the two springs, as such reduction must be the same else your pendulum will tend to wobble.

All that is required beyond being of sufficient safe strength to support the weight of the pendulum ball in a pendulum rod is enough rigidity so as not to bend or give when the impulse is given through the crutch fork.

ADJUSTING ANSONIA STRIKE

I have an 8-day Ansonia chime clock that had the chime spring broken and the coil spring on the chime lever missing. After repairing and making a new coil spring I cannot get the chime train to synchronize with the hour strike.

Please advise as to where to attach the free end of the coil spring and the amount of tension on the spring.

How do you set up the fly wheel trip and the chime train with the hour hand? I find that when the chime lever is tripped, the chime strike goes continuously.

A.

Judging from the sketch you sent me it appears that you may be calling a striking clock a chime clock—I have never seen this type of count finger in a quarter-hour chiming Ansonia.

The coil spring on the count finger serves to pull that count finger down into the locking (low) slot in the count wheel—I think that you are calling the outside end the "free" end. Since this spring must exert downward pressure on this arbor or count finger, the outside end is attached to the plate, front or back whichever is practical. The correct amount of tension is a matter of judgment on the part of the clockmaker—it must be enough to make the action positive and yet not enough to place a serious drag on the strike train.

The prime function of this count finger is to lock the strike train at the conclusion of the strike. Such locking is accomplished by another finger extending from this same arbor (your sketch indicates this) catching in the slot of the locking disc. During the strike the count finger falls in a shallow or high slot thereby holding the lock finger up above the slot in the locking disc; when the train completes the final stroke of the count, the count finger drops into a deep or low slot of the count wheel. This brings the lock finger down with it into the slot of the locking disc, thus locking (stopping) the strike train. Chapter 16 of Ward Goodrich's "The Modern Clock" goes into details and has half a dozen good drawings.

Your sketch indicated two other fingers on this same arbor in addition to the count and lock. One of these (the one nearest the back plate) is acted on by the center trip, i. e. it is by means of this finger that the center post raises the lock finger out of the locking disc and thereby releases the strike train—this action takes place near the fifty-five minute position of the minute hand. At the same time the center trip is turning this arbor, i. e. lifting all four fingers of the arbor, it therefore is raising the fourth finger, the warn-run lock finger.

There should be an arm on the fan-fly or a pin in that wheel that drives the fan-fly, and when raised this warn-run lock finger prevents the strike train from running. As said, the warn-run takes place about three to five minutes before the hour—the strike train stands unlocked, but held still by the warn-run lock finger.

Exactly on the hour (minute hand at 60) the lift finger drops off the center trip—this allows the arbor to turn all fingers downward, but during the warn-run the slot of the lock disc has moved past the locking finger. Therefore, the strike train must operate—the operation must continue until the count finger can drop into a low slot and lock it.

Now there are many adjustments you must look to in order to make this operation perform correctly. The relationship between the height of the lock finger and the count finger is critical; when the count finger rests in a high slot the lock finger must be just barely high enough to clear the slot in the lock disc as it revolves. On the other hand, when the count finger rests in the deep or low slot, it must lower the lock finger enough to catch into the lock disc. The count finger must drop clear—not touch either side—of the low or deep slot to make the action perfectly free. At the time the count finger drops into the low slot on the count wheel, the lock slot of the lock disc must come right under the lock finger in order for the train to lock. If the lock slot comes up too early or too late your train will not (cannot) lock properly, but will continue to strike.

Once the above is set, you must see that the warn-run is so set that it permits only a slight forward movement of the strike train—just enough to get the lock slot on the disc forward far enough so that when the center drops it, the lock finger falls just outside the slot and not in it.

CALCULATING S.T. TRAIN

I have in for repairs a Seth Thomas 8-day, hour strike wall clock that is giving me much trouble.

This clock runs ten minutes slow per hour. The movement seems to be original in every way, although when it was brought to me the pendulum bob was affixed about 1/3 up the distance of the pendulum rod (wood), but the rod does look original with the adjusting nut fixed to the bottom.

After putting the movement in order and returning the bob to its correct posi-

tion I timed the seconds hand (direct to the escape wheel) and it makes 80 beats per minute, one perfect rpm, but the clock runs slow, why? This seems to be a ¾ beat pendulum (22 inches long), escape wheel has 40 teeth, pinion (lantern), 8, next wheel 90 and 7, next 84 and 8—I did not count the main wheel.

A.

We fear that you have made some error, or else haven't given us the complete data on this clock. Wall clocks that strike are a bit rare, especially if it is a long pendulum —is it possible someone has installed a regular striking clock in this wall case?

The 40-tooth escape wheel in a regular wall clock generally indicates an 80 beat (22 inch pendulum); it should be 90 beats to be an exact three-quarter beat. You state that the wheel driving the escape has 90 teeth and a 7 leaf pinion, the wheel driving it has 84 teeth and 8 leaves, thus:

$$\frac{90 \times 84}{7 \times 8} = \frac{7,560}{56} = 135 \text{ revs. your escape}$$

arbor. 40 escape teeth times 135 revs. equals 5,400 teeth per one rev. of the 84 tooth wheel. 5,400 times 2 beats per tooth equals 10,800 beats per rev. of the 84. 10,800 beats per hour is 180 beats per minute; pendulum 4.3 inches long.

This calculation presumes the 84 wheel to be the hour wheel. If your hour wheel is auxiliary driven it could turn up almost anything, depending on which wheel drives it and what ratio. The 4.3 inch pendulum sounds like an ordinary mantel clock movement — please re-check your figures and give us a rough sketch showing the center and how driven.

To calculate the proper length pendulum for any clock one must know the required beats per minute — this you can determine by counting the train. That is, you wish to determine just how many escape wheel teeth past a fixed point in exactly one revolution of the hour post (wheel).

As each tooth makes two beats, multiply by two and the result is the number of beats per hour. Divide by 60 for the number of beats per minute, square the number of beats per minute, square the known length of the pendulum beating seconds 39.2 inches and divide.

SETH THOMAS #124

We have a Seth Thomas 'Legacy' clock for repair which has a No. 124 movement. After taking the movement down, we noticed that the time barrel arbor hole is not concentric with the barrel—by a long shot.

The time main wheel is smaller in diameter than the time barrel too, but because of the eccentricity of the arbor hole, the teeth extend far enough past the barrel to engage with the next wheel. The chime and the time trains have the same size barrels and apparently the two springs are the same length. The strike barrel is smaller.

Is it "kosher" to have the main arbor out of center with the barrel? Too, it seems to us that the time train in the No. 124 had the smaller barrel? Or haven't we been too observing?

A.

What you are referring to as a 'barrel' in the No. 124 S. T. chime clock is not a barrel at all, but rather a spring box. To all intents and purposes it only confines the spring as it unwinds, just the same as the pins attached to the plate do in the general run of open spring American clocks.

Since it is a box and not a barrel, there is no absolute necessity for it being concentric with the winding arbor. In the earlier model No. 124 chime, the main-spring boxes were mounted concentric (or nearly so) with the arbor. Now, since the engineers at S. T. saw fit to make this change, we take it that they must have seen no necessity for allowing (or making) the spring develop to one side.

If you have noted the pins mentioned above, usually two or three, they are never set equally distant from the arbor, but are placed so as to prevent the unwinding spring from developing against another arbor, the strike hammer, etc.

In general, in timepieces you have two types of barrels—1. the going barrel; in this type the driving gear is cut on the barrel and it turns (goes) as the piece runs—the arbor turns only when the spring is being wound. 2. the motor barrel; on this type the mainwheel is separate from the barrel and turns with the arbor as the piece runs, the barrel remaining stationary and turning only when the spring is being wound. Here we note that both types' barrel turn at some time or other; a spring box never turns at any time—it is riveted fast to the plate.

SILK SUSPENSION SPRING

The clock in question is a French clock, round movement, about 4 inches in diameter, 8-day strike. Name on the back plate is, "Guyenot A Paris, No. 740. This clock has no pendulum bob and no suspension spring (if that is what it takes). However, regarding the latter, I see no place to attach same, as on the very top there is a regulating rod coming through, with a hole on the rear end. This is about one-half inch higher than another rod riveted onto the rear plate. This has two small holes, henceforth I cannot understand where the suspension spring is to be hung, if that is what is needed in this instance.

Attached to the verge is a wire which extends out and down for about three inches. This is at the end, bent away from the movement. At right angles to the wire is a flat segment of brass with a long, recetangular slit cut in it. It is open at the end, no doubt to allow for entry of the suspension spring, or whatever it may be that should go through.

A.

You have a "French Silk Suspension." These clocks never had the conventional suspension spring. This was a popular method of manufacture with the French up until Achille Brocot, around 1833, invented his now very famous suspension spring with means for adjusting (regulating) from the front of the dial.

Take a small silk thread; pass it through the hole in the regulating staff, down through the hole in the post riveted to the plate. Form a loop approximately one inch long; bring the thread up and tie in the hole in the riveted staff back next to the back plate. Now turn the regulating staff and it will reel up the loop until it is only about a half-inch below the staff riveted to the back plate. Your pendulum merely hooks into this loop. Thus to regulate the

piece, you take up the loop to shorten (fast) the pendulum, or let out on it to lengthen (slow) the pendulum.

Quite naturally these pendulums show a wide difference in both length and weight. Anything I might say is just a "fair guess." The length you can (and will) determine by timing the clock. In the weight, you have a wide latitude, i. e., it is not critical. To one accustomed to handling American clocks, and even French clocks of later construction, all these silk suspended pendulums seem to be on the very light side. Generally the pendulum ball was a little larger than a quarter and a little less than the fifty-cent piece—the same goes for thickness. Turn up a piece of brass about that size, drill it from the edge to take a small wire, 20 or 22-gauge.

Take a small rectangular piece of brass about three-quarters of an inch long and file it to fit the crutch segment of your verge (a loose fit). Then polish it and drill from the end and slip it over the pendulum wire. Both this piece and the pendulum ball should fit friction-tight—tight enough to stay in place on the wire while you are timing the clock. Bend a little hook in the top end of the wire and hang the completed pendulum on the clock.

Position the rectangular piece on the pendulum wire so that the crutch segment of the verge will work about the midway point, and start the clock running. Bring it to time by raising or lowering the ball by sliding it on its wire. Now with the piece approximately "on time," take your pendulum off and lay the ball on an anvil. Take a pointed punch and strike one sharp blow right over the wire, to make the ball fast to the wire. Do the same (either extreme top or extreme bottom) to the little rectangle of brass. We now have the clock practically "on time" and there is no occasion for further moving of the ball.

The final (fine) regulation is had by taking up or letting out the silk loop. With the little brass square centered in the crutch-piece, a slight raising or lowering still keeps the crutch-piece upon it

Correcting faulty Revere strike

I have a Telechron motored Revere clock, Cincinnati, Ohio, model 161314, self adjusting, quarterly chime and strike. The chimes work O. K., but the strike does not work right. I am sending you a rough sketch of my trouble.

At two o'clock the clock strikes once. The rack does not fall accurately and the rack hook doesn't drop into the correct tooth. The hook drops into the first tooth at 10 'til 2. At two o'clock it's at the correct spot near the snail step, but it drops too soon in the first tooth and strikes once. I lift the rack and it drops into the second tooth and works O. K. I set the hour snail and wheel one tooth clockwise. It works O. K. at two, then I have the same trouble at 12 when it strikes only 11. Other hours the strike works all right. Can you please tell me where the trouble is?

A.

Your effort to advance the snail clockwise by one tooth of the hour wheel over the dividing wheel was indicated and a step in the right direction, but since by so doing it clipped the twelfth stroke off the 12, it is plain that the step was too big.

First, we think that your strike train is dropping the rack-arm a bit too early since you say at ten minutes before the hour. Make the strike train lock just a tiny bit deeper so that the dropping action takes place around five minutes to the hour, then there will be considerably less travel of the snail between the drop and the strike.

You may advance (or retard) the snail by smaller steps than one tooth of the hour-wheel by doing it between the dividing wheel and center (cannon) pinion instead of between the hour-wheel and the dividing wheel. After setting the strike train so that the drop takes place around five minutes to the hour, turn the hands to the twelve o'clock position; this allows the rack-arm to fall into the lowest (12) notch of the snail.

Slip both the hour-pipe and the dividing wheel forward 'til you can revolve the dividing wheel barely free of the center pinion and adjust the snail so that the tip of the rack-arm rests in the center of the low notch, press the hour-pipe and dividing wheel back into position, pin the dividing wheel washer and allow the clock to strike the 12. Advance the hands to one o'clock; the rack-arm should drop mid-way of the high or one o'clock notch.

Question of Regulating

Subject: Regulating Clocks.

I make a motion that your column instigate a movement to get the clock manufacturers to stamp the number of ticks per minute on all pendulum movements manufactured. The reason: Many hours of time lost by the repairman in regulation would be saved.

By using a stop-watch and knowing the number of ticks per minute, the time spent on regulation would only be about ten minutes at the most. We have learned this method and its usefulness regulating 400-day clocks.

No practical timing machine has been developed for regulating clocks due to the many variations of pendulum lengths.

I believe the stamping of the number of ticks per minute on the clock plate, where it is visible to the repairman, is just as important as the label on an electric motor which states the voltage and the number of revolutions per minute.

May I have your opinion?

A.

First, it can not apply to the millions of clocks now in circulation. Second, to all practical intents and purposes there are no pendulum clocks being manufactured in America today. Let's hope that someone will come up with a quick, sure and practical method of determining the beat of any clock. It might not be a bad idea if we clock repairers would make a practice of scratching upon the back plate of clocks which we do have occasion to determine the beat of, while repairing them. It could come in very handy when next the piece makes a trip to the shop.

Actually, one can now rate pendulum clocks by devious methods and some improvisation after determining the required "beat" on the watch rate recorder. It requires far more time than the results warrant because the workman can do a couple of other jobs while counting and improvising, so why not set the old clock upon the shelf and turn out those jobs, having a look-see at the rate 24 hours later?

Correcting old S. T. strike

However, my present trouble is a regular old eight-day Seth Thomas hour and half-hour strike. The clock is in excellent condition and runs well. I did not take it down to clean it—so I know I didn't disturb anything.

My problem is that the clock starts to strike on the hour and will not stop. I bent the finger on the count wheel to drop in the slot and now it just strikes once on each hour and half-hour. Can you give me some pointers on how to restore the strike to normal?

A.

Seth Thomas made many models of eight-day, spring driven, striking, mantel clocks. Many have slightly different striking trains, yet practically all operate along the same basic principle. You do not mention which movement you are having trouble with.

The No. 89 was very popular. This movement ran through many variations, all the way down to about "89-M." The letters or combinations of letters, such as 89-AD, 89-LA, etc., indicated a different center gearing to accomodate different pendulum lengths, different striking, etc.

The No. 89 was a five-arbor strike train. The count wheel operated concentric with the second arbor; locking plate and count advancing pin on the third arbor; warn-run latch pin on fourth arbor. Of course, the fifth arbor was the fan-fly.

When setting up these strike trains (any strike train) you should work from the lock position—the position of all members of the strike train as it rests in its locked position, beginning with the first or winding arbor. The first (main) arbor and the fifth (fan-fly) arbor do not enter into the run, strike and lock operation, and therefore may be set in any position. Thus, you are concerned only with setting (correctly) the second, third and fourth arbors. After placing the first, then the second arbor—on this wheel are the hammer lift pins. Revolve the second wheel until the hammer has just dropped off a lift-pin, this being the position it remains in while at "rest" (locked). Next, turn the count wheel so that the count-finger rests in the bottom of one of the deep lock-notches.

Now set in the third arbor so that the lift finger rests in the bottom of the notch in the locking plate. Next set in the fourth arbor so that the warn-run lock pin rests approximately one-fourth of a turn of the fourth wheel away from the warn-run lock wire. That is, when the center arbor raises the strike trip, this pin will permit the fourth wheel to turn about a fourth of a turn before it locks against the warn-run wire.

Naturally, all of the above takes for granted that your lift wire, count finger and warn-run lock wire have not been bent out of "true." Usually, they have, but that is no cause for despair. Actually, you have quite a bit of latitude in adjusting (bending) the wires. The lock-plate on the third arbor is friction tight, and may be advanced or retarded (slightly) to effect perfect locking.

The strike release wires (two on the same arbor—one raised by the center post, the other raises the lock-wire and count finger) may be bent to release early or later as the need may indicate. After all is said and done, setting in the strike train is still something of a "cut and try" operation. The main thing to do is study each member and make sure you know its precise function.

Vibrating second hand

I have a clock in my care I would like your advice on. It is a second beat pin wheel escape with sweep second. I have serviced this clock for the past ten or more years. It did not have the second hand on until just recently. I overhauled it and got a hand I could use by altering it somewhat.

The hand I installed is a counter balanced hand, but at each beat it bounces enough to be noticeable and I am at a loss to remedy the situation. It runs good and regulates to a good rate. The dial wheels run on a fixed post and the escape pinion is extended through this post to carry the sweep hand, and uses a screwed-in bushing for the front bearing. I will appreciate your advice.

A.

Vibration of these long sweep-second hands on pin regulators can (and often does) stop the clock, if it happens to be in exact tune with the escapement. That is, if it vibrates so as to be in the backward swing at the time the escape wheel should be impulsing the pendulum.

You say your clock runs and rates well, so evidently you are only bothered with the annoyance of seeing the hand oscillate between seconds marks.

Possibly the pointer portion of your hand is the same or very nearly the same size all the way out. Much of this whiplash effect can be overcome by having a tapered hand. Then, there is a certain relation between your counter balance and your pointer end. It is usually better to try shortening the counter balance end a little. This will require a little additional weight to have the hand in perfect poise. Either one or a combination of the above alterations should remedy your trouble.

Atmos principle

First, what is the principle on which the new Atmos so-called "perpetual motion clock" works? According to the sales literature, the change of room temperature provides the driving energy, but in a modern house where temperatures are thermostatically maintained at nearly a constant point, it seems difficult to believe that sufficient energy would be generated. Do you have any special advice on the repair of these clocks?

Second, what is the objection to using ordinary white gasoline for cleaning clocks where the movement is not exposed to view? If the movement is taken apart, scrubbed in gasoline, pivot-holes pegged out, pivots polished, and all parts dried in an oven, I cannot see any reason why brass and steel parts must be shined when they are never exposed to view. However, if you think the soap and ammonia formulas are essential, what rinse do you recommend?

A.

If you've examined the Atmos closely, you discovered a double ratchet-click, and that the teeth of the ratchet are pretty fine. Now, with two clicks (they are not synchronized) it is possible for this clock to wind by just one half ratchet tooth. The normal minimum running reservoir of spring power in the Atmos clock is one year. Put these two facts together and you can readily see that temperature variations can easily keep it running.

Regarding repairing: A. H. & J. published as lead article in the June, 1952 issue, "How to Repair Atmos—The Perpetual Motion Clock." Vacheron & Constantin, Le Coultre Watches, Inc., 580 Fifth Avenue, New York 19, New York publishes a little booklet for watch and clockmakers, "How to Repair Atmos."

White gasoline leaves a thin film on anything cleaned in it. This film does two things—it has a tendency to contaminate the fresh oil you apply and it has a tendency to make the oil crawl or creep away from the pivots. It does not matter whether the parts are exposed to view or not, the prime object of having steel and brass parts "shine" is that it indicates to the repairman that the piece is thoroughly clean, that there is no remaining parrafin or chemical to contaminate your lubricant.

Soap and ammonia formula do this much better than white gasoline, naphtha, etc. From these cleaners, the work should be quickly rinsed under hot running water, then in alcohol and dried in warm boxwood sawdust.

Has trouble regulating "Golden Vision" clock

May I have your advice on a clock which I have for repairs and which has proved a bit puzzling. This is a Haddon "Golden Vision" Model 70. The trouble I have is the minute hand will skip occasionally. I located the error by hearing a slight click and just by touching the hand it will slip into another notch on the ring which carries it. By increasing the friction on the little spring at the end of the hand it also increases the friction on the center post. If you can help me there it will be greatly appreciated.

A.

The trouble you have encountered in the "Golden Vision" clock is quite common due to its peculiar construction plus its running of like metals, (brass upon brass) together, and increasing the spring tension at the tip of the minute hand is adding fuel to the fire despite the fact it may make the hand keep up for a few days or weeks.

Friction at the hand center becomes greater than that of the spring upon the revolving rim and thus the rim being driven by the electric motor moves ahead of the hand.

Remove the base in order to allow taking out the retaining frame at the back— this releases the glass center, etc.; then take off the hands and inspect the bearings of both minute and hour hand—if scored, polish them. When replacing the hands use a good light grease   With the glass center out of the clock there is no contact (tension) upon the hands; they should turn so freely that with the dial in horizontal position you are able to blow the minute around with light breath.

The trade name of the battery clock you mention is "Elix."

PROBLEM WITH CHAIN

The name is not clear, but looks like "W. Mueller, Halifax." The sweep second hand turns counter-clockwise and it runs with one chain and one weight for both the time and the strike.

My problem is that the chain keeps jumping off the gears. What can be done to prevent this?

A.

Your "W. Mueller, Halifax" clock intrigues me because I fail to find this maker listed. The only Mueller located for the Western Hemisphere is "Frederick" at Savannah, Ga., about 1747. Very little is known about him save that his clocks were "rope drive" and he probably made the wood wag-on-wall type.

It is odd that your sweep-seconds should operate to the left; that one weight should operate two trains — what is generally known as the "Huygens Fall" system was used with both chain and rope. If the points in the main or sprocket wheels of your clock give any indication of having been real sharp, that could indicate that it was originally intended to operate by rope.

In most instances where the chain persists in jumping off, we find that a new chain whose links are incorrectly spaced to fit the sprocket has been substituted. Naturally, the overall size of the links must be such as to about fit the groove. In addition, the number of links per inch must match the prongs of the main-wheel. That is, when a prong or spike fits within a link the next link, being at right angles, works "free" and the next link by reason of size must come just right so that it fits upon the next spike. By bending a piece of paper around your main-wheel you can determine the number of spikes per inch as it turns, and thus deduce the number of links per inch that the proper chain should have.

ADJUSTING S.T. STRIKE

I have a Seth Thomas No. 4602, 8-day, pendlum, striking clock in for repair. It had a broken spring on the strike side to begin with. In assembling this clock everything went nicely until I came to the self-correcting device of the striking.

What is the striking sequence, how does it strike the quarters, etc.? This clock has three rods in the base of the case. On the back of the clock movement there is a cam on the center arbor and a lever on the gathering rack arbor that work in conjunction, each having a collar and set screw for adjustment upon their respective arbors. It seems to me that in adjusting these two is where I am having trouble, but I am not sure, it could be elsewhere.

What should the width, strength, and length of the springs be for striking and time for this clock. I am sure that you are very familiar with this Seth Thomas movement and can give me some information on adjusting the striking.

Also, what length of time do you think a clock spring can be carried in stock if it is well protected, and still be usable?

A.

Your clock is generally known as one that "ding-dongs" the quarters, i.e., at the first quarter (15 minutes after the hour) it should strike one "ding" and one "dong." At two quarters (the half-hour) it should ding-dong twice, and at the third quarter (45 minutes after the hour) it should ding-dong three times.

It does not have what we usually have in mind when we refer to a "self-corrector." The self-corrector is to be found upon chiming clocks and operates to correct the chiming mechanism so that it will chime the correct quarter tune at the correct time.

Your clock uses the rack-and-snail method for its hour and also for its quarter strokes since both are struck by the same train. The cam-like arrangement upon the back of the center-post serves to hold up the ding hammer so that same does not enter into the hour striking. The snail has three notches or steps between each hour notch for counting the quarters.

Place the minute hand upon the centerpost so that the long side of the cam is in position to hold up the ding hammer, and the hand points to the XII position. This puts the minute hand and cam in position for the hour stroke. Adjust the snail so that your strike rack falls freely into the deepest, or XII notch and make it fast there. Now, when you advance the minute hand to the 15-minute (III) position, the cam will have turned far enough forward to release the ding hammer; the rack will fall into the first or high little notch after the XII and your clock should strike "ding-dong." Advance it to the half spot (VI) and the rack drops into the second little notch, resulting in "ding-dong, ding-dong." At three quarters, the sound should be "ding-dong, ding-dong, ding-dong" and when the minute hand returns to XII the cam has raised the hammer, the rack drops into the highest hour notch and your clock strikes "dong" for 1 o'clock.

The same spring you've always used in the old No. 89 movement works in this model, $7/8$ inch by .018 inch thick by 10 feet long, loop-end.

How long a spring can be carried in stock is difficult to answer in a brief and concise way. Basically, age alone doesn't seem to hurt springs . . . springs lying dormant are less likely to crystalize than one in use being bent back and forth. I would think it would depend a great deal upon the particular texture of the steel, and how closely it is coiled. Anyone accustomed to handling springs, either watch or clock, pretty soon becomes adept at determing when a spring is "set." I'd lots rather trust such judgment instead of any rule trying to pin-point any certain period in which a spring must be used.

I've always advocated (and practiced) straightening springs out, save the last couple of inner coils, for cleaning and inspection. Same should be done with new springs right out of the clamp. The spring should be wiped thoroughly clean and any rough or rusty spots polished out. Your own better judgment should tell you pretty accurately whether of not the spring has lost any of its elasticity (become set).

Seeming lack of power in a strike spring is not always a sure-fire sign that your spring is set. Lubrication (oil) that is too light and quickly squeezed out from between the coils can be one trouble. A strike train set in so that it locks with the lifting pin in contact with the hammer tail-lift will act sluggish simply because the train has moved forward a tiny bit with the let-off run. Then when the trip drops for the hour strike, your train has to start from a dead stop with a full load upon it.

Check these two points before discarding any spring you may feel is too weak. Any time when replacing a new spring, if the spring taken out of the clamp seems sluggish enough to create a doubt, it is better to discard it and get another spring with more pep than to have to take the clock down again. Springs come cheaper than your time.

ADJUSTING ANSONIA STRIKE

Could you give me any information on how to straighten out this strike clock? It is a small Ansonia movement.

I cleaned and adjusted it; everything seems to be in line, but it won't kick-off on its own power. I can run the hour hand around with my finger, and it kicks off perfectly, but on its own it just doesn't strike.

I can't see anything out of place. What has me puzzled is why it will strike when I'm running the hand around, and won't strike when it gets to the half hour and hour marks on its own. This movement is a rack type with round plates. I can't find a number on it, but it has a mark, a large "A" in a diamond shaped frame, on the plate, and on the adjusting wheel is engraved "Pat. 1866."

A.

Practically all the round plate Ansonias were the same—minor changes were made over the years but the basic design remained the same. We shall mention one of those changes later.

Apparently your clock is "sticking" on the "warn" run. Or, your lift is so very shallow that when the clock operates itself it does not lift high enough to unlatch, whereas, when you chase the hands around with your finger at a faster clip the lift rises sufficiently to unlatch.

Set your clock in operation. Allow it to run past the strike point, then examine closely—if the lock-pin remains in the lock position then it hasn't been raised high enough to unlatch. If the lock-pin has passed beyond the lock posi-

tion then it must rest against the warn run latch, and since it did not strike, it must be because the warn run latch did not drop and permit completion of the strike operation.

In this Ansonia clock—as you face the front plate and look at the inside of the back plate—you will see a lever (of odd shape), pivoted in the back plate, just above and to your right of the center post.

As the hands (center post) turn, the strike lift upon the center post engages this lever underneath and to the left of center, raising it. It, in turn, raises the strike lock approximately three to five minutes before the hour. Now, the strike train being released, the lock-pin continues forward, but the clock can't strike because it comes to rest upon the end of the above lever. This is called the "warn run." The lever is held up against the lock pin until it (the lever) drops off at the exact warn run position.

In all the models, the lift lever was pivoted upon a post in the back plate, above, and to the right of center—held on the post by a friction boss (washer) staked on tight. This rarely is ever taken off for cleaning and thus gets sticky and will not fall by gravity after the lift pin passes under it. In many of the later models there was applied to this lever a light brass spring to throw it down. If your clock originally had this spring such will be indicated by a little hook extending out of the lever hub to your right.

In the older models without spring, the hub was perfectly round. You may attach a light spring to either model—in the one operating without a spring, generally removing the lever —cleaning the hub bearing thoroughly, and cleaning and polishing the post will remedy the trouble.

WINDING CORD NOT TRACKING

I am working on a Chauncey Jerome brass movement weight driven striking clock which has been causing me a lot of trouble. I repaired the lantern pinion as you instructed and am very pleased with the results.

Now my problem seems elementary (Dr. Watson!), but in all the years of reading your department since May of 1947, never have I seen this condition arise. . . . In winding the strike side, the gut cord does not follow nicely, but crowds toward the front of the movement, finally riding on the end of the drum, out on the arbor.

The time side causes no trouble.

I started out with a medium cord, but switched to a lighter, thinking it might perform better. If you can straighten this one out, I shall be very grateful.

A.

Either your movement tilts backward in its case, throwing the front end of the "spool" up, or the axial upon which the pulley runs is lower at the front, causing the pulley to drift forward.

Since the strike side spools on correctly, chances are the movement is level and your trouble lies with the time pulley axial.

Smooth spooling is basically a matter of alignment; the pulley axial should be both level and in line with the spool or drum. The pulley itself must be true and have a free run upon its axial.

Sometimes the hole-bearing in these wooden pulleys becomes worn allowing it to wobble; this can upset the spooling of the cord. We sometimes find it necessary to re-bush the old pulley or even make a new one. In either instance, the pulley should be forced, friction tight, upon a piece of stubbs steel wire, chucked in the lathe and have its groove touched up with a sharp graver just to make sure that it runs "true."

ERRATIC TIMEKEEPING

I have a regular Seth Thomas eight-day mantel clock. I have just cleaned and repaired it.

I find that for the first few days after winding it up tight the clock gains. After running for a while on toward the end of the week it will start losing. This is two eight-day clocks that have given me trouble in this respect.

I have "The Modern Clock" by Goodrich but find nothing in this book to indicate the trouble. Will you please tell me how this can be corrected.

A.

If you'll restudy Goodrich, we believe you may discover partial answers to your question at several spots. For instance, 3rd paragraph, page 274: "A rough mainspring will lose one-third of its power from coil friction, and in certain instances even one-half." Another, page 85: "In such a case thinning the spring (suspension) will require the bob to be raised a little, and also give a better motion."

Perhaps there is no one, specific answer to your problem simply because any one of several things can contribute to, or cause the effect you note.

First off, you rarely ever get one of these old clocks in anything near its original state — springs have been replaced, verges are worn (even replaced), new pendulum wires (and spring) put in, and then there is the wear evident at every point.

Begin with the mainspring—make sure it is not set, and above all, perfectly smooth. Springs in the common mantel always run "open"—they have plenty of room to expand, so a little over-length is better than being just barely long enough to drive the clock eight days. After all, you wind it every seventh day, and thus do not utilize the very weak end running.

We shall assume that your train is in good order and go on to the escapement. Check this closely; make sure that the verge is set "in" to the wheel to its full working depth; that the pallet angles are about correct and especially that they are smooth and polished (no pits). The escape-wheel bearing must fit snug—no "up and down" to absorb part of the power. Any looseness or wobble in the suspension spring anchor will cause trouble. Last but not least the crutch wire must fit snug and the pendulum wire at this point ought to be smooth and polished. Last reference to Goodrich, note page 84, 2nd paragraph, how it is possible to improve the isochronal action of the pendulum by thinning the suspension spring either above or below its center depending upon what action is desired. I've found that with the common, eight-day, mantel clock the same results may be obtained by trimming the edges a bit with good shears; since their suspension springs have no chocks, this is easy. Instead of thinning at the top, just taper it upwards. Instead of thinning it at bottom, taper it upwards.

FAN WHEEL RATTLE

The following is another "gimick" that we've used many · times, but, of entirely different type. The clockmaker is faced with problems that the watchmaker never hears, and, this is one of them. Many owners of fine old clocks who have them repaired and keep them running for sentimental reasons, etc., object to any excess noise the fan-fly may make or the speed at which the clock strikes (sometimes, both). I've always had the feeling that perhaps these old clocks did a good bit of "rattling" when they were new and nearly every experienced repairman has found for himself (the hard way) that the mere re-bushing of the strike train, i.e. getting the closest fit possible in the bearings will not, in many instances, eliminate the excess 'grinding' complained about.

After closing the bearings, look to the fan-fly pinion—99 & 44/100's of them are the lantern type, and, will show some wear. Most, definitely need re-filling; that is new staves. Never use needles—because they are not round—use common Stubbs steel wire: select a size fully as large as the old staves; a thousandth or two larger won't hurt. If the holes in the pinion heads show excessive wear, make new heads being careful to maintain the same pitch circle as the old pinion. See Fig. 1.

Making new lantern pinion heads may be a bit time consuming, but it is not at all difficult, and, does not require any special equipment. Your lathe already has a sixty (60) stop division located in the pulley, most fan-fly pinions are either 5 or 6 staves, thus it comes easy. Select a brass rod whose outside diameter is the same as the outside diameter of the desired head—chuck it up and scribe the correct pitch circle; drill the center hole (correct size for friction fit to fan-fly arbor), set the "T" rest to the exact center level and with a fine point scribe the five or six divisions across the pitch circle—set the point exactly where the division crosses the pitch circle and tap with hammer to make a sink for starting the drill accurately. Drill to a depth a little less than twice the thickness of one head, then, with the brass stock still in the lathe, mark the thickness of the first head and saw off with fine jewelers saw with lathe running slow—mark second head and saw off in the same way.

We've noted some repairmen with an idea that the pinions should roll. There is such a thing as "rolling" lantern pinions; they were only used upon the very early clocks and but few are around to-day. If the stave was meant to roll, it can always be noted because the rolling type stave had 'pivots' and/or stepped shoulders. Where the wire stave is the same diameter all the way it was meant to remain tight, thus when bradding the stave in at the open head do not hesitate to pound the brass in good and tight. Less there be some question about the pitch circle, see Fig. 1.

Fig. 1.
LANTERN PINION HEAD.
(ENLARGED)
PITCH CIRCLE INDICATED
BY DOTTED LINE.

Even with snug fitting bearings and a new lantern pinion the objectionable rattle still persists in some instances—if it does; try turning the wheel, that drives the fan-fly, over. Thus driving the fan-fly pinion with the un-worn side of the teeth. The center distances in the common garden variety of American clock were never ultra-accurate; regardless of whether or not they were accurate in the first place, bushing (or closing) and a new pinion may have altered them some—a bit of adjustment may be in order. See Fig. 2.

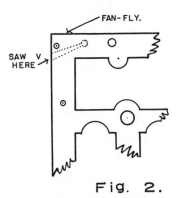

Fig. 2.
UPPER QUARTER OF S.T.
30 HOUR WT. FRONT PLATE.

This sketch was made from the familiar, Seth Thomas, 30-hour weight driven movement, however, most clocks have their fan-fly bearings located near the top, outside corner of the plate making the same type operation possible upon most clocks. Fortunately, the fan-fly pinion is always at one end of the arbor making only one center-distance adjustment necessary—the opposite bearing need not be touched.

Select a point well back of the fan-fly bearing, approximately three-sixteenths from the upper edge of the frame and drill a one eighth or three thirty-seconds hole. From the left-hand edge saw a narrow "V" in to this hole. Slight alteration of the center-distance by springing the fan-fly in or out are obvious.

Slowing down the strike speed always presents 'problems', and, in some instances there isn't very much one can do towards that end. NEVER use a mechanical brake. We've seen various attempts, such as riveting a flat spring to press against the end of the fan-fly pivot, or, rigging a spring to ride friction upon the lateral side of the fan-fly arbor. Any time you place a mechanical brake at this point you are bidding for trouble—the strike train of necessity must 'start' from a dead stop, like starting your car in low gear, the strike train must have sufficient power to set the fan-fly in motion; once it is turning the same power is still there—unlike the car, it isn't shifted to high.

The best and mechanically correct method, is to enlarge the fan, i.e. make a new one wider or longer (preferably both) often the existing fan pretty near covers or fills the available space it has to turn in, thus the new fan can be but a very little larger, upon the other hand a slight increase in fan surface will make considerable difference.

Where the fan-fly pinion has six staves, a new pinion of five can be made; this way, the train has to drive the fan-fly one-sixth faster and thereby slows down the strokes. In pure theory, changing a pinion from six down to five and thus increasing the speed of one of the mobiles alters the center-distance, etc., but, this type of clock repair is not to exact tolerance and while the pitch circle of the new five stave pinion should be reduced enough to give the five about the same spacing the original six had, we've seen new pinions of five whose pitch circle was approximately the same as original work very well; with the 'sawed V' a bit of adjustment can always be made. Just remember when scribing the new five pitch circle it should be a little smaller and thus work to the reducing side rather than larger.

Time Train Count

"THE COUNT OR SPEED of a train in horology is determined by the number of vibrations of the balance (pendulum) in one hour." so, says Donald de Carle, in his Watchmakers & Clockmakers Dictonary. Other similar volumes have almost identical wording.

Counting the train, seems difficult to many bench clockmakers if we are to judge from the number of comments, inquiries, etc. The latest concerns a clock familar to all; the old No. 89 Seth Thomas.

Thomas Reid, thought and so states in his letter of 27th January, 1826, to Prince Frederick, Duke of Sussex, that his "Treatise On Clock and Watch Making" was the first to be published in English. Quote: "The chief object which I have had in view, and which has not hitherto, that I am aware of, been attempted in the English language, ..."

Despite the fact that Reid's treatise of 1826 was preceeded in English by the Rev. William Durham's "The Artificial Clock-Maker," published in 1696 and Thomas Hatton's, "An Introduction to the Mechanical Part of Watch & Clock Work," in 1773, Reid was substantially correct—most horologists regard Durham as being far from a treatise and Hatton is mainly arithmetic and geometry.

The method of train counting is the same from all three 'original' writers, however, Reid, gives it in fewer words, and, perfectly clear. Quote: "The revolutions of the last pinion may be found without the use of fractions. Let the product of the wheel teeth, when multiplied into one another, be divided by the product of the pinions. The quotient will be the number of revolutions of the last pinion."

Britten (1881), Wright (1889), Hood (1903) my favorite Goodrich (1905) who merely quotes Britten, all give substantially the same.

All make it crystal clear, that: the "train count" is the number of revolutions of the last pinion (arbor carrying escape wheel) times the number of teeth in the escape wheel; times two-beats per tooth gives the number of "beats-per-hour." But, the simple fact that any and all members of the train below the center (hour) wheel do not enter into this calculation is not sufficiently stressed.

Since the center (hour) wheel revolves once per hour, the number of revolutions of the escape pinion and/or arbor must be counted from the center, forward. It makes no difference how many wheels may be behind the center or how many teeth they may have, they do not and can not enter into the calculation per hour. This seems to confuse some, more confusing, is the auxillary driven center and it is not mentioned at all.

In the early days, the center or hour wheel was directly within the train and thus the train count began with the number of teeth in that center wheel and went forward. Somewhere along the way; the date and place seemingly lost in the shuffle, the "auxillary" drive was introduced—perhaps in the Black Forest, about the mid 1700's —whereby the clock train was set up, and, the center or hour merely set along side it, being driven from what ever wheel that was convenient to the construction, by what ever number of teeth necessary to make it revolve once in sixty minutes. This auxilliary-drive method was, we might say, universally adopted by the American clock manufacturers.

Note our sketch of the No. 89 train layout. The second wheel of 60 drives the

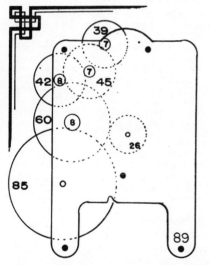

SETH THOMAS No. 89 TRAIN COUNT.

C. & O.

train and from it, the center is auxilliary driven via a 26-leaf pinion. Now, instead of the second of 60 making one revolution per sixty minutes, it takes only 26 of its teeth to revolve the 26 center through a full sixty minutes. So, when you come to

set down your calculation do NOT use 60. For one complete revolution of the center you are utilizing only 26 teeth and this is the figure to be used. Following Reid's instruction, we have: 26 teeth times 42 teeth times 45 teeth. Divided by 8 pinion leaves times 7 times 7.

$$\frac{26 \times 42 \times 45}{8 \times 7 \times 7} = \frac{49149}{392} \cdot = 125.35$$

$$125.35 \times 39 = 4888.65 \times 2 =$$

9777.30 beats per hour.

9777.30 ÷ 60 = 162.95 beats per minute.

This is one of the reasons—perhaps the main reason, we clockmakers do not have a rate recorder, or, can utilize our watch rate recorder to any degree of satisfaction for timing the common garden variety of eight-day mantel clock. The minute this gets circulated, somebody is going to give me the 'business' upon that 95/100 of a beat. Anything can happen via this auxilliary drive method; any slight discrepancy is very easily compensated for by the regulating nut.

The theoretical pendulum beating 160 times per minute is 5.5 inches long and that of one beating 170 is 4.8 thus .7 of an inch equals some ten beats per minute. By actual measurement, the travel of the regulating screw upon the No. 89 is a fat half-inch, or we might say .6 giving approximately a control of about ten beats per minutes from one extreme to the other. In time value this is roughly about three and one-half minutes per hour. One last caution, train count must be accurate—any error within that train is multiplied every time the wheel turns.

CHANGE OF PENDULUM

I recently acquired an old floor clock, seven feet, four inches tall, hand carved walnut case, put together with hand-made square nails. It's a seconds (60) beat French movement with a 12 inch porcelain dial, and it came with a mercury pendulum which I replaced with a huge brass grill type pendulum purely for looks. It kept good time with the mercury pendulum, and I now have the brass bob pendulum adjusted so it only is off five minutes in 48 hours—fast.

When I got it, the weight was missing, so at the present I'm using a container with pieces of lead in it until I find out how much weight I need. There is just one weight because it's a silent clock — not a striker or chimer.

Can you tell me about the weight; whether the weight has anything to do with the speed the clock runs: Should I try to get along with the least weight it takes to keep the clock running, or does it make any difference on the wear of the movement like I've been told by amateurs? Some informants tell me the lighter the weight, the easier it is on wear and tear of the clock.

The whole clock—case, movement, dial, and pendulum are all in very good condition. To make the permanent weight we will melt lead and pour into copper tubing after determining the amount needed.

A.

From the standpoint of accurate timekeeping, a well made, correctly compensated mercurial pendulum is to be desired above all others. However, I take it, from the way you say it, you desire the "effect" of the large brass ball over and above accuracy.

Be that as it may, a variation of 2½ minutes per day (5 min. 48 hrs.) can, and, ought to be bettered even with the brass ball.

The lightest possible weight is to be desired both from the angle of accuracy and the angle of wear the running of the clock will be subjected to. Your present method of determining correct amount of weight required is the best practical at hand. See the very smallest amount of weight that will operate the movement then add a small amount (5 to 10%) as a safety factor.

You do not tell us what type of escapement—since it is French, has 12-in. porcelain dial and no strike; I strongly suspect a "Laput" pin escapement. Excess driving weight is bad for these, (any other escapement for that matter) because once the escape wheel has delivered its impulse and the pin (or tooth) has dropped to the lock position upon the other pallet any excess pressure results in a "drag" upon the free swing of the pendulum. It is a mistaken idea that a long, vigorous swing of a pendulum indicated good timekeeping. If, yours is a "Laput" pin, three-quarters of an inch to an inch and a quarter, either side of dead-center is sufficient "swing" for the ball. With the escapement correctly set, the movement in good order, you should be able to adjust it to a minute per week with the ball you have added.

Ansonia Strike Gives Trouble

I now have an Ansonia half hour strike; the number on the back plate is A26. The trouble is in the strike; there are two hammers but the train stops before the last strike. In other words at 2 o'clock it strikes bong, bong, bong. On the half hour it strikes bong. This in turn sometimes affects the next succeeding hour. I would appreciate any information you may be able to give in order to correct this condition.

A.

Apparently you just have the common variety of "ding-dong" striker — since they make twice the number of hammer strokes that the straight striker makes, the setting up of the strike train is generally about twice as critical. Simply, because the distance traveled by the hammer-lift pin is so much less.

You will have to go over and re-set the strike train; as you describe it, it is now locking between the ding stroke and the dong stroke.

Set in your strike train at the exact completion of the XII stroke. Locked. It is now ready for the 12:30 stroke; setting in this locked position; the first or ding hammer lift-pin should not touch the hammer tail; it should be far enough away that it does not even touch after the warn-run has advanced it a tiny bit. Allow it to strike 12:30 (ding-dong). Then, so place the locking that it "locks" immediately after the dong hammer tail falls off the lift pin. Correctly position the warn-run so that it is just as short as possible with a "positive" un-lock. The very construction of the clock should give you a sufficient forward run of the strike train for a "positive-lock" between the last dong stroke of one hour and the beginning ding stroke of the next strike operation.

French Pendulum Locks on Snail

I experience a lot of trouble with a French pendulum clock. It stops on the 12 strike; seems to lock on the snail. Could you advise me how I could determine the cause of this trouble? Thank you.

A.

Apparently, you are not re-assembling your French dial trains correctly and when the rack drops for the 12 stroke at the warn-run, it falls against the edge of the high step jamming the dial train; shutting off the power and thus stopping the clock.

Most (90 to 95%) of the French, rack strike clocks you will get for repair will have their dial trains "marked" by the factory. Look closely at the rim of your hour-wheel; somewhere about 90 degrees from where the rack-finger drops on to the snail for the 12 stroke (depending upon the location of the dividing wheel) you should discover a small punch-dot. The cannon-pinion and the dividing-wheel are also dotted, see Fig. 1. To correctly set up the dial train; place the cannon pinion on; then the dividing wheel and match the dots as shown.

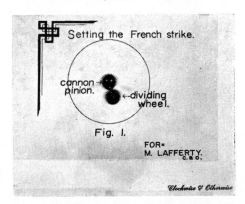

Setting the French strike.

cannon pinion.

←dividing wheel.

Fig. I.

FOR= M. LAFFERTY C.&O.

Clockwise & Otherwise

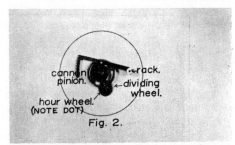

cannon pinion.

←rack.

←dividing wheel.

hour wheel. (NOTE DOT)

Fig. 2.

Now, place the hour-wheel on, seeing to it that the "dot" of its rim matches the pinion of the dividing wheel as shown in Fig. 2. The end result is you will have all three "dots" lined up, and, your clock is correctly set for the 12 stroke drop.

The warn run always takes place a minute or two before the final drop to start the strike operation. If, the rack finger drops against the edge of the high step on the snail, the forward travel of the snail during this minute or two jams the snail against the rack-finger; shutting off your power.

While we are upon the "dots", just a bit more. When setting-up your strike train you will note a separate bridge on the back plate for the third-wheel—this member carries the hammer-lift pins and on its back side you will discover another "dot". Set in your entire strike train; leaving off this bridge; now, revolve the

train with your finger til it locks; turn the third-wheel (still out through the open bridge) til you can make that dot on its rim match the spot where it meshes with the fourth-pinion as the fourth-wheel, fifth-wheel and fan fly remain in the locked position; put on the bridge and your clock will lock after the strike operation with the lift pin just the proper distance away from the hammer tail (no lock with hammer raised) You will see dots on the rim of the mainspring-barrel and on its cap. Match these dots when re-assembling the barrel — this keeps the barren turning true upon the winding arbor, etc.

Ansonia Swinging Ball Clock Needs Balance

Such a clock, made by the Ansonia Clock Company, was brought to me for repair and it is giving trouble. The figure with up-raised arm that should support the clock is missing, but the owner plans to use a pedestal as a substitute. By filing two flat faces at an angle of 60° upon a piece of ⅛" drill rod, I have made a knife-edge support.

The clock runs well, but does not keep time, in fact it gains several hours a day. Shortening the pendulum as much as possible does not bring it to time, but adding ¼ pound weight to the top of the clock does.

The pendulum ball contains a pie-shaped piece of lead, also a small amount of bird shot. Removing them makes possible a smaller weight at the top of the clock. Above the crossed springs on the pendulum is an opening, which seems to be the logical place for the knife-edge support.

If you will give me advice about this clock, I shall be deeply appreciative.

A.

We meet the Ansonia Swinging-Ball clock pretty often—it has been mentioned a number of times.

Does your clock have a decorative piece atop the big ball? Originally they did have such, and its weight would approximate a quarter pound. Enclosed photostat of page 85, of Ansonia factory catalogue for 1907 to show you how they originally looked.

No doubt about it, something has happened to "up-set" the balance of your clock. Apparently you are upon the right track and will just have to "play-it-by-ear". Eliminate the excess weight in the ball (small) below; set the reg. in the center; then add sufficient weight to top to bring you back to time (restore original balance).

You mention "knife-edge" support. It is NOT intended for this clock (compound-pendulum is what it really is) to pivot upon a knife edge. True, the hole in the upper member of the suspension vaguely indicates such. File the flats upon your drill rod to match that hole so that when you hang on the clock it will saddle snug to it. The top suspension member must remain level and stationary—allow all the swing in the crossed suspension springs —its proper action is a sort of up and down pumping type of motion quite similar to the way a youngster pumps himself in a swing. "That" card letting us know how well this covers your problem will be appreciated.

Setting Pallet Jewels In Brocot Escapement

Just yesterday, we listened—attentatively —to a lengthy complaint by a customer, a complaint so stereotyped I'm sure most of you have heard it many times. This housewife deposited a 'common-garden-variety' of eight-day, striking, mantel clock (Ansonia, Brocot escape.) on the counter and proceeded to relate how she carried it to Mr. "A"; paid him X dollars for a repair job. It was highly unsatisfactory, whereupon it was then carried to Mr. "B" with identically the same unsatisfactory results. While hearing her out, we glanced in the dial—standing out like a beacon light in pitch darkness were the two half-round pallet jewels with their FLAT sides turned to the escape teeth. "Who-done-it?" Your guess is as good as mine; in all likelihood the piece stopped from 'natural causes,' and Mr "A" thought some dumb joker had turned the round side to active position; proceeded to do a fair cleaning and turned the flat to the active side—Mr. "B" certainly did not know any better else he would have set them aright.

Less than five minutes after she left the clock, the postman deposited a packet from GHQ (Denver) on the counter—it was this letter from the clockmaker

Gentlemen:
Ref. Horologist & Jeweler magazine. Do you have a pamphlet on setting the pallet jewels in a French clock, mantel type. This is the exposed escape wheel with jewel pallets as per sketch.

Well, sir: we do not have such a pamphlet or spec sheet, but I'm reminded of what my old mentor used to say when I'd inquire for a needed piece of material. His terse reply was: "That one didn't grow on a bush." By that, he meant: someone made that one, you make one—so, since we don't have one, we shall just make it.

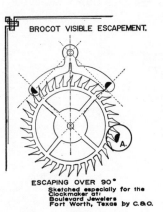

BROCOT VISIBLE ESCAPEMENT.

ESCAPING OVER 90°
Sketched especially for the
Clockmaker at:
Boulevard Jewelers
Fort Worth, Texas by C.&O.

This is generally known as the "Brocot" escapement because its invention is largely credited to Achile Brocot (b-1817, d. 1878) when he was about twenty years old. Actually, the pin pallet form was originated by "Pinchon" at Geneva, when Brocot was but three years old; it was popularized by Georges Frederic Roskopf (b-1813, d. 1889), a contemporary of Brocot's. It has been said that: "It (Brocot escapement) was invented by a boy, misunderstood by many, even despised by a few, yet, it revolutionized the clock industry of France and the U.S. and had a tremendous impact upon the U.S. watch industry."

As with all escapements, it is subject to numerous slight variations; that indicated in our sketch above is a sort of "in-the-middle" form for a short pendulum. The "Horological Journal" for September 1895 carried a splendid article titled "The Brocot Pin Pallet Escapement applied to English Clocks" by E. Herman Horstmann. In it he gave detailed instructions for drawing this escapement, and we've followed it pretty closely. In addition, we've thrown in, at the circle marked "A", the proper method for determining the correct pallet size; that is the over-all diameter of the pallet jewel should be just slightly less than the distance from one escape tooth tip to the next. Since this embraces 8½ teeth, 90 degrees of the escape wheel, it works out upon a "square" —the dotted line square enables one to definitely fix the whole setting and action in his mind.

The old method for setting pallets called for spacing the clock depthing tool to exactly the center distance (escape pivot to verge pivot) from the clock itself, and setting up the verge and escape wheel, as in Fig. 2.

This is convenient since the back of the verge is in the open and accessible to a small alcohol lamp for warming the shellac while the pallets are turned to the correct angle (flat side in line with escape wheel center) with pair of tweezers; further, it permits a 'trial' and correction if necessary before the parts are returned to the movement.

The job can be done equally as well with all parts in the movement by those clockmakers who do not own a depthing tool. Clamp the movement face up on the bench

Fig. 2

and make the verge fast in its 'center' position; this leaves both hands free for work. By using a small electric solder gun from which all solder has been wiped off, the end of the verge can be warmed enough to melt the shellac; the pallet is correctly aligned with tweezers and shellac allowed to cool (set).

To adjust the escapement, Horstmann says: "Three points must be noted: 1st, that the flat edges of the pallets are at their correct angles, viz. at right angles to lines drawn from the center of the pallet arbor. 2nd, that the drop should be even, not more on one pallet than the other. In this escapement like in the dead beat, the teeth will catch on the pallet if they are set too deep or too shallow: if they are set too deep, the teeth catch on the disengaging pallet; if too shallow, on the engaging, so that the drop on the pallets can never be excessive, and can be made even by correctly adjusting the depth. 3rd, when the teeth drop on the pallets their points should pitch just half way across the semi-circle; if they pitch beyond or within this point, the pallet brass must be opened (the jewel-pins brought further apart) or closed respectively. This is an important point, as a clock will often go with this incorrect, but will not give good results, for if the teeth pitch too far on, great loss of power is occasioned by the excessive unlocking, and if they pitch within this point, heavy engaging friction takes place." end quote.

Dr. Rawlings, in his "Science of Clocks and Watches" (2nd Ed.) says: "It (Brocot) is the cheapest form of jeweled escapement and its performance is nearly equal to that of any other." Maj. Chamberlain, in an article in the American Jeweler (July 1915) described the Brocot escapement as being 'unsymmetrical' because it is neither equidistant or equal locking. Perhaps, the 'unsymmetrical' feature may be one of the things that causes an experienced horologist a bit of confusion; we mentioned above various forms: in a little volume titled "Katschismus der Uhrmacherkunst" by F. W. Ruffert, published at Leipzig, Germany in 1885, he suggests flattening the impulse surface just a little. The Gilbert Clock Co. (Winstead, Conn.) produced many clocks with visible "Brocot" escapement, in the first portion of this century; their 1900 catalogue illustrates some 15 models, they used a triangular pallet, see Fig. 3. Mr. S. A. Ransom, long time Gilbert service manager and enthusiastic horological historian, tells me that this escapement was popular with Gilbert from around 1890 to about 1910; further, that during that period

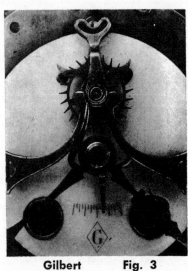

Gilbert　　　**Fig. 3**

they had a number of employees of German origin who must have gotten the idea from Ruffert.

Ward L. Goodrich in "The Modern Clock" suggests that flattening the curved impulse surface slightly, or flattening the tops (end) of the escape wheel teeth a little will avoid stoppage on stubborn movements.

What of this young genius who devised this escapement? In the 41 years that followed (he died at 61), he became one of France's noted horologists. Following the escapement under discussion he devised a form of "free" escapement which he termed: "d'mise d'aplomb seul." A year clock. The regulator-suspension which also bears his name, in 1839. By 1850 practically all French movements were equipped with it—it replaced the former one of silk thread, and that is why we generally date French clocks with silk suspension as being before 1850. A perpetual calendar mechanism, and, a new form of rack strike. He won the first class medal at the expositions of 1849, 1851, 1855, 1862 and 1867. In 1845 he traveled to London where the English horological fraternity received him warmly. With his success at the 1849 exposition his fame traveled to foreign countries and he moved to St. Petersburg (Russia) for a short time. While he produced a few papers, his only book was a 10½ X 6¾ in. 97-page volume, published at Paris, 1862, giving his new method for calculating trains by approximation—Fig. 4.

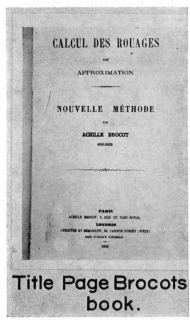

Title Page Brocots book.

Despite his having quit school at the age of 15 to work at the clockmakers' bench, we find the mature man well educated. His close friend Antoine Redier (b.-1817, d.-1892), famous French horologist, wrote in the "Revue Chronometrique" (1878): "To be a calculator and a man of taste are qualities not easily found together. Brocot possessed them to the highest degree. . . . His process for train calculations by approximation is of a genuine learned gentleman. . . . It follows that at the end of his life, there is great admiration for a gentleman who has fulfilled his life by doing many services for people, and by giving the best of himself to the art of horology."

The impact upon U.S. horology it attested by the fact that every major clock manufacturer (perhaps with the possible exception of Ingraham) made liberal use of it—we've already mentioned Gilbert; a 1902 catalogue shows Waterbury had 46 models that year with it; a 1907 Ansonia catalogue illustrates 302 models. We illustrate a few of them.

How did it effect the U.S. watch industry? This item alone would be good for a splendid paper. About 1912 Charles

E. DeLong (b.-1871, d.-1942) began experimenting with a variation of the Brocot escapement for application to high grade watches—in 1915 he formed and incorporated the "DeLong Escapement Co." Under DeLong's supervision, Illinois, Hamilton and Webb C. Ball produced a hundred

movements each; all performed satisfactorily and factories were about ready to adopt it permanently when trouble began to show up. It was observed that a high percentage of movements either did not function properly or failed to go at all after their first cleaning. This was a great blow to DeLong and he set about to determine, and,

remedy the fault—it was found to be "off center" jewels; Mr. DeLong then devised ways and means for insuring perfect concentric jewels, a method in use to this day.

The latest "Brocot" touch upon American horology was by Seth Thomas, shortly after World War II in their No. 125 Westminster Chime movement. The A-200 series is a modified Brocot, something on the order suggested by Ruffert and used by Gilbert. A thirty-tooth wheel; pallet span of 5½ teeth. So, my Texas friend (I wish you had used name instead of your firm), here is your Brocot Escapement 'pamphlet'.

Must Know Steps for Minute Repeater

I received a small French carriage clock It is a platform lever escapement, strike and alarm. I repivoted the escape wheel and made an insert tooth for the crown wheel.

The clock runs fine, but I am somewhat puzzled as to how it should strike. I will describe the striking mechanism the best I can and hope that you can understand it. It is a rack and snail type. In fact it has two racks and two snails of 12 steps each. One snail is attached to the hour wheel and naturally revolves once an hour. For identification I will letter this snail (A). As this snail turns, it trips a second snail, which I will call (B). At the half hour the clock strikes one, at the hour both racks drop and both are picked up to the number of steps on snail (B), but snail (A) is always in the same position. There are two wire coil gongs and three hammers. Of course one hammer is for the alarm. I believe if I knew how it should strike I could make it do so.

A.

Evidently you have a "minute repeater," since you say: "two snails of 12 steps each."

Did you actually count the steps of the second snail? or just assume that it has 12 steps?

One snail should have 12 steps, one for each of the 12 hours — this snail should revolve once in 12 hours. The second snail wheel should have 14 steps, and revolve once each quarter hour.

A minute repeater should, say at 10 minutes to eight o'clock, strike seven for the last hour; then, three (3) ding-dongs for the three quarters; then, five single strokes upon the highest toned gong for the five (5) minutes is past 7:45.

Naturally, different makers varied the mechanical details by which they accomplished this — basically, all are about the same but rarely ever two just alike. Not having had your particular clock in hand, it is most difficult to give you a step-by-step procedure. Once you've determined just "how" the clock was meant to strike, the function of each piece and lever should be obvious. Upon this type clock it is well to remember that no provision can be made for turning the hands backwards; also that no oil should be applied to the striking parts. Great care is necessary when handling them to make sure that none of the strike parts are bent. Above that, little or no difficulty should be met with. If convenient, have a look-see at "Practical Clock Repairing" by Donald de Carle — he goes into more detail than any other writer I know and has some splendid drawings that always help.

Needs Help To Repair Hereshede Clock

I have just received a Hereshede Chime Clock for repairs that was damaged in shipment. I have got it in running condition except that it stops after running three or four days, and the minute hand locks on the hour and you have to turn it back a half turn before it will strike the hour.

The clock is a Grandfather tubelar chime striking on five bass tubes.

I am not familiar with this type of clock and would appreciate any help you could give me in adjusting this clock.

A.

Evidently the strike is hanging up your time train rather than the hands locking up since you say you back it off half a turn before it will strike.

First, check your August Clockwise & Otherwise to familiarize yourself with the correct sequence of the chime operation. Herschede has many types in operation and thus we do not have the exact details of the construction of your clock.

Second, re-check your strike train to make sure that: when at the end of the striking operation, your clock locks with the warn-run lock pin about half a revolution away from the warn-run lock lever.

There are instances, where a strike train is so set up that when it locks at the finish of the strike, the warn-run lock pin is very near to the warn-run lock lever and because the train locks further back down its train upon another mem-

ber the exact position of the warn-run lock pin is rarely ever at the exact same position. That is: the portion of the train beyond the strike-lock is drifting free and the warn-run pin may come to rest a bit earlier or later. Now, when it happens to come to rest squarely over the warn-run lever and that lever is raised at the beginning of the strike un-lock comes jam against it stopping the center-post from turning further in its clockwise direction, ultimately stopping the clock by shutting off its power. Your description indicates just that situation.

With the warn-run pin half a rev away from the warn-run lock lever, the warn-run lock lever is perfectly free to be raised upwards til the strike train un-locks, then, the strike train is permitted a forward motion of the warn-run a half rev to lock against the warn-run lock lever. Here is remains locked until the completion of the hour-chime when the warn-run lock lever is permitted to drop out of the way of the warn-run lock pin and the strike train is free to strike the hour.

What Method Gives Correct Endshake?

I am working on parking meter timers with 360 beat movements and a problem has arisen regarding the amount of endshake required in a balance with conical pivot riding in V cone bearings similar to the type found in the majority of travel alarm clocks.

Two basic methods have been described to me—one, being with a slight amount of slop, and the other being twice the thickness of the hairspring. Could you advise as to the correctness of these or give a practical rule of thumb method for adjusting endshake in this type of balance assembly?

A.

You have practically answered it, i.e. it is strictly a "rule-of-thumb" adjustment.

Using the hair-springs thickness as a guage is strictly a new one to me, further, I can't see any direct relationship. A hairspring could be narrow, fairly thick and pretty long; another could be, say very thin, have a bit more width and maybe a couple less coils and yet both springs beat your balance to 360. It stands to reason the endshake should remain the same. Now if you use the thickness of the spring as a measurement of the endshake you would be bound to come up with two (2) different adjustments.

The ideal is the very smallest possible 'slop' you can get by with complete safety. After all, the best balance is the one running in a hole jewel—with which the V-cone should imitate this just as nearly as practical.

Most of these movements operate with the balance staff in the horizontal, thus gravity holds the pivot down. Where you have excessive endshake or slop as the roller pin strokes downward the re-action had a tendency to lift the staff upward; as it slops up a large percentage of the spring power as applied by the lever is consumed in this raising of the staff up instead of propelling the balance wheel forward on its stroke, giving you a rather poor motion.

Most certainly, the endshake must NOT be so small as to cause a friction on the staff—it has to operate freely. Another feature entering into the general problem is the rigidity of the frame; a movement with thin plates (easily pressed together) or insufficient pillar-posts which allow some give with excessive hard winding, etc., requires a little additional endshake to be safe. Lastly; IF we accept "Twice-the-thickness-of-the-hairspring" as being correct, how are you going to determine it? It all boils down to judgment based upon experience; you know you want the smallest possible slop that is safe—a little experience and you'll soon know what is too little and this brings us right back to rule-of-thumb.

German Elephant Clock Vibrates on Bars

I now have a clock in the shop and would appreciate some help in obtaining some information on it. It is a German Elephant clock with (inverted banjo-shaped) balanced mechanism. It has ..J.. on the dial, no other markings.

My problem is that it has been in another shop and they put lead on the pallet and removed weight on the balancing ball on the bottom. Also it has had spring replaced and possibly other alterations.

I would like to put it in good condition again, but I have no way of knowing what the various specifications are. If you can help me, I would appreciate it very much. Thank you in advance.

A.

Your clock was manufactured by the Junghans Clock Co., 23 Erhard Junghans-Strasse, Schramberg (Weurtt) Germany. Perhaps if you made a rough sketch and addressed an inquiry to them, enclosing an International Postal Reply Coupon, their technical dept. would supply specific answers.

It is noted, you say spring has been replaced, but you do not say for a certainty that it is the main-spring. Very often repairmen not familiar with the construction of these clocks have them come in with the "suspension" missing and try to "improvise" some sort of suspension-spring. The fact that you say weight has been added above, and subtracted from below would indicate this. i.e., an improvised spring to suspend it would off-set its true suspension point.

Fact is: they were not spring-suspended. The elephant holds in his trunk a little bar with two (2) cupped jewels set into it. Just under the dial is another bar with two (2) pointed, tempered steel pins — very much like phonograph needles (in fact, they'll do for replacement) that extend downward to rest in each of the cup jewels. The clock operates by vibrating back and forth upon these points.

Pendulum Ball Stoppage

I would appreciate it if you would answer the following question.

When I clean a clock, oil it, and screw it on a board, level it, I move the fork and rod and it starts to run and keeps running. When I put the pendulum ball on, it stops.

Will you please tell me where the trouble is most likely to be?

A.

With no more details than you give us, it is difficult to give you a general answer, and impossible to pin-point your particular trouble.

Let's look at it this way; with your motor as dead as old Nell, your car would still roll down hill—that is exactly what you are doing when you run your pendulum clock without its pendulum ball.

Now, since the clock stops when you hang on its load—ball—it must be from lack of power—it simply does not have enough "zip" to pull the full load. Assuming that you have the original power—mainspring—then we must conclude that "friction" is robbing you of power. This, you can look for just anywhere—bent pivots; scored pivots; verge fork binding upon the pendulum wire; plus a dozen faults in your escapement. If set too shallow it can rob you of a lot of power; if the pallets are pitted so that the escape teeth "dig" into the pits, that can kill a lot of power. Upon striking movements, an exceptionally hard to raise strike lift can absorb a lot of power.

Two spots generally overlooked, are: loose lantern-pinion staves where the hole in the pinion head has worn 'til the stave is loose—stave can drift toward the arbor center thereby reaching the wheel tooth a little high and late, causing a butting action. Most common garden variety of American mantel clocks can show wear at the main-wheel center since the winding arbor must turn in the main-wheel when the spring is being wound up. Such wear permits the main-wheel to shift off center; this is generally indicated by excessive wear showing up up front or drive side of the main-wheel teeth, again causing a butting action and robbing you of a lot of power right at the source. Check closely 'til you have located where you are losing power.

Model 89K Modified

I have clock problems with a Seth Thomas mantel Bing Bong clock Model 89K.

I have a factory list of Seth Thomas clocks in which the foreword is signed in your name. I note, in the 4th paragraph, you state that one of the No. 89 movements was modified for Florence Krober. I rather suspect that the clock I am writing you about may be one of that type.

This clock strikes Bing Bong at quarter past, and Bing Bong, Bing Bong at half past, but at quarter to any hour it strikes three, with only one of the hammers. The other hammer is held up by a single lobe cam on the hour shaft.

My customer, the owner of the clock, says it has always Bing Bong-ed six, or three pairs, at quarter to the hour. I claim that it could not do this on account of the cam.

I would appreciate a letter from you if you have information on this peculiar model. In the book it lists No. 89, A, B, C, D, E, F, and G, but no 89K.

I am making a special effort to get this matter straightened out and I hope you can help me.

I have written to the factory and have a letter from their service manager, who suggests that I have the minute hand on 90° off position. I am surprised that a man in his position would assume that a person who is a certified watchmaker with many years of experience with clocks and watches would make such an error.

A.

Always, I like to side with the watchmaker; I'll just have to side with both your customer and the man down at Seth Thomas this time, however.

No, your "quarter ding dong," the 89K, came along after the little booklet you refer to was published in 1907, and it is not the one made for Krober.

First, as to how this clock should strike. It sounds one "ding-dong" at 15 after the hour, for the one or first quarter. It ding-dongs twice at the half for the second quarter. Then, it ding-dongs three times at the 45 minutes for the three-quarters.

As the minute hand advances from the 45 to straight up, the cam you mention comes under one of the hammers, preventing that hammer from operating. Thus, when the strike train is tripped for the hour stroke, only one hammer operates and the clock strikes the hour just as any clock strikes it—the correct number of single strokes.

These movements were manufactured with both rack and snail type striking and count-wheel striking. You do not indicate which yours is, but you can easily line it up.

Turn your center-post until the cam is squarely under one hammer and the strike has just tripped. This is the hour position, so place the minute hand on, pointing UP. Now, if it is rack and snail, the snail is held upon the hour-pipe with a set screw. Set the snail so that the rack falls into an hour-strike slot—deep—and secure in that position with the set screw. If it is the count wheel type, set the count-wheel so that it strikes the hour. Once synchronized, either type, it should thereafter follow the correct sequence as noted in the 3rd paragraph above.

FRENCH CARRIAGE PLATFORM

I have a small French carriage clock which I undertook to repair. It had a cylinder escapement with the balance and scape wheel missing. I had difficulty finding a platform small enough and finally sent to A. Shoot & Son Ltd. in London, England, for one, which I adapted to this clock. It took nice motion and showed a near perfect line on the Watchmaster. I soon discovered it was running very fast and after counting teeth in the train, I find it is 13,500 beat in place of 18,000 which I believe is more usual for these clocks.

I would like to know if there is anything I can do, beside changing the wheels, so that I can use this platform escapement.

318

A.

You say "besides changing wheels." Then, the only course left open would be to make your balance beat slower.

One may make a balance-wheel beat slower by, 1: using a weaker hair spring, and 2: adding weight to the rim of the balance, or by doing a little of both. In this case you would have to slow the balance from 18,000 down to 13,500 or by 4,500 beats per hour. Divided by 60 minutes, this would give 75 beats per minute. Divide by 60 seconds and you get 1¼ beats per second. This is entirely too much to make a satisfactory timer by altering the wheel or spring.

What has happened is this: the escape wheel and pinion are a part of the platform assembly which was lost. So, it is here we look for the trouble. Now the 15-tooth escape sounds good; let's look to the pinion.

Re-calculating your train: 75 x 64 x 48 x 15 equals 3,456,000. The pinions: 8 x 8 x 6 equals 384. Divided into the wheels, or 3,456,000, we have 9,000 escape wheel teeth passing a given point per hour. Two beats per tooth, and there is your 18,000.

Thus, if you can substitute a six-leaf pinion for the eight now in your escape wheel, your clock should come within range of its regulator.

With reference to the near perfect rate shown by your Watchmaster: it must be remembered that the Watchmaster merely tells you how the balance wheel is "beating." It is always presumed that the timepiece is correctly geared to that beat, for that is something the rate recorder does not show.

Parts Becoming Magnetized

So often after I clean a watch and begin to assemble it I find either the escape wheel or the pallet or both badly magnetized. What would cause this?

A.

Do you test these parts when you first take the watch down? You imply that the parts become magnetized during your cleaning process. To be sure of this, you must know that they were not magnetized to begin with.

For a steel (iron) part to become magnetized, it must come within a fairly strong magnetic field. Thus, if you are doing the magnetizing, you must be bringing the parts within a magnetic field.

When, where, or how you could be doing this is difficult to determine from a distance. Most electrical mechanisms create a magnetic field, as motors, and even some ultrasonic cleaners. Generally these fields are mild, and, removed far enough from your work as not to magnetize it.

Check your operation close, see how close and how near it is to the motor. Check with your fellow watchmakers, especially with ones who are using the same equipment you are using. See if he has the same problem. This is one that has to be "played-by-ear."

TOBIAS CHRONOMETER

My second question concerns a conversation with a watchmaker friend of mine, when I mentioned that I had never seen a marine chronometer. It did not take him long to produce one of the most beautiful pieces I ever saw.

The inscription on the dial reads Morris Tobias, 31, Mindries, London 733.

It has an up and down indicator. The movement is approximately eight inches wide by 3½ inches deep. It is set in a ring which pivots; then the brass ring in turn pivots on its own set of gimbals. This is all in a mahogany box which has a glass top, over which a door rests on hinges, and which can be locked.

The balance is the most intricate part of the movement, as it is a split balance, but with three arms rather than two. The hairspring has ten coils, but instead of being flat, coiled up like a front coil spring in an auto.

I would love to work on this mechanism, but have been advised not to by a friend. Since it did not seem that complicated to me, I would still like to repair the clock as it is not running. Would you advise touching such a piece?

I would appreciate it if you would tell me about Mr. Morris Tobias. Is this the famous Tobias watchmaker, or a member of that family? Are their schematics of that type of clock available? Where can I obtain a book or books on the repair of chronometers? How would a clock of this type get into this country? Could it possibly have been donated voluntarily to the war effort? Do all these marine chronometers have the coiled vertical hairspring, and what is the purpose of such a type of spring? What is the purpose of the up and down regulator?

A.

By all means, do not go into a good marine chronometer until you have fully prepared yourself. The Chronometer tune is one you certainly can NOT play by ear; it requires adherence to the sheet music all the way.

We recently saw a very fine "Hodell" English marine chronometer that had literally been ruined by a "watchmaker." This man was a fair workman, careful and conscientious, with some 12 or 15 years at the bench with watches, but he was totally unfamiliar with chronometers. When this piece came to his hands, he looked for a way to let the mainspring down. No easy way being apparent to him, he decided to gently remove the balance and allow it to "run down." Accordingly, the balance cock screw was removed and he lifted the balance out with the cock; result, the broken locking-jewel, all teeth on the escape wheel bent back, both pivots of the escape arbor broken, and one escape jewel cracked. A method that will work with watches, yet it can do a hundred dollars worth of damage to a chronometer in about one second flat.

Write to the Superintendent of Documents, Government Printing Office, Washington, D.C. 20025, for a price upon the Navy manual for chronometer overhaul.

One of the best works upon the Marine Chronometer is "The Marine Chronometer, Its History and Development," by Lt. Com. Rupert T. Gould. This is NOT a repair manual, but it contains a wealth of practical information the successful chronometer maker must have. It is a six by nine inch volume, 287 pages, with 139 plates and 61 drawings. The Clock Tower Book Shop, 7801 E. State Street, Rockford, Ill. 61108, can probably locate one for you.

Practically all chronometers have the winding indicator. Its purpose is to show the observer when it was wound, or when it should be wound — just like the gasoline gauge on the dash of your car indicates to you about how much running time or miles you have left.

The purpose of the cylindrical type hair spring is to allow equal pinning of both the inner and outer terminals, to secure better isochronous action, i.e., have the balance make long and short strokes in the same time. This spring is credited to John Arnold, about 1770.

How did the "Tobias" chronometer get here? Your guess is as good as ours. Some are brought in by collectors. Others are bought by watchmakers and jewelers wishing a very accurate timepiece. Still others come via the surplus route and are picked up by those interested in a different type of timekeeper, and so on.

Chains for Dutch Clock

I have a problem which I hope you can help me with solving.

I have a Dutch Hooded clock which needs some repairs, but the biggest problem is the chains to run the movement. As you probably know, this type of clock runs off chains similar to a Cuckoo clock, with the striking train in front of the running train, as the movement is made square.

The front wheel has a gear the same as a cuckoo clock, which the chain fits into, but this gear is fastened to the wheel. The other gear which is back of this one has a ratchet, the same as a cuckoo clock. With this arrangement, one continuous chain is used instead of two chains, as used with a cuckoo clock.

I have been told this would have to be a double loop chain as a regular cuckoo clock chain would twist.

Would you by any chance have any of this type of chain, or could you tell me where I could locate some? I have written to several firms, but have been unable to obtain this chain. As a matter of fact, I have no idea just what this chain looks like. Could you give me some idea?

An help you can furnish me on this matter will be greatly appreciated.

There is no problem. I fear the joker who gave you the "double loop" story has merely confused you, and that confusion was passed on by you to your dealers. Most all dealers have chain for your clock.

The system you indicate is known as the "Huygens Fall," or as it is sometimes also called, "Huygens Endless Rope," so named for the celebrated Dutch mathematician and horologist Christiaan Juygens who devised it about 1657. He first used a rope. The chain came later.

This sometimes baffles modern workmen not familiar with it. In fact, it is a very "neat" arrangement. It not only permits you to drive two trains with one weight, it also serves instead of a maintaining power, since there is always a pull upon your time train, even while being wound. It is used to this day in the automatic winding for tower clocks.

This double loop thing is a mystery. Perhaps the fellow thought it ought to be a "ladder link" chain? The clock actually takes the plain, ordinary, oval link chain. Note your catalogues. These chains are listed at so many links per foot. Cut from a piece of limber cardboard, such as from a laundered shirt, a strip about a scant quarter inch wide. Bend it around one of your wheels, pressing each prong about half way through; that is, force the cardboard down half way upon the prong, taking them one at a time, in rotation, so that your cardboard strip will just about occupy the same position as the chain in action.

Take off the cardboard and measure it. You should get a space of at least three inches for an accurate measurement. Count the spike holes and multiply by two, because a prong or spike ought to hit every other chain link. As three inches is one fourth of a foot, multiply by four. This gives you the correct links per foot.

The action is: a link lying upon a spike is in the level, or 180 degrees. Its following link, which is at right angles, 90 degrees, does nothing but lie between two spikes. The next following link is back to 180, and ready for the next spike. Just tell your regular supplier how many links per foot and how many feet you require.

IMPERIAL ELECTRIC CLOCK

Recently, I acquired a battery-operated clock, called a self winding clock, with the following name on the dial: Imperial "Electric Clock". This following bit of additional information appears on the movement: Pat. 5-4-09. The clock is operated by two 1.5 Volt batteries, No. 6 by General Electric.

It has only one lever weight, or arm, which operates the clock for some seven minutes, when the electric contact is made and the weight is thrown upward to a forty-five degree angle, more or less, from whence it starts its downward "pull", operating the clock for another seven minute period. (I am assuming the seven minute period to be correct, since I saw a similar clock which operated in this manner). All the wires on the batteries and coils are intact except one.

The difficulty is that each time the end of the loose wire makes contact or is placed against any part of the clock movement, the lever will be thrown upward immediately to its highest position. I am unable to locate the correct point to which this wire should be attached. I have read the discussion relating to the self winding clocks in "The Modern Clock", by Goodrich, and deduct from reading his remarks that the electric contact should be made only when the lever reaches the lowest point of its downward course. Contact is thus made and the electric current causes the lever to rise to its highest position. Would you kindly tell me a little something about the clock and where the loose end of wire should be attached in order to make the clock function properly?

A.

To pin-point your exact trouble, and give step by step instructions to remedy it, would be well nigh impossible because we do not know the exact condition your movement is in, or what may have been removed or lost. Therefore, we must proceed along general principles.

The negative side of your circuit connects to the frame of the movement; the positive side connects to a pin located in the tail-piece of the armature. This pin (or piece) is of necessity insulated from the frame. When the weight descends to just about its lowest point, a pin located near the weight's pivot comes into contact with this insulated member, closing the circuit; this energized the coils kicking the weight upwards and breaking the circuit. This is the rewind style.

Enclosed are a copy of the patent and a copy of some notes I made several years ago. Combined, these completely cover this clock. I believe you can take them and "play it by ear."

A bit of history: The Imperial Electric Clock Co. was founded at Granite City, Ill. in 1908 by three Frenchmen, brothers, Francis, Joseph and August Feraud. The patent you refer to was filed Sept. 8, 1908 and granted May 4, 1909, No. 920,124 in the name of Frank H. Feraud, a citizen of France. Their first advertisement to the trade appeared in "The Keystone" for October 1909. The factory was later moved to St. Louis, Mo., where it was merged with the Sempire Clock Co. Sempire clocks were never manufactured after the merger. A little later, the factory was again moved, to Kimswich, Mo. Next it was moved to Imperial, Mo. (about 30 miles from St. Louis).

Again the factory became short of working capital and the St. Louis interest, to protect their holdings, leased a building on Rutger Street just east of Grand Avenue and moved the firm back to St. Louis. Meanwhile the Feraud Brothers had sold their interests to Imperial. This brings the operation up to World War I.

About 1920 the company became insolvent. Mr. A. W. Fowler purchased the assets of the Imperial Clock Co., organized a new company under the laws of the state of Illinois and moved it to Collinsville, Ill. It operated at Main Street and Morrison Avenue there for one year, and in 1922 Mr. Fowler moved it to Highland, Ill., where it is today under the name of C. J. Hug Co., Inc. They discontinued the manufacture of the type battery clock you have about 1928.

STRIKE TRAIN ANALYSIS

To analyze the strike train we can first break it down into two basic types: 1, the count wheel; 2, the rack and snail. Any further break-down leads to the many variations already mentioned — only one other mechanical feature is to be found in all models; namely the final strike release. In order to have the clock strike upon the exact hour the train has to be 'cocked' very much as you pull the hammer back upon a fire-arm, so that it will commence the strike operation the instant the lifting arm is dropped by the center-post lift-pin. This cocking or priming is called the "warn-run." As the center-post lift-pin revolves clockwise it lifts and unlocks the strike train, allowing it to run for a couple or three revs of the fan-fly, where it is temporarily locked by another stop-lever that the raising has brought up into the path of the warn-run stop pin. It is then held here in readiness until the center lift drops at the exact hour mark. The correct number of hammer strokes are dealt by the count wheel or the rack and snail; then, the train is locked at the permanent lock point till the next hour, when the cycle is repeated with one hour added.

Calculating the strike train has to be based upon 156 hammer strokes for each 24 hours — many clocks strike once at the half-hour — this adds 24 strokes. Some count wheel types have the half included in their count wheels, while some may have an additional hammer lift-tail on the hammer to drop off at the half point, tripped by an additional lift pin at the center-post set at 180-degrees from the hour trip. Despite the fact that all clocks — barring the ship's bell striker — deliver up the same results, the calculations of different strike trains can vary forty ways from Sunday. Depending to a large degree upon the number of lift pins the maker plants in the hammer lift member; and, where this member comes within the train — here again enters the half hour stroke and whether or not it is from the center post. Practically all of the rack and snail types strike their half via the train, because it is mechanically convenient to have the half lift just high enough to unlock the train, but not high enough to allow the rack to drop; thus it will perform one stroke and drop back to the permanent lock position.

Most French clocks have their strike trains 'marked'; if you will observe closely you will see a little spot — punch mark — at the base of the teeth of the strike train wheels. When setting in the strike train see that the tooth indicated by the mark extends into the pinion it drives and so on through the entire train and you will end up with a strike train CORRECTLY set in.

Often, the clockmaker can save some time by closely examining the strike train before taking a clock down. If he finds the train correctly set-in he may mark it in the permanent lock position with a little "V" scribed upon each wheel opposite that tooth then engaged in its pinion, thereby enabling him to reassemble the strike train correctly.

Unlike English and French clocks which utilize levers, most American clocks have their warn-runs and strike locks made with wires — to accurately adjust these every clockmaker should have a set of wire benders. Years ago, supply houses catalogued them; somewhere along the line they have dropped out, possibly during that great slump in clock repairing from the turn of this century to W. W. I. A quick check of to-day's catalogues shows them conspicuous by their absence. Fortunately, a set can be made at very little cost and equally little effort.

Secure from your five and dime, three screwdrivers — roughly nine inches long over all, with a shank of approximately quarter-inch diameter. Test with a file; chances are they will be soft enough to cut with your jeweler's saw without drawing the temper. Next, saw them off at the point where the flat begins. Then, saw into the end of one a slot about two m/m. wide by 5 m/m. deep and dress the slot out with a flat file to about a width of 2.5 m/m., but don't increase the depth. Your No. 1 wire bender is now complete.

Heat No. 2 and No.3 to a cherry-red at the tip and turn up a 'calk' about seven m/m. high; allow to cool and slot the calk with a cut same as No. 1.

On the No. 2 the slot should be straight-in-line with the shank, while the slot in the No. 3 should be at 45-degree angle to the shank.

After the slots are cut and dressed out, re-heat and quench in cold water to restore a good temper. The set is now complete and you will find them most helpful in bending strike wires while the movement is fully assembled.

Example: the center-post lift on most American clocks is merely a wire set into the post and bent at right angles; by inserting the No. 1 bender from the side and between the plates this trip wire can easily be slightly advanced or retarded to make the strike drop come exactly at the hour mark.

While the strike train differs upon many mechanical points from movement to movement, upon every one of both types the permanent lock should come immediately after the final stroke of the hammer — a feature that must be checked closely. If your train is not so set it may use up the free space between the hammer-lift pin and the hammer lift tail with the warn run; thus when the train drops for the strike run it will be starting under its load. In other words, there ought to be a couple or three revs of the fan-fly before the train picks up the load. Many clock strike trains will take off under the load and strike the hour and halves correctly when fully wound, but about the sixth day when the spring is a bit weaker, fail; some owners do not get them fully wound and the failure may come earlier. Then, there is the added friction from dried lub, etc., after a year or two of operation which increases the friction. That little run before the load is picked up is kind-a-like starting your car in low gear — they haven't yet come up with automatic drive for strike trains.

Practically all that has been said here re the strike train is also applicable to chime trains, especially that point of the fan-fly having a few revs before picking up the load. Study each strike train before you pull it down; understanding its operation will save time upon the reassembly.

We have pointed out that there are a blue-jillion different mechanical combinations — some have the permanent lock on one pin; the warn-run lock on that same pin; others with a separate pin for the warn-run; any number of hammer lift pins, depending upon which wheel of the train they are planted in and whether or not the halves are tripped from the center post. Another feature of striking trains often overlooked is that their wheels do not turn the same at every strike, yet they do repeat every twelve hours.

Those strike trains in quarter-hour chiming clocks operate exactly like those in the hour strikers with one general exception, they never strike one for the half-hour, and, they are tripped from the chime train instead of from the center post. The chime train is tripped from the center post at each quarter.

Most chimers are provided with a self corrector feature; usually, this is a deeper lock at the end of the third quarter chime operation making it necessary for a higher lift to trip the chime train before it will chime the fourth quarter. Then the chime train trips the strike at the end of its fourth quarter operation, insuring that the clock can only strike the hours when the minute hand points to the 60 minute mark. It therefore follows that you observe this high lift at the center and set on the minute hand so that it points to 60 when the high lift drops — one should examine this self-corrector feature carefully before disassembling a movement. As with the strike train it will show you HOW it performs, and, whether or not some workman before you has set it in incorrectly — a couple of moments spent here may save you half an hour when you come to assemble the movement. Perhaps we've only touched upon the high spots of the lowly strikers. The point is: the many inquiries we get indicate that the clockmaker is NOT familiarizing himself with the details of a movement's strike action before he pulls it down, thus, when he comes to setting it in again he encounters trouble.

Welch Patti Collector Has Unanswered Questions

The Patti clock leaves many questions unanswered. I would like to list a few of these questions and perhaps in your spare moments you could drop us a line and give us some additional information that we have been seeking.

1. Do you believe that the movements were American made?

The reason why I ask this question is that the Patti movement itself has a very strong resemblance to the French type movement. Although they are not quite as fine, they have some very strong similarities. The workmanship, the gearing, the brass floating barrel for the spring, and in the later models the pinions themselves seem to resemble the ones used in carriage clocks.

Also, I have owned a good many Patti clocks on and off and I have yet to find a movement that is signed. The only one I have found to be signed is the miniature Patti #2 model where I have found two that were nickel plated with Welch, Spring Company initials on the front and back plates. Other than that, I have not been able to find a Patti movement that

has any markings whatsoever or any indication of who made it. It would seem to me that if either Welch or Spring had made these movements completely they would have signed them because at the same time they were manufacturing the Patti clock they were also producing other clocks which movements they did sign Welch, Spring or Welch.

2. Was there any reason for lining the back of the clocks with the black flocked paper?

This practice was not duplicated on any other clock by any other maker. Welch and Spring also went to great extremes in having very elaborate cases which required considerable amount of workmanship in turning finials, etc. They also made the majority of the cases in rosewood with very little rosewood veneer, and made very few of the better clocks in walnut and mahogany. In some cases, they even used porcelain dials.

The finish on their clocks is one of the most outstanding I have ever found on any of the American clocks. The finish is extremely hard, it cleans well and seldom if ever needs to be stripped to be refinished. In most cases, the original finish is so well done and hand rubbed that only a slight amount of cleaning will recondition it to its original condition where it looks almost as though it came off the manufacturer's shelf.

3. What is the easy method of removing and replacing the springs in the barrel?

In your article in 1948, you go into great detail about removing the two springs from the barrel and I have yet to find an easy method of replacing the springs. You have written that it is an easy method to remove the springs and replace them; but of all the Patti clocks that I have repaired, I have yet to be able to say that it is an easy matter to replace the springs once they have been taken out of the barrel. If you know of any shortcuts or any method of doing this, I would certainly appreciate hearing about it.

I would like to see you write an article for either the Bulletin or for the American Horologist and go into much more detail on these Patti clocks Or, if you have any information or record material which you could loan to me, I would be more than glad to compile as much information as I can and maybe some day I can write an article for the Bulletin and let all of our members know the history and the differences and answer all the questions that have come up on these Welch, Spring clocks

I realize that this is a rather cumbersome letter; but I would genuinely appreciate an answer to the questions and any other information you would care to supply.

A.

1) Certainly their movements were Connecticut made — this is the first time I've ever heard it questioned. Frankly, I can't see that first French resemblance. If you are going back to basics, note the bent-strip verge and the clivis pendulum suspension a la the cuckoo . . . both stem back to the black forest of Germany.

2) Purely a decorator's whim — the "Patti" pendulum-ball was (is) exceptionally bright and thus shows to the best advantage against such a background.

That the "Patti" movement was extra well made is evidenced by the fact that it operates upon a relatively weak mainspring compared to other Connecticut, eight-day movements of that era. It is odd in that it is the only movement of that era that: 1) had most of its impulse delivered via clubbed-tooth escape teeth rather than pointed with all impulse from the verge plane: 2) it had no suspension spring: 3) carried its odd mainspring in a floating box.

As you point out, its case has much that can be described as "ginger-bread" work — typical of the styles of the era. This prohibited the use of veneer as well as entailed additional hand work. It must have added much to the cost. Just why the manufacturer did not stamp the frame of this movement is subject to conjecture. In the 1880's 'brand names' as we know them today had not been established, thus Welch, Spring & Co., meant very little or nothing to a buyer.

As you get into the proposed paper, I trust that you will identify the different "Patti" models along with good close-up photos of their movements together with wheel sizes, train count, and pendulum length. Much of this you can get from your own clocks. Enclosed are a couple of my Patti photos for your files; use in any way you see fit. The label upon the back of the No. 2 carries two patent dates — March 25. 1879 and May 20, 1879. The B. B. Lewis patent dates Nov. 22, 1881. All three are vital to any Patti paper. I do not have, nor have I seen either of these two patents. As you know, copies can be had from the U.S. Patent Office, Box 9, Washington, D.C. 20231. The price is now 50¢ per, up from the 25¢ quoted in the 1948 A.H.&J. article.

The Patti clock is a distinct type — one of a kind — well worth researching and writing about. I'm sure that you can get some valuable assistance from The American Clock Museum, 100 Maple St., Bristol, CT 06010 upon history of Welch and of Spring, as well as their joint operation, etc.

Now, to #3: use your mainspring winder; taking the spring out is the exact reverse of setting it in. There is no short-cut. As I recall, the Patti spring having two (2) to the box with their outer ends coupled and winding from one inner end and driving from the other does not necessarily alter the procedure. Set your winder in the vise — the ratchet of it will hold the end coupled to the square — grasp the other member, using a soft glove, with your free hand. Wind slightly until you have relieved the pressure against the box and allow the winder to hold while you gently slip off the box. Then flip your winder ratchet and gently let down via the winder crank.

VIENNA REGULATOR GAINS

In my letter to you on the 4th of September I told you about the Vienna regulator that I suspected had the wrong center wheel and that it gained about five minutes in a half hour. I figured the beats per minute as you did and came up with the same answer. I increased the length of the pendulum as far as the case will allow and still the clock gains five minutes in two hours. It is an improvement over the original time, but now I ran out of room.

I figured that if I can get a pendulum ball that is smaller in diameter I can by this means lower the center of gravity possibly an inch. The pendulum ball now is 6" in diameter; if I can get a 4" diameter ball I might be able to bring the clock to near correct time. It seems this is the only way left to me to slow it up.

I would appreciate your thoughts and comments on this problem and I thank you for the solution to the problem of figuring the approximate length of pendulums.

The pendulum now is 28" from point of suspension to regulating nut; that is considerably longer than the 21 plus inches according to the formula.

The pendulum rod is wood, oval shaped and 13/16" in width.

A.
That length arrived at by the formula is the theoretical length — that is from the point of suspension to the center of gravity of the pendulum assembly — not to the regulator nut.

Your reasoning that to lower the weight within the ball increased the length to the center of gravity is correct — however, in your case it will not be enough to slow the piece by five minutes in two hours.

Try replacing the 30 tooth escape wheel with one of thirty-two teeth; it should give you a theoretical pendulum of approximately twenty inches.

How to Alter Floating Balance Clocks

I would like information pertinent to altering the timing rate of Floating Balance Clocks. Conventional methods do not seem to work.

A.
Your floating balance escapement is equipped with a cylindrical hairspring which does not adapt itself to the orthodox regulator pins.

The timing rate is altered by moving weights in or out as required; exactly as you do with the 400-day clock. You have the same thing upon the ry grade pocket watch in the mean timing screws, and the marine chronometer.

There are several slight versions of this floating balance escapment; most have two little weights, spring loaded against a curved edge of the inside of the balance wheel. Moving them in one direction brings them closer to the center and for faster time — the other direction the opposite.

Fixing Vienna Regulator
A Problem

Again I turn in your direction for advice. I have a Vienna Regulator which has given me no end of trouble. This model is a Gustav Becker clock made in Austria. It chimes once at the quarter, twice on the half hour, etc., and strikes the hours. It is a rack and snail striking mechanism. Somewhere in its history the quarter chimes have been badly handled and I am unable to determine if it should chime on both rods at once or in sequence, bim-bam fashion. It does not have enough power to consistently operate both hammers at once, but will operate one at a time satisfactorily.

The clock is clean; bushings ok; and there appears to be no other problem, as the time and strike trains function ok. I tried getting more power by substituting a lead weight for the steel weight that was in use, but it did not help too much. In addition, I read-

justed the angle of the hammer tails with the chiming wheel pins, several times in fact, without achieving satisfactory results.

Also noted that as the weights fall, the center weight catches on the ones on either side. I wondered if this would indicate that the weights are not original and are perhaps too light for the clock?

I have had the clock for some time now and really need some fresh ideas . . . any suggestions?

A.

It is difficult to tell whether your Becker clock is a ding-dong at the quarters or if both hammers were to hit at the same time. That it has two independent acting hammers seems to vote in favor of the ding-dong or as you say, bim-bam. Also, the fact that it has sufficient power to operate them one at a time satisfactorily is still another vote for that system.

I have seen many G. B. clocks and not that first one has iron weights — all were lead-filled brass shells. Certainly your present weights must be of a different diameter than the originals, else the time weight in the center would not touch the others — the original weights were designed to clear in their downward decent.

Adjusting the hammer life (tails) should not be too difficult. If they are actuated by the same lift-pin, then to obtain the bim-bam effect one tail would have to be longer than the other provided that both hammers are pivoted concentrically. If their pivot center varied by a little, then one lift pin would provide the bim-bam from lift-tails of the same length, etc. Try a weight of a few more ounces than the one you presently have. Variations in weight, after enough to drive the chime has been reached, are not critical.

MOSHER & DAVIS G.F. CLOCK

Strike Pattern Falters Each Hour

A short while ago, I spoke to you regarding a problem I had encountered with the striking mechanism of an antique clock made by Mosher and Davis. The clock is said to have been made in the year 1820 in Hamilton, N Y. The movement is weight-driven, wood-framed, brass-wheeled and housed in a grandfather case.

The problem is with the strike pattern which is as follows: the clock strikes one time 15 minutes past the hour and once 15 minutes before the hour. This part is correct. In addition, it would appear from the way the strike count wheel is made, that the clock should strike once at the half hour and the correct number of hours at 12:00 o'clock. This is where my problem begins. The striking at the half hour and the hour is incorrect. The clock strikes as follows:

HOUR	NUMBER OF STRIKES
12:00	13
12:30	1
1:00	1
1:30	3
2:00	5
2:30	5
3:00	5
3:30	7
4:00	9
4:30	9
5:00	9
5:30	11

The strikes will then repeat from 6:00 through 11:30 beginning with 13 strikes and continuing the same pattern as from 12:00 through 5:30.

The weight which drives the strike mechanism will travel the full length of the chain in a 12-hour period. Consequently, it must be rewound every 12 hours for the clock to continue to strike.

I have checked the strike count wheel. Incidentally, it is handmade just like every other wheel in the clock and it seems to be correct. The wheel has not been altered and nothing appears broken. I am enclosing a sketch of the strike count wheel showing the number of teeth and its diameter. A sketch of the pinion adjacent to the strike count wheel has also been included. I have double checked the mechanism and see no other way of setting up the strike train so that it strikes properly on both the half hour and the hour. Interestingly enough, you will note that all the even strikes are not sounded. The clock does not strike 2, 4, 6, 8, 10 or 12.

Any information and assistance which you can

There was an S. Mosher advertising at Hamilton, NY in 1830 and Mosher & Davis advertising there in 1834.

Now, to your strike problem. It is one "Dilly" and I find it most difficult to tie into. First, you say that it performs one stroke at the first quarter — 15 past the hour — and one stroke at the third quarter — 45 min. — adding that "This is correct." This I doubt. There would certainly be some indication of a difference between the quarters if the clock was meant to be a quarter striker. To do so, you would have a clock sounding one time upon each quarter with absolutely no indication of which quarter one stroke would indicate. Furthermore, I'd think the clock was NOT constructed to be wound each 12 hours.

You make an excellent sketch of the count-wheel and its drive pinion but this tells me very little. It is how this relates to the entire strike train that counts. A clockmaker thoroughly familiar with the strike operation, will have to determine from his in-hand examination of this train and its action, or its failure to act properly.

First, one can determine from the strike trip what the clock was intended to do: if only the hour is to be struck, then only one trip; if the hour and half then two trips at the center; if it is to sound quarters then you will find four (4) trips, etc.

Now, once you have made this determination you can calculate the number of strokes that must be assigned to the count wheel, i.e. from 1 to 12 the count-wheel revolves once per twelve (12) hours, therefore if it only strikes the hours, then the train would perform seventy-eight strokes of the hammer per one rev. of the count-wheel. If the hours and halves, then ninety (90) strokes per rev. "If" as you say, it must strike one at the first quarter and another at the third quarter, then add 24 strokes and come up with 114 per rev of the count-wheel.

Start with this test; let us say, that the clock strikes the hours and halves — which I feel must be correct — then you require ninety (90) hammer strokes of the gong hammer to one complete revolution of the count-wheel. First: see that the strike train locks with the hammerlift tail slightly away from the lift pin; then, mark a point on the count wheel; hold up the count-finger thus allowing the strike train to run continuously, count the strokes until the count-wheel comes back to the marked spot—one exact revolution. If you do not get the required 90 hammer strokes then you have either the wrong count-wheel, wrong drive pinion or both.

Your sketch indicates a drive pinion of fourteen (14) driving a count-wheel of ninety (90). So far, so good, but we would have to have more data from the strike train to relate the drive pinion to the hammer strokes.

'If'' your clock strikes 90 per 12 hours . . . rev. count-wheel . . . and your count wheel has ninety (90) teeth, then each tooth represents one hammer stroke. This being the case, it has to mean one stroke per leaf of the drive pinion.

Mark the drive pinion so that you can accurately determine one complete rev. Strike the train and see if you get 14 hammer blows. If you do, then both the pinion and the count-wheel are correct, and your whole difficulty lies within the locking set-up in your strike train.

You should have the strike train locking — positive — every time the count finger drops below the rim steps. Locking is merely a matter of distance; i.e. the rim holds the count-finger up thereby preventing any lock until it can drop deeper as between rims.

At this point, a good test is: with the strike train securely locked, place on the count-wheel with the entering edge of the twelve (12) step right next to the count finger; trip the train; at the first stroke the count finger should drop on to the 12 step and thereby permit the train to continue to strike until it has performed 12 strokes. The count finger should drop off the leaving edge of the 12 step and lock the train. Next turn the minute hand to 12:30. One stroke should be performed and again the count finger drops below the rim and locks. The same should take place when you advance the minute hand up to 1:00 and again when you advance it to 1:30. With the completion of the 1:30 stroke, the strike train should lock with the count finger right near the entering edge of the two o'clock rim, then when you advance the minute hand to 2:00 the first stroke will drop the count finger onto the 2 o'clock step allowing the strike train to make a second stroke and lock as the count finger drops off the leaving edge of the two step. This is the correct action for a clock striking the hours and halves.

All this may seem a little confusing. I suggest that you go over it carefully with clock in hand and that you will point up the trouble and correct same. You always think of the strike train as "walking" i.e. the strike hammer falls on the gong and then the count finger falls on the rim just as one foot passes the other when you walk. As an apprentice, when I had strike troubles, my old mentor would say: "make her walk." I would like to hear IF you solve the problem.

Calendar Mechanism
Does Not Operate

I have a problem on an Ithaca Calendar Clock. I have consulted Catalog I, J. R. Oakley, page 92, explaining works of Ithaca Calendar movements.

When the crooked wire that works against the 8-year wheel is forced in position for 28 days or 30 days, it does not move back against 8-year wheel. Is

there any tension or spring placed on wire, or what makes it go back into position? The wire on the movement I have just stays there, but I think there should be something to make it move back.

I would greatly appreciate any information you can give me on this. I am enclosing a stamped, self-addressed envelope for a reply.

A.

Before answering a question about a calendar mechanism, one is almost compelled to review the whole calendar mechanical operation in order to make sure what is said is understood.

The SIMPLE calendar is one that indicates the day of the month via a pointer — hand — that is stepped around the circular dial one step each midnight. The wheel upon the arbor taking this hand, of necessity has to have 31 teeth to make 31 stops for the 31-day months, etc. Adjusting it for other months requires hand setting. The PERPETUAL calendar is one which automatically compensates (sets) for the 28, 29, 30 & 31 day months, as your Ithaca does.

In order for the perpetual calendar to work, it must have a mechanical device for accurately skipping over 29, 30 and 31 day positions to start the next month upon the 1st. What Oakley calls the "crooked" wire, my old mentor called the "skipper." This is the wire you inquire about. Examining your calendar, you will see that it is moved in and out, laterally within the slot it moves in, positioned by the 8-year wheel; that, its active end comes under a little three-step lug hinged onto the 31-tooth wheel: that, when all the way to the back it rides under the three-step thereby permitting the hand arbor to turn past three teeth, i.e. 29, 30 & 31 and landing into a lock on the 1st to start a new month. That, when back to the second position it rides under two steps to skip 30 and 31 — and — back only to the first position, the 31 will be skipped compensating for the 30 day months, etc.

Now, to your specific question: this skipper wire is held against the 8-year wheel by its own tension. That tension is applied via a little spring-wire located near where the tail and/or back end of the skipper is pivoted in a bearing in the iron frame, being bent here at a right angle, etc.

Oakley's instructions — we believe taken from original Ithaca specs, are very good, and so are the patent copies—however, neither mentions this little wire tension spring. If this little tension spring is missing, either from usage, break and/or some bumbling mechanic, you would not see where and how mounted. At the back of the frame — upon your right as you face it — is a coiled spring to pull down the lock on the 31-day wheel, this spring is anchored on a stud driven into the frame — before driving that stud home, your missing tension wire was inserted into that hole inside the frame — when broken next to that stud, nothing remains to show it has even been there. I would be interested to know: 1) if this answer is clear? 2) if you succeed in effecting the repair.

Clock Gains Five Minutes Per Half Hour

I have a Vienna regulator that I suspect someone has replaced the center wheel with the wrong one. The diameters of the wheel and pinion are correct but the number of teeth must be wrong, the clock gains approximately five minutes in a half hour.

When I removed the movement from the case I noticed that one of the pins holding the upper plate to the spacer posts was missing and the plate was bent, pushing upward in the center where the center wheel is. The wheel was wedged between the plates even with the plate being pushed out; the clock could not possibly run. This must have happened a long time ago because most of the wheel arbors and levers were caked with dust and rust which took some doing to get clean. Fortunately the pinions were not so badly rusted that I still could polish them up without affecting the meshing of the teeth.

I turned the upper shoulder of the center wheel back so it would fit properly between the plates after I had straightened the upper plate to where it should be. I also had to turn back the shoulder on which the canon pinion rides so that the minute wheel on the canon pinion would mesh properly with the ¼ hour count wheel.

After all this cleaning and polishing and getting the clock to run I find it gains this terrific amount. That is why I suspect the center wheel is not the right one.

I remember that in one of your Clockwise and Otherwise columns you had given the formula for figuring out the number of wheels, the number of teeth of the wheels and leaves of the pinions for each wheel and the length of the pendulum. I have the AH&J magazines from way back but no master index, so I can't pinpoint the issue or issues that this information is in.

So that I am sure of getting the information correct about the center wheel here are the number of teeth and leaves of the wheels and pinions in the time train:

main wheel . . . . 96 teeth

center wheel
                pinion . . . . 8 leaves
                wheel . . . . 72 teeth

3rd wheel
                pinion . . . . 8 leaves
                wheel . . . . 64 teeth

escape wheel
                pinion . . . . 8 leaves
                wheel . . . . 30 teeth

Length of pendulum from top of suspension spring to center of pendulum disk is 22¼ inches, from top of suspension spring to regulating nut is 25 inches. These distances can be varied by at least a half inch or more in either direction.

A.

If the train count be correct, then, any gain and/or loss in timekeeping of a pendulum clock has to lie within the length of its pendulum. As per your count, it appears that your movement has not been altered. Your center of 72 will revolve the 3rd pinion of 8 times; the 3rd, of 64 will revolve the escape pinion of 8 times; thus the escape wheel will be turned 72 times per hour. This we multiply by the 30 teeth in the escape wheel, 2, 160, at two beats per tooth we then get 4,320 beats per hour — divide by 60 and get 72 beats per minute.

We square the 72 — 5, 184 and divide into that fixed number 141, 120 and it comes out at 21-plus inches. That would be the theoretical length of a pendulum beating 72 times, or, from the point of suspension to the center of gravity in the pendulum.

Your pendulum rod may be rather heavy thus throwing the center of gravity well above the center of the ball. Many of these Vienna regulators are shipped over and get their pendulums changed, or, sometimes another movement may be put into the case. Just keep lowering the ball until you have it on time.

Ithica Clock Missing Part

I have an Ithica Two Dial Calendar clock with a part missing and I thought perhaps you could advise me how I could get this part. The clock is in good condition otherwise and I would appreciate any help you could give. The part in question is that which connects the time keeping movement to the calendar part, evidently a wire rod about 6 inches long which connects on to two rods one of which is fastened to the days of the week cylinder, the other to the days of the month cylinder. This part I have but the part that fits over the snail casting and down to these two rods is gone.

If you have a clock of this kind and would give me a description of this connecting device I would appreciate it very much.

The time part of the clock is made by Noah Pomeroy, and if you have any clock books I refer you to "American Clocks and Clock Makers" by Carl W. Dreppard, Page 154, the middle clock. Do you think it would be better to buy another complete calendar part?

A.

Noah Pomeroy, died about 1878 and the business was sold to Hiram C. Thompson, thus you see parts for your clock haven't been available for about 85 years.

Upon the back of your clock you should find a cam revolving once per twenty-four hours; hinged to one side and upon the back plate should be a little lever extending across the whole back of the movement; said lever has a little projection on it that rides upon this cam. As the cam turns; it raises this lever, at midnight the projection drops off the high portion of the cam allowing the lever to fall. This drop or fall, actuates your calendar mechanism by one step, i.e. the Wednesday is advanced to Thursday and the 20th this advanced to the 21st.

From the lever down to the brass piece at the top of your sketch, a piece of wire some six inches long, connects. As I recall, the top end of that wire has a hook riding in a hole in the end of the lever. The bottom end of that wire is threaded for about an inch; it should couple with brass piece by a hole in its center. Two nuts screw onto the wire; one above and one below the brass piece; the inch of threads enable you to adjust the drop so that the lever raises both members just barely enough to positively advance them by one step when it is let drop.

French Clock Needs Weights

I have in for repair a very old clock "French" for which I must furnish proper weights. Originals were destroyed by fire. The clock in question has a calendar dial and on top has three bells. It strikes two bells at fifteen after, four at thirty after, six at forty-five after and eight on the hour plus hour. Before all this takes place a bell rings once on the warning run. Approximate measurements are 10½ wide by 12¼ tall. There is a metal plate at top and bottom and the supporting rods are braided to them. The works are removed by unscrewing screws from top of upper plate. The bottom of the clock has basses that fit into holes in lower plate.

A.

Your description portrays a typical "French Provincial" quarter striker. My "Big Hoss" has two of them, one wall model, spring driven and one long-case weight driven, in her little collection.

First see that your clock is clean and in order; take an ordinary, fairly accurate spring tension scale, anchor the hook to the floor and your cable or pulley to the other end and crank the clock up 'til it registers 10 or a dozen pounds. Allow the clock to run upon this scale pull until it stops, then read the pounds on your scales; add 10% as a safety factor and you'll have about the correct weight.

It is noted that you say one stroke is made on the "warn-run"—this isn't right. Check and see if the strike train is locking at the end of a strike operation with the hammer raised. Also check, carefully, the entire setting of the strike train.

Exactly upon the hours, just when it has completed the four-quarter-ding-dong, it should strike the correct hour—then, between one and two minutes after, it should "repeat" the hour stroke, not the quarter ding-dong. Incidently, in the third part "La Pendule Francis" by Tardy, which we have mentioned, we found upwards of a dozen illustrations of these "Provincial" movements along with some sketches of their strike action, etc.

GEARING

I have for repair an 18S Waltham Watch, No. 1,980,828, 15-jewel. I can tell the watch has been tampered with because the hairspring is all fouled up, and because of broken staff and jewels. I cleaned the watch, put in two balance jewels, upper and lower, a staff, and had a new hairspring vibrated. I put the watch on an electric timing device and it rates out in the dial position 5 seconds fast, and 15 seconds fast in the pendant position. But the watch gains 6 hours in the course of 24 hours.

I took it all apart and this is what I found when figuring the ratio of the train:

Center Wh.	Third Wh.	Fourth Wh.
64 Teeth x	60 Teeth x	63 Teeth =

8 Leaves x	8 Leaves x	7 Leaves
Third Wh.	Fourth Wh.	Escape Wh.
Pinion	Pinion	Pinion

$$\frac{241920}{448} = 540$$

If the escape wheel turns per hour 540 revolutions, that gives me 16,200 beats per hour. Is there such a thing in 18S Waltham watches? Do I have to have the hairspring vibrated for that, or is it possible that someone has changed the wheel of the train?

I would appreciate very much if you could tell me how to proceed.

A.

Your watch was made sometime between 1880 and 1885. This date roughly coincides with the change-over from the old quarter-beat (14,400 train) to the modern five-beat (18,000 beats-per-hour train). During this transition, a number of different or odd beats were produced; a quick check indicates that your 16,200 calculation is correct.

In Charlie Purdom's "Scientific Timing," arranged and published by Orville R. Hagans in 1947, he records a 16,200-beat on page 135, and says it will show nine lines on the electric timing machine chart.

It is my guess that when you had the new hairspring vibrated, you did not tell your vibrator that the balance must beat 16,200, and he assumed it to be an 18,000-beat train, and fitted that spring for you.

This doesn't exactly jibe with your reported gaining rate of 15 minutes per hour. As I said, we are in the clock department, and I'm sorry that timing machines aren't readily adapted to clocks. Anyway, that is beside the point, because there isn't any question about a balance beating 16,200 times per hour keeping correct time with the train you describe.

"How does a lantern pinion differ from a leaf pinion?" The correct answer to that specific question is: "In design and calculation, there is *no* difference." He tells me that he hasn't found very much upon lantern pinion gearing, but has discovered that there is a difference. Actually this difference is not in pinion design, but in driving tooth profile.

First, you have a point in deciding upon lantern pinions, and are probably correct when you say you can make them easier than you can make cut or leaf pinions— you know your own equipment, etc., best. After you have calculated your train and made your drawing, select a brass rod of the proper diameter; chuck it and lay-out your pinion by turning a circle exact diameter of line of hole centers. Using the dividing head to space the *staves* (in cut pinions they are called leaves—in lantern pinions they are called staves), see drawing No. 1. You have already determined the proper diameter of stave wire, so drill your holes the correct size, and a little over twice as deep as you plan to have your pinion heads thick. With the stock turning, use your

jeweler's saw and cut off two heads after drilling the proper size center hole for staking on to your arbor. This way not only saves time, but gives you two perfectly matching heads.

When calculating your train, you have two known facts to work from: *A* the wheel size (more correctly, center distances), and *B* the ratio, that is the number of times you wish the wheel to turn the pinion. As an illustration, let us say you have a center distance of 80 m/m., and that you wish your wheel to turn the pinion 7 times—a ratio of 7 to 1. Lay out upon your drawing board, in any proportion you desire, your line of centers to represent the 80 m/m. Take your ratio of 7, add 1 and you get 8. Divide the center distance into eight parts, Fig. 2. Seven parts will be the radius of your wheel and one part will be the radius of your pinion. We presume you have found in your watch books and are familiar with: Addendum, dedundum, pitch circle, etc. With the radii mentioned above draw the two circles, these will be the *pitch* circles. A good rule to follow when making pinions is to divide your space into five equal parts; giving two parts to the stave or leaf and three parts to the space. Therefore, in our proposed pinion above, the pitch circle is first divided into eight parts for the eight leaves or staves, and each of these parts divided into five equal parts.

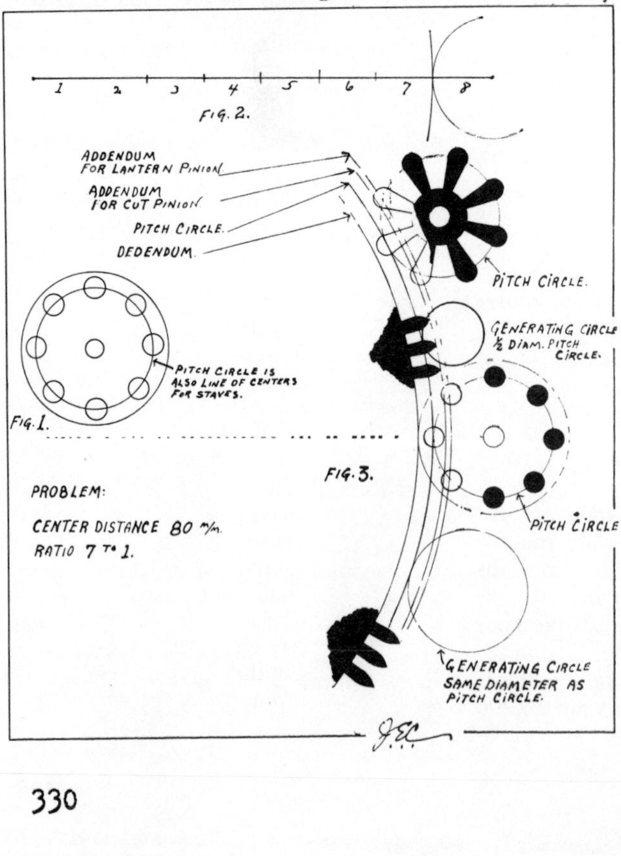

Since our ratio is 7 to 1 and the pinion has eight staves, your wheel must have seven times as many teeth—7 times 8 equals 56. Saunier recommends making tooth and space of equal width, however, recent practice tends to give more to the space and less to the tooth. Godrich suggests about 11/20ths to the space and 9/20ths to the tooth.

Now, we come to the actual difference, the profile or shape of the wheel teeth.

FIG. 2.

ADDENDUM FOR LANTERN PINION

ADDENDUM FOR CUT PINION

PITCH CIRCLE.

DEDENDUM.

PITCH CIRCLE IS ALSO LINE OF CENTERS FOR STAVES.

FIG. 1.

PROBLEM:

CENTER DISTANCE 80 m/m.
RATIO 7 TO 1.

PITCH CIRCLE.

GENERATING CIRCLE ½ DIAM. PITCH CIRCLE.

FIG. 3.

PITCH CIRCLE

GENERATING CIRCLE SAME DIAMETER AS PITCH CIRCLE.

As said before, both lantern and cut pinion are designed from the same method, but for teeth to drive a cut pinion, you would use a generating circle whose diameter would equal the radius of the pinion; while for teeth to drive a "lantern" pinion you would use a generating circle whose diameter would equal the diameter (not the radius) of the pinion. In different words, the diameter of your generating circle for lantern pinions is exactly twice as large as for cut pinions. We've tried to further clarify this in sketch No. 3.

After all, your main question might be re-phrased into: "What is the main difference between lantern and cut pinion gearing?" The essential difference lies in the fact that in the lantern pinion there is no radical flank for the curve of the wheel tooth to press against. Excepting in the very small numbers, the driving is all done on and after the line of centers; this is the feature that makes it an ideal gearing for clock work. You can readily see that if the pinion was the driver instead of the driven; this condition would be reversed, and the lantern pinion would not make an ideal driver.

"FRIESLAND" MISSING WHEEL

I have received a clock for repair which has no markings of any kind and is not familiar to me. Enclosed is a photo of this movement which may help in identifying it. This clock looks similar to the Zandam clock

The hour wheel is missing and I wonder if you can give me any information as to where one can be obtained or specifications for this wheel so that I can make one for it.

The pendulum is missing too, and I would like to know length, etc., for it. Also, this clock was received with only one weight. Should it have two or does the one weight run both the time and strike trains?

A.

Your clock is definitely Dutch and of the same type as the illustration you refer to. I've always called them "Friesland" clocks and believe this is the term generally used. However, I must remind you that my speciality has always been early American.

By all means make the hour wheel yourself. Fortunately in this case it is idler-driven

and therefore does not require precision mesh. I know of nothing that brings more lasting satisfaction than actually making parts with your own hands and tools.

Usually on these clocks, the dividing wheel is the driver. Your excellent photo indicates it to be in this case—the dividing wheel of 39 teeth drives the minute wheel

Photo of Mr. Schreur's clock.

of 26 teeth. The dividing pinion (on the dividing wheel) has 6 leaves; thus when the dividing wheel revolves two revolutions it will have turned the minute wheel three revolutions (three hours). Three hours of the 12-hour circle is one-fourth, then the two revolutions of the dividing pinion of 6 must turn the hour wheel one-fourth— four times twelve equals forty-eight. You can readily determine a workable diameter, general tooth profile and length of hour pipe from actually measuring the clock.

As a general rule, "Friesland" clocks are driven with one weight, Huygens fall, and it is quite likely this holds with your clock. I cannot determine from the photo but you

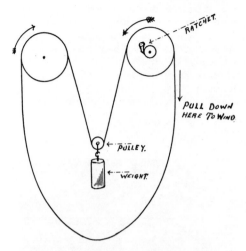

Sketch illustrates one-weight operation.

may easily tell from the clock. If it was de-signed for two weights, then both drums will have ratchets. If designed to go by Huy-gens fall and one weight only, one drum will be ratchet mounted; the other being made fast to the main wheel and arbor. The sketch above will serve to give you an idea of the one weight operation. The trick lies in the endless chain and having the single weight ride by pulley.

Calculating the Train

First of a mechanical necessity, there is no pinion on the first and/or main arbor therefore the 'first' pinion finds itself upon the 'second'

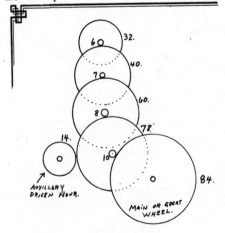

Figure 1

arbor — the second pinion on the third arbor and so on. Referring to pinions by their consecutive numbers can, and does, lead to some miscalculation and confusion. A more accurate designation is via the use of the arbor — axle or spindle — for when one says the pinion upon the second arbor, it is immediately clear which pinion regardless of what it's con-secutive number may be. When setting out to make a train calculation it is well to make a rough sketch of that train and place thereon the wheel teeth and pinion numbers as per Figure 1.

My old mentor insisted upon calling the wheel the driver and the pinion the driven, say-ing: multiply the drivers then multiply the dri-ven and divide—pointing out that the result-ant figure is that number of teeth driven past a fixed point in one hour — divided that by sixty minutes and get the number of teeth in the escape wheel that is driven past the fixed point in one minute — each tooth of your es-cape wheel delivers two beats to the pendulum; one as it enters the verge, the second as it leaves, so, we multiply by two and get the number of beats per minute. In many instances the train is calculated — counted — to ascer-tain the proper length pendulum for that clock — to translate the number of beats per minute to pendulum length, square it and divide into the fixed number 141,120. EXAMPLE: let us say that you have determined that 45 teeth of the escape wheel pass the fixed point; then, 2 times 45 equals 90 beats per minute — square 90 and get 8,100 divide into 141,120 and come up with a pendulum of 17.42 inches.

Let's go to area two — the auxiliary drive — and try out the clock sketched in Figure 1. The basic rule pre-supposes that the hour-post is an integral part of the train, in which case it might be arbor #2 or arbor #3 and you would of necessity calculate with all the teeth in that wheel. Not so in this illustration; the hour is auxiliary driven by the second arbor wheel via a 14 tooth wheel. This means that only 14 teeth of that wheel are required to revolve the hour post one complete turn, therefore we use four-teen instead of the 78 in the complete wheel: multiplying the drives and substituting the 14 we have:

$$\frac{14 \times 60 \times 40 \times 32}{8 \times 7 \times 6} = \frac{1,075,200}{336} = 3,200$$

3,200 what? Meaning that 3,200 escape wheel teeth pass a fixed point in one hour's run — divide by 60 minutes and get 53.66 teeth passing on one minute — we can't have a fraction of a tooth and since it is greater than a half we shall call it 54. At two beats per tooth that indicates that this movement is adaptable to a pendulum beating 108 times per minute. Square 108 and get 11,664 — divide that into the fixed number 141,120 and you get twelve plus inches for the correct pendulum length.

We have to keep in mind that: this is the pendulum of theory, NOT the over-all length of the practical, mechanical pendulum. The theoretical length is from the point of suspension down to the center of gravity — referring to the center of gravity, Reid says: "For this purpose the pendulum is laid across an edge, the edge of a knife for example . . . Often the pendulum assembly, ball, rod etc., are not one rigid item and can not be thus balanced. Wright, suggests that you suspend a small lead pellet by a thin silk thread even with the suspension point of the pendulum and adjust its length until it beats with your pendulum thus indicating the center of gravity of that pendulum close enough for all practical applications. Pendulum calculations are not an extra precise exercise for the simple reason you have a regulating nut enabling you to vary the beat considerably, that enables you to round off fractions — if less that .5 to the next low number; if more than .5 to the next high number, etc.

We often have questions for a lost escape wheel, or, lost escape arbor — such questions are incomplete and/or open ended — the questioner should ascertain from the case the approximate over-all length of the pendulum. That would complete the question and give us something to work toward. To ask "How many teeth in an escape wheel" without indicating what the clock should beat is like how high is up or how long is a string.

This brings us to area three — the length of the pendulum. The pendulum length per se is not an integral part of the train calculation, but is so very closely related to it that it is almost impossible to treat one without including the other.

Two major properties of the pendulum concern the clockmaker; one, the length; two, the number of times it will vibrate in one minute. In most instances he has one of these figures and only desires to calculate the other — this writer prefers the method — rule — as set forth by Thomas Reid in his "Treatise on Clock and Watchmaking," 1826, page 140; however, all the old masters stick very closely to the funda-mental physical laws as enunciated by Galileo, 1564-1642, and later confirmed by the Dutch mathematician Christian Huyghens, 1629-1695. Reid gave it thus: "The lengths of two pendulums are reciprocal to one another, as the squares of the numbers of vibrations made in the same time. If, then, the number of vibrations that a pendulum makes in a given time is known, and the length of the pendulum, we can deduct the length of any other pendulum if the number of vibrations it must give in a certain time is known; and reciprocally the length of the pendulum being given, we can find the number of vibrations which it must give in a certain time." End of quote.

To find the length of a pendulum for a given number of vibrations? RULE: "Multiply the number of vibrations made in a minute by the royal or seconds pendulum — 60 — by itself which is squaring it, and this being multiplied by the standard length of 39.2 inches, and the last product divided by the square of the number of vibrations given in a minute, by the pendulum whose length is required, the quotient will be the length of that pendulum, in inches and decimal parts of an inch."

EXAMPLE: Let us say that you have counted the train and found that 60 teeth of the escape wheel pass that fixed point in a minute — at two beats per tooth when your pendulum must beat 120 — let's utilize ratio and proportion route — I believe my old Grand-dad called it rule of thumb — you shall have: 120 squared is to 60 squared as 39.2 is to x then we get: 14,400 : 39.2 :: 3,600 : × 39.2 × 3,600 equals 141,120.0 — that divided by 14,400 gives 9.8 inches for the theoretical length of our pendulum. Since you always have the 60 squared times the 39.2 inches every time you make a calculation; it is convenient to set that number aside as your "fixed figure"—jot it upon the fly leaf of your repair book; the edge of the bench drawer or upon your wall calendar, then you will have only to square the beat and divide.

Now, let's take the problem the other way around; say you have a clock with a lost escape wheel — you will wish to match the new wheel to the pendulum therefore you will have to know the beat per minute — from the existing pendulum and/or the location of the movement in the case, ascertain as accurately as possible the theoretical length of it.

RULE: "Divide the fixed number 141,120 by that length, the square root extracted from the quotient will be the number of vibrations per minute."

EXAMPLE: Length of pendulum is 156.8 inches, what will it beat per minute? 156.8 into the fixed number 141,120 goes 900 times — square-root 30. A two-seconds pendulum from a tower clock — used only because figures come even — principle remains the same.

Over the years, I have discussed the pendulum theory with literally a "blue-jillion" clockmakers — it is amazing that only ONE man detected a slight difference between T. D. Wright and Thomas Reid where they suggested a "fixed number" — that we used, 141,120 is from Reid, Wright says: 140,904 that comes about because each authority utilized a different "standard" pendulum — Reid's was 39.2 inches long while Prof. Wright used 39.14 — Saunier, while employing the "ratio and proportion" method does not suggest a "fixed number," in fact, he gives the pendulum calculation short shrift, stating: "such calculations are almost quite useless, since a table is given, at the end of this volume, of the lengths of pendulums for all numbers of oscillations." Here he is referring to a "Table showing the length of a simple pendulum" as calculated by E. Gourdin — many writers have repeated this table; you will find it in your Goodrich, page 16. We are unable to locate Monsieur E. Gourdin, on any of several French listings therefore conclude that perhaps he was not a maker of timepeices but a physicist or mathematician.

I can never go through the train count drill without recalling an incident of several years back; one afternoon a tall man strode into the shop with a 30-hour steeple clock under his arm which he plunked down upon the counter and immediately began to explain that he did not wish it repaired, only, that he wished me to tell him what to do, etc. as he was a repairer of clocks. His demeanor and speech immediately identified him as a hill character — I have always divided clockmakers into three divisions, the self-taught; those that served an apprenticeship and those products of an horological school; so, I asked him "where did you learn your trade?" He drew himself up to his full height and waited what seemed like a full minute, then, said with the greatest air of authority, "My pap taught me." He then proceeded to explain just what was wanted; he said that the clock was clean and that the main-string — s-t-r-i-n-g his words — was okay as he had supplied a new one — he had cut a slot in the floor of the case to permit the pendulum to swing through — regulated to time; it extended below the floor of the case almost an inch. We calculated the train and found that the escape wheel of the wrong number had been substituted. After suggesting a wheel of 32 instead of 28 he was quite satisfied but asked if I'd go over it just once more to be sure he had it. This time I gave him the paper and let him push the pencil; he was as pleased as a child with a new toy and wanted to "recompense" me for my effort — I refused any pay and thought I had sent him upon his merry way, rejoicing. In about ten minutes he was back, — laid a big Tennessee Country ham upon the counter saying: "I was afeared you would not take my money, so I fotched you a ham."

CHIMES

GERMAN WESTMINSTER

This double decker German Westminster chime with hour strike has given us quite a time in setting up to chime properly. At present, we have it striking the full Westminster Chime at each quarter hour, followed by a single rod hour-strike at each hour.

Mr. Richard's double decker German Westminster chime clock.

Could you tell me how to make a correction so as to bring about the purposes of the manufacturers?

A.

We handled a number of these clocks and from remembering them it seems that every one varied in some detail from the others. In the first place, the prime reason for building such a clock (you call it "double decker" which is as good a name as I've heard) is to lower factory production costs. The lower section can be cased and sold as a straight striking clock; the second deck

can be cased in a larger case and sold as a chime clock. Many of them further cut factory production cost by not making the second deck a full Westminster chime; they only chime the first, second and third quarters then the chime skips the fourth quarter allowing the clock to strike the hour only. With this type construction the second deck only has to perform six cords per hour instead of ten—a saving of some 96 cords per 24-hour day or 672 cords in a seven day run, this requires less mainspring and train for the week's run.

Of necessity, the quarter trips have to be actuated from the center post where the clock strikes the full chime; there is usually a trip on the chime attachment to trip the strike train down in the main clock just as the fourth quarter is completed. On those omitting the fourth quarter chime there is a lever on the front plate generally actuated by a pin set in the dividing wheel; said lever serves to shift the fourth quarter or hour trip from the chime attachment to the main clock, allowing the chime to remain silent for this one trip. Like the center staff, the dividing wheel makes one revolution per hour, thus the lever shifting pin comes into position once per hour and only on the hour when properly set up. This is the point that confuses many. Either they endeavor to make the clock chime the full quarters or fail to set the dividing wheel so that it makes the shift from chime attachment to clock proper when the hour is indicated by the hands.

Your clock seems to be a "Ding-Dong" striker. That is, the hour is struck by two hammers actuated from the main movement.

When repairing clocks of this type, first determine just what the manufacturer intended for it to do: (i.e.) chime the full Westminster chime or only the first, second and third quarters and keep this in mind when assembling the movement. Since the chime, be it full or three-quarters, is an attachment added to the clock, the clock movement can be set up and the strike train synchronized for warn, run and latch without regard to the chiming. I don't know that this makes the task any easier but it definitely divides the problem into two separate parts for likewise the chime portion can be set up, tripped by hand and the warn, run and latch checked without regard for the clock, just as you would do with the old Sonora model Seth Thomas chime.

The first, second and third quarter chimers should have 24 pins in the drum, while the full chimer usually has 40 pins in its drum. Where the fourth quarter is not chimed and the strike trip is thrown back to the main clock movement by a lever and pin in the dividing wheel as indicated above, the warn latch is also in the main movement. As to those that chime the fourth quarter, both the trip and warn latch are actuated from and by the chime attachment. Such a warn latch sometimes consists of a wire or lever pulled down into a position to hold the strike fan-fly until the chiming operation is completed, then as the chime train locks at the completion of its fourth quarter this lever or wire raises to permit the strike fan-fly to turn freely.

Clocks of the type you indicate were manufactured in Schramburg, Germany by Junghans. Later several companies took it up. The notable example of an extra chime attachment by American manufacturers was the Sonora model by Seth Thomas. However, this model was a full Westminster chime—always with the chime attachment being tripped from the center post four times per hour and it in turn tripping the strike. The Sonora is not noted for giving the repairman trouble. Waterbury built a hall clock with extra added attachment for chimes but I don't recall ever seeing one in a mantel clock. It too, was a straight thru tripper and does not give any particular trouble.

S.T. CHIME ADJUSTMENT

An 8-day Seth Thomas chime clock, recently overhauled by the factory for us, fails to strike the full number of chimes before striking the hour. The chimes at 15, 30 and 45 minutes are perfect. The chimes at the hour are O.K. except for the last hammer

before the hour strike begins. This last chime will then sound at about 10 minutes past the hour.

A.

You do not specify which model Seth Thomas Westminster chime clock, but we shall presume it to be the No. 124.

From your letter I'd say that what is taking place is:

Your chiming operation ends and locks just an instant before the last hammer drops. The train being locked, that hammer remains in the raised position until the chime train is set in motion for the warn-run, as you say, about 10 minutes later. With the slight forward motion of the hammer lift drum, the raised hammer is allowed to drop with the warn-run; the train again being locked and remaining in that position until the minute hand reached the quarter point and completely releases it for the quarter-chime operation.

The toothed gear that drives the hammer-lift drum is outside the back plate and fits on its arbor by a set-screw. Grasp the hammer-lift drum between thumb and forefinger of your left hand and hold it steady while you unscrew the set-screw just a very little. Turn the hammer lift drum forward just enough to clear and let that hammer fall. Then retighten the set screw. Strike the clock around through one hour and when the strike train comes to the lock position at the end of the fourth quarter operation, that last hammer should clear and fall correctly.

PENDULUM WEIGHT

I have a modern chime clock that has the pendulum ball lost. I believe the clock is of foreign make. How can I find the proper weight for the pendulum ball, so as to get a new one?

A.

If there is a "sixty-four dollar question" in the whole of the clock repair industry, you've got it.

Let's divide the "weight of the pendulum ball question" in half: (1) the horological - engineer designing a complete clock. (2) the repairman with a completed movement, and the ball missing.

Naturally, we are concerned with and

shall confine ourselves to the latter half. About the *only* answer I can give you is the old standby—trial and error.

All too many repairers cling to an idea that the weight of the ball is the governing factor in the timing of the clock; no other idea he might have about the movement could be further amiss. It is the length of the pendulum that determines its period of vibration and not the weight. The weight idea as coupled with the rate or period of vibration is occasioned because when one makes a change in weight, he nearly always alters the length.

Reid's "Treatise" gives the following: "Between the weight of the pendulum ball of a clock and that of the weight or moving force applied to it, there ought to be some sort of proportion; for, if the moving force is too great, it will tend to increase the friction and wear the machine faster out; if it is too little, the clock will not get well through when the oil gets thick and foul. The far greater number of clocks have the moving force much more powerful that what is necessary, arising in some degree from the trouble of getting weights to any specific number of pounds . . . it is for this reason that we shall insert the rules and examples for finding this, so a clockmaker, when making trial with his clock, should give no more than motive force requisite for the pendulum."

Now which came first, the hen or the egg? From the above, it would seem that the clockmaker first builds his clock, then determines the driving weight by trial and error. This in no way contradicts the statement above, that weight does not determine the rate. The clockmaker chooses a pendulum ball of any size and weight (within limits, of course) that suits his fancy, and simply hangs on sufficient driving power to maintain its motion.

Your problem is just the reverse. The clock is completed, and pendulum length and driving force are already determined. So it remains for you to hang on a passable weight pendulum ball by trial and error. Experience with these matters is always a great help. Do you recall ever repairing the movement with about the same general construction, pendulum weight, etc., and roughly the size and weight ball it had? If you do not have a comparable clock in the shop, can you conveniently have a quick look-see in another shop? Such will only serve as a starting point for your "cut and try" work.

ADJUST NEW HAVEN CHIME

We have a New Haven 8-day shelf clock in for repairs which has the chime train out of index. At the hour-strike it is always one stroke short. About 20 minutes after the hour, when the stop is released, the hammer comes down completing the last hour chime. At the half-hour, there is one stroke of the hammer, and about 8 minutes to the hour, when the stop is released, the hammer comes down completing the half-hour chime.

A.

It's likely that you have a "rack" strike movement, and the gathering pin is so set as to allow the strike train to lock before it drops the hammer on the last stroke. However, we can't be sure of the type of strike from your description. The "count wheel" strike type can, under some conditions, evidence similar symptoms.

Since clocks strike the hours and halves, the strike trip must, of necessity, come off the center-post (minute post), and because it turns so slowly (1 r.p.h.), you cannot have the clock strike right on the correct minute with one simple trip from this slow motion. Both "rack" and "count-wheel" striking trains follow the same general pattern, i.e., as the center trip unlocks the strike train, it raises another locking piece (wire or lever) which again locks the train, generally one wheel further up (next fan-fly) the train. This part of the strike operation takes place anywhere from ten minutes to two minutes before the hour, depending on the clock and how it is set up. It is called the "Warn-run."

This warn-run should be just enough to positively unlock the train—one to three revs of the fan-fly, and very little forward motion of other members of the strike train. At the end of the warn-run, the hammer lifting pin should be spaced roughly one-fourth the distance between lifting pins away from the hammer tail. This space or "lead" permits the strike train to get well going before it picks up its load. Now your train remains in this warn lock position until the minute hand points exactly to the 60 mark. The trip drops off the lifting cam on the minute post, releasing the strike train, and it proceeds to strike the correct hour.

At the very instant of the last hammer stroke, your strike train should lock. This brings us through the complete strike operation. Besides locking immediately after the hammer tail has fallen off the last pin, that wheel upon which is situated the warn-lock pin should stop with that pin a very short distance from the warn-lock piece. This distance is what determines the amount of warn-run. Your clock is locking with the hammer raised; thus, when this warn-run takes place (several minutes before strike time) the hammer is allowed to fall, and you have that odd stroke.

You will have to let your mainspring down and re-set the entire strike train. Study it closely; keep the above in mind, and begin at the bottom (main wheel). Usually the second wheel has the hammer lift pins; set it in place and revolve till a stroke of the hammer is completed. Note or mark its position at the instant of the hammer fall (and keep it there). Next the third wheel which generally has the lock plate (or lock pin) should be set so it is locked. Then the fourth wheel with its warn-lock pin should be set in with that pin slightly behind the warn-lock piece.

Last, is the fan-fly. If it is the count-wheel type, it must be set as above, with the count hook resting on the very bottom of one of the deep (locking) slots. If it is the rack type, you set the stroke train up as above with the gathering pin just emerging from the rack. It is not always necessary for the positive lock to take place with the gathering pin entirely out of the rack, but it must be near enough out so that the warn-run moves it forward enough to clear the rack and allow it to fall.

WATERBURY SHIP'S BELL

Could you kindly give me some information about a Waterbury 8-day clock? This clock was made to strike the sequence of bells as used aboard ship, but unfortunately had been taken to pieces, and we think some of the parts are missing.

For your information, the striking mechanism is mounted on the back plate of the clock; attached to the extended center arbor friction tight is a two-pin lifting cam, and on the same arbor in front of this, running free, are the pinion and four-step snail. The 7-tooth rack and gathering pallet have been refitted, but as stated above, the lever to lift the releasing mechanism appears to be missing.

Information is also required on the sequence of bells struck in relation to time shown on the dial.

A.

I truly hope that no parts have been lost from your strike mechanism on the Waterbury ship's bell. I am sending you a photo of the complete movement, strike side (back) and by this, you can easily determine whether or not something is really missing.

In case some parts are missing, I believe we can supply accurate sizes, a sketch, etc., from our files—just write us indicating which part.

The answer to your question concerning sequence to bells struck in relation to time shown on the dial would be:

12:30—1 bell	4:30—1 bell	8:30—1 bell
1:00—2 bells	5:00—2 bells	9:00—2 bells
1:30—3 bells	5:30—3 bells	9:30—3 bells
2:00—4 bells	6:00—4 bells	10:00—4 bells
2:30—5 bells	6:30—5 bells	10:30—5 bells
3:00—6 bells	7:00—6 bells	11:00—6 bells
3:30—7 bells	7:30—7 bells	11:30—7 bells
4:00—8 bells	8:00—8 bells	12:00—8 bells

We suspect that possibly the 7-tooth rack maye be confusing, especially when one thinks of it in connection with 4-step snail. Actually the hammer makes one stroke for each tooth and the eighth for the locking notch at the bottom. It also makes two strokes for each step of the snail. There is a tail-piece extending downwards from the striking hammer pivot—a cam on the center engages a lever at the half-hour (odd strokes) allowing a pawl to catch the tail-piece on the last stroke and preventing the hammer from reaching the gong with its last' stroke. Thus, for seven bells, the rack drops into the lowest notch of the snail and the mechanism actually operates for eight strokes, but with the last one being locked off from touching the gong, only seven bells are sounded.

S.T. NO.124 CHIME

I am writing in regard to a Seth Thomas Kingsbury model chime, S. T. No. 124 chime. This clock runs a full eight days, but the train on the quarter and half-hour will not chime the full eight days. It will stop chiming and the hour hammer that strikes the hour hangs up at times and will not strike at all. Have you any advice to offer?

A.

When your No. 124 Seth Thomas chime fails to strike the full week or hangs up during striking operations, we look to the power. Either it does not have the correct mainspring, or friction (bind) prevents it from delivering its full power to the train.

No. 124 chime, strike and time springs are housed in non-going barrels. Any time you have the spring in a barrel, whether it is a going-barrel or not, that spring must be of the correct length and thickness. Springs too long are so crowded they can't uncoil or drive the train the full required time. Springs too short also fail to drive the full week.

In the new No. 124, the chime spring is approximately 5 feet, 10 inches long by 12/16 inches wide, and .015 inches thick. The time spring is 5 feet, 10 inches long by 11/16 inches wide, and .012 inches thick. The strike spring is 4 feet, 2 inches long by 11/16 inches wide and .015 inches thick.

Check first the two lower pillar posts. These movements are constructed with the barrel plate fitted on top of the train plate. All pillar posts are cut the same length so as to build up or lengthen the two lower pillars on which the barrel

plate fits. The factory places two (one upon each) spacers or washers to make them equal in height to the top of the train plate and thus fit the barrel plate level. Many workmen are without this knowledge, or are just plain careless, and when removing the barrel plate, lose these spacers and then replace it in the unlevel position. This absorbs all the winding arbor end shake. Your clock might continue to struggle on for a few days until the bind is sufficient to overcome the power of the partially unwound spring.

2 TRAIN GERMAN CHIME

I have an eight-day spring wound West-minster chime mantel clock about which I would like some information. It is German with the trade mark of a lion and under this the letters U. M. It has only two springs, one time and one for both strike and chime. The problem is, it only chimes on the quarters, on the hour it does not chime but just strikes the hour. You see the chiming cylinder moves out of action at the hour and the outer pins contact the hour strike hammer. By the first quarter the cylinder moves back in place, but the tune is not the conventional Westminster first quarter, neither are the other quarters as usual, and it takes three or four hours before it returns to the proper tune.

Is this a usual arrangement for this two-spring clock? Mechanically I can't see how it can be otherwise for the minute or reducing wheel carries the pin that moves the lever that shifts the chime pin barrel. Even if it does chime the fourth quarter before the hour strike, it still would not be the right tune on the following first quarter.

I would very much appreciate your opinion and advice on this clock. Is there something I should correct or leave as is? It has moon dial and calendar, parts all nicely finished and appears to be rather a good clock. About all the present owner knows is that it won't run. Thank you very much.

A.

The basic thought behind the construction of all these two-train chiming clocks was to produce a chiming clock cheaper.

You can readily see that not requiring that third mainspring and train, the factory could easily produce a movement much cheaper than the orthodox Westminster chime with three trains — the jeweler could offer his chime buying customer a chiming clock at a lower price.

Some of these two train German chimes were full Westminster chimers, i.e. they chimed one chord on the first quarter, two chords on the half (second quarter) hour, three chords on the three-quarter (45 minutes) and four chords on the hour, then the full hour stroke. These clocks of necessity had to have the shift (from chime to strike) on the chime drum, at the end of the fourth quarter.

Others were "cheaters"; i.e. the shifting was done by a pin in the hour wheel at some time between 45 minutes and the hour, and when it tripped at the hour it only struck the hour stroke, omitting (cheating out) entirely any chiming on the hour. A quick examination will immediately determine whether or not the movement is intended for a full chime, or is a "cheater." Evidently the movement in question is one of those that cheats its owner out of the hour chime.

Some of the better "cheaters" have the correct Westminster chime set up on its chime barrel so that the barrel has completed its full revolution at the end of the third chord at the three-quarter chime. In this way when it comes back into action at the first quarter it has to start with the proper four notes for the first quarter. We've seen a few of the poorer quality "cheaters" whose chime barrel did not make sense, and it simply gives the correct number of notes each time it chimes but does not, and can not, adhere to a regular hourly pattern.

Mark your chime barrel—start with the hour stroke and take the minute hand through one hour, after the chime barrel has operated through its hour-cycle, in your case, has chimed the first, second and third quarter, and note your mark. If the barrel has not made exactly one revolution, then the clock cannot follow an hourly pattern.

SETH THOMAS STRIKE

I have received for a repair a S. Thomas shelf clock on which my customer would like an approximate dating. It is a 30-hour, hour and a half hour strike, spring wound, pinned pillar posts, pin count wheel, plate stamped "S. Thomas, Plymouth Hollow, Connecticut," has a plate shaped like the sketch I'm including with my letter, and has a wire gong in the case.

The case is approximately 14½" high, 9½" wide at the base, bottom glass panel in the door is decorated in black and gold leaf designs with a 10 point star in red and yellow points surrounded by a blue circle in the center.

I have put the movement in order, but am having difficulty with the strike. When it strikes the half hour it is short one count on the hour strike, and when adjusted to strike correctly on the hour, it skips the half hour. Is there any trick to setting up this particular strike mechanism? Please advise.

A.

Seth Thomas built a good many models, both one and eight-day, on the lyre-type frame, and although various details of the striking mechanism were changed from time to time, basically all were essentially the same. All had the count wheel, and I'm sure that there is no trick involved in correctly adjusting any of them.

Many, if not most, of the little 30-hour (one-day) clocks did not strike the half hour at all, and from your description it would appear that somehow you are forcing a half hour strike. Since there are just enough strokes allowed for on the count wheel to strike the hours, one necessarily is subtracted if you force the clock to strike a stroke at the half hour point.

You can easily determine from the count wheel whether or not it provides for the half stroke—only 78 strokes are required to make the complete revolution of the count wheel or 12 hours. If you put in the halves, you add 12 single strokes— 78 plus 12 equals 90; just count the count wheel.

CHIME NOTES

We repair all types of clocks, but have just run into a snag. We are faced with a twelve tube, floor chime clock having five different chimes. Every twelve hours they automatically change the type of chimes; the first is Westminster, Trinity, Notre Dame, Carillon, and then St. Paul. What we are after is to get the true tones of the notes of the above chimes. We were told you would have all the combinations of note tones in some form.

A.

We do not know of a pamphlet containing all the information requested, but can supply the correct notes as follows:

WESTMINSTER
First quarter G - F - E - B (below mid-C)

Second Quarter
E - G - F - B
E - F - G - E

Third Quarter
G - E - F - B
B - F - G - E
G - F - E - B

Fourth Quarter
E - G - F - B
E - F - G - E
G - E - F - B
B - F - G - E

This chime is very familiar to most clock repairmen, and they generally work out most of their chime problems from it. Note: Ten chords are required to chime the entire hour—the No. 1 chord for the first quarter: G-F-E-B is repeated as the last chord of the third quarter, thus it occurs next following B-F-E-G the last chord of the fourth quarter or hour chime for the first quarter of the next hour.

TRINITY
First Quarter
D - C - B - A - G - D

Second Quarter
A - C - B - G - A - D
D - B - C - A - G - D

Third Quarter
C - B - A - G - D - A
D - D - C - B - A - G
D - C - B - A - G - D

Fourth Quarter
A - C - B - E - F - D
D - B - C - A - G - D
C - B - A - G - D - A
D - D - C - B - A - G

Again you will note that the number one chord for the first quarter is repeated as the third chord of the third quarter.

NOTRE DAME
First Quarter
B - C - D - D - E - F - A - G

Second Quarter
A - B - C - G - F - E - D - G
B - C - D - D - E - F - B - G

Third Quarter
C - B - G - G - F - E - D - D
A - B - C - D - F - E - F - G
B - C - D - D - E - F - A - G

Fourth Quarter
A - B - C - G - F - E - D - G
B - C - D - D - E - F - B - G
C - B - A - G - F - E - D - D
A - B - C - D - F - E - D - G

Despite the thirty-six different chimes in our files, we do not locate a St. Paul or Carillon, perhaps some of our readers can supply these. I suspect that your Carillon may be more of a "bell effect" rather than a true chime. No doubt all the chimes of your clock are set up on one drum, and if you can coordinate them to the three above, the other two, of necessity, must be correct.

S.T. NO.124 CHIME

I am writing you regarding a Seth Thomas Kingsbury model chime, S. T. No. 124 chime. This clock runs a full eight days, but the train on the quarter and half hour will not chime or strike at all. Have you any advice to offer on making the clock chime and strike?

A.

Since the hour strike of the Seth Thomas No. 124 Westminster chime clock is tripped by the chime train, any time the chime train fails to function there is nothing to release the strike and it always remains silent. With no more to go on than just the make and model of this clock, it is going to be difficult to actually pin-point your trouble.

These movements come equipped with an automatic chime corrector, which device very often gives trouble to those not fully familiar with it. Correction is accomplished by having a much longer lift for the fourth quarter stroke—you will note on the center-post a four-legged lift, three legs being the same length and the fourth being much longer—this long lift will point straight up when the minute hand points to XII.

Now, on the third arbor of the chime train affixed by a set-screw just in front of the front plate is a double locking disc; note that the front disc has four notches, one to stop the chime at the end of each quarter and the back disc has only one notch. On completion of the third quarter chime operation, the chime train locks in the one deep notch in the back disc. So locked it can only be tripped by the longest leg, or only when the minute hand points to XII—in other words, if the minute hand is carried past the III, the VI or the IX spot, the clock will not chime simply because these short trips do not raise the trip lever high enough.

The two locking levers at the extreme right and near the top of the movement extend through the front plate and have on their extended pivots the pawls which ride the locking plates. These pawls are affixed to the arbors by set screws. Assuming that you have set the chime train up correctly and the clock acts as you indicate, your whole trouble lies between these three set screws, one in the locking disc, one in the lock pawl and one in the safety pawl.

There is a pin extending forward in the front locking disc which engages a tail-piece from the strike lock lever and as the chime lock disc turns (R) this pin raises the tail-piece releasing both the strike train and the strike rack very near the end of the fourth quarter chime.

At the completion of the fourth chime operation the pin has just revolved from under the tail-piece and allows it to drop down at about the instant the chime train locks. Its dropping releases the strike train and it immediately starts to strike. There are six arbors in the chime train counting the mainspring arbor as number one, the fan fly being the sixth.

When setting the chime train up the procedure is the same as used for practically all strike trains, the warn run and the locking pin being located on the fifth wheel, but aside from this comes the automatic correcting device just mentioned. Part of it is a little disc with only one notch cut in it about midway distant between plates on the fourth arbor. With the chime train set up to the correct locking position, this single notch must be exactly under the little L-shaped locking lever that extends just above it.

Note a small pin in the back locking plate, on its back side and extending from it backwards towards the front plate. This pin is so located in the plate that about the end of the third quarter chime it acts against a short lever pulling the L-shaped lock lever down into the disc with single notch on the fourth arbor.

SESSIONS WESTMINSTER

Now here's my problem. I have a two-spring Sessions Westminster chime clock; it plays the melody correctly and strikes the hour, but I have had trouble getting mainsprings to drive it eight days.

I didn't have the original springs as they were gone when I procured the clock, and I have written to the company but have had no reply. There isn't any model or serial number on the movement or case; it is a rack and pinion affair with the chime roll being charged by the center pinion.

So please give me some help—I'm stuck! It sounds something like the cheater you spoke of in a past issue.

A.

Your two train Sessions Westminster chime clock is not a "cheater," for it gives you the full four quarters. The German clock I spoke of as a cheater because it cheats its owner out of the fourth quarter chime and only strikes on the hour. E. & J. Swigart Company, 34 West Sixth Street, Cincinnati 2, Ohio, can supply you with the correct spring for this clock.

Chime-reflecting back board

I am building a case for a grandmother clock. Could you advise what would be best suited for the back board for fastening the chime block to? It has 8 rod chimes. Would plyboard or a pressed wood back deaden the sound of the chimes?

A.

Yours is a problem of a sounding board or one of vibration and, frankly, one about which this writer does not know very much. I discussed it with three people whom I felt ought to know, or perhaps had had some experience.

All vetoed the pressed board idea; two felt that a good laminated plywood board would be as good as a well-seasoned piece of solid wood board. It was generally agreed that a heavy board would be better than a thin one. The more practical suggestion was that possibly the only sure way of obtaining maximum results would be by experimenting with the actual chime block you will use. Try it on two or three boards of different thicknesses, selecting the one that best reflects the chime sound.

Keep in mind that your chime block must be attached as rigidly as possible to the board. In effect, the chime rod vibrates and the vibrations are transmitted to the sound board by the block, and any loose or soft fastening tends to soften or kill the vibrations. Once you are getting all the sound or vibration transmitted to the board, then you are seeking a board that responds best to it.

Assembling a chime clock

I have a Seth Thomas chime clock for repair and I would like to know where I can get a chart or blueprint that would give me an idea as to how it is assembled.

A.

So far as we know, none of the factories have published an instruction chart for setting up chime trains, and neither has any individual devoted any effort to such.

To the watchmaker not familiar with clock work, and especially chime clocks, the first job or two presents a "problem." I can assure you that it isn't as big as you first thought. If you have a copy of Ward L. Goodrich's "Modern Clock," refer to Chapter XVI on striking trains. Then study the particular clock in hand (you failed to state the model) and you can "feel" your way so to speak, and assemble it step by step.

First, set in the time train. This is in the center of the movement. Then the two main-spring barrels for the strike and chime are set in. Put the front plate flat on your bench—top away from you—the chime train sits on your left and the strike on your right. As with the strike train of the eight-day clock, you will always work "to the lock position," that is, set it up just as if it had just completed the striking operation and locked.

With the quarter chime, you will see that the lift on the center post has four legs or trips—one for each quarter-hour of the circle. One of these trips is much longer than its three companions. This is the hour-trip and self-correcter. When the chime train has completed the third quarter chime and locks, it requires an additional high lift to unlock for the hour chime. Thus the fourth-quarter chime and the hour stroke can only be performed by the clock while the minute hand points to XII. In this connection, you will also note that it is the chime train which trips the strike (hour) train, and not the center post as in common striking clocks.

Now, the warning run latch, the train's operation, and its locking, are in general principle identical with all striking arrangements. Beginning with mainspring, you work toward the fan-fly, setting each member in the position it will be in when the train is locked. This goes for both chime and strike trains. On both the 113 and 124 Seth Thomas models, the chime hammer lift drums are auxiliary driven through an intermediate wheel, meaning that you may (and should) assemble the clock, check the trains, and have them working before setting on the chime drum. Make the movement chime through its fourth quarter and lock. Put on the chime drum and revolve it with your fingers, making it chime through the fourth quarter. Then while in that position, set in the intermediate drive wheel.

Though the problem as a whole may look large at first, look at it now. We have it split four times: 1. The time train. 2. The strike train. 3. The chime train. 4. The chime drum and its driver. Really four little problems. Each, worked individually, step by step, feeling your way as you go, becomes easy.

Scrambled chime drum

I have a watch and clock repair shop at the address below. About nine months ago, a customer brought me a German-made, quarter-hour chime, mantel clock to repair. When he first brought me the clock, he stated that someone had been tinkering around with it and it would not strike right. In my efforts to repair it, I found that the teeth or pins on the chime pin barrel do not make the hammers strike the chimes in the proper order. It is my personal conclusion that the pin barrel has been taken apart and reassembled in the wrong manner.

My problem is how, or in what order, do the pin wheels go back together? The pin barrel consists of ten pin wheels, each with a number—one to ten—a number of spacers, and two long screws which hold the pin wheels together.

I have tried putting them together in every form or order that I can think of and none of them seem to be right. The pin wheels do not seem to go together with the numbers in sequence or numerical order, such as one to ten, or ten to one. It seems that the numbers are staggered in some order, but I have yet to learn what that order is.

A.

Your deductions are probably correct, and I can assure you that a scrambled chime drum can be awfully mean. To give you minute details would require more information than you supplied.

We would have to know whether or not your chime rods set into the block in consecutive order—that is, straight from long to short, or whether the lengths are scrambled. Would have to know whether the long or short rod sets to the back of the case. However I am sure that the two of us working together can get your chime straight.

First, let's establish the correct notes and order of striking your chimes:

WESTMINSTER

G F E B—first quarter;

E G F B - E F G E—second quarter;

G E F B - B F G E—third quarter;

E G F B - E F G E - G E F B - B F G E—fourth quarter.

TRINITY

D C B A G D—first quarter;

A C B G A D - D B C A G D — second quarter;

C B A G D A - D D C B A G - D C B A G D—third quarter;

A C B G A D - D B C A G D - C B A G D A - D D C B A G—fourth quarter.

Where you have two chimes set up on the same barrel, it is only necessary to arrange one right. The other necessarily follows since the barrel makes the same turns for the quarters in both chimes. But, it is best to work from the chime using the greater number of notes.

Let us take the Trinity. Determine on the chime block which rod is "D," the first note of the Trinity chime. In this case, it should be the shortest rod, as this D is the highest note used in either chime.

Choose a section of the chime drum with 11 spaces between two points, because you will note that this high D is the first note, and does not reoccur until 11 other notes have been struck—the first note of the last chord of the second quarter. Place it in position of lifting the hammer to strike the first note of the first quarter. Now, choose a section whose point you can set ready to follow with the second note of the first quarter, namely "C," and have five spaces before the next point, as this C must be struck again for the second note of the first chord in the second quarter.

If you will observe carefully, you will

note that the first chord of the Westminster, G F E B, is repeated as the third chord of the third quarter, and that the first chord of the Trinity, D C B A G D, is repeated as the third chord of the third quarter again. This means that your chime drum is starting on its second revolution, or that only five chords are contained in one complete revolution of the drum. In other words, you proceed with other drum sections as outlined for one and two, and by the time you have worked through the second chord of the third quarter you are all the way around, and back to the starting point, and have used all the sections.

We know
that there are more chiming clocks in use
today than ever before and that there are
fewer "old timers" around to service them.
My thought is: perhaps, the great variety
of chiming mechanisms adds to the "confusion"—a bench clockmaker takes in one
today and the next possibly a week or ten
days later. Both do approximately the
same thing, yet on the one he will find a
drum turning two revolutions per hour,
while on the other a large drum revolving
only once per hour; one turns left, the
other turns right; the lapsed time between
jobs of identical construction being great
enough so that he never gets some of the
"basic" action firmly fixed within his thinking.

The most popular chime is the Westminster, and on those clocks having multiple chiming drums, Westminster is almost sure to be one of them, thus when
you have mastered the Westminster chime
you are ready to cope with about 98 percent of chiming clocks.

The chime, generally known as Westminster, was taken from the fifth bar of
Handel's aria from the Messiah: "I know
that my Redeemer liveth"; you will be
hearing the "Messiah" a lot around Christmas holidays; listen for it.

It gets its name from use by "Big Ben,"
the great clock on the abbey of Westminster, London. However, it is said to
have been used much earlier (1793-94)
in St. Mary's Church, Cambridge.

We find it written (sheet music) several
different ways: de Carle gives it:
G# F# E B—first quarter,
E   G# F# B—E F G E—second quarter.
G# E   F# B—B F G E—G F E B—third
                              quarter.
E   G# F# B—E F G E—G E F B—
                    B F G E—fourth quarter.
Whether this is a printer's error, or Mr.
de Carle intended to more accurately set
to paper the Westminster chime, we do
not know. In the average chime clock
only four hammers striking upon four rods
are used and it is therefore impossible to
have sharps one time and naturals another.

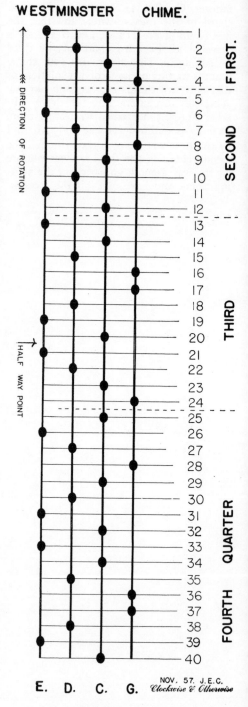

WESTMINSTER   CHIME.

DIRECTION OF ROTATION

HALF WAY POINT

FIRST

SECOND

THIRD

FOURTH QUARTER

E.   D.   C.   G.

NOV. 57. J.E.C.
Clockwise & Otherwise

346

At any rate, we are principally concerned with the sequence of strokes more than the tone—most chime clocks are as they left the factory and whatever note upon the scale is represented in the tone of each individual rod when struck by the hammer fortunately is not a part of the clockmaker's "problem."

The following is taken from an American clock catalog of several years back and we think is very near the average chime you will have for servicing. Anyway, it serves our purpose for this review:

E D C G—first quarter.

C E D G—C D E C—second quarter.

E C D G—G D E C—E D C G—third
quarter,

C E D G—C D E C—E C D G—G D E C
—fourth quarter.

Just how do we get these notes played mechanically, and at the proper times? See sketch Fig. 1. A chord of four tones represents each quarter—adding, we have one chord for the first quarter, plus two chords at the half-hour, plus three chords at the three-quarters (45 minutes) and four chords before the hour is struck; making a total of ten chords covering the hour.

Four notes to the chord times the ten chords gives a total of 40 notes struck to complete one hour's operation—in our sketch we have set down each note and opposite it is its individual number. Each of the four heavy black vertical lines represents one disc of the chime drum, if the construction at hand happens to be assembled from discs, or, a line around the drum if it is a solid drum with pins set in.

E being the highest note in our chord (line on left) is therefore the shortest rod in the block. G, the lowest tone is the longest rod.

One problem that has stumped a number of our questioners, has been the assembly of disc drums, i.e., some joker disassembles a drum, takes it to the bench clockmaker for correction and not being familiar with minute details, or able to locate it in his books, he has no end of trouble getting it assembled so his chime operates correctly.

A glance at the sketch shows that C, the short rod is struck ten times; D, the next

rod in length is also struck ten times; C, the next to longest rod gets 12 strokes, and G, the longest rod receives eight strokes. Now, you know immediately that an individual disc with eight lift-points goes to the long rod—which hammer the twelve point disc operates and by comparing the two ten point discs to see which has strokes coming close together (E), you can tell at a glance which operates the hammer for the shortest rod. After all, the problem is a simple one—fellows just allow it to bluff them.

Why do some clocks have a large drum and some a small one? It's equally simple. Another peep at the sketch and you will see that stroke (or note) 21 is the same as the first one—that stroke 22 is the same as the second and so on to the end at the 40th stroke.

In other words, of the 40-note hour duration operation the last 20 notes are duplicates of the first 20 in exactly the same sequence. Sketch is marked between the 20th and 21st stroke as the half way point. In such chime clocks as the Seth Thomas No. 124 model, the drum has only 20 strokes in its complete rotation; it merely turns twice per hour. Large drums have the complete 40 strokes set up for one revolution per hour.

Other variations in original design and construction are: a reversal of the order of rods, i.e., some have the short rod toward the front or dial side of the clock while others place the short rod towards the back; some chime drums rotate clockwise and some rotate to the left. Such points or differences are merely the idea of the designer; for some mechanical reason he wishes to build his movement that way. The playing of the Westminster chime is easily adapted; again to the sketch, the E disc is placed in the present G position; the D and C are reversed and the G put on last. Of course this is all easy enough for the factory because they are building the clock, but just a few months back one clockmaker was adapting a Seth Thomas 124 to another case wherein the chime block was reversed; after making the switch of movements he did not know that the S.T. disc drum could be disassembled and re-set to chime correctly with the short rod next to dial side and ruined a good chime block trying to drive out the rods and set them in reverse order. (The chime drum of the new S. T. A-400 German movement chime is almost a duplicate of the drum in the old No. 124.)

The "warn-run," "play," and "lock" action of chime trains are generally controlled from a locking plate, the action being like the count wheel of a strike train, having the ten chords stopped, 1, 2, 3, and 4 between locks. The lock plate always makes one rotation per hour's chiming regardless of whether the drum makes one or two revolutions. Of necessity the chime train must lock upon an arbor-wheel member of the chime train "between" chords—usually by a pin in that wheel coming against the stop when it is lowered into stop position by dropping in a slot of the chime locking plate. In most instances this will be the fourth arbor of the chime train—thus if the chime lock plate is carried upon the third chime arbor the ratio between that third wheel and the pinion upon the fourth arbor will be ten to one—ten chords to one revolution of the locking plate.

These references were based upon mantel clocks; basically grandfather clocks operate upon the same principle—many have multiple chimes played from a long drum located atop the movement. Some of these drums are rather small in diameter and revolve twice per hour—others large, making one revolution per hour's chiming. The fortunate feature of multiple chimes is: all the hammer lift pins are set in the drum, thus if one chime is correct the others have to be. You correct the Westminster and you have the others.

CORRECTING FAST CHIME

We have a new Seth Thomas electric Westminster Chimes clock and the chimes "chime" so fast all the beauty of them is lost. It also struck the hour so loud it could be heard a block.

Now I got that fixed but I can't slow the chimes. Could you please send me the solution?

A.

You do not mention the model number or otherwise indicate what kind of strike and chime the S. T. movement has.

Some S.T. electric strike and chime movements have their trains governed by a regular fan-fly—if this type, look to the fan-fly. Make sure that it has maximum friction against its arbor.

Other S.T. electric chime and strike movements utilize a little metal disc upon the last arbor instead of the regular fan. This disc turns between two permanent magnets which are adjustable via a screw setting arrangement either in or out. We suspect that since you have encountered trouble it is this latter type you have. Moving the magnet in or out controls the retarding effect the magnet has upon the disc; i.e., the speed at which it allows the train to spin off. A little "trial and error" method ought to enable you to set the chime to the proper speed.

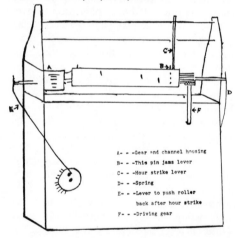

A- - -Gear and channel housing
B- - -This pin jams lever
C- - -Hour strike lever
D- - -Spring
E- - -Lever to push roller
        back after hour strike
F- - -Driving gear

Now, after the hour stroke is completed, the chime drum comes to rest in this position — i.e., that position where the strike pin remains in direct line of the strike hammer. Before the clock can chime the next (first quarter) quarter, the chime drum must be shifted back to the chime position—that one where the chime pins are in line with the chime hammers and the strike pin is to one side of the strike hammer.

The first shift, from chime to strike position, is done while the chime drum is in motion, but the second shift, from strike to chime position, is done by the movement as its hands travel from the hour to quarter past; and while the chime drum is dead at rest.

Evidently your strike train is so set up that when the drum comes to rest in the lock position, all pins are not CLEAR of their respective hammer lifts.

First, I'd look to the strike lock. Try setting that arbor-pinion one leaf forward (or one leaf back) from the position in which it now locks. Sight across the top of the drum to see when it is locked that all pins are clear of their lifts in order to permit the drum to shift laterally.

NEW HAVEN CHIME

I have a New Haven chime clock that does not strike the hour regularly. For instance, after it runs through the chime period it will strike the hour for several hours and then it will not strike the correct hour. It will strike like this, say, at 6, it will strike 7. When I correct the striking it will be okay for several hours then strike the wrong amount again. Why doesn't it strike the correct amount of times for the hour that is registered by the hands?

Why doesn't it miss the striking at other times? Why doesn't it always miss at the same amount of hours running time?

A.

Apparently your New Haven chime clock is a rack-striker, although you do not designate it as such (some New Heaven Chimes had count strikes). Any time a rack striker fails to strike the hour designated by the clock's hands, one of two things has happened. Either the rack did not drop all the way down, or the gathering pallet picks up a couple of teeth on one stroke. First see that your rack falls free and easy, that the stop finger rests against the snail as near the center of that step as possible, and last, that the gathering pallet cuts pretty near center between rack notches.

Look for looseness in the stop finger, wear in the bearing of the gathering pallet on the end nearest the rack. If I recall correctly, many of these New Haven gathering pallets were just a small disc with two steel pins set in it. Often these get bent or loosened in their settings. Sometimes a loose or bent pin will enter the rack and lift it about half the required distance. Flopping about in a bearing too large will do the same. The rack will not latch positively on that stroke, and will slip back, thus making an extra stroke. Many, if not most, rack strikers have a small spring to throw the rack down after it has been tripped. Yours could be bent, weak, or lost . . . check that point.

This "Junghans" puzzles repairman

We have in for repairs a "Junghans," no serial number, Chime clock, different from any we have ever had before. The movement has upper plates for the chime mechanism including mainspring, chime drum and wheels.

There are five strike hammers from front to rear. The first four do the chiming. These strike 16 times on the quarter hour, then hammers Nos. 5 and 6 ding dong once. On the half hour the chimes strike 16 times, and ding dong twice on the fourth and fifth rods. On the hour the chimes strike 16 times, and hammers ding dong the hour. The chimes are the same on every quarter hour. This is not a Westminster chime as one would think from the four chime rods at first observation as it strikes 4—8—12—16 times. This clock always strikes 16 times when the drum has made one revolution. The rotation of chime strikes on rods is 3—1—2—4—3—2—1—3—1—3—2—4—4—2—1—3. The long chime rod is at the rear and they get shorter as they go toward the front.

The rods are mounted on clock case back of movement like other Junghans. The question is, does this chime rotation have any meaning like Westminster and others and if so, what is it? I would be very grateful for a reply.

The time and strike are mounted in separate plates below the chime assembly, and are conventional except for a rod that goes up from the hour wheel trip, this trips the chime.

A.

You are correct, you do not have a true Westminster chime, however, the clock is supposed to imitate one. That is, it should chime one four-note chord upon the quarter after, two four-note chords at the half hour, three four-note chords at the 45-minutes, and four four-note chords at the hour just before striking.

This clock is one of several makes we see quite often "built down to a price." As you have noted, the quarter chiming mechanism is "added." By this arrangement the manufacturer was enabled to take one of his regular eight-day movements, add the strike attachment and come out with a chiming clock that cost less to produce than the regular, three-train, Westminster chime.

If your clock hits 16 notes and/or one complete revolution of the chime drum each and every quarter hour, that would mean four revolutions of the drum per hour, 96 per day, and 768 for the eight-day period. It would require one tremendous barrel and mainspring to do that. Don't you find your chime barrel very near the same size as the others?

Check the locking and check the drum size.

Full Westminster Has Three Trains

Since its inception, the full Westminster chime clock has, by its very nature posed a 'cost' problem to the manufacturer. It required three separate and distinct 'trains' i.e. one for timekeeping; one for chiming, and a third one for striking the hours. Over many years a great number of models have been produced with a view to having the clock chime on the quarters without having to build that third train; many ingenius devices—some practical and some not — have been marketed. Pretty often, we see one of the foreign models operating on two (2) trains—this is practical and a pretty good 'fooler' but it is not a "full" Westminster chime. It gives the correct Westminster chime upon 1st, 2nd, and 3rd., quarters, but, going from IX to XII the center-post shifts to a strike and upon the hour it merely strikes—no chime. Most experienced clockmakers have encountered various and sundry sorts of chiming clocks with only two trains.

So far as this writer's experience goes, the Sessions people produced the only practical 'full' Westminster chime, operating on two trains. This model came out in the 1920's and its practical operation is attested to by the fact so many are performing satisfactorily today.

Mr. Harry, writes, in part: "I need help on a Sessions Eight-day Chime clock. This clock has a small 7 rack on the front, and on the rear are five wheels with nibs on the rim to operate the hammers. My customer wants it to strike the hour, then chime. Is this the regular way for this clock to work? Tell me the correct procedure for this clock to strike and chime, AND HOW TO MAKE IT DO IT." (the caps are his).

The correct order for any Westminster chime clock is to chime one chord of four notes at the first quarter. Two chords of four notes each at the half-hour, and, three chords of four notes each at the three-quarter 45-min.) point. And four chords of four notes at the hour, then strike the correct hour.

This Sessions model, from the orthodox view point of the standard three-train type, is a bit weird in its performance; just watch the chime shaft continue to turn to pick up the hour strike etc., seems to baffle the repairman who sees it for the first time. Actually, the way it operates both chime and strike with one train and one source of power (mainspring) is rather simple when each seperate mechanical action is studied separately and apart from the whole.

There are four chiming wheels to operate the four chime hammers, plus a fifth wheel for operating the strike, all mounted upon one arbor. See Fig. 1.

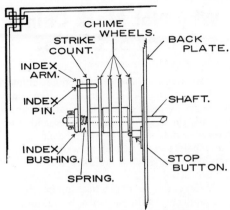

Fig. I During hour strike.

All five wheels 'float' loose upon the drive shaft, however, the strike wheel (one nearest the back of the clock) always revolves with the shaft since the index arm carries it around. The four chime-wheels are a solid unit (prevents a scrambled chime) and move, laterally upon the drive shaft when the stop-button drops into the hole in the back one (see Fig. 3), or, they are pushed outward upon the shaft by the unlocking-cam on the back end of the center (hour) post, as in Fig. 2.

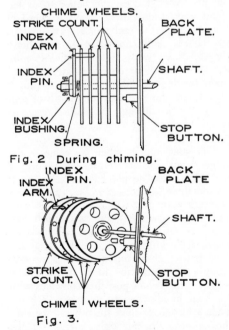

Fig. 2 During chiming.

Fig. 3.

Especially sketched by J. E. Coleman

This model clock is a 'self corrector' thus it is at this point we must start when setting up the chime and strike train. Located in front of the front plate and just under the dial are two racks; one for the chime operation and the other for the strike operation. Note the four lift pins -- like most other self-correctors, the operation at the hour (minute hand at XII) position is only released when a high lift pin has raised the trip an additional distance. In this particular instance, high enough to permit both the chime and the hour rack to fall. Turn the center post (forward) until this high lift has been observed; set on the minute hand pointing to XII. Then, set the chime snail to position for the chime rack (the one Mr. Harry refers to as 7) to drop into its lowest step—four. Set the hour snail as usual. When power is applied to the train, the gathering pallet which acts upon both the chime rack and the strike rack, will begin to pick up notches upon the strike rack only, it is slightly higher and the chime rack continues to fall back until all the notches of the strike rack are used up. When the gathering pallet drops off the strike rack it will still have the four notches of the chime rack to gather up. Suppose you are setting up at the VI position; the chime rack will drop down four steps and the strike rack will drop six steps— when the chiming operation commences the clock will execute the four chords by utilizing the first four steps upon the strike rack (one of the weird angles—chiming off the strike rack) at this point the hole in the chime wheel next to the plate (see Fig. 3.) drops on to the stop button; disengaging the index pin from the chiming wheels as in Fig. 1—as the chime wheels drop back toward the back plate the strike wheel is also moved in that direction by the spring; bring it over the tail piece of the strike hammer; the remaining two steps upon the strike rack count off two strokes; the gathering pallet drops on to the chime rack and its four steps count off four more hour strokes, for a total of six for the VI.

The one remaining item is: here you set the cam upon the back of the hour (center) post, so that it is just ready to begin engaging the chime shift lever. As the clock progresses from XII to III this cam which just covers 45 degrees of its circle, will lift the chiming wheels outward and off the stop button into mesh with the index pen; thus, recycling the chime operation for another full hour's chiming.

A little further observation of the chime wheels, etc. may lead to a fuller understanding of the entire operation. It is a mechanical necessity that any chiming device has to conform to the steps in the rack, i.e. if the clock is to chime just one chord when the rack drops just one step, then throughout its entire operation every step upon the rack necessarily represents one chord upon the chime drum (wheels). One chord for the 1st., quarter; two for the 2nd., three for the 3rd., and four for the hour totals ten (10) chords. The ten necessary chords are all set-up within the one complete revolution of the chiming wheels (drum) thus when the drum is pushed off the stop button it is the start of a complete hour cycle. Note: the strike wheel has only ten notches to trip the strike hammer—it has to be thus because every step of the racks have been proportioned to one-tenth the circumference of the drum.

However, this does not complicate the hour striking, simply because we are free to revolve the strike wheel any amount, just so long as it is by the tenths of the circle. At eleven o'clock, it is driven one and 1/10th. and·at twelve o'clock, one and 2/10ths., turns. There are ten holes on the outside chime wheel, so, from any position of the index pin the chime wheels can conveniently pickup when recycled by the cam on back center.

Despite its departure from orthodox construction, and its seeming weird action of chiming off the hour rack at the hour, then striking twelve strokes off a ten notch strike wheels, etc. it is quite simple when one takes one function at a time, in sequence—in fact, when the Sessions factory first put this chimer upon the market, they said: "Time required for assembly after cleaning is one-fifth of that required in other types of Westminister chimes, by reason of the elimination of all combination levers and discs and delicate adjustments common to other chime clocks."

Why Not Mark Chime Drums of Clocks?

First, a few of the older German chime clocks have their chime drums marked for the begining point of the first quarter strike. Second, there are so many makes and different models of those makes, coming to the repair bench that it is well nigh impossible to set down a definite procedure in minute detail.

Perhaps the best practical approach to the problem would be via a better understanding of the chiming operation— Mr. Donald de Carle, in his "Watch & Clock Encyclopedia" lists some three dozen different chimes; it is fortunate for the bench clockmaker that better than 95% of the mantel chime clocks coming to his bench, are "Westminister" chimers, or, combination chimers and the Westminister is included in that combination. Thus, if the repairer thoroughly understands the Westminister chime he will be equipped to handle nearly all chimers coming to his bench.

Let's analyze the Westminister chime and see just what it does, the better to understand how it does it. It plays a chord of four notes at the end of the first quarter; two chords (eight notes) at the half hour; three chords (twelve notes) at the 45 minute spot, and, four chords (sixteen notes) upon the hour. Adding we have 1 plus 2 plus 3 and plus 4 equals ten chords of four notes struck during the hour cycle. A grand total of 40 notes, or 40 hammer blows.

The same applies when we come to the chime train and its setting in. Many of the older clocks do not have a 'self-corrector' and those self-correctors that came along in recent years vary widely in their mechanical design though they accomplish the same net result. It generally comprises an auxilliary locking at the completion of the third-quarter chime operation thus necessitating a longer lift to unlock it; the chime lift upon the center post that coincides with the hour hand when it points to 12 being made a bit longer than the other three thus the chime train can only unlock for the fourth-quarter (hour) chime when the hand points to the hour (12).

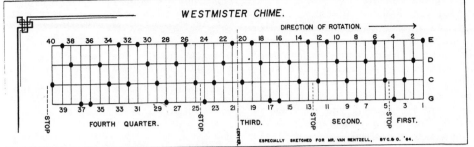

The warn-run, the play and the lock action of chime trains are generally activated with a locking plate—the basic action being the same as a count-wheel. This locking plate will make one revolution per hour; it is divided to permit one chord (4 notes); two chords; three chords and four chords between locks. In most instances, locking is accomplished by having a pin set parallel to the wheel-arbor in some wheel in the chime train; so long as the locking-plate holds a lever up allowing the lock pin to pass under it the chime train will run; when the lever drops into one of the lock-slots in the locking plate the lock-pin comes squarely against the lever thereby locking the chime train. When setting on the chime drum you must see to it that with the train locked, the drum comes to rest mid-way between chords.

Since ten chords comprise the hour chime cycle; the chime train must lock between chords and these ten chords are allotted to one revolution of the locking plate, it can be readily seen that the gear ratio between the locking plate and the arbor carrying the locking pin will have to be ten to one. Despite all the variables when one comes to try and cover the entire chime construction field; a good understanding of just what the Westminister chime is plus a basic understanding of how the chime train makes it chime as it should equips the workman to handle whatever peculiar type construction he has in hand at that moment.

These references are based upon mantel clocks; grandfather clocks operate along the same principles; many have multiple chimes, played by a long drum located atop the movement. Some of these drums are small; revolving twice per hour, others, large, making only one rev per hour's chiming. The fortunate feature of multiple chimes, they always contain Westminister,

and you can set up by it. All the hammer lift pins are permanently set into the drum so when you get the Westminister correct, the others will have to be.

The tones generally used are: E. D, C, and G. The order in which they are sounded is: E D C G for the first quarter; C E D G, C D E G for the second quarter; E C D G, G D E C, E D C G, for the third quarter and C E D G, C D E G, E C D G, G D E C, for the hour.

Now, should we plot these notes or tones upon a graph using the top line for E, the second line for D; the third line for C, and the bottom line for G; crossing that graph with a numbered line for each time performed (hammer stroke) it would show up as the sketch at the beginning of this article.

A study of this chart will firmly fix in your mind the entire operation of the Westminster chime. The center point is marked to show that the last 20 strokes are but duplicates of the first 20 strokes. Further, that shows why some clocks have a large chime drum while others have a much smaller one. Large drums make one revolution for the hour cycle while the small drums as that in the 124 Seth Thomas chime, make two revolutions per hour cycle. This is readily understood once you see that the last 20 strokes are the same as the first 20; you get them by simply revolving the small drum again.

At this point, we could inject some of the mechanical engineering problems involved in chime construction; it is quite clear that more power is required for the large drum—being large, the lift pin has to be farther from the arbor center, thus greater leverage. Another factor; the small drum making two revs. per hour, 48 per day, requires a mainspring twice as long if the gear ratio is the same; if the gear ratio is altered between the drum and drive arbor in order to allow a spring of less than twice the length then the spring strength must be increased to compensate for that increased gear ratio, etc. Injecting construction engineering is beside the point for here we are only concerned with a method of 'restoring' the chime train to operate as the manufacturer has already engineered it to function.

Many things become evident when considering the Westminster chime in its "chart" form — every so often, a chime clock is brought in whose chime drum is made up of discs and some not-so-understanding workman (or owner) has disassembled it— this often happens with the Session, two train chime which we sketched in the October 1962 column. Reassembling the discs becomes easy by following the chart.

First, you determine the direction of drum rotation. Second, from the chime-block whether "E" the high tone (shortest rod) is next to the front of the clock, or, back. Third, identify the discs; the G disc will have eight (8) lift-projections; the C disc twelve (12) and both D and E have ten (10). By comparison it is easy to note the E disc because it performs 11th & 13th, the 19th & 21st, and the 31st & 33rd hammer strokes just one stroke apart. Having correctly identified your discs; determined the direction of rotation and whether "E" or "G" goes next to the back plate, assembling it is easy.

Thus far, we've seen that: the chime drum can turn either clockwise or left; it can turn one rev per hour and have forty (40) lift notches or turn twice per hour and have twenty (20) lift notches; it can have the low tone (long rod) to the front or to the back—it is such variables as these which make it almost impossible to set down a pin-point, step by step procedure to be followed.

Has Chime Strike Problem

I would like to have some information concerning a Seth Thomas electric Westminster chime mantle clock.

I am having difficulty trying to adjust the chimes to operate properly. When the

hands are set manually for the complete twelve hours, the chimes work very well, but as soon as it is power-driven, the chimes will miss the last note on the ¾ hour, and consequently the last note will chime 15 minutes later, which is on the hour, and no other chime or strike follows. This does not happen every hour, but about twice in twelve hours, and it will take one hour each time it happens to correct itself.

A.

Let's analyze your chime strike problem this way: for some reason, your movement "locks" before it has completed the three-quarter chime operation, then, when the clock trips at the hour, it merely completes the three-quarter operation though it be but the one stroke, and locks again. This later time is at the point it should have locked at the end of the three-quarter operation. And, thus when the clock trips for the first-quarter, the chime drum is in the hour position—just one-quarter behind the hands.

Now, you have four "stops"—one for each quarter—upon the chime lock disc. Wherein does the third-quarter stop differ from the other three? It has a deeper notch to actuate the self-corrector. It is at this point I suspect you are going to find the real trouble.

At the completion of the third-quarter chime operation, the chime train should lock in exactly the same manner it locks at the end of the other chime operations, i.e. upon the same lock pin. Note that your hour lift is longer and that it therefore lifts the locking lever higher than the ¼, ½, and ¾ lifts. Upon the three-quarter chime lock a second disc (just behind the chime lock disc) presents a notch which permits the self corrector to come into play so that when the clock lifts upon the hour position the chime train is released just as at the quarter points; the lock pin advances a little bit to be stopped by the self-corrector lever; the additional raise at the hour also unlocks the self corrector, only permitting the clock to perform the full hour chime when the minute hand is at the XII position.

Check your third-quarter locking; see that it locks in the usual manner after the completion of the full 12 chime notes, upon the regular locking point, NOT upon the self corrector.

How Did Seth Thomas Chime System Work?

I have in my shop a Seth Thomas eight day clock with the words "Sonora Chimes" on the dial. Inside are four gong type chimes, but most of the hammers are missing as well as that part which releases the chime mechanism. Could you tell me how the chime system worked and if anyone might have parts for it?

A.

The Sonora was not a true chime clock mechanical-wise—rather, it utilized one of the Seth Thomas No. 89 eight day movements with a completely separate mechanism for sounding the Westminster chime, set in behind it. This chiming mechanism had an extra long winding arbor to reach past the movement, it came out just outside the minute circle at about the III o'clock mark.

The No. 89 movement was equipped with four angled lift wires on its center post, by which it tripped the chiming device every fifteen minutes. The hour strike was tripped by the chiming mechanism immediately as it completed the hour chime.

Since you mention that most of the hammers are missing, I'm wondering whether or not the entire chime device has not been removed. Re. material and parts, same have not been available for a good many years. The Sonora was a popular seller between the turn of the century and World War I. The Thomas people were able to produce and offer a clock that would chime the full Westminster chime and strike the hour at a much reduced figure—a 1917 catalog shows one Sonora model retailing for $32.50 while their orthodox Westminister chime clocks (three trains incorporatd between plates in regular manner) were retailing for double that. That was because they used the regular 89 movement and merely set in a chiming mechanism, etc.

How Do Chime Tubes Hang?

I have for repair a 1919 Herschede three-train chime, six-tube clock. I got a new escape wheel from the factory but they have no instructions for setting up the chime drum.

Someone else took it apart. I don't know for sure how to hang the tubes on the rack. The longest tube is the strike and this has a separate bracket and two pins to hang on. Then how do the five chime tubes hang?

And how do we mesh the gear on the chime drum? This clock has Westminster and Canterbury chimes. I have been looking for a place on the drum where the four hammers follow one after another in a row for the 15-minute chime but can find none.

Can you write me how to set this up correctly?

A.

If ever we had notes on this clock, I can't seem to locate them. There is a faint recollection of the trouble of setting one up. We are not going to be able to give you a "pat" how-to-do-it answer, only a couple of suggestions that may help.

As I recall, the tubes do not hang in either of the usual orders; i.e., shortest on the left and graduate to the right or longest tube on left and graduate to the right. They are scrambled, thus the lift pins of your drum are also scrambled and you will not find the four hammers for the first quarter chime of the Westminster coming in direct sequence on the drum.

First, set the clock to the Westminster chime because that is the one easiest worked out—once you have it correct, the Canterbury will automatically be correct. Next, hang up tubes; and by tapping them, determine which are "G", "F", "E" and "B"—the first four notes, struck in that order, for the first quarter Westminster.

Now, select a spot on the drum where four strokes are made in step, one right after the other. Then hang the four tubes selected so that it then strikes this first quarter. Then try for the half or second quarter stroke. It should be "E", "G", "F", "B"—"E", "F", "G", "E"—in exactly that order. If it hits, you've got it.

If it does not—select another four lift pins which strike in order and rehang your tubes in order to get the G-F-E-B of the first Westminster quarter; then try again for the second quarter. By this trial and error method, you will eventually strike the correct method for hanging the tubes. The remaining tubes then fill in the gaps left after the Westminster has been properly placed. Switch the chime indicator to Canterbury and by listening you will quickly determine whether or not you have filled the gaps correctly. If not, re-arrange. Be careful not to take down either of the Westminster tubes already correctly positioned.

Why the Extra Strike?

I've been having trouble with Revere and G.E. electric chimes giving an extra hour strike at the end of its regular sequence of striking the hour. I've checked and rechecked on spring tension and oiling the sliding parts.

This one clock is about 18 years old and doesn't seem to be worn. I wonder if you can give me any hints as to the cause. These clocks are new type self-adjusting chimes ¼-hour Westminster.

A.

Have you checked to see that the "rack" is not falling one tooth low each time? Getting an extra or one stroke too many each time would indicate that.

There is one possibility of getting that extra stroke, even when the rack is falling down through the correct number of teeth. Watch your rack closely at the finish of the strike operation. If you get the correct final stroke just as the gathering pawl drops off the bottom end of your rack and then get that additional stroke before the strike train locks, it indicates that the strike train is not properly set up.

Note the position of the strike-lock pin at the instant the gathering pawl drops off the bottom end of the rack—it (the lock pin) should be just a very little way from locking against the stop lever so that the strike train locks instantly.

If the lock pin is abreast of the locking lever, or slightly in advance of it, the locking wheel and arbor will have to make an additional revolution to bring the lock pin against the stop lever. During this additional rev., the strike train picks up the hammer tail for one more stroke. One other point to check—once you have the strike-lock properly set up, see that the hammer has just fallen and that the tail is not resting on the next lift pin. Generally, the gathering pawl falls off the end (lower) of the rack and the hammer falls against the gong about together, then, just a split second later the lock pin strikes the lock lever, stopping the strike train.

Chimes Not in Sequence

Needless to say I enjoy your articles every month in the American Horoligist and Jeweler.

My problem that I would appreciate your help on concerns Westminster chime clocks. Several times after cleaning them I find that the chimes do not play in even sequence. There seems to be a ⅛ note rest between some of the notes. This happens usually on Seth Thomas #124 movements. Could this be caused by slightly

oversize pivot? I would appreciate your advising me on how I may solve this problem.

A.

The setting up of any chime, and this includes the #124 Seth Thomas, can be a tedious affair. It isn't clear that your clock chimes in the proper sequence or that your only trouble is what you call a one/eighth rest upon one of the notes.

First check to see if it is that same note that temporarily hangs back every time? Chimes are musical and correct and/or smooth timing is very necessary. I seriously doubt that this hesitance is occasioned by worn bearings (oversize) unless it be the bearings of the chime drum.

There is a good chance that this trouble lies with the hammers and lift pins. Check to see that all the lift pins are straight and the same length. Check the hammer tails and their stops to see that every hammer has to be lifted exactly the same distance. On the 124 S. T. the hammer is raised by a drum pin acting against a flat pallet. See that this is not worn. It just could be that your hammers are gummed a bit and occasionally a hammer acts sluggish. We always dismantel the hammer assembly and clean it thoroughly. When reassembling make sure that the washer goes between each hammer and use a very little light oil in the hammer bearing. There are occasions where the fanfly gets shoved over or askew permitting it to touch lightly every once in a while, which would cause the chime to hesitate for an instant. All of this is quite general, and assumes that the chime train is functioning correctly and that the chime drum has been correctly set so that the clock chimes in proper sequence. Somehow I can't help but feel "we've not helped" and would like to hear from you again and more in detail.

HERSCHEDE TRIPLE CHIME

I have a Herschede Triple Chime Movement. The chimes will not remain synchronized with the time. I suspect the problem is in the mechanism. I think that the level and the single pin in the chime drum is a self-correcting device as it works in conjunction with the high pin on the cam. Is this correct?

Somebody had bent this lever at right angles so that it was underneath the chime drum, but I can't see how it can possibly work in that fashion. What is the correct method of adjusting this mechanism?

A.

When the quarter-chime gets out of step, sync, it has to be due to one of two things: 1) a failure to chime on a quarter: 2) over-run, striking more than one quarter at one trip. Either can be caused from a very light lock on the chime train, a too deep a lock, or, bent lift pins — check all these points.

If and when the quarter chime gets out of step, the self-corrector is supposed to realign it upon the hour. We think you are correct in saying that that simple pin on the chime drum is your self-corrector — just on the completion of the third-quarter chime this pin should act to so lock the chime train to a depth that will require additional lift to unlock it. That lift-pin in the hour-post set further from the center point than the other three, 1st, 2nd and 3rd quarter lift, does this additional lifting. Now, since the chime train is additionally locked at the completion of the third quarter and can only perform after it has received the additional lift which comes when your minute hand points to 60 it follows that the clock will chime the fourth quarter ONLY on the hour.

Sorry, we can't pin point a step by step instruction to make the correction you require — that you will have to work out via trial and error. It should present no particular problem once you have studied the operation of his train, and, understand how it is supposed to work — good luck.

Chime Problems

MANY BENCH REPAIRMEN are encountering difficulty with chiming clocks. Our contacts certainly indicate that the chime problem is definitely upon the increase rather than declining. Even taking into consideration the population explosion, does not completely cover the increase. Cataloguewise, it appears that the basic percentage of chimers has increased considerably.

Perhaps two other factors bear upon the problem: Available texts and manuals devote little or no space at all to the makeup of the chimes operation and watch repairers are getting more and more into clocks and their horological training and experience does not include the lovely chime.

Chiming clocks were once the proud possession of a few; today they are found in hundreds of thousands of homes. Our favorite treatise by Ward L. Goodrich devotes only seven and one-half brief pages—Chapter XX under the title of "Hammers, Gongs and Bells." If anything, Goodrich was practical and I am sure that when compiling it some 65 years ago, he little envisioned today's situation, and by the same token, today's demand upon the tender of the "144" to service chiming timepieces. Otherwise, he would most certainly have devoted more space to a dis-

cussion. Donald de Carle in his "Watchmakers & Clockmakers Encyclopedic Dictionary" (1950) lists and depicts some 37 different chimes upon their music bar scale.

Right here I hasten to confess that I'm getting into water well over my head and am a poor swimmer. Being no part of a musician, as I have difficulty playing a phonograph, I am not rightly qualified to come up with an explanation of how music (chimes) may be written in different keys. Should you take the trouble to check our music, Fig. 2, against that shown by Goodrich and de Carle, you will note a slight variation within all three. Goodrich writes it with three sharps, which I believe is the key of F-minor. De Carle sharps his G & F. American manufacturers—especially Herschede—stuck to the key of C, which we use on our chart. Sharps, flats, majors and minors are the very points we lose out musically while mechanically it makes no difference. Besides the "key" never concerns the clockmaker anyway and was determined by the manufacturer when he chose the sound item tube, rod or bell.

The following was taken from an American catalogue of several years back and we feel that it is very near the average Westminster chime you will have for servicing, Goodrich and de Carle's variations notwithstanding. Anyway, it serves the purpose of this review: E, D, C, G the first quarter; C, E, D, G,-C, D, E, C, the second quarter; E, C, D, G-G, D, E, C-E, D, C, G the third quarter; C, E, D,G, -C, D, E, C-E, C, D, G-G, D, E, C, the fourth quarter. Thus, a total of ten chords of four notes of 40 notes or 40 hammer strokes.

The most used chime by far is the "Westminster" and by its wide use is the basis from which nearly all of your chime problems can be solved. It gets its name from the great clock at Westminster. "Big Ben," after Sir Benjamin Hall, is the name given to the hour bell and has become the name of the clock by general usage. Westminster chime was taken from the fifth bar of Handel's aria from the Messiah: "I Know My Redeemer Liveth." The December 1941 issue of The Horological Journal records that it was selected and expanded into the present chime by Mr. Crotch and Dr. Jowett and first used in St. Mary's

357

Church, Cambridge, from 1793-'94. True, these are not repair facts, but, it is info you should have readily at your tongue's tip for discussion with your Westminster repair customer.

Reduced to its lowest common denominator we might say the Westminster chime simply strikes 40 hammer blows each hour, see Fig. 1. This covers the mechanical work, but, it alone does not make music. The complications set in with when, where, and how these strokes are performed.

The dotted line marked mid-point just between stroke 20 and stroke 21 divides the chime operation in exactly half. Now a look at Fig 1 shows the second half to be an exact duplicate of the first half. Blows No. 1, 2, 3, and 4 are identical to strokes 21, 22, 23, and 24.

Mechanically this means two things: (1) the manufacturer can construct a small drum upon which the lift pins execute the first twenty strokes and have that drum revolve twice per hour, (2) he can make a drum twice the size of the small one and plant thereon forty lift pins. In this latter case you as a repairman have two positions on the drum where you may install it during reassembly and still be correct.

Upon a few drums, the start point is marked by an arrow or some other indication on the end of the drum on those not marked, strokes 1, 2, 3, and 4 are easily located as it is the only spot upon the score where they come in that same order.

From the music score it is seen that the first beginning note is the high note. When setting up a grandfather clock with tubler chimes the repairman has to observe these first four notes. The high note is the shortest tube (shortest rod, or smalled bell) and indicates how the tubes are to be hung. The short tube may be on the left with the rest graduating down as you go to the right, or the long tube on the left graduating up.

A few clocks have their tube bar marked and their tubes marked which makes tube hanging easy, yet on unmarked tube bars you have to know your chime. In cases of clocks that need no repair (in order), merely calling for a set-up job, tube hanging alone can be a sticky problem. Just last week the column had a query from an experienced clockmaker who had been called upon to set up a very large g-f clock with 13 chime tubes. After trying a dozen combinations he gave up in disgust and called for assistance. We could only suggest the "Westminster" route and hope that that would solve the problem. Where the clockmaker takes down a g-f chimer either for transport or a trip into his shop, it is good practice to tag each tube as he takes it off, seeing that a similar marking is placed on the tube rail for easy, accurate, and quick re-hanging. Tube hanging, beyond the straight method of straight graduation either left or right, never seems to follow a "pattern" one might remember and go by at a later date. In nearly every instance, a thorough, working knowledge of the Westminster system, will enable the workman to spot those four tubes. It is fortunate that just about every multi-chime movement contains the Westminster.

Shift the chime drum to its Westminster position, hang E, D, C and G and operate the chime through the full four quarters to make sure you have it right. Next, shift the drum to another chime, preferably to one you are familiar with, one matching another clock then in the shop, or, to one which you can pick up the music score as in the de Carle volume (No. B-256, Roberts Book Co., $8.95) and proceed to hang on the additional tubes.

Each tube is suspended from two pegs, see Fig. 3. Make sure each hangs free and parallel to the next one. Hammers should strike tube about mid-way between the string holes and the top end. Tie each hammer to its respective lifter and adjust the hammer head with a 1/16th inch clearance off the tube. If you think the 37 catalogued chimes mentioned at the beginning is a goodly number, actually it's very little to the number of problems chiming makes for the clockmaker over and above those encountered in clocks that only strike the hours and halves. The latter only performs 180 hammer strokes in 24 hours, whereas on the Whitington Chime (American version) it has to perform 80 chiming strokes per hour. By the time you multiply this by 24 hours, then add the 156 hour strokes, as there is no single stroke at the half, you come up with a figure of 2,076 80 x 24 plus 156. This is a tremendous

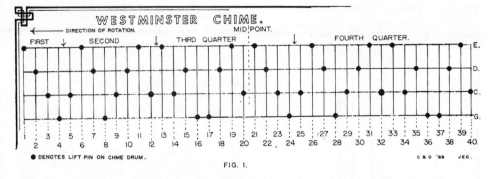

WESTMINSTER CHIME.

DIRECTION OF ROTATION. MID POINT.

FIRST SECOND THIRD QUARTER. FOURTH QUARTER.

● DENOTES LIFT PIN ON CHME DRUM.

FIG. I.

C & O '69   JEC.

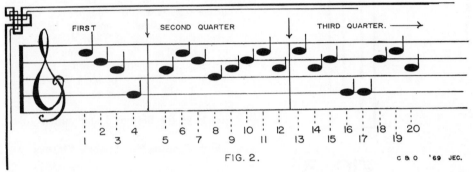

FIRST SECOND QUARTER THIRD QUARTER. ———→

FIG. 2.

C & O '69 JEC.

amount of work for the movement to perform every 24 hours.

No part of the clock has undergone greater changes in recent years than the chiming mechanism. Today's market brings to the "144" many ingenious devices. The designing of fool-proof and/or self-correcting mechanisms have come about through sheer necessity. While these devices render the clock more suitable for general use, they, at the very same time, bring new problems to the clockmaker in their assembly and adjustment. The purpose of the "self-corrector" is to make certain that no matter how the train is allowed to run down or become out of step, it will automatically correct itself at the hour.

The basis of these systems is virtually the same though there are a dozen ways to mechanically bring it about. Four trip or lift pins on the center, trip the chime at each quarter and simply allow the chime train to latch or lock at the completion of the third quarter into a deeper locked position. The lift pin for the hour—minute hand at twelve—is set further from the center than the other three pins and then only at the hour position will the clock

lift the chiming train high enough to unlock and then perform the fourth quarter. Since in practically every clock the completion of that fourth quarter trips the strike, this self-correcting device on the chime train also serves to keep the hour stroke in step.

The repairman should carefully check out the mechanical sequence of this operation before disassembling a movement. In most cases a clock comes to your bench undisturbed, but, for those few that are brought in which have been "mal-assembled" by some would be clockmaker who just plain did not know what he was doing is altogether a different problem. Solving it will require a thorough knowledge of the chiming operation, plus your past experience with chimers, plus all your "woman's intuition" and your "sixth sense."

One very sticky task is that of reassembling a chime drum made up of four discs which some some joker has pulled apart. The Fig. 1,chart comes in handy here. First, determine where the "E" (high note disc is located—if a mantel clock, or, a g-f with rods in a block, a reference to the short rod will indicate and if a g-f with tubes it makes no difference as you can

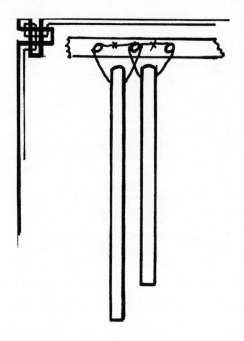

FIG. 3.

re-hang tubes to match.

How does one determine the "E" disc when the drum is disassembled? Count the lift pins first. If there are 8 it is the "G" disc. If 12 it is the "C" disc. Both "D" and "E" discs have 10 lift pins (cut these numbers in half if the drum makes 2 revs. per hour). By placing the two ten-pin discs upon each other you can easily determine which is which. Upon "E" strokes 11 and 13, 19 and 21, 31 and 33 have just one stroke space between them. At no point upon the "D" disc are pins located with just one space between. Having correctly identified the discs and determined whether you will assemble starting with "E" or "G" plus the direction of rotation, the rest is simple.

We repeat, problems bobing up in the servicing of chimes are seemingly without any limit, then, there is always the "finicky" customer, like a lady very much upset with her mantel chimer insisting that someone had ruined the chimes. It took a little time to calm her down and explain that we were not interested in names. The indicator

sat upon "Trinity." We switched to West-minister and tripped it and it was quickly evident the clock was correct. Allowing her to hear another Westminster to show the clock correct, she replied, Yes, I know but the Trinity is wrong." Turning the clock around so she could see the chime drum, it was pointed out that all the pins being in that drum, if one was correct the others necessarily had to also be correct. Having already admitted to the West-minster being right her reply, "Well, why didn't he tell me that?" For this we had no answer. It is my thinking he simply did not understand chimes else he would have. This brings us right back to the age old problem "it's one thing to repair a clock, but, sometimes another to satisfy the customer." This problem is one that has and will, continue to dog the heels of the clockmaker as long as he patches old clocks for his bread and butter.

Seth Thomas Has Speedy Chimes

The chime and strike are both too fast. I have cleaned, brushed, and lubricated the movement. This movement is the one with the copper discs and magnets instead of the usual flys. With the magnets moved all the way in toward the discs the chime and strike go like a fire engine. Thinking the springs were not slipping properly I have polished the inside of both barrels, but no change. The springs appear to be original.

A.

The copper discs you refer to perform the same function as the old orthodox fan-fly, and like it they are frictioned to their arbors, NOT permanently attached.

Moving the permanent magnets in and out increases or decreases the magnetic resistance and thus regulates the speed of that train, just as the size of the fan upon a fly does. Now, if that friction holding the disc is weak it may permit the arbor to revolve faster than the disc. Check this point and increase the tension. Next, look to the magnets. They should ride as close to the revolving disc as practical without touching it.

When a train — strike or chime — performs it is suddenly and positively locked. If the disc (or fan-fly) were permanently attached to the arbor the momentum gained during the operation would, via this sudden locking, exert an additional strain upon the lock, etc., thus they are frictioned on so that when the train is locked the disc (or fly) travels on a bit further til braked to a stop by that friction. With your discs properly frictioned and your magnets correctly positioned you ought to be able to control the speed of the operation to where you desire it.

ESCAPEMENTS

GRAHAM DEADBEAT

Perhaps you will be able to supply me with information regarding a certain type of clock escapement known as the Graham dead beat. We have been buying the necessary verges and escape wheels for years but now our supplier has gone out of business and we are confronted by the necessity of producing them in some other way.

What we require, is a drawing of the escapement showing all dimensions, curves, angles, etc. Verge and escape wheel arbors are on approximately 1-5/32 inches and the verge embraces eight teeth of a thirty-tooth wheel.

A.

The dead beat escapement is so called because when the tooth of the escape wheel drops on to the locking surface of the pallet, the wheel remains dead (is not forced backward) during the completion of the arc of vibration of the pendulum. It was invented by George Graham (1675 to 1751) in the latter part of the 18th century.

Several books describe it: Goodrich's "Modern Clock" now being reprinted, and "Horology" by Eric Haswell, obtainable from the *A. H. & J. Book Department.* Both give details for laying it out.

It is noted that your verges span eight teeth and since by the method of laying out this escapement the distance from escape wheel center to verge center automatically places itself it may be made to embrace almost any number of teeth. Graham originally designed it to span 138 degrees (11½ teeth on a 30-tooth wheel). Use over the years has proven the ninety degree escapement (7½ teeth on the 30-tooth wheel) to be the most efficient. With pallets embracing an arc of ninety degrees, power is applied to the pendulum rod at right angles, the most effective drive.

Pictured here are some sketches. *No. 1* is the line of centers *AB*. On this line of centers scribe the escape wheel with center at *C. No. 2*. Lay off two radii, *RR* as in *No. 3*, each 45 degrees (total 90 degrees) on either side line of centers. At the point where radius *R* cuts the primitive circle of escape wheel, draw tangents *TT* as in *No.*

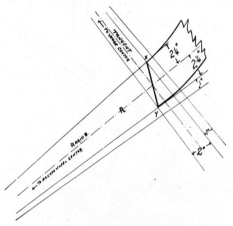

An enlarged sketch of the let-off pallet, drawn by J. E. Coleman.

4. If drawing is accurate, both tangents will meet line of centers at the same point *A*. This is your verge center.

On either side of the radii, lay off angles of 2¼ degrees each. On either side of the tangents, lay off angles of one degree each. Where the upper angle of radius cuts the outside angle of the tangent—point *X* on the enlarged sketch and the lower radius angle cuts the inside angle of tangent. Point *Y* represents the impulse plane. The front of the escape wheel teeth should be cut back about ten degrees; the back something like fifteen degrees. One degree from the pallet center is allowed for lock and two degrees for lift. The length of the impulse plane is 4½ degrees from the escape wheel center; one-half degree is allowed for tooth tip.

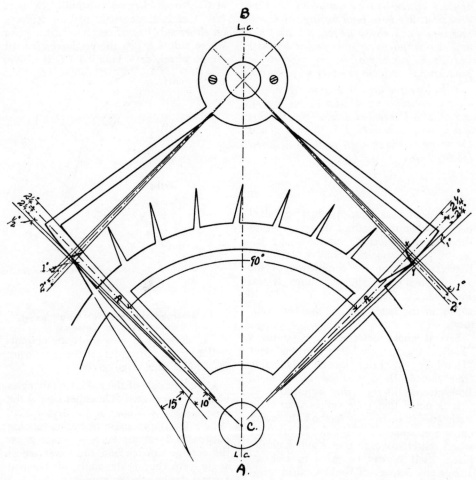

Graham 90° dead beat escapement

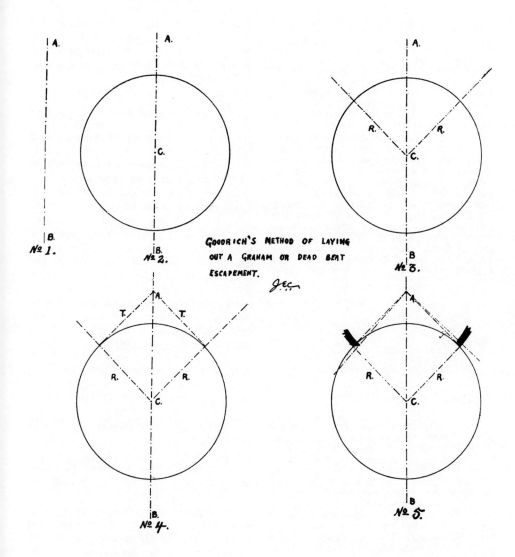

GOODRICH'S METHOD OF LAYING OUT A GRAHAM OR DEAD BEAT ESCAPEMENT.

N⁰ 1.

N⁰ 2.

N⁰ 3.

N⁰ 4.

N⁰ 5.

BROCOT ESCAPEMENT

We have an Ansonia clock which we are having trouble with in matching escapement. This is the type with exposed escapement, with pallet stones similar in shape to the roller jewel of a watch. Can you tell us how to set and what position to set them?

A.

You do not furnish any specific measurements, but the Brocot visible escapement most widely used by Ansonia was a 30-tooth escape wheel, 22 mm. in diameter with the pallet stone spanning 10 teeth, thus escaping over 120 degrees. The teeth on your wheel are slightly different from the pointed ones shown in our sketch, although the principle of setting the stones remains the same.

Let's hope that your escapement hasn't been disturbed, the center distance between verge pivot and escape wheel pivot altered, or the verge itself spread or closed. Assuming that it hasn't, you will be fairly safe in choosing stones that properly fit the holes of the verge. Set them so that the flat side practically lines up with the escape wheel center as shown in the sketch. When set to the proper depth, the point of the escape wheel tooth should drop on the center or a little beyond the center of the pallet stone.

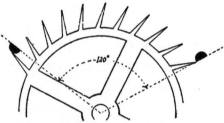

This escapement was first designed by a Frenchman, Achille Brocot, just about 100 years ago. However, he is better known by his suspension of regulator —two chops free to slide between guides, embracing the suspension spring and operated by a vertical screw running through the chops enabling the clock to be regulated with a key through the dial; the dial regulator found on so many mantel clocks today. The late Chas. DeLong adapted this escapement to watches about 1915 but at that time watch jewels were not perfectly enough centered and when they were taken down and cleaned there was considerable difficulty in again matching so close an escapement. It never came into general use but resulted in Mr. DeLong making great improvements in centering jewels.

ANGLE OF VERGE

I would like to know if there is a book containing information for making up an escapement for a clock, say an ordinary 8-day strike such as a Seth Thomas 89L or similar to it. The information I want is the angles on the verge if there is no verge for sample. How can you determine the entrance and exit angles and the contour of the verge? The idea applies to older clocks where there are no replacement parts to be had and must be made up sometimes without a sample.

A.

Abraham Lincoln, in answer to a question as to how long a man's legs ought to be, is reported to have replied: "Long enough to reach the ground." I fear that we shall have to answer you in much the same manner. The making of a recoil verge for an Early American clock seems to cover about as much territory as the Lincoln leg question.

To Eli Terry goes the credit for bringing the verge out from between the plates and possibly credit for some convenient adjustment feature about the year 1814. At this point the entrance and exit angles and contour of the verge you inquire about seems to have just about parted company with all the books and many of the fixed rules. The other notable example of moving the verge out and on the front plate and some center distance adjustment goes to the famous Achillie Brocot of Paris, France (b. 1817, d. 1878) who was only about three years old when Terry was building his first shelf clock with verge out front.

Following are some sketches which may be of help to you:

Fig. 1 shows the recoil verge as recommended by Thomas Reid and no doubt must have been the prevailing and accepted standard for that time.

Fig. 2 shows the method of laying out a dead beat escapement as suggested by Ward L. Goodrich (1905). Speaking of the difference between the Graham or dead beat and the escapement you have in mind, he said: "The sole difference is in the fact that there are no separate locking planes in the recoil, the locking and run take place on an extension of the lifting planes."

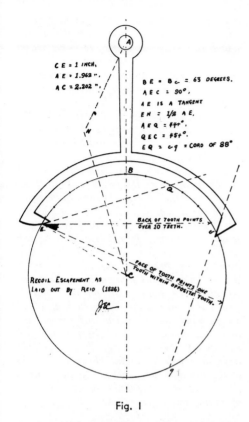

CE = 1 INCH,
AE = 1.962 ",
AC = 2.202 ".

BE = Bc = 63 DEGREES.
AEC = 90°,
AE IS A TANGENT
EN = 1/2 AE,
AEQ = 44°,
QEC = 45+°.
EQ = cq = CORD OF 88°

BACK OF TOOTH POINTS
OVER 10 TEETH.

FACE OF TOOTH POINTS ONE
TOOTH WITHIN OPPOSITE TOOTH.

RECOIL ESCAPEMENT AS
LAID OUT BY REID (1826)

Fig. 1

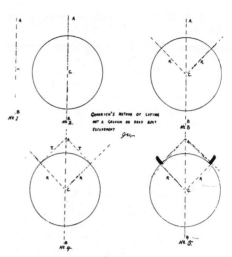

Goodrich's method of laying
out a Graham or dead beat
escapement

Fig. 2

In *Fig. 3* we have plotted your type of escapement from actual measurements taken from a 1-day Seth Thomas weight clock (about 1875).

In *Fig. 4* we take the same Seth Thomas escape wheel and measurements and adapt it to the Goodrich rule exactly. You will readily note that there is very little dif-

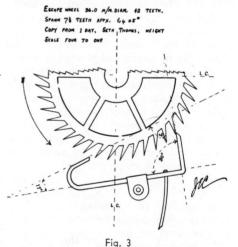

ESCAPE WHEEL 36.0 M/M. DIAM. 42 TEETH.
SPANN 7½ TEETH APPX. 64 05°
COPY FROM 1 DAY, SETH THOMAS, WEIGHT
SCALE FOUR TO ONE

Fig. 3

Note the similarity between Reid and Goodrich. Goodrich lays down the line of centers, *AB* as in No. 1. Scribes the escape wheel with the center at *C*. No. 2. From the center *C* one-half the angle your verge is to span is laid off by the radius *R* on your left of the line of centers. The other half on your right, No. 3. At the point where this line intersects the primitive diameter of the escape wheel a tangent is drawn, No. 4. This tangent will cut the line of centers at the point *A*, the correct center for your verge. Quoting further from Goodrich: (Comparing the recoil and dead beat) "Otherwise we have the same elements in our problem and it may, therefore, be laid out and handled in the same manner; indeed, if we were to set off on No. 5 the amount of angular motion of the pallet fork (verge) which is taken up by the run of the escape wheel teeth on the locking planes, by drawing dotted lines, above the tangent *T* we should then have measured all the angles necessary to intelligently set out the recoil escapement."

ference—also, that both Reid and Goodrich, by slightly different approaches, have divided the angle of span of the verge in half, laying out each half on either side of the line of centers and to all practical intents and purposes come up with the same verge.

We have always maintained that the drawing board is just about the clockmakers' most essential tool and here is one of its best uses: Supposing that you have in for repair one of these clocks which has a missing verge. I find that a four-to-one ratio is a good one to work with. Carefully and accurately measure the diameter of your escape wheel and count its teeth. These two figures are all you need to draw your escapement. Thus if the escape wheel is one inch in diameter, set it off on the board four inches

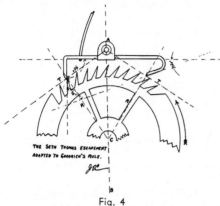

THE SETH THOMAS ESCAPEMENT
ADAPTED TO GOODRICH'S RULE.

Fig. 4

diameter; divide the number of teeth into 360 to obtain angle between teeth, decide upon the span—usually 5, 7, or 9½ teeth, multiply this figure by angle between teeth obtaining the total angular span of your verge, lay out one-half of this on either side of your line of centers and proceed to sketch the escapement as suggested by Goodrich. From your finished drawing you not only get a very accurate idea of how you want to make the desired verge but with dividers may obtain all desired measurements accurately enough for practical purposes such as correct center distance, actual distance from tip-to-tip of verge, etc.

When fitting the finished verge to the job, remember that closing the verge tips closer together or spreading them wider will only adjust the drop on one side, while the other drop can only be altered by shifting the center distance verge to escape wheel.

WEAK HAIRSPRING

I have a German Junghans clock which has a weak hairspring, but pulling the spring through the stud to tighten it does no good; the clock still runs about two hours slow a day. This clock has a rather large balance wheel and makes a full revolution each time. The escape wheel has 15 teeth, escape pinion six bars (lantern type) and is driven by the wheel which carries the second hand—this wheel has 40 teeth, so I figure that the balance should vibrate 100 times per minute. Is this correct? I intend to send the balance to the Charles Thomas Hairspring Vibrating Company as per your advice to Mr. Metzelfeld in the May issue of A. H. & J., but don't want to send it until I know that the vibration count is correct.

Some time ago, I repaired an old clock which at the time I thought was of either Spanish or Italian manufacture. The name on the dial was J. Altonaga, San Jacinto, 57. This clock had a (to me) rather odd striking sequence. It had two bells on top and struck the hour on one bell at each quarter, followed by one, two or three strikes on both bells to indicate the quarter after the hour; but, on the hour it struck the hour only. This clock also had a date hand and an alarm, and the pendulum was made of thin sheet brass and was about two feet long, about one foot wide at the bottom and about six inches at the top and was worked out in a raised figure design to represent harvest, a sheaf of grain, some grapes, etc.

A.

With an escape wheel of 15 teeth and a six-leaf pinion driven by a 40-tooth wheel carrying the seconds hand, you have correctly calculated that 100 teeth per minute must be let-off. The 40 drives the six-leaf pinion 6⅔. Fifteen by 6⅔ equals 100, but you failed to reckon that each tooth calls for two beats—one on each pallet; therefore, your clock should beat 200.

Your clock seems to be more of the German make. From the strike it could be French provencial. Dutch is possible, but Spanish or Italian are practically out.

It is my thought that J. Altonaga, San Jacinto, 57, could be the name of the jeweler who sold the piece—1857 would be the approximate date for clocks of this type. Can you check down at San Jacinto to see if a jeweler was in business about this time?

BROCOT ADJUSTMENT

I have in my possession an Ansonia clock. The only number I can find on this clock is 5½. This is an eight-day clock with half-hour and hour strike, and visible escapement in cast iron case, patented June 13, 1882.

This clock came to me with several holes badly worn. After bushing the holes and reassembling the clock, I find the escapement will not function. The verge will not unlock on the escape-wheel. The verge laps 11 teeth, but I noticed in a 1949 issue of the American Horologist and Jeweler that you stated a verge laps 10½ teeth. Therefore, I am inclined to believe that someone has replaced the escape-wheel with the wrong wheel. What makes me believe this is the sketch of the Ansonia escape-wheel that you had in the 1949 issue. I am sending you a sketch of the verge and escape-wheel. Please give me all the information you can concerning the escapement of this clock.

Is there more than one style of escape-wheel in the visible escapement? What is the diameter, and the distance between centers of verge jewels? What is the distance from the verge arbor pivot to the line drawn from one verge jewel to the other? If the wheel is wrong, where can I get one or have one made? This being my first Ansonia clock, my head is under water.

A.

It is unfortunate for you that in this particular instance you have a pretty mean escapement to "set up" or adjust; the Brocot visible escapement seems to be a trouble-maker for many repairmen.

It is difficult to give you much more than you already have from our articles you referred to. First, I think the 5½ you noted on your movement merely denoted the length of the pendulum and neither identifies the escapement nor enters into its adjustment. All escapement adjusting requires quite a lot of "feel and try," rather than setting it up to definite measurements, like distance from the verge center to the escape-wheel center, and distance from one pallet to the other, etc., that you asked for. Ansonia, during their course of manufac-

ture, varied their visible escapements some —just how many changes isn't recorded, and I doubt if anyone knows exactly.

I note that you say your verge spans 11 teeth; this probably means that it has at some time been "spread." For all practical purposes, one can say that the verge always spans a half-tooth space; that is, 10½, 11½, etc., and never exactly even-tooth spaces—with a little practice you will readily discover that when you make the pallets the exact width of even-tooth spaces, it cannot work.

Lock, drop and run on this escapement should be of the same amount on each pallet when it is correctly set up. One fact repairmen often get confused is (1) moving the pallets closer together, or opening them wider, will only adjust the drop on *one* side; (2) altering the distance between the pallet center and the escape-wheel only affects the drop on the *other* side.

In many of the fine French clocks with Brocot visible escapement, the verge is set with its bearings in eccentric buttons for fine adjustment of the pallet center to escape center adjustment, and the pallet itself is provided with a fine screw to alter the distance between pallets. In your Ansonia (and other American clocks) no method of adjustment is provided and you have to accomplish it by deftly bending the pallet arms and tilting the verge cock up or down. It was the general practice when building movements with short pendulums (3 to 5 inches) with this escapement, to build the escapement to 120 degrees; thus, your verge should span 10½ teeth.

First, check the pallets (they may be either jewels or steel). They should be half-round (cylinders cut exactly in half) and the over-all diameter of the pallet should be roughly just a little more than two-thirds the distance between tooth tips.

Second, make sure that they are properly set. When the escapement is on "center" their back or flat sides should be on a line with the escape-wheel center.

Third, make sure the escape wheel is perfectly round (no long or short teeth) and that all teeth are straight.

With these features correct, you are ready for the adjustment of pallet width and center distances, but not before. This final adjustment is strictly "cut and try," careful manipulations and close observation. This is sometimes time consuming, but there is nothing too difficult about it.

He has escapement problems

After cleaning a watch I usually check up on the escapement. In moving the pallet arm from left to right, I so often have the following experience. When I move the pallet arm to the left slowly, the escape tooth will drop off the pallet stone and the pallet will move slightly further before striking the left banking pin. That of course accounts for the slide.

However, when I move the pallet arm to the right, in many cases, will drop off the pallet stone. Then I cannot move the arm any further, as the minute the tooth drops off the pallet stone the arm is striking the right banking pin. In other words there is no slide on the right side.

This happens so often to me that I am somewhat confused as to what to do. I have always been told there should be slide on both sides. I try to correct this condition by opening the right banking pin to allow for slide. Then when I test for guard pin shake I find that I have too much guard pin shake on the right side so I have to push the banking pin back in place again which takes away the slide on the right side. This happens on new as well as old watches—I can't understand how the factories can turn out new watches this way.

What puzzles me most is how the watches can run and keep proper time when the slide is lacking on the one side. They seem to run alright but when I listen to them in my timing machine they have a knocking sound. What is the proper procedure in cases like this? I will admit that in some cases, when I open the banking pins, the knocking sound disappears, and when I test the guard pin shake it is O..K., but often I get too much guard pin shake when I open the banking pins.

A.

To adequately answer and explain your problem would require more space than even a long letter. In addition some drawings would be necessary to make it clear.

Basically, we have two quite different types of escapements—circular pallets, and equidistant pallets. In the equidistant locking pallets the discharging stone must embrace a greater angle than the receiving stone. You are primarily concerned with "slide" (sometimes called run). It is defined as: "the distance from the point at which the wheel tooth strikes the locking face of the stone at the instant of the drop to the point it reaches when the

motion of the pallet is stopped by the fork coming against the banking pin."

Slide is measured by lines radiating from the pallet center, etc. Now, the total angular action as measured from the pallet center must of necessity be the same on both sides, so where you have a stone presenting a greater angular lift surface, that difference has to be subtracted from another of the angles. At the moment I'm observing a large drawing of an Elgin 18-S equidistant pallet escapement—the total angular motion of the fork is 10 degrees. On the receiving stone the lift is 4 degrees, the lock is 1½ degrees and the slide is 4½—total 10. On the let-off stone a slide of 1½ degrees is indicated.

May I suggest a careful study of the escapement in some work with ample drawings. A good one is "Precision Time Measures" by Higgenbotham (B-280, $4.50, book department, American Horologist and Jeweler).

I believe you may purchase from the book department blueprints and charts section, individual lessons from the Science of Horology course. These are amply illustrated (drawings) and run, roughly, from $1.50 to $2.50 depending upon size. Lesson 16 covers drafting and lay-out of the lever escapement—very good.

The American Outside Clock Verge

WHEN CLOCKMAKING came to America in the early 1700's the clock per se had already reached a state approaching mechanical perfection. Prof. Robert Hooke had perfected the anchor escapement about 1676 and also made a wheel cutting engine using circular cutters; Honest George Graham devised the gridiron pendulum about 1715, etc. In a manner of speaking, the clock was handed to the American clockmaker 'full blown'.

Were we called upon to pin-point one small item that contributed the most to clockmaking by the American craft, we would have to say the lowly outside verge. It is as American as turkey on the Thanksgiving menu and without question the product of the fertile brain of Eli Terry. Very little has been said—in detail— about it and as I recall, minute details of it were not spelled out in any of Terry's patents though it is quite clear that it is a vital and integral part of Terry's "improvement". Typical of the omission of any specific reference to the minute details of the outside verge is to be found in the suit in Chancery filed by

Terry, in the Litchfield Superior Court, April 28, 1827, against Seth Thomas. Terry's petition covers some four, single spaced pages when typed and his attorneys went into much wordage, but never pin-pointing the outside verge, a portion of the third paragraph reads thus: " . . . that in the years 1815 and 1816 he formed the design and undertook the construction of a wooden wheeled thirty hour clock which should be of such a size, shape and confor-mation of parts as to be a cheap, convenient, portable and accurate timepiece, and at the same time retain the strength and other valuable properties of the common wooden clock, and unite utility with ornament, that in the year 1816 he completed the improve-ments so far as he had then discovered the same, and constructed a clock with a new combination and arrangement of the prin-ple parts of the same, (viz) the weights, hammer and bell, Dial wheels and Pendu-lum, and such a calculation and arrange-ment of the whole movement, and other parts, as to bring the same into the size, shape and appearance, designed, accom-panied with the other beforementioned advantages—and thereup the petitioner ob-

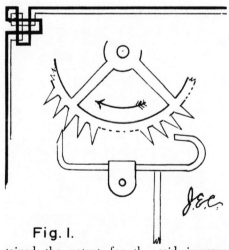

Fig. I.

tained the patent for the said improve-ments." Remembering that the common wooden clock prior to Terry's experimenting was long case, it is crystal clear that two of the points uppermost in his thinking were, 1, size, 2, cheapness. Assuredly the lowly outside verge—Fig. 1—was a most important factor.

The continental clockmaker, Achille Bro-cot, responsible for more clocks with the verge in front of the front plate than any other, was born some half dozen years after Terry first began his experiments. If any other clockmaker, foreign or domestic, had ever tried bringing the verge from between the plates prior to Terry, we haven't been able to locate him.

The impact of the outside verge upon the clock manufacturing industry was tre-mendous; the litigation referred to above Terry's petition alleges that Seth Thomas had already produced "fifteen thousand of said clocks"—some seventy-five years later in writing of this outside verge, Ward L. Goodrich, in his "Modern Clock", said: "One factory in the United States is turning out annually two million movements; there are four other larger factories and several with a less product; so it will readily be seen that any decrease in cost, however small it may be on a single movement, will run up enormously on a year's output." One may safely conclude that this little outside verge, which I think ought to be termed the 'Terry' verge, has been applied upon more clocks than any other one specific type.

One has to come on down through our horological history about sixty years before he can tie into pin-point by pin-point de-tails upon the "Terry" verge. Several years ago there came to the repair bench an un-usual little calendar clock made by S. E. Root, Bristol, Connecticut. In many re-spects it resembled the little E. N. Welch 'Parlor' calendar, yet there were some new features; its pendulum hung via a clivis like the Welch, but, the escapement dif-fered in that all the impulse was upon the verge rather than a portion of it being across the escape-wheel tooth. Upon it was a patent date—July 13, 1869—obtaining a copy showed that it dealt only with our favorite, the Terry verge. Patent No. 92,644 was issued to Noah Pomeroy, July 13, 1869. We took the actual verge from the clock and laid it upon the patent drawing for comparison and came up with the photo in Fig. 3.

Noah Pomeroy was actively engaged in clockmaking at Bristol for some thirty years, first in "Pomery & Robbins" organized in 1847. In 1849 it became Noah Pomeroy &

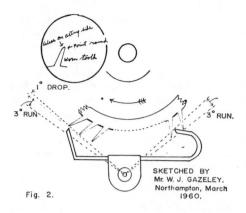

Fig. 2.

SKETCHED BY
Mr. W. J. GAZELEY.
Northampton, March
1960.

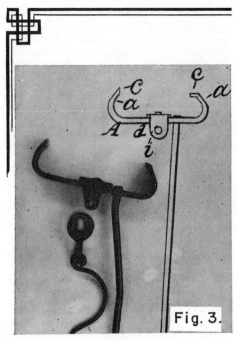

Fig. 3.

Co., then Pomeroy & Parker 1852 to 1857. After that he was alone until he sold out to Hiram C. Thompson in 1878. His patent reads: "To All Whom It May Concern: Be it known that I, Noah Pomeroy, of Hartford, in the county of Hartford, and State of Connecticut, have invented a new and useful Improvement in Dead Beat Verges; and I do hereby declare that the following is a full, clear, and exact description thereof, which will enable those skilled in the art to make and use the same, reference being had to the accompanying drawings, making a part of this specification in which—Fig. 1 is a front elevation of my invention (in our Fig. 3.) Fig. 2 is a side elevation of the same. Fig. 3. is a plan or top view of the blank of which the ears are formed (that refers to what we call the saddle). Fig. 4 is a plan or top view of the blank of which the verge is formed. Similar letters of reference indicate like parts. My invention consists in swaging the body of a dead-beat or four pallet verge, from a thin strip of metal, and attaching ears to the same, by which it is pivoted to the front side of the clock. It is well known that the ordinary springs for cheap clocks exert much more power when first wound than when nearly run down. The common recoil verge has but two pallets, both of which are impulse pallets; consequently, when one pallet has given the pendulum ball an impulse, the other pallet immediately begins to exert its power to throw the ball back, and soon hurries it in the other way; thus when the power of the spring is strongest, the arc described by the ball will be the shortest, and the number of vibrations per

minute the greatest, causing the clock to run too fast when first wound, and too slow when nearly run down.

When the teeth of the escapement-wheel strike the dead beat pallets a, a, the wheel remains stationary until the ball has described its full arc, and returned so far that the teeth of the escapement-wheel strike the impulse pallets c, c, when an impulse is given and the wheel moves. Thus it will be seen that a dead-beat verge does not shorten the arc of the pendulum ball, and consequently equalizes the power of the spring.

"The ordinary dead-beat verge is so expensive as to prevent its general use on cheap clocks. To make a better article of the common clock, without increasing its price is the object of my invention.

"To construct these verges, the metal is first cut across the grain into strips as wide as the verge blank, Fig. 4, is designed to be, and then cut into strips of the width designed for the verge. It is then swaged into shape, great care being taken to swage the dead-beat pallets a, a, Fig. 1, into nearly or quite the requisite shape. It is then filed to a gauge, or milled in a milling machine to shape the impulse pallets c, c, and take a slight dressing from the dead-beat pallets a, a, in case they are not properly swaged.

With a suitable die and punch are cut ear blanks Fig. 3 the body of which is riveted to the body of the verge A, and the ears d, d, swaged or bent into position as shown in Figs. 1, and 2. The verge rod is passed through a hole in the body of the verge A, and then upset to secure it in its place. The verge a is then hung to the front of the clock by a pin passing through the pin holes "i" in the ears d, d. The pallets a, a, and c, c, of the verge A, are of the same shape as the common dead-beat verge. The shape of the metal, however, opposite the pallets, is very different from the ordinary dead-beat verge, but as these are not the working parts it is immaterial what shape they are. To construct the ordinary style of dead-beat verge metal is selected which is as thick as it is desired to make the width of the verge. Then, with a suitable die and punch, the verge is cut into the desired shape. It is then trimmed to a gauge and polished, and then rigidly secured to an arbor passing through its body, which arbor is provided with a pivot at each end, and hung between the frames of the clock movement.

"The cheapest of this old style dead-beat verge costs six cents—each, and the other parts of the clock are generally made of a corresponding price. The cost of my improved verge can not exceed two cents each; therefore I produce a good dead-beat timer for about one third the usual cost. If desired, my style of dead-beat verge might be hung between the frames of the clock, securing the body of the verge A, to an arbor by means of a rivet; but I consider it preferable for cheap clocks, to hang it in front of the frame. I do not claim the common recoil verge, which has only two pallets, both of which are shaped by a file although the body of the verge is swaged. Neither do I claim the application of a dead-beat verge to a cheap clock, unless the verge is constructed as described; but What I claim as new and desire to secure by letter patent, is A dead-beat verge, constructed substantially as described, and for the purpose specified."

(s) NoahPomeroy.

Witnesses:

George W. Atkins,

Charles A. Roper."

Note: nowhere in his specifications does Mr. Pomeroy mention that the locking pallets a, and a, are sections of a circle whose center would rest at the verge pivot point. Both his patent drawing and the verge we handled clearly indicate that the locking plane of the receiving pallet is perfectly flat. We noted that there was, though somewhat reduced, a slight recoil—the locking plane of the exit pallet is 'curved' and showed only the slightest bit of recoil. While he calls it "dead-beat" we feel that it belongs into the half-dead-beat class.

It was our good fortune to discuss our favorite verge with a leading authority upon escapements, Mr. W. J. Gazeley, one of England's last escapement makers and author of "Watch and Clock Making and Repairing" (Roberts Book Co., No. B-283, 425 pages, $10) and "Clock & Watch Escapements" (Roberts, No. B-500, 294 pages). He thought higher of it than I expected from a man doing the ultra-precision work I knew him to be engaged in. Out of that discussion came several sketches, one of which we reproduce in Fig. 2. This sketch was based upon a Seth Thomas, 8-day, cabinet clock, escapement, escape wheel of 42-teeth, 36-m/m. diameter, quote: "The secret of the Seth Thomas, or as it appears to me, is that the impulse angle is only three degrees as against the average recoil escapement which has five degrees. That is why they appear to have excessive power. There is another point, which according to theory, is wrong. This applies to many Seth Thomas clocks and that is the pallets do not span a quarter of the wheel but only eight and one-half teeth. This is correct for a wheel of thirty teeth. With a wheel of 42 teeth the span should be ten and one-half teeth. One of my students quite sometime ago had one of these clocks where the wheel teeth were much worn. A new wheel was not available except by having it specially made, so I suggested reversing the wheel. The clock carried on with the wheel this way for a long time." end quote. This is our Fig 2. illustrating the wheel with the teeth reverse-slanted.

Our discussion went on through many letters and covered other escapements — I shant risk other quotes lest I get something out of proper context; with further regard to the American "Terry" type verge and a new one, he suggested first making a drawing, twice or four times actual size. Then another of actual size and measurement; then, forming and fitting the verge to this drawing, saying: "The principle I adopt is to leave the entrance pallet a little long, otherwise the same as the drawing. The object of this is to give a certain amount of scope; as you know with all pallets it is the inside freedom that is the difficulty. Thus if this pallet is long, the inside shake can be adjusted to be very close. The outside shake by the studded bar on the plate; deepening will reduce outside shake. The main thing is that the angles of impulse be correct." end quote.

This points up a fact we've observed that many clockmakers endeavoring to make a satisfactory verge seem to overlook, i.e. that adjusting the verge closer to the wheel does NOT alter the inside 'drop'.

Nearly always, we over here, look to the exit pallet as being a ninety degree angle as in our Fig. 1. Mr. Gazaley says lean it slightly outward for the reversed wheel—Fig. 2—and says a slight outward lean is desirable even when the teeth are at their normal slant. We followed this for a few years and found that there is a bit of improvement.

I am aware that this Otherwise leans pretty much toward the historical as we always have a tendency to do, but, believe that it contains some pointers that will be of material aid to the tender of the "144" both in making a new verge and the adjusting of it or an old one. For one thing, it points up the vast difference between the "Terry" type recoil verge and any form of dead-beat or half-dead-beat verge. Note: Mr. Pomeroy said "The common recoil verge has but two pallets." This emphasizes the fact that others have four; now-a-days we refer to them as 'planes', a locking plane and an impulse plane to each pallet, totalling four planes. Understanding this, plus the deepening altering only the outside shake (drop) should certainly make the manufacture of a new verge both faster and easier.

VERGE ASSEMBLY JIG

Another tool which so far as this column knows is the first and only one of its kind ever offered to the clockmaker is an outside verge "Assembly Jig", made of heavy tool steel with an extension so that it may be

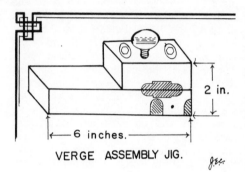

VERGE ASSEMBLY JIG.

clamped in your bench vice. It sells for $14.95.

This jig is constructed in such a way that the steel pallet portion will fit into a slot even after the saddle has already been riveted on. There is a "V" for holding the brass crutch wire enabling the operator to easily rivet it to the pallet using a flat punch and a couple of hammer strokes.

Designed to go with this jig, they have a verge kit of three steel pallets, three brass saddles pre-punched and pre-bent, three crutch wires and three rivets. Riveting the brass saddle to the pallet just isn't as easy as said if one is to come out with a professional looking job. Hall has designed a special punch for that purpose—when used with the special rivets of the "Easy-Way" verge kits one can attach the saddle to the steel with one blow of the hammer and have a "professional" looking finish. Price of special punch, $5.95. He is enthused over this new tool and so confident the mechanic will be pleased with it, he is offering it with a ten-day, return privilege.

ESCAPEMENT TERMS

That there is considerable confusion throughout the trade of "escapement terms" is amply proven by our mail. This is natural because each writer has some slight variation in his terms and/or his method of describing action, and so forth. "If" it is possible to set the record straight with a rough sketch we shall have a go at it.

Study—don't just read the words—this sketch and make sure you can correctly identify each function of the escapement. Some drawings identify the pallet-jewels as "R" and "L." If you interpret this as Left and Right it can become confusing so forget the left and right. "R" indicates "receiving" i.e. it is the first pallet to receive the escape wheel tooth. "L" is "Let-Off," the pallet that lets-off the tooth. On our sketch, the "R" stone is labeled "A" and the "L" is labeled "B." The only other jewel on the sketch is the roller-jewel, labeled "P".

When reading angles, the very first thing is to determine from WHERE that angle is measured. Upon the escapement there are three important such points, the escape-wheel center, the fork center and the balance center. There are others such as that indicated at "D"—it is known by two terms "tooth clearance angle" and "rake angle."

Measured from the escape-wheel center is the impulse angle across the face of the pallet "S"—the impulse angle of the "club" of the tooth is indicated by "R." Upon a 15 tooth escape-wheel, the angular distance between teeth must be 24 degrees—15 divided into 360—then it is mechanically clear that angle "S" for the R stone; plus "S" for the L stone; plus two times "R" for the club; plus a slight drop or clearance angle, all, added together can NOT exceed 24 degrees. It is at this very point one discovers the vast difference between the "clubbed-tooth" and the "pointed-tooth" escapement.

In clock work one rarely ever encounters a club-tooth, insofar as our experience goes, E. N. Welch was the only American manufacturer to employ a club-tooth escape wheel in his clocks. "K" is another angle not measured at one of the three prime points. Called the "draft" angle it is measured from the receiving point of the pallet stone. By leaning the pallet stone in the direction of the motion of the escape wheel by this angle, the pressure of escape power "draws" the lever fork against the banking pin "F" thus the term "draft." "O" indicates the safety crescent in the safety roller. "I" indicates the guard finger—this sketch portrays the double roller escapement.

In the single roller escapement, the safety crescent is cut in the one roller-table and the safety finger is a vertical pin erected upright in the lever fork. "E" represents the escape angle; again measured at the escape wheel center. "N" indicates the unlocking angle of the balance, here measured from the balance center. "J" is the lever action angle this time measured from the lever center. "L" is the lock or slide angle sometimes termed both as "lock and slide." This is measured from the lever center and encompasses that point where the tooth drops on to the pallet stone and that point where the tooth comes to rest as the lever stops on the banking pin. "G" is the roller-jewel table and "H" is the safety table. This particular sketch happens to portray the "equal distance locking" type of escapement; meaning if you place your compass at the lever center and scribe a circle beginning at the lock corner of the receiving pallet it would come through the lock corner of the let-off pallet. A popular type of escapement is termed "equi-distant centers"—in it, such a circle scribed from the center of the receiving stone face would then pass through the center of the let-off pallet.

Just this very simple variation involves a whole NEW set of figures and angles—the variations in escapements must be almost limitless—thus, we see a different set of measurements in about every escapement we run across. One of the best books specializing upon watch escapements is a 250 page work by T. J. Wilkerson, published at Philadelphia in 1916 and long since out of print. There are a good many around and book dealers occasionally come up with a good copy. Ours is from the late Major Chamberlain's library and we recall his saying that it was the best ever published in America.

Another good work is a volume by Dr. James C. Pellaton, "Watch Escapements" published at LeLocle, 1924, and also out of print but a bit easier to come by. Still another, and believe it or not, it is out of print, is: "Know The Escapement" by Homer & Sara Barkus, published at San Diego, 1945. There are a good many of these in circulation and it perhaps is the easiest to pick up. Just this week we had a letter from Mr. W. M. Borrow, editor of New Zealand Horological Journal, in which he mentioned that the Barkus work is used down there. He said, "I think it has many points in its favor compared with Swiss methods."

Just now slipping into the out-of-print category is: "The Watch Escapement" by Henry B. Fried, 164 pages, 111 drawings, published at N. Y. in 1959 and selling for $4.95. Both Roberts Book Co. and Adams-Brown include it in their 1969 catalogue, but we had a recent notice from Roberts that they are out. W. J. Gazeley's "Watch & Clock Escapements" covers as wide a range of escapements as any work we know and is also out of print. It was produced at London, 1956. Neither Roberts nor Adams-Brown mention it. Malcolm Gardner's latest catalogue lists it with this notation: "Temporarily (at least) out of print,

this book is extremely popular. There is no alternative for the same information in one book." This would indicate that republishing is under consideration, and, as soon as the decision is reached C. & O. will make an announcement. Publication costs are rising almost daily. We've just had a good phone chat with Bob Spence of American Reprints in which he mentioned this mounting cost a couple of times. It is something bordering upon the paradoxal that our craft does not support the re-printing of some of these very fine volumes and the "collectors" will literally gobble up the re-printing of some old catalogue of timepieces. The collector can merely thumb through an old catalogue and point out that such-and-such a clock sold for X number of dollars back in 1872, while the tender of the old "144" can actually put a work like that of Wilkinson into daily practice and increase the ring of his cash register. How does that figure?

ESCAPEMENT TERMS.

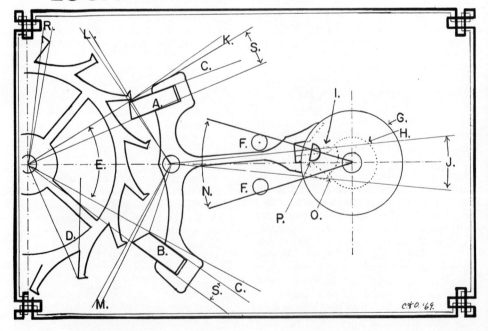

Floating Balance Escapement

SMITHS CLOCKS & WATCHES, LTD. recently announced that they have perfected a jeweled, balance escapement for application to their eight-day mantel clocks. The unit is primarily designed to replace the short pendulums used on their line of domestic clocks.

Radical—is not the proper description, but it represents a wide departure from conventional horological construction. Quite a while back, a German firm, Blesch and Hettich, announced a floating balance escapement, and when we saw the Smith announcement, a letter was immediately dispatched to Major R. A. Fell, Chief Research Engineer for Smiths. He asked Mr. C. Brook Flowers, of their New York office at 45 West 45th Street to send down a sample of this new escapement that "C. & O." might have a look-see. So, thanks to Major Fell, we could photograph and sketch its working parts.

These approximate measurements and a reference to the sketch will give our readers a practical idea of the size of this escapement. The over all height of the iron frame is one and 10/16 inches; the over all width is one and 1/16th; the diameter of the balance wheel is one and 1/32 inch; the pivot tube (in standard escapement this would be the balance staff) is one and 7/16 inches long. The cylindrical hairspring is exactly seven-eighths of an inch long.

One of the outstanding features of this escapement is that it is "free sprung." It follows that a smaller error of isochronism can be expected because of this than is generally found in the platform escapement with conventional regulator.

Note that on the sketch the pivot tube is just a straight brass tube with a jewel frictioned into each end. Through the jewels is passed a hard drawn, stainless steel wire. This wire is stretched tight across the iron frame, and in effect, serves as the balance pivot. The entire weight of the balance is supported by the hairspring, i.e., the balance literally floats around the stretched wire.

Close observation will reveal that the cylindrical hairspring is literally of two parts—the upper half being coiled counter clockwise while the lower half is coiled clockwise. This unusual construction eliminates any up and down or pumping motion, for while the one-half uncoils and lengthens, its counter half coils and contracts, automatically compensating itself.

We mentioned that it is free sprung, and this called for additional engineering to provide a means of regulation. A pair of regulating weights are provided on a spring member that fits friction tight in the balance wheel. The inner rim of the balance wheel is not concentric with the staff, but cut after a spiral form. When the weight carrier (or regulator) is turned, the weights move toward or away from the center of rotation, and thus alter the moment of inertia, to make the balance beat faster or slower just as you turn in or out the mean-timing screws of a watch or chronometer.

Probably the most unusual bit of construction is the safety action. It is a ring mounted at the bottom end of the two impulse pins. This ring is open at one point (just to the right of the pins in the sketch). This gap permits the guard pin, which is a tongue formed on the right side of the lever fork, to pass freely through the gap during the action of the escapement, and during the excursion of the balance, it will lie against the inside or the outside of the ring.

Last, but by no means least is the novel manner of the right angle turn converting the 180 degree action of the clock's train to the 90 degree action of this escapement. It is obvious that the balance goes upright. In conventional clocks with platform escapement, this is accomplished by the use of a contrate wheel.

Those of you who have battled trouble with contrate gearing will appreciate this feature. The lever is somewhat long and bent over at right angles, bringing the lever fork and tongue into the horizontal

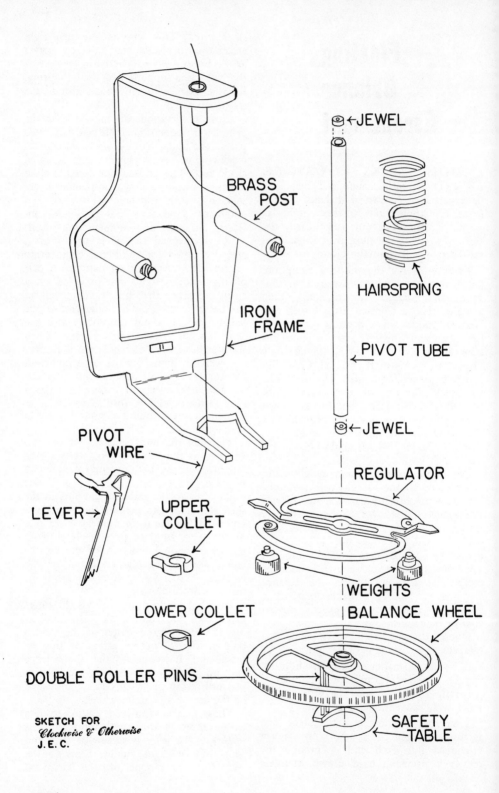

JEWEL

BRASS
POST

HAIRSPRING

IRON
FRAME

PIVOT TUBE

JEWEL

PIVOT
WIRE

REGULATOR

LEVER→

UPPER
COLLET

WEIGHTS

LOWER COLLET

BALANCE WHEEL

DOUBLE ROLLER PINS

SAFETY
TABLE

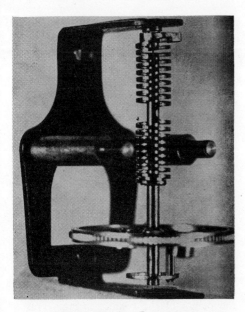

Smiths' Floating Escapement

plane.

Major Fell mentions that the novel form of safety locking was first suggested by Charles Gros of Paris in about 1913, and points out that the floating escapement is not intended for portable timekeepers, but as a substitute for short pendulums on domestic clocks.

We are grateful for his cooperation. It enables us to bring to you this brief description, and while we have only the escapement under actual examination, it is quite easy to see the sturdiness of construction, and the remarkable way in which the reverse coiled hairsprings compensate one another, maintaining the balance at a constant level. All in all, it is most practical—if it is a departure.

BATTERY CLOCKS

EUREKA BATTERY CLOCK

I have a clock operated by magnetism which is unfamiliar to me. Hence I come to you as a seeker after knowledge. The clock has no name or mark of any kind. I am sending some free-hand sketches.

I can understand a pull from the right side "A" to the left side "C," as indicated on my sketch, but that pull should cease at the midway point "B." But with this clock, after passing "B," it will pull back. When I get it okay in one direction it will be un-okay in the other. Occasionally it will act as a magnetized watch, changing rate.

There seem to be no poor connections. As the power is derived from a dry battery, the current is of course, direct, which means a polarity, positive and negative. I cannot see how this makes a difference in an electro-magnet, but on a c h a n c e, I changed the polarity and the movement seemed more smooth or regular. There is still, however, a change of rate, but not so sudden.

Question: Should an electro-magnetic core show a positive and negative at the ends when a compass is applied when the power is off?

I presume that the balance should be as finely poised as a watch. Should this be done by undercutting, or should it be by screwing the balance screws in or out, which someone seems to have done?

A.

You sketch a very good second model Eureka battery clock. We've handled a few over the years. In fact, I own one that was given to us by Friend Orville R. Hagans a while back.

This clock was patented in England by Kutnow Brothers of 853 Broadway, New York, New York, No. 14,614 application, filed June 26, 1906, and allowed February 14, 1907. They are designed to operate upon one cell (1½ volts) and once adjusted are fairly reliable.

The adjustments are about on par with most battery-driven clocks of that period, i.e., inclined to be upon the tricky side. First and foremost the balance impulses in only one direction. Basically, the polarity should not matter. However, if actual tests indicate a better and smoother motion with a certain connection, keep it that way.

The very important points in operation of any battery-impulsed clock are (1) time; (2) duration. On the Eureka, the time of impulse is determined or controlled by the height of the contact spring. This is the reason for the up-and-down spacing of that spring. Your clock should impulse (contact) on the clockwise stroke; thus it can be easily seen that to raise the contact spring, the contact pin will reach it later and conversely, if it is lowered, the contact will be made earlier in the clockwise stroke.

The duration of contact is determined by the length of the contact piece—that is, the L-part of the contact s p r i n g. The broader the L-piece, the longer the current is on the magnet. A slight curve cut into the steel strip under the wheel will be noted. This portion of the steel comes closer to the magnet than any other part, and the contact should break just before the magnet passes out of it. The contact should be broad enough to allow the current flow to begin several degrees before the magnet starts to enter this curve upon its clockwise stroke.

The contact pin in the balance wheel should be of two materials—conductor and a non-conductor. It is round, and should be about two-thirds of some non-conductor, like bakelite, and the remaining third, silver or platinum. The conductor third goes upon the top side so that it comes in contact with the L-piece upon the clockwise stroke, contact will be made and the balance impulsed. This L-piece sits at an angle and at such a position that the conductor element of the pin strikes it a little to the right of the midway point. Upon the upward (clockwise) stroke, the angle of the L-piece permits the contact spring to be bent or pushed aside (to your right as you face the clock) as the pin passes. On the return (counter clockwise) stroke, the non-conductor portion of the pin strikes the L-piece, again a little to the right of the midway point. This time the contact spring is forced to your left as the pin passes it.

Special attention must be given to the contact spring. I quote from the patent line 50, page 2: "The contact spring can be made of three laminae of different lengths well pressed together. The one on the left which has the L-shaped head, is the longest and therefore, the head moves easily to and fro. The middle one is of medium length and the one to the right is the shortest. By virtue of this arrangement, good contact is made and there is little resistance when the pin returns. This requires less power when the pin returns and gives high efficiency both electrically and mechanically, and the spring is quickly brought to rest."

You are quite correct in that the wheel should be well poised; however, you may find that the big screw heads already travel so close to the steel piece that it will be impractical to turn them out. We believe that upon the removal of the screws, you might find the heads already hollow and bits of lead inserted therein. Poise may be had by adding to or reducing this lead.

In answer to your last question, the poles of the core should not show any magnetism when the current is off.

In closing, let me point out that the hairspring conducts the current from the frame to the balance; therefore the spring itself and also the pin with which it is held should be clean and bright. So should the inside of the collet and that portion of the balance staff upon which it fits. Oxidation and corrosion at these points interfere with a free flow of the 1½-volt current, and that would vitally influence the performance of your clock, even when all other features are in order.

BATTERY CLOCKS have been with us far longer than most think. In fact, the first electric clocks were battery clocks. Electricity in timepieces dates back to the period 1840-1852 and those experiments of one Alexander Bain, of Edinburgh—b.-1811 d.-1877.

Folowing closely upon the heels of Bain's work was that of Dr. Mattaus Hipp, of Neuchatel—b.-1813 d.-1893. Thus the battery clocks we are today servicing are the sum total of better than a century of progress in the electric timekeeping field.

With the advent of synchronous electric clock in the late 1920's plus the many battery clocks that have hit the market, the term "electric clock" has, in this year of 1970, very little specific meaning beyond the fact that electricty in some form is utilized. Should an inquiring customer tell you he has an "electric" clock stopped, you haven't the foggiest idea of what kind of clock he has.

Webster defines "type": a kind, a class, or a group as distinguished by a particular character. In this light we have three distinct types of battery clocks.

There is no claim to originality here; the fact is, it is quite difficult to really discover what and where something original begins. Checking back, it probably belongs to Mr. C. B. Marble, an engineer with General Electric Co., in a paper he presented to the French and German Societies for Chronometrie at Colmar, France, on May 17, 1968, when he said: "The popular-priced mass-produced battery clock movements, manufactured during the last ten years, can generally be classified into three functional groups.

"One, the first group of battery clock movements is the mechanically driven, balance wheen-escapement type system with mainspring, wound electrically by an electric solenoid or motor.

"Two, the second group is based on the magnetically driven balance wheel-motor system, using either electrical contacts or transistor switching to drive the balance.

"Three, the third group represents a system using an electro-mechanical oscillator as a frequency generator to control a small synchronous motor through a transistorized electronic circuit." end quote.

In short, we would like to see this "system'" adopted by our trade by simply listing movements as "type 1," "type 2," etc. It is quite true that some trade names such as the Seth Thomas "acrotyne" implies a specific type, i. e. the tyne of a tuning fork, but, Westclox TT-1 does not in any way indicate that it is "type 2."

The fact is, the whole application of electricity to the timekeeping fields is in a very fluid state and very little understood; 99-44/100% of your customers will tell you that they have an "electric" clock in their automobile when you well know that it is "type 1" or merely a clock that is electrically wound. We vivdly recall when the sync clock first hit the retail market—in the early 1930's if you walked into a retail jewelry store to purchase a clock you would be shown one of the new electric creations. If you inquired about its timekeeping qualities, the clerk would lean forward bated breath —almost whisper—"it's electric". Truly, we live in an electric age; the sync clock gained immediate acceptance to the point where a renewned national monthly publication whose main claim to existance is that of testing, comparing and advising it's readers upon technical points, worth etc., of household appliances, a few years back when evaluting the battery clock, reported one to be about as good a timekeeper as the synchronous clock. From a publication leaning heavily upon the technical side, we considered this a clossal boo-boo and wrote to point out that it was impossible for a sync clock to be a true timekeeper, thus how could such a comparison be made? That brought, not one, but two letters "explaining", but they never got around to correcting it in their magazine. We would have liked to have seen that, but we are satisfied and will lay you dollars to donuts that it won't happen again.

The battery powered clock is rapidly increasing in popularity; it is most convenient simply because it does not require winding. It is also presenting the repairman with problems; "electric" though it may be called, it is mechanical and continued-operation means that somewhere along the line service is required. Some are so cheaply constructed they are not worthy of repairs but thanks to

the center mounting, a complete new movement is easily installed. This is a source of revenue the bench mechanic can't afford to overlook. The better ones will stand a reasonable—livable—repair charge.

We have two new ones this month—both "type 1". This type rarely requires any special technical repair pointers. The train is orthodox and therefore work such as cleaning, re-bushing worn gearings, etc. is standard procedure and already well known to the tender of the "144"—it only remains for the delineator to point out any new or different construction in them.

Direct from Mauthe Uhren KG, 722 Schwenningen/Neckar, Germany, comes their new W-371. This column illustrated and described their No. W-370, page 32, September 1964.

The principal difference between the W-370 and the W-371 is a re-designed winding switch. This enables the new movement to be mounted in any position. Like the first model, it winds every four minutes; the winding motor is started and stopped via a lever aplying or lifting the brush from the commutator thus insuring positive action in any position. The regulator is a new design eliminating any free play; cast in the plastic cover is a strong magnifying lens like those

MAUTHE   W-371.

seen upon the calendar window of some wrist-watch crystals. This with the elimination of the free play in the reg., Manthe says, increases the sensitivity of regulation by 50%. One mark upon the reg. scale gives five seconds per 24 hours. To remove the works only two capsule screws have to be removed. Thereby the plastic cover—capsule—can be removed and the works lifted off three support pillars enabling the repairer to observe all phases of the mechanism while it is still working. They stress the fact that this new movement is not only an important upon the W-370 but that they had in mind making the repair and adjustment easier for the repairman. We are grateful to "Mauthe" for their good cooperation.

The second movement was sent down by Bob Moses; it is the first battery powered pendulum movement we have had the opportunity to examine and test run. The model we have under observation has a pendulum that is twelve inches from hand center to bottom tip; I have the feeling that it may come in different lengths but haven't had time to check that, Bob—B. M. S. Materials, Box 1, Pleasantville, N. Y. 10570 is supplying it with hands to the repairman at $14.95. He pointed out that it is for installation in the drop ocagon—School House—clock. Either rear or hand set, it will operate hands up to a twelve inch dial.

Being 'type 1' it has no special instructions for cleaning and repair. However, there is embodied a new bit of construction which is quite neat in its action and should come in for some comment. There is no suspension spring. The pendulum hangs from a brass clivis directly upon the pallet-fork arbor rather loosely via an oval shaped hole; the weight of the pendulum pulling the clivis against the narrower portion of the oval creates just enough friction for the movement to maintain it in motion. The net result of this unusual feature is to make the clock "self-leveling"—one may slant the clock slightly upon the wall and it immediately puts itself "in-beat." This strikes us as being a feature well worth noting from the stand point of the ultimate owner—no stopped clock because it is a little out of plumb.

Furthermore, it is a feature the repairman must understand. When our movement came in it would not run; an examination indicated no malfunction, only a lack of power.

The drive spring is a cylindrical round-wire spring. When run down one (plus) revolution of the main spring wheel a contact is tripped; the wind motor winds it through one rev. (plus) of the wind wheel which wheel via loose arm—here is where the plus comes in—switches it off. What had happened, the clock laying upon it's side and no pendulum was free to kick around—down—with no battery. It thus ran down and passed by a couple of trip operations leaving the spring too weak to drive the pendulum. By hand tripping the wind switch through two windings the spring tension was brought to it's required strength—now, hanging upon the wall with its pendulum, the movement can not skip a wind. With that tension it has delivered a satisfactory performance for better than a month—there is no earthly reason why it will not continue to do so.

AMERICAN CLOCK CO.

I recently secured a battery type regulator. The name on the dial is the American Clock Company, Chicago, and the number of the works is B-10222. I wonder if you can give me any information as to what happened to this company and if possible where I could secure information as to the electrical end of the mechanism.

For your information, this has a standard clock movement with pendulum and is activated by two weights that operate on a cam arrangement. Every fifteen minutes the electrical contact causes the coils to pull these weights up and thus continue the flow of power to the clock movement.

The clock works fine but I cannot seem to activate the coils and I'd be particularly interested in finding where I could have these coils checked or replaced.

I regret that I can't give you any definite history on the American Clock Co., Chicago, Ill.

A.

As to your questions abount the electrical part—I trust we may be of more service. I do not know of any source of replacement for the coils and as for testing, you can easily do this yourself. These clocks were built to operate on three volts —two No. 6 dry cells, connected as shown in the sketch, the center carbon post (positive) to the coil terminal and the side zinc post (negative) to the frame of the clock. Secure two No. 6 dry cells and connect them up this way—complete the circuit by closing the contact points and the coil should energize the magnet. If it does your coils are okay. If it does not, check all the wiring and connections to make sure that your current failure is not outside the coil. If after this check the magnet will not energize we must conclude that the circuit is open somewhere within the coil. This being true the only thing to do is re-wind the coil with new wire. Any good electrician can do it for you, or you can do it yourself by simply duplicating the original coil. Take it apart carefully, observing the insulation and recording the number of turns in each layer, and the number of layers. Secure new wire of the same size, etc., and re-wind it as it was originally—same number of turns per layer, same number of layers.

I note that you say: "It winds every fifteen minutes" and suspect that this is exactly where your trouble sets in. All of these I've had wind every 7½ minutes. On the drive post (where your weighted levers are hinged) you should find two ratchet discs—one for each lever. Each of these

ratchet discs should have seven notches in it—if so then your clock definitely winds every 7½ minutes. You possibly have endeavored to work the weighted levers in "tandem" and thereby gained the every fifteen-minute winding idea. To start this clock: set one lever up until it is about horizontal, then set the other up in the next higher notch. As the clock runs, both levers come down. When the lower lever has reached approximately a 45-degree angle the top lever will be just about horizontal. In this position the cut portion of the hub of the upper lever will have pass-

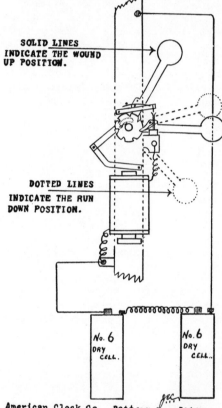

SOLID LINES INDICATE THE WOUND UP POSITION.

DOTTED LINES INDICATE THE RUN DOWN POSITION.

No. 6 DRY CELL.   No. 6 DRY CELL.

American Clock Co. Battery Regulator.

ed the top notch of the ratchet thereby allowing the contact arm to drop—closing the circuit. This energizes the magnet which in turn jerks the lower lever up one notch above the other or horizontal lever. When it reaches the bottom, contact is again made and the operation repeated.

These weighted levers that drive your clock should work just like a man's feet when he is walking—each contact or winding representing a step, and not in tandem.

POOLE CLOCK BATTERIES

I have in for repair a clock which gets its power from batteries. Are these batteries ordinary flashlight cells, or is a dry cell battery used? I have used flashlight batteries, but the power doesn't seem to go through to the coils. What can be wrong?

How long can the batteries be used for a clock of this sort? I would like very much to see this clock run; it is the first of this model that I've worked on, or for that matter seen.

The manufacturer's name is Poole of New York City. All the wiring looks very good, and the connections seem to be tight; yet for some reason it will not take the current.

A.

Yes, ordinary flashlight batteries are quite satisfactory in Poole clocks, it takes three "D" size cells. I have a "Poole" (wall model, 10 inch dial) right here in the office, which depends upon the batteries; they last from eleven months to fourteen months per set.

Now, your other question: "I have used flashlight batteries, but the power does not seem to go thru to the coils, what can be wrong?" If you mean to say that the current does not reach the coils, then only one thing can be out—the wiring. Check your wiring and contacts thoroughly. When your magnets fail to energize, the circuit must be open somewhere.

The operation of the Poole clock is sometimes puzzling, and it might be well for you to go over it again. It is just the reverse of spring-driven pendulum clocks; the pendulum drives the clock instead of the clock driving the pendulum—it in turn is driven (impulsed) by spring energy (not by the magnets). This spring is re-set (wound) by the electro-magnets. As a general rule, these clocks are good reliable timekeepers, giving no undue amount of trouble if left undisturbed.

In all likelihood, you will find your trouble in the contacts, see that these are clean and come together firmly and evenly. There are two contacts at the ends of thin springs at the top of the rocker-arm. When the stroke of the pendulum shortens enough for the extension finger to engage the rocking trigger, it releases the rocker-arm which in turn is forced down by spring tension. As the roller wheel of the rocker-arm rolls off the impulse pin on the pendulum rod, it imparts new force to the pendulum and as it (the rocker-arm) continues downward, the two contact springs come to rest on the fixed contacts; this closes the circuit, energizing the magnets and the magnets jerk the rocker-arm up where it is latched, to remain until again released. When the amplitude of the pendulum drops, then the cycle is repeated. In normal operation, the pendulum gets an impulse anywhere from every twenty-second stroke to twenty-eighth stroke. You will note that the fixed contacts are adjustable by being threaded, it is probably right here where you will find the trouble.

TIFFANY CLOCK BATTERY

I am in search of a battery, or to learn the voltage of the battery Eveready used to make, that ran the old Tiffany Neverwind clock. It was a square battery that fit into the bottom of the clock.

A.

The "Tiffany Neverwind" clocks were designed to operate on approximately four volts. You can easily assemble a satisfactory battery yourself. Get three regular flashlight batteries, "D" size, and connect them in series (center to side), cut a couple of pieces of cardboard slightly wider than the batteries are long and slightly longer than the three batteries laid side by side; place one on top, the other on the bottom, and bind the whole with Scotch tape or regular mailing tape. The finished product will be a battery about the right size to fit into the base of your clock. Insert it and make connections by soldering your lead wires to the brass terminals in the base.

HISTORICAL ANSONIA CLOCK

The Ansonia, cast iron case with "Brocot" type escapement was made about the turn of this century. I find this model illustrated in Ansonia's catalog for 1907.

Being a Tennessean, and an east Tennessean at that, you will be interested to know that Governor Robert L. Taylor (Our Bob), an east Tennessean, bought one of these clocks for the governor's office in 1897. This clock sat upon a mantel piece in the gov-

Governor Taylor clock

ernor's office from that date until the capitol offices were remodeled and decorated in 1938 under Governor Gordon Browning. At that time it was rescued from what almost amounted to a salvage sale, and turned over to the Tennessee State Library where today it rests upon a book case in back of Mrs. John Trotwood Moore's desk. The story is told that Governor Taylor personally selected this clock himself at the B. H. Stief Jewelry Store. Certainly the bas-relief scenes in the panels on either side of it are characteristic of the poetic nature of "Our Bob."

BULLE BATTERY CLOCK

Thought I might contact you for information about a clock which I received from friends in Belgium.

The clock is about two and one-half inches wide, six inches high and six inches long. The marking are as follows: Dial, CLOCKETTE—BREVETE, S. G. D. G.; rear plate, BULLE CLOCK, FRANCE, 277852. It seems to operate on the solonoid principle. I have searched the public library for information on the clock but all I have found is that it runs on a one and one-half volt dry cell battery and draws from .002 to .003 amperes. I have used such a battery but have difficulty keeping the clock going as a little vibration seems to disturb the oscillation of the pendulum and the clock stops. A three-volt battery (such as used in hearing aids) seems to provide a better oscillation of the pendulum but I am afraid it might burn out the pendulum coil. What can you tell me about this

A.

I don't think three-volts would burn out your pendulum coil, however, the clock is designed to operate on one and one-half volts and I'd say you must have some interference that is retarding your motion, rather than lack of current.

The pendulum contact pin at top of pendulum being held in place by set screw can easily be moved. Make sure that it rides in and out quite freely.

BULLE BATTERY CLOCK

We recently acquired a French battery-controlled clock. It is under a glass dome, about 18 inches high. The dial is labeled, "Bulle—Clock Brevete S. G. D. G. Movement No. 95615. It has a pendulum suspended by two rods; the bob is a short, hollow cylinder which swings along a horizontal rod passing through its center.

We would much appreciate any information regarding these clocks, the types of batteries required, and where obtainable.

A.

It is regretted that we cannot even approximate the date of manufacture of your Bulle clock from its serial number. This timepiece is the creation of two Frenchmen, Marcel Moulin and Favre Bulle. H. R. Langman, writing in his "Electrical Horology" (1935) says: "The Bulle clock is quite a new entry in the field of electrical horology."

It is an electro-magnetically maintained pendulum clock. That is, the pendulum is maintained in motion by magnetism; said magnetism being generated at the proper instant by electrical contact, etc. In turn, the pendulum drives the dial train, or registers the time by means of a rachet operation.

These clocks were designed to operate on a single dry-cell battery, one and a half volts. Now your clock will operate (if in order) on any single dry-cell you can get into the battery compartment; the larger the cell, the greater its capacity and the longer it will last. The "D" size flashlight cell will operate it 30 to 50 days; try one of your radio shops for an "A" battery for a portable radio. We believe you can locate a cell almost as large as the case which will run the clock 12 to 14 months.

WARREN BATTERY CLOCK

Antique clocks are my main interest. I recently added a Warren battery clock. The pendulum and rod are missing. I have written to Telechron for information or an illustration. They have sent me the following information which may be of interest to you and your readers. There are no sketches available.

WARREN BATTERY CLOCK: Mounted upon the pendulum rod in the small brass case is a device which sends electric impulses through the coil at every complete swing of the pendulum. These impulses are of such a nature as to maintain the swing of the pendulum in practically the same width of arc whether the battery be new or old. If the swing of the pendulum be increased or decreased by external means, the electric impulses will quickly restore it to its normal value. Thus we have the basis of a timekeeper, consisting of a pendulum swinging over a uniform arc and consequently at a uniform rate.

The oscillating motion of the pendulum is converted into a continuous rotating motion by means of two very small horse-shoe permanent magnets concealed upon the platform fastened to the pendulum. The poles of the magnets strongly attract a steel part mounted in sapphire jewels in the clock movement case. Because of the attraction and motion of the pendulum this part revolves. The motion is then transmitted by means of a screw thread at greatly reduced rate to the first gear of the clock train.

Regulation of the clock is accomplished by means of a small permanent magnet mounted beneath the hollow base of the clock and moved by the adjusting screw. By varying the distance between the permanent magnet and the bottom of the pendulum magnet the force of attraction can be varied which varies the rate of the pendulum and consequently the rate of the clock.

For the purpose of setting up this type clock correctly on a mantel or other surface, three levelling screws are provided beneath the base and a pointer and indicator on the column and pendulum rod respectively. Thus, the clock can easily be adjusted on a surface that is not level so the pendulum will hang true and the clock run properly.

A.

Normally, electric clocks are said to have their beginning with Alexander Bain's patent of October, 1840. Since that date practically every clockmaker of note has given some thought to driving a pendulum electrically, and no doubt Mr. Henry War-ren did it too. It was before World War I that he worked upon the frequency meter problem. As a rough guess, I'd say that possibly his battery clock dates before that.

In "Electrical Timekeeping" by F. Hope Jones, no mention is made of the Warren battery pendulum clock, while it has a full account of his work on the synchronous clock. In "Electrical Horology" by Langman and Ball, it is mentioned on page 25 . . . only one paragraph and a full-page sketch . . . and in principal, it is depicted as having a pendulum ball like a letter "C", or the greater portion of a ring. As the pendulum swings, the opening straddles a small coil. Fastened upon the rod, down near the ball, is a glass tube with a globule of mercury in it, and two contacts in one end. As the pendulum swings in the direction of the coil, the bit of mercury flows to that end of the glass tube (the end on that side with the contacts in it), thus briefly energizing the coil and giving to the pendulum a slight impulse.

Absolutely no idea is given as to date, size (length) of the pendulum, etc. Beyond this, the clock is merely described as driving the ratchet wheel by means of a pawl attached to the pendulum, the said ratchet wheel being mounted on the seconds arbor of a clockwork train. From this, we might guess it to be a half-seconds pendulum whose ratchet pawl engages a 60-tooth ratchet type of wheel.

RIEFLER CLOCK

I have a battery driven impulse pendulum clock of German manufacture. All the information on the clock is Riefler Munchen No. 374 and D.R.P. 50739. I am enclosing two photos of the clock, a front and a side view. The clock will only run for about an hour. Any information you can give me will be very much appreciated, particularly about the escapement.

A.

Before getting into a meager description of the escapement and its action, allow me to suggest that you study both it and your clock closely, then reduce further questions to specific points. Mr. Hamilton Pease, 51 Empire Street, Providence 3, Rhode Island,

and Mr. H. E. Reum, 1103 Woodbine Avenue, Oak Park, Illinois, both have this type clock in operation and I am sure would be glad to assist on specific points.

Aberdeen is, I believe, very near Washington, D. C., and if convenient, I suggest you contact in person, Mr. John Early Jackson, 4440 "Q" Street, for I am sure he can supply any answer on the Riefler clock.

This is generally called the "Riefler Free Pendulum" precision clock, and its very high accuracy is attained because its pendulum receives the impulse through its suspension spring and is, therefore, as free as a mechanically propelled pendulum can be. Oddly enough, the thought is prevalent that Sigmund Riefler originated this idea, possibly because he patented it in Germany shortly before the turn of the century. It rightfully belongs to Abraham Louis Breguet (1747-1823) who made a fine clock with its pendulum so impulsed for the royal house of England nearly a hundred years before Riefler began using it.

Let's take three views—front, side and top—of the Riefler clock and split its workings three ways. 1. How the pendulum is impulsed. 2. Description of the escapement parts. 3. Action of the escapement.

One: In this clock the pendulum swings perfectly free, being connected with the clock work solely through its suspension from which it receives the impulse; this impulse being communicated in the axis of oscillation and at the instant when the pendulum swings through the dead point (center of gravity). The impulse is imparted by the escape wheels bending the suspension spring a little at each oscillation of the pendulum, which produces a slight tension in the spring. This tension-force of the suspension spring gives the pendulum its impulse.

As this bending takes place around an axis which is identical with the axis of oscillation of the pendulum, and further, occurs every time at the instant in which the pendulum is swinging through the dead point or center of gravity, there is gained thereby perfect freedom of the pendulum and also the great advantage that irregularities in the communication of

force from the train and escape wheels, and resistance to the escape can exert no detrimental influence on the uniformity of the motion of the pendulum.

Two: T.T., figures one and two, is a heavy hanger of brass securely fastened to the back plate of the movement W by means of four screws uu; the flat and highly polished agate stones PP which are in a perfect horizontal plane and form together a bearing between which is the opening for the suspension spring FF'. On this horizontal plane or bearing is the axis aa of the verge or anchor AA', of which the knife edges CC' form the axis. The screws KK center the verge so that it engages properly with the escape wheels H and R. These screws are withdrawn slightly after the pendulum has been hung in position so as to allow the verge to act freely on the knife edges without friction on the points of KK'.

FF' is the suspension spring resting on the verge of frame AA' and the springs ii, the axis of which coincides exactly with the axis of motion of the verge. The escape wheel is a double wheel composed of an impulse wheel H, and a somewhat larger-locking wheel R. The teeth h and h' on the wheel H are cut tangent or ratchet-shaped, and do the lifting or make the impulse, and the teeth r and r' on the larger wheel R, do the locking. S and S' would be the lifting and locking pallets of the anchor or verge—these are cylindrical and the front ends are cut away to the center of their axis just like the pallet stones of the Brocot escapement.

The verge receives its lifting motion on the cylindrical part of the pallets from the teeth of the escape wheel H, and the locking is accomplished by the teeth of the wheel R resting on the flat (cut away) portion of the pallet stones.

Three: For the action of the escapement, refer to Fig. 1. The instant the pendulum is on or near the center of gravity, the tooth r of the locking wheel R is locked on the pallet S. If the pendulum swings in the direction of the arrow (the left), then the suspension spring ii, being vertical and taut by weight of the pendulum, follows its swing and causes the

Fig. 1

MIELE ILLUSTRATION OF RIEFLER CLOCK

TOP VIEW FROM IX SIDE MIELE RIEFLER MOVEMENT.

verge A to swing or turn on its knife edges owing to its being on the same axis aa (see Fig. 2), and attached to same to also follow the swing of the pendulum until the pallet S′ has passed the tip of the locking tooth r, disengaging itself. When accomplishing this, the pendulum has described an arc of approximately one-quarter of a degree. By this time the cylin-

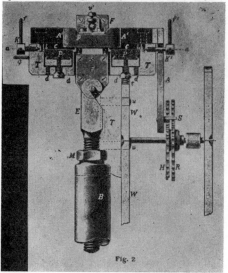

Fig. 2

drical part of the pallet S has approached and been engaged by the inclined plane of the tooth h′ of the ratchet type impulse wheel H, up to the necessary nearness for play or drop, and has been raised by the revolving of the escape wheels; (in Fig. 1, the wheels revolve in the direction of the arrow, clockwise) until the locking tooth r′ of the wheel R has engaged the

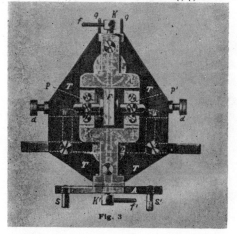

Fig. 3

flat face of the pallet S′, the action of the tooth h′ on the cylindrical part of the pallet S′ raising the pallet and moving the verge A to the right; this causes a slight bend in the suspension spring through the axis aa to the right. This slight bending of the suspension spring has taken place before the pendulum has made its full swing to the left, and on its return swing to the right, gives it a slight impulse or motion to the right, the same operation of the suspension spring carrying anchor A with it disengaging the pallet S′ from the locking tooth r′ and receiving a new impulse through the tooth to the left. It is quite evident that these impulses are very gentle and gradual, and makes really the ideal escapement for precision pendulum clocks. To avoid any confusion, I should point out that the screws d of Figures 2 and 3 are to clamp the lower chock of the suspension F′ secure so that the pendulum can be put on or taken off without damage to the suspension spring, and that they have nothing at all to do with the escapement or its adjustment.

HAMILTON BATTERY CLOCK

The battery movement (see illustration Fig. 1) is powered by a single "C" size cell and requires no special tools in its servicing. Round, $2\frac{1}{2}$ inches in diameter, it comes housed within a plastic case (cap was removed for our photo), $2\frac{3}{4}x3\frac{7}{8}x1\frac{1}{4}$ inches—additional size of case is for holding the battery. The solid balance is 1 1/16 inches in diameter and when you recall that a "C" size cell is but $1\frac{7}{8}$ inches tall, correct proportions may be drawn from our photo.

Calculations from laboratory tests show that the capacity of a single "C" size cell is sufficient to drive this movement for five years, its actual current consumption being so small. However, the common garden variety of cell we pick up at the corner cigar store or 5 & 10 just doesn't have a 5-year shelf life, so the lab fellows play it safe and say one cell will drive the clock for about two years.

Basically, this new movement shows no radical changes, it has the conventional

Fig. I   J. E. Coleman

balance, jeweled bearings and a flat hairspring from the "Elinvar" family. The balance is magnetically impulsed and in turn ratchets the dial train forward via a most efficient yet simple method.

Staff breakage and/or damage upon jeweled clocks happens less often than in watches. When it becomes necessary to replace a staff, Fig. 2 shows the proper alignment for the impulse-rotor and the index spring retainer as they relate to the balance wheel, also the proper in-beat position for the hairspring stud. This stud is slotted and snaps into the balance bridge friction tight.

To remove the balance assembly from the clock

1—Use a roller remover such as HR #39-520 to pull the balance from the pillar posts.
2—Rotate the bridge clockwise to free the rotor from between its pole pieces.
3—Raise bridge and withdraw unit away from clock.
4—Pry the hairspring stud from the bottom side of balance bridge using small screwdriver or pointed round stock rod.

To disassemble the balance unit

1—Remove hairspring in usual manner.
2—Remove the rotor with a roller remover such as the HR #39-520.

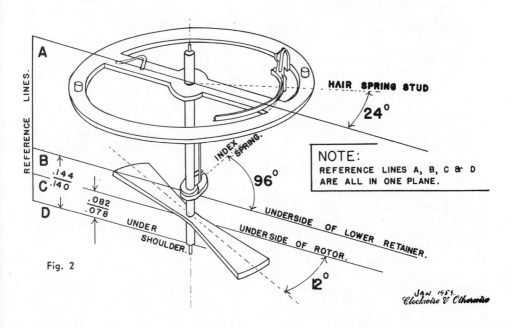

Fig. 2

389

3—Remove balance wheel and retainers in the same manner.
4—Remove the index spring with tweezers; inserting points between the large and small coils forcing the small coils to top of staff.

To put in new staff

A—Assemble index spring loosely on new staff.
B—Partially press balance wheel on.
C—Align spring to approximate location as it relates to balance wheel.
D—Press wheel to the shoulder.
E—Partially press upper retainer on staff using staking tool and punch like K&D #85.
F—Align retainer to proper angular location with respect to balance wheel.
G—Partially press lower retainer on staff.
H—Align retainer to proper angle.
I—Press both retainers to proper depth.
J—Place rotor on; align to correct angle and press to proper depth.
K—Feed index spring leg into the slot formed by the two retainers.
L—Stake on hairspring collet, aligning the stud 24 degrees from reference line A.

To replace the completed job

1—Lay balance bridge inside up and press hairspring stud in slot using long nose pliers.
2—Back up jewel screw couple of turns.
3—Feed balance assembly into the movement so that the rotor end passes through opening between pole pieces.
4—Carefully set lower pivot into jewel hole.
5—Press balance bridge onto posts—down firm on the shoulders.
6—Rotate balance counter-clockwise so that rotor is working between pole pieces.
7—Gently raise balance until rotor hits top pole piece, then in this position turn jewel screw down while feeding upper pivot into jewel hole.
8—Endshake staff to position where rotor is free but cannot touch pole pieces, and the job is finished.

The electrical circuit portrayed in Fig. 3 is simplest imaginable and so is the contacting system. The contact spring serves a dual purpose—slotted across it, slightly beyond the center point is a round jewel just like a roller jewel; the spring tension holds this jewel against the train ratchet wheel thereby retaining the train in place. When the balance strokes (counter-clockwise), its attached index spring moves the train ratchet wheel forward by one tooth; as this tooth travels forward it lifts the

locking roller-like jewel up, pressing the contacts closed. You can note that cir-

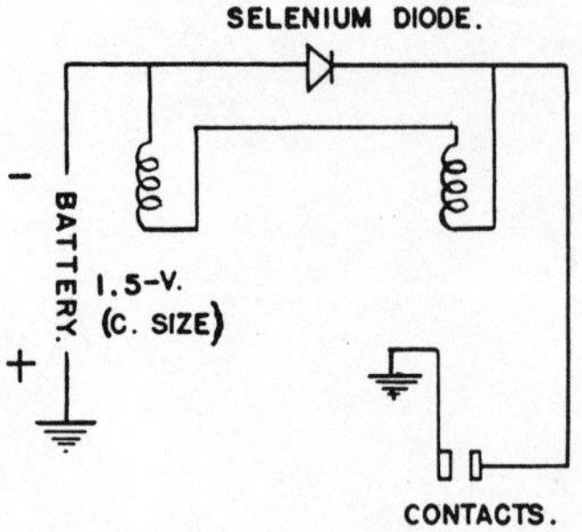

SCHEMATIC CIRCUIT. *Clockwise & Otherwise JAN. 1959*

cuit closure takes place just before the rotor wings enter the pole pieces and opens when they are half-way of their excursion through them.

The movement has a 14,000 beat balance—quarters—but since the train is advanced by only the left rotation, the center-seconds hand is advanced by the half-second just like a ship's chronometer.

As shown on the circuit diagram there is cut into the minus line supplying the two coils, a diode. It is the tiny green object with a small red spot upon it you will see at the top of the movement. It acts as a spark suppressor between the contacts. While a cheap resistor would serve this purpose it would not serve so well. Hamilton chose to use a selenium diode costing much more and this bespeaks the refinement of construction evident throughout this clock. As we said before, it does not embody any radical basic operating principle. It's smooth operation, very low current consumption and excellent qualities therefore must be attributed to superb engineering. I don't feel that I'm going far afield if I deduce that perhaps the construction of this movement went along with that of the electric wrist watch.

Is Tiffany clock practical?

Any information you can supply concerning the Tiffany Electric clock, manufactured in the United States, and patented 1904, will be appreciated.

This clock appears on first examination to need only routine care and batteries, but the batteries and their brackets are gone. What is the proper battery voltage and capacity? Is this a practical clock, and feasible to restore?

The finish is streaked and rough. Apparently it was gilded. If you have knowledge of the material in the base and pendulum, that would be useful.

A.

From about 1900 to the Kaiser's War, the Tiffany Battery Clock enjoyed a measure of successful sales and went through several changes; both in management and models.

Nothing in your letter indicates which model you have. It IS a practical clock; in our opinion it is feasible to restore. Collectors (especially those looking for as many different battery clocks as possible) are seeking them. Back to the practical; it is a torsion pendulum type (short, at that), and therefore must not be expected to keep "observatory" time.

These clocks were first made in New York City, later in Buffalo, N. Y., and then moved to Dunkirk, N. Y. The first models came in wood cases (glass sides), were quite a bit taller than following models and impulsed the torsion pendulum on both strokes. Later models were on brass bases, covered by a glass dome, and impulsed their pendulums in only one direction. The first model was designed to run upon two No. 6 dry cells, therefore 3 volts. I've been told that some short later models were designed for 3 volts, but, those I've handled work fine on 4½ volts, i.e., a battery made up of four "D" size flashlight cells. Most of these models take a Horolovar, .005 suspension spring; 6¼ inches long, with the contact finger set for just 12 mm. clearance down from the top chock. Most bases were solid brass, most pendulums were lead filled brass shells which will stand a lot of polishing and buffing—a few were outright lead just gilded. You can readily determine this—if lead, just clean and spray with "Krylon" bright-gold.

"Orion" Distinction is 9-V Battery

So far as we are aware, this is the first nine-volt battery movement upon the American market, and, since the little 9-v. battery as used in small transistor radios has become as popular as the old "D" size cell (and almost as cheap) power replacement every twelve or fourteen months is quite nominal.

Basically, the power application in the "Orion" is totally different from the method we generally meet in the little jeweled, 1.5-volt movements. Where the 1.5-volt makes contact and wind) and set-up tension in a spiral spring; the Orion's train is driven by an orthodox mainspring, quite like those in the self-winding wrist watches only it is motor wound.

The complete movement is a four-deck affair; round, 1 and 11/16ths., in. diameter by one inch deep. The time train is located between the two plates next to the dial and the winding mechanism; two additional plates behind them. The battery fits into a clip on the back side of the back plate of the wind mechanism. The time movement is orthodox in construction; seven-jeweled, shock-resistant balance, solid with 'flat' temperature comp. hairspring — nothing radically different and therefore needs no comment. We show it in Fig. 1. Note the posts at A and A. These fit into the holes

Note: how, when fitted together, the hand set pinion extends through the large hole at bottom of time movement to engage a pinion coupled with the dial train to effect hand setting. That: the spiral grooved disc at top of wind mechanism fits over a pin in the tail piece of the regulator giving micrometer adjustment when moving the regulator.

The ORION. 7-jewel 9-volt.

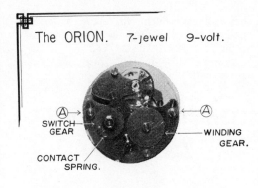

Time Movement   Back Plate.

Fig. 1.

B and B in Fig. 2 of the wind mechanism.

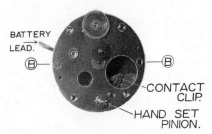

Wind Mechanism   Front Plate.

Fig. 2.

The very small 8-leaf pinion at the center of the wind mechanism is located upon the outer end of the 9-v. three-pole motor arbor and performs two functions: i.e. 1, it drives the intermediate wheel as shown engaged whose pinion drives the winding gear Fig. 1.) and 2, it also meshes with the intermediate gear which by it's pinion in turn drives the switch gear Fig. 1.). This winding gear is frictioned on to the end of the winding arbor; in the center of the mainspring barrel.

The time train, proper, consists of three wheels, main, center (seconds) and escape wheel. Backwards, or, behind the main (barrel) are two other wheels; the first, driven by the barrel carries the hand-friction and it's arbor extends through the front-plate to drive the hour and minute hand via the intermediate dial wheel. The No. 2 wheel behind the barrel is driven by a pinion on the No. 1 arbor; it's arbor extends through the back plate; riding idle

over this extension is the switch gear (Fig. 1.) and screwed upon it's end is the switch cam. Note: the very large hole at the right in Fig. 2, when the two sections are coupled together, the switch cam extends into it and against the contact clip (Fig.4).

Now, let's assume that the clock is wound and running—as the time train runs forward, the switch cam turns while the switch gear sits still; the contact spring rides in the groove of the open circuit (off) cam (black) until the beveled notch reaches it; it's spring tension flips it on to the closed circuit (on) cam (white) starting the wind motor. While it is winding the mainspring, it is also turning the switch gear; when the switch gear has been turned through 180 degrees the contact spring (Fig. 3.) has reached the beveled notch of the closed circuit (on) cam (white) flipping on to the open circuit (off) cam (black) and stopping the wind motor. The motor remains stopped until the time train has turned the switch cam through 180 degrees and the cycle is repeated. See the two sketches at bottom of Fig. 4.

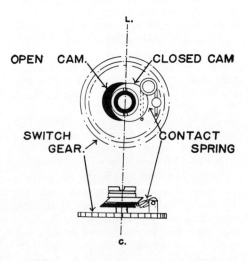

Fig. 3.

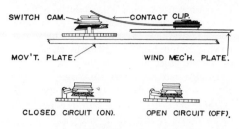

SWITCH CAM. — — CONTACT CLIP.

MOV'T. PLATE.   WIND MEC'H. PLATE.

CLOSED CIRCUIT (ON).   OPEN CIRCUIT (OFF).

Fig. 4.

Detailed procedures for servicing the Orion, as suggested by the makers: "Remove setting knob by holding setting shaft at slot and unscrewing knob.

Remove 3 case back screws, located immediately behind bezel.

Dial, movement and battery are attached to bezel. Holding bezel, remove case by lifting straight off.

The pliable strip seal located between case and bezel can be reused if kept clean and not overstretched.

Disconnect and remove battery.

Remove 3 flat head bezel screws and lift dial plate and movement unit from bezel.

Remove rubber sleeve from setting shaft.

Remove hands in usual manner using a dial protector to avoid damage to the dial.

Remove dial by carefully bending dial tabs perpendicular to dial plate.

Remove 3 pillar screws and lift battery plate from pillars.

Remove setting wheel. This is a light press fit and can be removed by prying evenly against hub, between hub and movement housing.

Remove dial plate by unscrewing 4 small flat head screws.

Remove 2 movement housing screws, located to left of regulator screw and to the right of setting shaft. (Located counterclockwise from these parts).

Remove movement housing.

The battery lead can be removed by inserting a screw driver thru clearance hole in motor plate and partly unscrewing the terminal screw. The battery lead can then be unhooked.

Remove two blue clips, holding the motor to the movement, by prying them from the posts with a screw driver. With the clips removed, the motor can be separated from the movement.

It is usually not necessary to disassemble the motor.

Remove the switch cam.

The switch cam can be disassembled by unscrewing it by the cross slot provided. It is necessary to remove the switch cam gear in order to remove the balance cock screw nearest it.

The movement is essentially a watch movement and disassembly, cleaning and reassembly can be carried out in the usual manner.

After reassembling the movement, reassemble the switch cam and its gear. Be sure to place the switch spring in a groove of the cam before the cam is firmly seated.

The cam must then be turned with respect to the switch spring so as to pre-load the mainspring. This is necessary so that the mainspring is never completely run down before the switch spring moves to the "on" position to cause the motor to wind the mainspring.

Proceed as follows: After seating the switch cam, turn the cam until the switch spring moves to the off position. It will then rest on the colored plastic part of the cam. Continue turning one quarter turn or 90°. The switch spring will then be in the groove of the colored plastic cam, half way between the "off" and "on" bevels. See Fig. 1, page 32. With a pair of tweezers, lift the switch spring and place it in the groove of the metal section of the cam. Then when power is applied, the motor will run and wind the mainspring while the switch cam moves three quarters of a turn before the spring reaches the off position. Since each winding occurs every half turn of the cam, there will always be one quarter turn of the cam reserve power in the mainspring, guaranteeing that the movement will run long enough to reach the 'on" position again.

Replace the motor, being careful not to move the switch cam in the process, and to be sure the contact clip rests on the top of the switch cam. See Fig. 2, page 32. It may be necessary to guide the gears into mesh with the pinions of the winding system. This may be done with tweezers point or long thin tool.

Place the hook of the battery lead thru its slot in the movement housing, and place the hook in its terminal, fastening the terminal screw thru the motor plate clearance hole. The winding may be checked by placing the lead terminal on the + terminal of the battery and touching the − terminal to any part of the movement. If it does not run, check the terminal clip on top of the switch cam to make sure of its contact. Some adjustment may be necessary, if it has been damaged or displaced in assembly.

Assembly

Replace movement housing and screws.

Replace dial plate with 4 small flat head screws.

Replace setting wheel, slotted end of hub first, so hub is flush with movement housing.

Replace battery plate and 3 pillar screws.

Replace dial and hands.

Replace rubber sleeve on setting shaft and apply a small amount of Hamilton PML stem grease to tube opening.

Bezel unit should consist of a bezel, gasket, crystal and reflector in the order given.

Place dial plate and movement unit into bezel unit and fasten with 3 flat head screws.

Replace and connect battery.

Replace strip seal evenly against stepped shoulder of bezel, directly behind spokes. Overstretched seals may require reshaping by pressing into shoulder with fingers.

Replace case, making sure screw holes of bezel and case are aligned before pressing case over seal.

Replace case back screws.

Replace setting knob.

Ingraham Develops Direct Current Clock

The Ingraham Clock Co. (Bristol, Conn.) announced Model "44," the only direct drive D.C. motor-operated clock on the American market.

Perhaps there are undesirable features to be found in every mechanism—the principal ones generally attached to the sync clocks are: 1. the dangling cord; 2. outlet-plug not always handy; 3. stoppage with every current interruption. Heretofore the battery driven clock has eliminated all three of those objections, but, it introduced some of its own: 1. periodical noise at re-wind; 2. contact troubles; 3. ratchet troubles. Evidently, "Model 44" is aimed at elimination of all six objections.

Being battery driven naturally cancels the sync objections; it has no contacts, no ratchet, and does not re-wind periodically cancelling out the latter three.

Fig. 1 shows the dial-side of the front

Fig. I.

plate, the movement is cased in a medium impact, plastic case upon rubber for a very quiet tick. Approximate over-all dimensions: 3.7 inches wide by 4¾ in. high by 1.4 in. thick. The "standard" movement is not jeweled; and is set by advancing the hands—it can be had with a jeweled balance, and, rear set, at slight increased cost.

The hairspring is temperature compensated; hands are interchangeable with Ingraham, 8-day spring-wound and Ingraham sync hands; the motor has ample strength to carry all normal size clock hands; has been used with dials up as large as fifteen (15) inches diameter.

Fig. 2 shows the back plate; location of

Fig. 2.

easily detached motor, etc. note the micro-meter screw regulator affording easy, positive adjustment—½ turn equals approximately one (1) minute per day (24 hours).

Fig. 3 is our rough sketch of the train lay-out. Each detail of the mechanical construction is quite orthodox and needs no special comment because the bench repairman is already familiar with it. However, the actual "drive" is unique and can come in for some explanation. Direction of motion (drive) is indicated by the curved arrows. The main drive arbor of the 1.5-volt, continuous running motor turns right (clockwise) as you face the back plate; it has short hairspring engaging a small pinion via crank style, concentric with it. The pinion revolves the large wheel numbered 2 to the left; this No. 2 wheel has no

pinion but engages directly into pinion No. 3 which it drives to the right. This No. 3 arbor has a smaller pinion driving the fourth wheel to the left. Now here is the unique feature, the drive power branches off in a "Y"—this fourth wheel directly driving the pinion of the fifth (escape) wheel to the right; simultaneously its (4th) pinion is driving the No. 5-A wheel to the right. 5-A in turn drives the center-wheel, 6-B to the left (remember you are looking at the back). The third arbor having two pinions carries a coiled spring between its pinions, i.e. one pinion floats loose upon the arbor and is only driven forward as this coiled spring exerts pressure in that direction. In substance, the 1.5-volt D.C. motor is continuously running forward with all its might but as we all know, direct current motors can not be made to revolve with any degree of accuracy approaching time keeping—in the "44" the balance and hairspring perform that function.

This being the case, it automatically follows that the turning of the escape wheel never "exactly" matches the turns of the No. 1 pinion. Such a variation is absorbed in an amazingly smooth manner by the combined give and take of the little hairspring upon the motor arbor plus that of the little cylindrical spring upon the No. 3 arbor.

Here is the one point of caution you as a repairman must observe and also caution the owner must observe. Make sure, when inserting a new battery that it goes into the case exactly as indicated by the case-marking—any time the current is reversed upon a D.C. motor the motor reverses—turning this motor the wrong way then "un-winds" the little hairspring instead of winding it up—there is the possibility of damaging, or, tangling it. And, of course the clock can't run backward.

We've found it to be a good timer; responds well to the regulator and runs very quietly. Mr. Wilson tells us that any standard "D" size flashlight cell will operate the clock for its shelf-life—12 to 14 months. We are grateful to the Ingraham organization for their co-operation—C. & O. is always anxious to present readers with details and information upon new clocks.

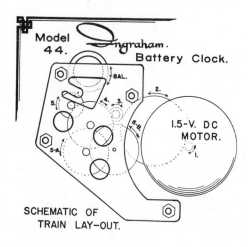

SCHEMATIC OF
TRAIN LAY-OUT.

Fig. 3.   C. & O. 1-63.

SCHATZ BATTERY CLOCK

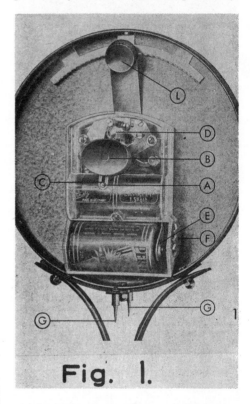

Fig. I.

Since the entire clock was a compound pendulum; the Ansonia swinging by a crossed suspension arrangement and the Junghans pivoted upon two fine points, trouble was sooner or later occasioned at these points because winding placed undue strain there. Shatz has overcome this feature by using their "Elexacta-P" movement, powered by one "D" size flash-light battery.

One new clock this month; Mr. Fred J. Koch (1115 Broadway, New York 10, N. Y.) sent down one of the new "Schatz" "Queen Anne" models for our look-see. Many repairmen are familar with the old "Ansonia" swinging ball clock and a smaller version marketed by "Junghans"—both were spring driven; the first had to be wound weekly and the latter was a one-day piece.

The "Queen Anne" is a wall clock as may be seen from the side view, Fig 2. It is 21½ inches high; diameter of dial without adornments 6¾ inches. It swings (beats) approximately 48 to the minute; winds about every two minutes. Basically, the movement is the same as those already familar to bench horologists, namely, it is spring driven (coil spring) electro-magnetically wound, with orthodox train and escapement. The major exception being the "Elexacta-P" movement has a short heavy pendulum rather than a balance-wheel.

We've watched this one closely for a full month; it is an excellent timekeeper and one point of particular test was to observe whether or not wind currents would stop it as was sometimes experienced with the two models mentioned. Perhaps because they were supported by statues and thus often placed out in the room where they got the full impact from air currents accounts for their stoppage. The Queen Anne is rather heavy; it swings close to the wall—approximately 1½ inches—rather swift air currents do not affect it, so it is not going to stop from the ordinary ones.

Appearing as a "sort of decoration" is a small brass chain shown at 'K' in Fig. 2. In

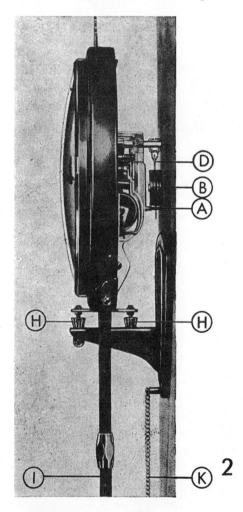

Fig. 2.

reality it is a plomb-bob from which the clock is to be leveled (aligned). After the bracket is mounted upon the wall, hang on the clock; back side outward as in Fig. 1, then note whether or not the pendulum-rod hangs perfectly vertical (in line with brass chain), if not, correct it by moving the counterweight "L" Fig. 1, either left or right as necessary.

With a slight push set the clock in motion and listen to see if it is in-beat—if out of beat, correct by bending the critch wire "A" as on any pendulum clock.

Servicing the "Elexacta-P" movement presents no unusual problems at all—to detach the mechanical part, remove the two pillar screws and movement holding screw. It is so constructed that this in no way interferes with the electrical part of the clock—proceed as with any mechanical clock.

When checking for trouble, first see whether the clock stopped in the 'rundown' position with contacts closed or in a 'wound-up' position with the contacts open. If your clock stops with the contacts open and wound, look for the trouble in the movement part (train & escapement). If the contacts are closed, check the electric part for: a battery exhausted. b. dirty battery holding brackets at "E" Fig. 1. c. dirty contacts. d. disengaged click on the winding rotor. e. faulty electric circuit. f. dust between coil case and lid. These should be corrected by. a. new battery. b. & c. clean contacts with a cotton swab on a piece of peg wood dipped in gasoline or alcohol. NEVER use a file or sand-paper and make sure to keep contacts free of any grease or oil. d. readjust click. If necessary, replace the center wheel or winding rotor—this should be part No. 58-07 and 61-016 respectively. e. inspect all cables making certain they have good contact at every connecting point. See that the positive cable is fully insulated and not shorting out on the movement or front plate. f. remove dust and/or dirt.

If, at the instant of re-wind a short buzzing noise should be heard, correct it by loosening the two screws on the bottom of coil, then press the lid firmly against the coil case at the same time tightening the screws again. This done, the coil lid should automatically lift to its normal position. A correction of the lid tension can be made by removing the screws and carefully bending the bronze spring. When the rewind action is functioning correctly, it should take place at intervals of from 90 to 120 seconds.

Mr. Koch remarked that on the Queen Anne you make the pendulum shorter to go 'slower'—this is always true of such compound pendulum pieces. These clocks are adjusted (regulated) at the factory and marked by two little marks upon the pendulum rod, however, if the regulating nut is moved during shipment, or, the battery supplied happens to be of a different weight from that with which the clock was originally regulated, some regulation must be necessary. The front side of the pendulum rod is graduated—two marks on this scale will vary the clock about ten (10) minutes in 24 hours. As we've already said, it is an excellent timer. Being battery powered, the winding chore and/or current failures are eliminated. Like every other clock with anything different about its motion other than that of the orthodox pendulum, it is an attention getter. Suggested retail price $43.95.

BATTERY MOVEMENT.

Mauthe Battery Strike Movement W-370

From Mr. Fred J. Koch, 1115 Broadway, N.Y.C. 10010, we have one of the new "Mauthe" W-370 battery movements under test-run for over a month; it has proven an excellent timer.

It is spring driven, electrically wound by 1.5 v. "C" battery, and center mounted. It is 2⅜ inches wide by 2 3/16 inches high, 1¼ inches thick, exclusive of the battery case under it. Basically, it follows the general pattern of battery wound movements and thus the unique feature of its design has to be its major difference.

Fig. 2, shows the movement with both back-plates removed. The section under the lower right plate is the clock proper; it consists of the center-wheel; escape-wheel, lever and balance assembly; any repair adjustment or cleaning will be handled by the clockmaker in the usual way and needs no comment here.

Located under the upper left plate is the

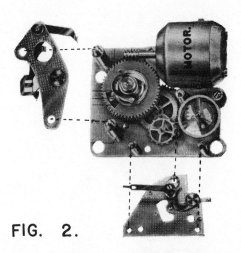

FIG. 2.

complete driving mechanism consisting of the main-wheel and the worm-wind wheel (fiber) with the main-spring in between them, this and the motor are the new construction which the repairer must familiarize himself with in order to be able to repair and service these clocks.

The motor is switched on and off by shifting the rotor axis-wise as indicated on Fig. 7. At 1.5-v. the motor will make about 900 revolutions per minute. Its rotor shaft is shiftable in the axial direction by about 0.8 mm. For this reason it is desirable to see that when set into the case the motor axis is approximately level. The following forces act upon the rotor: 1. In switch-on direction there is a permanent magnetic force between the stator and the rotor inside the motor. 2. Also in switch-on direc-

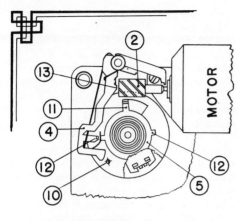

FIG. 3.

tion the switch actuating lever (13 in Fig. 3.) by its spring washer presses on the end of the worm gear. 3. In the switch-off direction another permanent force comes from the mainspring through the worm wheel and the worm gear.

The mainspring is rewound at constant intervals by the motor every four minutes. The effective average torque on the mainspring always remains the same, irrespective of battery voltage, and this is given as the main reason for its good timekeeping.

During the clock's run-off, the worm wheel remains stationary while the mainwheel is turning. At the same time the release pin 10 moves toward the cam 11 which is bent toward the front side of the movement, and pushes along the cam plate, after having reached it (Fig. 3). One of the two cams 12 which are bent in the opposite direction rests during the run-off under the switch actuating lever 4. Its spring now moves in a clockwise direction beyond the release edge, where the switch actuating lever drops and with its bent flap 13 pushes the worm gear 2 in the switch-on direction. This force together with the magnetic force within the motor moves the rotor in the switch-on direction and holds it there during the whole winding process of one-half revolution of the worm-wheel.

The winding operation is over when one of the two cams 12, which are bent toward the back plate, reaches the switch actuating lever 4, thereby the rotor shaft moves under the force of the fully wound main-

spring in the switch-off direction—to avoid any shock to the movement from the winding operation, the worm-gear is attached to the rotor shaft by means of a friction.

Care must be exercised when disassembling the winding mechanism, the mainspring is pre-loaded and must not be bent. The mainspring is pressed into the mainwheel locking plate in a pre-determined position and therefore should not be removed. When reassembling always apply a little grease to the worm-wheel teeth.

When reassembling the W-370 first secure the mainspring with screw to the worm-wheel. Then put the latter on the cleaned and oiled bearing bushing, and insert the spring washer into the slot of the worm-wheel bushing. Check the endshake

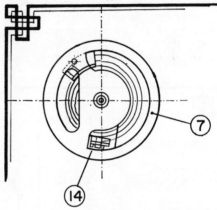

FIG. 4.

of the worm-wheel. Pre-load the mainspring by turning the main-wheel three half revolutions. The mainspring fastening arm 14 must be in the large cut of the main-wheel 7—see Fig. 4.

The release pin of the main-wheel 10 has to move toward the cam 11 of the cam plate—see Fig. 5. And has to contact it during the run-off.

If necessary, adjust cam. Check flat and centered condition of the pre-loaded mainspring. Make the same test wth the mainspring fully wound (additional half revolution of the wheel).

Here is a suggested procedure for locating trouble and correcting it: "A" Clock comes in stopped and battery is not discharged. First, check whether movement is

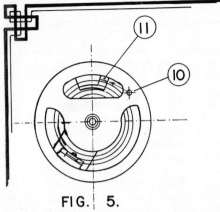

FIG. 5.

run-off and whether switching lever has dropped. If this is not the case then the trouble must be in the mechanical part of the movement and can be corrected in the usual way. If the movement is run-off and its switching lever has dropped, look for the following failures: A, 1, if the motor shaft

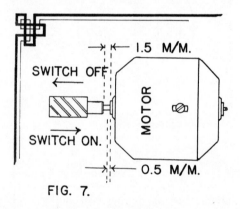

FIG. 7.

is not in the switch on position (Fig. 7) although the switch actuating lever has dropped and presses against the worm gear; check to see if the worm-wheel jams? Motor shaft jams? A, 2, check all contacts between battery and motor for sufficient contact pressure and current supply. A, 3, in case the motor won't start although the rotor shaft is in switch-on position (Fig. 7) the motor is at fault and should be exchanged.

"B" Clock comes in stopped and battery is untimely discharged; B, 1, Bent switch actuating lever causes faulty cooperation between cam plate and the switch actuating lever and its spring. Motor is not cor-

rectly switched off. To correct: adjust switch lever and spring. B, 2, Cam plate and release pin of the main-wheel are not right position as shown as Fig. 5. B, 3, Friction between rotor shaft and worm-gear is insufficient. Motor does not switch-off. This is evident by a slight vibration even though the worm-gear is not turning, or a slight noise—sometimes both.

To correct you generally have to exchange motor. B, 4, Motor does not start normally. Take off motor and connect it with an almost discharged battery whose voltages register between 1.1 and 1.2 volts. Check starting several times. If motor continues with faulty starting, exchange. B, 5, Check all contacts for current flow and short circuits. B, 6, If none of the foregoing faults are observed but you still have trouble: change the motor.

Mauthe regulates the W-370 on the "Vibrograph" to plus 20 or minus 20 seconds per day—the repairer can easily obtain better time by his individual hand-regulation method and should easily reach plus 5 or minus five seconds per day.

Mauthe W-470

L AST COLUMN we dealt in a few pointers upon the Mauthe W-370 and pointed out that much of it would apply to the W-470. One and a half volt, battery clocks have been coming to the repair bench for several years; in a great many instances we find them to be quite similar in construction or at least in basic principle; all have been straight timekeepers. The major difference found in the W-470 is: it strikes the hour and half-hour.

By means of a planetary gear one mainspring drives both the time and strike trains, this arrangement simplifies the winding since only one spring has to be wound. Because this spring has the additional chore of propelling the strike, it must be wound more often then the W-370. Where it (370) winds every four minutes, the striker winds every three minutes.

Worm wheel 3 on Fig. 2, with its cam plate 5, and main-spring fastening arm; winding limit plate with its release pin 10 and drive pinion; main-spring 6 plus two drive wheels, one for time and one for strike, comprise the complete power and winding unit, all working off one single arbor.

Its switching arrangement is identical to the 370, contained within the motor, however, instead of being fastened to the front via two screws, the 470 motor is held to the movement by a tension strap. The battery box is connected with the terminal nuts on the motor by two pole tipped wires; the pole tip of the red wire must be connected to the terminal nut marked red. When disconnecting the wires from the motor, do NOT loosen the connection nuts.

When the assembled mechanism is mounted, the main-spring must be preloaded by three half revolutions. The winding limit plate has to touch the main-spring fastening arm. Before mounting the preassembled differential into the clock movement, check to make sure that they are

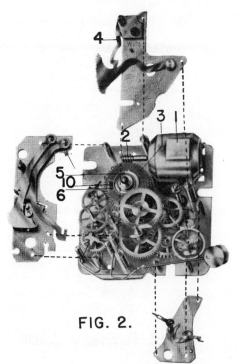

FIG. 2.

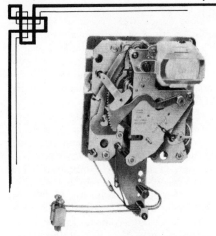

W-470 MAUTHE 1.5-V. STRIKING MOVEMENT.

clean and properly oiled for friction free running.

The shut-off lever of the strike mechanism is mounted in the correct position and need not be taken off when repairing the movement. Also, it should never touch the movement cover in order to avoid any noise transfer.

During the storage and transportation, make sure that the circuit is off either by

removing the battery or by insulating with a cardboard tag over one pole of the battery.

From power application onward, the strike train is completely orthodox and is thus handled in the same manner in which you are accustomed to handling light strike trains. It is the rack and snail type with a five-arbor train; the gathering pallet being located on No. 2 arbor.

Both the rack and gathering pallet show plainly in the photo and Fig. 2, as does the locking lever. The half-hour lift is shorter than the hour lift and thus the rack never falls at the half-hour stroke; the train is merely unlocked; one hammer stroke is executed and the locking lever falls back to lock position.

The hammer-tail lift is located upon the No. 2 arbor the same as the gathering pallet, thus making the strike adjustment simple and easy. This strike train, while having ample power to execute the strike operation, is not over powered thus when setting it in you want to make sure that it locks with the hammer-tail lift a short distance from the hammer tail, giving the fan-fly a couple or three turns before the lift begins to raise the hammer.

Like the 370 the striker movement is equipped with a Nivarox spring; its motor is easily interchangeable from the rear without removing hands, etc. There is no flow of current if the battery is inserted the reversed way—the near constant torque held by the battery even at a decreasing voltage accounts for its high accuracy. It has no center seconds hand.

We are grateful to Mr. Koch and the good people in the Mauthe factory for their cooperation. In closing, a word about the complete clock might be well since it will give you some idea of the size of this movement— it (the clock) is eight inches high, by nine inches wide. As you've noted the double hammers in our movement photo, it is a 'bim-bam' striker upon two rods. The case is a high polished, dark walnut and the dial has embossed figures and batons—as of this moment we do not have the U.S.A. price.

Imperial Battery Clock

FROM NORTH DAKOTA, Ohio, Arizona and most recently from Riverside, Calif., this column has received queries about the Imperial battery clock. In view of the fact the makers do not appear on any of the listings and the demand for data for the repairman, it might be well to combine a bit of history along with the technical and get the whole into the record.

As with the "Stray Bits" articles we sometimes do on these pages, we like to have "first-hand" information that has never before been published. Our "Imperial" file dates back to 1954. We were fortunate enough to locate and correspond with a Mr. August Feraud, Granite City, Ill., the last of the three Feraud brothers who founded Imperial in 1908. A bit later we were honored by a visit of Mr. A. W. Fowler, the man who purchased the assets of The Imperial Clock in 1920 and moved it to Highland, Illinois, some 25 miles from where it was originally founded.

Normally one might think that a couple of "contact" sources as those indicated above make research very easy—practically it does not and there are certain detail gaps in our "Imperial" history. First, we have practically nothing on the activity of the Feraud Brothers—Francis, Joseph and Frank—prior to their application for the patent, Sept. 8th, 1908. Evidently, all three were clockmakers and the resultant patent No. 920,124 is the net result of their combined efforts, though it was filed in the name of Frank.

Mr. August Feraud wrote: "We opened a factory in Granite City, Ill. about 1908 and after a few years we organized a company and moved to St. Louis, Mo." (Year ?) Mr. Fowler related that when the move was made to St. Louis, they purchased the assets of the "Sempire Clock Co." and combined it into Imperial and that no more "Sempire" clocks were produced.

After the St. Louis operation was started, there was a need for additional capital and some people in Kimswick, Mo., became interested. They put up some funds but had the factory moved to Kimswick (date ?) where it operated for a short time before more funds were needed. This time some St. Louis men became interested and evolved a great program to build a factory and found a town around it. They went some 30 miles from St. Louis and founded Imperial, Mo. The town prospered but the clock factory did not.

It was about this period that the Feraud Brothers sold all their interests in Imperial. After the factory was built and the town established, the company was again in embarrasing financial circumstances. The St. Louis people in order to protect their interests, removed the company back to St. Louis, leasing a building on Rutger Street just east of Grand Avenue. Shortly thereafter came World War I and the manufacture of clocks was discontinued. They secured some war orders that kept them operating during the war. However, for some reason, that venture was not profitable and after the war additional capital was needed.

A Mr. George A. Abell invested in the company and became its manager; he operated the company through 1920 when it became insolvent and Mr. Abell was appointed Trustee. Mr. A. W. Fowler purchased all the assets of The Imperial Clock Company, organized a new company under the laws of Illinois, secured a factory building at the intersection of Main Street and

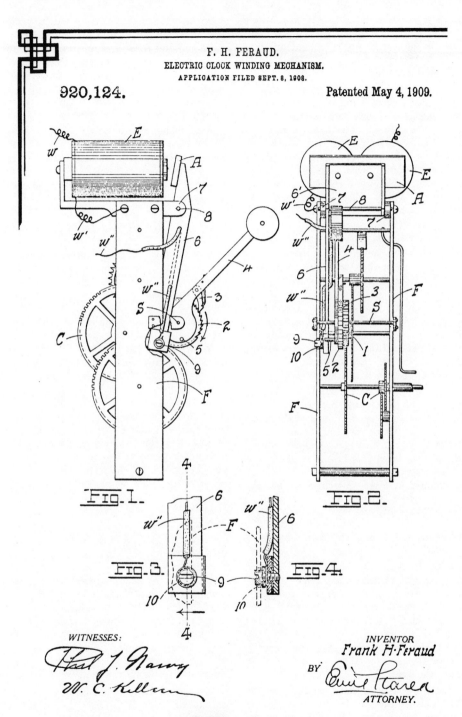

Fig.1.

Fig.2.

Fig.3.

Fig.4.

WITNESSES:

INVENTOR

Frank H. Feraud

BY

ATTORNEY.

FIG. I.

403

Morrison Avenue, in Collinsville, Ill., where he built clocks for approximately one year; then he moved again to Highland, Ill., about 1922 where the battery wall clocks were produced until 1928.

At this time Mr. Fowler invented a different type of electric wind clock, still pendulum controlled. These were produced for a year or two then, in order to market a clock in a smaller case, the pendulum was discarded for a lever escapement. The first of this production utilized an eleven jeweled escapement which they contracted for from Tavannes Watch Co., Switzerland. Because of high duty, distance, etc., that contract was dropped and Imperial bought escapements first from Waltham Watch Co. and then from Illinois Watch Co.

During this period Mr. Fowler continued to work on design and with the synchronous motor fast coming in, he devised and patented a striking mechanism and a Westminster chime mechanism. They purchased "sync" motors from the Hansen Manufacturing Co., Princeton, Ind., and proceeded to produce and market the smallest, full Westminster chime clock on the market.

Right after World War II, Mr. C. J. Hug and his son, J. C. Hug, became interested, bought the company and changed the name to C. J. Hug Company, Inc., retaining Mr. Fowler as general manager. The clocks were still labeled Imperial. This was the status of the operation when Mr. Fowler visited the column in 1954. A glance at the map will show that with all its moves—Granite City, to St. Louis, to Kimswick, to Imperial, back to St. Louis, to Collinsville and finally to Highland, it was never more than about 40 miles from St. Louis.

Thus the immediate subject of this story, the "Imperial" battery clock was produced from 1908 to 1928—a twenty-year period—in which Mr. August Feraud said many thousand clocks were manufactured. He last wrote: "I still have two of these clocks; they have been running since 1909 and seem to be good for another 100 years as they show very little wear."

The Imperial was first introduced to the trade with a little 2½ by 4-inch ad in the Keystone for October 1909. So much for the history; now, for the technical and those pointers which will assist the re-

pairman. In many instances, patent specifications are a bit confusing to the bench mechanic and thus of very little help. This is an exception; Mr. Feraud has set forth an excellent account of the 'working' of the Imperial and we doubt we could improve on it so we give a verbatim copy of his specs.

United States Patent Office
Frank H. Feraud, of Granite City, Illinois. Electric clock winding mechanism.
No. 920,124 Specification of Letters Patent. Patented May 4, 1909. Application filed September 8th, 1908. Serial No. 452,012
To all whom it may concern:

Be it known that I, Frank H. Feraud, citizen of the Republic of France, residing at Granite City, in the county of Madison and State of Illinois, have invented certain new and useful improvements in Electric Clock Winding Mechanism, of which the following is a full, clear, and exact description, reference being had to the accompanying drawings, forming a part hereof.

My invention has relation to the improvement in Electric-clock winding mechanism; and it consists in the novel arrangement and construction of parts more fully set forth in the specification and pointed out in the claim.

In the drawings, Fig. 1 is a side elevation of the clock with driving lever about half descended; Fig. 2 is a rear elevation of the same; Fig. 3 is an enlarged side elevational detail of the end of the long arm of the armature-lever, and Fig. 4 is a sectional detail on line 4—4 of Fig. 3.

The object of my invention is to construct an electric clock winding mechanism made of a simple set of electro-magnets; one having no expensive contacts; one possessing a minimum number of parts; one which is simple and positive in action, and one having further and other advantages better apparent from the detailed description of the invention which is as follows: Referring to the drawings, C represents a clock of any conventional design having a winding shaft or arbor S as usual.

Connected to it or forming an integral part of the gear 1 on shaft S, is a ratchet disc 2 with which cooperates a pawl 3 carried by the weighted driving lever 4. The lever is loosely pivoted at one end about the shaft S, the basal enlargement of the lever carrying an impact pin 5 which, when the lever 4 has dropped to its lowest position in the normal operation of the clock comes in contact with or engages the long arm of the armature lever 6, the latter being pivoted between the lugs 7, 7, on a shaft 8 immediately below the adjacent ends of the energizing coils E, E, and the armature A, being secured to a plate 6' forming the short member or arm of the armature lever.

One of the terminal wires w of the coils E, E, leads to one pole or terminal of a suitable battery or other source of electric energy (not shown). The other terminal w' is connected to the metal frame F of the clock the said frame conducting the current through the lever 4, pin 5, armature lever 6, and wire w" back to the opposite pole or terminal of the said battery or source of electric energy.

When the driving lever 4 is in its highest position (Fig. 1,) the pin 5 is disengaged from the lever 6 but as soon as the clock runs down, that is when the lever 4 has dropped to its lowest position, the contact between the pin 5 thereof and the armature lever 6, at once closes the circuit. This suddenly energizes the coils E, E. These, in turn, suddenly draw the armature inwardly which has the effect of suddenly throwing the long arm of the armature lever outwardly. This sudden outward movement or oscillation of the long arm of the armature lever contacting as this arm does with the pin 5 has the effect of tripping or throwing the drive lever 4, upwardly, in which upward movement the pawl 3 thereof simply over the teeth of the ratchet 2, the lever 4, again being brought to its highest position and in readiness to again propel the clock.

This action is repeated indefinitely. It is to be noted, of course, that the armature lever is properly insulated from the clock frame so it is only serviceable as an electric conductor when the pin 5 of the drive lever comes in contact therewith as the clock runs down. The armature lever is so mounted and weighted as to normally keep the armature A a slight distance from the coils E, E, the base of the armature lever being provided with a laterally binding screw 9, (for the wire w") which rests in a notch 10, formed for its reception in the clock frame.

Having described my invention, what I claim is: in combination with a clock mechanism having a weight shaft and a weighted driving lever loosely pivoted at one end about the shaft, a pawl on the lever, a ratchet disc carried by the shaft and engaged by the pawl, a laterally projecting impact pin at the base of the driving lever, an energizing coil, an insulate armature lever, an energizing coil, an insulate armature lever having a long and a short arm, the short arm carrying an armature in front of the coil, a conducting wire coupled to the end of the long arm of the armature lever, a binding screw to secure the wire, the frame of the clock having a notch for receiving the head of the binding screw, the pin on the driving lever being adapted to contact with the long arm of the armature lever, whereby the circuit is closed and the coil energized, and the armature lever is suddenly oscillated thereby throwing the driving lever about its axis of rotation upwardly thus restoring it to its highest position, substantially as set forth.

In testimony whereof I affix my signature, in the presence of two witnesses.

Frank H. Feraud"

To this, we added our own sketch & notes, see Fig. 2, page 43.

It will be noted that it covers the seconds pendulum regulator; as indicated in the first ad, which appeared in Keystone, Fig. 3, that clock is housed in a 24-inch case and thus a shorter pendulum. Different pendulum lengths were attained by varying the gearing, most often in the pinions. On this, Fig. 2, 'royal' pendulum, the escape and third pinions were lantern type; on the shorter pendulums these points were cut style. Sorry we do not have wheel and

FIG. 3.

405

pinion, size and count for a short pendulum model. The impression is that they were substantially the same as apparently the very same plates were used.

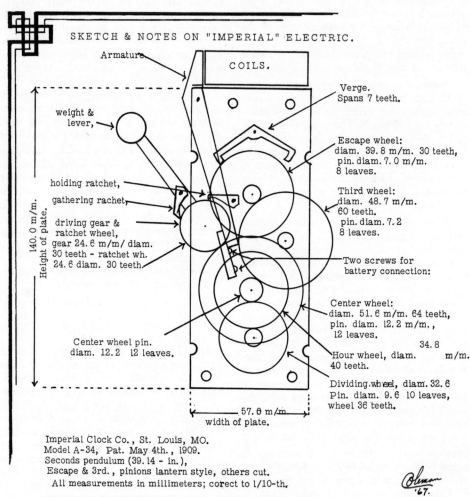

SKETCH & NOTES ON "IMPERIAL" ELECTRIC.

Armature

COILS.

Verge.
Spans 7 teeth.

weight & lever,

Escape wheel:
diam. 39.8 m/m. 30 teeth.
pin. diam. 7.0 m/m.
8 leaves.

Third wheel:
diam. 48.7 m/m.
60 teeth.
pin. diam. 7.2
8 leaves.

holding ratchet,
gathering rachet,
driving gear &
ratchet wheel,
gear 24.6 m/m/ diam.
30 teeth - ratchet wh.
24.6 diam. 30 teeth.

Two screws for
battery connection:

Height of plate. 140.0 m/m.

Center wheel:
diam. 51.6 m/m. 64 teeth,
pin. diam. 12.2 m/m.,
12 leaves.

34.8

Center wheel pin.
diam. 12.2 12 leaves.

Hour wheel, diam.   m/m.
40 teeth.

Dividing wheel, diam. 32.6
Pin. diam. 9.6 10 leaves,
wheel 36 teeth.

|← 57.0 m/m →|
width of plate.

Imperial Clock Co., St. Louis, MO.
Model A-34, Pat. May 4th., 1909.
Seconds pendulum (39.14 - in.),
Escape & 3rd., pinions lantern style, others cut.
All measurements in millimeters; corect to 1/10-th.

Coleman
'67.

FIG. 2.

VOLTAGE FOR BAIN CLOCK

Concerning the question of voltage for the Bain clock: At the time this clock was built, there were two sources of electric power in common use, the dynamo and the dry or wet cell battery. The dynamo is ruled out because of size. The wet cell is ruled out, because of the mess, which leaves us with only the dry cell. The #6 dry cell which was used for doorbells and telephone was very popular in the early days. The flashlight battery which we now call the "D" size also came along at an early date. Both of these sources of electric power produced about 1½ volts each. As I recollect, it was common practice to use the cells in batteries of two, in series connection, giving a total voltage of about 3.

If I were given a small electrical device, such as clock concerned, I would first put it in good mechanical order, being sure the electrical circuit is clean and all insulation is in good condition. Then I would trace the electric circuit to see that there is a continuous line of wiring through the contact mechanism, back to the battery. The contact mechanism should close the electric circuit through the coil to energize it at the proper time so that the magnetic pull produced is applied to the mechanism at a point in the travel of the rotor or armature where is will be most effective to keep it running continuously. The contact should open the circuit before the moving part reaches the end of its travel to save electric power and also not to slow the travel of the rotor.

The electric power impulse can be compared with the power of an overshot water wheel. If the water spills into the buckets before they reach the top, some power is wastd in lifting the water to the top before it can start down to do the work intended. The same applies if the contacts remain closed too long. It would be the same as if the buckets did not empty by the time they get to the bottom of the wheel. So much for that.

Now back to voltage: if there is no case, or no evidence in the case of an arrangemnt to hold the battery, which might give a clue as to the number of dry cells intended, I would start out with one dry cell and observe the motion just as you observe the travel of a balance to detect trouble. If one dry cell does give ample motion, I would stop there. I can't conceive of a clock builder using more than two or three dry cells to power a clock. I would start with a 1½ dry cell (penlight battery).

One more thought I might mention. In the early days there was considerable thought given to perpetual magnet for the rotor or armature. In this case you would need to observe the polarity. For this reason, it may be worth while to try reversing the battery connections which would change the polarity, and observe which produces the greatest motion. Of course you would leave the connection which produced the greatest motion.

ELGIN BATTERY CLOCK

Most of these clocks are equipped with the "Kienzle" 606 battery movements. There are two types, the monocell, Fig. 1 and the minicell, Fig. 2.

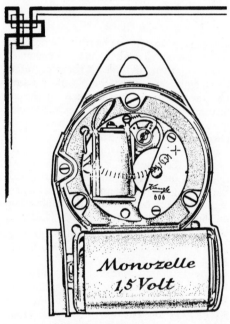

Fig. 1

— both are the same basic 606 movement, the first operates on a standard "D" size flashlight battery and the second uses a penlight size battery. Kienzle, recommends their own "Monocell" saying that it will last about three years; and for the second they recommend their "Minicell" or a Mallory ZM-12. Both operate well upon regular flashlight cells (leak-proof) but the active life is from 11 to 14 months.

These movements can easily be broken down into three separate and distinct parts: 1, the electrical assembly, 2, the mechan-

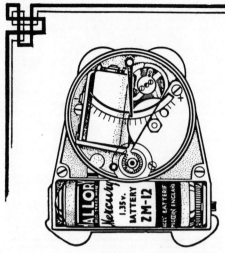

Fig. 2

ical energy storage mechanism (barrel and spring assembly) and, 3, the movement.

Taking them in order, "Kienzle" offers these repair hints: On the electrical assembly; the two fine silver contacts on the armature and barrel are best cleaned with methylated spirits and a clean cloth — never use an abrasive material or a file. To check the magnet armature, turn the movement so that the coil is in a vertical position with the magnet armature on top; with the driving spring wound up, the magnet armature must bear against the rubber stop on the plate by its return spring. Under no condition should the magnet armature rest upon the magnet casing by its own weight when in this position.

The returning force may be increased by carefully bending the return spring outwards after having slacked off its two screws. The gap between the magnet armature and the magnet casing is not super critical; it should be anywhere from .9 to 1.2 m/m., and is adjusted by shifting the guide plate. Make sure that the magnet armature does not touch or rub either the barrel, its spindle, or the ratchet support when performing the winding operation for to do so will short-circuit.

The Mechanical Storage part: 1, in case of a broken mainspring the whole barrel should be renewed. 2, the barrel is inserted without pre-winding. When movement is assembled, the spring is wound by turning the adjuster on the plate in a clockwise di-

rection, 2½ or 3 turns. 3, the time interval between windings should be two to two and one-half minutes.

This brings us to the movement part: here there is no more problem than with any ordinary mechanical movement. The hairspring stud is held by a clip and is removed by pressing it out, lightly. The balance wheel comes as a complete unit with spring and stud attached; evidently they do not suggest staffing it and as of now we have not had that experience. When in order, the balance amplitude should be from 250 to 270 degrees; that is, its total oscillation 500 to 540 degrees. See Fig. 3. If your balance does not reach this motion when the clock is in order try in-

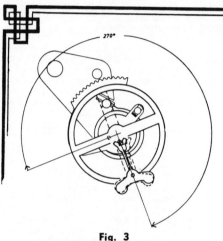

Fig. 3

creasing the drive force by winding the mainspring a little more—should that not correct it, look for some other mechanical fault.

As with other battery clocks, the first check when one comes in for service is to see whether the clock has stopped in the "wound-up" or "run-down" position. If it has stopped in the wound-up position, the fault is generally mechanical and will be found in the movement portion. If in the run-down position, look for: 1, dead battery. 2, dirt etc. between contacts or battery holder. 3, driving pawl slipped out. 4, magnet armature touching the barrel or barrel spindle.

Either of the sub-assemblies are available as replacements; Elgin suggests that you observe closely the works number in full as it appears on the winding bridge, i.e. 606, 606-b or 606-c. If you wish to time it on your timer, the balance beats 16,200. Fig. 4, illustrates the different application of the winding systems—the top diagram being for the 606-B and the lower, for the 606-C. Note that the drive wheel 1-a

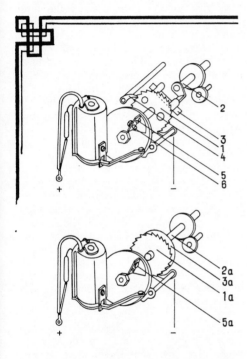

with its rotating mass 3-a is rigidly fixed to the third wheel spindle 2-a; in this manner the principle of the mass moment of inertia is being turned to practical use.

Staiger 'Chrometron'

A COMPLETELY NEW, 1.5-volt, type two battery movement, 70 mm wide by 80 mm high by 37 mm thick, center mounted and powered by a "C" size flashlight cell, of radical design and new material, is just now hitting the American market.

Horology is replete with the theory of the constant force escapement and also the principle that the time-train being mathematically correct, any error registered by the hands has to reside within the "standard"—balance or pendulum—and thus the fewer the beats the fewer the accumulated errors at the end of any period of run.

To pinpoint the very first application of either theory would be quite difficult since any initial application of a principle or theory has a way of getting completely lost in the passage of time. Perhaps the most notable application of the combining of the two theories would be the building of "Big Ben"—finished in 1854—whose chief designer was E. B. Denison. He lengthened the pendulum from one to two seconds with the thought that in a minutes run only thirty errors would be accumulated instead of sixty, drove his pendulum by the fall of a little gravity arm—constant force—hoping to eliminate all possible mechanical errors, and come up with as near a perfect timekeeper as mechanically possible.

The Column is grateful to Mr. F. W. Schubert, of Gebr Staiger Co., 7742 St Georgen, Schwarzwald, Germany, for air mailing one of these movements over for observation and test run. Since this test is of less than one month's duration, certain features, such as battery life, material durability etc. can not be commented upon from it. Such features to be derived from actual test of a necessity require much more time.

The factory engineers say: the "C" size cell is good for eighteen months operation which can very well be as the contact is practically instantaneous and only once per second. This contact and/or current consumption results in a far less drain upon the battery life than those required to drive a motor for winding a drive spring.

This design, combining a slow beat with a constant force, is definitely an aim for accuracy and apparently this little movement will turn up a pretty accurate rate. Any manufacturer aiming for a high degree of accuracy is of necessity faced with a cost problem—of course he can build an accurate timekeeper; even a marine chronometer, "if" the consumer will meet the price. Staiger attacks that problem by: 1, utilizing the new DuPont acetal resin "Delrin". 2, reducing the number of conventional parts from the approximately 155 to 45. 3, injection molding of the Derilin makes it possible to produce plates complete with all bushings, stops, integral springs, and locating surfaces without resort to subsequent machining, etc.

This clock contains more plastic than any movement we've seen since the famous Waterbury plastic alarm shortly after WW 2. Even the reg pins, the regulator, and the little sweep-seconds hand are made of plastic. Aside from the balance-wheel, the hairspring, the gathering ratchet—shows in black in Fig. 1—and one brass wheel, the whole is made in plastic, even to the retaining pawl.

As per the "one", "two" and "three" type classification suggested in this column for March, the "Chrometron" is type two. It's balance is electro-magnetically impulsed and in turn drives the hands ratchetwise. Any old timer, brought up on brass and so accustomed to view movements of metal is bound to do a double-take when he first views this movement of pure white. Such first impression can be misleading until you learn that two of the main plates, Nos. 1 and 2 on Fig. 2 have been molded with a steel insert; this reinforcement permits optimum plate thickness as well as insures freedom from corrosion. It allows axial load to be borne by the metal while the radial bearing load is carried by the plastic, etc. The movement is a three plate construction, the third and very back plate is shown at No. 5. Under this plate—between it and middle plate No. 2—is located the balance and lever, plus the "C" shaped permanent magnet.

The balance-wheel: solid, three spoke and overly large—diameter 31 mm—is a necessity for the slow beat. The hairspring, also large, 13 coils, flat, though the outer coil is off-set to accommodate the thick plastic reg pins, gives it an over-all appearance of the Breguet over-coil. The lever is of the chronometer or detent type from which the movement gets its name, "Chrometron". Even the unlocking spring is "Delrin".

In the true Marine Chronometer power of the drive train is imparted to the balance-wheel when the train is unlocked by the detent, thereby maintaining the balance in motion. In the "Chrometron" there is no train and/or train power; it's drive power is derived from and applied by the detent lever via a conventional roller pin set in the balance-wheel exactly like the orthodox roller jewel. Viewing the movement from its back: as the balance-wheel makes the counterclockwise stroke, this roller pin is brought against the passing spring on its no-pass side bringing the lever downward; as it comes down a little metal finger carrying one leg of the current contacts the roller pin closing the circuit. This energizes the coil upon the back of the lever causing it to align within the "C" magnet and impart a thrust to the balance-wheel. The balance continues in its counterclockwise excursion breaking the circuit; the lever is immediately restored to the up position by a little coil spring. This spring also serves as a leg in the circuit carrying the current from the coil back to the negative side of the battery.

As the balance makes the clockwise stroke, the roller pin strikes the plastic passing spring on its pass side so nothing happens. We do not have a wiring diagram. Fact is, it is so simple one is not necessary because it is so easily traced. The lead from the positive pole of the cell goes to the hairspring so to the roller pin; when the roller pin contacts the metal lever finger, current flows to the coil and, as explained, via the coil spring that returns the lever to the top position, back to the negative side of the battery.

Apparently our trade has not been very specific in correctly distinguishing between these three types—catalogs, PR releases, and ad flyers seems to be thoroughly content with the simple term battery clock and in most cases leave you to "guess" as to the details of mechanical construction. It's just like saying "escapement" a term and/or type which definately requires something more added to adequately inform the horologist exactly what it is. It may well be a cylinder, duplex, detent, or plain lever. One is forced to read further with his guess until possibly coming across a word or indication that may pin-point it; a full understanding is certainly necessary if one is to assimilate the info he is seeking. Without it, the mechanical or electro action can not be crystal clear.

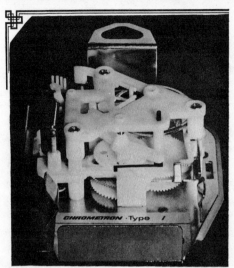

FIG. I.

Fig. 1 is looking at the movement from the bottom side, battery removed. It is marked "Two Jewels — Unadjusted." The hairspring is temperature compensated and supposed to deliver satisfactory rate between minus four degrees and 140 degrees Fahrenheit. The beat is 120 per minute. Since the hand is advanced by ratchet action only at every other stroke, the sweep seconds hand "walks" around by one second steps giving the same pleasing appearance of the seconds beat regulator. As of this moment, no info upon spare parts or service instructions; I am reasonably sure they will be easily available in due course; going to press without them is just one of the risks encountered when grabbing items hot off the production line.

"Clockwise", we see very little in the "service" angle here, the resilient banking for the lever; the retaining pawl for the seconds wheel, the lever etc., being plastic—should one break or become damaged from accident—I don't think it might be cemented as in so doing would alter their elasticity.

We get the impression that "Delrin" is one of those self-lubrication materials. However, the information supplied by Mr. Frank Zumbro, of DuPont, at Wilmington, Del., did not specifically point out that it is.

The "Chrometron" is being installed in more than thirty different table, wall, office and kitchen clocks. The Gebr Staiger is already well-known to the U.S. horological trade through their clocks that have been in this market for quite some years. It is a safe bet, the bench horologist will be seeing this new type movement in the future.

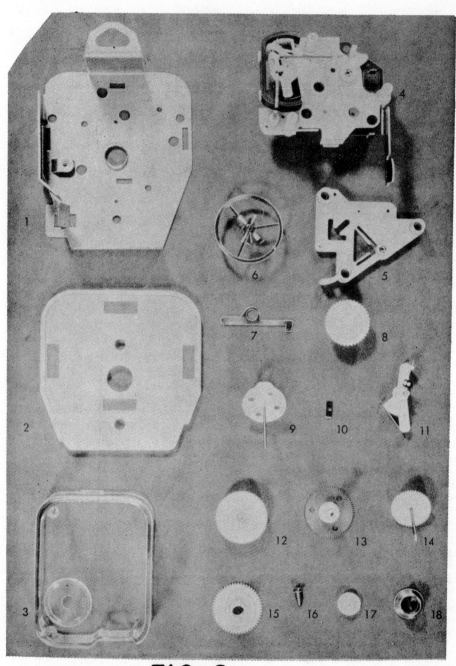

FIG. 2.

French Battery Clock Economizes
On Power Utilization

ANCIENS ETABLISMENTS Duverdrey & Bloquel, 22 Rue Reaumur, Paris 3, France, producers of the "Bayard" line of timepieces, announce a new battery powered clock.

M. Boquet, their Commercial Director, air-mailed a movement for photos, study and observation. He tells us that L. Harris Company Inc., 1 Park Ave. (at 33rd St.) New York, N.Y., will be the U.S. Importer.

Mr. G. Jones, of the L. Harris Co., writes that for the time being, the sale of the "Bayard R" movement is being restricted to quantity sales to a few wall clock manufacturers in the U.S.A. To date, no provisions have been made for single unit sales to repairmen, etc., but he feels sure that manufacturers using this movement will have provisions for the sale of repair parts for use by repairmen.

We are grateful to M. Boquet and Mr. Jonas for splendid co-operation enabling us to both observe this clock and bring to the readers of A. H. & J. some technical pointers upon its construction.

The engineers at "Bayard" have come up with a completely new design in battery powered clocks—they have eliminated the 'contact' and thus the usual troubles that have accompanied same. Also they have designed a most unique wind system eliminating any re-wind noise; reduced the gearing by using a couple of pinions with only two staves each; designed a new safety-

roller, and, combined the whole into a battery unit that ought to delight the repairer because he can take out the motor and/or any vital part without having to take the movement apart from its casing.

BACK PLATE.
Fig. 4.

The case is 3¼ inches wide, 4½ inches high and ¾ inch thick; the battery "C" size is located very near the hand center, under the movement, permitting the smallest radius of 2-⅝ inches centered on the hand-center.

FRONT PLATE.
A.H. & J. Photo.
Fig. 3.

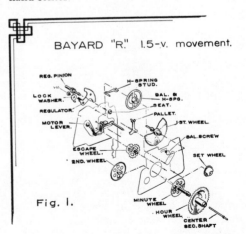

BAYARD "R." 1.5-v. movement.

REG. PINION
H-SPRING STUD.
LOCK WASHER.
BAL. & H-SPG.
REGULATOR.
SEAT.
MOTOR LEVER.
PALLET.
1ST. WHEEL.
BAL. SCREW
ESCAPE WHEEL.
2ND. WHEEL.
SET WHEEL
MINUTE WHEEL
HOUR WHEEL
CENTER SEC. SHAFT

Fig. 1.

Fig. 1 is an exploded sketch of the movement-train, and Fig. 2, an exploded sketch of the plates and entire clock. Combined, they give almost the whole mechanical 'story' and being lettered are practically self-explanatory.

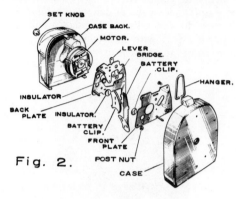

Fig. 2.

Fig. 5 is a detailed sketch of the escapement and winding, and Fig. 6 illustrates that removal of the motor is as easy as pulling out an electric plug.

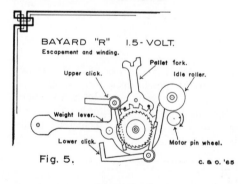

BAYARD "R" 1.5-VOLT.
Escapement and winding.

Fig. 5.

C. & O. '65

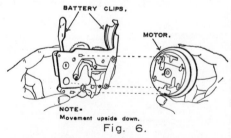

NOTE-
Movement upside down.
Fig. 6.

The motor is 1¾ inches diameter by ½ inch thick; attached by three studs in its back plate—to remove, first turn the clock upside down; take out the battery by spreading the spring clips; then, simply pull it out. The weight lever (Fig. 5) is gravity operated as will be seen later; turning the clock bottom up allows this lever to fall away from the motor pin wheel while removing the motor.

Bayard engineers call this motor a "technical miracle." They say it would require about 100,000 of them to consume as much current as a standard 30-watt light bulb—its current consumption is so small that it has practically no influence on a standard flashlight battery, thus batteries should last over a year.

The escapement is the pin lever type, jeweled balance—the hairspring stud (a Bayard patent) is an automatic closing pincer that is very easy to open. The 'safety-roller' is a ring or crown with a single opening; also a Bayard patent (See Fig. 1.). Note the pallet fork in Fig. 5; the little flat at the top right is simply bent back at a 90-degree angle to the fork proper. As the balance strokes clockwise, this little projection enters the opening of the safety-crown; as it strokes counter clockwise the projection passes out through the opening and rides against the outside of the safety-crown just as a guard-pin rides the regular roller table.

Fig. 5 holds the key to the whole unique construction. Actually, there are but two wheels in the train proper; the escape-wheel drives the center-seconds wheel and thus all that remains is 'hand' gearing, seconds to minutes to hours. Upon the back end of the escape arbor is the ratchet wheel shown in Fig. 5. This ratchet wheel rides "free" upon the arbor but is coupled to the escape-wheel via a cone type little wire spring which is the drive power.

The weight lever is pivoted at the extreme left; it stradles the ratchet wheel with its "U" shaped end, carrying the upper click on its left and the lower click on the right. The right side of the "U" extends upward and terminates with a little nylon idle roller. Note the pin at the right on the motor pin wheel; this idle roller rides the motor pin imparting an up and down motion to the weight lever thus winding the cone drive spring.

The upper click and the lower click with their counter-balances are made from nylon

—one piece. When the weight lever descends by its own weight (it is brass) the lower click engages the ratchet wheel and ratchets forward (clockwise) by one ratchet-tooth. When the weight lever is raised by the pin in the motor pin wheel, the upper click advances the ratchet wheel forward by one tooth. Now—when the tension in the drive spring builds up to the point it overcomes the gravitational pull on the weight lever, the weight lever will not descend; thus the winding stops automatically while the motor continues to turn as usual. This not only makes the winding independent of the speed of the motor or tension in the battery, it makes for almost constant power and as the motor has no load during a goodly part of its revolutions, accounts for the small power consumed.

The regulator is a toothed sector geared to a very small pinion, enabling very fine regulation—our test of this one movement shows it to be an excellent timekeeper. The one point to remember, since the wind is partially by gravity, this movement must always operate in an upright position.

Checking Auto Clocks

Could you tell me how to fix up a 12-Volt system that's not expensive to check automobile clocks after they've been repaired?

Also, I thought you might like to know that I lost a S. S. tension spring and temporarily used a dial washer between the second hand and the minute hand. It worked fine.

A.

Nothing beats a battery for supplying current to run auto clocks and other d.c. clocks. There are a number of rectifiers, converters, etc., upon the market — some half wave, some full wave. Even some full-wave instruments show a ripple in the delivered current.

New 12-Volt auto batteries may be purchased upon today's market very reasonably. Good used batteries may be had in the neighborhood of half the advertised prices. Since the load upon it, when only using it as you intend, is exceptionally light when compared with what is required to start the average car, a good "used" battery should serve you for several years.

Most auto parts stores are advertising little chargers. Let us say you invest a few dollars in a used battery and charger. You may then build yourself a very serviceable system. Any man servicing battery electric clocks must have enough electrical know-how to do it.

Locate your battery and charger in the back room or some distance from your bench, as battery fumes can create rust. With suitable wire, run four lines to the bench. One wire common; one tapped off the first cell for 1½ volt clocks; one tapped off the middle for 6-volt clocks; and the fourth off the other end for the 12-volt line. Thus, you are ready to test and run three different types of battery clocks with a good, steady current. Depending upon how much you use it, a battery can usually be kept well up with a few hours of charging per month. The charger is good for many years of service and you should have three or more years of service from a good, used battery, so you can maintain satisfactory current for all your clock needs for about two bucks per year — cheap enough.

Transistor Clock Has Battery Problems

I have in my shop for repair, a battery-operated transistor pendulum clock made by Aug. Schatz & Sohne, Germany. No jewels; it has 5 60 on back plate. Also takes a size D flashlight battery.

The clock is clean, field coil checks okay, but the pendulum will not go. Could it be a bad transistor?

A.

From any angle, long distance diagnosis is quite difficult. As a general rule transistors do not fail — upon any battery powered clock giving trouble, the first point to check is to see that the battery is inserted correctly. The transistor can not function where the polarity is reversed.

You state that the coil checks out okay — are you sure?

Most of these transistor switched and/or contacted clocks utilize a magnetized pendulum swinging within the coil housing. Actually there is within this housing, two (2) coils — a magnet traveling through a coil generates some current — that current generated in the first coil serves to bias your transistor thereby enabling it to act as a contact for energizing the second (big) coil with current from your battery with a polarity the same as that portion of the pendulum at that instant within the coil thereby repelling or giving the kick impulse to maintain the pendulum in motion.

If you have a tape recorder and a phone pick-up; fire it up and hold the pick-up next to the clock coil. If the transistor is working, it will give off a bark much like a small dog each time it closes the circuit. If this test indicates that the transistor is functioning but your pendulum gets no impulse, I'd think that the big coil is open. Should the transistor not function I'd think that the small coil is open. In either instance we believe that the coil assembly comes complete therefore a new one would contain both coils.

One last caution: oftimes when replacing a battery, either one or both points of the metal where contact is had may be covered with a coating — oxidation; preventing full or complete contact. With a knife, scrape all four places down to bright, bare metal.

ELECTRIC CLOCKS

Factual info and data on the synchronous electric, the type data much in demand by the bench repair man, and similar to that supplied by the Herschede Clock Company in their booklet remains very difficult to lay hands on. We've just completed a long distance phone call to Seth Thomas in an effort to get something on their new line. I use the "new" advisedly as actually I do not know the exact date it came out, at least it has been on the general market long enough to reach the repair bench. For a number of years their striking clocks (synchronous, that is) were equipped with the Sangamo motor; a 2.6 watt, 450 R.P.M. hysteresis type motor. The new line has a completely new motor very similar in construction to Westclox models.

Judging from the inquiries we get and frank discussions where we ask the pointed question, the one greatest need is still a better understanding of the basic principals of the synchronous motor. Practically everyone of us can well remember the non self-starting clocks of just a few years back. These were really just phonic wheels, developed and used extensively in printing telegraph instruments the latter part of the century.

In addition to being very simple, one is quite easy to build—a rough experimental model, that is.

I guarantee you will find it interesting. Obtain a sheet of soft iron two or three 32nds. thick; the thicker the better but harder to saw out. First, cut a rectangle 3½ by 5¼ inches, an inch and one-half from the end and equal distance from either side. Spot the center for your rotor. From this center, scribe a circle 2¼ inches in diameter, divide it equally into twelve parts (an old clock dial as template will come in handy) and drill ⅜-inch holes as per sketch. With a jewelers saw, cut along scribed circle between holes. This will give you a twelve-pole rotor with quarter-inch poles. Three-eighths inch apart and 1¼ inches from the side, scribe a line and saw—this gives you two stator pieces with four poles each.

We will skip the technical details of winding a coil. First, because repairmen won't be winding coils, at least for a while yet; second, any old coil from a discarded clock

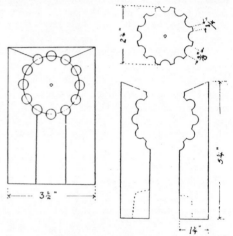

Shown here are the sketches for making the non-self-starting clocks   Drawings are by Mr. Coleman.

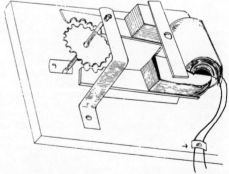

or toy train transformer, just so it will take 110 volts, will serve the purpose. Mount as per the prospective sketch. Select from an old alarm clock a balance staff and bearing screws that are in good condition. Drill the rotor just right to stake on with plenty of friction and mount the staffed rotor vertically as indicated; connect and spin in the direction you wish it to turn.

Now, as the 60-cycle current shifts from positive to negative sixty times per second—3,600 times per minute, the poles of the stator are energized just that many times, each energizing attracts the next pole upon the rotor you have already set in motion. Since the rotor has twelve poles, twelve steps will be required to pull it around through one revolution or twelve divided into 3,600 equals 300 R.P.M. once every fifth second.

From this it is easily seen that by various combinations of poles, several different R.P.M.'s may be obtained. Also, that the speed of the rotor is governed solely by the cycles. For example, the timekeeping of a clock so constructed depends only on the regulation of the cycles. Commercial current of today is regulated to a tolerance quite satisfactory for household timekeeping purposes but not close enough for high precision purposes. To bridge this gap your watch rate recorder has a device, either a tuning fork or a quartz crystal tied into the electric line whereby it regulates the cycles to the desired precision.

This is merely a practical experiment but demonstrates clearly the fundamentals. It is limited only to your imagination and may be carried further if you care to indulge. Since your rotor travels fifth seconds, it is easy to drill a small hole near the rim (remove weight on opposite side to keep it in poise) place a small flashlight underneath and permit the transmitted beam to fall on a watch balance wheel beating fifths. Revolve the watch until the light beam strikes at the instant the wheel is reversing; it will appear to be standing still.

Possibly you have noticed that in some of the early clocks the rotor had a floating washer held to it by very light friction or weak coiled spring. This allowed the rotor additional forward inertia and had a tendency to drag it forward while the magnetic pull was on the pole. Such additional weight may be added to this motor by simply laying a washer, brass or any nonmagnetic, drilled to fit loosely over the staff on top of it, and will give your motor some additional power. With enough power, a pin may be set near the edge of the rotor and made to operate a light electrical contact; connected to a very light telegraph sounder or similar instrument you get fifth-second ticks. A small pinion may be staked on the lower side of the rotor and be made to mesh with a wheel from some old alarm clock, ratio five-to-one and you get a wheel with one revolution per second. A hole through it and your light beam and a mirror to reflect it on a seconds beat pendulum makes an interesting experiment. It naturally follows that two holes will work for a half-seconds pendulum; also, that a contact pin and the sounder will give seconds ticks. Either the fifth ticks or half and seconds ticks can be registered on your rate recorder by setting the sounder where you usually place the watch. Use your short wave radio and compare the seconds ticks with the Bureau of Standards ticks via W. W.V.

The contact on the one R.P.S. wheel may be coupled to an old minute jumper and made to operate a giant seconds hand. We recently saw such an arrangement with a three-foot dial—the 18-inch seconds hand being ratcheted forward regularly each second.

"MINUTE JUMPER" CLOCK

We have a large pendulum clock in our store which we use as a timer; and we would like to fix this clock with an electrical impulse arrangement so that we could put an electrical impulse dial movement in front of our store in place of a street clock that we have there now.

Can you explain how the master clock is fixed so these "jump clocks" can be used; and also, give us the names and addresses of some places where we can obtain the "jump clock" itself?

We would like to connect several of these clocks, so will you please explain the procedure for this?

A.

Relative to "Minute Jumper" clocks which you wish to connect with your store regulator, a make and break contact must be placed upon your master clock (regulator); secondary movements come in minute and half-minute "jumpers"—this will have to be determined in advance so you will know whether to make your contacts every thirty seconds, or every minute. Making and placing such a contact on your present clock should not prove a very difficult job. The most satisfactory and probably the easiest to construct is the spiral-cam type.

Select a spot on the seconds arbor where you have the most space. Cut and stake on friction tight, a brass spiral-cam (it is sometimes called "snail"). Two arms or fingers, one above the other, of a size convenient to the movement you are working to, are pivoted to ride upon this snail to the lower arm you make, and firmly attach a small "U" shaped piece to ride with the unattached end over the upper arm. Now, the difference in length of your arms determine the length of your contact (closed circuit). The snail revolving once per minute permits the lower (shorter) arm to drop first; making contact with the upper arm through the portion extending above it (the upper arm). As the snail continues to revolve, the top arm drops, thereby breaking contact as it falls away. Two seconds, or thereabouts is a good positive contact. You may readily see that the length of contact (time circuit is closed) is from the time the short or lower arm drops until the upper arm drops; and can govern it easily by the difference in length.

NEW HAVEN, CALVIN MODEL

I have a New Haven, Calvin Model NH611-905 strike and manual - start which stops, and would like to know how this clock can be made usable. The New Haven Clock Co. says the motor is beyond repair and that they no longer make that model. Have you any suggestions as to how I can substitute another type motor?

A.

An adequate answer concerning a substitute motor for the New Haven electric clock will have to be more in the nature of encouragement than instruction. Such alterations require quite a bit of cleverness and inventive skill on the part of the one doing the altering. I don't have a clock of the model indicated at hand, and don't recall just exactly the train. Neither does the N. H. Catalog give the correct speed of the motor. I feel sure that it must be one of those equipped with an Elm City motor, manual-starting with the lever through the dial.

Naturally, if you have an arbor within the time train turning 1 rpm, you will have little trouble adapting one of the many 1 rpm motors now available on the market—provided you can find room within the case to attach the new motor— provided you can find room within the case to attach the new motor. Telechron makes and sells a special motor, their type 1M-9 for powering various instruments. This motor comes in 15, 30 or 60 minutes for 1 rev.; also 1, 2, 3, 4, 6, 8 or 12 hours for 1 rev. Overall dimensions: 3½x3½x2 11/16 inches. Net weight, 18 oz., either left or right rotation. Terminal shaft to set horizontal as normal operating position.

From the above different rotations you may with the aid of a properly figured-out toothed gear attach one of these motors somewhere in the train for satisfactory operation of the clock. Check and recheck your calculations to be sure the timing is right before you try it.

SETH THOMAS CHIME

I have a problem clock that you may be able to help me adjust. It is a Seth Thomas electric mantel clock, and I can get it to run all right, but I can't get the chimes adjusted properly. It chimes four times on the quarter-hour, eight times on the half-hour, twelve times on the three-quarter hour and sixteen times on the full-hour when properly adjusted. I wrote in to the Seth Thomas Co. to see if they could send me any diagrams or blueprints on how to adjust the chimes and they referred me to a man in San Francisco, who wanted me to send him the clock for adjustment. Well, I want to learn how to adjust it myself as I am a student in watchmaking. If you could tell me how to adjust the chimes, I will be very much obliged to you.

A.

You do not state which model your electric chime is, or just what your particular difficulty is. In all likelihood you have reference to one of the 1700 series, self-starting electric Westminster chime movements. If you are familiar with the 124 spring-wound Westminster chime, the working of the electric—that is so far as the adjustment is concerned—is exactly the same.

I note that you count the strokes; these are chords when taken together. Thus, the one chord for the quarter-hour, two for the half-hour and three for the three-quarters, etc. All Westminster chimes strike, or as some like to call it, "play," these same chords in the same sequence.

You have probably noted that the strike train is tripped by the chime train just at the finish of the fourth quarter. This feature eliminates all strike trouble since your clock can only strike the hours at the completion of the fourth quarter. While the hour strike is rack-and-snail controlled, you will observe that the chimes are on a count disc. The notch at the end of the third quarter is deeper than the others. Of the four lifts placed upon the hour-post (to trip each quarter), that which corresponds with the minute hand is longer than the rest of them. Now, it requires the extra-long lift of this long one to lift (unlatch) the chiming train after it has chimed the third quarter. In other words, the fourth quarter can only be let off by the long lift when the minute hand points to twelve. As the clock cannot strike except by being released by the fourth quarter, and the fourth quarter can only be released when the minute hand points to twelve, you should always have the four-quarter chime followed by the correct hour only when the hand is at twelve. The chime drum is driven by an auxiliary gear on the back plate.

Is it possible that when re-assembling the movement these gears weren't set or synchronized properly? If you will drop me a line giving me the correct model of the movement and specifically the trouble you are having, I'm sure that with a few pointers you can correct it.

HOWARD ELECT. MASTER CLOCK

I have repaired a Howard master clock with a ½-minute jump clock. The contacts are on escape wheel and are platinum; they arc and sometimes the jump clock will get a minute or so ahead in a week. Did this have a condenser across

points at one time—if so could you tell me what capacity it should be? If that is not the trouble, please advise me how to correct same. I am told that this trouble has occurred for the last 10 years.

A.

Shunting a small condenser across the line is usually a great help to prevent arcing, and the firing that blackens your points.

Back about the time Howard was building jumpers, condensers were not so popular as at present and I seriously doubt if he used one. Arcing is due to heavy voltage—clock circuits are generally designed to work on very low voltage and point troubles are many times introduced by altering the circuit, or using a higher voltage than it was designed to operate on.

Many times we run across jumpers intended to work on 1½ volts—two dry cells connected parallel. Some mechanic gets hold of the clock who doesn't know any more than the two cells, and connects them in series, giving him three volts instead of 1½. I'd suggest that you check this angle; if your clock is now operating on 3 volts, series connected, try 1½ volts, parallel connection, and observe if there is sufficient power for positive jumps.

SESSIONS CLOCK MOTOR

Fellows, your "Clockwise" division always puts forth an extra effort to keep both feet on the rock. Your "Otherwise" division sometimes ventures out a very short way but this time we are heading for the deep water sure enough. I wish it might be the other way around because technical data and instructions definitely belong in the other section, but lack of cooperation from the manufacturer makes it necessary that we run wholly on our own. There is a dearth of data regarding the servicing and lubrication of electric clocks. Repairmen are constantly writing in for it and it is becoming quite a problem.

Compared to the regular clock, the problems encountered in electric clocks are as different as night and day. There is one similarity however, the need for lubrication, but with that need the similarity stops. For years the clockmaker has used oil. There were different weights and grades; tower clock oil, mainspring oil, clock oil, watch oil and bracelet watch oil, but still it was oil.

For the reason that the electric coil generates heat (the greatest enemy of oil) many electric clocks are designed for grease lubrication. Lot of repairmen have reached this conclusion and turned to vaseline only to discover that it lasted no longer than the oil they used.

One motor about which we have had many inquiries is the Sessions. Herewith is an exploded sketch of the Sessions motor. We gave Mr. Michael J. Zubler, Garfield, N. J., all the data obtainable from the manufacturer in the June issue. Namely, that the average repairman would find it more economical to install a new motor.

The "barb" on this hook is that the average repairman does not so find it. First, there is the cost of the motor. Second, he has to turn in the old motor in order to buy a new one. This prevents his stocking up on them and therefore increases his ultimate price to the clock owner. We believe that experience will prove (1) that the average clockmaker *can* properly lubricate a Sessions motor, and (2) that he can make a livable wage by so doing.

First, it is inconceivable that any workman accustomed to setting jewels, and working to position adjustment tolerances, cannot remove and replace the bearings— parts 5 & 7 on sketch—satisfactorily.

Second, he can easily do from four to six of these jobs per hour. Figure your overhead and your profit, then see what is economical.

To do this job you will need three tools, two of which are easily made:

    1. Punch
    2. Staking block
    3. Grease gun

The "Durex" bearings, No. 7, are roughly 8.2 mm. diameter. A punch to drive them out need only be slightly less. We find 7.5 mm. diameter to work quite

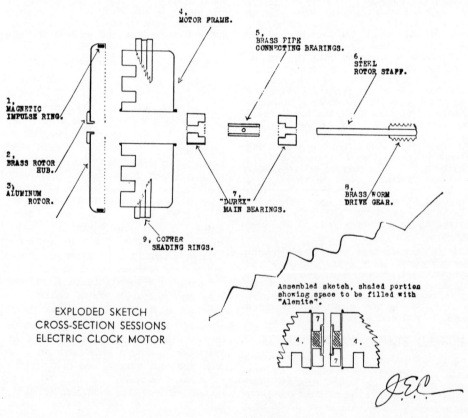

1, MAGNETIC IMPULSE RING.

2, BRASS ROTOR HUB.

3) ALUMINUM ROTOR.

4, MOTOR FRAME.

5, BRASS PIPE CONNECTING BEARINGS.

6, STEEL ROTOR STAFF.

7, "DUREX" MAIN BEARINGS.

8, BRASS WORM DRIVE GEAR.

9, COPPER SHADING RINGS.

EXPLODED SKETCH
CROSS-SECTION SESSIONS
ELECTRIC CLOCK MOTOR

Assembled sketch, shaded portion showing space to be filled with "Alemite".

well. Select a Stubbs rod of about this diameter, chuck in your lathe and drill to take an old "Rotor Staff," No. 6, from which you have removed the old worm gear, No. 8. Drive this old staff, worm gear end, into your punch to about the depth the worm gear originally occupied. This fits your bearing assembly and serves as a guide, both when driving out and driving back into position.

A block of hickory or good hard maple (metal is better) roughly two inches thick by two and three-quarters diameter may be turned up on your lathe, drill clear thru center with 7/16th drill, turn step rings in one end to fit rotor side of motor frame. In the other end turn step ring to fit back side of motor frame, countersinking two holes to take the two stud screws.

A common hypo glass syringe, 20-C.C. size, obtainable from your druggist, makes an excellent grease gun. Good ones can be had from $3.00 to $5.00 each and needles at 25c each. No. 17-2 is a good size for grease.

Remove motor from frame of clock, end up your staking block to take the back side of the motor, gently drive rotor staff from brass hub, No. 2, then with your special punch drive out the Durex bearing assembly.

Never immerse these bearings in any cleaning solution. Dry clean them by thoroughly wiping with clean soft cloth and a good pegging out. Reverse your stake block to take rotor side of motor frame and drive in first bearing to its original position, set in the brass connecting pipe making sure the little hole in the side is clear and open, and that it will face downward (to VI o'clock) when the motor is replaced in the clock. With your grease gun fill the space between this tube and the outside wall with Alemite No. 33. Now, stake in the last bearing. The guide pin in your punch will align the brass tube and make it fit into its proper place. Next try the rotor staff; you can quickly judge whether or not it will spin freely, should it fit tight or bind try to determine where (front or back), then open slightly with a round broach—never a cutting broach. Drive on the rotor and your motor lube job is completed.

Lubricate the clock movement with Alemite No. 33 instead of oil after cleaning it

as you usually clean clocks. Replace motor and case the clock. If you'd like to test for time without a trial run, secure a G.E. neon bulb—the little bulb with vertical elements, not horizontal. Paint one half of it black, in line with the elements so that in effect you get the light from only one element. Shine this on the opening holes of the rotor —if they appear to stand still, the clock is keeping time.

Like all other instructions, the above will require a little time and practice to perfect.

FRENCH ELECTRIC

I have a French clock which I would like you to give me some information on. The only information I am able to give you is that it is an electric clock and has the name Henry Le Paute printed on it. Also, can you tell me how much electricity it takes to run it?

A.

Baillie lists a Henry LePaute as clockmaker to Louis Phillippe and Napoleon III, stating that he made a clock for the Palais de Justice and the Bourse. He was born in Paris in 1800 and died in 1885.

Your clock evidently has a "Brocot" escapement (Achille Brocot, Paris, 1817-1878). Thus, LePaute could have easily had access to its use. Further, electric clocks can easily date back that far. Alexander Bain, Edinburgh, (b. 1811, d. 1877) first began to experiment with electric timekeepers about 1840; his first clock was exhibited at the Polytechnic Institute in 1840. A long series of experiments by this maker from about 1840 through 1852 resulted in the production of many ingenious forms of electrically controlled and electrically driven clocks. From the above it appears possible that this Henry LePaute could have constructed such a clock in the very early 1880's at least, but we can't be sure of this being the correct Henry or the date or the voltage required to operate it.

MOTOR HUM

What causes an electric clock (coil with magnetic field) to hum? and what is the remedy? I have oiled the pivot holes of the wheel in the magnetic field, tried from light to very heavy oil, and still that hum.

A.

Oiling never eliminates hum or noise in electric clocks for any appreciable length of time.

Your synchronous electric clock is driven from the regular sixty-cycle mains. Alternating current is so named because it alternates polarity—usually sixty times per second. When changing from positive to negative there is a point where the magnetic field is dead. It is thus dead sixty times per second on 60 cycle current. Any loose steel or iron within the field of the coil is thereby caused to vibrate or hum.

Very often this is occasioned by worn rotor bearings, and sometimes by pieces of metal close to the field. Examine your clock closely, first to see that no adjacent piece is loose enough to hum. If this isn't it, close the rotor bearings to a good snug fit and lubricate with a good heavy grease

BURNED OUT COIL – HAMMOND

I have a problem and thought you might help me. I have in for repairs a Hammond electric clock with the coil burned out. Here is the problem: the new coil that I obtained has two wires coming out the end of the coil, possibly two inches in length. I don't know where to attach these wires. I can see no evidence of similar wires coming from the old coil, although the lead in wire was burned completely loose from the coil. I thought possibly these wires could have burned up since they are quite small.

If you could enlighten me on this, I would be very appreciative. As it stands now, I don't know if I have the right coil or not, and I'm afraid to experiment since they are rather expensive.

A.

You say you do not know whether or not you have the correct coil—this is probably occasioned because you did not see the two leads on the old coil as they were either pulled or burned off.

Barring electric alarms or lights tied into the coil, all electric clocks can have but two connections. Your plug-in cord is merely a "straight two" wires; thus at each end two ends or connections—that plugs into the wall socket terminates in the two prongs of the plug; the remaining two ends connect directly to your coil. Two leads on the coil, two ends on the cord, solder and wrap separately with electrician's tape for insulation. Your current is alternating so it does not matter which wire is soldered to which lead.

TELECHRON MOTOR REPAIR

Turning to electric clocks, perhaps I have overlooked it, but I have never seen much reference to Telechron sealed rotors. I know the maker says to put in a new one and turn the old one in for credit. I would like to outline the procedure I have used occasionally over the past three years on noisy and non-operating rotors, and ask if you approve or disapprove.

First, I drill two number 60 holes one-quarter inch apart on the bottom side opposite the word, "top." Then with a hypodermic syringe, I fill the case with carbon tet; I have a field coil on the bench to operate the rotor for a moment while the carbon tet is in. Then I drain and flush again, and dry with heat for an hour. I then refill with 1½ cc. electric clock oil and seal the holes with flat-head copper rivets and a quick touch of the soldering iron.

Of the fifty rotors I have tried this way, none have come back so far. By careful use of time, I find it much cheaper than new rotors. From time to time, I cut open a rotor I know to be ten years old, and I have found little or no wear in pivots, plates or gear teeth. It strikes me that with fresh lubrication they would have been good for another ten years.

I would like your frank appraisal of this procedure. Is it "botch work" or poor practice?

A.

Glad you brought up the sealed electric motor question and outlined the method you are trying. I would like to hear of more experiences along this line.

Who am I to say what is botch work and what is not—especially in the face of so little data on electrics and their comparatively short time with the repairman. I'm reminded of the time I asked my pastor a few years back for his thoughts on evolution. He replied that I'd first have to furnish a definition of evolution. The same, I think, should hold here—you will first have to supply a definition of "botch work." We must remember that all "poor" work can't be classified "botch"; for example, say that one of your customers brought in an eight-day mantel striking clock that had stopped running, and that you merely take out the movement, wipe it off a bit with a dry cloth (especially the verge) and give it a liberal oiling. Chances are, it will plod along for a few more months, maybe ten or fourteen. Could one call this botch work? Poor it may be, but you haven't materially harmed it, disfigured it, or damaged it.

Much of our work, the methods, etc., have been established over many years, to the extent that certain operations like cleaning, bushing, etc., have certain standards set up. The electric clock has been in use such a short time, comparatively, with absolutely *no* repair suggestions or standards from the manufacturers that almost any treatment you might administer to it could be defended as proper repairing if the clock is restored to service for a reasonable length of time.

What we need is to hear from more repairmen who have done serious experimenting, who have devised a practical method, followed that method and kept records until they know what they may reasonably expect from it.

A few years back, I chanced to take in a clock of this type and I found the whole back cut from the motor case, leaving the rotor completely exposed. Upon inquiry, it was determined that the person bringing it in was a building engineer, and that this timepiece was in use in the boiler room when he took over about five years before. He said he was absolutely sure that it had not been touched during his office, and that it had operated satisfactorily up to a couple of days before. I sent this motor in to the manufacturer with the story and asked pointedly (1) what they thought, (2) whether or not they had records of, or had experimented with these motors dry.

You guessed it—up to date, no reply. I'm running one of these motors now with the whole back of the case cut away and practically dry (it was stood on end overnight to drain). It has been so operating about 13 months, and has recently got a bit noisy, but is still registering the time. It is doubted whether or not such an experiment will prove very much; nevertheless, I'll have the consolation of seeing how many months it will go before stopping completely.

It is true the manufacturers want you to install a new unit, but I have several questions here. Does he protect you as a repairman? By that, I mean do you get a proper discount when buying that unit for re-sale? Haven't you found that any joker, whether in the trade or not, can go to these depots and get the same unit at the same price you have to pay for it? We've had word that some distributors even offer to install the unit while the customer waits— no extra charge. Does the manufacturer price his unit in keeping with the retail price of the clock, thereby enabling you to install a new unit and make a living wage?

TELECHRON QUESTIONS

I am writing to you for your answers on a few questions, all on the Telechron electric clock containing the M1313 rotor:

(1) What causes the humming sound in electric clocks?

(2) What is the correction to make to stop this humming?

(3) What should one do when the flat pieces that are held together with shellac come apart?

(4) What is the best way to tell that a coil is no good?

A. (1-2) We are dealing with synchronous electric clocks, all of which, of necessity, operate on an alternating current. Most alternating current is 60-cycle, that is, it alternates its polarity sixty times per second. At the zero point between changing from positive to negative, the current must be nil, magnetically. This is the basic cause of what you refer to as a "humming sound." Anything loose or affected by magnetism within or attached to the movement ceases to be attracted when the magnetism is nil. A sort of vibration sets up, and those accustomed to the 60-cycle-per-second alternation will instantly recognize it. Most call it the 60-cycle hum. See that all parts of the clock are tight, that no iron or small steel objects are near the clock. If it comes from, or by the motor, it could be due to wear, and the motor should be replaced. In aggravated cases, it may be necessary to suggest to your customer that the clock be set upon a piece of felt, dresser scarf or other soft material, and not set directly on solid wood.

(3) We do not fully get your meaning here. Probably you refer to the laminated core through the coil. These pieces are held firmly together by bolts. While cores generally have coatings of lacquer or shellac, that is not intended to hold them together.

(4) Rig up a probing line. Secure a regular light socket and a 5-watt or 7-watt bulb from your current outlet. Run one wire to one socket terminal, and take off the other terminal with about a single 3-foot length of drop cord. Let the other wire come directly to about the same length and solder to the two remaining terminals a short piece of stiff copper wire. Now if you place these pieces of copper wire touching, it will complete the circuit and your bulb will burn with full brightness, but placing one piece at one coil terminal and one to the other, current will have to pass through the coil to reach the light and it will burn very dimly. Where the coil is "open" (bad) no current can pass through it and the bulb will not light up.

WALTHAM ELECTRIC CHATTERS

We have a Herman Miller electric clock that we overhauled, and it runs fine. The ends that support the rotor pivots are stamped "Waltham W. Co."

Is it possible to eliminate the chatter sound when this clock runs. It is not very loud, but the customer has a very quiet house and good hearing. She uses the clock on her bedroom dresser.

A.
If the clock in question was manufactured by Waltham, and it evidently was, it has been running for enough years to wear the rotor pivot bearings. It has been several years since Waltham manufactured electric clock motors.

Just as quickly as the rotor pivot bearings wear enough to permit the pivots excess play or freedom, the alternating current causes them to "chatter" or set up an unpleasant hum.

We believe that you will find this particular motor with caps over the ends of the pivot bearings, and under this cap, a light felt washer. The bearing hole should be closed, or if the wear is excessive, it should be bushed to a comparative tight tolerance. See that they are perfectly clean—throw away the old felt washers and put in new ones. Do not lubricate with an oil, but use Alemite No. 33.

Sometimes these noises from an electric clock used in the bedroom can be most troublesome. Often these clocks had, or can have, attached to their base a felt piece that helps deaden any noise. Even after you have seen that the bearings fit properly, it is well to check this felt angle. Years of use will pack the felt, impairing its deadening qualities. Renew it. If it never had a felt-coated base, you can add one. Some prefer to cut little discs about the size of a ten-cent piece and glue one on each corner, like miniature feet. Be sparing with the adhesive, for if the piece of felt is saturated with it, the sound-deadening qualities are lost.

How Sangamo winding works

I have a Hamilton Sangamo clock to repair. It is an electric clock that will run on electricity and at the same time wind a spring which will run the clock if the current should go off. I am not the first person to get this clock to repair. The owner tells me that the other repairmen told him that there is something missing, but they didn't know what. I have never seen one of these clocks before, so my question is: Do you have any information that you can give me?

The trouble is in the winding. It doesn't stop winding the spring.

A.

The sale of the Sangamo Hamilton clock to General Time Instruments Corporation was in 1930 and parts have not been available for about 20 years. These clocks were generally equipped with an Illinois 7-jewel watch escapement, which escapement was driven by a regular mainspring. This spring was wound by an electric motor.

Many repairmen encountered trouble with the winding, yet that winding was sound mechanically and fairly simple if only the repairman would take the time to study it out. It is noted that your clock does not stop winding. Either the brake isn't correctly set, or some former repairman has lost the little single ball end bearing under the wheel brake. More than likely, it is both.

First, you will observe that the motor winds the spring by turning the arbor. Fitted into this arbor is a threaded collar. Now when correctly set up with the spring all the way down, this threaded collar is out or farthest from the barrel proper. There is a lever pivoted to the plate, which lever ends in a "Y" or fork that rests right under the flange of this threaded collar, also on this lever, back nearer the pivot point is a leather-faced shoe riding just above one of the wheels of the motor winding train which I called the brake wheel above.

As the motor turns the arbor to wind the spring up, the turning of the arbor at the same operation screws in on the threaded collar and this collar pulls the pivoted lever down bringing the leather shoe against the brake wheel. The travel, in and out, of the threaded collar is calculated to equal the number of turns required to wind the spring fully, thus when all the way down (spring) the collar is farthest out and when fully wound up, it has been screwed down next to the barrel head.

You therefore adjust the leather brake shoe which is inserted into the lever by means of a threaded post so that when the collar is screwed almost completely in, the lever will press the shoe against the brake wheel hard enough to stop the motor. The clock running down reverses this procedure and as soon as the mainspring unwinds enough to release the pressure on the brake shoe, the motor takes over and commences winding.

Now observe the bearing under the brake wheel; it is capped with a metal cap. There belongs in this bearing just one very small ball. The end of the brake wheel arbor pivot works against this ball. Many repairmen not familiar with these clocks do not know of this construction, and pull the clock down losing this ball.

If the trade has any tricks, here is one of them. You may obtain a practical, workable ball from an old ball point pen. With the bearing under the brake wheel in proper order (the bearing on the opposite end of this pivot is just an ordinary hole bearing in the plate) and the threaded collar properly set with the brake shoe adjusted so as to exert enough pressure on the brake shoe to overcome the pull of the motor, just about the time the threaded collar reaches a couple of threads before the end you will find the winding is functioning as the manufacturer intended.

Remember, there are no switches—the current remains on the field coil at all times. The winding motor turns only when the pressure is released on the brake shoe. It is best to place the movement up in a movement holder, connect it and watch the operation. Most of these clocks are strikers and the same spring powers the strike through a differential gearing, thus when striking the spring goes down enough to allow the motor to wind some, it takes over.

It is easy to place on the minute hand and advance it one operation of the strike train at the time and see for a certainty that the winding operation starts and stops properly. Possibly we should cover another feature of the threaded collar in order to make its operation perfectly clear because the turning of the arbor turns or screws this collar in, yet the running of the piece does not turn the winding arbor in the opposite direction to screw it out There is a slot cut laterally with the collar and through the threading in which works a polished pin in a close-fitting hole in the flange. The actual mechanics are that when winding, the arbor turns the collar by means of this pin thus screwing the collar down and into the threading which is on the barrel proper.

When the winding operation ceases, the arbor sits still and holds the collar still by the same pin. It is the running (turning) of the barrel which screws the collar out. Make sure that this little pin has not been broken out, as the entire operation depends on it.

Postal Telegraph electric clock

I have several of these clocks that need repair

The holes have been bushed and the clock cleaned but sometimes it runs so fast it gets to speeding. At times I can slow it down by touching the rotor and then it will keep time. Now, occasionally the current is shut off here and when it is turned on again the clock will race.

On the dial is the word "Synchronous" and below it "Postal Telegraph." That is all the identification I can find. It does have a mainspring and it is my opinion that it is to be used if the current is shut off temporarily because the clock will continue to run. The trouble may be located here because it seems the mainspring work-

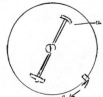

ing along with the motor (rotor) picks up momentum. The back of the clock looks like this: a-weight and adjustment screw. If it runs too fast "a" will hit "b."

Any information you can give me will be appreciated

A.
The clock you indicate was built by the Hammond Clock Co., for the Postal Telegraph Co. I don't recall when production first began but it ceased in 1932.

These Postal clocks were equipped with the Hammond bi-chronous movement . . . bi for two, and chrono for time . . . two times, i.e., the two trains you found and its two ways of keeping time.

In normal operation, that is, with the 60-cycle current on, both trains operate, and in step. This you can note by looking across any of the double wheels and seeing the teeth keep even. When the current goes off, the mainspring is supposed to drive the clock for 60 or 70 minutes.

Now, any timepiece when driven by a spring has to have an escapement ·or other regulating device to control its speed. The rotating spider you sketch at the back of the movement performs this function; it is a form of a centrifugal governor. Built in one end of it is a small spring upon whose end is a small weight; this is adjusted via a little screw to increase or decrease the tension of the spring. If, and when, this spider governor is accelerated beyond correct time speed, centrifugal force overcomes the tension of the weight-spring and the weight is thrown outward where it strikes a little flipper at the lower right. This impact slows down the governor. See that the mainspring is fully wound . . . allow the clock to run without being plugged in; start its sweep second-hand exactly with the hand of a clock you know is keeping time and you can observe in a few minutes whether it is running correctly or not.

A light tension upon the governor spring permits it to come out often and thus get retarded often and cause your clock to keep slow time. Excess tension on the governor spring holds the weight in, permitting the governor to turn too fast, resulting in clock keeping fast time. The little flipper at the lower right has its own coiled spring around the arbor for adjustment. When this is strong, it exerts excessive force when struck by the weight . . . this flipper-spring should be just barely strong enough to retain the flipper in its inward position . . . no stronger.

To your statement that with the current on, both rotors running the governor seem to pick up speed. This is NOT normal. Note that one rotor is smooth on its edges while the other is notched. The smooth rotor merely winds the mainspring and is NOT synchronous. The notched rotor (nearest the back) is synchronous, i.e., these notches run in step with the alternations of the current.

In normal operation, this synchronous or step feature acts as a brake preventing the spring from driving the spider governor faster than synchronous speed. As you know, upon these manual-starting synchronous motors, one notch upon the rotor steps to the next notch on the stator at each reversal (cycle) of the current and there is no adjustment for altering the speed. If your sync motor is failing to act as a retard or brake, the rotor must be out of line with its stator.

See to this alignment, also, to the bearing of that rotor. They could be so worn as to allow the rotor to wobble out of line.

Most of the bearings in the Bi-chronous clock were made of a phenol product and vacuum-impregnated with mineral oil . . . when re-oiling you should use a good grade of light mineral oil.

Normal current consumption of the Bi-chronous clock is 3.2 watts.

WESTCLOX GAINS TIME

I have an electric clock to repair. It is rather an old one that the owner thinks a lot of, since it was a gift from a friend now deceased.

On the dial is "Westclox, La Salle, Ill." The sweep second hand has a lever through the side of the case; this starts the hand when the lever is pressed down. On the back are the figures 50 or 60 cycle. The clock is driven by a fiber gear about two inches in diameter, and show Pat. No. 20462660. Just below the patent number is inscribed "G. T. Brittain, 462660, Made in U. S. A."

A.

Apparently you have an old manual-start synchronous clock designed for 50-cycle tied onto a 60-cycle current. If this is correct, at the end of a 50-minute run, the hands will have traveled 60 minutes; i.e., a gain of 10 minutes in 50.

Merely changing coils upon clocks of this type will not "do the trick." Determine the speed of your motor—count the leaves in the motor pinion—count the teeth on the fiber wheel, and see if this clock is designed for 50-cycle. Altering these clocks from 50 to 60 cycles is done right in that ratio, and can't be accomplished by changing coils.

Upon these old, non-self-starting motors, the rotor has a number of nodes or bumps. In effect, these are impulsed forward at each cycle—if your main is feeding out 50 cycles, you have 50 impulses per second. Regardless of the coil used, the main continues to supply 50 cycle alternations and you continue to get 50 impulses per second. We trust this will enable you to remedy the situation and satisfy your customer.

AMERICAN CLOCK CO.
ADJUST DRIVING WEIGHTS

Would you kindly send me some of your information on a very lovely wall clock on which I have completely refinished the case and repaired the movement. Dial and brass parts refinished, too. It was made by the American Clock Company in Chicago and the movement shows as being patented in November, 1899 and July, 1900, serial number B-12386. It is electrically weight lifted by two 1½ volt number 6 dry cells which actuate a magnet coil which in turn pulls up two lever weights to a near vertical position (or presumably supposed to do so). There is a knife switch which causes the circuit to close for this purpose as the lever weights descend by gravity to a certain given point.

The apparent problem (?): when the descended weights reach the limit of downward travel, the knife switch closes and the magnet, which is connected to a rachet on the central pinion, snaps the lever weights back upward—but only to a horizontal position, the knife switch momentarily staying in a closed position until the weights descend a fraction of an inch. Now there is a metal, leather covered stop on the stop right side which has all the appearances of impact indentations from the lever weights striking it. However, try as I have, new batteries, clean electrical connections, freedom from mechanical friction, etc., the weights will only snap to the mentioned horizontal position. The clock is running and otherwise seems to be correct but the above detail concerns me a lot. Where have I missed the boat?

Presume this clock is no longer made—can you figure when it was manufactured —are parts available?

A.

Let's take your question in reverse order answering the last first. Yes, the Seth Thomas Co. is active; the only address you need is Thomaston, Conn.

No, your clock hasn't been manufactured for years. Since it is stamped with a "1900" patent date, it must have been made since that date—we believe this type went out about World War I, therefore your clock must have been made during the first dozen years of this century.

We think that your trouble is: you are letting the two driving weights work in unison, thus you do not have sufficient magnetic pull to "jerk" both at the same instant up against the leather buffer. Separate them, i.e. when one weighted arm extends horizontally, see that the other is up at 45 degrees—as the horizontal weight completes the circuit, the electro-magnet should "jerk" it (only) up and past the other descending weight.

Action of these weight arms should be exactly as the legs of a man walking—they alternately pass each other. A full and complete description of your clock may be found along with wiring diagram, etc., pages 393-397 of Ward L. Goodrich's "The Modern Clock."

Fig. 132 is a schematic of the circuit and Fig. 133 working drawing of the movement. Fig. 134 showing the working of the contact and Fig. 135 the mechanics of the electrowind. Goodrich's instructions plus these drawings ought to lick your problem.

Synchronous Motor Has Great Impact

THERE CAN BE NO DOUBT about it, the greatest single impact on the American timepiece industry was the synchronous motor in the latter 1920's—it enabled man to manufacture a 'practical' time 'indicator' for literally pennies. It has been said that some manufacturers were producing 'units' (sans dial train, hands, glass and case) for under fifty cents and while I haven't documented this, I'm prepared to completely believe it from some examples that were plentiful in the early 1930s. Truly, it seemed as though everybody was getting into the act; little manufacturers sprung up overnight like mushrooms; names of towns never before heard of began showing up on dials.

Note that we said time 'indicators' for that is exactly what they were (are). Mr. Henry Warren gave the name "Telechron" to his motor because it literally means time from a distance. The sync motor does *not* keep time; it merely indicates time as kept at the control center of the generating grid-system. The basic principal of the synchronous motor was known several years before the advent of the sync. clock but it was of no value clockwise because electric current was generated and distributed on an individual generator basis and not regulated to anything like time indicating accuracy.

It was about this era that generating plants began hooking-up, combining their output in what we know today as the grid system. In order for two or more generators to combine their current in one system, each producer must regulate (time) the alternations of their generators to a very accurate degree. Our standard current alternates sixty times per second. Should generator 'A' couple up with generator 'B' with a portion of his plus cycle overlapping the minus cycle of generator 'B', just that portion of the output of both generators would be cancelled out. Thus, it was only when our homes began to receive "regulated" current that the sync time indicator became practical. That impact was so great that, for all practical purposes, we might say: that today no pendulum clocks are being produced in America (the relative small production of g-f movements being the exception).

In passing, we might also note that the sync indicator also occasioned the largest clock repair job in the U.S. When Los Angeles County went from 50 cycles to 60 cycles. Power companies converted owners clocks to the new 60 cycle current without charge. This involved clocks by the tens of thousands. That operation alone with its details would make a whole and interesting story by itself.

Another thought in passing, Mr. Henry Warren, founder of the Warren Telechron Co., who was instrumental in devising ways and means for synchronizing generators for the grid system, was first a 'clockmaker'. About 1911 he was engaged in manufacturing a pendulum clock, battery driven. Several of these unique clocks are around today; they are much sought after by collectors. His manufacturing operation was interrupted by WW-1 and by the time it was over he was working on the regulated generator principle, etc.

Shortly after the little sync indicators got their show on the road, their impact was followed by a couple of lesser shocks in quick succession—so quick in fact it is difficult to pinpoint which came first. One was the changeover from a manual start motor to the self-starting motor; the second was strike. No sooner had John Q. Public begun to enjoy the convenience and reliability of his new sync clock than he noted that it was not striking the hours and halves. Many of the smaller manufacturers never made any effort to add a striking mechanism though some of them did add an alarm. Most of the larger and old established clock manufacturers began to add a

strike. In this, they were not handicapped by price since they were producing a better, larger and higher priced clock in the first place.

Adding a strike train to the new sync clock posed many new mechanical problems and there were equally as many new and different solutions offered. Some kept an orthodox strike train, spring driven, and simply hooked the spring up to the sync motor so that it kept the spring wound sufficient to perform the strike; some added a second motor to do the work of striking, hooking it on at the fan-fly arbor and thereby driving the strike train from its other end, relying on the stall principle. The motor was simply stalled when the strike train locked at the end of a strike operation. Two motors called for not only additional manufacturing expense but also made for a greater current consumption.

At about this stage many new forms of strike mechanisms began to appear; design engineers were striving for a strike that would work off the one motor and at the same time eliminate the mainspring thus not only saving the cost of the second motor or spring but eliminating for owner the hazard of a broken mainspring in his strike. That effort produced many completely new forms of strike mechanisms; many were patented and tried. As always, the 'lemons' were quickly eliminated and the more satisfactory ones prevailed.

Today, the tender of the old "144" is occasionally called on to repair and/or restore one of these strikers—30- and 35-year-old electric clocks that come in for service are nearly all heirlooms, wedding presents or for some other reason have much sentimetal value attached.

Here the experienced repairman will immediately recognize three areas: (1) it's owner is willing, yea, anxious to pay 'top' price' if only he can get the piece restored; (2) it is outmode and therefore spare parts ar non-extant; (3) if he can do the job, he has made a customer for life. Chances are he may not be thoroughly familiar with some odd mechanism and has no place (except C.&.O.) to turn for a few pointers that will enable him to restore a piece others have turned away. For this reason, we propose to jot down some brief descriptions from time to time. There is only space for one this trip.

One of the most completely revolutionary and unique strikers was brought out by The E. Ingraham Company about 1934 as we first find it described in their '34 catalog. Here is what it said: "Self-starting synchronous motor strike clocks. — the striking unit is a development of years of experimentation — it is a clever camming mechanism with all count-hook and rack and snail striking parts eliminated. No additional motor is required to operate the strike, resulting in a simplification and economy of operation. Furthermore, the hands may be turned backward without injuring the strike and the clock will always automatically adjust itself to strike the exact hour at which the hour hand points. In addition, the tone of the strike may be adjusted in volume and clarity by turning the screw marked 'strike adjustment' which is located at the back of the clock."

With the servicing of this strike in mind, we contacted the good folk up at Ingraham. They were most cooperative but had nothing. Mr. John Holland, their chief engineer, wrote: "The Model "P" motor was introduced in 1938. A search of our files did not reveal much data for this 30-year-old mechanism. Enclosed you will find a reproduction of one of our service publications which shows the motor and associate strike mechanism. Unfortunately we do not have detailed drawings of this unique unit."

We appreciate his good cooperation — but— his Zerox sheet dealt more on the "P" motor than on the strike and did not detail the strike operation at all. This left us with no other alternative than to dig out our movement, photograph it and have 'a-go' with our own brand of "specs". Figurse 1 shows the complete movement — back side — with the "P" type motor removed. From 1934 to 1938 they came with the old style, self-starting motor — you may recall the one with two coils. Figure 2

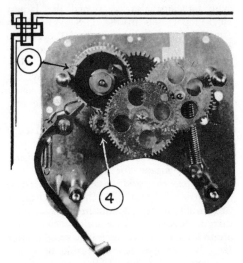

FIG. 2.

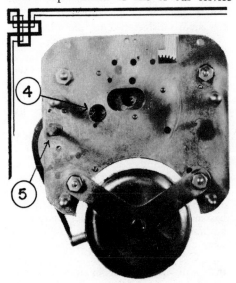

FIG I

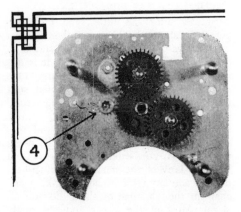

FIG. 3.

shows the movement with bell and back plate removed. Figure 3 is the same, with train and members removed. And, Figure 4 is the strike mechanism — all mounted on one single arbor.

In Figure 4, "A" is the drive wheel made fast to the arbor; "C" is the strike-trip pinion, loose on the arbor and driven by the dividing wheel. Shown uppermost in Figure 3, this dividing wheel, sometimes termed intermediate dial wheel, serves a dual purpose; it is driven by the cannon or center pinion and its pinion drives both the hour wheel shown at center in Figure 3, and wheel "A", turning each one rev. in twelve hours. This same dividing wheel

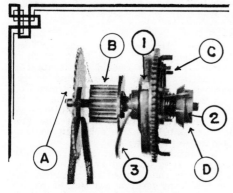

FIG. 4.

also drives the pinion "B" one rev. per hour. Note the width of pinion "B"; this allows it to shift forward or backward on the arbor and still remain in mesh.

Wheel "C" is also free on the arbor; it is driven by pinion 4 which shows on Figures 1, 2, and 3. This pinion is hollow and its hollow end fits over the drive pinion of the sync. motor; therefore it turns continuously—never stops. The portion of the sync. motor pinion remaining after it is inserted into pinion "4" serves to drive the center wheel (center of Figure 2.) This takes care of the hands and time.

Member "D" is a brass hub staked tight to the arbor and therefore turning with wheel "A", one rev. per 12 hours. Note the slot "1" in the flange of wheel "C" and still another slot "2" in the brass hub. Wheel "C" is studded with twelve hammer-tail lift pins. Between "C" and brass hub

"D" is a coiled spring pressing "C" towards the front plate (to your left in Figure 4). Since wheel "A" is staked fast to the arbor and brass hub "D" is staked fast to the other end of that arbor, there is no chance of upsetting this unique strike when you pull the clock down for cleaning. Furthermore, there is only one adjustment to look to when re-assembling the clock. That is: wheel "A" must be positioned and meshed with its drive pinion so that slot "2" will correspond with the hour-hand; this will become self-evident as we describe the strike operation.

There is a spring-loaded lever (the coil spring on your right in Figure 2) which rides on strike trip "3"—this trip raises the lever and at the same time moves it toward the back-plate (your right in Figure 4.) Then when this lever drops off the trip at the hour, it drops on to the flange of wheel "C", but is prevented from dropping all the way down by the flange. Remember that wheel "C" turns continuously; it rides the flange until the slot "1" reaches the 12 o'clock high position, then the slot allows the lever to drop all the way down. This downward travel of the lever presses wheel "C" toward the back plate (right) bringing the hammer lift pins over the hammer tail. "C" is held in this position via a trigger-hook which the backward move had latched over brass hub "D"—here it rides until the trigger-hook reached slot "2" of the hub, then the coiled spring over the arbor pushes wheel "C" back to the neutral position.

Now, it can readily be seen that, if at the time the spring loaded trip lever drops and latches "C" for the strike operation with slot "2" positioned half-way between the 12 o'clock high and one o'clock, just one lift pin will pass over the hammer tail before "C" is released via "2" to go back to neutral and the clock will have struck one for one o'clock. After an hour's run, the hour hand will indicate 2 and wheel "A" will have turned 1/12th of a rev. thus positioning slot "2" half way between 1 o'clock and 2 o'clock position.

The cycle is repeated when the lever drops through slot "1", two hammer lift pins will pass over the hammer tail before slot "2" releases it back to neutral thus two strokes for 2 o'clock. And, thus on around the circle for the correct stroke on each hour. There is a second tail to the strike hammer which ends at the 6 o'clock position (straight down). This drops off "3" after pinion "B" has made a half rev.; this gives one stroke at the half-hour.

On Figure 1, "5" indicates the tone adjustment mentioned in the catalog description. It so happened we varied the camera a bit and the plates in Figures 1, 2, and 3 vary a little in size but the plates are 3 1/16th inches across and the bell, as shown in Figure 1, is 1¾th. inches diameter to give you a more accurate idea of the size. Figure 4 is enlarged. It goes without saying, there is no material available for this model.

Generally it is strike trouble that brings them to the repair bench so once you are familiar with this strike operation you can quickly check it out — malfunction is usually at brass hub "D"; either the trigger hook after some 30 years wear has worn til it does not hold "C" in the strike position or its latching spring has broken. In some instances we find the brass hub well worn to the point "C" is released before the hook reaches slot "2". Measurements are not super-critical; you can easily turn a new hub and slot it with a jeweler's saw. The making of complete new trigger-hook or a spring for it is not at all difficult—one should never hesitate to take one of these 'oldies' just because no material is to be had.

BLODGETT BROS. & CO.

I have in my possession an old electric clock. I am very curious to find out something about it. Many of my friends suggested that I take it to a watch repairman and let him examine it. That I did and all he could tell me was that he was very surprised that the mechanism, as old as it is, is original.

He told me it was at least 65 to 70 years old. I will describe it to you. It is about 2¼ inches in diameter. It is made by Blodgett Bros. & Co., Boston. The mechanical works inside are originally electric and the frame work structure is stamped, imbedded, and reads A. D. Blodgett, Pat. May 24, '98. The face of the clock is 19 inches in diameter and white with Roman numerals with the name of Blodgett Bros. & Co., Boston, under the center of the face just below the shaft that holds the hands.

The clock housing is of sectional royal oak wood and made up of many pieces to form a complete circle. The front glass door hinges at the top and has a simple catch at the bottom.

As far as I know and hear, this clock was used in some old school house in Boston. The two electrical leads coming from the clock top were cut short and I added an electric cord to them. I plugged this cord into our conventional wall outlet and all I heard from the clock was a growl and saw a bit of smoke. I tried this for only a few seconds for fear of doing any serious damage.

If it would not trouble you too much, certainly would appreciate any information you could offer me in finding out anything about this clock. Could you give me the name of anyone that could help me? Would a picture help if I sent one to anybody?

A.

Neither "Drepperd" or "Palmer" include "Blodgett Bros. & Co." on their listings—in fact, we could not locate any information at all. While trying to research it, in came from Adams-Brown Co., their new book catalog #87; one of its offerings was a "Blodgett" catalog—we now have that catalog in our file and this accounts for the delay in getting some answers to you.

This catalog is rather small and only 16 pages. It is undated but definitely belongs about the turn of the century. Inside the front cover is a letter of recommendation from the Mechanic Arts High School, Boston, dated March 20, 1896. Thus, it (catalog) must have been published after that date. The final three pages are given over to "A Few Buildings where our Electric Clocks Are in Use." It lists 101 of them, about 90% are in Massachusetts. The balance are in Rhode Island, Connecticut and New Hampshire. This would indicate that they must have distributed only in the New England states. Their address was 141 Franklin St., Boston. Very little technical info can be obtained from this catalog— it lists a couple of "school systems" using a tape in their program clocks; says their system is also good in factories, banks, etc., and suggests a home system whereby the "master" clock is a grandfather clock (strike or chiming) with units for each room; said units can be installed in already owned clock cases with an allowance for "your present clock movement."

Here is a verbatim paragraph from page 2: "Our clock is driven by a fine spring same as many high grade mechanical clocks. The term self winding results from the following: two small cells of battery are placed in the clock case and connected with a motor attached to the movement. As the center spindle which is driven by the fine spring makes one revolution, it brings up a loose arm, which passes under a stationary projection secured to the back plate. When these two are in contact, the circuit is closed through the battery and motor. The motor is thus actuated and winds the fine spring from left to right one turn, which was just the amount used to run the clock during the last sixty minutes. When this has taken place, another arm carried by the winding wheel slips the loose arm from under the projection opening the circuit. This action is repeated in exactly sixty minutes more and so on."

That paragraph is the extent of technical data, save, that one gathers by the over-all look at the little catalog that the units are "jumpers." It does not even indicate whether half or minute jumpers.

Since it says "two cells" and the time is around the turn of the century its pretty certain that they were No. 6, 1½-v. cells, i.e., the master clock was wound by a three volt d.c. current.

Perhaps the "system" also operated on 3 volts? Again, if a number of units were hooked onto one line, they may have used 6 volts (4 batteries) in their jumper circuits.

Their master clocks had quite a pendulum; since apparently your piece does not have one, I'd guess that you have one of the jumper units. As you have applied 110-v a.c. current to it, I fear you may have burned out the coils. Your best bet is to take your piece to a "clockmaker" experienced in servicing jumper systems—Cincinnati, I.B.M., Simplex, et al, and let him have a look-see. He can, by a simple test, tell and show you whether or not your coil (coils) are serviceable.

Several people have come up with old school and/or jumper units which they desire to operate for sentimental or other reasons. This can be easily done by utilizing a sync motor to contact it at the ½ or minute as required with a battery circuit of the proper voltage. Results are generally satisfactory and not too expensive.

Sorry we can't give beginning and end dated on Blodgett Bros. & Co., maybe some of our readers can supply—we'd certainly appreciate that card.

Inconsistent Striking

I have a Seth Thomas electric self-correcting clock.

This clock will strike the hours for a day or longer but will not strike the half hours. Then it will change and strike the half hours and will not strike the hours.

Could you tell me where I should look

for this trouble. I have never had a clock do this before.

A.

The term "self-corrector" is more generally applied to that device upon a quarter-hour chime clock employing a high trip at the hour position in order that the clock will only chime the fourth quarter at that point and then strike the hour. However, some workmen apply this term to the common rack and snail system.

Since you do not say your problem is a chimer I take it that you have a rack and snail. It is difficult to spot the exact performance you describe and it is odd that your clock will switch its mal-performance from the hour to the half hour position and then back again.

It must be that the strike train "sticks". First, make sure that the strike train is set-up correctly, making sure that the warn-run pin is as far from the lock position as possible. If there is only one warn-run pin it should lock with that pin approximately 180 degrees from the warn-run lock position. If the particular clock you have happens to be equipped with two warn-run lock pins upon the same wheel then it should lock with the pin 90 degrees from the warn-run lock position.

Next make sure that the warn-run lock pin is riveted tight in the wheel as sometimes a loose pin will cause the train to bind and fail to unlock. Make sure all levers are free and will drop freely. It could be a sticking lever. Conceivably a lever could stick upon the hour trip remaining until the half-hour trip and then turns loose and strikes or sticks upon the half hour trip to be loosed when next the clock trips to strike the hour. Make sure that the fan-fly is perfectly free and that it's bearings are not worn to excess and that the staves, or pinion leaves, are not worn enough to stick.

With a completely free train properly set up with perfectly free levers and the proper lift upon those levers your clock should function correctly as the manufacturer intended.

Wiring Diagram

I have a large electric clock made by Self Winding Clock Co., Brooklyn, N.Y. This clock is shown on page 324 of Time and Timekeepers by Professor Milham published by the Macmillan Co., N.Y. in 1944.

I have the clock in first class condition mechanically, but it fails to wind 50% of the time. Do you know if a wiring diagram for this clock can be obtained?

I found that the trouble is in the exact sequence of the brushes and six lobe contact cam. If the motor stops at a certain point it will start, but there is no exact stopping position.

In Fig. 217, page 324, fingers are shown which prevent backlash. My movement does not have this finger. I assume that these are an addition to a later model than what I have. I can make and add a finger if you think it would solve my problem.

I might add that I am using a small AC-DC converter that gives 6V-DC in place of the old wet batteries. It has worked fine so far as power is concerned in that I have arranged a cam on the hour shaft which turns on 110V-AC for winding time only. This seems to work fine.

A.

Your reference to Milham, p. 324, helps to identify your movement as "Style A." You will note that Prof. Milham got his illustration from Ward L Goodrich's "The Modern Clock". Mr. Goodrich devotes some half dozen pages to detailing the action and working of this clock. We find it illustrated in a Self Winding Clock Company 1908 catalog, but no wiring diagram.

The fact that your clock winds better than 50% of the time must indicate to you that your wiring is correct. Your trouble being that it occasionally fails to wind indicates a faulty contact or contact system. The finger or fingers you refer to as preventing back-lash are exactly that. Goodrich, calls it "back stop spring" and has this to say: "The back stop spring S, Fig. 137 (exactly the Fig. 217 in Milham) must be adjusted so that the brush O is in full contact with a point of the commutator when the motor is at rest and with a tooth of the ratchet touching the end of the spring S. Sometimes the stop spring S becomes broken or bent. When this occurs, it is usually from overwinding. It must be repaired by a new spring or by straightening the old one by burnishing with a screwdriver. Set the spring so that it will catch about half-way down the last tooth," end quote.

You mentioned a later model. All Self-Winding Co.'s clocks with this "motor" wind device had that stop spring. Later models were wound by a vibrator type mechanism. I think perhaps you have just about diagnosed your own problem but have failed to note the operation of this particular motor. Examine it closely and you will see that at the end of a wind operation it has to stop in an exact position so that it will be able to start next time a contact is made. The stop spring holds it in that position. All this assumes is that your circuit is alive, that the contact is positive, and that your 6-volt converter is okay. Make sure your failure is not in the switch you have for turning on the 110-AC.

BARR ELECTRIC STOPS

I have a Barr electric clock and it won't run. It has a glass dome, the base is round, 10 inches in diameter, with a drawer in the base. It has three flashlight batteries, a lever mounted in the front of the base, Serial No. or Patent No. 1945069 mounted just back of the level, and Barr Electric Clock on the dial. My current meter shows the current is present at each end of the coil, also at the two contact points located high up on the left side. Also, the batteries are not shorted as they remain clean. The pendulum will not continue after a very short time, which indicates the current is not doing its job. I cannot find a short, nor can I find where the current is doing anything at all.

A.

With no more to go upon than you give us, i.e., the "make" and the fact it does not run, it is practically impossible to arrive at any ideas as to the why of its not running. Perhaps if we can outline the basic action of this clock, it will aid you in locating the trouble.

This clock was first built by the Poole Clock Co. 2 at Westport, Conn., then later transferred to the Barr Mfg. Co. at Weedsport, N.Y.; several years ago, Barr discontinued the manufacture of clocks and we understood that the residue of parts, etc., were purchased by Mr. Raymond F. Clancey, 25 East Brutus Street, Weedsport. We've had no direct contact within the last few years and do not know if the latter still holds good.

First off: the Barr or Poole is a "reversed" clock. That is, the pendulum drives the clock, instead of the clock driving the pendulum. Thus, we may divide it into two separate mechanisms, the prime apparatus being the driving device and the secondary unit designated to the ratchet mechanism whereby the pendulum ratchets the hands forward.

Since your clock does not run, it is a safe bet that your point of trouble lies in the prime mechanism. It is the type known as "remontoire," a French term usually referring to a timepiece in which the driving spring or weight is lifted or wound periodically to drive the actual mechanism. The Barr utilizes the Hipp system, sometimes called butterfly, of toggle tripping to apply the power to the pendulum.

Located about the center of your pendulum you will find a little box-like frame holding this little vane-toggle which trails backwards and forwards across or under a notched block which is attached to the trigger-latch holding up the impulse lever. Again, upon the pendulum is a pin. When the pendulum's motion drops off enough that the vane-toggle is not carried all the way across the notched block, its knife edge top portion catches onto one of the little notches, lifting the latch and thereby allowing the impulse lever to drop. Mounted upon the impulse lever is a small wheel or roller. When the impulse lever is released, it is pulled downward by gravity and a spring. This roller rolls off the pin in the pendulum, giving the pendulum an impulse in the forward direction.

As all the above action takes place and the impulse lever drops, two contact fingers upon its end fall on two contact points, closing the electric circuit, energizing the coil. Thus the impulse lever is jerked or remounted up to be caught by the trigger latch.

The pendulum will continue to swing free for 5, 6 or 7 strokes until the amplitude dies down enough for the toggle vane to again catch and raise the trigger latch, releasing the impulse lever and the cycle starts all over again.

The box-like frame holding the toggle is attached to the pendulum rod by two screws. Look to this, first. It must be clean and dry, no oil, because the toggle has to be free to swing by gravity. Check the upper edge of the toggle. It should be knife sharp in order to positively engage the notched block. Note: that it is sharpened on only one side and that the beveled side is toward the 3 o'clock side of the dial, your right as you face the clock.

The bevel is faced in this direction because the pendulum is impulsed in this direction, toward 3 o'clock.

If you will examine the clock closely with this before you, taking it through its operation very slowly by hand, seeing that each item functions or why it does not function as outlined, we believe you will locate your trouble. Our experience has been that where the batteries are good, the electric circuit working correctly, 99-44/100ths of the trouble was encountered with the toggle. About half the time it is a dulled or worn knife-edge, the other half, worn bearings, which interfere with its free swinging.

These clocks must be perfectly level, both fore and aft, and abeam. The little level built in the floor of the clock takes care of the abeam leveling. You will note a line on the metal plate immediately under the pendulum. The pendulum's tip should swing directly over it. This takes care of the fore and aft leveling.

The Hamilton-Sangamo Clock

The Sangamo Electric Company, of Springfield, was organized in 1926 when the Illinois Watch Company, at Springfield, failed. It was bought by Hamilton in 1927; then in 1928 Hamilton combined with the Sangamo Electric Co. to form the Sangamo-Hamilton Corporation to manufacture and market this clock. In 1931 this corporation was merged with the General Time Instruments Corp. to become a part of the Seth Thomas Company.

Though the operation at Springfield was short lived—1926 to 1931—it produced a great many high grade clocks that are now showing up for service and repair; this is indicated from the number of questions being received about it and by the same token indicates that some "pointers" are in order.

In 1929 the Lancaster office issued an eight-page "Service Bulletin." As of that date the servicing of clocks was at a very low ebb. Evidently, it was never widely distributed, and a fast check of horological journals of the period shows they did not pick it up. During that period this writer was busily engaged in gathering and filing technical data but never saw one of these service bulletins until a couple of months ago when one of our readers fired in one for the files. While I am familiar with this clock from having serviced many of them and am the proud owner of one with a "Tompion" style mahogany case, I must credit this bulletin for the "frame-work" of this "Otherwise."

Sangamo Electric Co. produced a few synchronous clocks; it appears that they were discontinued when Hamilton came in. The Hamilton-Sangamo is NOT a sync clock—rather, it is a spring driven clock, electrically wound.

They produced a few wall models—non strike—and several mantel styles, some with English type cases but most in the "Tambour" style. Many have a little window located just under the XII o'clock figure through which the balance wheel can be viewed.

The mantel clocks come with two movement models; the earlier models were powered by two motors—one for winding the mainspring and the other to perform the strike operation. Later models were equipped with only one motor and had their strike trains powered from the mainspring via a planetary gearing arrangment —all models employed the same wind device.

Figure 2, shows the two motor strike movement and Fig. 3, the single motor strike movement. Fig. 1, which is seen later in this article, is a side view of the non-strike movement to illustrate the wind device.

These movements easily divide into three principal functioning components: 1) The Escapement; 2) The Motor and 3) The Movement.

The escapement is from a Hamilton watch, mounted as a readily detachable unit on the front of the front plate. The round 11-jeweled escapement with a bi-metalic balance as seen in Fig. 2; another escape-

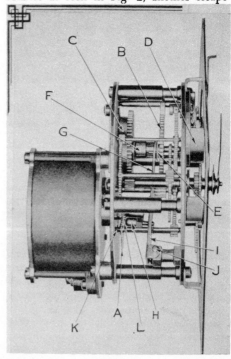

Figure 1.

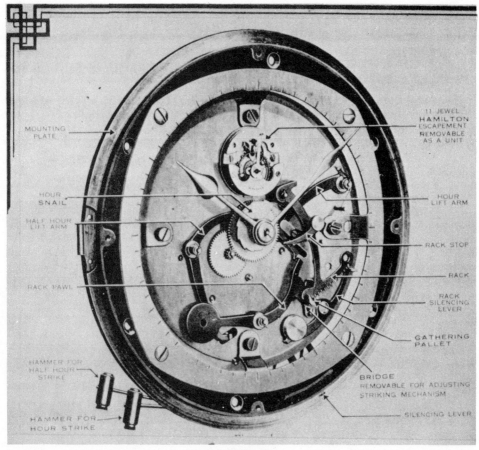

Figure 2.

ment is upon an oval plate, seven-jewel with a mono-metallic balance. Servicing of these escapements requires no comment here since it is identical with the servicing of jeweled watches; neither does the servicing of the next unit—the motor—call for any service instruction since all you do is lubricate it.

Motors of two models were used. The first was designated as "Type A" and two of them were used in the Fig. 2 movement. The staff or arbor of the rotor of this "A" type motor had cone pivots running in ball bearings, when excessively dry they can cause an objectionable noise—rattle—easily remedied by proper lubrication. The motor utilized in the single motor movement—Fig. 3—was designated as "Type C;" this same motor was utilized in some Seth Thomas clocks—as of a year or two back.

Replacement "C" motors were available from Sangamo Electric Co. but the "A" type has not been available for several years. They are after a fashion repairable, i.e. in case of an open coil, a new one can be hand wound; pivots can be hand ground; even a new arbor hand-made.

So much for the first two units, now to unit three, the movement: because of some new and unusual mechanical construction not met with in other timepieces, it calls for some detailed description.

The wind system of all models is the same and has to be thoroughly understood to correctly service the clock; Fig. 1 accurately portrays the mechanical action.

Parts lettered here are as follows:

    A—Fourth winding wheel
    B—First winding wheel
    C—Mainspring barrel

D—Escapement
E—Barrel sleeve
F—Barrel hub
G—Governor arm
H—Governor arm screw
I—Governor arm spring
J—Fulcrum pin
K—Ball bearing

As Fig. 1, shows, the motor pinion engages the fourth winding wheel "A" which in turn, through a train of wheels, rotates the barrel arbor through the first winding wheel "B", the mainspring is thus wound up in the barrel "C" and in the usual way supplies power to the hands and escapement "D." In order to govern the number of turns to which the mainspring is wound up, a governing mechanism is utilized to stop the motor when the mainspring is properly up; as the first winding wheel revolves, it winds the sleeve "E" into the barrel hug "F," causing the governor arm "G" to be pressed toward the back of the clock, and thereby forcing the governor arm screw "H" closer to the fourth winding wheel. By adjusting the screw in the arm it is made to act as a brake on the fourth winding wheel when the mainspring has been wound to any desired number of turns. Stopping the winding wheel stalls the motor and thus ends the winding operation. All motors are built for "stall" operation; the current is always on the motor thereby eliminating any troublesome contacts.

Now, as the barrel unwinds as it drives the clock, the sleeve "E" from its screw thread action unscrews permitting the governor arm "G" to lift the brake shoe at bottom of governor arm screw off the winding wheel; when this happens the wind motor goes into action to again wind the spring. As the winding train turns the screw thread on the barrel sleeve pulls the governor arm "G" toward the back of the movement thereby pressing the break-shoe against the fourth winding wheel "A" 'til the break pressure exceeds the motor torque and brings the motor to a stall stop.

This is one of the most satisfactory electro-wind systems we have ever examined, and that is borne out by its many years of satisfactory operation; yet it has given a number of good clockmakers considerable trouble. Over the years, we've heard from 50 or more good men who have carefully serviced one of these clocks and encountered trouble they could not locate.

Note:: "K" on Fig. 1; this ball bearing designation needs explanation. It is not a ball bearing in the orthodox sense of the term; rather, it is a closed bearing with a small ball at its bottom. As the governor arm brake presses the fourth winding wheel, the end of that wheel arbor pivot is thrust against this single ball to attain the friction necessary to stall the wind motor.

What happens in these cases where trouble comes after a careful overhaul job is: the clockmaker did not know of this single ball lying at the bottom of the back fourth wheel bearing; it becomes lost in the dismanteling, because it is so small and light it can drop and one does not hear it fall. He re-assembles the movement without it. Then, the stall friction comes when the pressure of the break shoe presses the shoulder of the fourth wind wheel arbor against the side of the bearing which is much greater than when pressed against a single ball, thus ending the wind cycle too early. The clock was not engineered for this type friction stall and no amount of adjustment of the governor arm screw can correct it. Naturally, the proper correction is to replace the ball—you will find that a ball from a ball-point pen will do the "trick."

Servicing the Hamilton-Sangamo movement is made easy as the motor, the escapement, and the mainspring barrel are removable as units. The movement is attached to a sub-frame which is released by removing four screws.

To disassemble this movement first take off the escapement—hold the time train with a finger between the plates to allow the spring to slowly run down; then place the movement face down upon the bench. Next remove the motor (S) and then take off the barrel bridge—two screws. Pull the fulcrum pin marked "J" on Fig. 1, and remove the governor arm "G;" then the whole mainspring barrel assembly can be brought up and out the back plate.

The earlier striking clocks were built with two motors—Fig. 2—one to wind the mainspring and the other to supply power to the strike train for the strike operation.

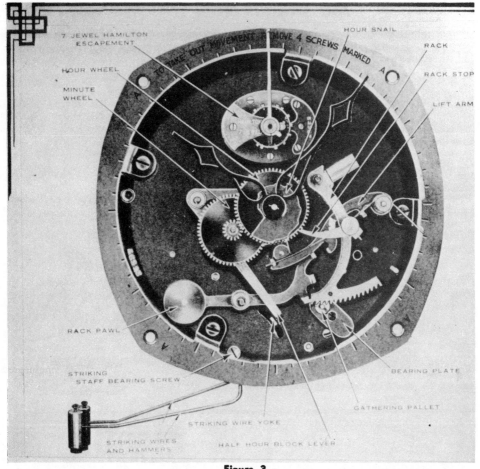

7 JEWEL HAMILTON ESCAPEMENT

HOUR WHEEL

MINUTE WHEEL

TO TAKE OUT MOVEMENT—REMOVE 4 SCREWS MARKED A

HOUR SNAIL

RACK

RACK STOP

LIFT ARM

RACK PAWL

STRIKING STAFF BEARING SCREW

STRIKING WIRES AND HAMMERS

STRIKING WIRE YOKE

HALF HOUR BLOCK LEVER

BEARING PLATE

GATHERING PALLET

Figure 3.

The strike mechanism is essentially the "standard" rack and snail system as used for years on all types of striking clocks; thus any repair or adjustment of same is not greatly different from those upon key wound striking clocks with which all clock-makers are familiar. The rack, gathering pallet, and levers are all mounted on the front of the front plate—easily accessible. While this strike mechanism is completely orthodox both in principle and mechanical action, it should be pointed out that it works "inverted;" that is, up-side-down from what you usually see. In order that it may still be gravity actuated, the rack pawl and the rack are counterbalanced with a small weight. The hour is struck upon two gong-rods by two hammers. Note on Fig. 2, there is designated a "half hour lift

arm," and on Fig. 3, "half hour block lever." These are operated from a cam under the hour wheel which cam must be positioned so that it holds up or blocks one hammer when the minute hand is at the 6 o'clock—half hour—spot. By this means the halves are struck on only one gong-rod.

The single motor striking clock—see Fig. 3—was supplied with the type "C" motor only. The reason for that change in design was to obtain a carry-over of both striking and timing with the current off. Single motor operation was accomplished by introducing a differential in the winding train of the clock mechanism, which serves to distribute power from the motor to both the mainspring and the strike train. In the event the current is off for a short period, the mainspring will supply power through the differential to actuate the hammers.

The movement has the usual type of rack and release levers all mounted in front of the front plate whith an ingenious spring action on the lift arm lever which allows the hands to be set forward or backward as fast as desired without injury to the movement, and without disturbing the strike sequence. The strike levers are actuated by the common type cam and pin arrangement, with an adjustable fan-fly to regulate the speed of the strike operation. As usual, your "C. & O." relies heavily upon the picture being worth a thousand words, it is hoped that these three illustrations and this brief delineation will be of substantial help in case one of these clocks comes to your bench.

HAMMOND POSTAL TELEGRAPH CLOCK, POWER PROBLEM

I have a Hammond Bichronous Postal Telegraph Clock that is giving me a problem. This clock when the power is turned off should keep time for thirty minutes, but instead the hands spin for five or ten

```
U.S. Pat.              Start
1787912         Pull Out — Turn
Others pend.     Left — Let Go

        HAMMOND
        Bichronous
While running synchronously clock also slowly stores energy
    to run through half hour current interruptions.

 [115]  VAC   [60]  CYCLE  [3] WATTS

                   Ser.
Set turn right     No.   [B 195784]
Time OB left       Type
                   No.   [B-3]

    THE HAMMOND CLOCK CO.
         CHICAGO, IL
        Made in U.S.A.
```

minutes; then when the power is turned on the clock begins to spin again.

Could you please inform me as to how I can disconnect this device or repair it?

I would appreciate any help or advise you could give me.

A. The "Hammond" Bichronous is just what the name implies — bi for two and chronous for time, thus two times. One via its sync motor and the other by mainspring when the power goes off. None were produced after 1932; thus no parts are available.

Check at the back of your movement — you will locate a little centrifugal governor. Said governor is held to its arbor via a little cross pin. Your saying that the clock spins when the current is again applied leads to the thought that this pin is broken or lost and thus the applied current will "spin" because the governor does not turn.

These clocks were made with one large field coil embodying two armature members, one to drive the sync motor (the motor with the notched edge) and the second to drive the free running variable speed induction motor. This latter is the one to the centrifugal governor — in normal operation, the sync motor is designed to keep time at the cycle indicated upon the clock — in your case 60 — it holds the governor back and thus the clock time. Now, when the current is interrupted the spring drive takes over propelling the governor. At the tip of this governor is a little spring-loaded weight. Any time this governor is urged forward by the spring power to a speed of 60 per second, the centrifugal force brings this little weight into the path of a flipper spring arm which knocks it back down to a speed of 55 per s.; sixty being the timekeeping speed this is as far below 60 as 65 was above averaging out the time kept by the mainspring.

You asked about disconnecting the free motor. Such is not practical and I would not recommend a try. Check this governor — once you get it right your clock will perform as before, provided the rest of the clock is in order.

STANDARD ELECT. TIME CO.

I have recently acquired a school clock. It is one of the room clocks which are controlled from the principal's office. I need some type of control motor to activate the current, D.C. each minute.

It is made by the Standard Electric Time Co., Springfield, Mass. I wrote to them but received no answer. Does anyone supply a moderately priced unit to operate this?

I believe I need a small unit that lets current activate the coil and hands every minute. Putting a D.C. battery to the coil in back of the clock lets the hands jump forward one minute each time it is touched as long as the battery touches it, it hums and doesn't move forward until the current stops or battery is taken away.

A.

Apparently, you have a "minute jumper" i.e. a dial indicating unit which jumps forward once every sixty seconds. In a factory, school or similar building, it is much more economical to buy one masterclock to "keep-the-time" and have it impulse, say ten or twenty "jumpers" than it is to buy ten or twenty clocks. It isn't economical to buy one clock just to have it impulse one "jumper" since that one clock would serve in the first place.

In case your "jumper" does not have the voltage marked upon it; you can determine its required voltage by adding 1½ volt cells until you get a positive, satisfactory jump — the chances are, you will find it to be six volts, four, 1½ No. 6 dry-cells connected in series.

Your most economical as well as easiest minute contactor will be from a Telechron or any sync motor making one r.p.m.

Devise and attach to the rotor-shaft of the one r.p.m. motor a simple contact that will positively close the circuit at each revolution and you've got it made.

CUCKOO CLOCKS

REPAIR BELLOWS

Can you advise me as to where I can get leather called Imported French Kidskin for releathering Cuckoo Clock bellows? Also, would it be possible to get a book or pamphlet showing the procedure for relining Cuckoo Clock bellows?

A.

All of the old timers were experts at relining bellows as there usually is quite a bit of it to be done. It's not difficult once you have one of them demonstrate the trick for you. They use a skin which is called Puma skin, imported from South America.

You should be able to obtain this skin from one of the organ houses. While you are at it buy a bit of the glue they use, it works fine.

REPAIR BELLOWS

We would like to know if you can tell us exactly what kind of leather is used in cuckoo clock bellows and where we might obtain it. Would also appreciate any other information you might give us in repairing bellows.

A.

We can't recall ever seeing anything in print that would answer your questions, thus our answer shall have to be based solely upon experience. It is said that the original makers use a "kid" skin for cuckoo clock bellows, but I've never located a source of supply.

About the best bellows leather I know of is a Puma skin, imported from South America and more generally used in pipe organs. This may be obtained from The Organ Supply Company, Erie, Pennsylvania. It is available in three weights, i.e. light, medium and heavy. Of course, you will want the light weight for cuckoo clocks. The skins vary in size and price, roughly about $6.00 each. It will be about half the size of a door, so you see it

would recover a good many bellows.

The latter part of your question—"any other information you might give on repairing bellows"—covers quite a lot of ground, other than cutting new leather to proper size and shape and correctly cementing it on. If it is possible, contact an old time pipe organ repairman near you. Usually they have had a great deal of experience along this particular line and will be glad to discuss it with you.

AGE OF CUCKOO CLOCK

A customer of mine would like information on a cuckoo clock she owns, such as its age, where it was made and by what company. The cuckoo is of conventional size, with leaf design about the roof and side of the case, and a round pendulum bob. Stamped on the movement is "G.H.S." All the levers are held in place by steel pins.

A.

Since you do not mention any unusual construction, such as wood wheels, etc., we think your clock may not be among the oldest cuckoo clocks. Frankly, we have very little on German Black Forest clocks and are unable to locate the trademark you indicate. We do have a 1925 catalogue of one of the Black Forest museums, plus a 1950 publication—a 105-page book covering 100 years, 1850 to 1950—of one of the state clockmaking schools of Furtwangen. Neither identifies this mark.

A Benjamin Allen catalogue of 1917 advertises these clocks without indicating what manufacturer used this trademark. Their listing reads: "Imported direct from the Black Forest, Germany. The carving of these clocks is done by hand by natives of the Black Forest, and is especially fine. The figures are accurate and lifelike. The movements are made of the best tempered steel and brass, and are well finished and adjusted. The same are guaranteed to be good timekeepers."

ADJUSTING CUCKOO

I have on hand a cuckoo clock which bothers me some since it is the first of its kind to come my way. I have it running all right but the question is how to make it strike right. There are two pins on the main staff which raise and trip a lever every 30 minutes; when released it strikes until it runs down. The lever that releases the cuckoo does not work either, and the leathers on the bellows are worn out. I wonder if anything is missing or just out of adjustment.

The clock was manufactured in Storz, Germany; I don't know when. Can you give me any information on how to put this clock in operation?

A.

It is almost impossible to answer your question without a sketch, so we've whipped up a rough one. It shows your typical

CUCKOO
STRIKE TRAIN

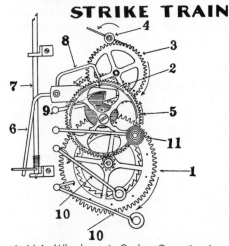

1. Main Wheel	6. Cuckoo Operating Lever
2. Second Wheel	7. Cuckoo Support Rod
3. Third Wheel	8. Count Finger
4. Fan Fly	9. Hour Trip Arbor
5. Count Wheel	10. Bellows Pushers
	11. Strike Hammer

cuckoo strike train from the back side, back plate removed.

The trip lever referred to in your second paragraph is mounted on arbor No. 9. Thus, when the minute hand revolves for-

ward it is raised, and in so doing rotates the arbor raising the wire shown in the sketch behind the shaded cam. When raising upward this wire comes in contact with the locking lever. Note that this locking lever is mounted upon the arbor next above 9, and that count-finger No. 8 and bird-operating lever No. 6 are mounted fast in the same arbor.

The strike-locking pin is mounted in the side of the third wheel—in the sketch, the strike train lacks about one eighth turn of the third wheel being locked. When locked, this pin comes to rest on the end of the locking lever referred to above.

Now, as the locking lever is raised the pin slips under it, making about 1/10 of a revolution before it is stopped by the bent hump in the wire from arbor No. 9 which lifts the locking-lever. This is called the "warn" or "warn run." It is the warning the strike train gives about three or four minutes before the hour. When your minute hand reaches the exact hour, the trip lever drops off allowing arbor No. 9 to fall, this drops the hump below the path of the lock-pin and the third wheel (No. 3) can revolve freely.

The train would stop, correctly locked at the end of each stroke, since the shaded locking-cam revolves once with each stroke, IF something did not hold the locking-lever up so the locking-pin could pass under it. This function is accomplished with the count-wheel No. 5 and the count-finger No. 8. The count-finger being attached to the same arbor as the locking-lever, comes to rest upon the solid portion of the count-wheel holding the locking-lever up until a stroke is made where the finger drops thru, then the train correctly locks and remains so until tripped again. The sketch is a bit on the rough side, so is my explanation, but I hope it will enable you to set your strike up correctly. From your letter, I'd take it that you have so placed the third wheel that: when the lock pin reaches the place to lock, the cam is holding the lock-lever up. It must be synchronized so that the lock-pin reaches the end of the lock-lever just after it (the lock-lever) has dropped off the high point of the cam.

ADJUSTING STRIKE MECHANISM

At present, I have on hand a cuckoo clock of the Black Forest type. It plays musical notes after the cuckoo and strike. When I disconnect the strike, the clock runs without stopping, but when I connect it, the clock will run two or three days and usually stops at 20 minutes after or 10 to the hour. I believe the trouble is in the striking mechanism, but I cannot locate it.

A.

I'm afraid we won't be of much help on this one, simply because this sort of thing is on the difficult side even when one has the movement in his own hands.

You have noted stopping time as 20 minutes after and 10 minutes to the hour. This would indicate that the additional power required to lift the strike trip is the trouble.

One point many repairmen overlook, especially on cuckoo clocks, is the polishing of the pivots. They seem to think any kind of pivot will do for the cuckoo. I've always thought this might be because of the total lack of finish on the plates, etc.

First, make sure that your time train is in perfect order—pivots polished, bearing holes fitted correctly, end-shake of arbors right, etc. Then look to the strike lift and also the lock. After years of service, the locking plate or cam wears a spot in the locking lever; thus when the time train comes to lift the locking lever, additional effort is required to pull it out of the worn spot.

The strike lift is actuated by two pins in the cannon pinion. These extend back toward the front plate, and as your clock approaches the hour and half, these pins lift a bent wire. By manipulating this, you may be able to lighten the lift a bit, even shorten its duration, and yet have it lift high enough to positively unlock.

Further, check the arbor the bird rides on, and the spring that brings him back. This arbor's bearings are secured to the front plate by screws and are supposed to also have a steady pin to insure their alignment. The bird isn't supposed to swing outward enough to open the door during the lift and warn-run, but is sometimes pretty much involved with the lift, and a bind on the bird arbor can cause the clock to stop.

ADJUST FOR SOUND

I have an old cuckoo clock in which I have installed new bellows, but I am unable to get the right sound from them. The clock strikes about as fast as one is likely to count, but it does not sound right. I have tried slowing up the strike on another cuckoo clock, but found that it had to strike fast in order to get the proper sound effect.

I have no idea how old this clock is, and the only markings are the letters, "G. K." The plates are cast brass, and also the gears. The strike or gong lever is missing, also the gong itself, but the parts that operate the bellows are all there—except that I had to make my own wire push rods that operate the bellows. Perhaps my trouble can be in the length of these push rods. I will appreciate any information you can give me on the subject.

A.

Speed is only one of the many factors in the call of the cuckoo—in fact, when everything else is in order you have quite a bit of latitude in the actual speed of the cuckoo strike train.

First, the push wires (or rods) must be of the correct length. If too short, they will not raise the bellows their full height. If too long, they prevent the bellows from falling the full stroke. Second, the top or movable section of the bellows usually has inserted in it, a weight. This weight serves to make the bellows close faster, thereby increasing the exhaust air pressure, giving a louder and more distinct note. Third, it is well to see that your clock has not been tampered with. Sometimes we find that the tail-piece (that wire in the push rod arbor lifted by the pins upon the wheel) in the push rod arbor has been filed or clipped off, preventing the lifting pins from giving the push rod its full stroke. Further, as both bellows are operated from the same pin lift wheel, alteration of either or both the tail-pieces can make a difference in the bellows' drop, resulting in a difference of the timing of the two notes of the call.

Maybe that can be explained this way: for example, we wish the clock to call 3 o'clock. Each call consists of two notes, the high note coming first. Now if the clock is in order, you will get the high note followed immediately by the low note, then a slight pause or lapse before the high note of the second call, thus: cuc - koo - - - cuc - koo - - - cuc - koo.

If the tail-pieces have been altered, it can allow the lifting of the low notes bellows immediately after the dropping of the high note bellows, and instead of getting a true cuckoo call, you'd have something like this: cuc - koo - cuc - koo - cuc - koo.

LEAKY BELLOWS

(1) I have a German cuckoo clock with an hour and half-hour strike. After about four weeks' running, it seems that the sound of the cuckoo is changing. What causes this? If I were to remove the movement from the case, what would be the best step to take to keep from tearing up the bellows? How do you cut bellows tubes from the case without tearing them? Are replaced bellows easy to put in without getting out of sound?

A.

(1) In its final mechanical analysis, the cuckoo sounds emitted by the clock are just a couple of whistles. If one of the bellows springs a small leak, the whistle gets less air volume and the sound is altered. If a leak develops within the whistle (pipe) itself, the air is lost and the sound is altered; otherwise, if the clock movement is performing its mechanical functions properly, I can see no other spot to alter the sound.

There is no trick to removing the bellows. First you disconnect the push wire. You will note that these wires have a peculiar S-shaped hook turned in their top ends which engages the wire eye at the back of the bellows, and it is easily sprung out of the eye with a little side pressure.

Practically all bellows tubes are secured to the case by a screw and a steady

pin near the bottom. First remove the screw and pull the tube off the steady pin.

If replaced in the same (old) position, there is no occasion for the sound to be altered. Of course, if the tube happened to be seated in a new location, whereby the orifice or vent was not centered with the opening in the case, it would interfere with the normal operation of the whistle.

TIGHT HANDS

I have a cuckoo clock whose hands are giving trouble, as many of them do. The nut that holds the hands gets so tight it stops the clock till it is loosened up again.

Just how shall I go about fixing it so this top nut won't tighten up? I can't figure out what makes it do that.

A.

Nearly all cuckoo clocks have a dead center; that is, the center post is made fast to the front plate (does not turn) and the member carrying the hour hand is made pipe-style to turn free upon it.

The hour hand generally fits friction tight upon the hour pipe. The minute hand is square-fitted to the minute pipe and held thereon by a nut screwed down tight. Upon all this is a nut screwed on the dead center post.

Use either a French closing hole punch, or the three-faced pointed punch from your staking tool on the outside of this nut. This makes the nut get tight just as the last threads try to turn onto the post and thus it will remain in place, not turning on down to the point where it interferes with the freedom of the minute members on the dead center.

Check the play (freedom) under the nut closely, for sometimes one encounters trouble even after making sure that the nut cannot turn all the way down. The nut just under it, holding the minute hand, is upon right-hand threads. If this minute nut drags, it will have a tendency to unscrew, thus coming up against the stationary nut and creating a binding friction that will stop the hands. The whole of cuckoo construction permits excessive play and adjustments. A full sixteenth-inch between minute hand nut and stationary nut is not too much.

Music, cuckoo, separate mechanisms

I have to repair a Cuckoo clock which has a music motor in it which is attached to ceiling of the small wood case. The box or case is 6 inches by 4½ inches by 4 inches. The clock and music motor with all wire connections are crowded into this small space.

My problem is to adjust the timing of this music motor so that the music will start to play, open the door and expose the figure of a man who plays the guitar and stops music before or after the cuckoo. I don't know which operation takes place first. My difficulty is that when I adjust the music to operate, the music continues until it is run down. When adjusted to stop music it seldom will play.

Please tell me how to correct the timing of this piece of machinery.

A.

These little cuckoo, music models can be—and usually are—pretty mean to handle. Mechanically, the construction is poor and the case is always a couple of numbers too small, allowing almost no space for adjustment, etc.

The clock is intended to cuckoo and strike in the usual manner, then at the end of that operation and closing of the cuckoo door, the little figure moves forward, plays one tune and the door closes.

The two operations are independent and separate.

To exactly pin-point your particular problem and give you detailed instructions as to exactly what to do would of necessity require an intimate knowledge of the exact clock you have. There are many of these in circulation; their different mechanical workings practically makes every job an "individual" problem, yet the net performance of all of them follows the same pattern.

Unlike the strike of the average clock; also that of this very cuckoo strike, the little music box is never provided with a "warn run." The equivalent of such is generally achieved via a little wire from the cuckoo side; said wire coming into the path of the music mechanism's fan-fly thus preventing it from any further run 'til the cuckoo operation is finished and the bird has assumed its rest position.

The music is stopped when a little pin or finger against the head of the prick-barrel drops into a hole therein bringing against the fan-fly another finger and thus stopping and holding the music mechanism inoperative. Generally, the same lifting action that trips the cuckoo train, pulls this lever out; the fan-fly will make three or four revolutions before being stopped by the little wire from the cuckoo side being brought into its path as the cuckoo comes out. The music mechanism, already unlatched and having turned a couple of revolutions of its fan-fly is prevented from further operation until the cuckoo operation is completed, then as the bird returns this little holding wire is removed from the path of the fan-fly; the music operation proceeds 'til the stop lever again drops into the hole in the end of the prick-drum.

We do not know of any book or pamphlet covering this particular clock.

On the Cuckoo and Quail, and chime clocks (three train) in general the last or following operation has the benefit of a "warn run" as mentioned before, incorporated within it. Upon your clock, we only have it in effect—the music mechanism is separate.

To eliminate cuckoo squeak

I have just cleaned and oiled a cuckoo clock. The entrance pallet squeaks each time it raises over a tooth in the escape wheel. When an extra drop of oil is applied to entrance pallet, the squeaking stops for about two days. The exit pallet never bothers.

How can I stop the squeak?

A.

If, as you suspect, this squeaking actually comes from the escape tooth sliding off the receiving pallet it must be due to a roughness upon this pallet. Polishing the pallet should eliminate the squeak. Attached is a little polishing wheel, mount it on arbor and turn your lathe or hand motor at high speed. Polish the pallet in question to a perfect mirror finish and see if that will "do the trick."

More often than not, squeaks from the running of a cuckoo movement originate with the crutch rubbing against the pendulum rod (wire), or from the clevis suspension. A bit of oil always eliminates it.

It seems possible that a rough pallet could set up a vibration (squeak) which vibration could cause the friction (rubbing) at either or both points mentioned above to emit even a louder squeak. Someone has said "expect the worst from a cuckoo clock for it always happens."

Squeaking Cuckoo

In overhauling Cuckoo Clocks I have had trouble with two or three that persist in making a squeaking noise. The last one is very annoying.

The squeak occurs when the pendulum swings to the right facing the clock.

I polished the pallet face to eliminate the indentation from escape wheel teeth, but this did not eliminate the noise.

I have overhauled many cuckoo clocks over the years without the squeak showing up. The last one I recently did resulted in the customer complaining.

Have you any suggestion on the above trouble?

A.

In some instances, a "squeaky" Cuckoo clock can become pretty annoying, and, I suspect your customer has one of them.

It would indeed be rare, if your squeak came from the point you've worked on, i.e. the pallet face, because the action against that face is by brass, an unlike metal. Practically all squeaks come from like metals rubbing together.

You will find it in the pendulum assembly. There, you have a steel clivis swinging on a steel wire. There, is the steel pendulum wire swinging upon the clevis. Lastly you have a steel pendulum wire working in a steel crutch. Your squeak must be coming from one or more of these three points. First look for a slight bit of rust; generally that indicates the "spot". Clean and polish that "spot"; then add just a bit of good clock oil.

Cuckoo Clocks

I am having trouble with Cuckoo Clocks and as they are coming in very frequently I need to know all about them. I have one thing that is puzzeling me.

After cleaning and setting the movement it runs smoothly with the cukoo door open or unlocked. However, if I lock the bird in, it stops at 1:15 or there abouts. If I open the door at that time the bird comes out and stays out. After working the striking chain several times it will start up again. I think the trouble is in the small shifting weight that moves with the rod holding the bird which seems to lock up. Can you tell me how this can be remedied?

I have a Goodrich book on clocks and although I think it is very good it does not tell me about some of the American clocks which do not have the cam locking devices. Can you tell me of some American book that includes this?

A.

Sorry, no point by point detailed solution to your problem. There literally seems to be a blue-jillion different types and variations for bringing the bird out and then back again after completion of the strike.

At the time Goodrich compiled his book the cam device you mention wasn't coming on cuckoo clocks. Fact is I think they were introduced with the WW-2 influx of clocks.

Basically the strike is tripped and held with a warn-run until the hand reaches XII when it drops off and releases. This release pushes the bird out and he in turn with that little connecting wire pushes the door open. At the conclusion of the strike operation that cam is made to release its pressure on the bird arm to allow it to be brought back by its spring-loaded power.

About all I can tell you is simply follow each item of this bird-in and bird-out action to see just what does it and how it does it and most important of all when it does it. I refer to that timing in relation to the raising of the hammer and bellows as a matter of synchronizing the strike train. On the cuckoo the strike train first pushes the bird out and then there are three trips. It must trip two bellows and a strike hammer. Thus it is most important that the strike train be synchronized so that no trip in action occurs at the same instant the bird is being pushed out, thus it will not perform two of its functions at the same instant. Some are the count-wheel system and some are rack & snail. Some lock one way and some another. All these combined to make "variations" so numerous that actual pin-point details are practically impossible unless one has the clock in-hand to demonstrate. Take it "slow and easy" to analyze each action separately. Note the sequence in which you wish them to come, even if it is the hard, time-killing way. I believe you can work it out

Cuckoo Clocks

A complete mechanical departure from the orthodox ratchet wheel and pawl method — despite being in the third decade of general use — it has not yet attained a generic name universally accepted and consistantly used by all catalogue makers listing our materials. It has been called a 'clutch,' 'coiled-spring-ratchet,' 'gripper spring,' or 'cuckoo wheel coil spring,' and none seem to automatically give one an instant concept of it's mechanical function.

A ratchet, of which it is not, definitely implies a toothed wheel gear into which a pawl drops or catches; and it performs this function. It is quite evident that this new method is much cheaper to construct for it is far easier to wind a little coiled spring instead of cutting a toothed wheel, a pawl, a revit for that pawl and attaching both to the chain wheel and main wheel. One point in common is in both methods is that there are lefts and rights. Some catalogues designate lefts for the time train and rights for the strike train. As a general rule that is accurate, but, not in every case. The clockmaker should note this when installing a new spring, i.e., make sure that the spring is coiled in the same direction as the old one.

Installing a new spring is time consuming, even a bit tedious but not especially difficult, particularly if the clockmaker is completely familar with the construction. Customers like their cuckoos' and seem quite willing to meet the service fee to place it back into operation. No special tool is required as many do it with those bench tools at hand. It can be done quicker and easier with a little anvil you can easily make.

Secure a piece of tubing, preferably brass, with outside diameter 1″ x 1⅝″ inches long and with a wall about 2 m/m. thick. Scribe a line around it a fat half-inch from the top with your jewelers' saw, cut down to this line; move over seven m/m. and make a second cut and join these cuts at the line thus leaving a slot 7 m/m. wide by a half inch deep. Now, move on around the tube thirteen m/m. for the next saw cut, then 7 m/m. for the fourth saw cut for a second slot. Repeat two more times and you ought to come out just 13 m/m. from the first cut with

your tube slotted four times. Naturally the cuts can be dressed out with a file straight through; two cuts at a time, however, this is only necessary if you desire a good looking and well finished anvil. One with rough saw edges is just as practical.

When you have occasion to replace a broken spring, remove the main arbor from the clock and set it wheel down upon your anvil. Practically all main wheels are four spoked thus the spokes fit within the slots and allow the top of the anvil to rest against the chain wheel. Next, take a flat faced punch from your stake with a hole larger than the arbor pivot so that it rests against the shoulder of the arbor. Drive the wheel and arbor down thereby removing the brass collar that holds the chain wheel against the main wheel; with that collar removed you can lift off the chain wheel again making sure you have noted the direction in which the old spring is coiled, and select, one of that same direction.

At this point comes the 'ticklish' portion, these springs attach to the chain wheel by two little tabs that have been pressed up out of the first layer of metal in the chain wheel. These have to be bent up to remove the old spring loop and to take the new. Unless you are very careful in bending these tabs they will break off. Grasp the outter end of the tab with flat-nosed plyers and make sure that your bend comes at the spot where it was originaaly bent and NOT at the line at the base of the tab. One tab can be raised just a wee bit while the other has to come straight up; then, the old loop can be raised off the straightened tab and slipped out from under the other one. Replace the loop of the new spring in reverse order, that is, slide one side of the loop under the slightly raised tab and the other over the straightened one. Lastly be extra careful when bending back the straight tab seeing to it that you bend it at the old bend point and NOT at the base line.

The tab that was slightly raised can be pressed down to its original position without fear of breakage. Having properly replaced the broken spring you are ready to reassemble this unit. Turn the anvil over and rest the main wheel upon it after first placing the chain wheel into position. As you replace the chain wheel slowly turn the arbor in the un-coil direction so that it goes down easily. With another flat faced punch with hole large enough to take the arbor, tap the brass collar into place and the repair is ready for reassembly.

Sometimes these jobs come in where the spring fails of a positive hold because it has worn the arbor to a diameter too small to grip. A new unit — wheel and arbor assembly — is indicated and most are available in the LaRose catalogue showing some 24 that range in price from $2.00 to $2.50 each. This point should be carefully checked when taking in a job since a broken spring is indicated if the chain wheel turns freely in either direction and your cost for a replacement spring is $1.20 per doz. But, if the wheel shows a tendency to grip once in a while it usually indicates a worn arbor; then your replacement cost may run as high as $2.50 all of which must be taken in for your estimate.

Sometimes the clockmaker attempts a repair here by turning down the main arbor. It CAN be done and satisfactorily, but nearly always consumes more of your repair time than the $2.00 or $2.50 for a new one for once you turn down the arbor to the extent of cutting down the wear to a smooth finish you have reduced it's diameter to where it does NOT fit the spring or the brass collar. The new spring has to be re-coiled and a new brass collar made and both consume your job time, thereby running up your cost. All in all, the new unit is the best answer and you will just have to pass the cost along to the job.

We have noted a tendency among the craft to shy away from cuckoo repairing and can see no valid reason for it. True, the build of the cuckoo is far from 'precision' construction and they are notoriously poor timers. Upon the other hand you are in businesss to sell your time and skill, and our experience has been that it, time and skill, will bring just as much in the lowly cuckoo as in the general run of clock repariing. Most cuckoo owners want their clock operating for some reason or other, maybe just to let the grandchildren see the birdy come out, and are quite willing to pay a reasonable fee for the servicing. Too many bench horologists are inhibited by original cost, this era referred to in the first paragraph has long since left that behind. When a prospective customer walks into your shop with a cuckoo he certainly expects to PAY for the required service. Not one out of a hundred is looking for something for nothing and if that one happens to be that type you are better off not having him for a customer for you will NEVER satisfy him even if you give him the job for free, he'll likely find something to complain about.

Four hours of your bench time is worth just as much spent upon a three dollar alarm clock as a clock selling for a hundred bucks. While the subject of cuckoo clocks is before the house; there is one other comment that C. & O. regularly gets inquiries for material to re-leather cuckoo bellows. That, also has passed with time since material houses no longer stock a cuckoo bellows leather — instead, they have the complete bellows listed as "cuckoo bellows tops." They come in about four sizes and cost the repairman about 75¢ each. It is impossible to tell from a questioner whether he is an old-timer who re-leathered bellows years ago, or, from a late commer to the bench who sees a leaky bellows and thinks only of replacing the leather.

The best, quickest, and cheapest repair on this point is a new "top." The bellows is cemented to the whistle part; don't try and break it loose, seperate it with your jewelers' saw and cement the new top on with Elmers' glue-all or epoxy cement. This takes very little of your time and the result is completely satisfactory. Even better than installing a complete new unit because you turn back to the owner the exact same tone whereas a new unit is generally a different tone — sometimes noted by a customer with a keen ear.

The aversion of the averaged clockmaker toward the lowly cuckoo is a bit difficult to understand — the same may be because of its poor, rough construction or that most treatises give it very little or no mention. Goodrich's "The Modern Cock" is an exception, he devoted a full chapter to it.

My guess is that writers omit the cuckoo because it does not present any particular mechanical problem and excepting the whistles and that action of bringing the bird out, the principals of construction and thus the repair is the same as for the common run of weight driven, pendulum clocks. Our experience has been that servicing of cuckoo clocks can command the same hourly shop rate as the general run of work — so, why turn it away? If the customer is one of your regulars, already familiar with your work and charges, it's okay to take in a cuckoo without that estimate out front. If a new one, make a close examination and give that estimate; at the same time drop the word that it is NOT a precision timekeeper as all too many proud owners think that it is. The cold, mechanical truth is that the cuckoo construction is just about as far from precision as one could possibly get and still have a continous running piece. One clockmaker said: "I've noted a higher percentage of 'come backs' in cuckoos and I know that it is not my work.'' Many, many come backs in all clocks rarely are ever the result of poor workmanship but rather the care the clock gets from its owner and what that owner expects of the piece. Some of the best moments, profitable that is, you can spend when delivering a completed job is to educate your customer upon two points: 1) What to rightfully expect in performance; and 2) proper management of the piece in daily use. In the old days when practically all cuckoos came with the count-wheel strike system, grandpappy made the birdy come out for the kids and goofed up the strike. If the clock has been recently serviced and in the warranty period, the clockmaker got a 'squak' happily, most of those coming today have the rack and snail system and thus that little bit of 'flack' has been eliminated.

Questions About Cuckoo Clocks

I need to ask you a few more questions concerning cuckoo clocks. These are as follows:
1. How can I tell from a movement inspection as to how long a clock will run before it runs down? Some will run for a week and some a day, as you know. For instance, I have two clocks with a rate of 132 beats/min., yet one runs around a week, while the other would be a 24 or 30 hour clock.
2. What is the purpose of the cuckoo wheel coil spring illustrated on page 172 of the LaRose catalogue I have?

A.

Generally, those eight day cuckoo clocks have an additional wheel and arbor, sometimes two, in the time train. Naturally, the strike train has additional gears to make the week.

All cuckoo clocks since World War II have the same type of ratchet. This spring arrangement is so new that it has not fully acquired a trade "term." It is variously called gripper, coiled spring ratchet, and clutch. You will note that these clocks do NOT have the orthodox ratchet gear and pawl at the winding drum. Instead, there is fitted into the center of the winding drum this coiled spring; when you pull the chain to wind it turns the wind drum in the opposite direction to the way this spring is coiled. Therefore, it slips easily; then when the weight takes over to pull in the direction of the coil, the coil grips the arbor and holds just like the ratchet. Also, from this you will see the need for lefts and rights.

Gripper springs often break and you have to replace them. Take the main wheel and arbor out. Note that the chain wheel is held to the main wheel via a brass collar staked friction tight on the arbor; stake the collar off, thereby leaving you free to remove the chain wheel; observe the direction of wind for the old broken spring so that you can replace it correctly. The spring is fast to the chain wheel via two little tabs punched up out of the wheel. Gently straighten these up with pliers to remove the old spring and to take the new. Once you get into this you will easily see how to do it.

Cuckoo Clock Presents Dilemma

I repair clocks as a hobby and have worked on many cuckoo clocks; however, I have two now that I cannot adjust to keep time. They both lose about 40 minutes a day with the pendulum bob as high as it will go. I have made every adjustment I can think of.
Since this has happened to me twice I feel that I am overlooking something simple. Could you offer any advice which may help me solve my problem?
I am sure that one of the clocks has all the original parts including weights; it is fairly new.

A.

Now, on any pendulum clock that is in order running forty minutes per day slow, the pendulum just is NOT short enough, because when the piece is in order, any variation in time has to lie within the pendulum.

Check to see whether you may have a faulty hand-set friction. A clock with a fault at this point, can run till it begins to lift the strike; then, the clock may run at the correct rate — BUT — the register as shown by the hands can be delayed (slowed) a little, etc.

Sometimes, a repairer replaces that wire by which the wood-rod pendulum hangs and does not have the original or does not correctly measure, coming up with a wire too long. Apparently your clock runs consistently; that is, it does not stop, so run it for three or four days, check it carefully at the same time each morning, and if the loss is the same within say a minute or so, then it's NOT a slip in friction for it is not constant. Should you get the same positive rate each 24 hours, then you know you need a shorter pendulum wire.

Setting Ship's Bell Striker

This is in reference to the setting of the striking on Seth Thomas ship's bell No. 354. It is probably a count wheel with long and short hammer. The wheels have red marks evidently for the setting of the bells, but were probably marked wrong. There is a little plate with two screws that can be removed to set the wheels without taking the clock apart.

If you can tell me the proper procedure in setting these bells, I would greatly appreciate it.

A.

The basic patent for it was first issued to Mr. Dudley W. Bradley, of Brooklyn, New York, March 22, 1879. Mr. Bradley assigned it to the Seth Thomas Clock Co., New York.

The setting of the strike should not make undue trouble. We must keep clearly in mind just what the clock is expected to strike, i.e. one stroke (bell) for 12:30; a double stroke (2 bells) for 1:00; three strokes (double and one single stroke) for 1:30; four strokes (two double bells) for 2:00; five strokes (two double and one single bell) for 2:30; six strokes (three double bells) for 3:00; seven strokes (three double and one single bell) for 3:30 and eight strokes (four double bells) for 4:00.

This identical cycle is repeated for 4:30 through 8:00 and again from 8:30 through 12:00. Thus one bell is 12:30, 4:30 and 9:30 and so on.

The main strike wheel is both the "main wheel" and the "count wheel." It is 69 mm. in diameter and has 80 teeth. The count slots are cut as follows: 2,2,4,4,6,6,8 and eight teeth apart. Adding this will give us 40 teeth or half-way around the wheel—the other half being cut the same. Thus this combination main and count wheel turns exactly one-half revolution

each four hours, or, three whole revolutions per 24 hours.

Now, the wheel having the lift pins in it rides concentric on the main arbor. It is 64 mm. in diameter and also has 80 teeth. It is driven by a 16-leaf pinion on the second strike arbor (cut brass). Also on the second strike arbor is an eight-stave lantern pinion which is driven by the "main-count" wheel. There are 20 lift pins set in the side of this wheel, parallel to its arbor, or course. Twenty pins in an 80-tooth wheel means four teeth per pin.

Let's go back to the main-count wheel. The smallest lock notch in it is cut two teeth apart, and this necessarily must be the one-bell stroke. These two teeth of the main-count wheel will drive its eight-stave lantern pinion through two staves or one-fourth of a revolution. The 16-tooth brass pinion turning one-fourth will revolve through four leaves, turning the lift-pin wheel four teeth forward, and we've already seen that the 20 lift pins set in the 80-tooth wheel are exactly four teeth apart. This means that the two-tooth or beginning lock of the main-count wheel will drive the hammer lift-pin wheel past one pin for the one bell stroke.

To take this same mechanical feature a bit further, you will immediately note that a half revolution of the main-count wheel driving the lantern pinion of eight staves will turn the lift-pin wheel a complete revolution because the cut brass pinion of 16 leaves is mounted on the same or second arbor and both wheels, main and lift, have 80 teeth.

At the half of the main-count, the lock notches begin all over again, and since the lift pin wheel has completed its revolution it is again ready to start the eight-bell series all over again.

The lock, warn-run and latch is the same in this strike train as in any other strike train using the count-wheel system, and should be set up accordingly.

The principal difficulty when setting up the ship's bell striker is that the hammer-lift pins can be confusing because each pin passes both the double hammer tails and of the 20 pins set into the wheel, four are short, actuating only one hammer while the remaining 16 pins are long and actuate both hammers.

Adding 1,2,3,4,5,6,7 and 8, we get 36 actual strokes for the four-hour, eight-bell period. The 16 long pins actuating both hammers will give 32 strokes, and the four pins actuating only one hammer give an additional four strokes. Thirty-two pins plus four equal 36 strokes, the correct number for the period and one revolution of the lift-pin wheel.

The only thing left to do is to see that the lift-pin wheel is set correctly with the main-count wheel, i.e. that both begin at their beginning points. Naturally, the beginning point on the main-count wheel is with the first two-tooth lock, or that

FIG. I.

SETH THOMAS   SHIP'S BELL STRIKE.

J. E. C.

immediately following the last eight-tooth notch of the other half of the wheel. The beginning point on the lift-pin wheel is that single short pin that sets between four long and two short pins. (The *only* short pin so located). Once set "in step" your clock is bound to strike correctly.

Let's imagine the lift-pin wheel cut and stretched out straight. It would look something like the sketch—Figure 1, on which I've indicated the strokes below in numerals.

Seth Thomas Ship's Bell

I've written you asking if you know where I can obtain a strike mainspring for an old Seth Thomas ship's bell. I've had this clock so long I'm feeling ashamed to keep telling the customer I'm still trying to get it. I think you know the movement with a pin wheel strike. It has the regular balance wheel No. 12-40 on the plate. The material houses can't still supply it as the ones they have are too short.

The spring was missing altogether. However, the width is 5/16. Please let me know as soon as possible as to the source of this spring.

A.

We can't identify your Seth Thomas ship's bell from the marking "No. 12-40." From a Seth Thomas factory listing published in 1907 we have all the S. T. movements (supposedly) from No. 1 up through 101. Many have several variations, generally designated by a letter, such as No. 89-A. (Incidentally, that old 89 ran all the way down to 89-G). No. 12 was a metronome without bell. No. 40 was a small 8-day, pendulum movement.

The first Seth Thomas ship's bell striker was No. 7, and it is described thus: "No. 7—1 day, lever, New Ship's Bell. Crown 15, center ⅞ths. Length 7¾, width 5½, depth 2-14. Time mainspring No. 54, 6' x ⅝' by .018. Strike mainspring No. 73 6' x 5/16" x .016."

Seth did not make any radical change in this movement for many years. In fact, it is my thought that it will hold good for all the S.T. Ship's Bell strikers using the pins to lift the double hammers. It went through several "slight" modifications, but remained a ONE DAY piece. Could it be that you are trying to make this one into an eight-day? Enclosed three photos (keep them for your files). Note that neither place is numbered. The movement with hands upon it is the older. It goes into the case in the cased photo. Upon both photos you will note that the strike trip is in front of the front plate, yet wholly different. On the newer movement the main-strike wheel has been spoked-out, and the hammer-drop is adjustable by eccentric buttons. Upon both movements the strike has a 'going arbor'; that is, the ratchet is on the wheel and the arbor revolves as the clock strikes, while the time side has a stationary arbor, the click is upon the plate and the arbor remains still as the clock runs. I'm reasonably sure that: 1, yours is a ONE DAY movement; 2, that six feet is sufficient to drive it 30 hours; 3, that .016 thick is plenty strong. Would be glad to hear further from you on this.

MISSING PARTS

We have an 8-day, spring driven, no jewel Waterbury ship's bell clock in our shop for repair. Apparently there is a part missing in the striking mechanism as it will only strike an even number of bells.

I am enclosing a rough sketch of the back plate of the clock in hopes that you can tell me what part or parts are missing, their shape and purpose.

A.

Accompanying this answer are a photo of the Waterbury ship's bell clock, and a sketch of the missing part that you need.

The locking lever, marked No. 1 on the photo, carries an adjusting lever, No. 2, which is attached with a free-moving swivel connection. The bottom end of adjusting lever 2 rests against the curved tip of stop lever, No. 3, upon which it slides as the locking lever is raised and lowered. The cam behind the snail presents its high side to the lower end of adjusting lever 2 when the hands of your clock point to the half-hour. When striking the half (odd bells) the locking lever drops to its low position and the lower end of the adjusting lever 2 will strike the high side of the cam, thus crowding it over against the point of the adjusting stop lever 3, which brings the left hand end of this lever into the path of the hammer tail, No. 4, holding up the hammer and thereby preventing it from touching the gong on that last stroke.

You may obtain additional, illustrated details on the operation of this clock and also the Chelsea ship's bell striking mechanism assembly from the U.H.A.A. Technical Release No. 7, the Clockmaker's Issue.

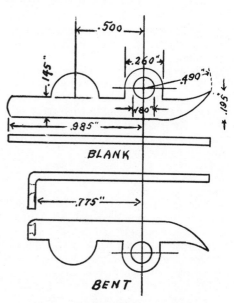

BLANK

BENT

Ship strike clock in error

I am seeking help on a Seth Thomas ship strike clock, 8-day model 115-C, which I have recently repaired and cleaned.

My trouble is the clock not striking correctly. It will strike correctly, but it repeats the same strike on the half-hour. The owner tells me it should strike 1 bell at 4:30 o'clock, 2 bells at 5 o'clock, 3 bells at 5:30 o'clock, 4 bells at 6 o'clock, 7 bells at 7:30 o'clock, 8 bells at 8 o'clock, and then it repeats the same from 8:30 to 12 o'clock, and 12:30 to 4 o'clock. I think my trouble may be the position of the starwheel to the hammer.

A.

The owner is entirely correct. As outlined in your letter it is the correct striking for ship's bell clocks. I'm not sure I understand when you say "I think my trouble may be the position of the star wheel to the hammer."

With nothing more specific to go on we shall have to quickly go over the basic strike system: note on your clock that it

is a "rack and snail" system; that the snail-wheel has three sets of steps; four steps to the set, and that it revolves once per 12 hours. Now, you can see that one set (or group) of steps will correspond to 12 to 4, the next from 4 to 8 and the third, 8 to 12, when it is ready to start the new revolution.

When the clock trips for the 1-bell stroke (12:30), the rack tail-piece should fall against the highest step and just far enough past its beginning edge to be positive. The strike train will take the hammer through two strokes, BUT the hammer stop lever drops to catch the hammer preventing it touching the gong on the final stroke and you hear just 1 bell. The minute hand now travels from 6 to 12 (12:30 to 1) and you must have 2 bells for 1 o'clock; this time the rack tailpiece falls on the highest step again and as the strike train takes the hammer through two strokes. The hammer stop lever does not act so you hear 2 bells.

Next, the minute hand travels from 12 to 6 (1:00 to 1:30) and you wish 3 bells for 1:30. The rack tailpiece falls upon the first edge of the second step and the strike train takes the hammer through four strokes, BUT, again the hammer stop lever cuts off the final stroke and the hammer reaches the bell only three times. By now you have observed the pin in the back of the wheel driving the snail. This wheel revolves once per hour, thus this pin is presented to the hammer stop lever once per hour—only at the half-hour stroke.

In other words, the four steps give you two, four, six, and eight strokes per step so far as the actual train operates; the hammer stop lever operates at the half-hour to cut off the final stroke and you actually hear 1, 2, 3, 4, 5, 6, 7, and 8 bells struck.

The New Seth Thomas Ship's Bell Movement

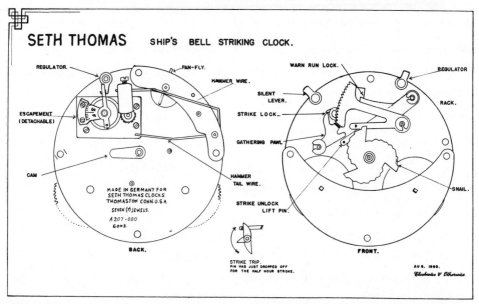

SETH THOMAS   SHIP'S BELL STRIKING CLOCK.

SEVERAL MONTHS AGO, Seth Thomas Clocks announced a new ship's bell striker. We mentioned it, then, and now have had opportunity to examine and study this new movement. Their new catalog (June 15, 1960) lists and illustrates four models equipped with movement No. "A-207-000"—the "Helmsman" 8¾ inches diameter, 3 inches deep with 4-inch silver-plated dial retails for $79.50 in the brass; $85 in chrome, has screw type waterproof bezel and special flange adjustable for front or flush mounting. For base mounting they provide a base 3⅝ inches high by 2½ inches deep by 10⅝ inches wide, retail $14.95.

The "Helmsman" clock-barometer combination has same clock with matching high-grade compensating barometer by Taylor for $181.50 in the brass and $192.50 in chrome. Base for combination may be had for $22.50.

The "Corsair" model has same case sans the ship's wheel, it is 5¾ inches in diameter by 3 inches deep with a 2¼-inch dial—retail $69.50 in brass and $75.00 in chrome. Base 3 inches high by 8 inches wide by 2¼ inches deep comes for $10.95.

The "Corsair" clock-barometer combination has matching Taylor barometer and retails for $153.95 in brass and $164.95 in chrome. Base, $14.95.

The A-207 movement has detachable, seven (7) jewel escapement mounted upon outside of back plate as indicated by sketch; solid balance, shock resistant jewels, temperature compensating hairspring; regulator coupled through the movement to dial and is adjustable just outside the minute track at 1 o'clock. Excellent construction but conventional and requires no detailed comment, neither does the rest of the time train whose second, third (center) and fourth wheels are contained between plates with 10 mm. inside clearance. Both the time and the strike barrels are located under a separate removeable bridge—clearance with back plate 21 mm. Ratchet wheels go next to inside of back plate, clicks held to inside of back plate by screws, both springs wind clockwise.

Basically, the principal problem encountered when designing a ship's bell striker comes in having the strokes executed in "pairs." Back around the turn of the century or shortly before, when Seth

455

Thomas produced the company's first Ship's Bell Striker, in order to get the double strokes they employed the "count" wheel system and double hammers (see page 313 Goodrich's Modern Clock). This necessitated lift-pins of two lengths, some actuating both hammers and the short ones just one hammer.

Such arrangement was fairly satisfactory but like all count-wheel strikers was not a self-corrector. Starting around the lifting wheel with the first short pin, we find six long ones; one short; four long ones; one short; two long ones; one short, and three long ones which brings us completely around the wheel and through four hours or full eight bells. This is not a "trick" arrangement but to say the least is odd, and has afforded many a headache to repairmen not accustomed to handling them.

Merely striking double strokes would be simple, but we must have odd numbers, 1, 3, 5 and 7, upon the half-hours and thus the problem boils down to what and how we do away with that last double of which we've used only one-half, in order to start the new (hour) stroke off with a clean double. The self-correcting feature of the rack and snail type strike was desirable and somewhere along the line, Waterbury, Seth Thomas and Chelsea all began to use it. They all obtained good results in the same way, i.e., building a clock that struck nothing but double strokes; by ingenious methods of catching the last stroke of the last double and preventing the hammer from reaching the gong they were able to get the "odd" strokes. The snail was cut with only four steps and in actual performance the time train executed 2, 4, 6 and 8 strokes, thus at one bell (12:30) the strike train did a double stroke but the last was prevented from reaching the gong and only one bell was heard. At 1 it did another double stroke and this time the hammer struck the bell both times for the two bells.

The A-207 is a plain, conventional, rack and snail striker; the strike train is the conventional six-member affair—main or barrelwheel; plus four wheels and fanfly. The hammer lift is a disc upon which is located 16 points by "pairs." It is carried upon the third arbor. The fourth arbor pivot extends through the front plate

and carries a double-pin disc type gathering pallet with two extra projections upon its edge extending at 90 degree angles from the pins. When the train has struck off the strokes allowed by the rack the gathering pawl drops under the end of the rack bringing the strike lock under one of these extra projections and thereby locking the train. The warn-run lock pin is located in the front side of the fifth-wheel.

The snail, located upon, and carried by the hour-pipe is a three section snail of eight steps upon each section—since the hour pipe revolves once in 12 hours, each 8-step section takes care of four hours.

Let us assume that your clock indicates 12:30 and our strike train has just tripped, the rack will fall upon the first, or, highest step and the train will perform one stroke for the "one bell." Now, as the points upon the hammer lift disc are in "pairs" this one stroke is the first stroke of a "pair." Note the inset sketch between the front and back sketches, the strike trip has three lift points, also our sketch shows the strike lift in its exact position at the instant of completing the one bell (12:30, 4:30 and 8:30) stroke.

Here is where the third lift (or strike trip) point comes into play and here is where we eliminate that left-over stroke from the "pair." As the minute hand progresses up to the 45-minute mark the third or short lift trips the strike in exactly the same manner French clocks do at the half-hour—it rises just enough to unlock the strike train but not far enough to permit the rack to fall; thus making the strike train perform just one stroke at 45 minutes. In the 45-minute position the cam indicated in the back sketch extends straight up, catching the hammer tail wire and preventing the hammer from reaching the gong on this stroke.

When the minute hand progresses on up to the hour stroke, the cam will have also progressed 90 degrees counter-clockwise and be in the exact position indicated upon the back sketch—entirely out from under the hammer tail wire, the rack will drop onto the second step of the snail; the clock will make one double stroke—two bells—for 1 (5 and 9) o'clock. It will be a full thirty minutes before the minute

456

hand will reach the half-hour point but there is no need for any action in the strike train because the hour stroke always completes the doubles and is ready to begin with doubles.

At this moment, the earliest date we have is: a clock in the C.A. Ilbert collection, dated ca. 1812 made by Morris Tobias, London, Baillie, says Tobias was granted a patent for a clock to strike ship's bells.

Ward L. Goodrich, said: "Of all the count wheel striking work which comes to the watchmaker, the ship's bell is most apt to give him trouble." He (Goodrich) devotes four pages plus two detailed drawings to explaining it and does not mention a rack and snail ship's bell striker at all; from this we could conclude that rack and snail ship's bell strikers weren't made before about 1900, at least in the U.S.A.

Seth Thomas was making them—count wheel system — in the 1880's, possibly earlier, and it seems pretty certain that Waterbury Clock Co., produced some before the turn of the century. It is logical to reason clockmakers turned to the rack and snail system in their efforts to construct a simpler and more satisfactory strike. Again, the who and the when is evasive, but it was here the half-pair, fraction problem set in.

One of the earlier U.S. patents went to H. H. Ham Jr., of Portsmouth, N. Y., May 6, 1879. We've encountered difficulty obtaining patent copy, but, feel sure that it must be a "count wheel" type—the late Paul Lux, patented a rack and snail strike in the early 1900's while with Waterbury.

The new Seth Thomas, A-207 was patented by Mr. Richard Kramer, to whom we are indebted for a patent copy as well as the opportunity of examining and photographing a movement, see figs. 1 and 2.

The front plate or under dial view, Fig. 1, plainly shows the three-section, eight-step snail as mounted upon the hour-pipe, and the regulating lever "E". Both the time and strike barrels are located under one single bridge; removable by backing off three hex nuts. The strike lock is indicated at "H"; the strike silencing lever at "F"; while the action of the rack as it falls upon the snail is plainly indicated.

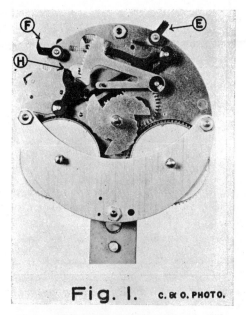

Fig. I. C. & O. PHOTO.

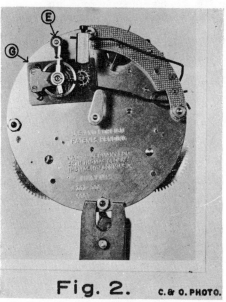

Fig. 2. C. & O. PHOTO.

Fig. 2, is our back view. The seven jeweled, shock-proof escapement is indicated at "G"; it is removable—by four screws; completely orthodox in its construction, and needs neither description or pointers for servicing. Again; the regulating lever is indicated by "E"—this photo was made with the clock's hands at the forty-five minute position (the same as in our drawing) and plainly shows how the silencing cam holds up the hammer tail piece when that last "half-pair" is struck at forty-five minutes.

The strike train is a "straight" six member, i.e. six arbor, train; in action the same as all straight trains. In our drawing the main or barrel arbor and the 2nd arbor have been omitted for the sake of clarity since they are only a pure power application; the sixth, or fan-fly has been left off for that same reason. Thus, those wheels indicated are: the number three arbor carrying the hammer-lift pins; the number four arbor with strike-lock and gathering pallets, and number five arbor carrying the warn-run lock pins.

Mr. Kramer, has solved the fraction problem; that of eliminating the last half of a pair, left over from the half-hour strike with a completely orthodox rack and snail strike, one operating in both principle and mechanically, exactly like all rack and snail strikers, i.e. the gathering pawl lifts up and clear of the rack at the hour, permitting the clock to make one stroke for each tooth of the rack that has to be gathered up. At the

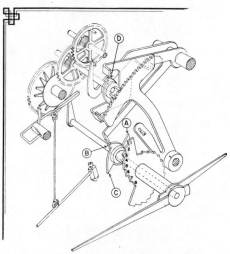

Strike Train Of The New SETH THOMAS Ship's Bell Clock Nº. A-207.

half hour the gathering pawl is actuated by a short lift raised just high enough to release the warn-run but not high enough to allow the rack to fall. Thus the clock performs one stroke and is again locked since the gathering pawl drops back behind the rack's end.

That, in principle and practice is exactly what the A-207 does. As indicated on both the photo and drawing, the snail is affixed to the hour-pipe and is divided into three snails of eight steps each; the hour-pipe revolving once per twelve hours gives the eight bells every four hours. While the hammer-lift pins are set by pairs, the train is so geared that each tooth or notch of the rack gathered-up accounts for just one stroke of the hammer.

The one and only deviation from the rack and snail strikers you are accustomed to handling is, a third short lift at the forty-five minute position. Now, let us say that strike lift "A" has tripped the strike train; and it has completed seven strokes for three-thirty. In that position your strike train is locked between a "pair" of strokes, or it has a "half-pair" left over. As the minute hand approaches the forty-five minute position the silencing cam comes under the hammer-tail; the short lift "B" unlocks the train but does not raise high enough to permit the rack to fall; just one stroke is performed; the hammer falls against the silencing cam; no sound is made but you throw away the "half-pair" left over from the seven stroke. Your minute hand advances to the sixty minute (hour position) and trip "C" raises the gathering pawl all the way up allowing the rack to drop into the eight step of the snail; the silencing cam, having advanced 90 degrees, is now out from under the hammer tail piece and the clock performs eight strokes of four-pairs— correctly—for four o'clock.

The cycle commences over again; there being no trip between the hour and the half-hour because at four-thirty, the rack will fall onto the one step and you'll get "one" bell, the half of a pair—the other half is again eliminated when the hand trips at the silent forty-five minute position.

The strike-train lock on the number four arbor at "D" is a double lock because the clock is geared to make two strokes for each revolution of number four; likewise it carries two gathering pallets; one for each stroke. Now by making one lock deep and the other short we have an "automatic" corrector —it can readily be seen that if the strike train were setting upon an even pair and ready to strike the hour that the short lift

"B" would not raise the locking lever high enough to clear the deep lock and thus the strike train would remain locked until the minute hand reaches sixty minute (hour) position when the long lift "C" would bring the locking lever high enough to clear the deep lock.

After a clean and overhaul job; setting in this strike train is just as simple as any other rack and snail—set the minute hand "almost" to the forty-five minute position; stake the strike lock (it and the gathering pallets are on one brass boss) on with the "short" lock in the locking position after making sure that the hammer lift is halfway between two close lift-pins, and, that the warn-run lock pin is about 45 degrees from the warn-run lock lever. Push the hand past the short trip (45) allowing the clock to strike off the half-pair; advance the minute hand to the hour position and set the snail on so that the rack falls squarely into the eight step—that's all.

A Battery Powered, Ship's Bell Striker

When Seth Thomas introduced a battery powered, hour and half-hour striker over a year ago, this column tested, photographed and wrote it up for the November 1967 "Otherwise." Its successful performance and immediate acceptance by the clock buying public made a Ship's Bell striker powered by a battery as natural as day follows the night.

The one major difference aside from the method by which the hammer strokes are delivered — in pairs — is: the regular hour and half-hour striker makes 180 strokes every 24 hour day, whereas the Ship's Bell striker operating via the subtractor system must lift the hammer forty times each watch, or, 240 times each 24 hours, thus it must perform a total of 60 strokes more than the orthodox striker each day. These additional strokes presented no mechanical problem at all; only the consumption of a very little more energy and since it was to be cell powered the only question remaining was a cell to last for the full twelve months. The good folk up at Thomaston solved that one with a mercury cell.

The orthodox striker was designated "A-209-000" (see page 37 Otherwise, November 1967). The new Ship's Bell striker has been given the number A-210-000. We are indebted to Mr. Richard Kramer, Special Projects Manager for General Time Corp., for a movement which we've had under test for a month.

Fig. I. Photo by J. E. Coleman

Fig. 1 is the front view of the movement and Fig. 2 is the back plate. It is the same caliber as the A-209-000 and operates upon the same principles. That is: the time is spring driven by a bridled spring which is wound by the strike motor a little each time the clock strikes. Both are powered by the same type motor and while there is a marked difference between the front and back bridges of these two movements, much of the material is interchangeable. Instead of the Smith floating balance the A-210 as a Swiss seven jeweled escapement, Incabloc shocks, and temp. compensated hairspring. The other major difference being the Ship's Bell count.

The contacting systems are identical; when the movement trips for a strike the spring contact "G" falls on to the round boss "C", Fig. 3, completing the electric circuit for the drive motor, which in turn drives the strike train for the number of strokes allotted to it by the step on strike snail. As the retaining pawl drops under

MOTOR→

Fig. 2.

Photo by
J. E. Coleman

Fig. 3

Photo by
J. E. Coleman

the strike rack at the last stroke the tail-piece "I" presses against the insulated pin "K" lifting the contact point "J" off the round boss and breaking the circuit. The Ship's Bell count is effected via the 'sub-tractor' system, that is the snail located upon the hour-pipe is divided into thirds so the strike cycle is repeated every third of a revolution; since the hour-pipe turns one rev. per twelve hours we get a repeat cycle each four hours, or, each eight bells. Each one-third section is a complete count snail con-sisting of four planes or steps spaced to allow the count-rack to drop for 2, 4, 6, and 8 strokes of the hammer. Each step is broad enough to have the count-rack fall upon its forward edge when the minute hand points to XII and still drop on its rear edge when the minute hand points to VI. The odd strokes for the half hours are had by simply

subtracting the final stroke. At 12:30, 4:30 and 8:30 the count rack drops on to the highest step near the forward edge; the strike train performs two strokes but the 'subtractor' has been brought into play and the final stroke is cut off so only one bell is heard.

At 1:00, 5:00 and 9:00 the count rack is again dropped on the highest step near its rear edge, again the strike train performs two strokes, the advance of the minute hand from pointing to VI to pointing to XII has turned the subtractor wheel by a quarter rev.—45 degree clockwise—bringing one pin "E" on that wheel under the subtractor lever raising it above the hammer tail piece thus allowing the hammer to make its full two strokes. By the time the hand has advanced another half-hour it has turned the sub-tractor wheel another quarter turn. This quarter removed the pin from holding the subtractor lever up, allowing it to descend to the cut-off position and subtract the last stroke. The count rack has dropped to the second, or four stroke step so with the last one eliminated the clock strikes the bell three times for 1:30, 5:30 and 9:30. This action is repeated on the third and fourth steps of the snail bringing the clock to the end of a four hour period when the next one-third section of the count snail is pre-sented to the count rack to begin a new cycle of eight bells for the next four hours.

An enlarged view of the strike side of No. A-210-000 is shown in Fig. 4. The subtractor wheel at "A" is driven by the dividing wheel, one half revolution per hour. Note the two pins set into this wheel — as it revolves to the right — clockwise — when the minute hand points to XII one of these pins has turned up under the tail piece of the subtractor lever "B" raising that lever up and out of the way of the strike hammer tail piece, thereby permitting all blows made by the strike hammer to sound upon the bell. When the clock progresses the next half-hour — minute hand pointing to VI — this lift pin has revolved forward by a quarter turn to bring it out from under the tail piece of the subtractor lever allow-ing that lever to drop under the tail piece of the strike hammer. When the strike is tripped, the strike train starts the strike operation; a pin set into the count rack

Fig. 4.

Photo by J. E. Coleman

shown at "C" comes up under the subtractor lever at the precise instant the gathering pallet raises the strike rack for the final stroke thereby bringing the end of the subtractor lever in line with the hammer tail piece, and when the hammer falls, the tail strikes the subtractor lever preventing the bell from being struck.

Fig. 2 is a back view of complete movement; the cell case is shown at "A". This clock takes the 1.4-volt mercury cell; Neda 1115, Mallory ZM-9, Eveready E-9, Burgess HG-9 or Ray-o-vac 15-M. A cell is inserted under a pry-off cap in the back of the case — make sure that the negative end is up (out) — mercury cells are all plainly marked by a plus on one and a minus on the other, the Eveready E-9 we have is also marked "neg." upon the end. This must show before pressing the cap home. The clock has a well made brass case, screw bezel; this is not as objectionable as with the spring-wind since you do not have to unscrew it once a week for winding.

To start the clock: Remove front bezel, check and make sure that the silentstrike lever protruding through the dial at the XI position is pushed to the strike position, marked "str." Then slowly turn the minute hand in the clockwise direction, pausing at the hour and half hour for the strike to complete its operation. Do this for a minimum of 36 bells. This action is necessary to wind the clock spring. Once this has been done further starting should not be required. It is set to the correct time in the usual manner, since this model is self correcting; it is not necessary to wait upon the strike when setting — it is regulated in the usual manner, a lever protrudes through the dial at the I o'clock position, marked s. and f. The strike may be shut off at any time by moving that lever to "sil." A well made brass case, dial is silver with black Arabic numerals, 13 to 00 inside the twelve. Comes in the "Corsair" model — plain bezel — and the "Helmsman" model with ship's wheel bezel, either for bulkhead mounting, or with a base for shelf use. For a semi-flush bulkhead mounting, Corsair model only, remove three screws in back of front bezel; remove three screws in back flange; slide flange forward to front holes and remount. Use remaining three screws in the back holes.

The Waterbury Ship's Bell Striker

Ship's time divides the 24-hour day into six watches of four hours each. A watch is further sub-divided into eight bells each, the odd bells indicating the half-hour. Thus, the "forenoon" watch from eight to twelve a.m. is struck: eight bells for 8 o'clock, four pairs of double strokes. 8:30 o'clock 1 bell, 9 o'clock 2 bells, 9:30 o'clock 3 bells, 10 o'clock 4 bells, 10:30 o'clock 5 bells, 11 o'clock 6 bells, 11:30 o'clock 7 bells—here the strike cycle has been completed and 12 o'clock is 8 bells to begin a new cycle—repeating again at 4 o'clock, 8 o'clock, etc.

Once understood, the first thing mechanically indicated is that the cycle is repeated each four hours; then the clockmaker will see that his striking device has "come full circle" and starts the system all over again.

Ever watchful to pin down some of those dates in horology that are either unknown or questionable, we have, for more years than I care to recall, tried to establish the origin of the ship's bell striker—who? when? and where? No real luck. Their origin could be German but I would not rule out the possibility of the U.S. to be first.

Turning to that volume researched and produced by the late George H. Eckhardt —privately printed, 1960—titled: "United States Watch & Clock Patents 1790 to 1890" we find that only one patent is listed under the heading of Ship's Bell Strike, listed as: No. 215,057, issued May 6, 1879, to one H. H. Ham Jr., of Portsmouth, N. H. One of the fascinating features of all research being that same is far from an exact exercise; one never knows when all the precincts have been heard from and thus all the votes in and counted. We can NOT accept this Eckhardt, single listing as being the one and only U.S. patent for the very simple reason others are known. Neither can we chalk it up as any error upon his part. In the early 1930's we endeavored to research the first half century—1790 to 1840—of the horological patents issued by the Patent Office. Publishing same in June of 1938. Mr. Eckhardt, had this list and wrote about it at the beginning of his project, thus we were "hep" to his project and know that a great deal of time went into

it over nearly a decade before the m/s. went to the printer. His single ship's bell listing appears upon page 23 while a section devoted to clock striking mechanisms begins at page 42. In this section is patent No. 221,210 issued just six months later, November 4, 1879, to one Dudley W. Bradley, of Brooklyn, N. Y., and assigned to Seth Thomas Clock Co.

This patent deals solely with the bell system and should have been in the page 23 listing. The fault here lies with the Patent Office, they so listed it and chances are Mr. Eckhardt had no way of knowing its particular nature. We have been told that the Patent Office has been adapting its listings to the computer; it is hoped that sub-heading will be elaborated upon as well as the computer kicking out a more accurate listing.

Engineering the 'bells' system involved more than merely making the clock revert back to one after having struck eight; the strokes of necessity to follow the on-board method had to be delivered in "pairs." Every strike system must be a "counter," and the counting falls into two divisions; the first a count wheel and/or disc wherein each successive operation increases the strokes by one each time tripped until this count wheel had completed one revolution to start the cycle all over again. The common hour and half-hour striker must perform 78 hammer blows to strike twelve hours with an additional twelve blows for the halves, making a total of 90 hammer strokes every twelve hours, or, one revolution of the count wheel. The second system, we know as the rack and snail. A twelve-step snail revolving once per twelve hours is utilized; the count-rack is permitted to fall upon these steps thereby counting the strokes. This system also performs the same ninety hammer blows per twelve hours.

The Ship's Bell system, striking from one to eight, each four hours must deliver thirty-six hammer blows in pairs. This totals 108 strokes for the twelve hours, or eighteen more strokes than the orthodox striker. When you multiply this by two for

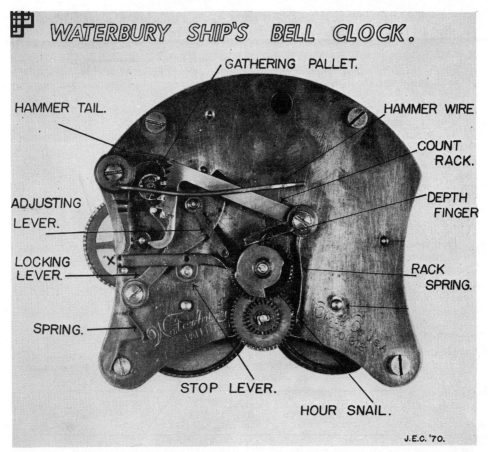

WATERBURY SHIP'S BELL CLOCK.

GATHERING PALLET.

HAMMER TAIL.

HAMMER WIRE

COUNT RACK.

DEPTH FINGER

ADJUSTING LEVER.

LOCKING LEVER.

RACK SPRING.

SPRING.

STOP LEVER.

HOUR SNAIL.

J.E.C. '70.

the 24-hour day, it comes out 36 more strokes. Herein lies the reason that early Ship's Bell strikers were one-day. Take the modern, eight-day clock and you can see that in it's eight-day run it has to deliver 156 more blows, requiring a different gearing as well as a longer or stronger mainspring.

Seth Thomas was the first American manufacturer to market a ship's bell striker and for the lack of any better date we shall have to take the 1879 patent as approximate. The Bradley system employed a count wheel and used two hammers to obtain the "pair" stroking. To achieve correct stroking by pairs, this system utilizes hammer-lift pins of different lengths, some pins acting upon both hammers while others can actuate only one hammer, the end result being a rather "complicated" strike set-up. One that has given many a clockmaker a pulsing headache and we suspect may be

the root cause of some of the shyness seen among bench clockmakers for servicing them. And, plenty lengthy for an article all its own, which we shall take up at a later date.

So far as we are able to determine, only four U.S. manufacturers have produced ship's bell strikers—Seth Thomas, Waterbury, and Chelsea; with G.E. producing some sync ship's bell.

Waterbury and Chelsea only one model each, both utilizing the rack and snail, while Seth Thomas, has produced three and one half models, the first the count-wheel the second and third the rack and snail, and assigning the half to the same rack and snail model but battery powered.

Back to our subject illustrated here. Patent No. 892,067, granted to Mr. Paul Lux, June 30, 1908, and assigned to The Waterbury Clock Co., we believe to be the first of the rack and snail types. Mr. Paul Lux was the father of Mr. Fred Lux, founder of the Lux Clock Co. It is said that when Superintendent of the Waterbury factory, Mr. Paul, posted upon the bulletin board, "Our clocks go, or we go." both father and son were employed by Waterbury at one time.

When Mr. Fred, returned from World War I, he founded his company and his father came with him. In 1954 The Lux Company opened a second factory at Lebanon, Tenn.; it was at that branch opening we enjoyed the privilege of discussing this clock with Mr. Fred Lux. He was most familiar with it and I gained the idea that he had bench serviced many of them, etc.

Our photo of this movement is practically self-explanatory. Some 25 or 30 years back, we took in one of these clocks from which some "joker" had removed—and lost—several of the strike parts—the factory could not supply parts, but, were kind enough to furnish detailed drawings of five of these items. We have "copied" each of them and reproduce them through this article as Figs. 1, 2, 3 and 4. These sketches are not to scale, but, correct measurements are thereon noted. These sketches should enable the bench clockmaker to make such parts as he may need as well as to better fully understand the mechanical action.

Note: first, that the snail is outside and upon the back of the movement; that it revolves counter-clockwise; one revolution each four hours. Upon the back side of the hour snail wheel is a cam, this cam

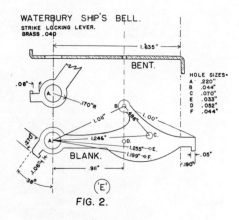

WATERBURY SHIP'S BELL.
STRIKE LOCKING LEVER.
BRASS .040

HOLE SIZES·
A .220"
B .044"
C .070"
D .052"
E .033"
F .044"

FIG. 2.

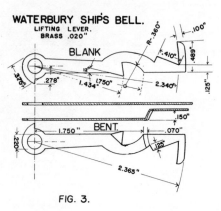

WATERBURY SHIP'S BELL.
LIFTING LEVER.
BRASS .020"

FIG. 3.

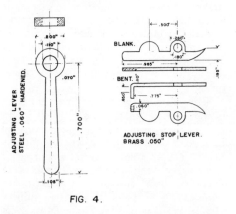

WATERBURY SHIP'S BELL.

FIG. 4.

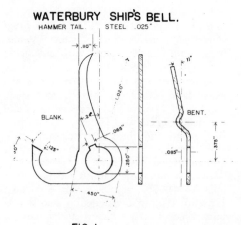

WATERBURY SHIP'S BELL.
HAMMER TAIL.   STEEL .025"

FIG. I.

is presented to the adjusting lever Fig. 4, at the half-hour position. In this position; when the clock trips for the strike as the final pair is executed, one stroke hits the bell, the locking lever drops behind the low lock notch of the count rack; the free end of the adjusting lever strikes this cam thus throwing it against the inner end of the stop lever pushing that end of the lever down making its other end move up into the path of the little extension on the strike hammer thereby preventing that last stroke from striking the bell at "X" on the photo.

SCHATZ SHIP'S BELL

Having a deuce of a time with a Schatz Marine Clock. I cannot get it to strike the odd number bells on the half hour. It strikes the even number of bells on the hour and then strikes the same number of bells on the following half hour. Do you have any suggestions? Ego-wise, I'm happy to say that three other local watchmakers couldn't find the trouble.

A.

Now, to your Ship's bell striker: the construction of various models very a little, but in the main the basic principal is the same. Note that you have a four-step snail; that it strikes two on the high step, four on the next step; six on the next and eight on the lowest step. The clock should be set up so that the rack falls upon the front edge of the high step. With the hands at 12:30 it will strike two, but there is a pin or lifting lever so connected to that half-hour position that it flips up just after the first stroke and the second stroke does not hit the gong, allowing you ONE Bell. When the hands advance to the 1:00 position, the rack falls upon the back (last) edge of the high step of the snail— again two strikes, but the pin at the half hour has advanced by 180 degrees and is out of the way of the hammer, thereby permitting two bells. By the time the hands reach 1:30 the pin has advanced another 180 degrees and is in position to cut off that last stroke. The rack falls to the front edge of the second step, the strike train performs four strikes, again the flip cuts off the last hammer from touching the gong and you get the correct three bells for 1:30, etc.

SHIP'S BELL GENERAL INFO.

THE ACTUAL ORIGIN of the Ship's Bell striker is quite clouded in horological history; whether in England, on the continent, or in the U.S.A., we have not been able to pinpoint after much effort towards that end.

Ship's Bell strikers are quite popular, especially among seafaring folk and have been manufactured by most large manufacturers. Two tower clocks that sound ships bells were built by Seth Thomas— we've heard of at least two watches, both specially built, Swiss—they are popular with some folk simply for the "novelty" or that one is enabled to ascertain the correct hour from its half-hour strike.

Seth Thomas began building them in the 1870s upon a plan patented by Dudley W. Bradley, No. 221,210 November 4, 1879; this was a count-wheel system utilizing two separate hammers to obtain the double stroke effect. Mechanically, it was simple enough to have two hammers lifted by the same pin give the double stroke effect by merely making the lift tail of one a bit shorter than the other. This system prevailed in the industry for about thirty years or until Mr. Fred Lux, of the Waterbury Clock Co. adapted the rack and snail method to the double stroke system, patent No. 892,067 June 30, 1908—see this column for January 1971—by permitting the strike train to perform an even number of strokes at each operation and by providing an ingenious device that would prevent the hammer from striking the bell upon the final stroke at the half hour to obtain the odd number.

Seth Thomas stuck by the old double hammer, count wheel method 'til about 1920 when one of their model makers, a Mr. Frank X. Wehrle, patented a rack and snail system—patent No. 1,394,957 Oct. 25, 1921—substantially like the Lux method, by eliminating the final stroke to attain the odd numbers. Seth Thomas designated this movement with the number 115, and it is now coming to the repair bench for servicing and is the subject of this Otherwise.

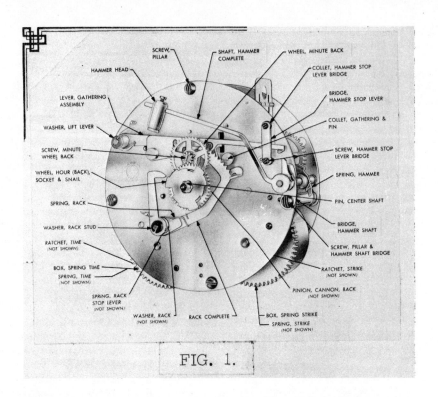

SCREW, PILLAR

HAMMER HEAD

LEVER, GATHERING ASSEMBLY

WASHER, LIFT LEVER

SCREW, MINUTE WHEEL BACK

WHEEL, HOUR (BACK), SOCKET & SNAIL

SPRING, RACK

WASHER, RACK STUD

RATCHET, TIME (NOT SHOWN)

BOX, SPRING TIME

SPRING, TIME (NOT SHOWN)

SPRING, RACK STOP LEVER (NOT SHOWN)

WASHER, RACK (NOT SHOWN)

RACK COMPLETE

SHAFT, HAMMER COMPLETE

WHEEL, MINUTE BACK

COLLET, HAMMER STOP LEVER BRIDGE

BRIDGE, HAMMER STOP LEVER

COLLET, GATHERING & PIN

SCREW, HAMMER STOP LEVER BRIDGE

SPRING, HAMMER

PIN, CENTER SHAFT

BRIDGE, HAMMER SHAFT

SCREW, PILLAR & HAMMER SHAFT BRIDGE

RATCHET, STRIKE (NOT SHOWN)

PINION, CANNON, BACK (NOT SHOWN)

BOX, SPRING STRIKE

SPRING, STRIKE (NOT SHOWN)

FIG. 1.

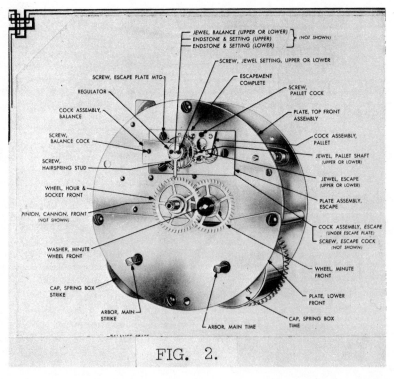

JEWEL, BALANCE (UPPER OR LOWER)
ENDSTONE & SETTING (UPPER) ⎤ (NOT SHOWN)
ENDSTONE & SETTING (LOWER) ⎦

SCREW, JEWEL SETTING, UPPER OR LOWER

SCREW, ESCAPE PLATE MTG.

REGULATOR

COCK ASSEMBLY, BALANCE

SCREW, BALANCE COCK

SCREW, HAIRSPRING STUD

WHEEL, HOUR & SOCKET FRONT

PINION, CANNON, FRONT (NOT SHOWN)

WASHER, MINUTE WHEEL FRONT

CAP, SPRING BOX STRIKE

ARBOR, MAIN STRIKE

ESCAPEMENT COMPLETE

SCREW, PALLET COCK

PLATE, TOP FRONT ASSEMBLY

COCK ASSEMBLY, PALLET

JEWEL, PALLET SHAFT (UPPER OR LOWER)

JEWEL, ESCAPE (UPPER OR LOWER)

PLATE ASSEMBLY, ESCAPE

COCK ASSEMBLY, ESCAPE (UNDER ESCAPE PLATE)

SCREW, ESCAPE COCK (NOT SHOWN)

WHEEL, MINUTE FRONT

PLATE, LOWER FRONT

ARBOR, MAIN TIME

CAP, SPRING BOX TIME

FIG. 2.

466

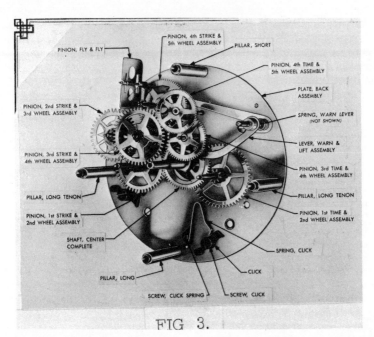

FIG 3.

It was produced in goodly numbers over a forty year period until superseded by their present ship's bell striker which was invented by Mr. Richard Kramer—patent No. 2,974,473 March 14, 1961—which came on the market as model A-207, detailed in this column June 1964. Shortly thereafter, it was altered to a battery power but the exact same striking arrangement retained—today, both the spring wound and the battery models are available.

Checking back over those questions we've received upon the ship's bell striker during the past two years indicated that nine out of every ten were occasioned by the bench horologist not knowing what his movement was supposed to strike, thus repeat it here seems in order.

On board ship, the day is divided into six watches of four hours each—a "watch" of four hours is struck on the ship's bell one to eight strokes; the strokes are by pairs, thereby making it easy to distinguish the halves from the hours—12:30 being one bell; 1:00 two bells; 1:30 three bells; 2:00 four bells; 2:30 five bells; 3:00 six bells; 3:30 seven bells and 4:00 o'clock eight bells. The cycle being repeated each four hours.

The S. T. 115 and 115-A movements execute this strike system with a rack and snail strike mechanism with a single hammer, all of which would be simple enough but for the fact that this hammer has to deliver its blows in pairs. The odd bells are had by simply having the strike train always deliver even strokes but having that final stroke locked from reaching the bell; thus the strike train actually trips the hammer an even number of times, but the final blow is prevented from reaching the bell and only an odd number is heard by the listener.

The three illustrations shown here are practically self-explanatory and by reason of that warrant careful and special study. Practically every detail of the 115 is plainly portrayed and thus our "One Picture—One Thousand Words" title. Fig. 2 is a view of the front of the front plate; shows the dial train and the jeweled escapement, neither of which calls for any special comment and/or instructions as they are identical with those encountered every day on the repair bench.

Fig. 3, shows the strike train set in upon front plate, i.e. the lower plate when the movement is down upon your bench, again no special comment as it is all clearly laid out.

Fig. 1, is a view of the back plate—equally well laid out, but, since this is the one that portrays the "subtractor" device some further explanations are called for.

Note the snail pivoted at the center, revolving as the hour-hand, once per twelve hours—this really is three snails, each with four steps. Divide your three snails into the twelve hours per rev. and you get each snail serving for four hours, or eight bells. Off the first step—the highest one—the strike train performs two hammer strokes; from the second one four hammer strokes; the third one six, and the fourth eight.

At 12:30 the rack falls on to the first step—near its forward edge and the strike train performs two hammer strokes; the second or final stroke is interrupted by the hammer stop lever and only one bell is heard. At 1:00 the rack falls to the same first step back near its heel, the same two strokes are performed and both are permitted to strike the bell so two bells are heard, etc.

What has happened between 12:30 and 1:00? At the cannon pinion behind the snail is a cam; at 12:30 this cam was straight up, that is pointing to the XII o'clock position. When it is in this spot the gathering lever assembly, falling behind the rack, strikes this cam raising the little stop lever upon the end of the gathering lever assembly and catches the tail piece of the hammer thus preventing it striking the bell so that you hear only one bell sounded. Comes 1:00 o'clock, the cannon pinion has revolved by 180 degrees and the cam is pointing downward—the two strokes are again performed and this time the stop lever is held up by gravity—note the little counter-balance at the back of the gathering lever—out of the path of the hammer and two bells are heard.

This bit of mechanical operation may seem a bit upon the "tricky" side, yet it is quite simple and once the clockmaker knows exactly what he wishes the strike train to perform he encounters no trouble. Once you have your movement assembled, place the minute hand—opposite side from Fig. 1—to the 6:00 o'clock position, pointing straight down; then place on the back cannon pinion with its cam straight up. Next set in the snail to that position where

the rack just drops positive to the forward edge of the high step; you are in position for the one stroke. Advance the minute hand forward to the hour position and note that the rack drops positive on to the heel of the high step, and you have it correctly set up. Check the little hammer stop lever to make sure that it is perfectly free upon its pivot; NEVER place any oil at this point, it will eventually gum and stick and cause the clock to deliver erratic strokes.

Once understood by the bench mechanic, servicing the ship's bell striker is a pleasure and we have never understood why some clockmakers shy away from them—generally, they are better constructed than the lowly eight-day striker, and their owners seem to give them better attention—a point that favors the repairman for no matter how well you execute your service job, the clock must get the proper and regular attention to perform properly.

Schatz Clock Has Quirks

I am writing about a Schatz Ship Bell Clock; 2 Jewel; No. 14400. It has a caged escapement — 2 screws remove the escapement from the movement. It was bought about two years ago and was running fast for about 1 year. It now stops and will start when I touch the minute hand, but it then only goes a little while and stops. This is a new experience with me although I have been repairing watches for a number of years.

The Schatz movement stops between hours – say 12:15 p.m. to 12:45 p.m. and between other hours, too.

The Schatz clock was bought in Bermuda about two years ago. Can you give me any information about this clock? I have cleaned and oiled the clock which does not seem to help any.

A.

It is difficult to spot the stoppage in your Schatz ship's bell striker and I fear we may not be as successful as last time.

Apparently the stoppage is due to lack of power. To locate what is shutting the power off is the problem. Since the stops come at any and odd points, the chances are it is NOT the strike lift, etc. because that comes with regularity.

Remove the hands, the dial, the hour-wheel and the dividing wheel and see how long it will run. It just could be a bind within the dial train. This would tell. If it continues to stop, mark the last three wheels of the train at the point of tooth entry, re-start it and allow to run until next stop; observe your marks to note if a tooth is ready to enter, etc. Try this three or four times to make sure that you do not have a bent and/or rough tooth.

BULOVA SHIP'S BELL

Two new clocks this month — the good folk up in Bulova Park have added the ship's bell striker to the "Bulova" clock line. The "Shipmate" illustrated above, is a simple circle in shape, overall diameter seven inches; dial 5¼, and a depth of 3¾ inches. It is a hinged, port-hole type bezel, four-jewel movement with compensating hairspring priced at $135 for bulk-head mounting, or may be placed upon individual mahogany stand for shelf or mantel placement.

The individual mahogany base is priced at $16.50. A matching aneroid barometer with a double thermometer — Fahrenheit and Centigrade — may be had for $85; the individual mahogany base for the barometer is also $16.50 or if it is desired to mount both instruments upon a double mahogany stand it is available at $23.50.

Bulova has given this model the designation of "Style B-1850" for the clock, and for the barometer "B-1840."

The second model, the "Yachtsman," is designated "Style B-1851 for the clock, and "B-1841" for the barometer. The "Yachtsman" is in the style of a ship's wheel, overall diameter 6½ inches; dial 3¼ inches, depth 2 inches; seven jeweled movement priced at $140. It too may be mounted as with the "Shipmate" upon either a double mahogany base, or, single bases — the barometer is priced at $85 — the double mahogany base at $21, while a single base comes for $16.50. Both the time and strike trains of these clocks closely follow orthodox construction and thus do not require any special instructions for servicing. Both movements are provided with a strike hammer lock device. On the model B-1850 there is located a slotted screw at the top of the back of the clock underneath which are two bells and the words "On" and "Off." The hammer should NEVER be locked while the strike train is in operation — wait until the strokes are completed and the train is latched of itself. It should always be locked to transport and/or ship. To silence the strike-train: on the B-1850 there is a slot and a lever — identified by the engraving of a bell — located upon the clock dial opposite the three o'clock position.

When ship's bell strike is desired the lever is moved upward toward the bell — to silence, the lever is moved downward. This lever should also be in the down position for ship and transport. Upon model B-1851 the control lever is opposite the eleven o'clock spot and should be handled as on the B-1850.

"Repairwise", servicing these clocks is going to be easy as Mr. George Doerr, of the clock division tells us that Bulova will have a complete line of parts — that such parts as cases and dials, etc., are upon a 24-hour turnabout. Movement parts ordered will require a little bit longer; if you can supply the specific part number it will help to cut down on the elapsed time. A self-addressed, stamped envelope to Mr. Doerr, Clock Division, 58-51 Maspeth Ave., Maspeth, NY 11378, will bring you parts list for both models as well as a little instruction booklet. The ship's bell strike is had by the subtracter system, i.e. each time the strike train is tripped for operation, the hammer is lifted 2, 4, 6, or 8 times. The odd bells, 1, 3, 5, and 7 at the half-hour are had by simply subtracting the last hammer blow from the even operation — there being a little cam upon the hour-post. When the minute hand points to VI o'clock where you require an "odd" bell, this cam actuates a little lever that flips up to prevent that last hammer blow from reaching the bell. At 12:30 the strike rack drops on to the toe of the high section of the strike snail; the minute hand points to VI, the train performs two hammer lifts, but the final blow is prevented from reaching the bell as the subtracter lever flips up. At 1:00 the strike rack drops on to the heel of the same high segment of the snail. Having turned 180 degrees, the cam at the center-post is out of the way and both strokes reach the bell giving you two bells for one o'clock, etc.

It is necessary that this system be completely understood when reassembling the clock. The minute hand must be positioned so that the cam is brought into the operation when it points to VI, and the snail must be positioned so that the rack falls upon the toe of the step. Otherwise no sweat.

Though radically different from the orthodox twelve-hour striker, the ship's bell system is easily understood from an inhand examination — where the twelve hour striker has just one snail revolving with the hour hand once per twelve hours, the ship's bell system has a triple snail still revolving once per twelve hours thus dividing it into three segments of four hours each — 12 to 4:00, 4:00 to 8:00 and 8:00 back to 12.

ADJUSTING S.T. SHIP'S BELL STRIKE

I received a Seth Thomas Ships Clock to be put into running order. This clock was in a loose parts condition I assembled it, and it is keeping good time. I have the hours striking fine, the half hours, I am having trouble, with the right strike. The strike the same as the hour. Could you give me any advice. What may I be overlooking or am doing wrong. Any advice or suggestions will be appreciated. I am sure that there are no missing parts.

A.

You do not indicate which model S.T. ships bell striker you have; thus we can't reach into minute details. Anyway, since you say that your clock strikes the same number of strokes on the half hour as it strikes on the hour, indicates that you have a rack strike with a 'pick-up' which takes care of the halves—odd strokes.

There should be a four step snail wheel geared to revolve once every four hours. The first or high step allows the strike train to perform two strokes. Now your rack should drop on to this snail upon the front edge of the high step at 12:30, minute hand at 6. The strike train will actually perform two strokes-—BUT—with the minute hand at the half-hour point there should be a little cam on the center-post just outside the back plate which cam brings a spring and lever into play and as the hammer falls for the second stroke this lever prevents the hammer from reaching the gong, thus only one stroke is heard.

When the clock advances to 1:00, minute hand at 12, this cam has advanced by a half turn and is upon the opposite side from high step, exactly the same distance down it did at the half-hour and your strike train again performs two strokes. Since the cam is on the opposite side from the spring and lever it does NOT cut off that last stroke and two strokes are heard upon the gong.

Again, when the hand has advanced to 1:30 the cam is back on the spring side; the rack falls on to the second step; a depth correct for four strokes—the train performs four strokes and the cam cutting of that last one, only three are heard. It then advances to 2:00; the rack falls upon the back edge of second step of the snail and all four strokes are heard for the two o'clock.

This same cycle is repeated every hour until you get your full eight strokes, bells at four o'clock. The snail has completed its full revolution by the time the minute hand reaches 3:30 where exactly the same action takes place as of 12:30 giving you one bell.

Either your cam is out of place—or for some reason the lever fails to cut off that last stroke. We hope that this will enable you to correct the trouble—if not, write again and we'll have another go at it.

GRANDFATHER CLOCKS

JOEL WHITE

I have a grandfather clock made by Joel White, marked Woodstock. The works are brass and the face is brass. The cabinet is made of white pine and maple.

Could you tell me anything about Joel White, when he lived and the probable age of this clock?

There is a Woodstock in New Hampshire and I presume this is the Woodstock where Joel White lived, although it is possible the clock works could have come from England.

A.

Since we cannot locate a "Joel White" in any of the lists, we can't be sure that your guess of Woodstock, New Hampshire, is either right or wrong.

There is a Woodstock in Windham County, Connecticut. (Northeast corner of the state.)

Mr. Brooks Palmer lists a Peregrine White, 1747-1837, Woodstock, Connecticut, as the son of Joseph and Martha Sawyer White, having a shop west of Muddy Brook village well equipped with metal working tools. He was a maker of tall clocks with excellent brass movements for many years. Some dials engraved; later he used enameled iron dials.

E. UNDERWOOD

The only markings or clues of any sort that we have been able to discover on the dial are "High Water at Bristol Key" and "Underwood, 35 Old Market St., Bristol." The clock is a grandfather clock with an eagle and brass bull on the top. It has just two weights. It is wound with a key and has a pendulum. The case has a tiny bit of inlay.

The clock books list four Underwoods in England, but not this one. In fact, we
have not been able to uncover any information at all about this timepiece.

A.

Baillie lists, "Ebenezer Underwood, Bristol, 1818." The directory (Bristol) for the year 1818 contains the following entry: "Underwood, Ebenezer, Clockmaker, Upper Easton (parish of St. Philip and Jacob)."

By 1830 he had moved out to Britton, Glos., a village not far from Bristol. By 1835 entries relating to him in the directories cease.

Ebenezer Underwood was the son of Stephen William Underwood, a schoolmaster, and was apprenticed on Jan. 5, 1811, to John Edgecumber and Ann, his wife. He became a burgess of Bristol on June 11, 1818. The Edgecumbers lived in Old Market Street, a street which exists in Bristol to this day. While the city directories do not give that address for Underwood, those addresses given could be his residence rather than his shop.

From the above, it is safe to conclude that your clock was made between 1818 and about 1835. Further, about this period it was popular to add various things to the grandfather clock. Many had calendars, showed the moon phases, etc., and some showed the tides. It is my thought that the scale at the top of your dial marked, "High Water at Bristol Key" possibly was intended to show the tides there. Naturally these were not too plentiful, and possibly in that way, adds to the rarity of your piece.

J. E. MILLIKEN

I have for repair a grandfather clock made by J. E. Milliken, Concord. The notation inside the case is "Sot up May 1800."

During what period was Milliken active?

The numerals on the clock face are faded. Can these best be restored with drawing ink and lettering pen, or what do you recommend?

The moon-phase dial carries two moons which rise and disappear behind two semicircular discs. Did this type come into use prior to the Brocot type? I note that Brocot is shown by Millison to have lived between 1817 and 1878, which raises some doubt as to the date this clock was "sot up;" unless the moon-phase setup used here antedates Brocot's.

A.

Your grandfather clock becomes interesting since none of the American writers list a "Milliken." Baillie (English) lists one Jonathan Milliken at Newbury Port, U. S. A., about 1790.

Newbury Port is some seventy-five miles from Concord, and Jonathan could be the same as "J. E." A check of the Massachusetts Historical Society, by writing to Boston, might determine this.

If J. E. and Jonathan were one and the same, then your clock could have easily been "Sot up May 1800."

Faded lettering (numerals) can be helped with India ink, however, I prefer paint. I'm reasonably sure that the type of moon dial you mention is much earlier than the "Brocot" type. (Brocot was born in Paris in 1817 and died in 1878). Evidently the two moons are used in this construction for convenience. The two hemispheres on your dial are nothing more than decorative; the fact that they are circular and the moon rose from behind the left one and set behind the right one, creates a very good imitation of the movement of the moon.

The lunar month is 29½ days; this is usually laid out on the circle just above the moon disc. This disc will have one hundred and eighteen teeth (ratchet style) cut into its outer rim, and is advanced by a pin in the hour-pipe, one tooth each revolution of the hour-pipe or two teeth per twenty-four hour day. Thus the moon disc makes one complete revolution every fifty-

nine days; split that in half by using two moons and you have the necessary 29½ days for the lunar month. After all, this shows the age of the moon rather than being built to simulate the various moon phases.

REQUIRED WEIGHT

I recently took a seven-foot hall clock into my shop for repairs. It has no trade name or frame number. It has a Graham escapement. As I dismantled the works from the case, I noticed the unusually large, heavy weights that hung on the chains. The clock had been in the shop of a clock quack posing as a clockmaker, previously. The clock shows that all over in the repair. The weight on the time chain is 2¼ inches in diameter and 12 inches long. Both weights are of solid iron and are very heavy. The repairman had obviously put this heavier weight on to overcome some fault that he himself could not locate or repair. I have worked on a number of hall and grandfather clocks, but I have never run into this situation before. I want to do a first-class repair job on this clock but I don't think these weights are the correct size. Can you give me information concerning the method of calculating the correct size in pounds and ounces of weights for weight-driven clocks?

A.

You are going to be disappointed in our answer to your question: How to determine the correct weight for your clock. First, we can't give you any simple, direct rule, and second, we are going to say that in all probability the weights you have are the originals. This is based on the fact that you say the weights go by chain, which indicates that your movement does not fall within the precision class. We've seen many long-case movements, weights going by ladder-link chain over a sprocket which weights (as supplied by the factory) were rough as any pig-iron and much in excess of the required weight.

The most practical shop method for determining the required weight is by trial and error. Put the movement in order, place it on your timing rack and secure some convenient container — an old tin can (diameter small enough to prevent its touching the

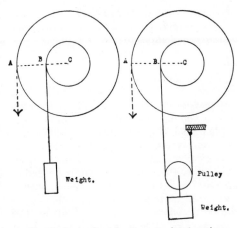

Sketch drawn for Mr. Rayman showing the methods of weight application.

You can readily see that: if the weight is ten pounds, in the single fall the gravitational pull at B will be ten pounds while in double fall the gravitational pull at B will be only five pounds. Also that if the radius of the drum, BC is one-half the radius of the main wheel AC, the moment of force at A will be just one-half of that at B. Thus in the case of the double fall, a ten-pound weight is only exerting 2½ pounds at A.

Throughout your clock train, you apply the force to the pinion, or, at the smallest radius; thus that force is in the same manner reduced, and you have this problem again for each wheel in the train. Aside from that feature, you have the ever present problem of friction.

Friction, in the train of a given clock, may be determined by rigging a counterbalanced lever to your escape wheel arbor; placing a given weight at a given distance from the center and determining how much weight is required to lift it, yet with all the above done, you still have to account for the diameter of your escape wheel, the distance the impulse faces are from their pivoted center, the length of your crutch wire, and, at what point it applies power to the pendulum, etc. It should now be clear that for speed and practical results the tin can trial and error method is probably best for general shop use.

Calculating d r i v i n g weights centers around the mechanical "Principal of Work" contained in the axiom "What is gained in force is lost in speed and what is gained in speed is lost in force." In clocks we maintain the motion of the pendulum by a small force delivered from a relatively fast moving part.

This small force is the outcome of a series of varying forces and speeds from the original driving weight which is slow motion at high pressure. At any step in this process, the actual amount of work done is the same (except for loss by friction), because as the force is reduced the distance traveled by the acting part is proportionately greater for any given length of time.

pendulum ball or the other weight) to which you can attach a wire bail to hook onto the line. Load this container with scrap metal or any convenient weight. Set the pendulum in motion and listen to the beat; adjust the amount of weight to the point you think is about right. By trying the timing for 24 hours you may determine whether or not you have sufficient driving weight to maintain operation. Take out a little and try again until you determine just about the required amount. Place your can on the scales and weigh — add about 10 per cent for a safety factor and you will have a passable, practical job. After determining the number of pounds, most repairmen cast their weights of lead. Where the case is wood (the weights do not show) without glass windows, rough weights are passable and may be poured into heavy cardboard mailing tubes. Where brass weights are wanted, the molten lead can be poured into brass tubes of the approximate diameter and length and caps for top and bottom turned out of sheet brass.

Now for a few words about determining weight required which will be of interest to you and a host of our readers who occasionally meet this problem.

The sketch shows the methods of weight application most usually encountered. The one on the left goes "single" and the one on the right is a "double" fall or once compounded. A is the diameter of the great or main wheel. B is the diameter of the drum and C is the center.

TABLE FOR CLOCK WEIGHT SHELLS IN INCHES AND POUNDS OF LEAD REQUIRED TO FILL THEM.

Length.	Diameter.	Cubic inches.	Pounds.
4.	2.	12.57	5.15
4.25	2.	13.35	5.48
4.50	2.	14.13	5.80
4.75	2.	14.92	6.12
5.	2.	15.71	6.44
5.25	2.	16.50	6.77
5.50	2.	17.27	7.09
5.75	2.	18.06	7.58
6.	2.	18.85	7.73
6.25	2.	19.64	8.06
6.50	2.	20.42	8.38
6.75	2.	21.70	8.90
6.	2.25	23.85	9.79
6.25	2.25	24.85	10.20
6.50	2.25	25.84	10.61
6.75	2.25	26.83	11.02
6.	2.50	29.45	12.09
6.25	2.50	30.67	12.59
6.50	2.50	31.90	13.10
6.75	2.50	33.13	13.60
6.	2.75	35.63	14.63
6.25	2.75	37.12	15.25
6.50	2.75	38.60	15.85
6.75	2.75	40.09	16.46
6.	3.	42.41	17.41
6.25	3.	44.17	18.12
6.50	3.	45.94	18.86
6.75	3.	47.71	19.59
7.	3.	49.48	20.31
7.25	3.	51.34	21.04
7.50	3.	53.01	21.76
7.75	3.	54.78	22.50
8.	3.	56.54	23.21

RELEATHER HAMMERS

A customer has a grandfather clock she wants repaired. The clock was made by the Colonial Mfg. Co., at Zeeland, Michigan. After a rather quick examination I believe the clock is about 80" tall, has 3 weights and plays the Westminster chime—5 tubular bells.

Examination shows that the rubber tips on the striking hammers are worn through, giving too strong a metallic tone. I would like to get these if possible before I start overhauling the clock but can't find anyone who can supply them. Would an eraser from a lead pencil substitute?

A.

The Colonial Manufacturing Company, Zeeland, Michigan, is active in the clock business today. No street address is necessary if you care to write to them.

Hall clock chime hammers are cushioned in various ways. Some are two-piece wherein a piece of leather is inserted in the front half before the hammer is screwed together and attached to its spring. Some have a method of clamping a strip of leather across the front and some are simply drilled out to have a piece of leather inserted. I take it your type is the latter since you asked about pencil erasers.

Regardless of the type hammer, leather is the best. If it is the latter type, secure from your most convenient shoe repairman some scraps of "Oak Sole" leather. With a sharp knife, shape and trim it to fit the hole in the hammer, drive in and allow about a full ⅛" extension.

FOUNDRY NAME, NOT MAKER

I have just repaired a grandfather's clock and would like to know its age. The only marking I can find on it is: Kempson & Felton, Birm., which is on a cast iron plate just behind the regular brass plates which carry the train. I have had two of these for repair recently and I understand both came from England.

A.

We do not locate the firm "Kempson & Felton, Birmingham" in any of the clockmakers' lists, and think it to be a firm of ironmongers rather than clockmakers.

About the turn of the last century many English clockmakers were buying such parts as the iron frame to support the dial already made up. I recall seeing several times these iron supporting plates marked "Osborn Foundry, Birmingham" and on investigation learned that the Osborn firm ran a foundry and made such clock parts as these frames, weights, etc., especially for the clock trade. Like yours, these clocks bore no other name.

MAKE PENDULUM & WEIGHT

I have a Tiffany & Co. grandfather clock with the trade stamping on back plate of B. & W. This may be Boardman & Wells. Required are the weights and pendulum with ball. I wish to substitute the missing parts, including chain. It appears to be of a 30-hour movement in brass plates with pins to pillars. I wish to know the size of chain, weight of time and strike weights, length of pendulum, diameter of pendulum ball and weight.

A.

I can't go along with your guess that your grandfather clock trademarked B. & W., and marketed by Tiffany & Co., was manufactured by Boardman & Wells.

That firm was made up of Chauncey Boardman and Col. Joseph A. Wells, Bristol, Connecticut, active about 1832 to 1843, under that firm label. It is my thought that they made only wood movements up to 1837, and that they never made any tall or grandfather clocks.

Chances are in favor of the pendulum beating seconds. Your pendulum length is determined by counting the train and thereby ascertaining the clocks beat. By counting the pinion leaves and wheel teeth, you determine the number of revolutions the escape wheel makes to one exact revolution of the center post (one hour). Multiply by the number of teeth in the escape wheel and by two since each tooth makes two beats, one on the receiving pallet and one on the release pallet. This last figure gives you the number of beats per hour. Divide by sixty and you have the number of beats per minute.

You may calculate any desired pendulum by the following rule: Multiply the number of vibrations in one minute of the seconds pendulum (60) by itself which is squaring it. Multiply this by the seconds pendulum length (39.2 inches). 60 times 60 equals 3,600. 3,600 times 39.2 equals 141,120.0. Divide by the square of the number of vibrations required per minute and the result is the length in inches and decimal parts of the pendulum required. Example: suppose you require a pendulum to beat 120 times per minute. 120 times

120 equals 14,400. 141,120.0 divided by 14,400 equals 9.8, the required pendulum length to beat 120 times per minute. This should enable you to determine the length of the pendulum for your B. & W. clock.

I suspect the chain size will have to be determined by actual trial and error. You must have some pieces of chain about the shop. Try one. Determine if links are too long or too short. A few trials and you will soon determine size and number of links per inch.

When counting the train you will find the number of hours one revolution of the main wheel will drive the clock after you've determined the correct chain size and number of links to turn main wheel one revolution. Knowing the height of case and maximum length of chain you can use, you can then determine the number of hours (30 hours or 8-day) one winding will drive the clock.

With no more data than you give, the best we can say as to how much each weight ought to weigh and the size and weight of pendulum ball is again by trial and error. Luckily, you have a pretty wide latitude in both.

Once you have the movement cleaned and in good order and well lubricated, calculated and built good pendulum of correct length, you may pattern and judge roughly size and weight of ball from a similar clock. Hang on to the weight end of each chain an open end can or container and place therein some weight— scraps of iron, lead, bolts, washers and what-have-you to about the amount you think required to drive that train. Try the train. From experience and observation you will have a pretty good idea of what to begin with. By actual operation (either time or strike) determine just the amount of weight required for safe, positive operation. Take it off and weigh it. Add about ten per cent for a safety factor and cast your weight accordingly.

In as much as most of this, boiled down, amounts to trial and error, don't feel that all of it was occasioned by the fact that your query contained so little specific data, for it is just about what an experienced clockmaker would do if he had the actual clock in hand for repair.

SLOW DOWN CHIMES

I recently acquired a Hall or Grand-father's Clock. It is not an antique, being only about 40 years old, but is in wonder-ful condition and a source of pride to the family. The movement was made by The Colonial Mfg. Company, which company I am unable to locate, and is beautifully constructed. It has Westminster tubular chimes with the hammers actuated by a brass cylinder with small spokes, similar to a Swiss music box, which is mounted above the movement.

In its old location this clock had a slow, stately chime but since being moved to my home the chimes strike very quickly . . . sort of "jazzing it up" if you know what I mean. The chimes strike on the quarter hours, starting on the first quarter with four notes and increasing each quar-ter until sixteen notes are struck on the hour.

If at all possible I do not wish to dis-assemble this clock but would appreciate any information you might be able to give me as to the possibility of slowing down the chimes. The clock was set very care-fully, using a level to see that it was per-fectly level. I had some slight difficulty with the pendulum wobbling but overcame that by inserting a new suspension spring. Although I have the bob lowered as far as it will go the clock still gains about five minutes a day.

I am particularly interested in slowing the chimes and if you can give me some information that would enable me to do this I will be very grateful.

A.

We think your clock has a German movement in a case made by the Colonial Manufacturing Company of Zeeland, Michigan.

Have you checked the fan-fly? It sounds as if the blade may be slipping on its arbor. Some of their movements were equipped with an adjustable fan-fly; they extend back beyond the back plate, the radius of the blade being too great to permit including between the plates. The blade (or fan) is of two vanes mounted on the ends of short arms; you will find that the crossmember (or arm) is secured to the arbor by being pinned against a friction washer, that each of the vanes is mounted friction tight in the arm ends. This is the adjustable feature; one may turn these vanes to cut more or less air and thereby control the speed of the chime train.

All fan-flys should be constructed so that there is a "slip" or "give" between the blade and its arbor; this is attained by friction. The friction is stiff enough to prevent the blade from slipping during the chime operation, but when the train comes to a sudden stop, on being locked at the end of the operation, it isn't stiff enough to prevent the blade or vanes from slipping a quarter or half revolution be-fore it stops. This relieves the fan-fly arbor of the strain of the sudden lock which would result if the blade were fast to its arbor. This "cushioning" feature is not so evident in small clocks, but is no less necessary. Some tower clocks whose strike train carries a rather heavy fan-fly have some pretty elaborate mechanisms to answer this purpose—generally, a set of large double ratchets which will permit the fan to coast on through several revolu-tions after the train has been locked.

Again, check this feature of your chime. If it's the 2-vane, adjustable type men-tioned above, the friction washer will be found just back of the arm. Remove the pin, then the arm, and you will see a cupped or dished washer works between the back of the arm and a shoulder on the arbor. With a round-faced punch, give this washer a bit more "dish" and replace it. This should give sufficient tension to prevent further slipping while the clock is chiming.

CHRISTIAN BIXLER CLOCK

I would appreciate some information on an old G.F. clock I recently had apart and repaired.

The name on the clock was written in very Old English lettering, and as near as I can make it out, it is, "Shriftian Gixler, Safton." The clock dial is the regular size over-all, with conventional moon-age dial at the top. It's a calendar clock with four dials, time, day of month, day of week, and month of the year, with a beautiful sweep-second hand covering the whole dial.

A.

If your clock is what I think it is, it deserves much better treatment than I am able to give it. I'm pretty sure that the engraving on the dial has you confused. Instead of "Shriftian Gixler, Safton," let's substitute a "C" for the first letter of the word. Then, one of the easiest mistakes to make is taking an engrarved "s" as an "f"—so we make the "f" an "s," and have C-h-r-i-s-t-i-a-n. In the second word, a "B" instead of "G," and we get B-i-x-l-e-r. In the third word, an "E" for the first letter, and again the "f" for your "s," making it E-a-s-t-o-n.

There is listed a Christian Bixler at Easton, Northampton County, Pennsylvania. In fact, three of them—the first at Lancaster County, Pennsylvania, the second at Reading, Pennsylvania, and Christian III, being the only one listed at Easton. There is no record of the first two actually making clocks. Christian III learned clock-making in his father's store and from John Keim in Reading. He had a shop in Easton by 1785, and records show that by 1812, he had made some 465 clocks.

Mr. Samuel Barrington is probably the best authority on Bixler clocks, having made a special study of them, and also having obtained access to the original Bixler records. Bixler must have been an exceptional mechanic. First, he had drawings of all the styles of clock movements he made, showing all the details, lay-out, dimensions, number of leaves in pinions, number of teeth in wheels, date of manufacture and serial number. Mr. Barrington says: "He was very particular about the pivot holes, which he drilled with drills of his own making and then polished to such a smoothness that they were equal to jewels for frictionless running."

RILEY WHITING

I have a grandfather clock for restoration, and I would like all the information I can get on it. It is an all-wooden movement, except for steel pinions and verge wheel and verge, which are of brass. It is a striking clock with an iron bell mounted on top of the movement and suspended from a wooden dolly or rod, which in turn is fastened to the movement by two metal rods. The striking wheel is mounted on the back of the movement and looks very much like the striking wheel in a cuckoo clock. This wheel is mounted on a wooden pinion, and the two main ratchets or winding wheels are of wooden pinions.

The weights are crude metal shells with wooden tops and are suspended by cable, and wound by a heavy cord on which is attached a small lead weight. The movement measures $6\frac{1}{2}$ inches wide by $9\frac{1}{8}$ inches long. The hands are of metal and the wooden dial has "R. Whiting, Winchester" on it. The movement seems to be made of cherry or rosewood, and the case is all pine and completely enclosed except for the dial opening.

A.

Riley Whiting is first recorded in the clockmaking business with Samuel and Luther Hoadley at Winchester, Connecticut, as early as 1807. Samuel Hoadley went into the army about 1813 and we find Mr. Whiting in business for himself. Evidently he continued making the hang-up or long case clock as made by the firm. Just a few years later the wood-movement shelf clock came into prominence, and he also began making them. His business prospered with the clock boom, and he built several shops. He died in 1835, causing something of a lull in the Winstead (or Winchester) clock business. In 1841 William L. Gilbert, with Ezra Baldwin and Lucius Clarke, acquired the Whiting properties and organized Clarke, Gilbert and Co. About 1850, it became the Wm. L. Gilbert Co., in 1871, the William L. Gilbert Clock Co., and then in 1934, the William L. Gilbert Clock Corp., a firm which is in business today.

It is possible that the plates of your movement may be mahogany, a few were so made, but most were oak. The wheels were generally made from apple wood and the pinions from laurel. This type movement or construction is generally referred to as the pull wind, hang-up, or long case clock.

No doubt you have already observed that there are no winding squares or key holes in the dial. Each drum has attached, two cords wound in opposite directions. When the weight is run down, the other cord with the small lead pellet on it is wound up; to wind the driving weight, one simply "pulls" the little lead weight cord, thus the name "pull wind".

30 HOUR OR 8 DAY

I would like to know a quick way to determine whether a grandfather clock is an 8-day or 30-hour. I wish to purchase a few and I would like to know a way to determine this.

A.

As a rough rule, one might say the 30-hour grandfather movements have only three wheels in their time trains, while the 8-day ones have four and usually five arbors in the time train.

The verge-arbor of most grandfather clocks sits under an easily detachable bridge. You can remove the verge and permit the train to run through 12 hours. Either from the number of coils reeled off the drum, or the distance the weight travels through this 12-hour run, you can easily tell whether it is one or eight days.

AGE OF LUMAN WATSON CLOCK

I have in my possession an old antique grandfather's clock, the works of which are made of wood. Besides the minute and hour hands, the clock also has a small dial approximitely 3 inches in diameter which gives the seconds. It also has another dial of the same diameter which shows the day of the month. On the face of the clock is printed "L. Watson, Cincinnati, Ohio."

I would appreciate any information you could give me as to the age of this clock. On the inside of the case where the pendulum swings, some person (presumably a person who had at one time repaired the clock) had written his name and then dated it 1823.

A.

Luman Watson, son of Thomas C. Watson, was born at Harwinton, Connecticut. Thomas C. was the Watson of the firm of Read & Watson that was producing woden movement clocks at Cincinnati as early as 1809. Son Luman seems to have struck out upon his own in the very early '20s. He died November 28, 1834. This is a revised date and is substantiated by cemetery records—the date formerly was given as 1841.

Mr. Watson was quite a character. He served as president of the Episcopal Singing Society, and in 1919, was elected to the highest office of the Masonic lodge. About 1824, with John Keating, he helped to found the Owenite colony at Yellow Springs. About 1826, he returned to Cincinnati, and was one of the founders of the Ohio Mechanics Institute.

In one of the early lists of American clockmakers by Wallace Nutting, the author said that Ephriam Downs was associated with Watson. Incidentally, this listing misspelled Watson's given name, making it "Lumas." The Downs association was subjected to question for many years, and recently Mr. Edward Ingraham confirmed it from some original Downs accounts and papers. They would indicate that Downs was in Cincinnati in 1817, 1818 and 1819.

The column has just received information that the quarterly publication of the Historical and Philosophical Society of Ohio (Cincinnati) will shortly carry a full-length article on Luman Watson. The article is written by Miss Annie Hoge Lockett, a resident of Springfield, Ohio, who spent several years of research on the Watson story, and it will be documented in every detail.

GRANDFATHER CLOCK STOPS

Here is a problem that might be of some interest for your column, which as far as I am concerned, is the most interesting of them all. I have a Seth Thomas, eight-day, weight driven, striking old grandfather case clock with the old lyre-shaped movement plates. I have overhauled it especially carefully because the case is in such good condition, and the painted glass original, etc. I closed the holes, checked depths, and end shakes, the trains run freely, the strike trips easily, and the clock runs perfectly without hands or with the hour hand only. But when I put the minute hand on, it soon stops, though not always immediately, and I cannot see that the hands foul each other.

I have tried putting a tight collar washer behind the minute hand, but that seems to make the trouble worse. The stoppage is not periodic, and can happen at any position on the dial. Well, there's the problem—I hope it has a solution because we are deeply attached to Old Seth and want him to run like the normal clock he otherwise is.

I had an interesting grandfather clock to overhaul the other day. The case was mahogany in perfect condition, seemingly fairly recent, for instance, the seat board supports were cast iron with two slots and recessed square head bolts like Herschede was using as late as 1929. The striking, hour and half hour, is on a spiral gong six inches in diameter, made of square wire, fixed to the back of the case; there is no evidence that there was ever a bell bracket on the movement plates. The dial is the conventional engraved brass-silver plated, arched moon dial with a calendar circlet below, and a seconds dial above the center. Both calendar and moon dials are in working order, the movement itself is the conventional English grandfather workings such as they made around 1750-1850, except for the missing bell. There is no sign of a maker name or mark anywhere, although the work is of excellent quality, and all handmade.

The pendulum is a cast brass disc on a wooden rod, its suspension conventional and old—long narrow spring with brass blocks riveted to the end, resting between the jaws of a brass suspension bracket that also bears the escape arbor hole.

Is it old or isn't it? The first thing that occurred to me was that it was a hodge-podge assembled from junk and put in a new case, but being all hand work except for the cast iron seat board brackets, my final impression is that one man, and a good one, designed and made the whole thing. And he was as modest as he was good—when did he live?

A.

That old story of the medic who gave the patient something to make him have "fits" because he had a remedy for fits is applicable in this case—yours is one of the mean problems we encounter in repairing old clocks.

First, your clock must be running upon very little power, most of these weight movements have sufficient reserve force to put them through little rough spots and take care of such minute additional loads as one hand. In the Seth Thomas, eight-day, lyre type movement the hand train is auxiliary driven, i. e., it is not an integral part of the train, but instead runs idle. This is a double bearing—the center arbor turning within the hour pipe, which hour pipe turns in its plate bearing—excess play in the fit between center arbor is added to any that may exist between the hour pipe and the bearing in the front plate to give a "double play" to the complete assemblage.

The next spot to look is the bearing of the main-wheel upon the winding drum. The winding drum is made of brass and so is the main wheel, thus we have two like metals wearing upon each other—a bad situation. To aggravate it further, there is the ratchet and spring to give excess pressure from that side while the weight is being wound (the only time this main wheel winding drum bearing comes into play). Wear and looseness soon develop here and the main wheel gets off center, even shifts its center sometimes while the clock is running. It's quite easy for a main-wheel off center, driving the clock train directly above it and also driving a loose idle center at your left, to form various and sundry "binds" without any periodic pattern at all.

With this condition it is quite possible for the mere additional weight of a hand to cause enough bind or friction to stop the clock. Generally when we suspect that the hands have something to do with stopping, we first look to the "dividing" wheel —the wheel that divides hours and minutes—reduces the one R.P.H. of the center arbor to one revolution in twelve hours for the hour pipe. In this action, the center or cannon pinion drives the dividing wheel. Fast to the dividing wheel is the dividing pinion, which drives the hour wheel. Excess wear or play in the hour pipe, front plate bearing, or the pivot holes for the dividing arbor can easily cause a bind.

Any by-letter or long distance trouble diagnosis is practically a guess—my guess is that your trouble will be located between the three bearings, main-wheel, center and dividing. Would like a card to know if you find it there. Some of these grandfather clocks like you describe can be pretty old, and are explained as being "bootleg" clocks, that is, a clock made by an apprentice and slipped out and sold on the side without name or identifying markings.

There is another story about these "unmarked" movements being imported in Colonial days — seconds or movements slightly below the requirements for standard upon which the better known makers did not wish to have their names being bought in shrewd Yankee trading, etc.

E. HOWARD G.F. CLOCK

I have a grandfather clock to repair which has no trademark whatsoever on the movement. On the dial is marked "E. Howards Company, Boston"; and it has a beautiful hand-carved case. Can you give me any idea how old this clock is?

I have a sixty-beat master clock in my store, mercury pendulum. I would like to clean the mercury—have you any method of doing so? We washed the mercury with nitric acid, but it is still not clean.

A.

It is a bit difficult to accurately spot a Howard clock from your letter. Mr. Edward Howard was born 1813 and died 1904. He was one of the most colorful characters in the timepiece manufacturing field, and it covered just about every known device for timing from watches to large tower clocks. Mr. Howard retired in 1882 and we believe the firm name became "E. Howard and Company" about that time. Since that is the name on your clock, it's a pretty safe bet that it was probably made between then and the turn of the century, however, it could have been a wee bit later.

We do not know of a satisfactory method for washing mercury. The one way to properly purify it is by distillation, and I suggest that you contact the science teacher of your nearby High School—chances are he has a pupil in charge of the physics lab who will run it through for you.

WATERBURY REGULATOR NO. 71

I own an old Grandfather clock some eight feet tall. It is in mahogany and has a large brass pendulum. It is powered by a weight filled with mercury.

It was made by the Waterbury Clock Co. We are unable to locate any numbers, other than in the bottom of the case there is a black nameplate showing "Regulator No. 71."

I was just wondering if there might be any way to determine how old the clock is. I think my father bought it in 1908 but I do not know whether or not it was new then. I shall appreciate a reply.

A.

For all practical purposes Waterbury Regulator No. 71 can be dated around the turn of the century. We've located it in their 1902 catalog, page 87. It is listed as follows:

Regulator No. 71, Quartered oak or mahogany
8-day time, Brass weight
Finely finished movement of best quality
encased in iron box
Dead beat escapement, sweep second,
Retaining power
12-inch porcelain dial

	Oak	Mahogany
With gridiron pendulum, Oval rods	$105.00	115.00
With compensating mercurial pendulum	143.50	153.50

Are you sure about your weight being filled with mercury? This is indeed unusual because there is no point in it; weight only supplies the driving force and lead (rocks or scrap iron) would do as well. In the pendulum there is a difference; mercury is used in pendulums to "compensate" temperature changes. Note that the same clock with mercurial pendulum is some $38.50 higher. It could very well have been a new clock when your father bought it in 1908.

Which weight drives which train?

I have a small but important problem. Recently I serviced an old Waltham Grandfather clock with three weights. One is extremely heavy; the next is about half the weight of the first, and the third one is still lighter than the second one. In other words, three weights in three different sizes.

The customer and I do not agree on which weight drives which. He has the heavy weight on the time, the next on the chime, and the light one on the hour strike. In this arrangement the chimes and the hour strike very slowly, even if the windmills are set as fast as they permit. I would welcome your suggestion as soon as possible.

A.

The heaviest load in your Waltham Grandfather chiming clock is the chime train, therefore it requires the greatest driving power, and uses the weight you refer to as extremely heavy.

Next is the strike train. The medium or "middle" weight is used to drive it. This leaves the lightest weight for the time train and that is just where it should go. No rule is completely inflexible, but the above holds good in about 99 out of every 100 cases.

With the movement in order and the weights so hung, the adjustable vanes on the "fan-fly" should set something near two-thirds full-open, give or take a little, depending upon how your customer likes the speed of the hammer strokes.

This clock may be a "Bryson"

The clock came into my family in England, presumably from Scotland, and we brought it here in August. A few days ago we found a scrap of old newspaper deep inside the base—it was an Edinburgh paper dated in June, 1867.

The clock stands about 6 feet, 5 inches high and is made of mahogany. It has little fancy work and really is quite plain. Enclosed is a drawing of the clock face. It is round, with a round wooden covering. It has the usual two weights hanging inside and a pendulum. I am unable to find any numbers on the works but have probably looked in the wrong place. The clock face is painted gold and bears the inscription "Bryson, Edinburgh."

Peculiarly (as you can see in the drawing) the small dial at the bottom has progressive numbers from 5 through 31, instead of the expected 30.

The clock case is in excellent condition except for a crack in the wood, and the many pieces of wood making the covering for the face and top have become unglued because of the trip from England.

The works of the clock are of brass, have recently been cleaned, and are operative. I confess that it hasn't worked since we came from England since I don't know how to set it properly and we don't have a winding key. The clock does not have chimes but does have a bell that is operative.

A.

It is noted that you use the term "expected 30." Evidently you must be thinking in terms of a seconds hand, yet a seconds-bit should be calibrated to 50, the hand making one revolution per minute. We think this is the calendar dial and that if you will examine it closely, you will discover four marks or dots between the 31 and the beginning "5." Each of these indicates a day, and that is the reason for the 31—i.e. to indicate the 31st day of the month. When in working order, the hand on this dial should advance by one calibration each night around midnight.

Only three "Bryson's" are listed for Edinburgh in Baillie's list. Robert, B-1778, D-1852, was a Fellow in the Royal Society of Edinburgh, a very fine horologist and made a sidereal clock for the Edinburgh Observatory. Alexander, B-1816, D-1866 was his son. Another son, Robert, D-1886, had carried on the business as Robert Bryson & Son.

Apparently you have a fine old Grandfather clock made in the early 1800's, quite a bit earlier than your 1867 newspaper clipping. Sorry we can't pinpoint the date any closer than above. Much more to be desired than a pinpointed date is the fact your piece came from a famous clockmaker family. Alexander was a Fellow of the Royal Society, and Clockmaker for Scotland to the Queen. He invented many devices for electrical and other clocks.

Regarding Augustine Neisser

My question for you is about a grandfather clock I recently worked on. It had the maker's name, Augustine Neisser, on the dial, and the owner would like to know if any information is available concerning this man.

A.

Augustine Neisser was born in Sehlen, Moravia, in 1717. He imigrated to America when 19, landing in Georgia and a few years later moved to Philadelphia. He settled in Germantown, married Catherine Reisinger in 1770, and they had three sons. Augustine Neisser died in 1780.

An advertisement is of r e c o r d for a stolen clock:

"$8.00 reward, a repeating 30-hour clock with alarm, by some British troops on September 25, 1777, with maker's name engraved on the face 'Augustine Neisser'; 11 inches square, taken without pendulum and weights.''

In 1746, Neisser was engaged to build a church clock for the Moravian congregation at Bethlehem, Penna.; it was completed the next year. From the map, you are located in Salem county, not very far from Bethlehem. Perhaps, if and when your customer happens to be in that city he just might pick up further data upon this man from the old church records.

HERSCHEDE STRIKE ADJUSTMENT

I have a Herschedes Grandfather clock to repair. It runs and strikes okay, except occasionally the chime roller seems to advance a tooth or two, causing the pin which actuates the hour strike to jam against the hour strike lever as the roller slides to chime position in preparation for striking the first quarter chime.

This clock was patented in 1909, No. 8723. All parts are tight and the gears seem to mesh properly. Please explain my dilemma.

A.

Patent dates and/or numbers very rarely convey any detailed information about all mechanical construction even if one had a copy in file—your sketch does help a lot.

Apparently you have one of those clocks striking the full quarter chimes plus the hour all from the same driving weight. To accomplish this, the chime drum, located across the top of the movement, was constructed to shift to one side at the end of the chime operation. This lateral shift permitted the chime lift pins to miss their respective chime hammers but at the same instant brought the strike lift pins directly in line with the strike hammer.

Hands Won't Turn

I am a watchmaker and not a clock-maker of any sort, but I got myself into trouble. My neighbor has a very old grandfather clock that has been in his family for years and he can not even remember the day that it ran. So I decided I would do him a favor and try to get it running. Well I got the clock to run fine, but the hands don't turn. I have been through it top to bottom and still the same result. The clock ticks away for eight days just like an old trooper, but the hands stay just where you put them.

I am stumped. There are no clockmakers around here that I can go to for advice so I am hoping you can help me.

There is no wheel missing or anything like that, because when you put back pressure on the hands, you can stop the clock. The clock and case were made by a Sam Harford in Suffock County, Conn. It appears to be an entirely hand made piece, and very well made too. But the hands still don't turn.

A.

We do not find your man "Harford" listed, nor do we readily locate a "Suffock" county Connecticut—quick look—thus, it is difficult to visualize just what the detailed construction may be.

Apparently, your problem is that of "center friction."

Being a "watchmaker" your basic thinking upon center friction is bound to be that of a cannon pinion frictioned—squeezed—against the sides of the center post. In many g.f. clocks, the cannon pinion fits the center post rather loosely, and, the center friction is had by pinning the minute hand and cannon pinion back against a washer; next to the front side of the front plate and behind the cannon pinion.

In instances where that back washer is lost and/or left off; pinning on the hands can press the cannon pinion back against the back plate, thus a definite drag upon the plate holding the hands still while the clock turns on.

Minute details of center friction vary according to the whim of each individual maker—your center post may be square-shouldered, indicating that the washer behind the cannon pinion had a square hole; most square-hole washers were not round, but, elongated so that the two long prongs would friction against the cannon pinion well out from the center. Those with a round shoulder were generally cupped washers of a size large enough to extend well out toward the edge of the pinion. In both instances, the hand washer is a cupped one so that when the taper pin is forced in, you get sufficient "canter-friction". In a few rare instances, the hands may be driven by or from the dividing wheel; in these instances you will find the frection escentially the same, i.e. between a washer, shouldered at its back and a cupped washer pinned on in front of the dividing pinion. With this arrangement, the center-post is generally "dead", does not turn—so your hands have to pin on it free.

The mere fact that your hands do not "carry" indicates a drag greater than the friction—a careful examination to locate this drag and you have located your trouble.

WOOD CLOCKS

CASE, WILLARD & CO.

Can you please give me a little information on how old the clock I have is? It is an all wood wheel except the escape wheel, with metal verge and metal pendulum rod. The movement plates are 6½ by 8 inches, made by Case Willard and Company, Wilmington, North Carolina. Do you know the year this clock factory started making clocks, and when they stopped making them?

A.

We can very accurately date your all wood clock from the fact that this type of movement came in the early 1820's, and stopped in 1837, with the great panic of that year, which completely wrecked the wood clock industry.

This firm name is a new one and not found in any of the lists.

In the 1820's and 1830's the South was over-run with Yankee clock peddlers. Several states became alarmed by the amount of money going out by this method, and endeavored to check it by passing "tax acts." In the Fall of 1829, some nineteen citizens of Knox county drafted, signed and sent to the Legislature a petition which reads in part as follows: "We your humble petitioners have with no ordinary feeling of regret, viewed the injury that accrued and is now daily accruing to the people of this state by the vending of wooden clocks. Speculators from the North are sweeping the country of what little money remains, and we feel ourselves supported by truth and reason in asserting that $100,000.00 is carried out of our State (Tenn.) annually. Trusting to the wisdom of your honorable body, we say no more, believing that something will be done to check the rapidly growing evil, by laying certain duties on said vendors or by any other plan compatible with the will of your Honorable Body, and we your humble petitioners as in duty bound, will ever pray." (Petitions, 1829 State Archives of Tennessee.)

Responding to this petition, the Tennessee legislature passed on January 30, 1830, a special act levying special taxes upon clock peddlers. Other Southern states did the same, but the enterprising Connecticut clock manufacturer just as quickly devised means of circumventing these new laws. He established "so called factories" within the states. I quote from Chauncey Jerome's "American Clockmaking" page 55: "We carried on this kind of business for two or three years and did very well at it, though it was unpleasant. Everyone knew it was all a humbug trying to stop the peddlers from coming to their states. We moved from Richmond to Hamburg, South Carolina, and manufactured in the same way. This was in 1835 and '36. There was another company doing the same kind of business at Augusta, Georgia, by the name of Case, Dyer, Wadsworth & Company."

No doubt, the firm of Case, Willard & Co., Wilmington, N. C. was operating there under the same conditions and for the same reason. It is possible that the "Case" of the Augusta firm and the "Case" of the Wilmington firm could have been the same man.

Wallace Nutting lists Case & Birge (Erastus and Harvey Case, and John Birge) as making clocks at Bristol, Connecticut from 1830 to 1837. In all likelihood one or both of these was your "Case." Jerome says: "Their clocks were sold mostly in the South."

May I suggest that the first time you drive up to Raleigh, you drop in at the state house and check the archives from 1825 thru 1835, for any tax act passed to curb clock peddling? If you should happen to drive down to Wilmington, check with County Court Clerk for any tax records on the Case, Willard & Company between 1825 and 1835. If you should spade up anything, drop me a line. You don't happen to have a photo of this clock's label do you? Look at the lower right corner of the label and see if it wasn't printed in Hartford, Connecticut.

S.T. WOOD STRAP DATA

Front Plate Sketch, Seth Thomas Pillar and Scroll Case, One-day, Wood, Strap-Type Movement

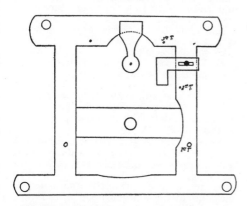

DATA: Front plate Mahogany, back plate Oak, distance between plates 36 m/m.

TIME TRAIN.

Main time wheel, 88.5 m/m. diam. 54 teeth. Actual cord surface on drum 25.5 diam. X 15.

2nd time wheel, 74 m/m. diam. 48 teeth. Pinion 16 m/m. diam. 9 leaves.

3rd time wheel, 63 m/m. diam. 40 teeth. Pinion 14m/m. diam. 8 leaves.

Escape wheel, 50 m/m. diam. 60 teeth. Pinion 13.5 m/m. diam. 8 leaves.

The escape arbor is 51.5 m/m. long.

Verge 19 m/m. wide, embraces 8 teeth. Over-all length of pendulum, 11 inches.

STRIKE TRAIN.

Main strike wheel, 88.5 m/m. diam. 54 teeth, Drum 25.5 m/m. diam. X 15 m/m. long. Set in the front side, near base of teeth are 18 hammer lift pins.

2nd strike wheel, 78 m/m. diam. 48 teeth, Pinion 16 m/m. diam. 9 leaves. Set near the hub in front side, 3 pins for advancing count wheel. In back of 2nd. S. Wh. very small locking plate, 3 locking notches.

3rd strike wheel, 65 m/m. diam. 42 teeth, Pinion 15 m/m. diam. 8 leaves. 1 warn lock pin set about half way from center to edge.

Fan fly, 23 m/m. X 63 m/m. Pinion 12 m/m. diam. 6 leaves.

NOTE: Count wheel mounted concentric with and over the center post.

DIAL TRAIN.

Center post, 80 m/m. long, two pinions mounted at back, one next to back plate engages the diam. Back one 18 leaves—front one 20 leaves and drives the dividing wheel.
Main time wheel. Both pinions are 30 m/m.

Dividing wheel, 57 m/m. diam. 40 teeth. Pinion 15 m/m. diam. 8 leaves.

Hour wheel, 72 m/m. diam. 48 teeth. Count wheel, 91 m/m. diam. 78 teeth, turns right.

J.E.C.

WOOD MOVT. FOR TALL CASE

I would like to have some information about an old wooden clock movement in my possession. The frame is 9¼ by 7⅛ inches, has three gears for weight, and three square shafts, key-wind. The hands gear is 3¾ by 3/16 and has 48 teeth. There are 10 wooden gears, 2½ to 4 inches in diameter, two fans to slow it down, the gear that swings the pendulum is right in the clockwork, and the striking wire is in upper left hand corner looking at the face.

Can you tell me how old the movement is? It was taken from a tall-case clock many years ago, and I would like to restore it. There are no broken gears in the movement, just bad bearings. A jeweler friend of mine suggested that I get in touch with you for detailed information on this subject.

A.

From your description you have a fine old wood clock. By all means preserve and restore it, for this type is growing very scarce.

Roughly the wooden clock era extends from 1797 to 1837 when it abruptly ended with the great panic of that year and the advent of rolled brass. Eli Terry devised the "shelf" wooden clock in 1816, and it is generally understood that very few wooden tall-case (grandfather) clocks were made after about 1820.

It is noted that you mention three winding squares and two fan-flys. I'm pretty sure that your clock was an alarm clock —a few of the wooden clocks had alarm trains and this would account for the third winding arbor. Also, that you say it was removed because of worn bearings. This can easily be remedied as it isn't too difficult to re-bush wood clocks and the procedure differs very little from the way you would re-bush a brass clock.

Get some boxwood or well-seasoned maple—cherry also makes good bearings —locate and mark the center distances in the usual way, drill the plate 5/16 or ⅜, and let in a new piece of your bushing wood (it should be slightly tapered), moisten lightly with casamite or any good wood glue and tap in fairly tight. Give it 24 hours to dry hard, then cut off smooth with the surfaces of the plate and finish with very fine sandpaper. Drill the new bearing-hole at the correct point and correct size to fit your pivot. You will note that practically all your old pivots are rusted—these are relatively short, just driven into the end of the wood arbor. Pull them out and replace with new pivots.

Your wood movement can be rebuilt or restored to practically new condition this way since you say that the wheels and pinions are in good condition. Don't fit the pivots too tight, and when finished *do not oil* the bearings—just allow them to run dry.

CLEANING WOOD MOVEMENTS

I have noticed instructions in A. H. & J. several times on how to clean clocks—giving formulae for cleaning solutions, etc. However, this covers only the brass movements. Occasionally we get one of the ancient wooden movements (I have had two recently). Reason would say that they should not be treated in the same way as the brass movements. Have you any suggestions as to how they can best be cleaned?

A.

So far as I know nothing has been published about cleaning wood clocks. Even my favorite volume, Goodrich's "The Modern Clock," has nothing on it and I don't recall ever seeing anything in any of the publications; so here goes—from scratch.

The procedure should be a "dry" one if possible. However, I can tell you that wood movements—both wheels and plates —can be scrubbed with a hand brush in the oleic-acetone-ammonia cleaning solution very practically.

You'd best secure a couple of round bristle brushes and a couple of fine wire brushes, round. To be used in the lathe of hand motor or flexible cable, for your dry cleaning. Naturally you want a good hole-pegging job on any cleaning. An inch and a half diameter is plenty large and you may have to obtain these brushes from a dental supply house. The wire brushes should be *brass*.

Most of the accumulation you will have to remove will be found around the shoulders of the arbors—the circular bristle brush used in a jeweler's flexible shaft is ideal for this work and only in the most stubborn cases will you have to resort to the wire brush. Around the pivot holes in the plates can be cleaned in the same manner.

One great trouble you will encounter in these jobs is *rusty* pivots. This is easily remedied by simply pulling out the old ones and inserting new wires—bright polished, of course. Once the new pivot has been driven in, chuck it in your lathe and revolve slowly (by hand) to see that it is *true*. If not, true it by hand, using your tailstock as an indicator.

Now, for the real bad ones—those that have been soaked with oil, etc. These will require a good scrubbing. This isn't at all difficult and with a little practice you

can learn to do it quickly enough to be finished before the wood is thoroughly soaked, in which case you will rarely be troubled with warping of the plates. I know, now, of wood movements running and giving good service, where the plates were so soaked, etc., that they had to be actually boiled in the cleaning solution. If it has reached this stage, it is best to take some precautions against the warping. I remove the pillar post from the back plate, the escape wheel potence and verge pin from the front plate, and as soon as finished, wipe them as dry as possible with soft cloth and place in a press (an old fashioned letter press) until thoroughly dry.

Washing the wheels and pinions do not require soaking. This can be done quickly—before your liquid cleaner penetrates the wood too far. The instant finished wipe dry with a soft cloth and place to one side to dry—never upon a radiator, or near heat.

Possibly this is aside from "cleaning" and could be under the head of repairs. Anyway, it can be done satisfactorily. You may find some of the pinions, especially the escape pinion, show considerable wear. The wheel driving the worn pinion can usually be moved down a bit on its arbor, thereby giving it a new driving surface on the pinion. Carefully pull the little spikes (sometimes two) that hold the wheel on its arbor, and remove the wheels. Chuck the arbor in the lathe, using the tailstock to support the other pivot and cut the hub back with graver the distance you have previously determined the wheel can be moved back, being careful in your turning to leave a good snug fit when the wheel is replaced.

Be sure that all your clock—wheels and plates—is thoroughly dry, bone dry, before you assemble it. Any moisture will rust your pivots. *Never* oil the bearings in the wood plates if they are wood. If they have been bushed with brass, use the barest amount possible—just what will remain in the bearing.

RILEY WHITING WOOD CLOCK

I have, in the repair shop, an old wooden clock, and the customer wants the date of manufacture if it is possible to get same. The plates are 6⅝ inches by 8⅛ inches. It has a strike mechanism that uses a heavy brass hammer, which strikes the half-hour and the hour. The clock was made and sold by Riley Whiting, Winchester, Connecticut. It has the caption "Modern Improved Clocks" above the name.

A.

To borrow from Ivory soap: 99 and 44/100% of all wood-shelf clocks can be placed in a twenty year period—1817 to 1837.

The present Gilbert Clock Co. at Winstead, Connecticut, is the outgrowth of a clock manufacturing business founded there about 1807 by Riley Whiting, Samuel Hoadley and Luther Hoadley. Luther Hoadley died in 1813, and Samuel entered the army after retiring from business. Mr. Whiting continued successfully; he enlarged the business, built new shops and made eight-day clocks. He died in 1835. The remainder of the business, shops, etc., was purchased by Lucius Clarke in 1841. Mr. Clarke was associated with William L. Gilbert, the firm name becoming Clarke, Gilbert & Co. Later the firm became W. L. Gilbert, and in 1866 was incorporated as the Gilbert Manufacturing Co.; in 1871, it was reorganized as the William L. Gilbert Clock Co.

It is noted that you say this clock strikes on half-hour. Wood clocks with the half-hour strike are so very rare, I'm tempted to ask if you are sure about this. If it does, we'd appreciate you letting us know if is from an additional lift on the center post, or is included in the strike train and taken off the count-wheel.

GEO. MARSH & CO.

Can you give me any information as to when a clock with the following inscription was manufactured: Manufactured and sold by George Marsh & Company, Farmington, Connecticut.

The clock case is wood and is 17 inches wide, 29½ inches high and 5 inches deep. It has two weights. The wooden plates have ivory bearings and the wheels and pinions are wood.

A.

You can always place wooden movement shelf clocks in the period between 1817 and 1837. Eli Terry first began with his shelf clock of wood idea in 1814, however, it was about 1817 when they actually got into production. The great panic of 1837 wrecked the whole clock industry and when it was revived rolled brass took the place of wood. Better than 99 per cent of the wood shelf clock production was turned

out during that twenty year period.

George Marsh is listed at Bristol, Connecticut from 1828 to 1830, then at Walcottville, Connecticut (now Torrington) in the 1830's. I've never seen a Farmington label. It is in Hartford county, only about ten miles from Bristol and it could indicate the same location as the Bristol labels.

MAKE WOOD CALENDAR PART

I have two clocks of the grandfather 30-hour type. They have wooden works and are almost identical only one is an S. Hoadly and the other a Seth Thomas. There is a dial on each to indicate the number of the day of the month, however, the mechanism for operating the indicating hand has been removed. Now, how can I restore this part of the works as near as possible?

A.

Inasmuch as the exact measurements are not necessary to the last tenth of a m/m, we'll describe it to the best of our memory. I am sure you will be able to work it out with the following sketch:

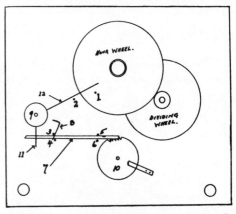

Calendar for one-day wood movement grandfather clock.

No. 1, Short wire pin set into the hour wheel,
No. 2, 3, 4, 5, & 6, wire pins set into the front plate,
No. 7, thin, flat metal strip (old alarm clock spring will work),
No. 8, keeper, similar to verge keeper found on wood shelf movements; it rests on top of pins 3 and 4 to hold strip 7 next to plate,
No. 9, wood hub, riding free on a pin set into front plate,
No. 10, brass wheel, sixty-two ratchet teeth,
No. 11 & 12, two wires mounted in wood hub 9.

You can readily see that pin No. 1 on the hour wheel will lift wire No. 12 once for each revolution of the hour hand or twice each 24-hour day. This is the reason for the sixty-two teeth on the calendar wheel; for the thirty-one day month it moves forward sixty-two times. When up and adjusted, your clock should be set so that this ratchet action takes place about six o'clock, thus the calendar hand (on wheel #10) points directly to the proper day numeral during the active part of the day and half a notch forward after 6:00 p.m.

After pin No. 1 lifts wire 12, it drops to rest on pin No. 2 as a stop. The length of wire 12 and distance from center of hour wheel pin No. 1 is set, plus length of wire No. 11 entirely controls the horizontal slide of strip No. 7. This horizontal action must equal about one and one-half the space between tooth tips of your calendar wheel 10. Make a small pipe for the calendar wheel of correct length to extend through the dial and mount the calendar hand thereon. Set the calendar wheel over a pin driven into the front plate and hold it down by a small flat friction spring with enough tension to hold the wheel in place during the backward stroke of No. 7.

ATKINS & DOWNS

I would appreciate receiving any information you might be able to supply concerning a clock manufactured by Atkins and Downs for George Mitchell of Bristol, Connecticut. The movement is made of wood.

A.

The firm of Atkins and Downs consisted of Irenus and Rolin Atkins and Anson Downs, Bristol, Connecticut, 1831 to 1832. Mr. Edward Ingraham tells me that he is pretty sure George Mitchell never made any clocks himself but that he was sort of an entrepreneur for the Bristol clockmakers.

George Mitchell was the brother-in-law of Irenus Atkins, having married the latter's sister. Irenus Atkins was the leading Baptist preacher in the Bristol community during the time he was the leading spirit in clockmaking. Mitchell was born in Bristol on April 19, 1774. He was brought up in his father's general mercantile store and became a shrewd trader and good business

manager in addition to being a typical promoter. He was the owner of a large amount of property and for years was one of the leading figures in Bristol. Mitchell was responsible for Chauncey Jerome coming to Bristol, selling him a home, taking in exchange clock movements. He also brought Ephraim Downs to Bristol, selling him a large tract of land, a mill, buildings, etc., taking half in cash and half in clocks. It was quite natural for him to form several companies and sales organizations to market the clocks he was taking in trade.

The firm of Mitchell and Atkins consisted of George Mitchell and his two brothers-in-law, Irenus Atkins and Rolin Atkins. They bought the old Baptist church building in 1830, moved it to a location on a brook and began building clocks. In 1831 Irenus Atkins formed the firm of Atkins and Downs, with Anson Downs, brother of the famous Ephraim Downs.

M & E BLAKESLEE, 1830

I have recently acquired a wooden works clock which has been very much abused, but I should like to put it in running condition. One of the gears which controls the striking is missing. Do you know of any place having these gears for sale?

This clock was invented by Eli Terry, made and sold at Plymouth, Conn., by "M. & E. B—akes—ee." The paper is torn and letters are missing where the dashes are. Can you give me the approximate date of manufacture and approximate length of pendulum rod and weight of pendulum?

A.

Re your "Blakeslee" wood works clock: Drepperd lists **M. & E. Blakeslee**, Plymouth, Conn., as working in the 1830's. Since the manufacture of wooden clocks ceased abruptly in 1837 you can be sure that it was made before that date. Thus it would be practical to date the clock in the early thirties.

"The first five hundred clocks ever to be made by machinery in the country were started at one time by Mr. Terry, in this old mill in 1808." Quoted from Chauncey Jerome, page 36. Further down, he says: "Capt. Riley Blakeslee, of this city, lived with Mr. Terry at that time, and worked on this lot of clocks, cutting the teeth." We must remember that this was the tall case (seconds pendulum) clock and that the shelf clock (short case) did not come in until after 1814. Nutting records Marvin and Edward Blakeslee as working in 1832, Heathenville, Conn. It isn't quite clear just what the relationship between Captain Riley and Marvin and Edward was. However, there were some dozen or more Blakeslee's in the clockmaking business during the first half of the century. One Milo Blakeslee worked for Eli Terry, Jr. in 1824 and later became a partner in the firm. Several of them moved to Ohio, and it is thought they are responsible for Plymouth, Ohio's being named that, for the Connecticut town. It is quite reasonable to conclude that Capt. Riley was probably father of the clan.

I feel sure you cannot locate any jobber with wood parts for sale; in fact, it is difficult to find a man to make up one to match.

WILLIAMS, ORTON, PRESTON'S

I have just received an all-wooden weight clock (strikes the hours—no half hours) which has brass bushings. The glass in the case is of the old bubbly type and looks like some of the first glass made.

This clock was manufactured and sold by Williams, Orton, Preston's & Co. of Farmington, Connecticut. Could you give me any information as to date when the clock was manufactured?

A.

This clock was made about 1820.

No doubt you have heard the old pun about the weather prophet who said "All signs fail in dry weather." This should also apply to any predictions made about a wooden clock. During the wooden clock era—about 1800 to 1837—there was so much trading in wooden movements, so many companies formed, etc., that it is very difficult to determine the movement from the wording of the label.

Most wooden movements found in cases with either of the following labels bear a close resemblance: Orton, Preston & Co., Farmington, Conn., about 1810; Williams, Orton, Preston's & Co., Farmington, about 1820; Seymour, Williams & Porter, Farmington, about 1835-1837.

Most of these were eight-day shelf clocks and the mechanical design differed quite a bit from the "Terry" type, the principal differences being (1) the strike train is laid out downward, ending with the fan-fly projecting below the bottom of the plates; (2) the count-wheel is between the plates instead of outside the front plate; (3) the plates were mahogany instead of oak; (4) weights, square, about 9 and 11 pounds, go compounded; (5) plates 11 inches high by 7 inches wide.

Seymour, Williams & Porter Clock.

489

COLUMBUS CLOCK

A customer brought in a wooden antique clock which he would like someone to repair. It has a picture of Columbus on the front and the word (Anno) 1492. The wheels are all wood but two are missing. It has only one hand, the hour hand.

I would appreciate it if you can give me the data on the above

A.

The clock you describe is known as the Columbus clock.

made by the Bostick and Burgess Mfg. Co., Norwalk, Ohio, for the Columbian Exposition at Chicago, in 1893, and later for prizes at the Garden theater in New York. The initial price was $5.00 but toward the end of the fair the price declined to $1.00.

A. HOPKINS, LITCHFIELD

Will you please give me information regarding an A. Hopkins Litchfield wooden movement, grandfather clock which is known to be over a hundred years old? I am concerned mainly about what weights to use as the originals are lost.

A. The original weights on these clocks were merely tin tubes with wooden tops and bottoms filled with sand, small stones, or scrap metal.

The time weight was the smaller. They are generally about 2⅛ inches in diameter, 7¼ inches long and weighed an ounce or more than three pounds. The strike weight is usually about 2½ inches in diameter, 7½ inches long and weighs 5 pounds.

You will find it quite easy to make these up. Use any tin handy. Cut two discs 2⅛ inches in diameter for the top and bottom weight. Cut two more 2½ inches in diameter for the strike weight from quarter inch ply-wood. Cut your tin 7¼ and 7½ inches respectively and roll around the proper disc. Cut the tin to allow about a quarter-inch lap, nail in the bottom with five or six cigar box nails, set in the top and secure with binding wire until you can wipe the seam up the side with soft solder; then, set it on the scales and fill with enough weight to bring it up to the desired point. Insert wire for the bail or loop through the top disc

from its top side and bend ends to prevent it pulling out; then nail top in as you did the bottom. This produces a very close copy of the original weights.

BOARDMAN & WELLS

I have a Boardman & Wells, wooden movement, striker weight clock that I would like to know the age of. Can you give me any information on this clock?

A.

You do not state whether or not the clock in question is a long-case or shelf clock. However, I'm pretty sure it is a shelf clock, as I've never seen a Boardman & Wells long-case clock.

Wood movement shelf clocks can always be dated between Eli Terry's improved clock of 1814 and the end of the wood movement era in 1837.

Carl Drepperd lists Boardman & Wells at Bristol, Connecticut from 1832 to 1843. Mrs. N. Hudson Moore lists this firm at Bristol, Connecticut, 1815, while Wallace Nutting says the firm of Boardman & Wells was made up of Chauncey Boardman and Joseph A. Wells at Bristol, 1815. Soon after 1820 they built a factory in North Forrestville, one of the most important of that time.

EPHRAIM DOWNS

I would like some information about a clock. It is a weight-driven wooden movement and all we can make out of the maker's name is Ephraim Bow— (rest illegible) Bristol, Connecticut, and the name Goodwin & Company. I would like to know the approximate age and if it is something out of the ordinary or just a run-of-the-mill timepiece.

A.

We think that you have a clock by Ephraim Downs. Take another look at the label and see if what you thought was Bow— could be Dow—.

Goodwin & Company is probably the printer of that label and their name should be found in the very bottom, right corner in small type.

Ephraim Downs was at Bristol, Connecticut from 1825 to 1842. Since wood clockmaking ceased abruptly in 1837, any Ephraim Downs clock labelled Bristol, Connecticut, would fall between 1825 and 1837.

With no more description than you gave us, this clock could easily be a common run-of-the-mill piece.

E. TERRY–SETH THOMAS

I have an Eli Terry clock made and sold by Seth Thomas at Plymouth, Connecticut. It is a shelf or wall clock, 17½ by 25½ inches, two weights, all wooden gears. It has been in my father's family since I can remember and I will be 87 next November. Can you give me any further information on this clock?

A.

All wood movement shelf clocks can be dated between 1814 and 1837.

On October 2, 1818, Thomas entered into a contract with Eli Terry to manufacture Terry's improved wood clock. April 28, 1827, Terry filed suit (friendly) against Thomas under this contract; thus, those clocks bearing a label stating invented by Eli Terry, made and sold by Seth Thomas, are generally placed between the dates October 1818 to April 1827. Some students are of the opinion that Thomas was omitting the Terry data from his labels some two or three years before the 1827 court action.

In a paper read before the Clock Club, Boston, several years ago by Albert L. Partridge about Terry's wood clock patents, referring to the action mentioned above, Mr. Partridge said: "That this was a friendly suit, there can be small doubt. The only possible reason for bringing a suit against Thomas instead of against a real offender, which suggests itself to me, is that he could not lose, because it was understood that Thomas would not force him to prosecute the action and he might win by causing others to withdraw from manufacture because of fear of similar action against themselves."

WOOD DIAL, 3 WINDING HOLES

I have a question I wish to ask you. I recently saw a hand-painted wooden clock dial on which I was unable to obtain any information. This dial is the same size and has the same type of decoration as the pillar and scroll wooden wheel shelf clock.

This dial has three winding holes, bound with brass grommets, positioned as follows: the lower two in conventional positions at 4 and 8 o'clock respectively; the third hole is directly about the 4 o'clock position or approximately in 2 o'clock position. I know of no wooden wheel movements, either shelf or grandfather, that use three winding holes. I wonder if it is possible this dial may have been used originally for an early brass movement having chime mechanism or quarterhour strike.

Can you give me any information as to the purpose of this third winding hole?

Eli Terry and Sons wooden movement clock.

A.

Your question is an interesting one and your deduction that the dial was from a wooden movement clock must be correct. There is such a similarity in these dials that one can hardly go wrong.

I seriously doubt, because of the odd position of the key holes, that that dial was ever fitted to any brass movement chime clock. Did you observe that the brass grommet in the added hole was the same as the other two? One can usually tell whether or not one of these dials has been altered. Alterations just don't look as old as original work.

My guess is that the dial in question was from a wooden movement which has an alarm and that your key-hole at the 2 o'clock position was for winding the alarm. Does it come as a surprise that the wooden clocks had alarms? We are illustrating herewith two, one by Eli Terry and Sons and one by Silas Hoadley. Note that the Terry is in Pillar and Scroll case and that its alarm release is of the same type as used in the common kitchen clock of the 1890's. In principal, the release used by Hoadley is identical with that being used today on the Big Ben the alarm indicator hand being concentric with the hour and minute hands two friction springs (photo clearly shows) holds the alarm hand at the position desired.

A Silas Hoadley movement.

CLEANING & BUSHING

Now and again we get wooden movement clocks for repairs which we accept only if the movement is not too worn. I have three questions:

(A) How best to repair when the holes or bushings are worn and need attention?

(B) What kind of lubrication should be used on the train pivots and throughout the whole clock?

A.

Your query re repairing "wooden" clocks must of a necessity be answered from experience. I've never noted in any publication anything near the required answers. In fact, the wood movement clock just isn't mentioned. I'm told that not too many years ago they were not considered "worth" repairing at all, and this probably accounts for their not being mentioned. Today the picture has completely changed—these rare old antiques are treasured—no one would begin to listen to substituting a new brass movement—and they have become an item with the clock repairman.

(A) Bush very much as you would a brass movement; any good hard wood— maple, hickory or cherry (well seasoned, of course)—will serve as your bushing stock. Just as with any clock, the main point is to maintain the "original" center. Being careful to do this, drill or cut out the old hole large enough to take a tapered reamer. Ream from the inside and, of course, insert the new plug from the inside. Most wood clocks have their bearings counter-sunk to approximately half the thickness of the plate and this counter-sink hole is several times the size of the bearing hole. I like to ream the new hole until it is slightly larger than the outside ring around the counter-sink. Chuck-up a piece of your fresh stock and turn it for a very tight fit; cut the counter-sink and drill while the piece is still in chuck. The hole drilled should be slightly less than the pivot, or at least a tight fit. Cut off about 1/64th longer than the plate is thick and drive in (from inside). Both the outside and inside should then be finished off smooth with the plate with fine sandpaper. If the hole has been drilled too small, you may use cutting broach to open it up to a tight fit; then, substitute a smooth or burnishing broach and open to the desired size. Remember that wooden clocks weren't built like a jeweled watch—a fairly loose fit is to be desired.

(B) I've found that wood clocks work quite satisfactorily without any lubricant at all in their wood bearings. Where you have metal against metal as with the pallets, escape wheel bearing (front) and the crotch wire against the pendulum rod, oil with a good clock oil as you always do on brass clocks. When cleaning as well as bushing wood movements, one should examine the time train pivots closely for rust and wear. These pivots do not extend the full length of the arbor as many suppose, but are slightly deeper in than their length protruding. Where you find a damaged pivot, pull it out and replace it. Pivots should always be burnished—bright.

LUMAN WATSON

I purchased an old mantel or wall clock from an antique dealer in Tennessee. I have been able to contact one of its previous owners who informs me the clock is about 150 years old. Is there any way the exact age of this clock can be determined?

I haven't been able to find a serial number on the clock. The works are all wooden except the verge wheel which operates from the lower center of the clock. The clock was made by Luman Watson, Cincinnati, Ohio.

There is a printed sheet on the inside back giving instructions for operating and care of the clock. The center of this sheet reads: "Improved clocks, made and sold by Luman Watson, Cincinnati, Ohio." This sheet was printed by W. J. Ferris, Printer.

The clock is run by two weights. It is about 2½ feet tall. Its face has the natural figures instead of the Roman numerals. It strikes on the hour and not on the half hour.

If you can give me any information concerning the age of this clock, I shall be most grateful.

A.
Wooden movement clocks were not as a rule numbered with serial numbers. This accounts for your not finding same. Wooden movement shelf clocks (as distinguished from the Grandfather clocks that stand on the floor) came into use about 1816, and into general use about 1820. Thus, your wood-movement shelf clock must date since 1820.

Luman Watson, born October 10, 1790, died November 28, 1834, was the son of Thomas Watson. Thomas was the Watson of the firm of Read & Watson, a clock firm dating from about 1809, possibly first at Springfield and Xenia, Ohio, and later at Cincinnati.

The first Cincinnati directory was published by Oliver Farnsworth in the year 1819. It lists,, "Luman Watson, wood and ivory clockmaker, residence 253 Main Street, factory located on 7th between Main and Sycamore." Further it lists, "Clock industry, ivory and wood clock factory employing fourteen hands. Machinery driven by horsepower. Value of clocks annually made, $30,000.00."

In that same year, 1819, he was elected president of The Episcopal Singing Society, and to the highest office of Miami Lodge No. 46, Royal Arch Masons. Mr. Watson was also an organ builder and at one time employed Hiran Powers (about 1822) who later became the famous sculptor. It was Watson who recommended his employee for modeling figures to the French scientist Dorfeuille at the Western museum.

This column has long endeavored to collect and correlate history on this clockmaker. If and when it were properly arranged and illustrated it would make a most interesting booklet. We've written to a great-grandson and great-granddaughter, and to Miss Annie Locket, Ohio historian, lodges, historical societies, etc. Miss Lillian Wuest, reference librarian writes, "Very little material can be found on Luman Watson, and it is in the most obscure places." The great-granddaughter owns his tall, wooden works clock, and I'm told that this clock was in Chattanooga, Tennessee, during the Civil War. Because of feeling, the words "Cincinnati, O." were removed from its dial and today only the "L. Watson" remains.

Luman Watson

He was a very religious man and was active in that field. On May 18, 1817, with twenty-one other men he signed the following document: "We whose name are underwritten, deeply impressed with the truth and importance of Christian religion, and anxiously desirous to promote its influence in the hearts and lives of ourselves, our families and our neighbours, do hereby associate ourselves together, and thus form a parish by the name, style, and title of the Parish of Christ Church in Cincinnati, Hamilton County, state of Ohio, in communion with the Protestant Episcopal Church in the United States of America, whose Liturgy, Constitution and Canons, we do hereby adopt."

He was a vestryman of Christ Church in 1819, 1821, 1822 and 1823. About 1824 according to Miss Lockett, Watson had become acquainted with an organ builder by the name of Adam Hurdus, who was also a cotton manufacturer, dry goods store owner and ordained Swedenborgian minister. Hurdus organized the Church of the New Jerusalem in Cincinnati and brought in a speaker, Robert Owen. Watson and others of the Swedenborgians became interested in Owen's ideas on Christian Communes and started their own "Owenite" pattern colony at Yellow Springs. Watson and one John Keiting signed in 1825 for 750 acres on which to develop the colony. They released their rights in 1826.

We find that Watson was buried in the Episcopal Cemetery but on December 15, 1856, was transferred to the Spring Grove Cemetery. Thus I assume that after leaving the "Owenites" he must have come back to the Episcopal church. He was one of the founders of the Ohio Mechanics Institute (chartered early in 1829), the oldest technical school west of the Allegheny mountains.

Evidently Watson was in the clock business (for himself) less than twenty years, but today clocks with his name or label are to be found scattered over the entire 48 states. We've had inquiries from as far west as Washington state, east to New Hampshire and yours is not the first from Texas.

WOOD CLOCKS

I have in my possession two all-wood clocks but know nothing of their history except one of them has the following name and date written on one wheel with a pencil: "A. Anson, Jr., May 26, 1882." Can you give me any information on how to learn if that was the original maker's name or if it might have possibly been a date of repair, as I believe the clock to be much older than that.

A.

You supply no information from which we might determine anything specific about your two wooden movement clocks. No doubt the penciled date of May 26, 1882 is by some repairman. The wood clock era ceased with the great panic of 1837 when all makers turned to brass.

A relatively small number of tall, floor or grandfather, wooden movement clocks were made in America prior to the advent of the shelf or short clock roughly about 1820.

In that seventeen year period, 1820 to 1837, untold thousands of wooden clocks were made. By far the most of them were made in the state of Connecticut although some were made in adjoining states. Mass production brought the price down and just about everyone was in the clock business in some form or other. The industry enjoyed a phenomenal boom—new companies or combinations were formed almost over night either to manufacture movements or cases or to sell them. It is said that wooden movements became a medium of exchange and were often used instead of money. In this rapid and vigorous expansion many clocks were marketed without any label or name brand on them at all. Possibly you just happen to own a couple of these unmarked pieces.

TWISS BROS. WOOD CLOCKS

Do you have any information regarding the country starting the manufacture of clocks with wood works? In this district there are quite a number of grandfather clocks with wood works. (I restored many of them to working condition.) The vintage would be 1825-1835 and the name is Twiss Bros. They were from Connecticut and moved to Montreal where the cases were made and works imported, I am sure, from Connecticut, as some details differ. So the works were not all from the same factory.

The odd clock, shelf or tall, is from England, but most of the dozen or so shelf clocks with wood works are American, the vertical type. I take my hat off to the men who made them. Lots of fancy touches were put on that would be hidden from appreciation, except by repairmen.

By the way, was it bone or real ivory that was used for bearings in the tall clocks? In shelf clocks no bushings were used.

I take it that wood was used for its cheapness and availability. Rolled brass came into use later and spelled the doom of wood.

A.

The origin of the wood clock is somewhat obscure. It is quite possible that clockmakers in several different parts of the world could have turned to the use of wood for building timepieces wholly without knowledge of any outside activities, and also possible that the use of wood cropped up in about the same general period. Wooden clocks are known to have existed in Germany as early as 1667; roughly somewhere about the same period wooden clocks appeared in Scotland.

The fact that some of the early clocks built by the celebrated John Harrison (1693-1776) were of wood is generally overlooked by horologists.

No doubt you are correct regarding Twiss Bros. clocks, and they must have come about the height of the wood clock production. J. and H. Twiss are listed as operating in Montreal, Canada. Active about 1828 was the firm of B. & H. Twiss of Meriden, Connecticut. It seems that there may have been three brothers in this firm, Benjamin, Ira and Hiram. There are also wooden clocks with "Hiram Twiss, Meriden, Connecticut," in them. Hiram was granted two patents on clocks about 1834. No doubt the Canadian firm made the very best use of its Connecticut connection.

Your general description of the Mac-Donald clock sounds very much like German work. It is quite possible that some Dutch trader could sell a German clock. However, we know very little about the Dutch using wood in clock work. Perhaps some of our readers could tell us something. Three hundred years takes it quite a ways back. Does it have two hands and the full 60 minutes marked within the minute track?

I'd hesitate to question the record of a Scot, leastways a MacDonald. I believe the clan is reckoned the oldest and most famous of the Scottish clans, descending from Donald, the grandson of Somerled, King of the Isles in the 12th century.

You mention modern lantern pinions—that all depends, for the lantern pinion was suggested by Leonardo da Vinci (1452-1519).

JEROMES & DARROW

I have a wooden-works clock that is about 2 feet high and 18 inches wide. It is brass-bushed and is labeled "Jeromes & Darrow." Could you tell me when it was made?

In my own collection, I have a set of wooden works which have either bone or ivory bearings. It is a 6½-inch by 8-inch plate, and has steel pivots. It is in very good shape. With this information, could you tell me who could have made this clock and if the bearings are ivory or regular bone?

A.

Jeromes & Darrow of Bristol, Connecticut, were operating under this firm name for the years 1824-1833, according to the Bristol tax records. The firm members were Chauncey Jerome (born June 10, 1793, died April 20, 1868); Noble Jerome (born December 20, 1800, died May 1, 1861); and Elijah Darrow. Noble Jerome made the movements, Chauncey made the cases, and Darrow, the dials and tablets (glasses).

Ivory, strictly speaking, is the tusk of an elephant. And we think this was never used for bearings in wooden clocks. When prefaced by a descriptive word, such as bone ivory, walrus ivory, etc., it may be applied to many substances which resemble ivory. Beef bone was used in the wooden clocks.

As to the wood movement in your collection, it is practically impossible to determine the actual maker of a wood movement unless it may have some very unusual feature used by only one man, such as the inverted pallet-verge between the plates as used by Silas Hoadley. During the wood clock "boom" (about 1827-1837) there were literally hundreds of men making wood movements. They were bartered in every conceivable manner, and even some were borrowed to complete pressing orders, etc., and later returned. Movements were never marked, numbered or dated.

REPAIR OF WOOD MOVEMENT

I have done quite a bit of clock work, but have never had the occasion to work on or repair the wooden movement Terry clock. I would like to know what peculiarities I should be on the lookout for. Also, the cleaning solution to be used, the drying process and what to do about rebushing if it needs it. If it calls for a particular type of oil, of course I would like to know what type.

A.

There has been so little written on cleaning the lowly wood clock, that I doubt anyone could point to any particular method or action as being standard procedure and prove it. First off, the mechanical action does not differ from any found in the brass movement. You look for the same things, i. e., broken parts, wear and butcher work.

On the cleaning, I can only give you my own method despite the fact I may be sticking my neck out. However, it is based on experience and I guess I average between 30 and 40 wooden movements per year. I'm not too enthusiastic about wetting either the plates or the wheels, and upwards of 50% of my jobs get "dry cleaned." We run into many of them that have been well cared for—plates not soaked with oil, etc., and a good dry brushing (sometimes includes the use of fine wire wheel brush on polishing motor) mixed with razor blade scraping, turns up a practical job good for years of satisfactory running.

With movements ultra dirty and/or oil soaked, sometimes both the plates and wheels get the full treatment, that is, through the regular cleaning solution and a quick hot water rinse. Both the cleaning and the rinse should be as quick as possible. There is no point in soaking, and it is surprising how little moisture they take up if you do the operation fast enough. I use a bone handle scrubbing brush with the cleaning, etc.

As to bushing, some say to use a hard wood like close-grained maple, but I generally use brass, but in using brass I vary the method a bit. Namely, I do not insert from the inside as with brass plates, and never let it come flush with the inside surface of the plate. My reason for that is the lubrication. If wood is used, it is finished flush with the inside of plate and the bearing run dry (without oil). With a brass bush, you have the steel pivot running against metal and some lubrication is definitely indicated. Brass bushes are turned up on the lathe leaving a flange to go against the back side of the plate. This flange is made as small as possible and drilled with three holes to pin it against and in the plate. The bush is countersunk so that the actual bearing surface is approximately ½ the thickness or slightly less of the plate. The inside end of the bush is tapered so that at its very inside end, it is but slightly larger than the pivot hole. By having this inside end set slightly below the surface of the inside and by its being tapered, the hole in the plate at this point remains much smaller than the shoulder of your wood arbor. Whatever thrust takes place is no greater than when the clock was new. Now you can readily see that when your arbor thrusts or works against that plate by reason of the inside end of the new brass bushing being below the plane of the inside of the plate, the end of the wood arbor cannot work against the bushing and siphon out the oil. When oiling these bearings, always do it sparingly, never too much.

The greatest trouble you will encounter will be broken teeth in wheels and broken leaves in pinions. In most instances with broken pinions, it is best to turn-up and make new arbor and pinion. With wheels, unless there is more than, say, half a dozen teeth broken off, a new piece of wood can be dove-tailed in and new teeth cut. This is a simple operation and with a little practice you can become quite proficient. Obtain one or two small screw C-clamps from your 5 & 10 or hardware store, select the piece of wood (I use apple that has been seasoned for more than 20 years), cut it to the thickness of the wheel or just a little thicker, turn it so the grain runs with the teeth you intend inserting and clamp it to the wheel with one or both clamps. Take a very fine jeweler's saw and cut your dove-tail plug through both the piece and the wheel at one sawing, then the new plug fits. Insert the plug with a good cabinetmaker's glue, preferably hot (though some cold water glues are good), and allow to dry thoroughly, at least overnight, but 24 hours is better.

Saw the plug to the full diameter plus. Mark and saw the teeth (get pattern from the other side of the wheel) still using the fine jeweler's saw, and finish with file. Smooth each side with fine sandpaper. As all the escapement is metal, those problems are identical with the brass movement clock. Generally you will find the pallets cut and the bearings in the verge saddle worn, and in most cases it pays to make

a new verge. Check and make sure that: 1. The brass escape wheel is not loose on its arbor. 2. Check the escape wheel for truth in the round.

FRICTION HOUR HAND

Here is something I might pass on—I own a Seth Thomas one-day wooden case and movement clock which isn't so unusual as to be a collector's item, but of all the wooden movements I've seen, this one differs in one respect. The pinion in the minute or change wheel is free wheeling or mounted in the wheel like the center pinion with a clutch affair—this allows the hour hand to be moved in either direction independent of the minute hand. It appears to be an original idea.

The clock is an Eli Terry patent, is running every day, is an excellent timekeeper, and the hour hand is mounted with a square hole on a square hour wheel tube. I had trouble with this clock stopping in a cold, damp room, so to correct this I set small bronze bushings on each pivot in the time and strike trains. It hasn't stopped in over a year now and I have tried it in a cold place—probably not the proper repair, but it has proven out.

A.

I differ with you on the wood movement clock not being a collector's item— they are pretty much in demand and not too plentiful. Practically every collector wants at least one example of the wood movement clock—why wouldn't one, if in the original case and in fair condition, be a collector's piece?

The friction hour hand is not entirely new to the wood clock; we've seen a few. Very, very little has been written about the wood movement, somehow they never seem to go into these small details. It is my thought that this feature may have been introduced to enable the owner to coordinate the hour hand and strike easier. Remember these were nearly all one-day clocks and the time side generally outran the strike side; thus, if an owner was away from home or forgot to wind his clock, he had only to pull the little trip wire and bring the strike up to the hour hand's indication.

If the strike got ahead of the hand, he had to strike the clock around to get them together. With this friction on the hour hand, anytime the clock struck six and pointed to five he could move the hour hand to six. Further, I believe that this hour friction appeared only on the earlier clocks where the hour hand fitted on a square. Pretty early in the game they began to fit the hour hand on a round pipe with a sleeve, and this within itself permitted slipping the hand forward (or backward) and thus the friction between the dividing wheel and its pinion was not necessary any longer.

Here is still another thought on the long case wood movements where the hour hand was fitted on a square — the dial train was located between the front plate and dial, and the repairman or assembler had no trouble in marking the square point exactly to the hour mark. With the shelf type movement the dial train went inside the plates, thus without the hour friction special care was required to set the hour wheel so that the square would be right for the hand to point exactly to the hour.

Repairing a Riley Whiting clock

I have a Riley Whiting Grandfather's clock with wooden works in my collection and have decided to re-bush the well-worn pivot holes. I have read many articles on this subject and am confused as to bushing material. Some use brass, others ivory, and still others, wood. I think I would like to use wood because it would be close to the original. What kind of wood would you suggest?

A.

Your point to use wood because the clock was originally wood bearings, is well taken; however, we may remember that many of the wood clockmakers used and advertised ivory bearings, calling it "an improvement."

For the simple reason that one can not use oil (the wood arbor soaks it away) I do not favor the use of brass. Personally, I prefer ivory, and find that graphite is a very satisfactory lubrication.

Background for a "Read & Watson" long case, wooden wheel clock

I have just finished rehabilitating a "Read and Watson" long clock, with a wooden wheel works.

I'd like to know something of the background of the clock, approximate date of manufacture, place, etc.

A.

We are familiar with "Read & Watson" wood movement, long case clocks, having repaired several of them. Yours is one of very few which failed to carry "Cincinnati, Ohio," along with the name on the dial.

That answers the "place" portion of your question. Your clock probably dates between 1809 and 1817. The firm of Read & Watson was a partnership of Ezra Read and Luman Watson, at Cincinnati. It is known that they were selling clocks in the Mad River, Ohio, country as early as 1809. This is recorded in the History of Clark County, along with the price of $20. I am inclined to think that this may mean just the movement since (1) $20 seems cheap for a "complete" clock; (2) it was quite common to purchase clock movements those days and either make or have a cabinet maker make the case. The firm of Read & Watson was dissolved in 1817.

Ezra Read was born in Northbridge, Worcester Co., Mass., Sept. 11, 1773. Luman Watson was born in Harwinton, Conn., Oct. 10, 1790. Perhaps both Watson and Read came to Ohio selling Connecticut wood clocks; that they were in actual production in Cincinnati by 1815 is proven by an entry in the account books of Ephraim Downs, for on Oct. 8 that year he (Downs) set down 10½ days work at the engine, meaning that he spent 10½ days cutting wheels. Downs was one of the well-known Connecticut clockworkers at work from about 1810 to 1842. He is supposed to have made two trips by horseback to Cincinnati, working for a while each time. His brother, Anson Downs, also a clockmaker having served his apprenticeship under the famous Seth

Thomas, was with him during his time in Cincinnati.

After the dissolution of the firm, Luman Watson continued the manufacture of clocks under his own name. By 1819 he was listed in the city directory as operating an "Ivory and Wood Clock Factory," between Main and Sycamore streets, employing 14 hands with machinery driven by horsepower, annually producing clocks valued at $30,000.

About 1821 a depression was felt in Cincinnati and Mr. Watson began to make pipe organs along with his clocks. By 1834 the directory stated that Watson's clock factory was worked by steam and employed 25 hands. I am inclined to believe that this covered the manufacture of both clocks and organs. Mr. Watson, a very energetic and civic minded man, took part in many of the community activities. He was an active Mason, took a leading part in the religious life of the community, and was also one of the organizers of the Cincinnati Chamber of Commerce. He died Nov. 28, 1834.

Wood-Movement Clock Predates Year 1837

I am sending you some pictures hoping you can help me.

Can you give me any info on this man or clock and would you have a picture of the case? I would like to put the top and bottom back on.

The movement in the clock is like Fig. 187 in "Book of American Clocks" by Palmer.

I enjoy working on these old clocks. I have a small shop, but if you are ever up this way stop in and see me.

This winter I would like to make a large grandfather clock to put in front of my shop. I have the formula for the gears of an eight day clock, Royal Pendulum, but I can not get it to come out right for a seven and one-half foot pendulum. Can you help me on this?

A.
You have a splendid example of the Early American wood-movement clock. Being a wooden movement, shelf clock definitely places it in the 1816 to 1837 era.

It is rather difficult to come by any detailed info upon its label — "H. Blakeslee, Cincinnati, O." — for H. Blakeslee isn't listed. Palmer does list a "Harper Blakesly" at Cincinnati as being active

about 1830, and, I feel sure that he is "your boy" — the slight alteration in spelling is often encountered in old records.

Annie Lockett did some research upon Cincinnati clockmakers and published it in the Bulletin of the Ohio Historical Society for April of 1953 along with a list of makers. H. Blakeslee (or Blakesly) is not listed. It is my 'guess' that she must have run across mention of him, but, that she did not consider him a real maker.

In one of her footnotes she points out that one Luke Kent Jr. was a jeweler and dealer in clocks and watches (he was not included in her list). During this wood clock era — 1816 to 1837 — Cincinnati undoubtedly had some pretty close connections with the Connecticut clock industry — the Downs brothers Ephriam and Anson, of Bristol, had made trips to Cincinnati, back in the long case wood clock days and were connected with Luman Watson, etc. While perhaps a clockmaker in his own right, Harper Blakeslee may have been more of a "trader."

This thinking is strengthened by his going west to Cincinnati; it is a pretty sure bet that the wood movement of your clock was actually made in the Connecticut Valley — perhaps he carried out with him a number of movements, and knocked-down cases, assembled them there (in Cincinnati), placing therein labels he had printed there (Chronicle Office, Cincinnati, O.) and did more 'trading' than clockmaking.

Now, to your pendulum problem: you do not state exact train count, but the accepted train for the Royal pendulum has its escape wheel revolving once per minute, i.e. the seconds hand works upon the escape wheel arbor. The Royal pendulum beats 60 per m. and thus 30 teeth in the wheel for the complete rev. in 60 beats. Your 90-inch (7½ ft.) pendulum is going to beat near the order of 40 per m. so, if you apply an escape wheel of 20 teeth; 40 beats will make your complete rev. in one minute, (actually, it does not come out even 40 — but — you will have considerable latitude screwing the ball up or down that will take care of the fraction.

Cleaning Wooden Movements

I have been searching for an article, once read, relative to the method and/or material one should use in the cleaning process of a Terry wooden movement. It seems that it once appeared in the American Horologist and Jeweler, but I've searched to no avail. Can you enlighten me, please?

A.

About the cleaning of wooden movements: there is a little booklet "Restoration of Wooden Movements and Cases" by J. V. Darnall, 5½" by 8½", flex cover, 31 pages, priced at $2 from Roberts Book Co. which stocks it under No. B-662.

He devotes one half of a page to "cleaning." The facts are: the cleaning of wooden movements depends to some extent upon one's definition of cleaning. With brass movements one naturally wishes to restore the bright finish to the wheels and plates. This, definitely is a part of wood movement cleaning. In other words the restoration of a new-like finish is definitely NOT a part of it. Darnall, says: "No water should be used" and I agree 100%, but, I go even further than that; no liquid should be used. I have yet to see a wooden movement I can't "dry-clean" to the point where it will render years of satisfactory service. The word "clean" has different connotations to different people. Whatever it may be, it is a cinch that from the standpoint of the repairman it must be measured in terms of the service the piece delivers for its owner after he has "cleaned" it.

A good stiff hand-brush, a brass wire brush, and even a circular brass-wire wheel brush upon your motor (polishing) can be used. Bearings should be "pegged" out until they are perfectly clean. Pivots and shoulders can be wiped clean with a soft cloth between the thumb and forefinger. Do not oil. A bit of oil upon each pallet and the crutch wire-loop (metal against metal) are the only points requiring lubrication. Good pivots are necessary. They do not extend the whole length of the wood arbor and can be pulled out and new ones inserted if rusty or worn. Sometimes, where the wire is bright and smooth merely swapping ends will do the trick. In a wood bearing that is clean there is very little friction and your wood clock is amply powered in the first place. Should one wish to be a little fancy, I can see no objection to wiping the pillar posts with a cloth moistened with spar varnish, or linseed oil diluted with mineral spirits to impart a shine, but I certainly do not wish to use it on the wheels and plates.

'Conventional' 30-hour wood movement.

Were Wooden Clocks Ever Made In Tennessee?

From Kansas to North Carolina and as far south as Mobile, Alabama, there occasionally turns-up a wooden clock neatly labeled "Made and Sold" by a firm in Tennessee. Every such event again raises the question: Were wooden clocks made in Tennessee?

"The 'wooden clock' era barely covers seventy years in American history—it extends from the 1760's to 1837. Relatively, not many were produced during the first fifty of that seventy year period in proportion to the thousands that were manufactured and marketed during the final twenty years 1817 to 1837.

Contrary to popular stories, clocks made of wood did not originate in America along with the wooden nutmeg and wooden cucumber seed; they were being made in Europe before clocks were ever produced in the western hemisphere. The first production were the grandfather type, i.e. long pendulum; approximately forty ·inches; beating seconds, intended to go into long cases that stood upon the floor. As was the custom of that day, the head of a household desiring a clock 'bespoke' a movement of his clockmaker and when it was finished, he, the new owner carried it to his cabinet-maker and had a case made for it. Some movements never got a case made for them; the proud owner merely hung it upon the wall to run, strike and keep time sans any case whatsoever; these became known as "Wag-on-the-Wall" clocks; both the custom and the term were borrowed from Scotland.

About 1816, Eli Terry of Plymouth, Connecticut, conceived the idea for a 'short' pendulum clock to set upon a shelf and began to experiment with a movement adaptable to a shelf or short case. Basically, Terry did not alter existing horological principle or introduce any new ones; his problem was: 1, to simply reduce the size of the movement (miniaturization), and 2, an increase in the gearing so that the hands of the shelf clock would make as many revolutions (30 for thirty hours) while the driving weights had descended about one

Same movement with its front plate removed to show working parts.

third as far as they did in the long-case clock.

Terry's first patent was granted June 12th, 1816—it is reasonable to assume that it was 1817 by the time he really got into production. This assumption is also good for 'round' figures since the manufacture of wooden clocks suddenly ceased with the great depression of 1837 and the perfection of a system of rolling sheet brass in that same year; this brackets the "wood shelf clock era" to 1817 to 1837—the last twenty years of the aforementioned seventy year period.

Being a native-borned Tennessean; intensely interested in clocks, any clock with a Tennessee label always rings a bell. Over a period extending beyond forty years, we've encountered in one way and another, some 35 or 40 such clocks but not that first single bit of evidence to support a belief or theory that wooden clocks were ever actually "made" in Tennessee. Not even a single isolated clock—one of a kind, to say nothing of quantity production as a manufacturing venture.

Another "popular" story about wooden clocks would have one believe they were whittled out with a pocket knife by unlearned farmers while sitting by the fireside at night; it's origin is a bit dim but it has been told and retold until accepted. That story seems to live on and on like a legend. Nothing could be farther from actual fact.

The construction of a clock to keep accurate time and correctly strike the hours required a high degree of mechanical and mathematical skill; that skill was only acquired via a long period of instruction and practice; generally an apprenticeship of four to seven years. The 30-hour wooden movement consisted of upwards of a hundred parts; correctly calculated; correctly cut; each tooth angled so that it drives the next pinion smoothly and evenly with a minimum of drive power. The end product had to meet a fixed standard, i.e. keep correct time, thus the completed machine presented a construction problem the unlearned and unskilled did not tackle.

It may be quite true our pioneer forefathers were pretty deft with the pocket knife—he whittled out some pretty remarkable things. One item often pointed to is a violin—these he made, but, not to a precise standard. He had never heard a Strad; neither had his listeners. At the outset his problem was to construct something from which he could get a sound. This he did and that sound 'passed' because it did not have to measure up to a standard—old sol hitting the zenith at noon neither proved him right or wrong, so, he could still enjoy the effort of his own handwork, regardless of a few mistakes.

Research has established that all our early clockmakers were well trained; their tools, their books and their clocks are the living proof. While the 'Indians' were pitching the tea overboard in Boston harbor an English clockmaker was debarking from that same ship; one Thomas Harland who moved on to Norwich, Connecticut, and set-up-shop; among his apprentices was Daniel Burnap. Later to take on Eli Terry as one of his apprentices, at the age of fourteen for a seven year period. Thus was Terry's training in the "latest English methods". One of my proudest possessions is a "Treatise on Clock and Watch Making Theoretical and Practical" by Thomas Read (England), a 476 page volume with 19 plates, which came directly from Eli Terry's library.

It is pretty definite that these clocks bearing Tennessee labels were manufactured in the Connecticut valley; that their labels were especially printed (in Conn.) and placed therein for the Tennessee distributors. One school of thought among lovers of Early American clocks and collectors; admits that the clock and the label originated in Connecticut, but were so used to avoid payment of special local taxes. Several southern states passed special tax acts placing a levy upon clock pedlars; Chanucey Jerome, the only one of our early clockmakers to leave us a full volume upon American clockmaking, in his "History of the American Clock Business" (New Haven, Conn., 1960) wrote: "The southern people were greatly opposed to Yankee pedlars coming into their states, especially the clock pedlars, and licenses were raised so high by their legislatures that it almost amounted to a prohibition." He relates how he and his brother went to Richmond, Virginia, and operated for three years; later moving to Hamburg, S. C., and that Case, Wadsworth & Co. went to Augusta, Georgia, etc.

None of these 'localized' operations involved any actual manufacture, both the movements and the cases were manufactured in Connecticut, and, in most instances the local address labels were printed in Connecticut and carried their Connecticut printer's address. One exception: an outfit operating out of Columbia, S. C., did use some locally printed labels.

Whether the 'domestic' label by itself saved a clock pedlar from the payment of $25.75 in each county, or not, is open to question since the act does not specifically exempt such—centainly the local merchant, with an established location, selling merchandise (including clocks) from a fixed address would not qualify as a 'pedlar'.

Perhaps the shrewd Yankee Clock Pedlar was motivated by other ideas—brand names were not then established; the name of an unknown Connecticut manufacturer did not mean a thing to the prospective Tennessee buyer, whereas the name of his own merchant whom he knew and trusted, meant a great deal.

In the fall of 1829, nineteen citizens of Knox county petitioned the Tennessee legislature for protection against what they termed a "growing evil"—in their petition, they said: "We your humble petitioners have with no ordinary feeling of regret, viewed the injury that has accrued and is now daily accruing to the people of this state by the vending of wooden clocks. Speculators from the north are sweeping the country of what little money remains, and we feel ourselves supported by truth and reason in asserting that $100,000.00 is carried out of our state annually. Trusting to the wisdom of your honourable body, we say no more, believing that something will be done in order to check the rapid growing evil, by laying certain duties on said vendors, or by any other plan more compatible with the will of your honourable body and we your humble petitioners as in duty bound will ever pray." (Petitioners of Tennessee, 1829).

In response to this petition, an obliging legislature promptly passed—January 5th, 1830—"An Act to Tax Clock Pedlars." It reads:

"An Act to Tax Clock Pedlars.

Sect. 1st. Be it enacted by the General Assembly of the state of Tennessee that every person or persons who may wish to peddle in the article of clocks shall apply to the Clerk of each County Court wherein he may wish to sell the same. Whose duty it shall be to issue to said applicant a license authorizing him to sell said article for the term of twelve months provided said applicant shall pay to said Clerk the sum of twenty-five dollars tax and the sum of seventy-five cents fees of office.

Sect. 2nd. Be it enacted that if any person or persons shall refuse or neglect to comply with the provisions of this act, he shall forfeit and pay the sum of one-hundred dollars, and it shall be the duty of said Clerk to institute suits by warrant before a Justice of the Peace in an action of debt in behalf of the state for the penalty prescribed by this act.

Sect. 3rd. Be it enacted that it shall be the duty of said Clerk to account for and pay over all monies by them collected by virtue of this act in the same manner that they are required by law to pay over and account for the state tax, and shall be liable in the same manner."

(s.) Ephriam W. Foster,
Speaker of the House of Representatives.

(s.) Joel Walker,
Speaker of the Senate.
Passed Jan. 5th, 1830.

One-hundred-thousand dollars is a huge sum today; tradewise, in the 1820's it was a terrific figure—considering that the states population was about 500,000 and that families were large in those days plus the fact that many families coming into Tennessee brought a clock with them cuts the number of homes that might be prospective clock purchasers to a relatively small figure. From that figure we must further deduct a substantial number of households that simply could not afford a clock—the net certainly does not indicate a hundred-thousand-dollar yearly sale and/or market. That the good folk of Knox County felt they were supported by "truth and reason" gave this writer some concern for that was not the time nor were they the type for gross exaggerations—researching the whys and wherefores behind community thinking is not always the easiest type; after some search it was found that one Birds Eye Pickett, a clock trader from the Connecticut Valley, had moved into Knoxville in the 20's and made it his headquarters for a sizeable clock operation. He was operating wagon trains driven by slaves to the Valley, hauling back clocks in great numbers. No doubt it was Pickett's operation that prompted the action as well as the one-hundred-thousand dollar figure, by the nineteen citizens signing the petition. Apparently they failed to take into consideration that Pickett was supplying clock pedlars in South Carolina, Alabama, Georgia and as far south as Louisiana.

Known Tennessee labels are: "Couch, Stowe & Co., Rock Springs, Tenn." "Reeveses & Co., Youngstown, Tenn." and "Pettybone & Co., near Nashville, Tenn."

Couch, Stowe & Co. operated a general merchandise store; Rock Springs was located in Wilson County, Tenn., according to Post Office records, it (Rock Springs) had a post office established there Nov. 28th, 1831, with one Nathanial Sparks as postmaster. The name of the office was changed to Sparks on Sept. 26th, 1832, and to Mount Carmel on November 27, 1844; discontinued Sept. 22nd, 1866; reestablished on July 21st, 1869, discontinued February 7th, 1870; reestablished August 31st, 1871, and finally discontinued April 1st, 1875.

We know nothing of "Youngtown" or where it was—it was never a post office, and, there is no record by the Census Bureau of such a village. The late Sterling Brown, of Woodbury, lawyer and historian (he wrote "History of Woodbury and Cannon County" for their centennial celebration 1936) owned a "Youngtown" labeled clock (now owned by James Foster, clock collector of Huntsville, Ala.) and spent many hours of research to come up with nothing upon either "Reeves" or "Youngstown."

Pettybone & Co. is even more elusive, as is "near Nashville"; it is quite reasonable to assume that both "Reeves" and "Pettybone" were country merchants, operating a general merchandise store as did Couch and Stowe. With a post office and its backing by the Federal Government having such a hectic career as the one at Rock Springs; that of a local merchant must have been "more so"—the post office got recorded but the merchant did not. Of the three labels mentioned, "Couch, Stowe & Co.," outnumber the other two combined; further, they continued on in the clock business after the wood clock era—clock collector, David Kivett, of Speedwell, Tenn., owns an eight-day, brass clock with their label

400 DAY CLOCKS

KIENINGER & OBERGFELL

A Kieninger & Obergfell 400-day clock, model 2EG, is in for repair and I am having trouble obtaining the proper lock to keep the train from skipping.

With a .0032 Horolovar suspension spring and the mainspring about one-third wound up, I got the clock to run within a couple of minutes a day, but upon winding the mainspring fully, the left pellet would develop light lock and skipping would occur, causing the clock to run fast from 30 minutes to 2 hours a day. By pushing the left pallet out slightly, the pallet would catch on the radius of the escape wheel and in time, the clock would come to a stop.

With a .0035 suspension spring, the action of the anchor was improved, giving me the proper lock and slide, but the time was 50 minutes to one hour a day fast, using the longest suspension spring possible and the pendulum fully expanded to slow.

A.

One cannot interpret the action of the 400-day clock escapement in terms of the suspension spring. You have absolutely no choice of suspension spring, for there is one, and only one, suspension spring for each individual clock. It is that spring that will permit the pendulum to beat exactly eight times per minute.

First, fit the proper suspension spring to your clock by "beating it in," i.e., with the fork left off (the fork is that member attached onto the suspension spring just a few millimeters below the top chock—it is sometimes called the crutch, and you must not confuse it with the anchor). Put on a Horolovar spring about the strength you think right, and of the correct length. Turn the pendulum a turn-and-a-quarter or a turn-and-a-half, and release. Give it a minute or so to settle

down, then time very carefully with a stop watch or a regulator with long-sweep seconds hand.

Start the stop watch from the dead stop or reversal point, counting "one" when it reaches the next reversal stop. It should come out *exactly* even "eight" upon the 60th second. If your pendulum beats eight in less than one minute, it's too strong. Take it off and use the next weaker spring. If more than one minute is required to complete the exact eight beats, your spring is too weak, so try the next stronger. strength. This beating-in is always done with the screw regulator setting in center. Naturally, when your count comes out very near the minute, you move the regulator a little in the indicated direction and re-count.

Now that you have vibrated the correct suspension spring, that feature can be checked off your mind, for such further errors as may show up can be looked for in every place except here.

Assuming that your clock is in order—clean, mainspring not coned, hands perfectly free, properly oiled, etc.,—there should remain but two features to be attended (1) setting the escapement and (2) setting the fork.

The 400-day clocks are "dead-beat." They do not have the draft or draw one finds in watches. In other clocks, your anchor is rigidly connected with the pendulum, but in the 400-day clock this connection is flexible. This flexibility allows your anchor to race or chatter when the escapement is set for light locking, or the fork placed on too low down from the top chock, giving the connection excess flexibility.

I wish I could say to you and others: Set the fork "X" millimeters below the top chock, but there are several variable factors, and this can't be done; 270 degrees pendulum motion between unlocking and locking is considered correct. This is just three-quarters of a circle, and I've found that if one will make a paper disc with the 270-degree angle marked thereon, and center it under the pendulum, it can be a great help in locating and setting the fork at the correct height on the suspension spring,

Before proceeding to locate the fork, you must see that the clock is in beat. From the practical mechanical point of view, "in beat" for the 400-day is the same as in other clocks. However, to put the 400-day in beat you shift the top suspension chock instead of bending a crutch wire.

To place it in beat, have the clock operating and closely observe the pendulum's rotation. Let's say the stroke is clockwise. Note an arm of the pendulum the instant the escape wheel drops, and see how much farther it rotates in the clockwise direction before reversing (an eighth to a quarter of a turn). Now, upon the counterclockwise stroke, make the same observation. The distance the pendulum travels counterclockwise from the drop of the escape wheel tooth to the reversal point should be the same as on the other stroke. Turning or shifting the top chock in the desired direction will equalize the stroke, i.e., put the clock in beat.

Have the fork fit the anchor tailpin snugly—not tight enough for friction or loose enough to permit play. Oil at this point, lightly—too much is as bad as none. Then you are ready to locate and set the fork. Place the paper disc under the pendulum—angle centered—set the pendulum in motion, allowing a minute or so for it to settle down. Shift the disc until one leg of the angle is directly under an observed arm of the pendulum at the instant the escapement unlocks.

If the fork is set at the corrected height upon the suspension spring, the observed arm of the pendulum should be exactly over the other leg of the angle at the unlocking point of the other pallet. By a little experimenting, you will readily find that lowering the fork brings the unlocking points within, and less than the 270-degree angle, while raising it throws the unlocking points outside the angle. I have found this the best method of setting the

fork when correct conditions exist in all parts of the clock.

Roughly, the 400-day escapement is built with equidistant centers, with about 4.5 degrees of run on the face of each pallet and is intended to have 1.5 degrees of lock. Thus, 4.5 plus 1.5 equals 6 degrees of motion for each pallet. So for the two pallets, we get a total of about 12 degrees of motion. It follows that the correct point for locating the fork on the suspension spring would be that spot where the pendulum, in its normal swing, would revolve or turn the anchor through 12 degrees of arc.

STANDARD 400 DAY CLOCK

At present I have a 400-day clock I have been unable to make run but a short time then it stops. When it came in it had a broken suspension spring. I replaced it with one of the same thickness and it would not run. I cleaned it, checking all working parts; then it ran for a short time, but only with 1/3 motion. I checked the pallet and escape wheel and found that it was not functioning as it should. There was no drop lock—it was striking the impulse face of the supposed-to-be stones.

The pallet does not have stones, the arms are curved and work as stones. There is no way to change them. There is a screw in the plate, and one pivot of the escape wheel works in it. The screw can be turned. I turned the screw to see if I could get any drop lock, and when I did it would not let off. If I set it so that it will pass both stones, it will have no drop lock and on the discharge side the stone will catch on the teeth of the escape wheel. On the receiving side, there will be plenty of drop but no lock.

It seems to me the escapement is set up off center. I would like to have your opinion as to what I might do to the clock.

A.

400-Day clocks never come with jeweled pallets, and you can't supply the correct suspension spring by simply measuring the old one. The off-center verge arbor bearing you mention is for the purpose of adjusting (changing) the center distance between it and the escape wheel. If, as indicated, the clock you have is the fixed pallet type, i. e., the verge is one piece and therefore pallets are not movable, and if it and the escape wheel have not been altered, proper depthing of escape to verge can easily take care of all the adjustment necessary.

Either you have fitted a suspension spring that is too strong or you have the fork set too low on the bridge. Quite possibly it may be some of both. Mr. Charles Terwilliger, Box 299, Bronxville, New York, publishes and sells the "Horolovar Suspension Spring Guide" (A.H.&J. Book Department, $2.00 plus 8 cents postage), which book gives all the correct Horolovar

suspension springs for the various 400-day makes. Your next best bet is to "beat" the suspension spring to determine whether or not you have the strength intended by the maker—with the exception of a very few of the late miniature 400-day, all of them beat eight to the minute. Put in a spring you think the correct strength, leave off the fork, swing the pendulum through about a turn, allow it to swing for a minute or so and count the beats with a stop watch, or in view of a regulator with long sweep seconds hand. It if makes more than eight (even) beats in 60 seconds, it is too strong.

After you have the correct spring set on the fork—most repairmen have a tendency to set it too low—so that the escapement barely locks and unlocks within 3/4 (270 degrees) of a turn of the pendulum. We've observed a number of workmen who jump to the conclusion that the escape wheel tooth is dropping onto the impulse face of the pallet simply because the escapement acts that way. Instead of allowing the pendulum to swing the verge, move it slowly but firmly with your finger and watch the tooth action through your loupe. Chances are you will discover that the tip of the tooth strikes the locking surface of the pallet and not the impulse face. Normally the locking is light, and while the escapement is dead-beat, the blow has a tendency to unlock it when the fork is set low. You can readily see that the nearer the fork is to the top chock, the shorter, and therefore stiffer than that portion of the suspension spring is—it must be stiff or strong enough to resist the drop and therefore keep the action locked.

Clock Runs Too Fast

I have in my shop a Kundo 6 jewel battery operated Pendulum clock.

I have installed a new battery power pack, cleaned and oiled the movement and made the necessary adjustments to the escapement.

My problem is that the clock is running exceedingly fast ten or eleven hours fast in 24 hours.

A.

Your 686 "Kundo" beats 180 times per minute. Any good timepiece with a sweep-seconds hand, count it for exactly sixty seconds — the best way is to count and observe only one side, every other stroke, your count should come out 90.

A gain of eleven hours in twenty-four, is far too much for any pendulum alternation — practically two to one.

NOTE: that this clock is ratcheted forward upon each stroke to your left; also that the pawl which performs this function is located near the top of the pendulum rod, and, is adjustable by two separate screws.

What is happening with your piece, the pawl is picking up two teeth; thus the tremendous gain. The horizontal screw nearer the front is simply a "stop." That is, it determined the distance the pawl drops down. Study these actions until you are familar with the whole action of the pawl as the pendulum swings then proceed to adjust until the pawl picks up only ONE tooth on it's excursion to the left.

With the clock picking up one tooth every other stroke — that to the left — you will find it will register time pretty close to correct — whatever small variation is easily corrected with the reg. Screwing the ball just above the pendulum assembly, up or down, etc.

Kundo Clock Creates Problems

I have a Kundo 400-day clock which is causing us no end of trouble. It came in for a new suspension wire – the orginal enclosed, minus bottom block which has an open hole. According to the book by Charles Terwilliger, the clock requires Kundo 5E.

I ordered the complete unit for this. After cleaning the clock and mainspring and oiling the pivots well, I found the clock would run only a short time and then stop. After lowering the fork on the block several times I finally got the clock to run. Finally I put the dial and hands on hoping that was it. The clock is doing the same thing as it did before I reduced the lock – stopping. It would seem that the wire is too weak to keep the escapements locking and moving the wire along in its cycle of locking on each side L-R etc. Would you advise a stronger suspension spring? This unit doesn't have large plates, but I would hesitate calling it miniature in spite of its call for a small suspension wire and blocks.

I have enclosed the original spring; the replacement is not curled. Please advise us what could be done further.

A.

NEVER increase the strength of the suspension spring to make the 400-day clock run — the strength of that spring does not enter into the continuity of the clock's run — it enters only into the regulation. Your clock is driven via the main spring.

We often see these tightly curled suspension springs because some "nut" gets the idea that the clock should be wound that way and simply twists the very heck out of it. The suspension spring is always straight and smooth.

Match your back plate to the proper cut in your 400-Day Repair Guide; it will give you the correct suspension strength and unit. That complete unit will come to you with the fork properly set.

Evidently, you have escapement trouble — re-read and study closely that chapter upon the escapement. With the escapement correctly set, and the clock "in-beat" it should deliver continuous running. With the correct suspension unit, the timing should be well within the reg. nut travel. Assemble the movement, leaving out the verge arbor — crank-up the spring about a quarter turn and note the freedom of the train. Pivots upon the 400-day are easily bent and a slightly bent pivot can cause a lot of stoppage — some workmen are not careful enough when putting the 400-day in-beat. The drop of the escape tooth upon the pallet is so light it is difficult to rely upon sound — take your loupe and eye-ball it. Note when a tooth drops and observe how much further the pendulum swings before it reverses. Check the overswing on the reverse stroke and equalize the overswing on both strokes, then your block is in-beat.

IIII vs. IV

I repair many old clocks and am wondering why the four is made with four IIII instead of the standard IV.

Also, could you please tell me why stationary clock faces used in advertising, etc., usually show the time at 8:18?

A.

Possibly backed up by more serious study than any other similar article on the subject was a paper titled "Numerals On Clock and Watch Dials," by Prof. D. W. Hering, and published after his death in the Scientific Monthly for October, 1939. In answer to your first question we quote therefrom: "Why IIII instead of IV for four? A feature in the dial marking that has often aroused comment is the use of IIII instead of IV for four. The later is undoubtedly the proper form in Roman notation, but the former is so general on clock and watch dials that IV looks odd. Two explanations of this singular alteration of the numerals are current: the first, a story ingenious and apt enough to be plausible though probably only a story, and the second an attempt at rational explanation on the ground of good taste. We give both. (1) When Henri de Vick had about completed his famous clock for the Royal palace of King Charles V at Paris, 1370, he submitted to His Majesty a design of the dial for his approval. It was marked with IV. The king objected to that and preferred IIII; de Vick defended IV as the correct Roman form for four. The king testily replied that that made no difference—he would not have it. Was he not 'Charles the Wise'? What was to gainsay him? So IIII it became, and IIII it has been ever since.

(2) Many early clockmakers as well as later ones possessed both inventive talent and artistic sense. They were not slow to perceive that the ring of numerals with IIII presented a better balance than one with IV—so much better that it won general sustained preference."

This latter answer almost answers your second question too. Painted and printed dials for ads and signs have the hands pointed to 8:18 and 8:20 because (1) It balances. (2) It gives the best division of space within the hour-numeral circle for lettering ads, name, etc. There are stories that it indicates the time President Lincoln was shot . . . others that it indicates the time of his death. Neither are correct and it has been established that it was the custom even before Lincoln's day.

"The Day of Two Noons" — November 18, 1883, when the railroads adopted standard time.

Many of us who tend the "144" and deal with 'time' day after day do not realize the confusion that prevailed throughout the nation prior to the railroads adopting a 'standard' time; and it is an odd fact that this time 'standard' was not official until some thirty-five years after it had been in general operation. Though cities, states and even the Federal government recognized and used it, it was NOT official until the "Standard Time Act" was passed by our Congress on March 19, 1918. Tell any of your clients that: Standard Time is only fifty-six years old and he'll give you an argument.

At the time it was put into effect by the railroads there was considerable opposition to it. Studying and researching this tremendous time change, one sees that the news media took it up and extracted all the mileage possible from the question. One is reminded that the scriptures tell us that there is no new thing under the sun, all the great papers of the nation belabored it in a manner that reminds you of the Watergate affair this date. Typical of how far afield they went would be a quote from the New York Herald on the day following the change: "Of course, no good comes along in this selfish and ungreatful world without having its motives suspected. And some people were unkind enough to believe that the whole affair was a mean and sordid device of the watchmakers. It is notorious that scores of people have never managed to arrange the operation of a watch yet without putting it out of order, and everyone knows that a timepiece once sent to the watchmaker for repairs is irretrievably ruined, and spends the rest of its days passing between his hands and those of the owners. It was but natural then, to suppose that an alteration of time which would necessitate the setting of thousands of watches, and their subsequent subjection to the malignant arts of the watchmaker, was only a gigantic scheme of plunder contrived in his interest." end quote. Too bad this 'brilliant' bit did not carry a by-line—be that as it may, it does show that our friends of the fourth estate have not altered their thinking a great deal in these past ninety-one years, 1883-1974, they simply can't miss an opportunity to take a swat at the lowly watchmaker.

Despite the opposition voiced by the great papers of the nation — Chicago Tribune, Indianapolis Sentinel, New York Herald, Detroit Evening Journal, et. al. — the American public came to accept standard time without question and today it is in almost universal use. They did however, succeed in winning one point — that of having a continuous count of one to twenty-four hours excluded. Only one railroad published their timetable on the 24-hour schedule but shortly fell into the style as always used.

Sometime, close to the day of "Two Noons" railroads ceased to run by 'clocks' mounted in the cab and went to the pocket watch. Shortly thereafter the system of watch inspection was established and the faithful clock disappeared from the locomotive cab.

During the "Civil War Centennial" when one of the great railroads toured the country with their famous "General" locomotive I was fortunate to enjoy a ride with some of their top officials, upon our inspecting the cab, I asked: "Where is the clock?" and was amazed to learn that with all their effort to restore it to its original 1855 building none knew that it was originally equipped with a clock. In this transition era, watches to clocks, and, use of a locomotive being assigned to any crew that came on duty rather than to one designated engineer, the railroads generally gifted the old engineer with the clock he had been accustomed to using. That is our reason for this mention here — occasionally these old locomotive clocks hit the "144" this date — they either belong to a decendent of the engineer, or, to a collector; in any case it is a 'desirable' job for two reasons, on one hand, they are definitely in the antique range thus one of the 'cream' jobs; on the other, they are well constructed, meant to keep time, therefore relatively easy to overhaul and put in order. Both E. Howard and Seth Thomas, supplied them — perhaps others but we don't recall them at the moment.

In the earlier days, perhaps when the "General" was built in 1855, contract specifications for the cab of locomotives called for a 'shelf' for the clock — a little later these clocks were encased in metal cases matching the steam pressure gauge. The Crosby Steam Gauge & Valve Co., at Wrentham, Mass., was very active in the locomotive accessory field, so was Ashton Valve Company — both cast cases for locomotive clocks. Several years back when researching the locomotive clock, Mr. J. J. Bresnahm, Vice-President for Crosby, wrote: "Neither Ashton nor Crosby supplied cases to clock manufacturers, but we purchased clock movements from the clock manufacturers and installed them in cases matching the pressure gauge case."

Since our above headline is 'questions' one might well ask; "Why this reminiscencing about locomotive clocks''? It is very simply that we have always maintained that when a repair is presented to the bench clockmaker, the owner expects him to know 'all' about the timepiece. With these older pieces they are so closely tied into history, it is almost impossible to separate the historical from the mechanical. The proud owner automatically feels that if you have the history you certainly have the mechanical, etc.; thus, you instantly enhance your repair image in his thinking if you can supply a bit of history. It is an established fact that the common run of clock repairs is a ''bread and butter'' operation — that is: if you can make expenses plus a wee bit for groceries from it you are lucky. This covers the cheaper, mantel strikers, alarms and non-strike battery movements — it is at this point that competition is the greatest; thereby the price is hammered down to the minimum — it is the 'oldies' — the antiques requiring parts to be hand-made that command the 'premium' fees. They are the jobs I refer to as carrying a bit of cream; now, I realize full well that perhaps I'm climbing out on a limb for there are those, particularly many outside the craft, who are wont to argue that a mechanic's time is worth a 'fixed' figure per hour regardless of whether he may be working upon a $1.98 alarm clock or a $3,000 grandpappy chimer. That, very simply is NOT a valid viewpoint for reasons that could fill the rest of this volume — one is the responsibility; suppose the dollar-ninety-eighter gets burned up or stolen; he can replace it for $1.98 — if the same happened to the grandfather, it is quite another cup of tea — your insurance company never hesitates to up the rate when the responsibility goes up.

Attorneys, doctors and what have you, have a different and higher rate for specialized services — even your TV repairman has a different rate where he services a color set. The system is too well established for anyone to saw off my limb. No two ways about it, the name of the game is m-o-n-e-y. I hope that you truly love your clock work, but, you are not running that ''144'' for the love of it, you are faced with taxes, the house mortgage, the car notes and supplying the table with groceries — I need not say here that *that* takes money. Or, that you owe it to yourself and family to market your skills at the top figure.

J. E. Coleman Honored
As "Man of Many Years"

JESSE E. COLEMAN, author of Clockwise and Otherwise in American Horologist and Jeweler, was honored in his home town of Nashville, Tenn., by this magazine with its first "Man of Many Years" award plaque.

Presentation was made May 25 on behalf of American Horologist and Jeweler by officers of the Nashville Chamber of Commerce at the Chamber offices in downtown Nashville a block away from the site of Mr. Coleman's clock shop.

As shown in the accompanying illustration John S. Bransford, Nashville Chamber, president, left, presents the plaque to Mr. Coleman while Edward J. Shea, executive vice president, right, witnesses the event and extends his congratulations. Ceremony was conducted in Chamber lobby with a photograph of Nashville's Central Business District in the background.

American Horologist and Jeweler editors set up the "Man of Many Years" award earlier this year to honor individuals in the horological and jewelry industry who have given outstanding service to others in the industry in depth over a period of many years. This is not an annual or a periodic award, but one which can be given as frequently as publication personnel receive nominations of outstanding individuals within the industry.

Nature of Mr. Coleman's service as one of American Horologist and Jeweler's technical editors is that for more than 20 years in addition to conducting writings of horological interest, he has carried on a continuing and extensive personal correspondence within the industry to help watchmakers and jewelers who were in need of specific answers to technical and historical questions on clocks and watches.

Legend on Mr. Coleman's walnut and bronze plaque reads: "Man of Many Years Award—Presented to J. E. Coleman. Researcher, writer, and technical editor in horology; specialist in clocks from the earliest to the latest. For service to his fellow craftsmen."

Nashville Chamber officials said they were happy to participate in the award program because Mr. Coleman's work in his field had brought distinction to Nashville over the years and had placed the Nashville postmark on letter of interest to people all over the United States and throughout the world.

J. E. Coleman is Named Craft Member of BHI

A N INTERESTING international honor recently was given to Jesse E. Coleman, 1116 East Granada Avenue, Nashville, Tenn., senior technical editor of American Horologist and Jeweler and writer of the Clockwise and Otherwise department in this journal every month.

Mr. Coleman was elected a craft member of the British Horological Institute by the membership committee of that society; received word of it and congratulations from F. West, the organization's secretary.

Within a week after he received notice of his election, which is based on skill as a horologist, he received Certificate No. 8979 which he framed to hang in his home workshop next to two other certificates he values highly. One is his designation as a Fellow of the National Watch and Clock Collectors Association; the other a Distinguished Achievement Award presented to him in 1955 by the United Horological Association of America one of the Forerunners of the American Watchmakers Institute.

Writes Mr. Coleman of his election in BHI: "Craft membership in the world's oldest horological organization is something to be cherished and believe you me, I do."

COLEMAN'S 301st COLUMN

T HIS, OUR THREE-HUNDRED AND FIRST column launches it upon it's twenty-sixth year of continuous publication without a single miss. In this quarter century, a whole new generation of horologists have come to the "144," thus a wee bit of reminiscing may be in order though I am not particularly keen upon just going back to that May issue of 1947, because, when so doing it has that tendency to sort of peg our association with this journal to that year. Naturally, we like to take that connection and/or association back to it's real beginning. That would be year 1935 . . . which makes it thirty-seven years instead of just twenty-six.

In the fall of 1935 Mr. O. R. Hagans, then Secretary of The United Horological Associations of America, came to Nashville, and among other things for the good of the bench horologist we discussed was the founding and publishing of a trade journal; at that time I had been writing a bit for "Horology" a publication headquartered at 747 South Hill Street, Los Angeles, Calif., published by the father and son team—Samuel and Louis Levine. When Volume one, Number one came out January of 1936 the mast-head listed Mr. W. H. Samelius, Technical Editor, with the Entire Technical Board—U. H. A. of A.—as assistants—yours truly was one of that Board. It was not until Volume four, Number 10—October 1939—that the full individual name went on the mast-head as Clock Technical Editor. Thanks to the editors, publishers, and all the good folk at Denver, it remains there to this day—also, I am grateful to all our readers for making it possible, for I love our craft and derive much genuine pleasure from any small effort to assist a fellow clockmaker with his repair problems.

At that time—1939—Mr. Hagans, was Editor and Publisher. The publication grew steadily until Mr. Hagan brought in Mr. Allan Clevenger, as editor; he was succeeded by Mr. Vern Kurtz followed by George Martin, and then by our present editor Mr. Walter Woolfson, sixteen years ago.

"Clockwise and Otherwise" in reality, was borned at the thirteenth annual convention of U. H. A. of A. at the Hollenden Hotel, Cleveland, Ohio, in October of 1946. It was there Allan Clevenger, and the late Emanuel Seibel, then Dean of the American Academy of Horology, and I, held a couple of sessions upon updating our question and answer service—plans were perfected for making it a regular monthly feature and to this day I am not sure just who it was that suggested the name. Lastly, we called in Mr. Hagans and laid the plans before him. I do recall his saying: "Don't confuse me with details, I'm too busy;" then he turned to me and said: "Jess, you write and I'll print it."

We shook hands upon it and that has been my "contract" for all these years. May I add, one I consider more binding than any an attorney can set to paper over a notarized signature. If you like, you may chalk this up as just an old man reminiscing —recalling the good old days—and you would be right. But, it is more, it is the history of the beginning of this column and we were just suddenly aware that it is also news to many of our readers who have come into the craft in recent years.

The publication has grown and the column has grown with it. No other journal in the U.S. or abroad devotes as much time and research free to its questioners as does "C. & O." Those answers published in the Clockwise section represent a very, very small percentage of correspondence received and answered. Every effort is made to get an adequate reply into the mails within 24 hours after its receipt; each question is treated as if it were the ONLY one received; we try to understand the problem from the view point of the repairman regardless of how it may be worded and all we ask is that stamped, addressed return.

So much for the column, its history and production, and anniversaries. With your continued support and your loyalty to our advertisers we hope to be right here serving YOU for another quarter century.

Jesse E. Coleman

JESSE E. COLEMAN, founder of this column 28 years ago last month; a bench horologist of international stature; a man fully versed in the history of watchmaking and clockmaking covering the inception of man-made inventions in timekeeping, and a long-lived source of wisdom for clockmakers and watchmakers all over the world, died in Nashville, TN, the morning of May 12 in his anniversary month as an American Horologist and Jeweler technical editor after a prolonged illness.

Born on a farm that was granted to his English forebears at Kittrell, Rutherford County, TN, while it was still a Territory of the United States South of the Ohio River — land that was never sold — Mr. Coleman was 77 years old. His birth was on Dec. 7, 1897.

He attended Kittrell High School in his native city, and Middle State Teachers' College, Murphreesboro, TN, before enlisting in the Navy to serve in World War I.

Mr. Coleman spent four years apprenticeship with a competent French-trained watchmaker who gave him full indoctrination into Claudius Saunier's contributions to horology. He went to work as clockmaker-watchmaker in 1919 for a Murphreesboro retail jeweler and remained there 10 years before opening his own clock shop in Nashville.

With his first job, he began a life-long study to its deepest roots in all aspects of horology from the disciplines of theory, mathematics and mechanics that he got from books and from doing constant research as a letter writer who made the entire world his classroom. When his researches and his own experimentation took him far beyond the requirements of a Certified Master Watchmaker, his knowledgeable writing . . . pursued with vigor and true constancy to an American Horologist and Jeweler audience of thousands of readers . . . established him at the level of a master teacher in a jargon and a vernacular of an inimitable standard.

His early inspirations for article writing were the late P. M. Chamberlain and the late William H. Samelius. He began writing for Horology Magazine in 1934.

Mr. Coleman's erudition in combination with his unpretentious Southern style of writing answers to the most complex technical questions on small parts or miniature master mechanics from the days when watchmakers were seeking know-how on how to mill and finish components for small clocks and watches to just yester-year when questions about quartz crystal clocks and watches began to surface, brought love and respect from fellow craftsmen throughout the U.S., Canada, and in a total of 68 countries abroad.

He was conversant with reference to mechanics of every type of clock ever invented in the total range from what he sometimes referred to as "the lowly synchronous electric movement;" to the grandfathers and grandmothers with various chime patterns; to the 17th Century automata; to the huge tower clocks that sounded their chimes across many a city on both sides of the Atlantic Ocean, and to railroad station clocks that were important Americana.

In May of 1947 American Horologist and Jeweler Vol. 14, No. 5, carried a small box on its bright yellow cover with this legend: "Clockwise and Otherwise." A new Question and Answer Department by J.E. Coleman. Page 57.

When readers of that issue reached Page 57 they found the accompanying modest one-column heading introducing the first writings of J. E. Coleman as technical clock editor of American Horologist and Jeweler.

And in a tradition from which his column never faltered there were lines under the heading inviting readers to send their questions with a self-addressed envelope. Exact words of that invitation follow:

MAY, 1947

Mr. Coleman invites your questions. If your question requires a direct answer, please enclose a self-addressed, stamped envelope. It is impossible through correspondence to give valuations of antique timepieces, and questions of this na-

ture cannot be answered.

Mr. Coleman's first letter was from an S. Rodick and had reference to a free-lance article Jesse had written for American Horologist and Jeweler as a non-staff member. That article dealt with chime clocks. Mr. Rodick also made reference to another such article in which Mr. Coleman had expounded on clock weights.

Birth of the Clockwise and Otherwise Column was in many free-lance articles which were of such broad and deep interest to American Horologist and Jeweler readers that their responses from the field became a signal to make the author a permanent fixture with this publication.

For more years even — 40 — than he conducted his unique column in American Horolgist and Jeweler, Jesse Coleman was the proprietor of Coleman's Clock Shop, the Arcade Building, Nashville, TN, where he practiced what he preached in professionalism at the bench when engaged in performance of the most difficult restorations and repairs. When he retired from his clock shop in 1969, he continued to pursue his horological research and monthly column in this magazine.

And even as he told subscribers of American Horologist and Jeweler over and over again that their true values as horologists could only be fulfilled to the degree that they worked with proficiency in their "144-square-inch world" — at the bench, but nonetheless escaped those limitations in their quest for universal knowledge about their field, he never permitted his own "144-square-inches" to become his boundaries.

A man with no borderlines when it came to knowledge and to contributions to a trade he made his profession, he was a member, director, and technial advisor to the United Horological Association of America which was organized in 1933; a member of the National Association of Watch and Clock Collectors and a frequent contributor to that organization's quarterly NAWCC Bulletin in the field of historic timepieces and their makers; a member and technical advisor to the American Watchmakers Institute and one of its founding committee members when it was organized in 1960 as a consolidation of UHA of A and the Horological Institute of America, and a Craft Member of the British Horological Institute — an honor and a mark of actual proficiency through testing achieved by a relatively small number of American clockmakers and watchmakers in the entire history of that Institute.

He also was active in organizing the Tennessee Watchmakers and Jewelers Association which he served as a state secretary and as president, and he was a member of the Boston Clock Club.

As a Baptist of the Southern Baptist Convention and a member of the Inglewood Baptist Church, Nashville, Mr. Coleman's funeral was conducted by the pastor of that church — the Rev. Mr. James B. Hopkins. Readers of American Horologist and Jeweler who desire to honor Mr. Coleman's memory are asked by his family to make their donations either to the American Cancer Society, or to the educational ELM Trust Fund of the American Watchmakers' Institute, PO Box 11011, Cincinnati, OH 45211.

Mr. Coleman was married in 1919 to the late Erin Jacobs. They were the parents of a son born in 1920 who preceded them in death.

Survivors of Mr. Coleman are a sister, Mrs. Grace White, Chattanooga, TN, and two granddaughters, Miss Janet Diane Coleman, Atlanta, GA., and Miss Jacqueline Erin Coleman, Chamblee, GA.

In the spirit of a man whose fidelity to this column was unwavering in the face of all the difficulties that profuse and profound writings created for him in his good times and bad . . . there is only one way to conclude this June, 1975, "Otherwise" section of J. E. Coleman's Clockwise and Otherwise column before starting with the regular questions and answers from which his major writings in this magazine stemmed . . .

J.&J.&J.

Jesse E. Coleman
Dec. 7, 1897 — May 12, 1975

by Orville R. Hagans

ANOTHER AGE in horology has passed with the death of my close personal friend, Jesse E. Coleman, on May 12, 1975. Although his passing is a very great loss to all of us who knew him either personally or as one of his thousands of correspondents, it is more so to me because my close personal association with Jesse goes back forty-three years to when we met in Elgin, IL in 1932.

It was at this first meeting that the two of us fell under the influence of the late William H. Samelius, "Dean of American Watchmakers," who convinced us that we could best serve our fellow craftsmen by dedicating our lives to the advancement of horology in all its phases. We both accepted his guidance and pledged to him we would devote our lives to improving ourselves and others. With this as a beginning of our friendship, our mutual bonds of respect for each other strengthened each passing year.

Jesse Coleman did not confine his writings to his well-known column Clockwise & Otherwise in AH&J, he contributed articles to HIA Journal, Horology, NAWCC Bulletin, BHI Journal, AWI News and many others too numerous to mention. In addition to his writing of articles, he personally answered thousands of letters from individual correspondents.

His quiet, unassuming but authoritative and positive acts were extremely beneficial in association work. He was among the first few individuals who created UHAA; he was a sparkplug in founding NAWCC; he organized Tennessee Watchmakers Association; and served as its President and Secretary-Treasurer.

He was one of a committee of six of UHAA who brought about the unification of HIA and UHAA, forming AWI, now the only professional horological association in America.

As was just stated in a letter from our mutual friend, Henry Fried, "He will go down as one of America's 'greats' in horology. He, probably more than anyone else, should have been the author of an authoritative book on American clocks and repairs. He was so reticent about writing such a book, yet his columns are so informatively original." How true this is, and it may help to know that under contract four books were started several years back.

Jesse was a most ardent and serious researcher and once he started on a phase of research he never gave up regardless of time and expense. Two months ago he turned over to me a research file of 25 years on the South Bend Watch Company, stating he could not put it together but "the profession must know what I have searched out authentically." And so his request will be fulfilled.

His faith and trust in his fellow man was quite unusual, particularly if compared to today's standard. In October 1946 at a UHAA Convention in Cleveland, OH, Jesse and the then Asst. Editor of AH&J, Allen Clevenger, perfected and agreed upon plans for a monthly column in that publication to be titled Clockwise & Otherwise. On Oct. 20th, Jesse, Allen and I went over the plans. At the conclusion of the conference, I said, "Jess you write it and I'll publish it." We shook hands upon that statement and 'that' virtually was the contract between the publication and Jesse Coleman. When the publication was sold to Mr. Bell there was no signed contract with Jesse and one was suggested. Jesse's reply to this suggestion was "Hagans and my gentleman's agreement was more binding than any an attorney could write" and thus the hand shake in October 1946 held until his passing.

From my files of correspondence with Jesse, there is one letter which I feel should be published. In Nov. 1973 in a letter to Jesse, I asked what caused him to become interested in "wheels" and writing. In a letter dated Jan. 29, 1974, he answers with the following:

"Now, why wheels? I suppose that you might say my father was a blacksmith; thus raised in a blacksmith shop my basic training was mechanical. I learned to work in and with metals as a mere lad. Rough though it was, welding and tempering was basic. Cutting threads and some lathe work was permitted a kid just hanging around because his dad owned the shop. Being fairly apt (If I do say so) I picked up a great deal that has stuck by me. About that time, Popular Mechanics magazine was founded and one of my country school teachers subscribed to it — when he had finished, he passed it on to me. That was my FIRST introduction to accuracy; in the shop about 1/32 inch was all you heard. There was no micrometer and I doubt my dad or those mechanics he employed could have used one if we'd had it. Repairing windmills, farm machinery and an occasional steam engine just did not come any closer than about a 32nd. Right along here at some spot I got the idea that the pocket watch was the acme of mechanical construction and accuracy.

Sneaked into the U.S. Navy in April of 1917 and when I got out, jobs were scarce, particularly to a youngster without a trade or skill. By sheer luck I happened upon this watchmaker-jeweler who wanted an apprentice. The rest of the story you know; a lad in a small town jewelry establishment was supposed to do everything from play a trombone to mik a cow. Repairing watches — very little attention to clocks in those days — repairing jewelry, sizing rings, etc., plus a bit of hand engraving was the order of the day.

My luck was that my mentor had been trained by a watchmaker straight from Paris who thought Abraham Breguet hung the moon and that Saunier's treatise was the bible. As to the writing, it came about from old NRA days; we had organized the watchmakers of Tennessee and as Secretary I was issuing a little "News Letter" from a Sears duplicator. Major Chamberlain suggested that I write a bit for the Levine's and then I was further encouraged by Mr. Samelius. I hope that this does NOT sound boastful, and, that I have fully covered your point. J.E.C."

Tribute to Jesse Coleman

THIS WEEK marked another heavy loss in our church in the "home going" of Jesse Coleman. Many of our newer members do not know Mr. Coleman because of his inability to attend services during these last few years. Jesse is responsible for the unique tower structure and witness of Inglewood. He installed the tower clock system (the only church in Tennessee to have such an installation). There are one or two other similar installations on college campuses in Tennessee. I remember my first visit to the tower years ago as he explained how the system worked. Jesse has been my friend. He always had a good and kind word to share with me. As he put it . . . "drive careful preacher." We will miss his wit and his love.

J. E. Coleman Educational Memorial

A MEMORIAL TO A MAN who devoted his life to education and helping thousands — professional watch and clockmakers, students, writers, researchers, industry, and collectors. A man who deprived himself in order to help his fellow man. A man who shall go down in the history of horology as one of America's "greats."

It is felt that the creation of a "J. E. Coleman Educational Memorial" would be his fondest wish to perpetuate his life's work.

The A.W.I., Educational, Library and Museum Trust is in the most favorable position to handle such a memorial. The ELM Trust is entirely separate from A.W.I. — it is administered separately and under I.R.S. rules and regulations.

The "J. E. Coleman Educational Memorial" has been set up within the ELM Trust and contributions already are being received in substantial number.

All moneys received will be used to help finance students of horology who are worthy and hopefully carry on Mr. Coleman's work as top flight mechanics.

We ask individuals and companies who were recipients of his help and admire his learned counsel to make donations to this Memorial. All contributions are tax-deductible and donors will receive a proper letter for tax credit purposes.

Send your contributions to:

A.W.I., ELM Coleman Memorial; P.O. Box 11011; Cincinnati, OH 45211

Let us keep our benefactor and friend's name alive, the greatest honor we can bestow upon him.

Orville R. Hagans
CMW, CMC, FBHI

519

525